Archie Bongiovanni

GREASE BATS ™

BOOM! BOX ™

Designer **Jillian Crab**

Associate Editor **Sophie Philips-Roberts**

Editor **Shannon Watters**

Ross Richie CEO & Founder
Joy Huffman CFO
Matt Gagnon Editor-in-Chief
Filip Sablik President, Publishing & Marketing
Stephen Christy President, Development
Lance Kreiter Vice President, Licensing & Merchandising
Phil Barbaro Vice President, Finance & Human Resources
Arune Singh Vice President, Marketing
Bryce Carlson Vice President, Editorial & Creative Strategy
Scott Newman Manager, Production Design
Kate Henning Manager, Operations
Spencer Simpson Manager, Sales
Sierra Hahn Executive Editor
Jeanine Schaefer Executive Editor
Dafna Pleban Senior Editor
Shannon Watters Senior Editor
Eric Harburn Senior Editor
Chris Rosa Editor
Matthew Levine Editor
Sophie Philips-Roberts Associate Editor
Gavin Gronenthal Assistant Editor

Michael Moccio Assistant Editor
Gwen Waller Assistant Editor
Amanda LaFranco Executive Assistant
Jillian Crab Design Coordinator
Michelle Ankley Design Coordinator
Kara Leopard Production Designer
Marie Krupina Production Designer
Grace Park Production Designer
Chelsea Roberts Production Design Assistant
Samantha Knapp Production Design Assistant
Elizabeth Loughridge Accounting Coordinator
José Meza Live Events Lead
Stephanie Hocutt Digital Marketing Lead
Esther Kim Marketing Coordinator
Cat O'Grady Digital Marketing Coordinator
Holly Aitchison Digital Sales Coordinator
Morgan Perry Retail Sales Coordinator
Megan Christopher Operations Coordinator
Rodrigo Hernandez Mailroom Assistant
Breanna Sarpy Executive Assistant

BOOM! BOX™

GREASE BATS, August 2019. Published by BOOM! Box, a division of Boom Entertainment, Inc. Grease Bats is ™ & © 2019 Archie Bongiovanni. Originally published on Autostraddle.com. ™ & © 2013-2018 Archie Bongiovanni. All rights reserved. BOOM! Box™ and the BOOM! Box logo are trademarks of Boom Entertainment, Inc., registered in various countries and categories. All characters, events, and institutions depicted herein are fictional. Any similarity between any of the names, characters, persons, events, and/or institutions in this publication to actual names, characters, and persons, whether living or dead, events, and/or institutions is unintended and purely coincidental. BOOM! Box does not read or accept unsolicited submissions of ideas, stories, or artwork.

BOOM! Studios, 5670 Wilshire Boulevard, Suite 400, Los Angeles, CA 90036-5679. Printed in China. First Printing.

ISBN: 978-1-68415-411-1, eISBN: 978-1-68415-412-8

Dedicated to Casey, Tristan, and Christina for letting me drag you to all those gay bars. Dedicated to Brie and Jess for always dragging me home again.

Created, Written & Illustrated by

Archie Bongiovanni

Introduction

When I first asked Archie Bongiovanni to write a comic for Autostraddle.com, I figured they'd already had *Grease Bats* ready to go, given how fast they were ready and willing to run with it. I only learned recently over breakfast burritos that this wasn't true, that after I'd asked, they went to their office (which is a drawing table in a closet, a space they love and I have heard much about), sat down and made it up.

I couldn't believe it—the original two characters, Scout and Andy, arrived so fully formed on the page that I thought Bongiovanni must have had these two bumping around their head for months or years. But at the same time, I could believe it. Because Archie Bongiovanni is a genius with their finger on the pulse of what it means to move through the world as a whole person and a member of a tightly-knit (and oft marginalized) community. It stands to reason, then, that they put their pen to paper and the *Grease Bats*—a fictional gang of friends known for supporting each other, slinging witty retorts, and riding their bicycles around a fictional Minneapolis—sprang onto the internet and into our world.

There is little you have to know about this comic before starting to read; Bongiovanni's superpower is to make anything accessible to nearly any reader. That means I get to spend a thousand words on praise, which is a fun time for me, personally. It's a spiritual successor to Alison Bechdel's *Dykes to Watch Out For*, for one thing. It centers the queer reader, speaks directly to us. You may find something familiar in the ways Scout, Andy, Gwen, Taylor and Ari speak with each other; you may find yourself reading a few of them in your dear friends' voices, laughing when you swear that Bongiovanni has been following you around, lifting scenes from your life, pieces of dialogue you heard at the bar, or at brunch, or said with your own mouth.

Or perhaps where you are right now looks nothing like the world of *Grease Bats*. And perhaps you hate that. Or love it! No matter what, it's all good, pal. As Andy says: "Being queer comes from the heart! And the head! And occasionally sometimes the groin!" There isn't one way to be, or look, or act queer; there are so many ways to be a person and your life may look nothing at all like what you'll find in the coming pages. But you will find likable, fallible characters here. Glorious trash gremlins who love the shit out of one another, who take care of each other, who, even as they are donking up royally in the goofiest of ways, try their damndest to be family. In the face of the buckwild racism, sexism, homophobia, and transphobia we're all faced with every day (in the U.S. and elsewhere), the friendships between these five queers might feel healing for you; they have for me.

The first *Grease Bats* strip ran on January 25th, 2014. I am writing this introduction in January of 2019, five years later. It feels appropriate for the *Grease Bats* to get their time in print now, as we spend so much of our lives in digital space, interacting with folks through screens and reaching as hard as we can for empathy. In the era of #MeToo and anti-trans memos and ICE raids and, dare I write his name, Trump, whether we are queer or not, we are all re-figuring out what it means to be a part of a community. There is still so much work to be done in the ways we love and care for each other. It is right, it seems, for the *Grease Bats* to crystalize into an object, a book, that we can hold in our hands and gift to each other, that we can read in a bar with our friends if we are Andy or at home by ourselves on Solitude Sunday if we are Ari. It feels like we need it in physical space now. Right now. As usual, Bongiovanni's work arrives precisely when it is most necessary. And Archie Bongiovanni should be praised until they blush all the way up to their hairline for taking our hands in theirs and leading us into a kinder, goofier version of reality.

I will stop getting serious for a moment and leave you with this very ridiculous thing: I had the pleasure of hosting Archie in New York City at the end of last year. While they were in my living room, we talked about which characters we were most like; it has been among my greatest dreams to con them into designing a quiz, like in the teen magazines of yore, so that I might take it and find out if I truly am Scout or not. But upon a closer examination, and with Bongiovanni as the authority on all things *Grease Bats*, we found we could not ascribe one character to either one of us, or to our partners or our friends. We were all a mix of several. So instead, we treated them like astrology, assigning each one of us a Sun character, a Moon character and Rising character. It was a rollicking good time.

Later that evening, Archie hosted a *Grease Bats* Live reading at Bluestockings Bookstore, a queer feminist touchstone on the Lower East Side. I had never seen them do this before—they picked audience volunteers to read for each *Grease Bats* character, based entirely on whoever raised their hands, whoever felt moved to voice each one. I cannot adequately describe to you how perfect it was; everyone sounded exactly as they ought to, and we all laughed together in the dark of the bookstore, the comic projected onto the screen before us all, a giant mirror reflecting us as we are on our best days. It was a hopeful thing, to embody the *Grease Bats*, to feel this close to the best versions of ourselves, of our community. We are all the *Grease Bats*, and the *Grease Bats* are all of us.

I hope you enjoy this book as much as I have.

A.E. Osworth
Scout Sun/Gwen Moon/Taylor Rising

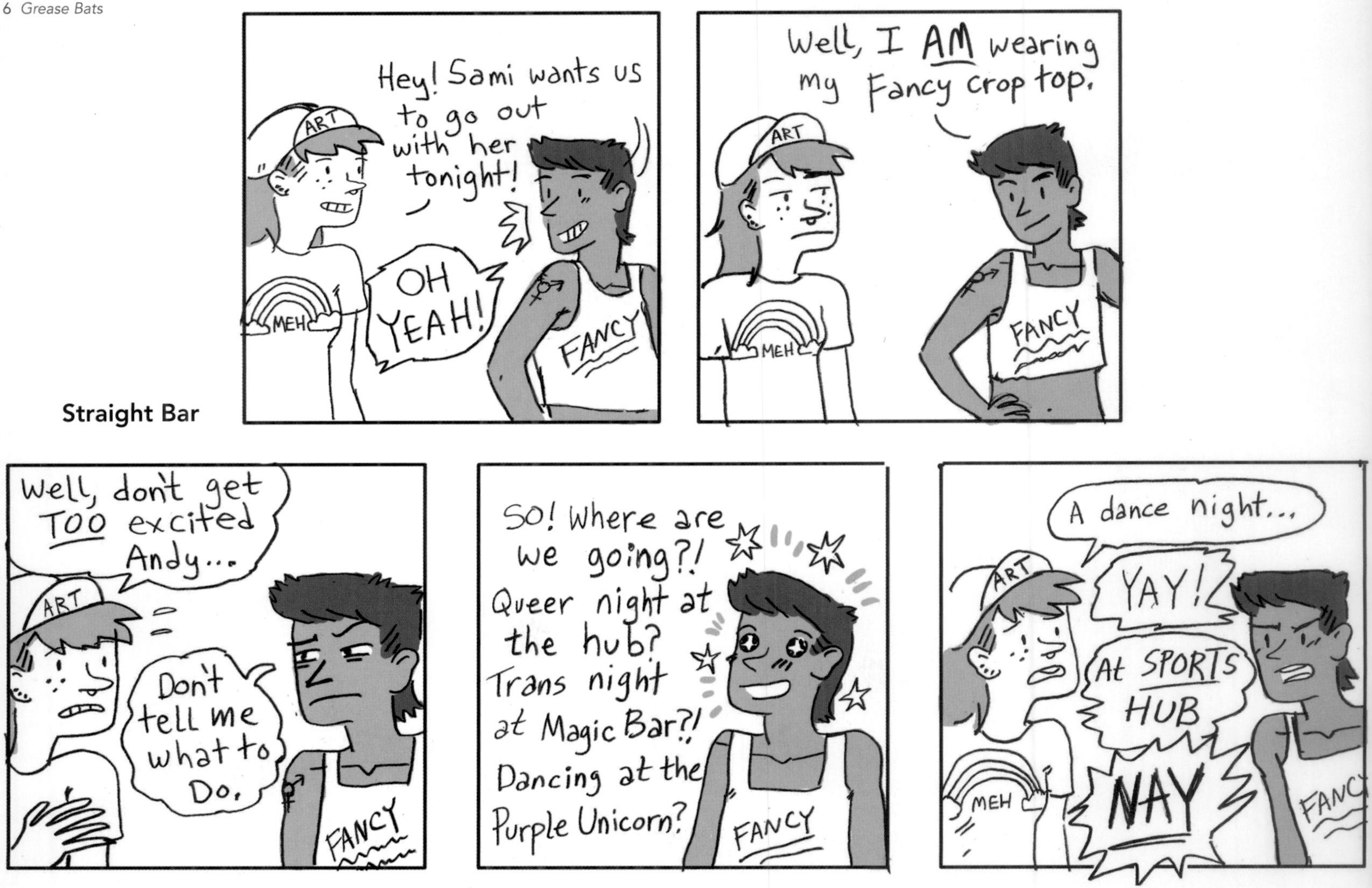
Hey! Sami wants us to go out with her tonight!
OH YEAH!
ART
MEH
FANCY
Well, I AM wearing my Fancy crop top.
Well, don't get TOO excited Andy...
Don't tell me what to Do.
SO! Where are we going?! Queer night at the hub? Trans night at Magic Bar?! Dancing at the Purple Unicorn?
A dance night...
YAY!
At SPORTS HUB
NAY

Straight Bar

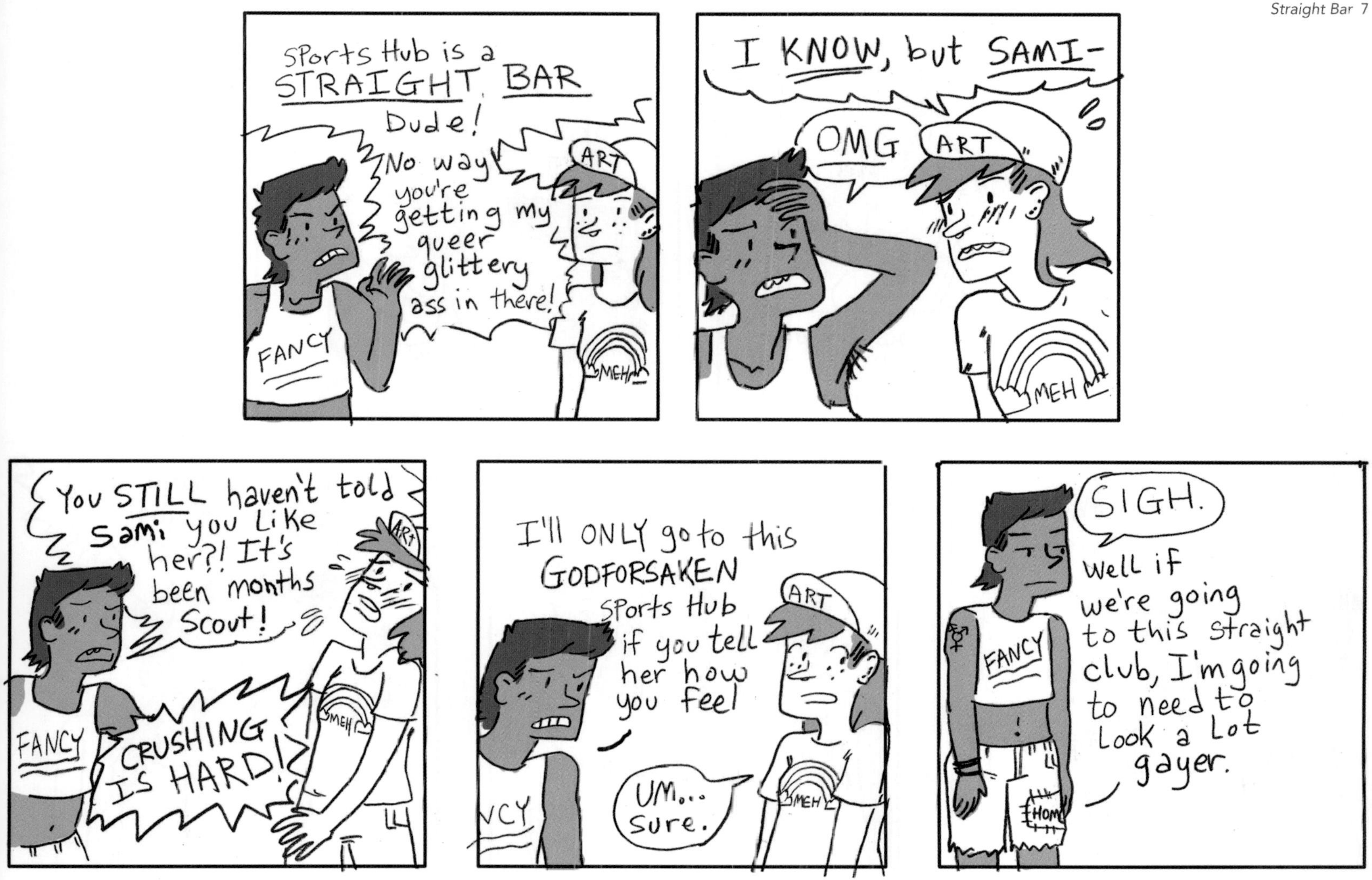
Sports Hub is a STRAIGHT BAR Dude!
No way you're getting my queer glittery ass in there!
ART
FANCY
MEH
I KNOW, but SAMI-
OMG
You STILL haven't told Sami you like her?! It's been months Scout!
CRUSHING IS HARD!
I'll ONLY go to this GODFORSAKEN Sports Hub if you tell her how you feel
UM... sure.
SIGH.
Well if we're going to this straight club, I'm going to need to look a lot gayer.
HOM

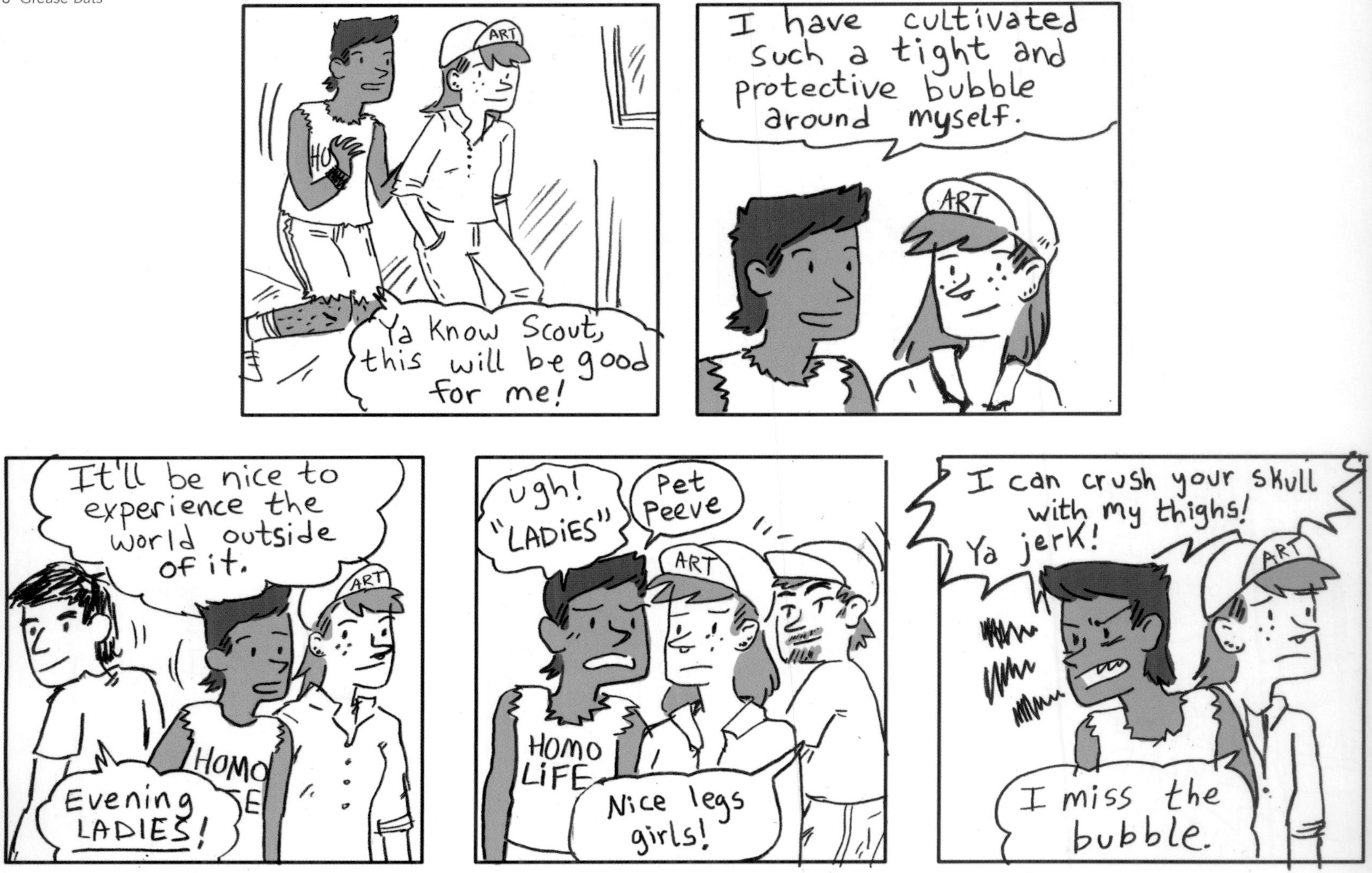
HO
Ya Know Scout, this will be good for me!
ART
I have cultivated such a tight and protective bubble around myself.
ART
It'll be nice to experience the world outside of it.
ART
HOMO
Evening LADIES!
Ugh! "LADIES"
Pet Peeve
ART
HOMO LIFE
Nice legs girls!
I can crush your skull with my thighs! Ya jerk!
ART
I miss the bubble.

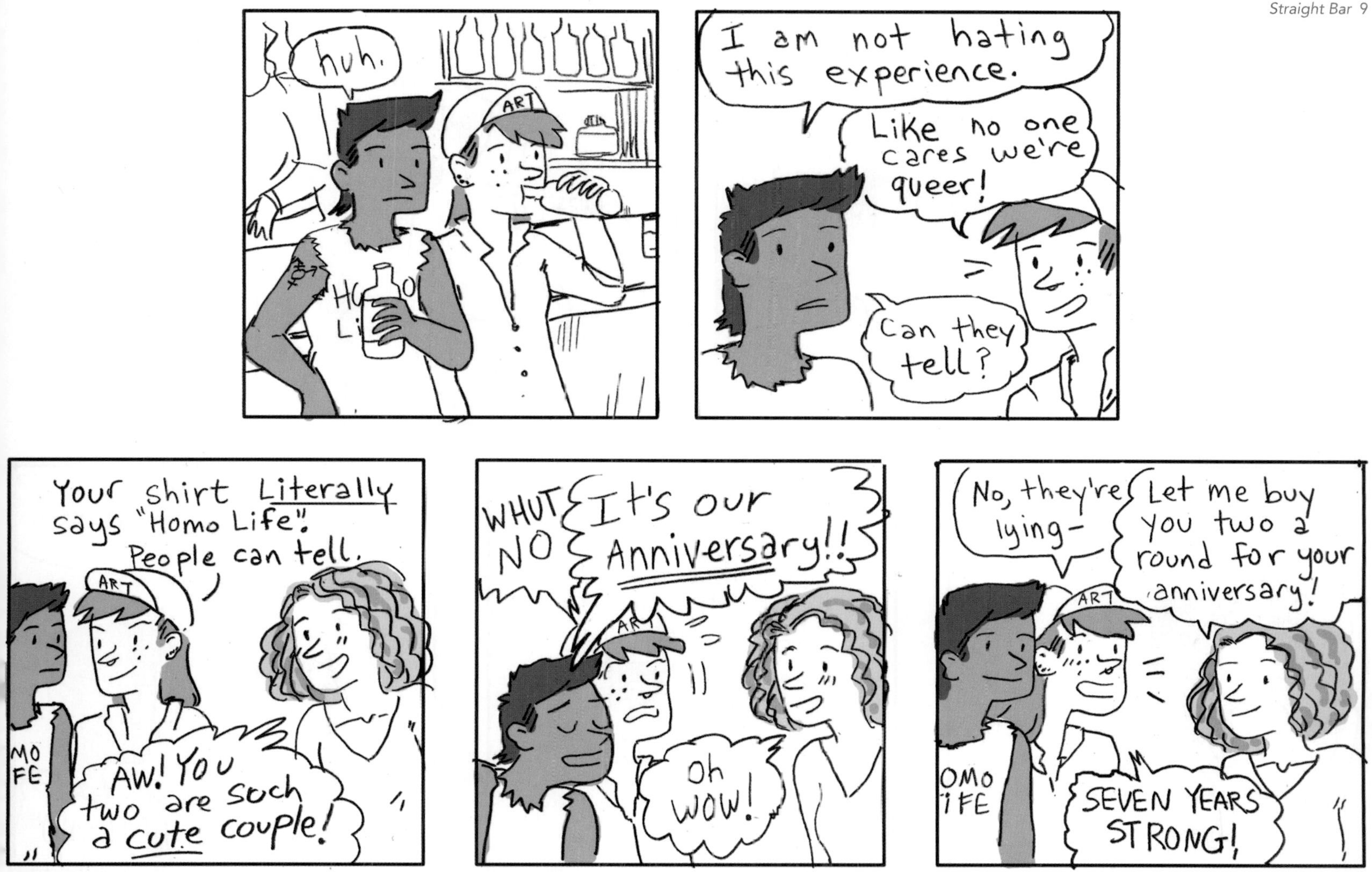
huh.
HO
LI
ART
I am not hating this experience.
Like no one cares we're queer!
Can they tell?
Your shirt Literally says "Homo Life"! People can tell.
ART
MO
FE
AW! YOU two are such a cute couple!
WHUT NO
It's our Anniversary!!
ART
Oh WOW!
No, they're lying-
Let me buy you two a round for your anniversary!
ART
OMO
IFE
SEVEN YEARS STRONG!

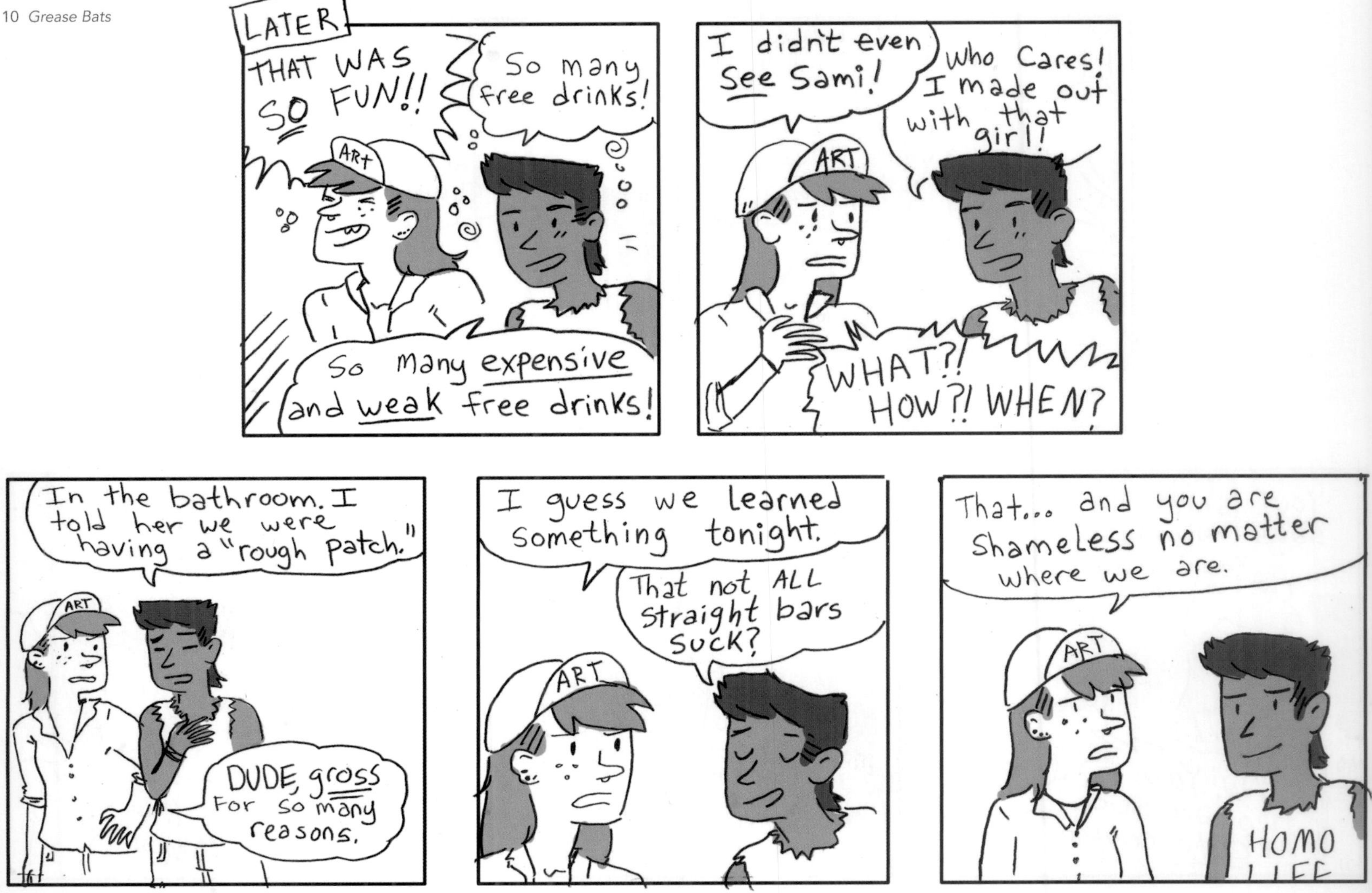
LATER
THAT WAS SO FUN!!
So many free drinks!
So many expensive and weak free drinks!
I didn't even see Sami!
Who cares! I made out with that girl!
WHAT?! HOW?! WHEN?
In the bathroom. I told her we were having a "rough patch."
DUDE, gross For so many reasons.
I guess we learned something tonight.
That not ALL straight bars suck?
That... and you are shameless no matter where we are.
HOMO LIFE

Queeroke

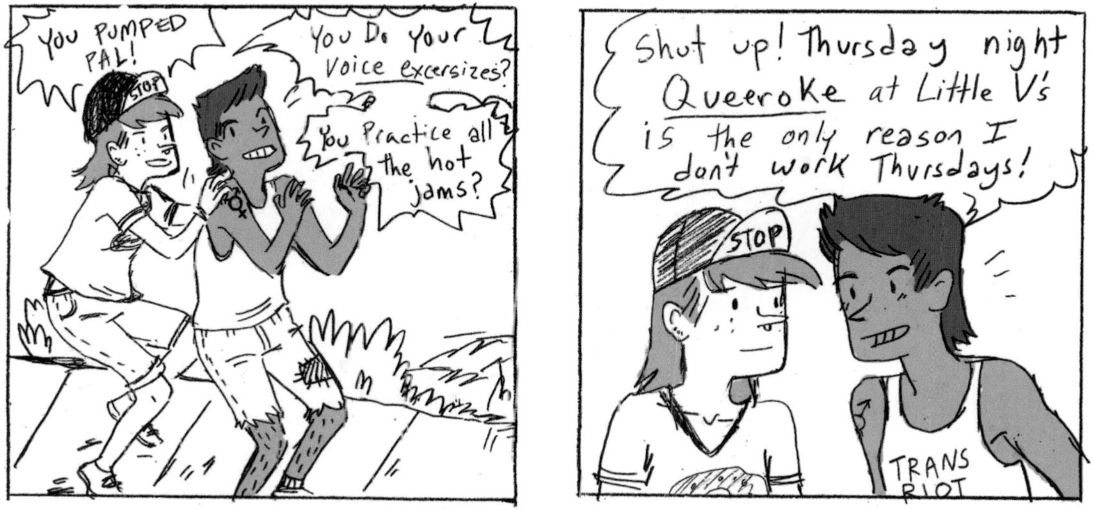
You PUMPED PAL!
You Do your Voice excersizes?
You Practice all the hot jams?
Shut up! Thursday night Queeroke at Little V's is the only reason I don't work Thursdays!
STOP
TRANS RIOT

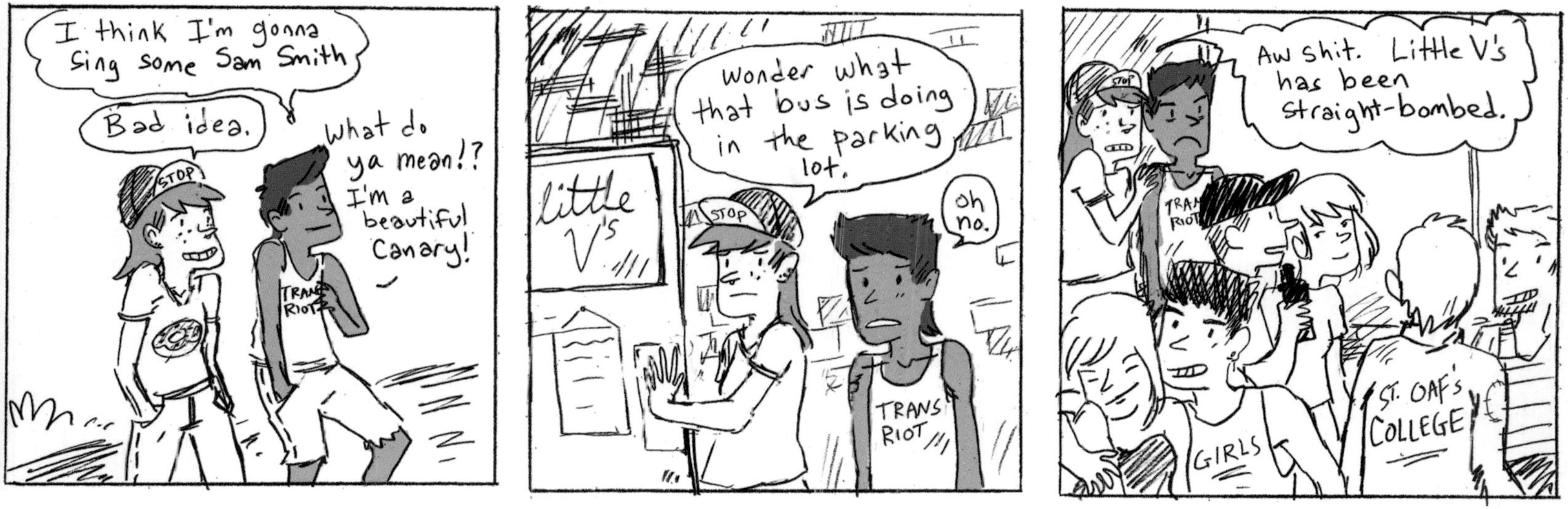
I think I'm gonna sing some Sam Smith
Bad idea.
What do ya mean!? I'm a beautiful Canary!
STOP
TRANS RIOT
little V's
wonder what that bus is doing in the parking lot.
oh no.
Aw shit. Little V's has been straight-bombed.
GIRLS
ST. OAF'S COLLEGE

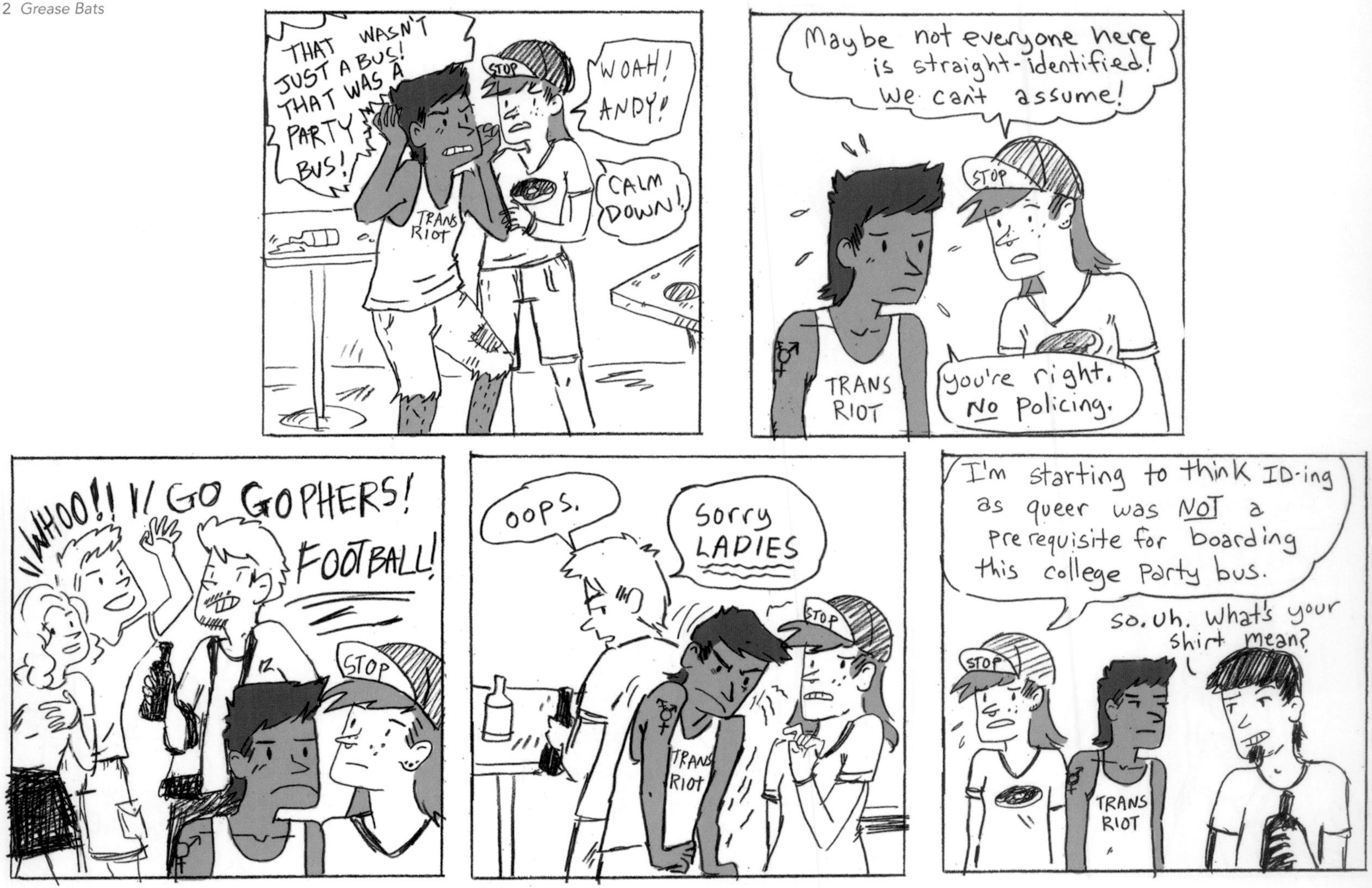
THAT WASN'T JUST A BUS! THAT WAS A PARTY BUS!
WOAH! ANDY!
CALM DOWN!
TRANS RIOT
Maybe not everyone here is straight-identified! We can't assume!
STOP
You're right. NO Policing.
TRANS RIOT
WHOO!!
GO GOPHERS!
FOOTBALL!
STOP
oops.
Sorry LADIES
STOP
TRANS RIOT
I'm starting to think ID-ing as queer was NOT a prerequisite for boarding this college party bus.
So. uh. What's your shirt mean?
STOP
TRANS RIOT

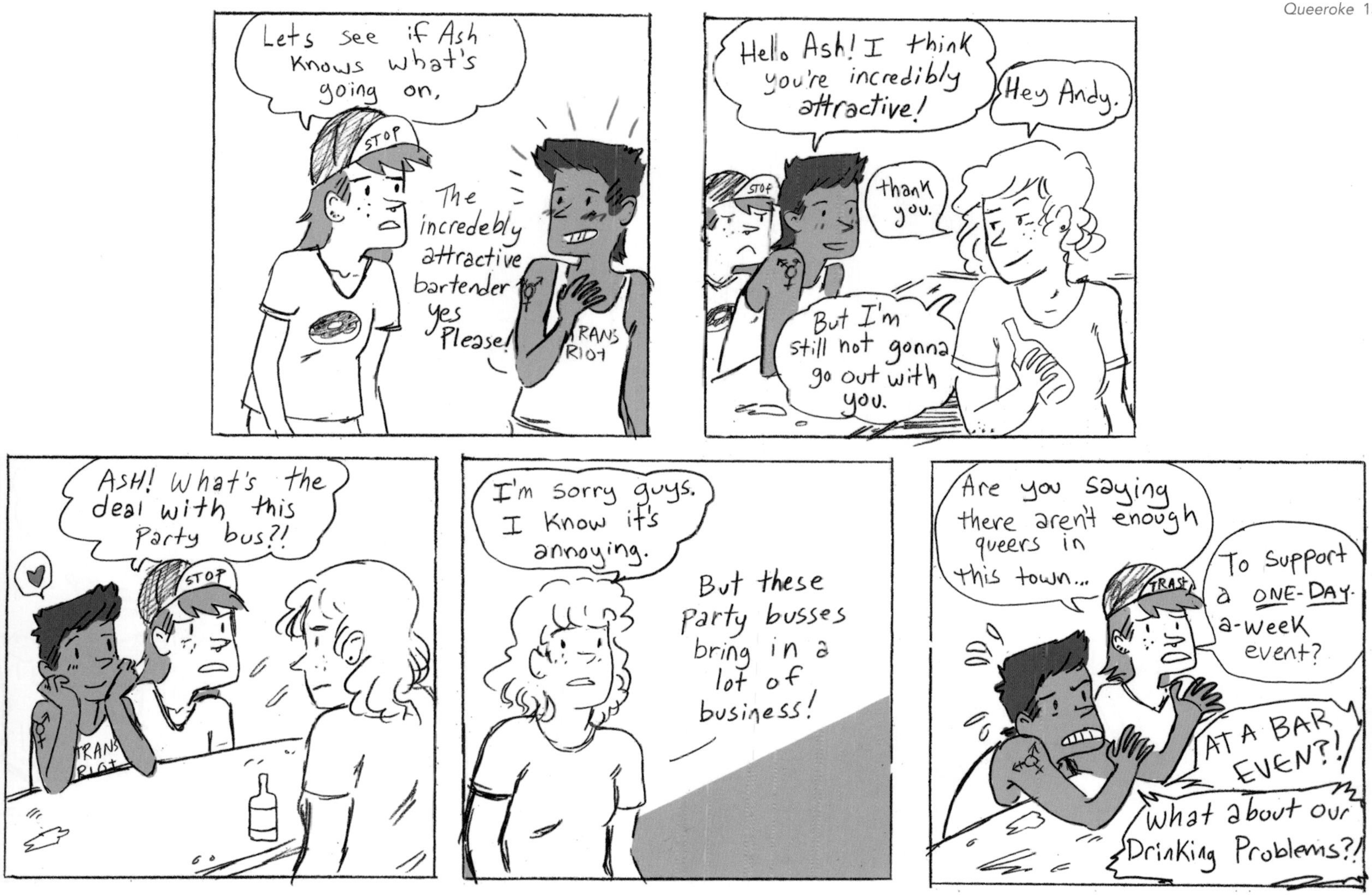
Lets see if Ash Knows what's going on,
The incredebly attractive bartender yes Please!
STOP
TRANS RIOT
Hello Ash! I think you're incredibly attractive!
Hey Andy.
thank you.
But I'm still not gonna go out with you.
ASH! What's the deal with this Party bus?!
STOP
TRANS RIOT
I'm sorry guys. I Know it's annoying.
But these Party busses bring in a lot of business!
Are you saying there aren't enough queers in this town...
To support a ONE-DAY-a-week event?
AT A BAR EVEN?!
What about our Drinking Problems?!

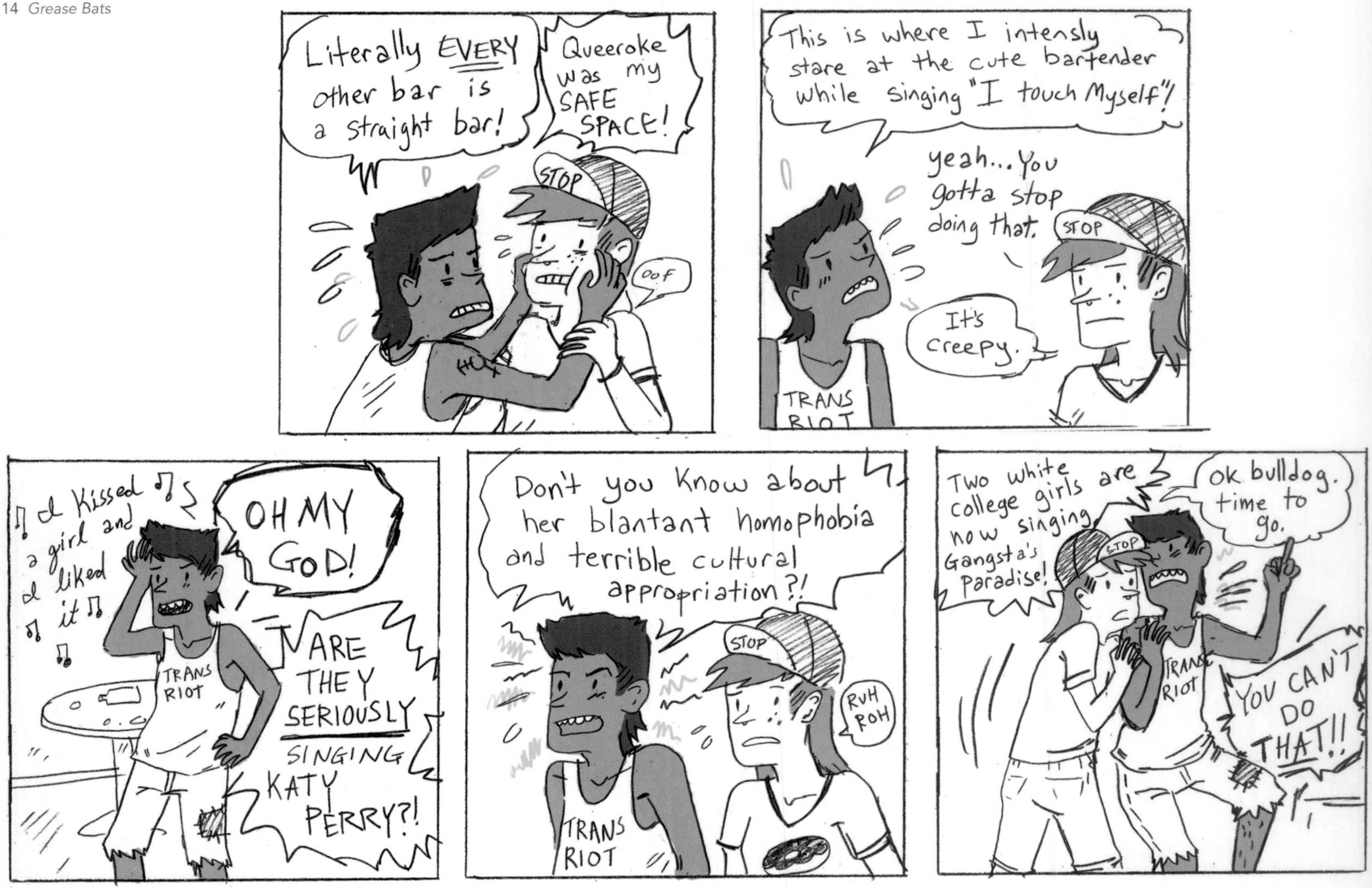
Literally EVERY other bar is a straight bar!
Queeroke was my SAFE SPACE!
STOP
OOF
This is where I intensly stare at the cute bartender while singing "I touch Myself"!
yeah... You gotta stop doing that.
STOP
It's creepy.
TRANS RIOT
I kissed a girl and I liked it
OH MY GOD!
ARE THEY SERIOUSLY SINGING KATY PERRY?!
TRANS RIOT
Don't you know about her blantant homophobia and terrible cultural appropriation?!
STOP
RUH ROH
TRANS RIOT
Two white college girls are now singing Gangsta's Paradise!
ok bulldog. time to go.
STOP
TRANS RIOT
YOU CAN'T DO THAT!!

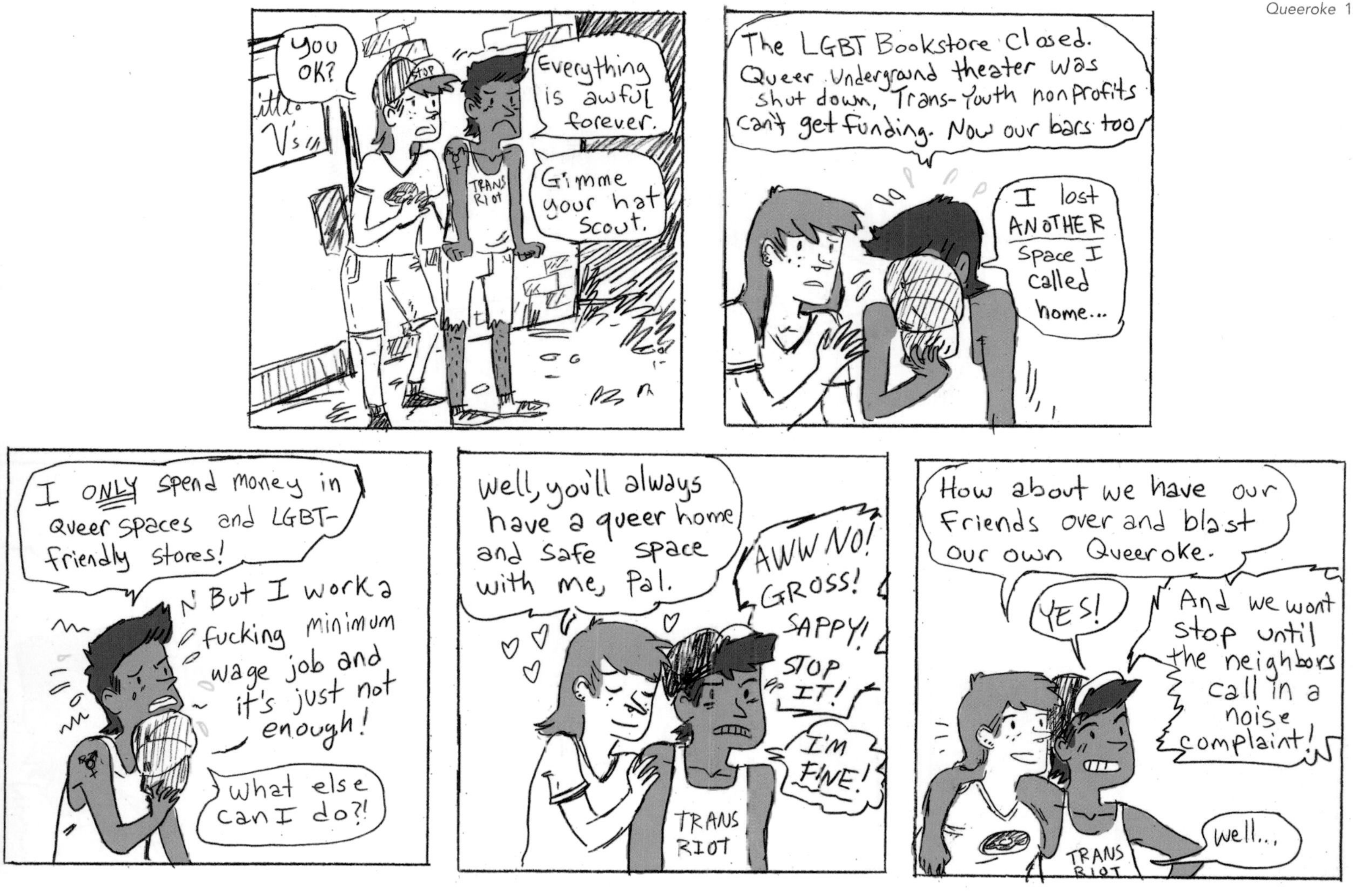
You OK?
STOP
Everything is awful forever.
Gimme your hat Scout.
TRANS RIOT
The LGBT Bookstore Closed. Queer Underground theater was shut down, Trans-Youth nonprofits can't get funding. Now our bars too
I lost ANOTHER Space I called home...
I ONLY spend money in Queer Spaces and LGBT-friendly stores!
But I work a fucking minimum wage job and it's just not enough!
What else can I do?!
Well, you'll always have a queer home and safe space with me, Pal.
AWW NO! GROSS! SAPPY! STOP IT!
I'M FINE!
TRANS RIOT
How about we have our Friends over and blast our own Queeroke.
YES!
And we wont stop until the neighbors call in a noise complaint!
Well...
TRANS RIOT

The Flirt

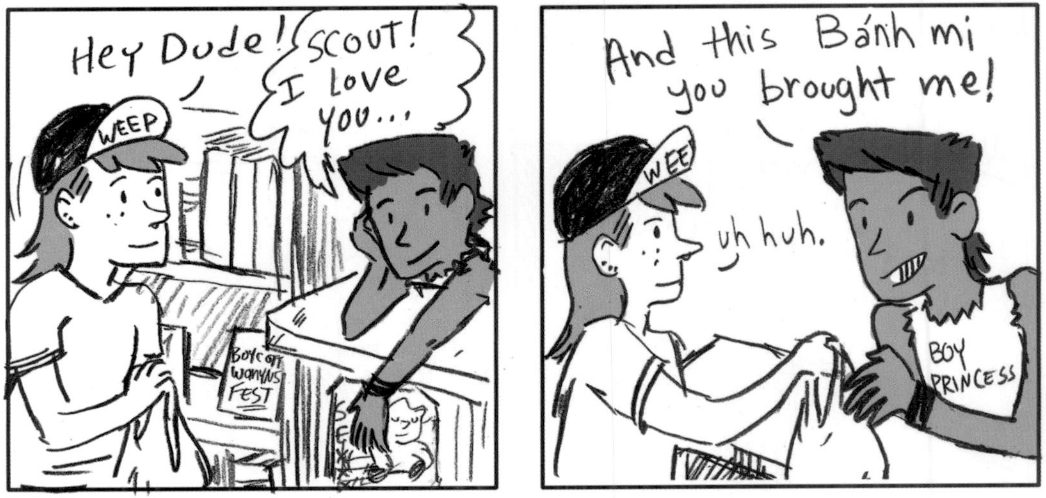
Hey Dude!
SCOUT! I love you...
WEEP
BOYCOTT WOMYNS FEST
And this Bánh mi you brought me!
uh huh.
BOY PRINCESS

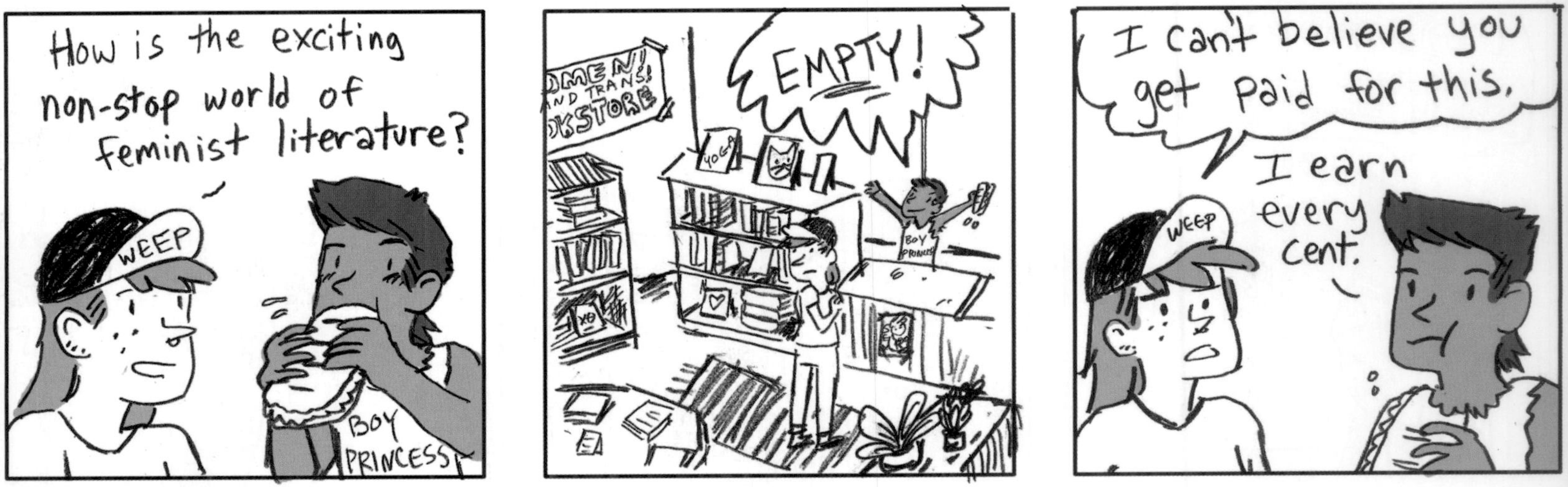
How is the exciting non-stop world of feminist literature?
WEEP
BOY PRINCESS
EMPTY!
YOGA
I can't believe you get paid for this.
I earn every cent.
WEEP

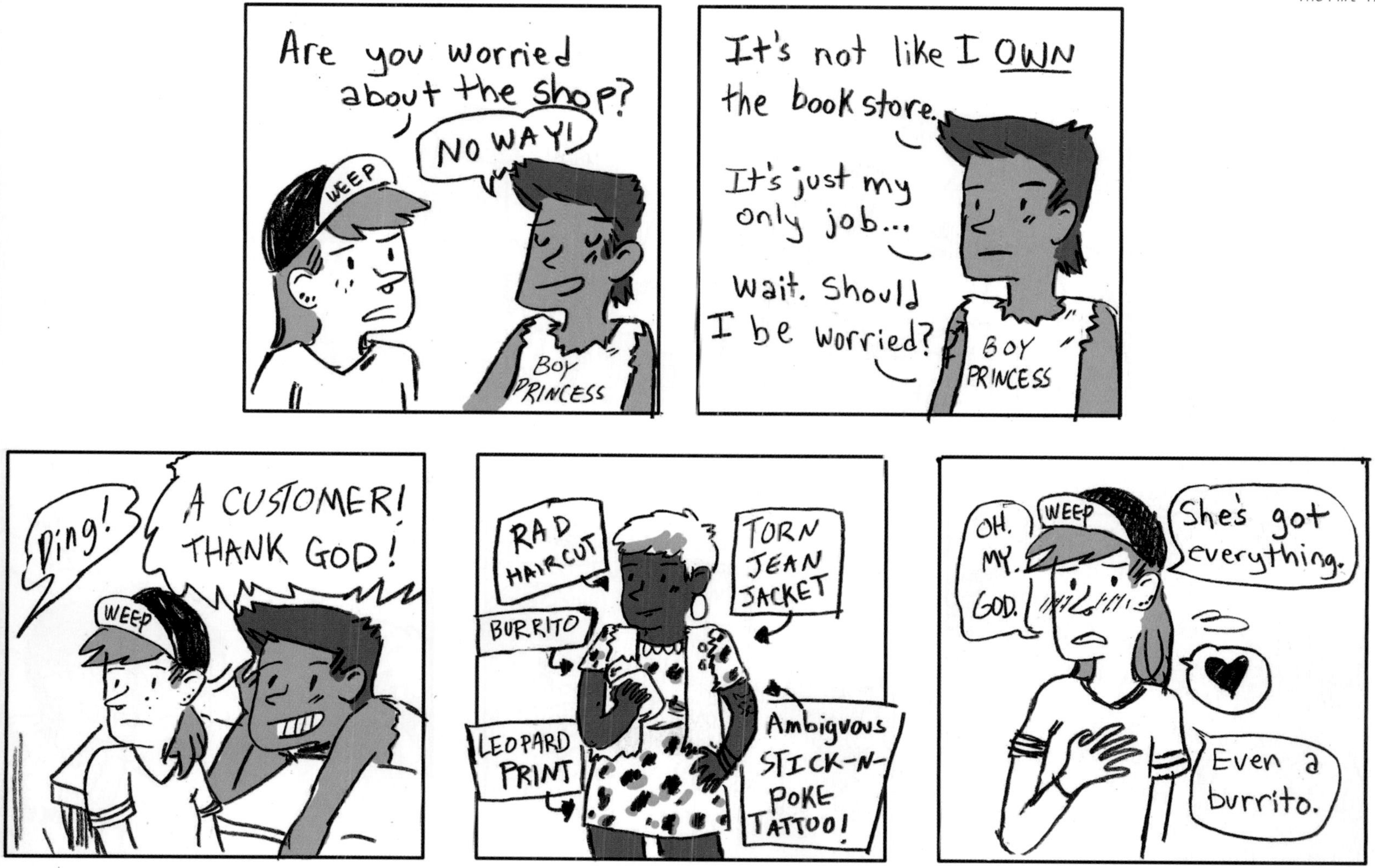
Are you worried about the shop?
NO WAY!
WEEP
BOY PRINCESS
It's not like I OWN the book store.
It's just my only job...
Wait. Should I be worried?
BOY PRINCESS
Ding!
A CUSTOMER! THANK GOD!
WEEP
RAD HAIRCUT
TORN JEAN JACKET
BURRITO
LEOPARD PRINT
Ambiguous STICK-N-POKE TATTOO!
OH. MY. GOD.
WEEP
She's got everything.
Even a burrito.

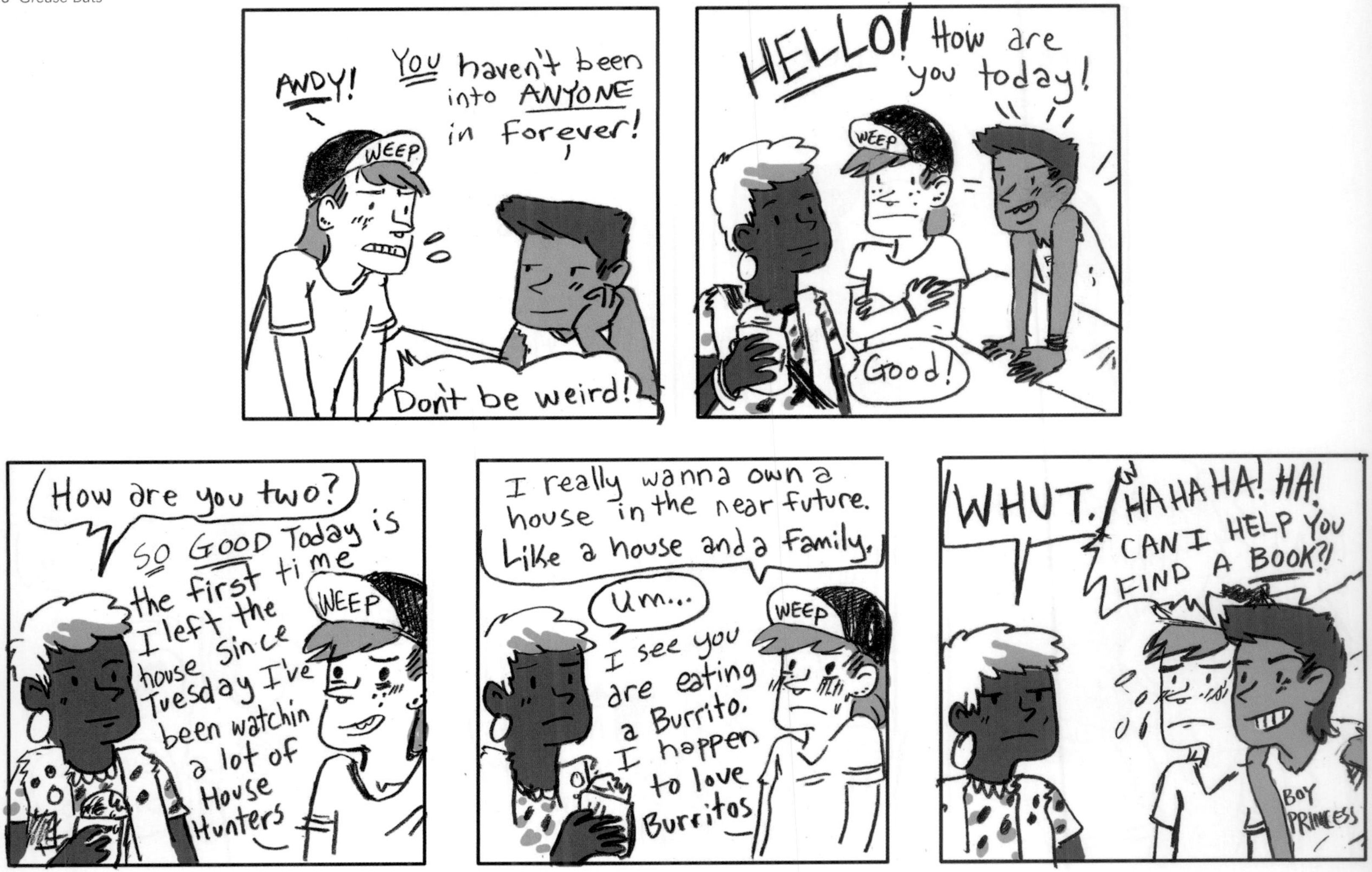
ANDY! YOU haven't been into ANYONE in Forever!
Don't be weird!
HELLO! How are you today!
Good!
How are you two?
SO GOOD Today is the first time I left the house Since Tuesday I've been watchin a lot of House Hunters
WEEP
I really wanna own a house in the near future. Like a house and a family.
Um...
I see you are eating a Burrito. I happen to love Burritos
WHUT.
HAHAHA! HA! CAN I HELP YOU FIND A BOOK?!
BOY PRINCESS

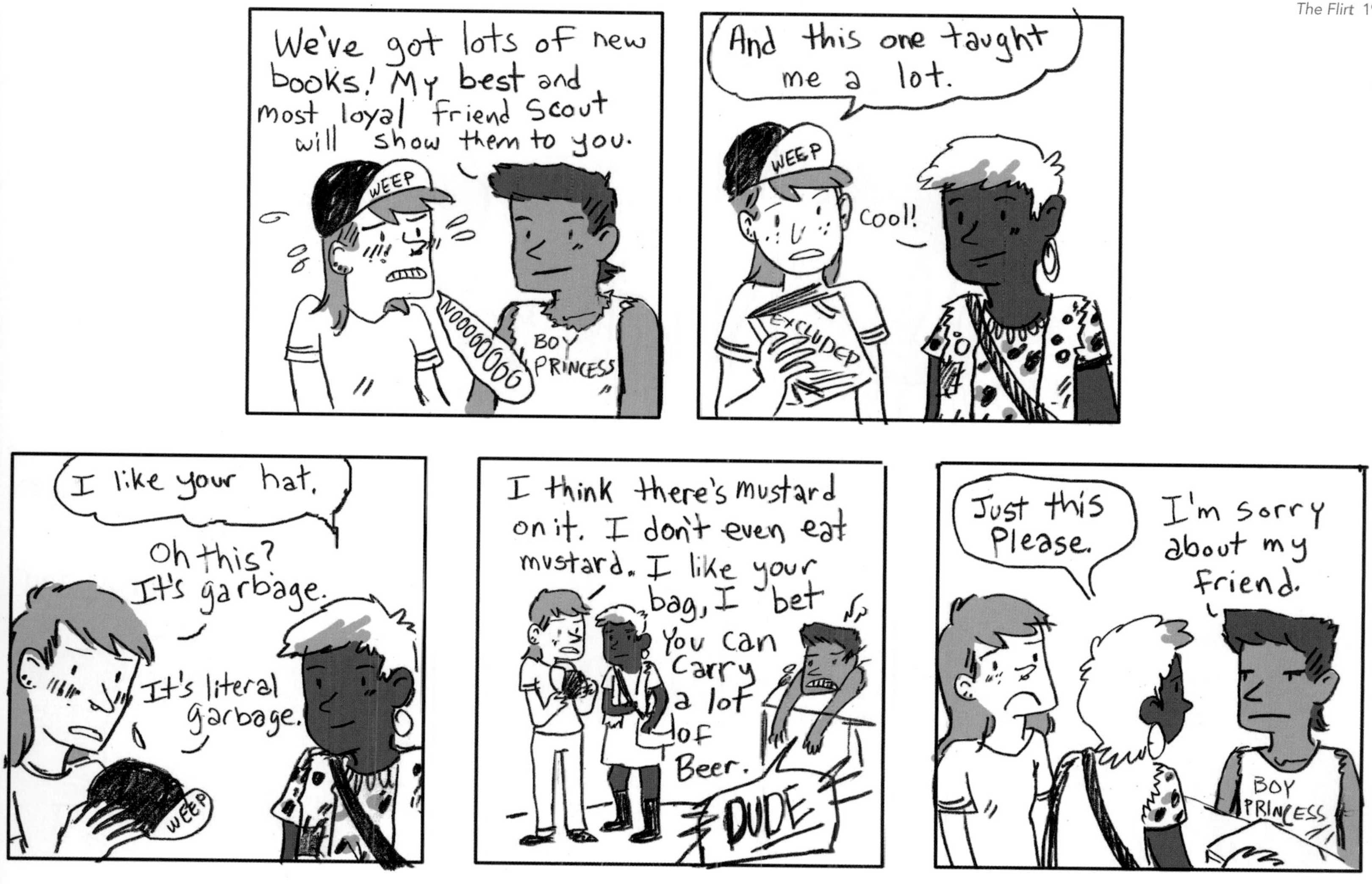
We've got lots of new books! My best and most loyal friend Scout will show them to you.
WEEP
NOOOOOOOO
BOY PRINCESS
And this one taught me a lot.
WEEP
EXCLUDED
Cool!
I like your hat.
Oh this? It's garbage.
It's literal garbage.
WEEP
I think there's mustard on it. I don't even eat mustard. I like your bag, I bet you can carry a lot of Beer.
DUDE
Just this please.
I'm sorry about my friend.
BOY PRINCESS

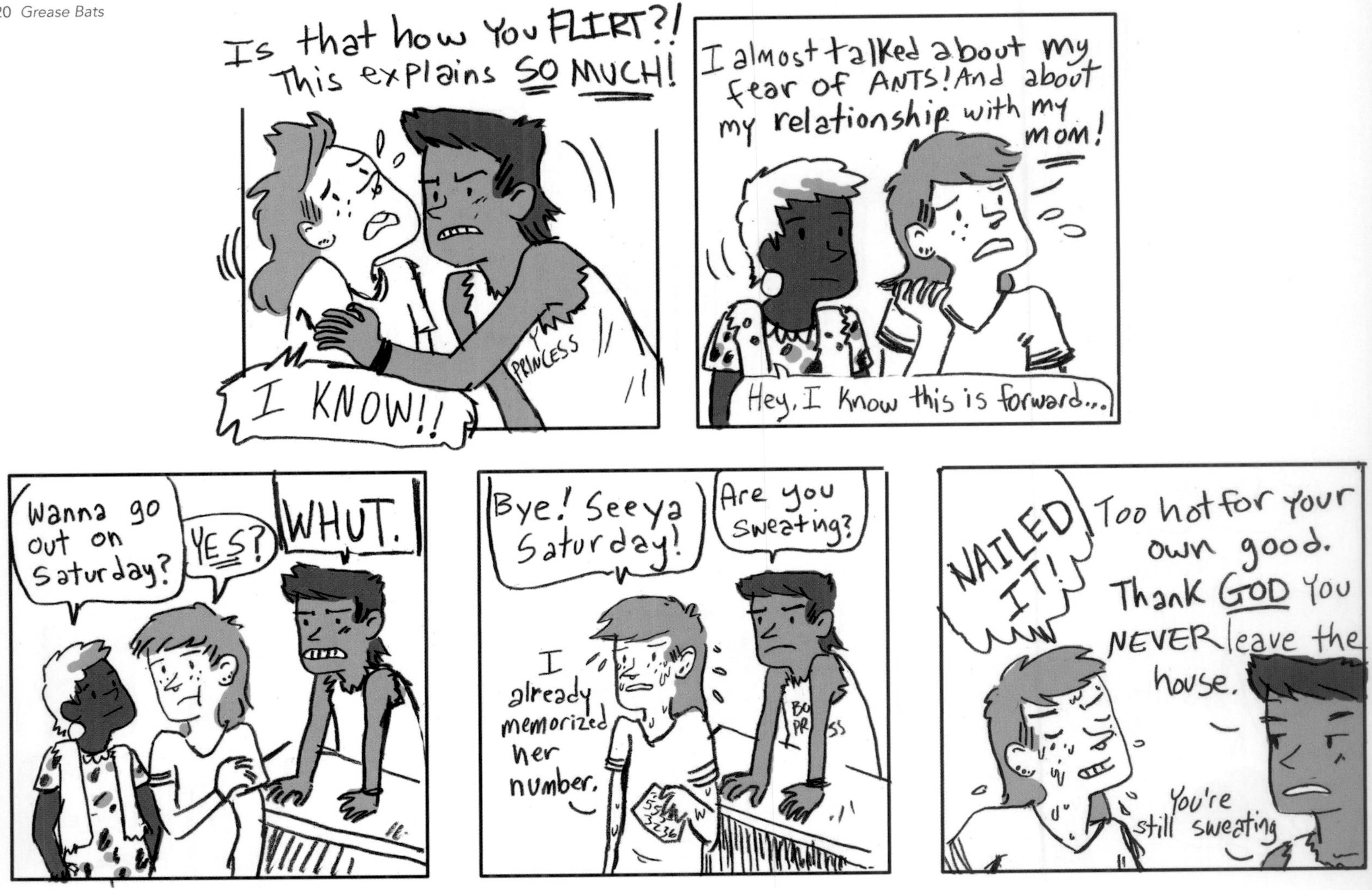
Is that how You FLIRT?! This explains SO MUCH!
I KNOW!!
YOU'RE MY PRINCESS
I almost talked about my fear of ANTS! And about my relationship with my mom!
Hey, I know this is forward...
Wanna go out on Saturday?
YES?
WHUT.
Bye! Seeya Saturday!
Are you sweating?
I already memorized her number.
555 3236
NAILED IT!
Too hot for your own good. Thank GOD You NEVER leave the house.
You're still sweating

A Case of the Floppies

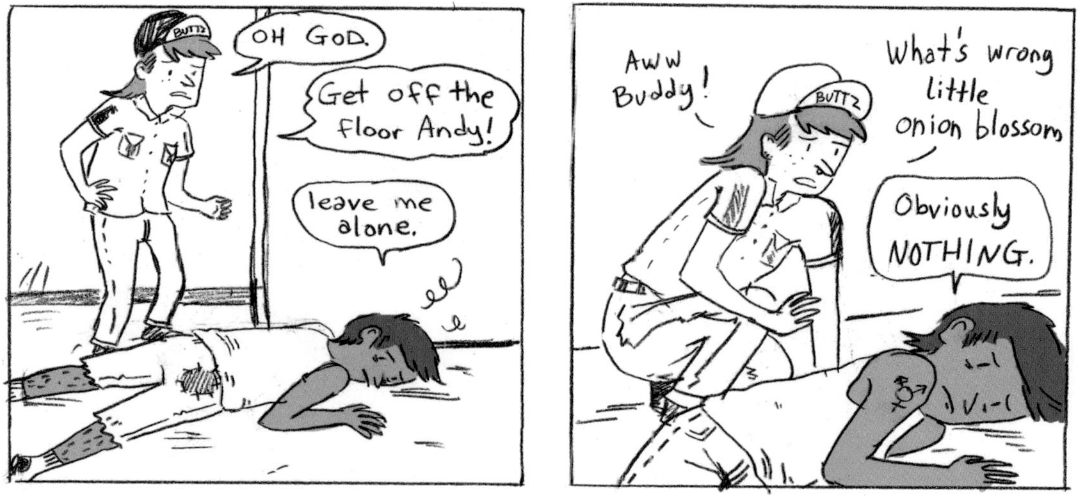
OH GOD.
Get off the floor Andy!
leave me alone.
AWW Buddy!
What's wrong little onion blossom
Obviously NOTHING.

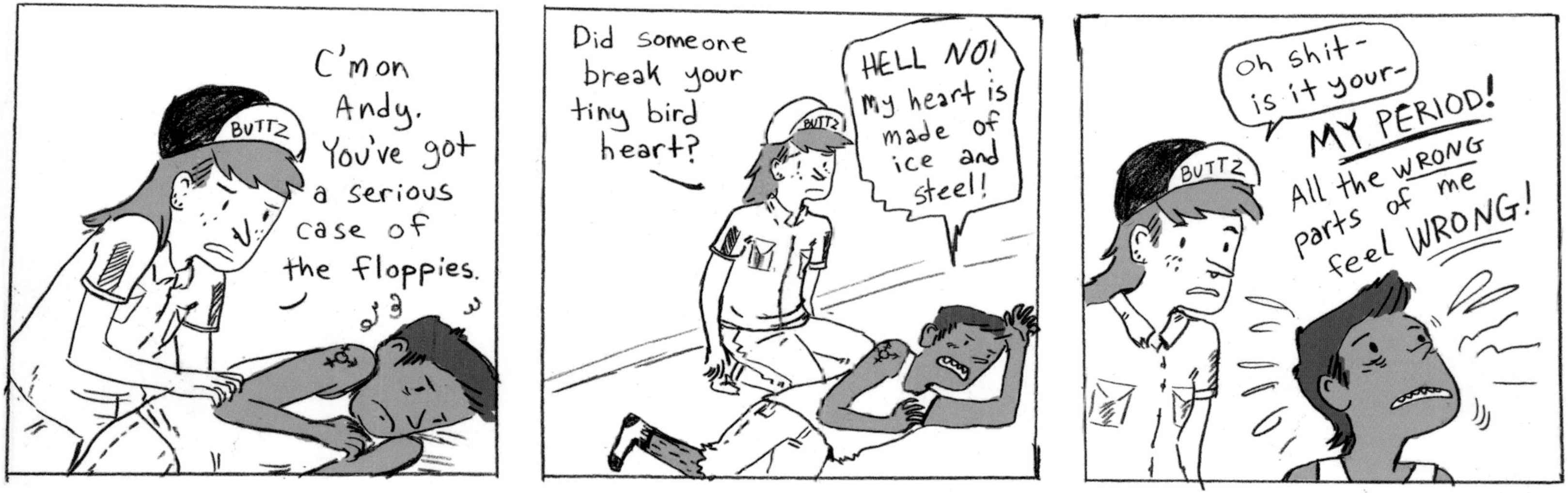
C'mon Andy. You've got a serious case of the floppies.
Did someone break your tiny bird heart?
HELL NO! My heart is made of ice and steel!
Oh shit- is it your-
MY PERIOD! All the WRONG parts of me feel WRONG!

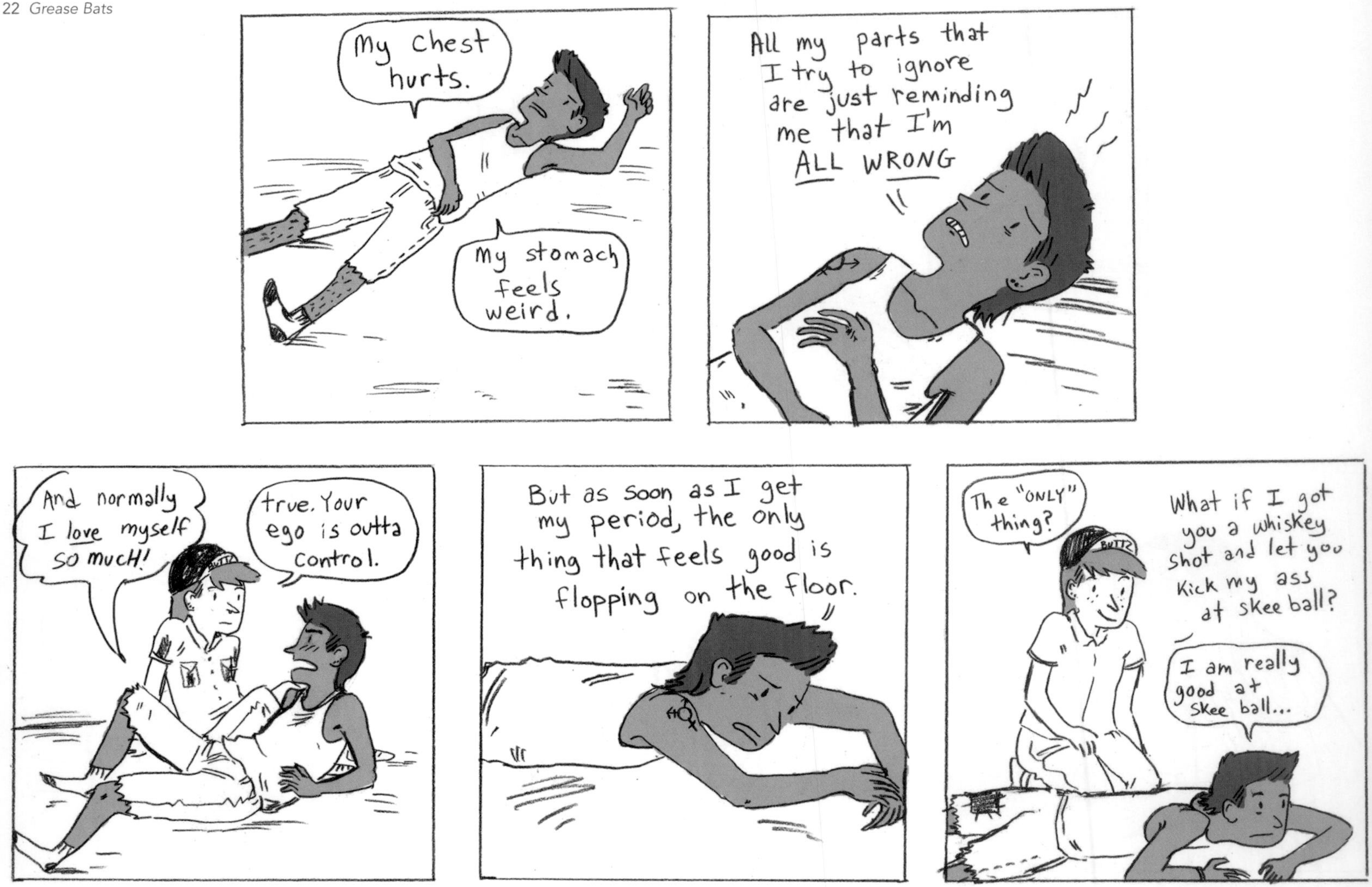
My chest hurts.
My stomach feels weird.
All my parts that I try to ignore are just reminding me that I'm ALL WRONG
And normally I love myself so much!
true. Your ego is outta control.
But as soon as I get my period, the only thing that feels good is flopping on the floor.
The "ONLY" thing?
What if I got you a whiskey shot and let you kick my ass at skee ball?
I am really good at skee ball...
BUTTZ

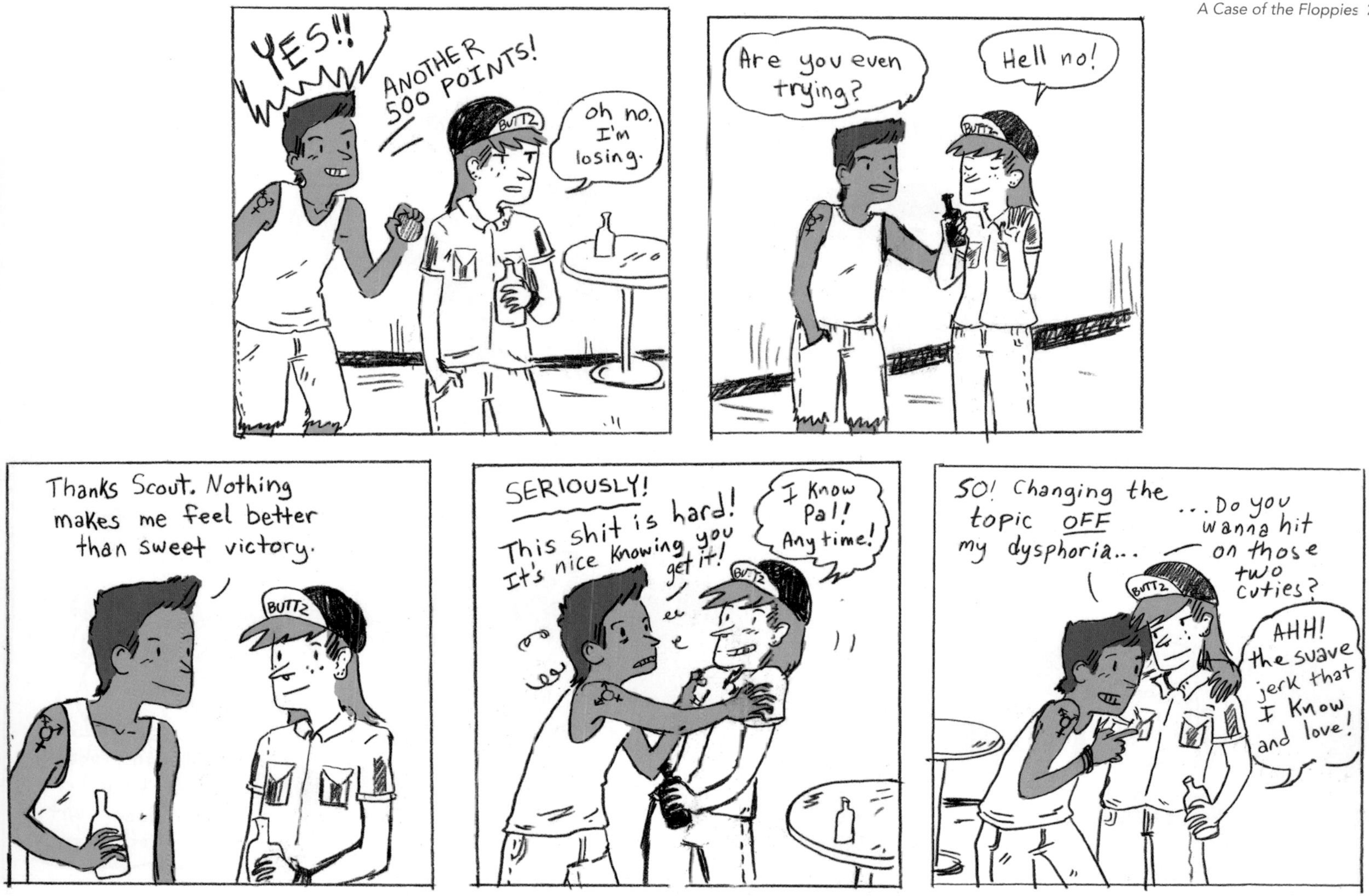
YES!!
ANOTHER 500 POINTS!
oh no. I'm losing.
Are you even trying?
Hell no!
Thanks Scout. Nothing makes me feel better than sweet victory.
SERIOUSLY! This shit is hard! It's nice knowing you get it!
I know Pal! Any time!
SO! Changing the topic OFF my dysphoria...
...Do you wanna hit on those two cuties?
AHH! the suave jerk that I know and love!

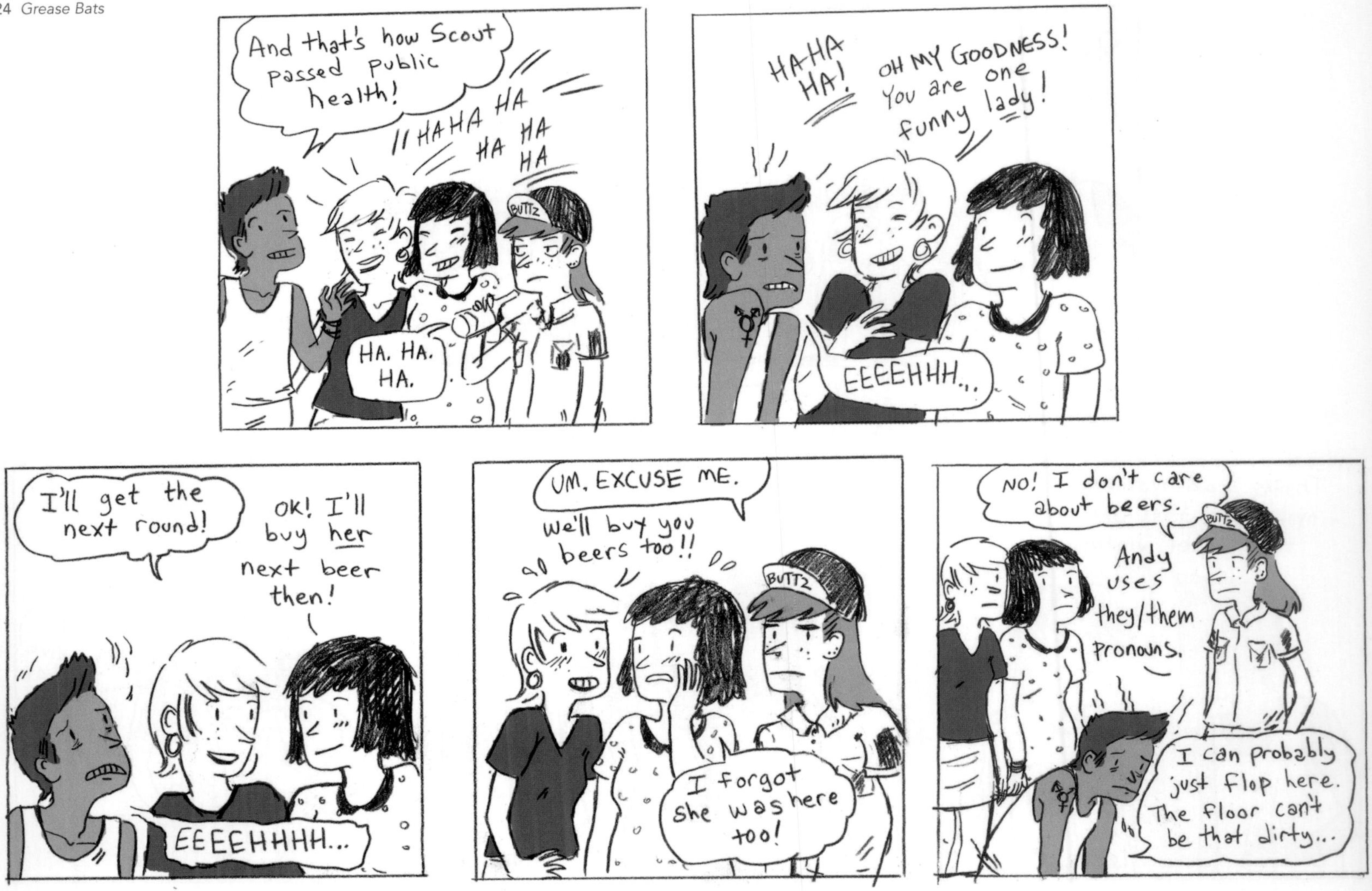
And that's how Scout passed public health!
HAHA HA HA HA HA HA
HA. HA. HA.
HAHA HA!
OH MY GOODNESS! You are one funny lady!
EEEEHHH...
I'll get the next round!
OK! I'll buy her next beer then!
EEEEHHHH...
UM, EXCUSE ME.
We'll buy you beers too!!
I forgot she was here too!
NO! I don't care about beers.
Andy uses they/them pronouns.
I can probably just flop here. The floor can't be that dirty...

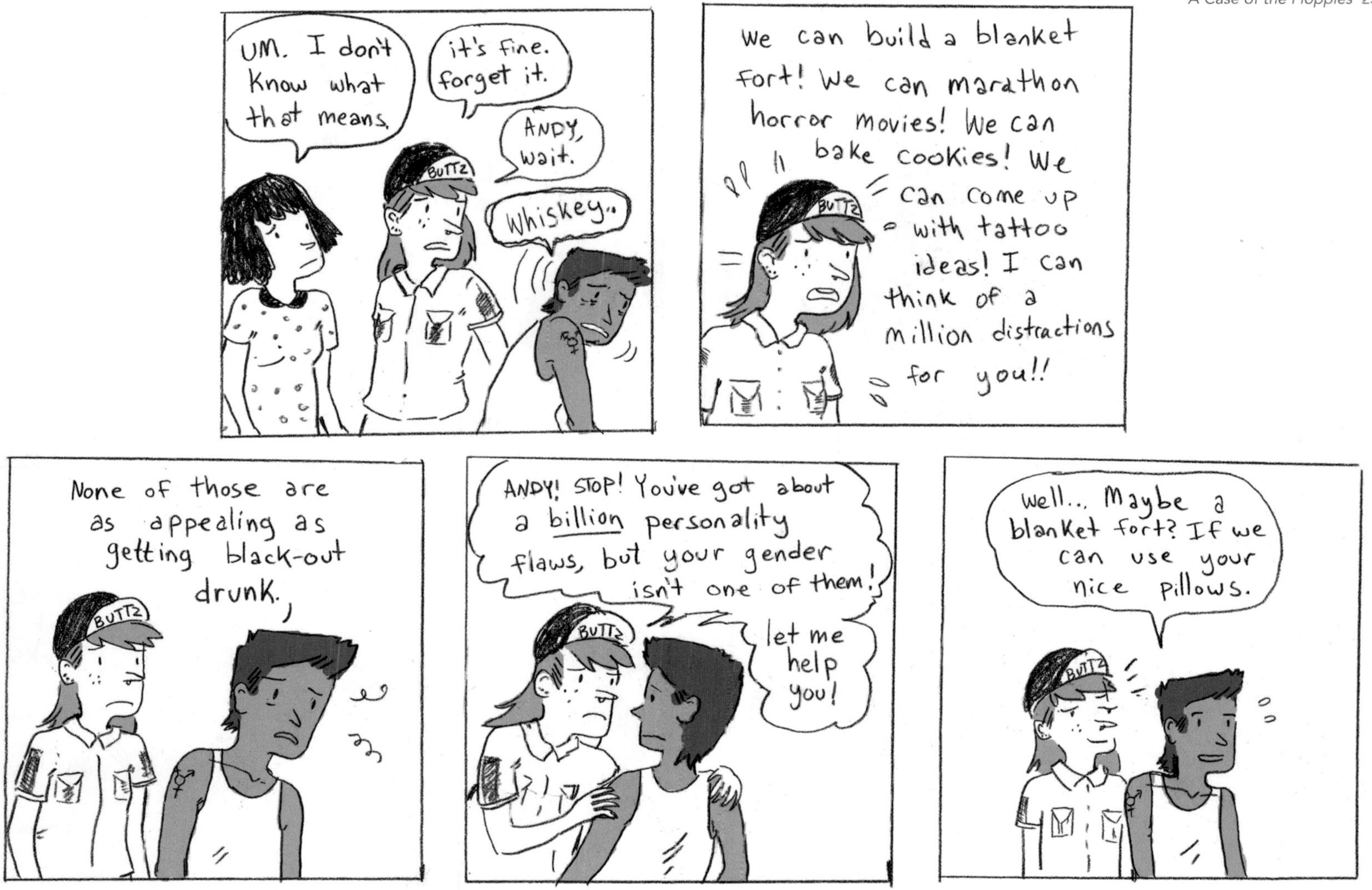
UM. I don't Know what that means.
it's fine. forget it.
ANDY, wait.
Whiskey..
We can build a blanket fort! We can marathon horror movies! We can bake cookies! We can come up with tattoo ideas! I can think of a million distractions for you!!
None of those are as appealing as getting black-out drunk.
ANDY! STOP! You've got about a billion personality flaws, but your gender isn't one of them!
let me help you!
Well... Maybe a blanket fort? If we can use your nice pillows.
BUTTZ

V-Day

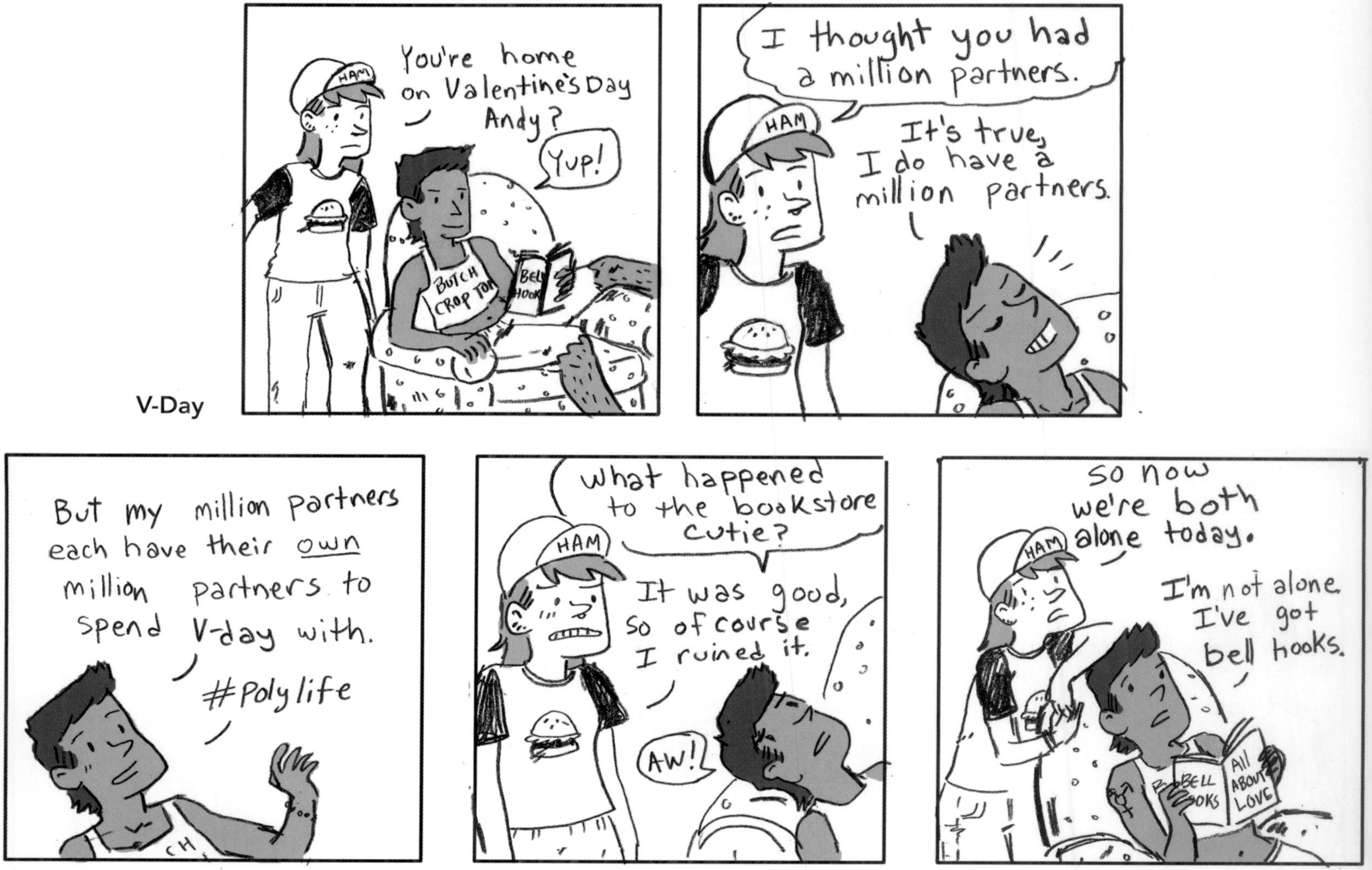
HAM
You're home on Valentine's Day Andy?
Yup!
BUTCH CROP TOP
I thought you had a million partners.
HAM
It's true, I do have a million partners.
But my million partners each have their own million partners to spend V-day with.
#Polylife
HAM
What happened to the bookstore cutie?
It was good, so of course I ruined it.
AW!
HAM
So now we're both alone today.
I'm not alone. I've got bell hooks.
ALL ABOUT LOVE

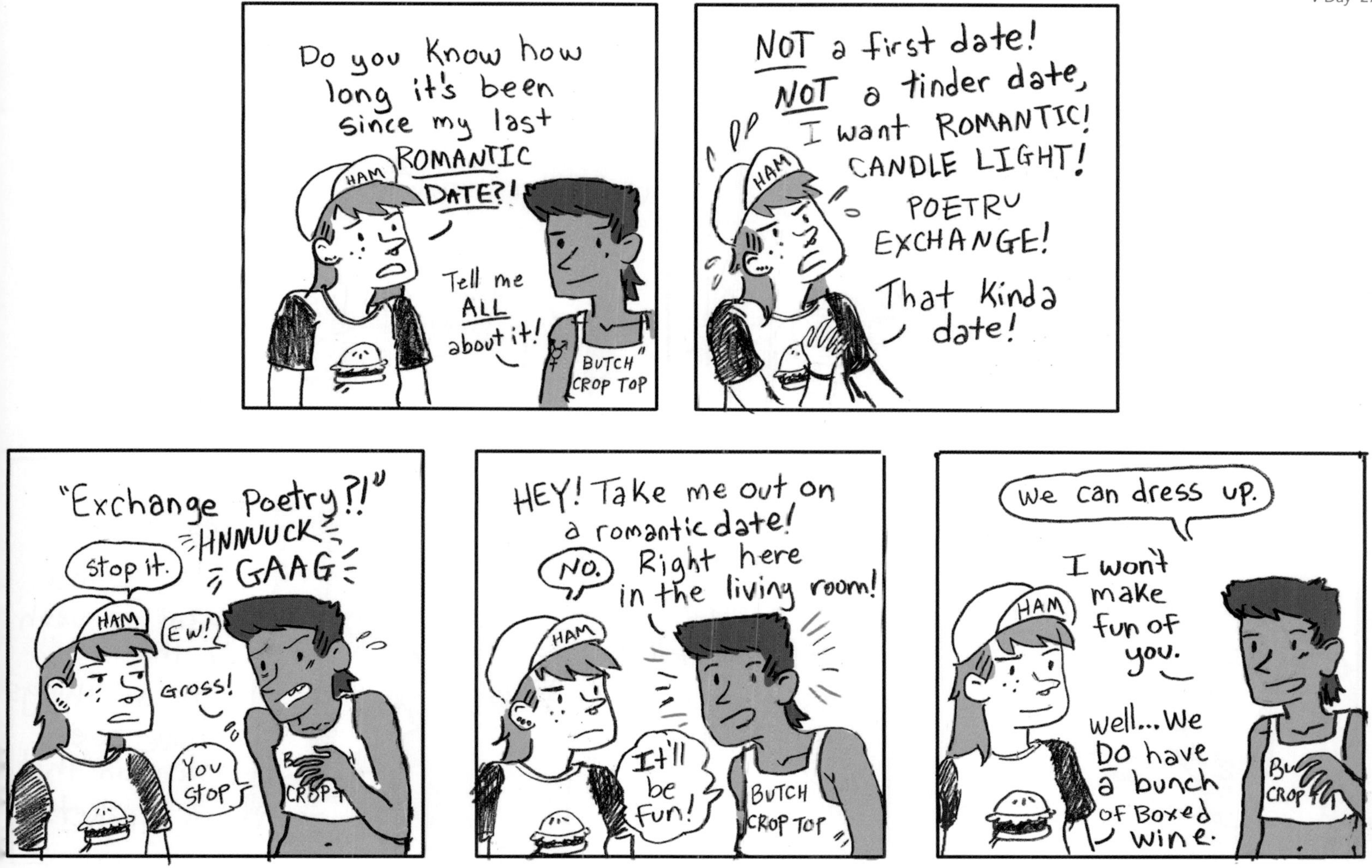
Do you Know how long it's been since my last ROMANTIC DATE?!
HAM
Tell me ALL about it!
"BUTCH" CROP TOP
NOT a first date! NOT a tinder date, I want ROMANTIC! CANDLE LIGHT! POETRU EXCHANGE!
That Kinda date!
HAM
"Exchange Poetry?!"
HNNUUCK GAAG
Stop it.
HAM
Ew!
Gross!
You stop
CROP-T
HEY! Take me out on a romantic date!
NO.
Right here in the living room!
HAM
It'll be fun!
BUTCH CROP TOP
We can dress up.
I won't make fun of you.
HAM
well... We DO have a bunch of Boxed wine.
BU CROP

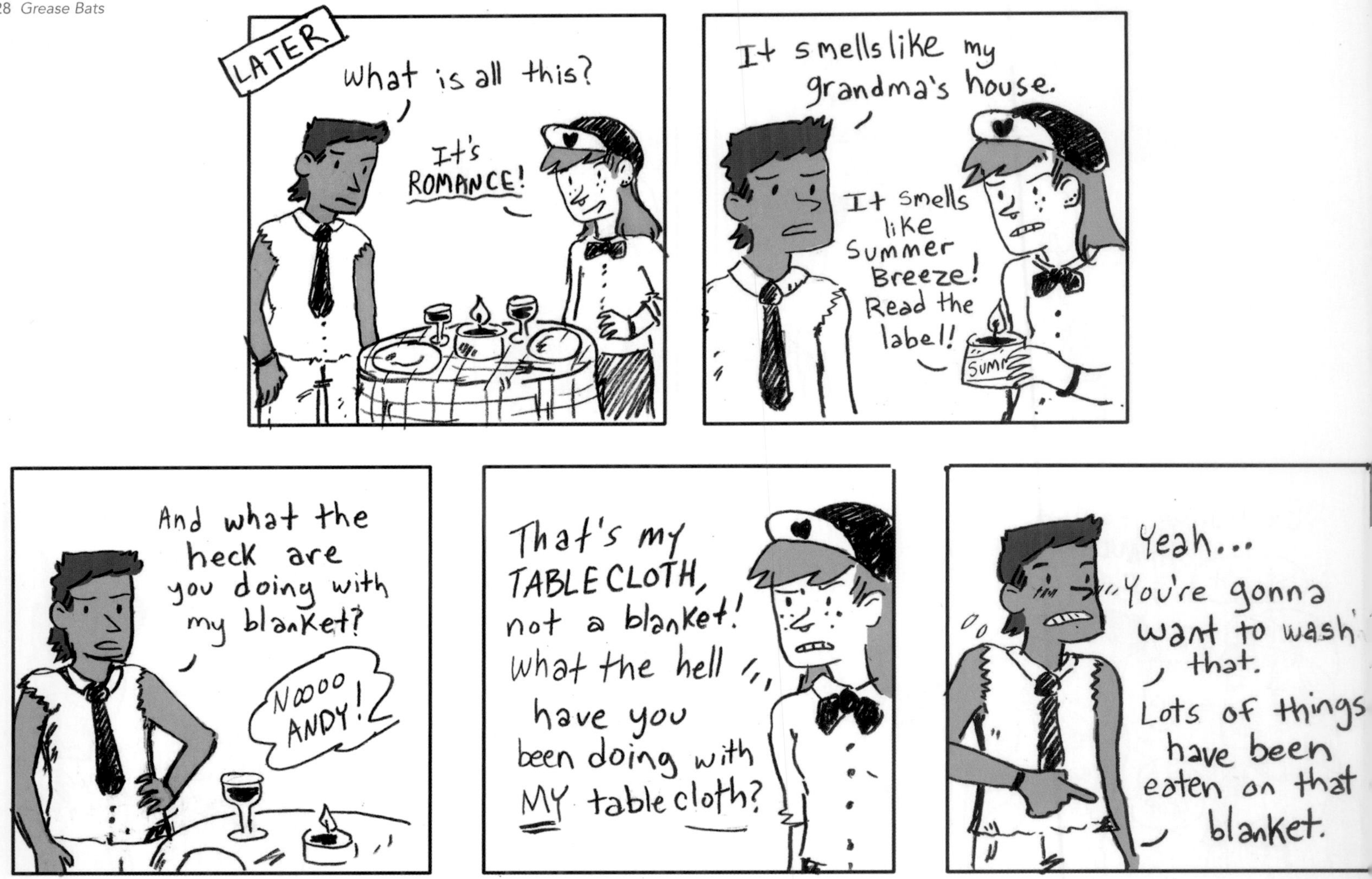
LATER
What is all this?
It's ROMANCE!
It smells like my grandma's house.
It smells like Summer Breeze! Read the label!!
SUMM
And what the heck are you doing with my blanket?
NOOOO ANDY!
That's my TABLECLOTH, not a blanket! What the hell have you been doing with MY tablecloth?
Yeah... You're gonna want to wash that.
Lots of things have been eaten on that blanket.

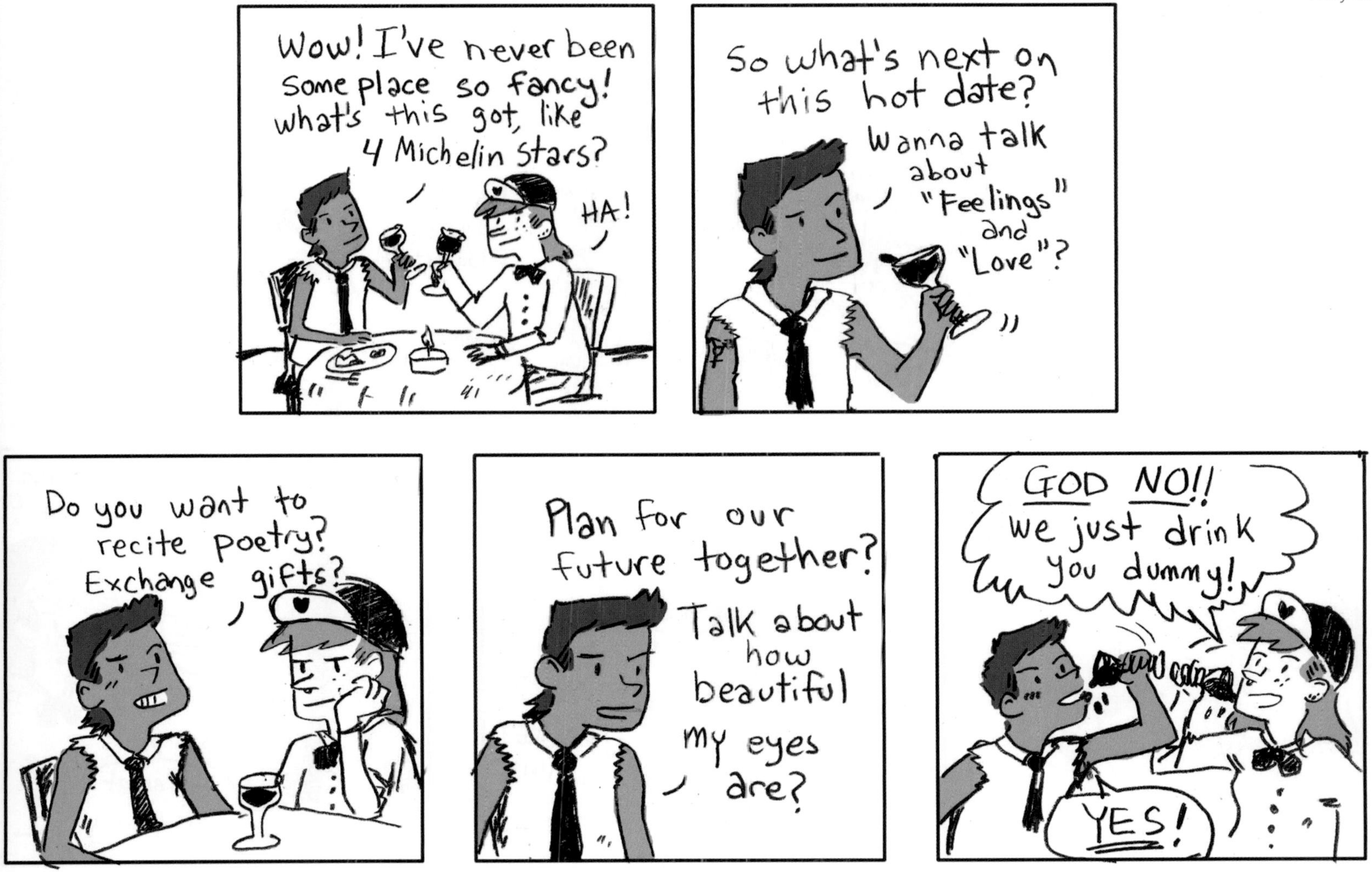

Wow! I've never been some place so fancy! what's this got, like 4 Michelin stars?
HA!
So what's next on this hot date?
Wanna talk about "Feelings" and "Love"?
Do you want to recite poetry? Exchange gifts?
Plan for our future together?
Talk about how beautiful my eyes are?
GOD NO!! We just drink you dummy!
YES!

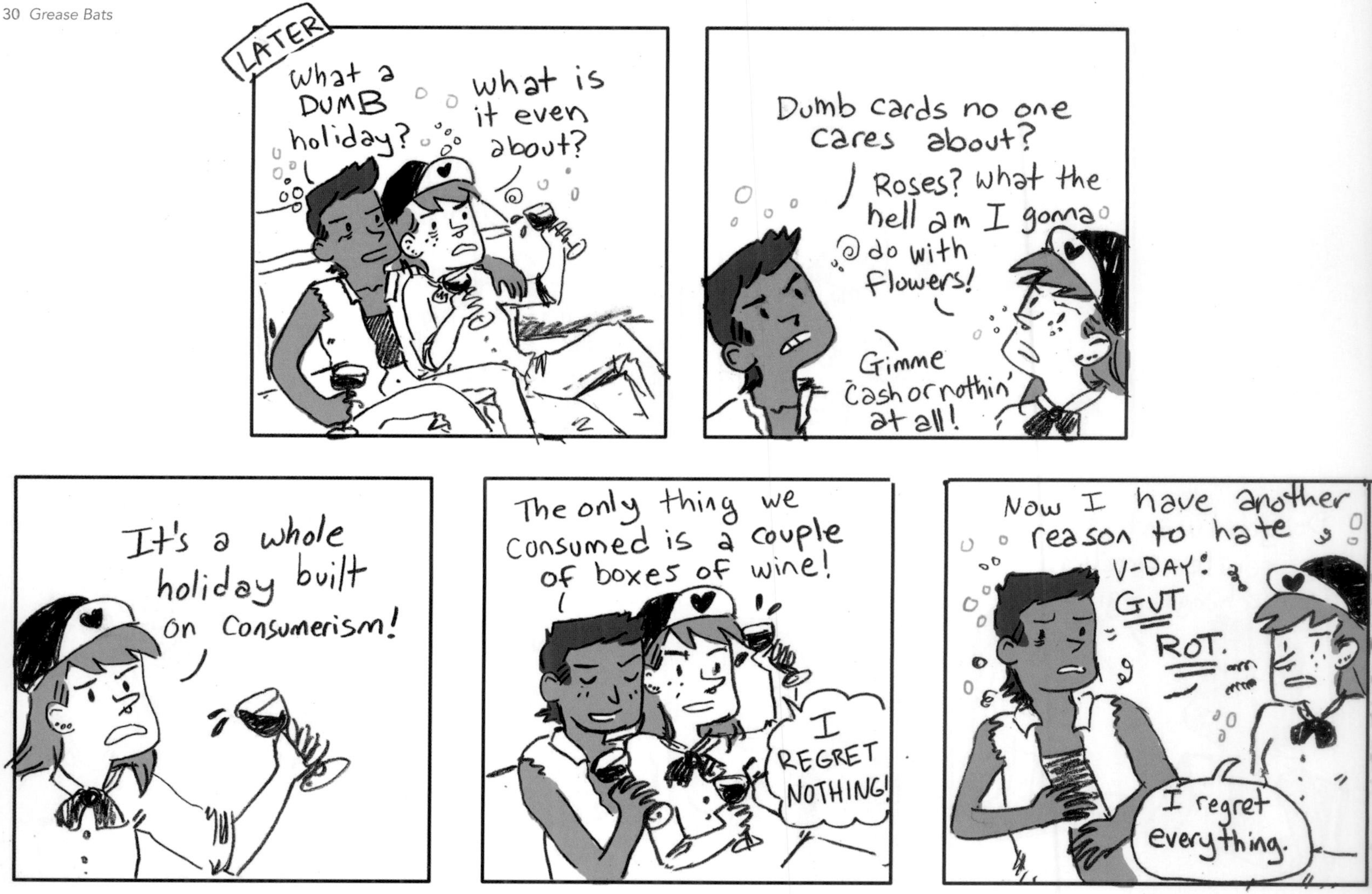
LATER
What a DUMB holiday?
what is it even about?
Dumb cards no one cares about?
Roses? what the hell am I gonna do with flowers!
Gimme cash or nothin' at all!
It's a whole holiday built on consumerism!
The only thing we consumed is a couple of boxes of wine!
I REGRET NOTHING!
Now I have another reason to hate V-DAY: GUT ROT.
I regret everything.

Puzzle

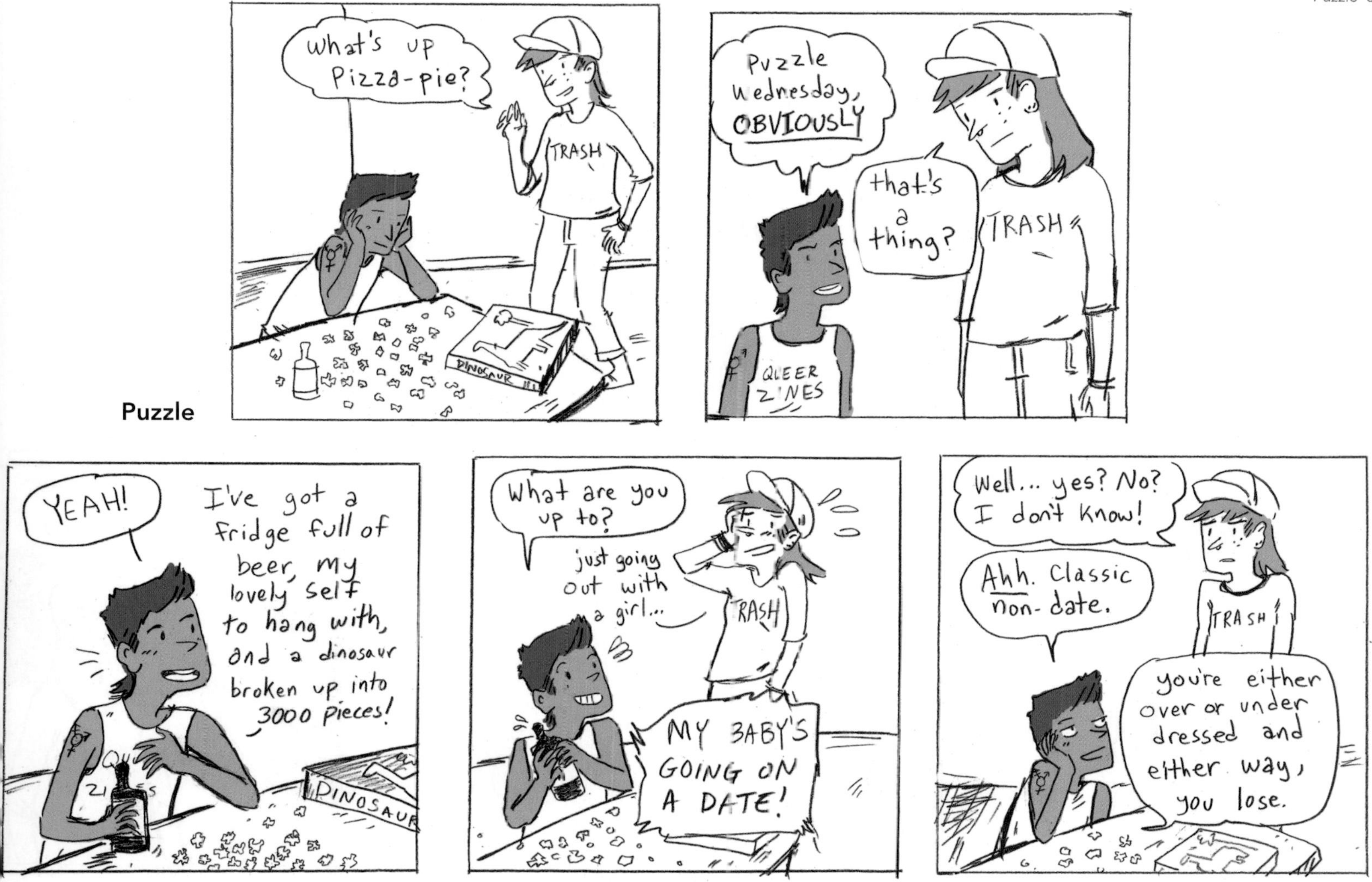
what's up Pizza-pie?
TRASH
DINOSAUR
Puzzle wednesday, OBVIOUSLY
that's a thing?
TRASH
QUEER ZINES
YEAH!
I've got a fridge full of beer, my lovely self to hang with, and a dinosaur broken up into 3000 pieces!
DINOSAUR
What are you up to?
just going out with a girl...
TRASH
MY BABY'S GOING ON A DATE!
Well... yes? No? I don't know!
Ahh. Classic non-date.
TRASH
you're either over or under dressed and either way, you lose.

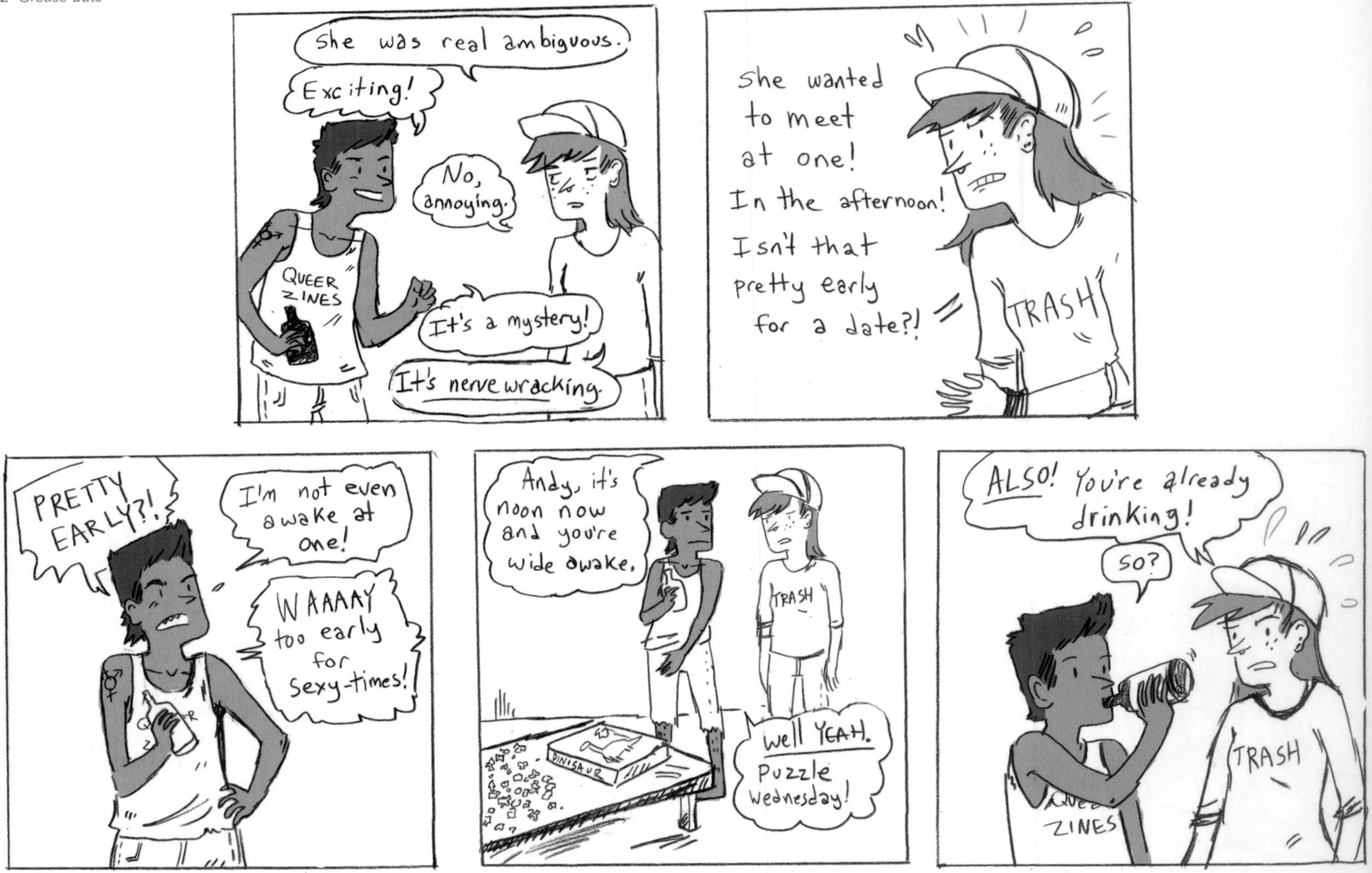
She was real ambiguous.
Exciting!
No, annoying.
It's a mystery!
It's nerve wracking.
QUEER ZINES
She wanted to meet at one! In the afternoon! Isn't that pretty early for a date?!
TRASH
PRETTY EARLY?!
I'm not even awake at one!
WAAAAY too early for sexy-times!
Andy, it's noon now and you're wide awake.
well YEAH. Puzzle Wednesday!
DINISAUR
TRASH
ALSO! You're already drinking!
SO?
ZINES
TRASH

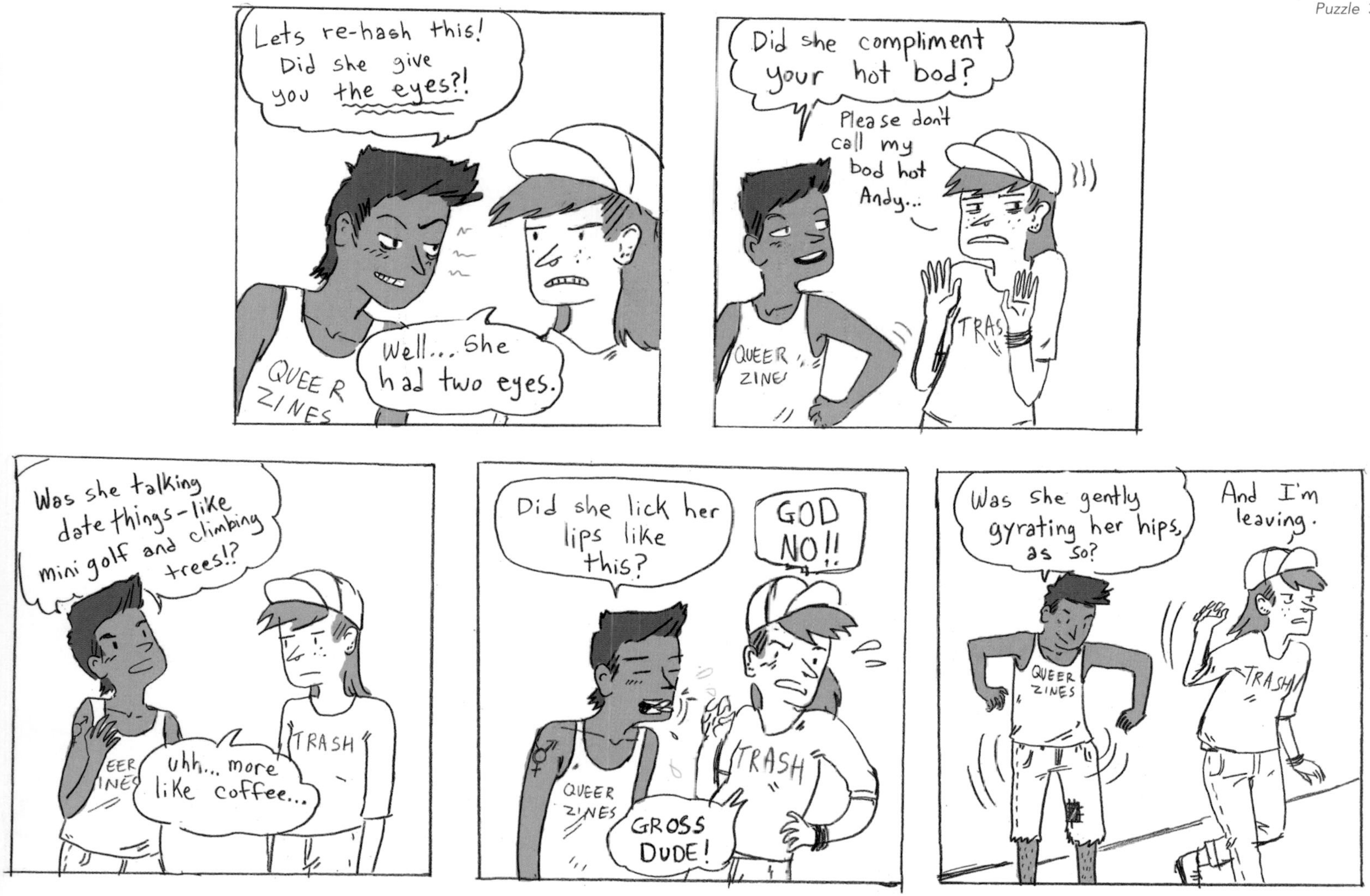
Lets re-hash this! Did she give you the eyes?!
Well... She had two eyes.
Did she compliment your hot bod?
Please don't call my bod hot Andy...
TRAS
QUEER ZINES
Was she talking date things - like mini golf and climbing trees!?
uhh... more like coffee...
TRASH
Did she lick her lips like this?
GOD NO!!
GROSS DUDE!
TRASH
QUEER ZINES
Was she gently gyrating her hips, as so?
And I'm leaving.
QUEER ZINES
TRASH

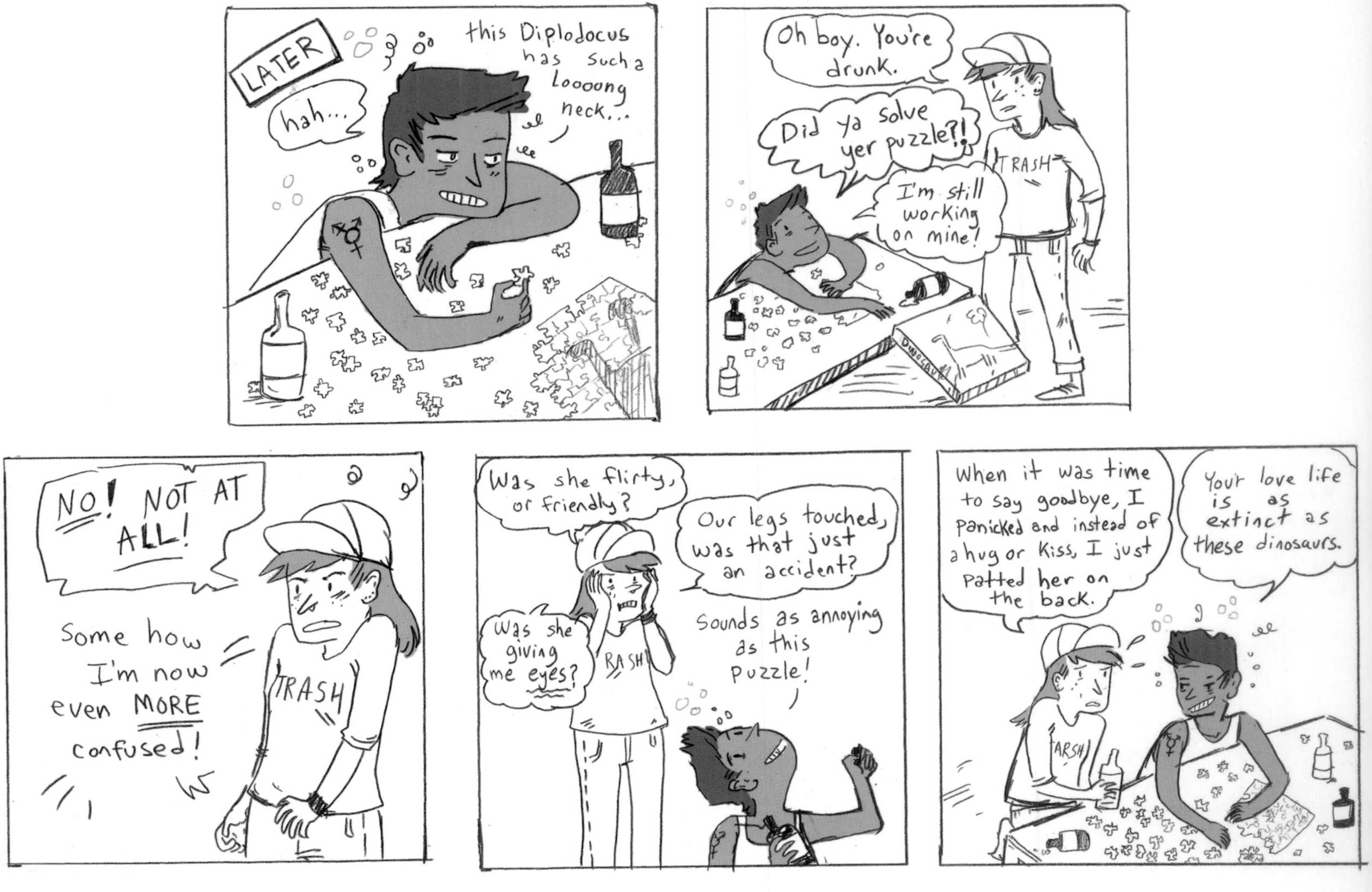
LATER
hah...
this Diplodocus has such a loooong neck...
Oh boy. You're drunk.
Did ya solve yer puzzle?!
I'm still working on mine!
TRASH
NO! NOT AT ALL!
Some how I'm now even MORE confused!
TRASH
Was she flirty, or friendly?
Our legs touched, was that just an accident?
Was she giving me eyes?
Sounds as annoying as this puzzle!
When it was time to say goodbye, I panicked and instead of a hug or kiss, I just patted her on the back.
Your love life is as extinct as these dinosaurs.

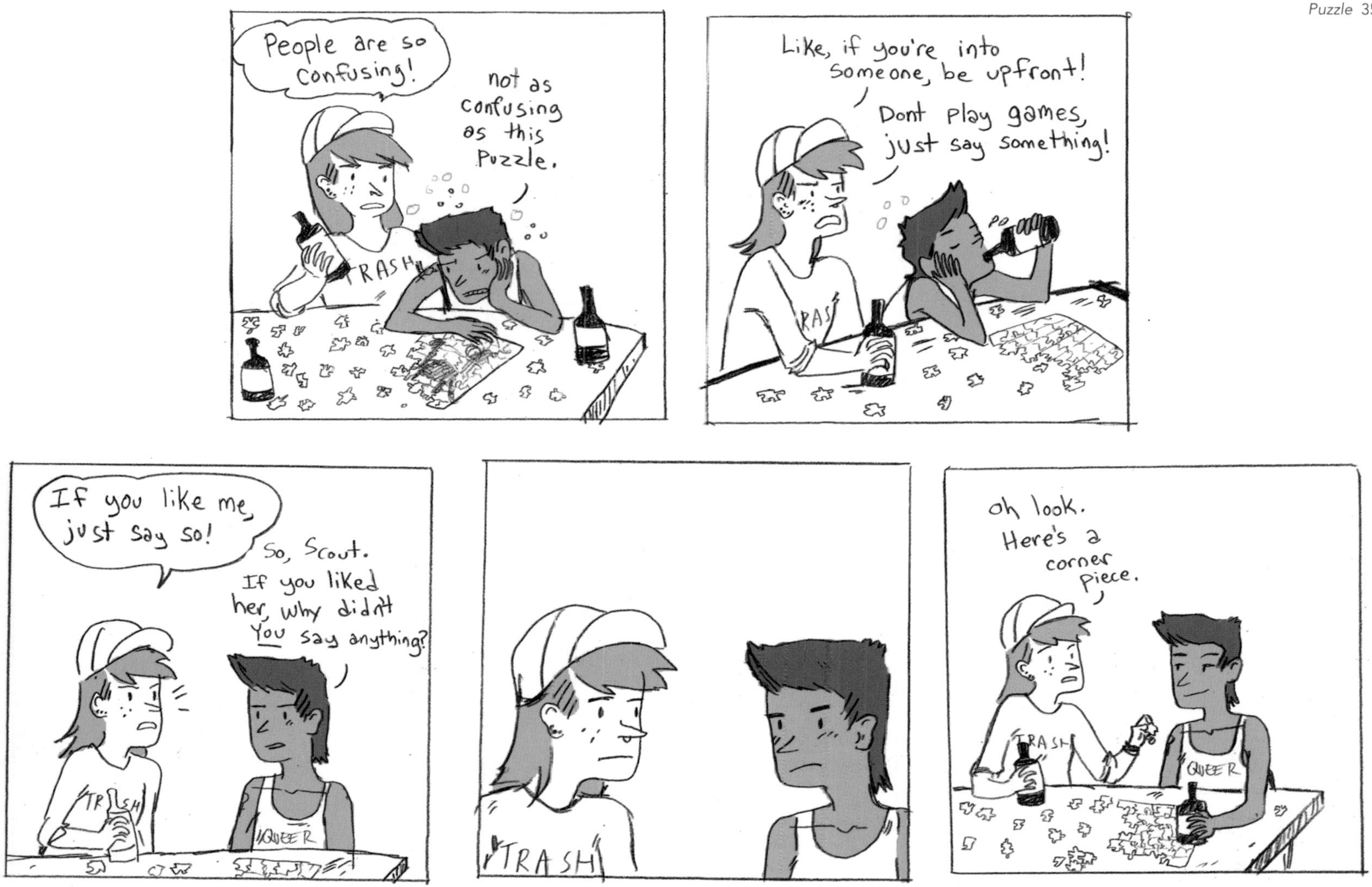
People are so confusing!
not as confusing as this Puzzle.
TRASH
Like, if you're into someone, be upfront!
Dont play games, just say something!
RAS
If you like me, just say so!
So, Scout. If you liked her, why didn't YOU say anything?
TR SH
QUEER
TRASH
oh look. Here's a corner piece.
TRASH
QUEER

Sexy Cowboy

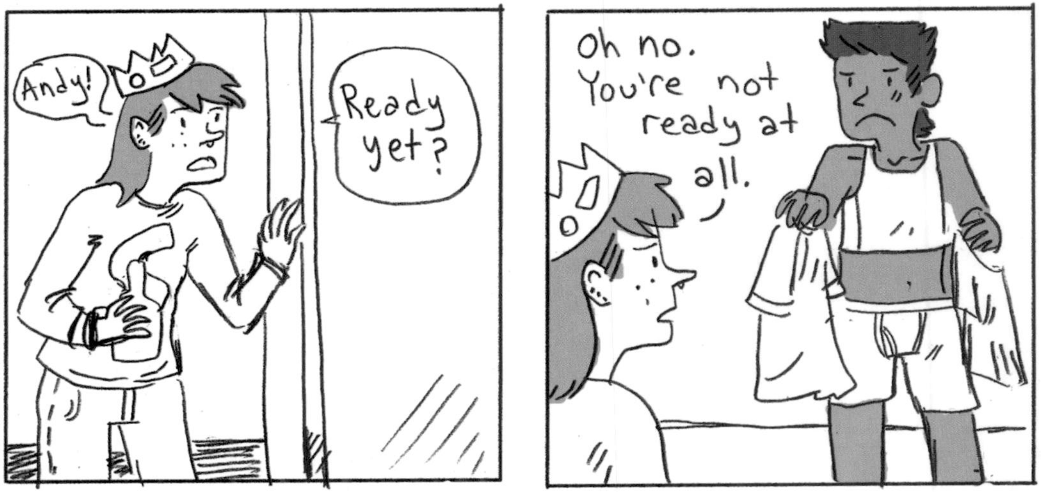
Andy!
Ready yet?
Oh no. You're not ready at all.

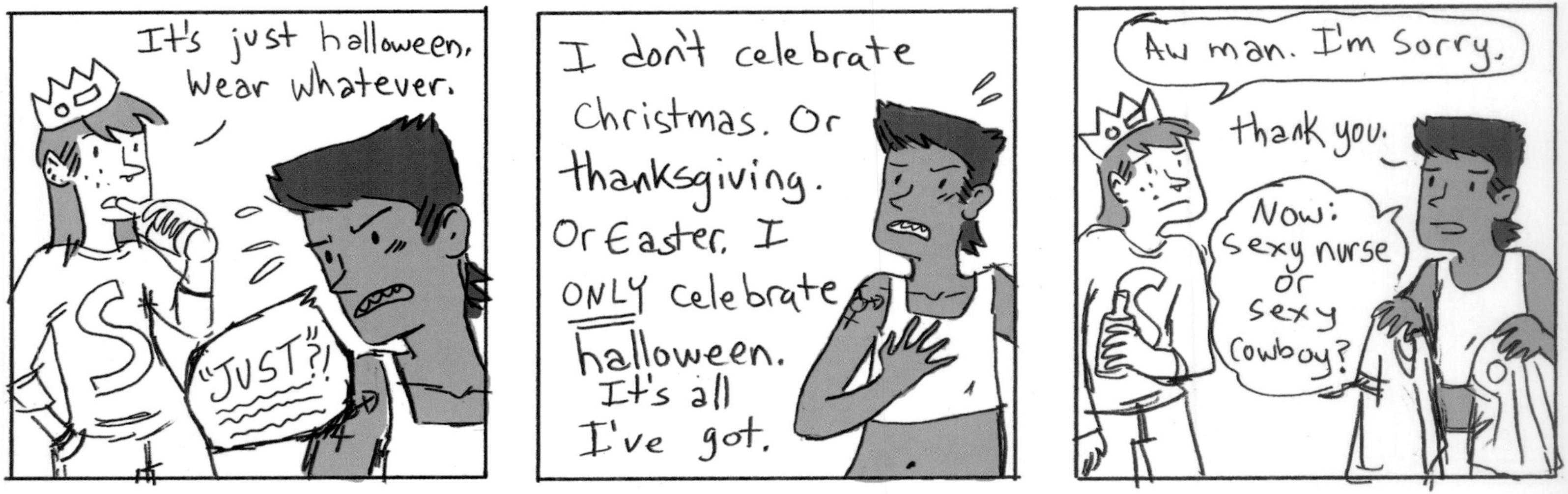
It's just halloween, wear whatever.
"JUST?!"
I don't celebrate Christmas. Or thanksgiving. Or Easter. I ONLY celebrate halloween. It's all I've got.
Aw man. I'm sorry.
thank you.
Now: sexy nurse or sexy cowboy?

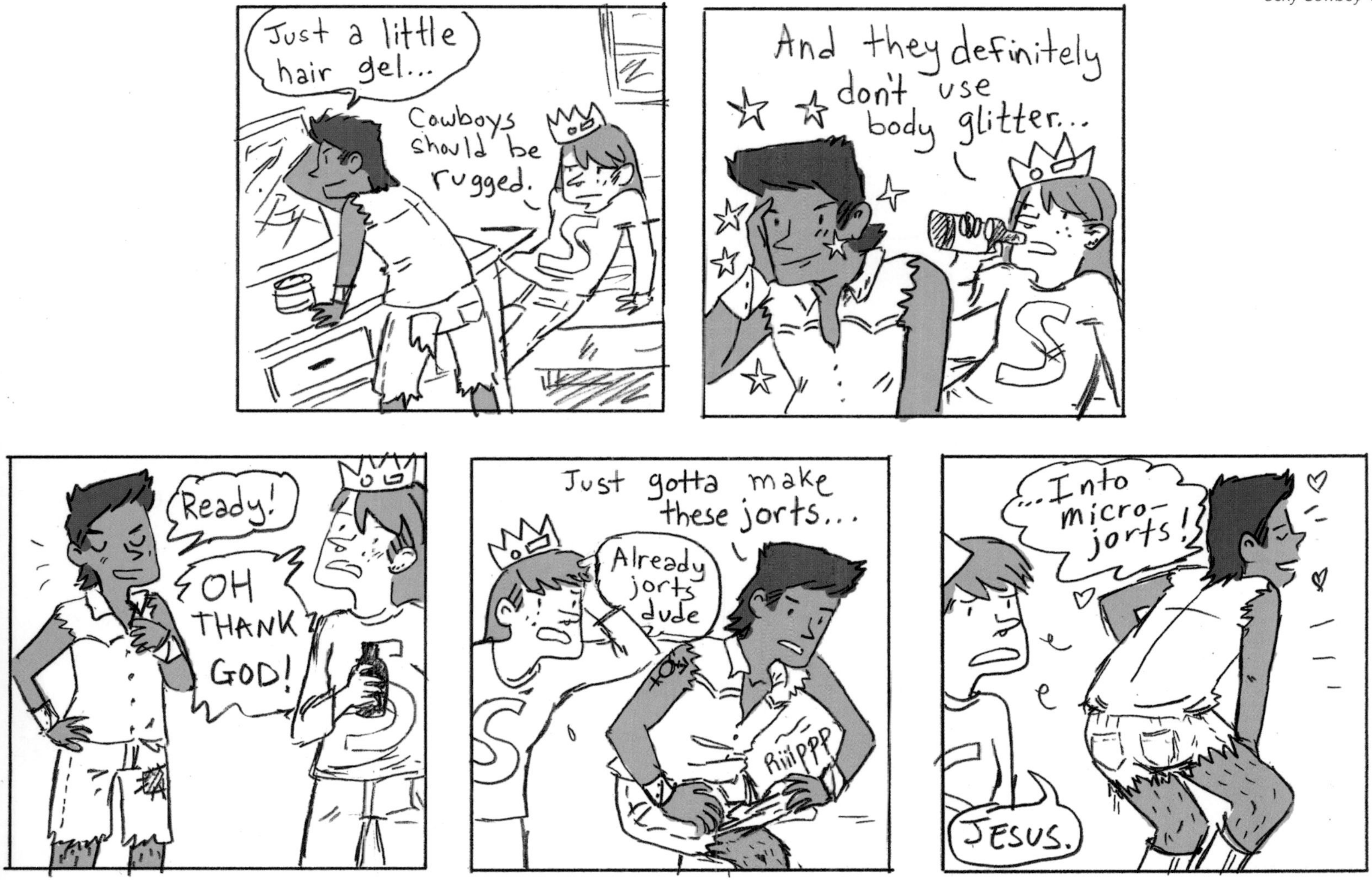
Just a little hair gel...
Cowboys should be rugged.
And they definitely don't use body glitter...
Ready!
OH THANK GOD!
Just gotta make these jorts...
Already jorts dude
Riiippp
...Into micro-jorts!
JESUS.

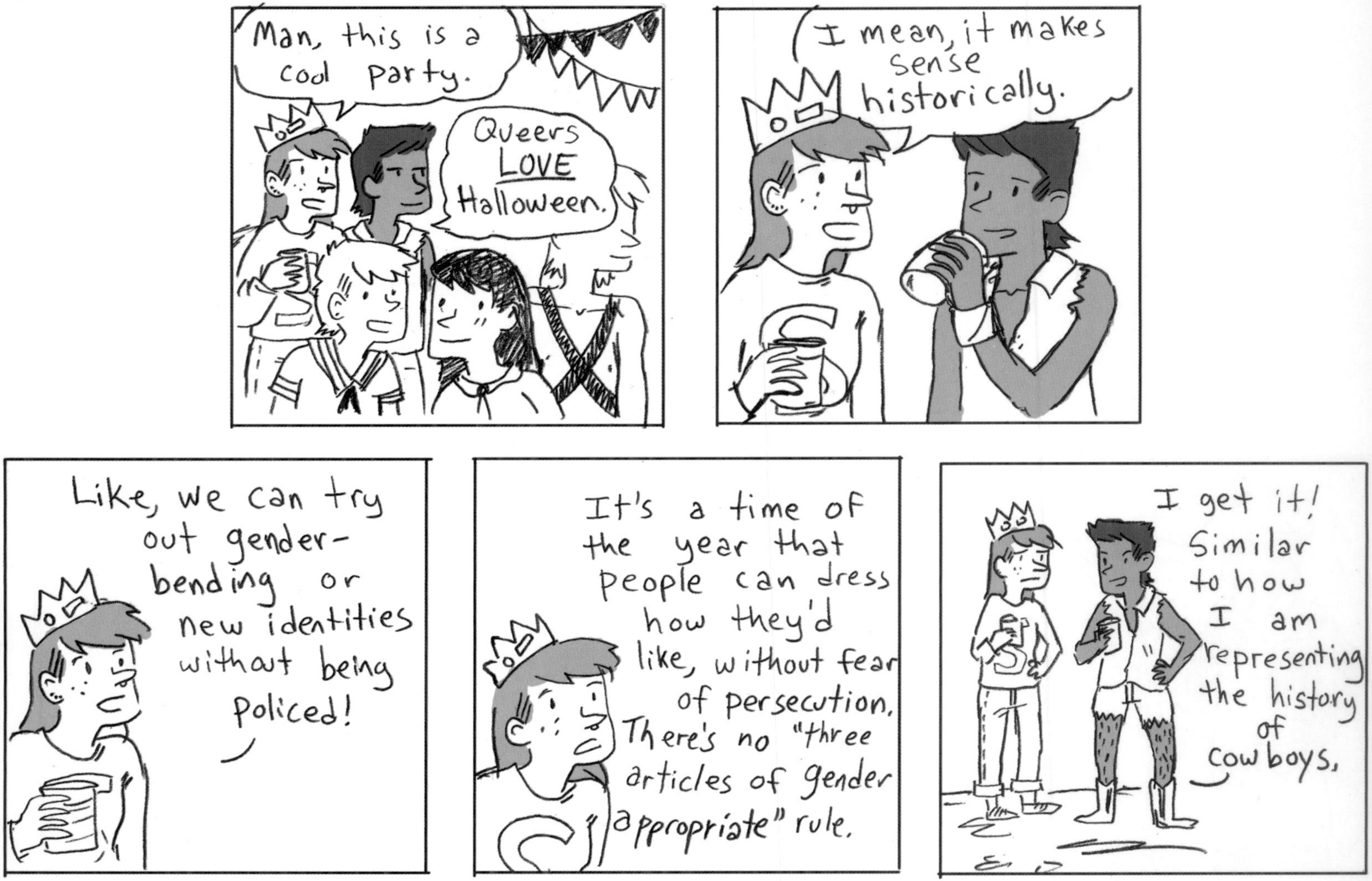
Man, this is a cool party.
Queers LOVE Halloween.
I mean, it makes sense historically.
Like, we can try out gender-bending or new identities without being policed!
It's a time of the year that people can dress how they'd like, without fear of persecution. There's no "three articles of gender appropriate" rule.
I get it! Similar to how I am representing the history of cowboys,

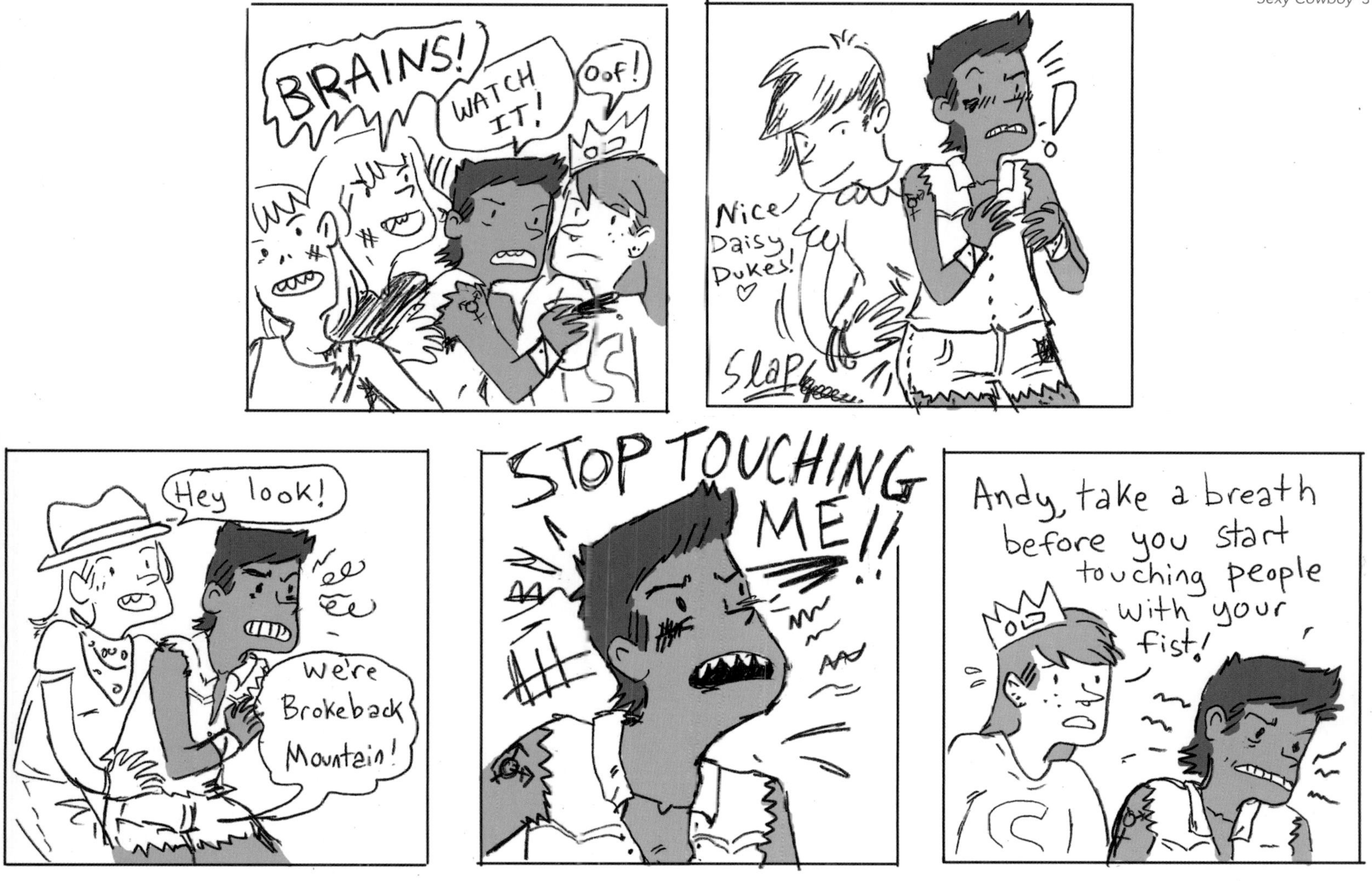
BRAINS!
WATCH IT!
Oof!
Nice Daisy Dukes! ♡
Slap
Hey look!
We're Brokeback Mountain!
STOP TOUCHING ME!!
Andy, take a breath before you start touching people with your fist!

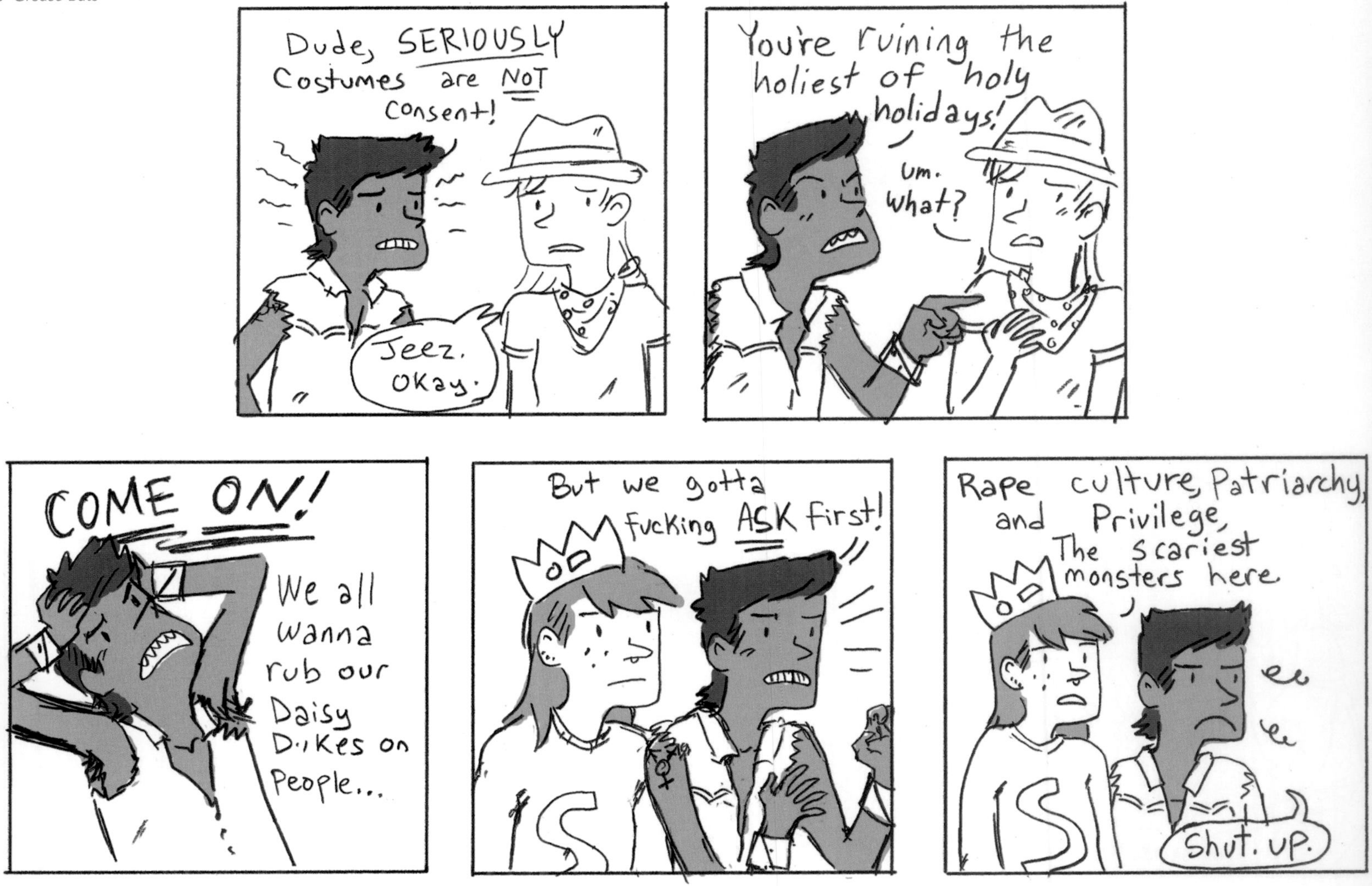
Dude, SERIOUSLY Costumes are NOT consent!
Jeez. Okay.
You're ruining the holiest of holy holidays!
Um. What?
COME ON!
We all wanna rub our Daisy D.ikes on People...
But we gotta fucking ASK first!
Rape culture, Patriarchy, and Privilege, The scariest monsters here.
Shut. up.

Love Letters

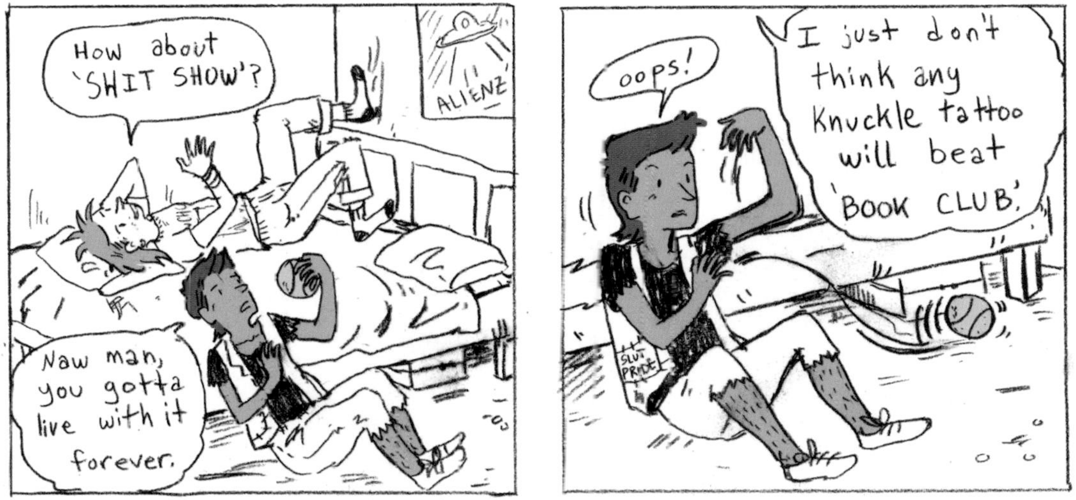
How about 'SHIT SHOW'?
ALIENZ
Naw man, you gotta live with it forever.
oops!
I just don't think any Knuckle tattoo will beat 'BOOK CLUB.'
SLUT PRIDE

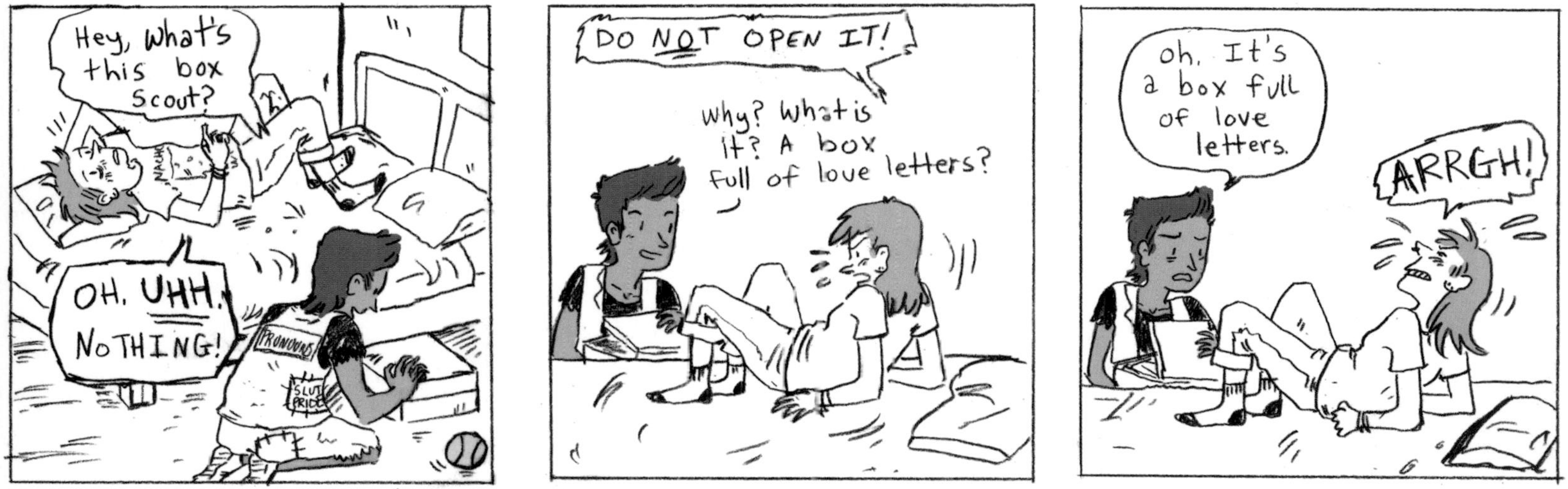
Hey, what's this box Scout?
OH. UHH. NOTHING!
PRONOUNS
SLUT PRIDE
DO NOT OPEN IT!
Why? What is it? A box full of love letters?
Oh. It's a box full of love letters.
ARRGH!

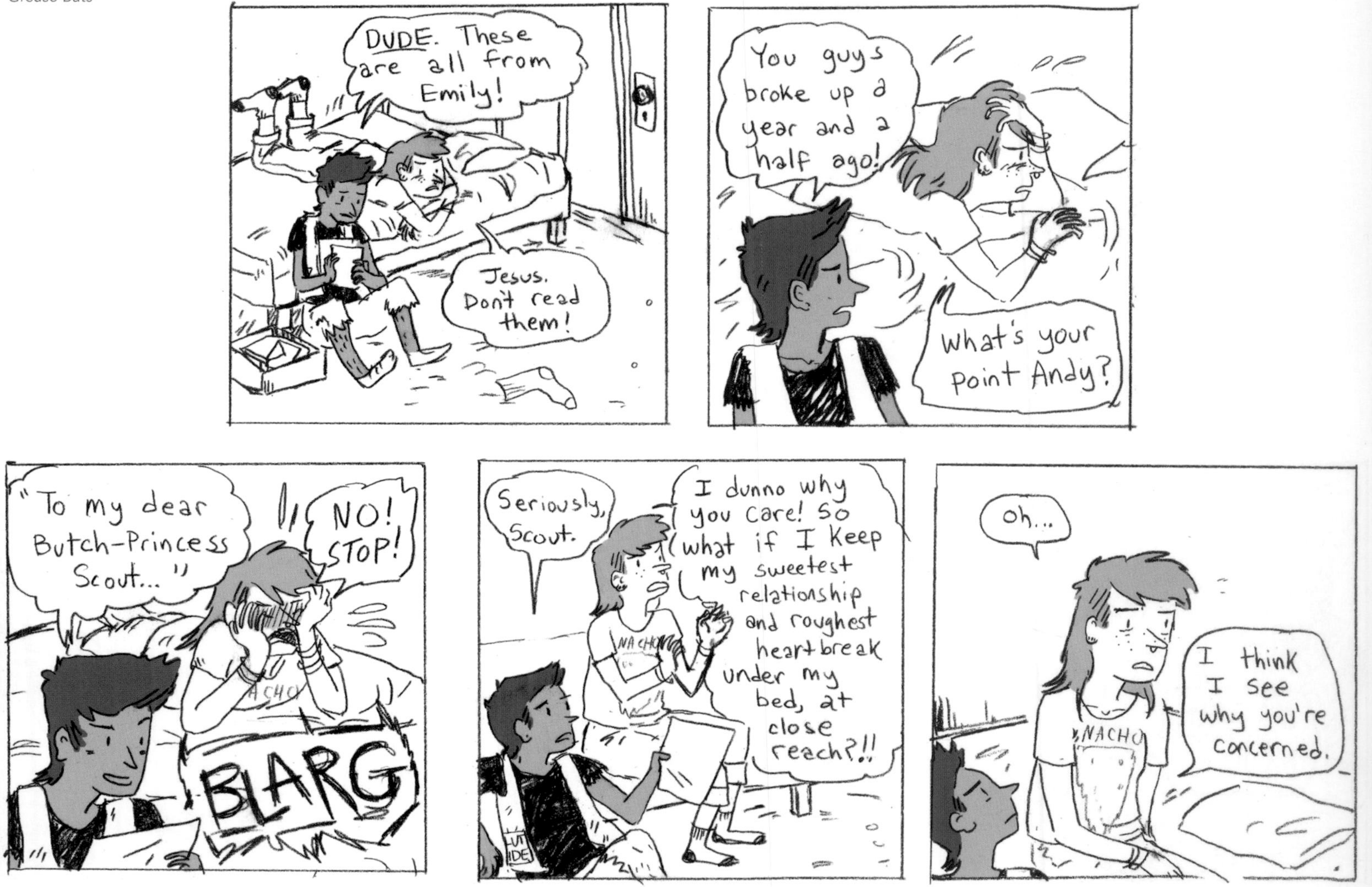
DUDE. These are all from Emily!
Jesus. Don't read them!
You guys broke up a year and a half ago!
What's your point Andy?
"To my dear Butch-Princess Scout..."
NO! STOP!
BLARG
Seriously, Scout.
I dunno why you care! So what if I Keep my sweetest relationship and roughest heartbreak under my bed, at close reach?!!
Oh...
I think I see why you're concerned.

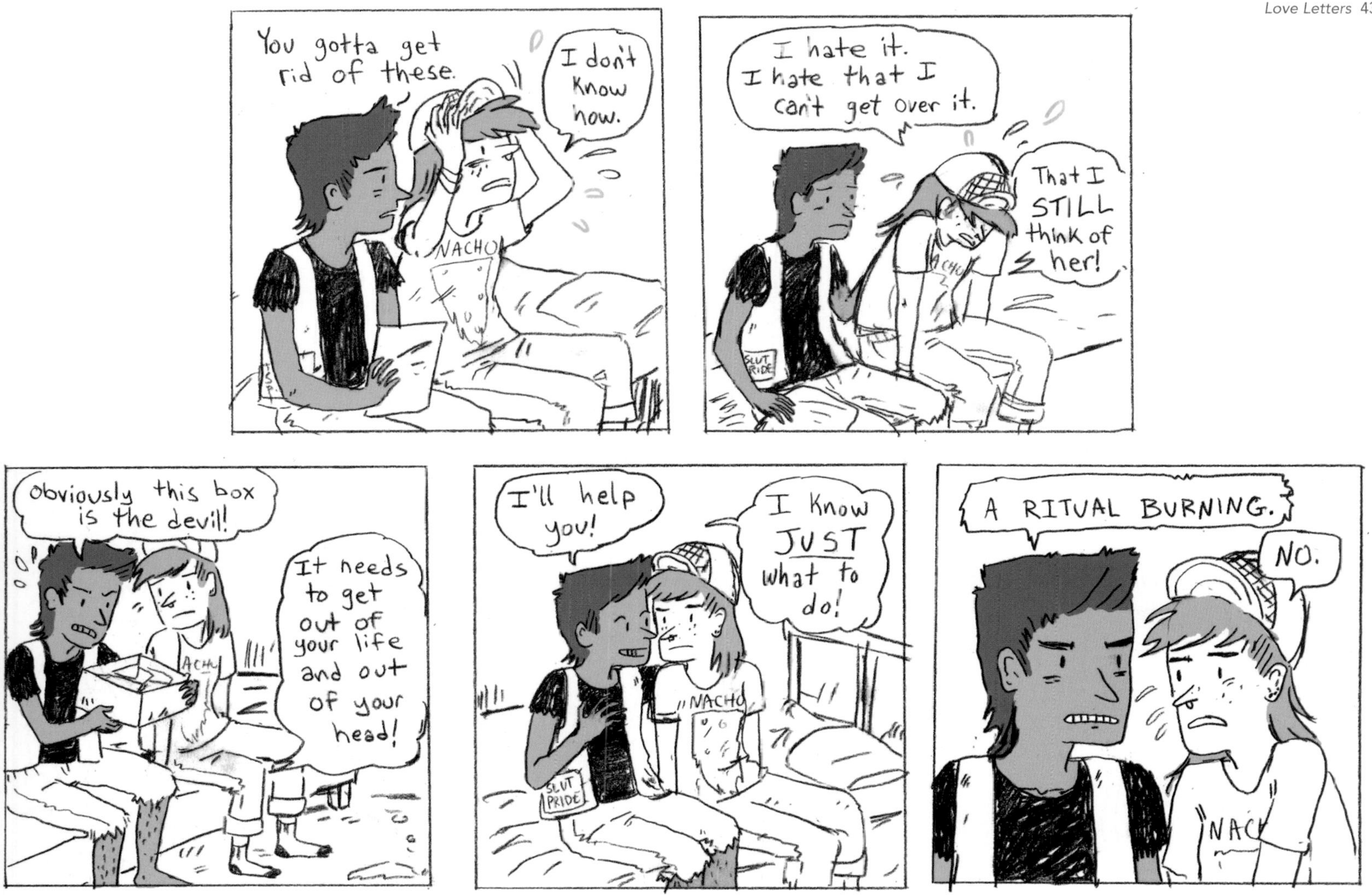
You gotta get rid of these.
I don't know how.
I hate it. I hate that I can't get over it.
That I STILL think of her!
obviously this box is the devil!
It needs to get out of your life and out of your head!
I'll help you!
I know JUST what to do!
A RITUAL BURNING.
NO.

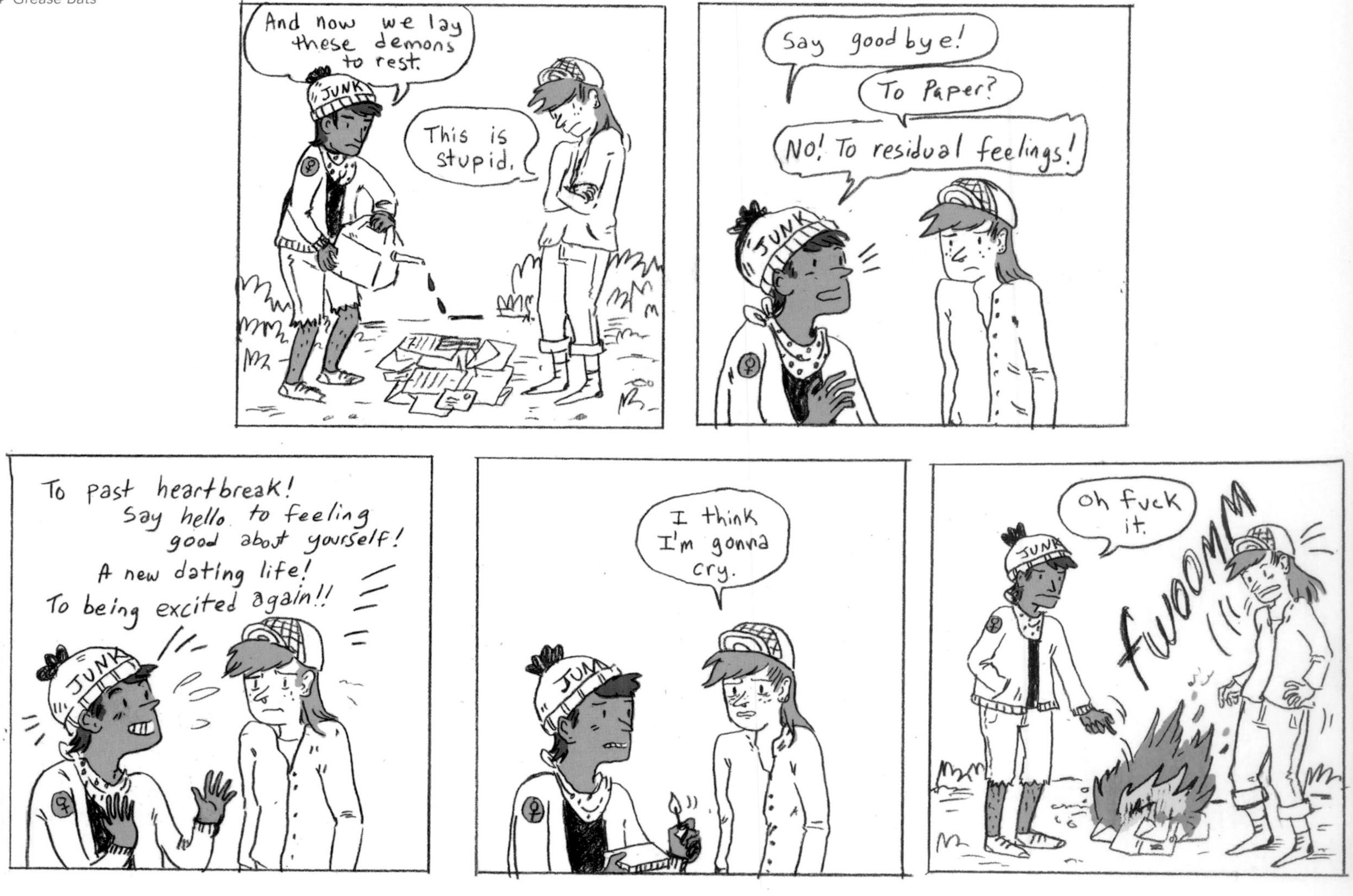
And now we lay these demons to rest.
This is stupid.
Say goodbye!
To Paper?
No! To residual feelings!
To past heartbreak! Say hello to feeling good about yourself! A new dating life! To being excited again!!
I think I'm gonna cry.
Oh fuck it.
FWOOM
JUNK

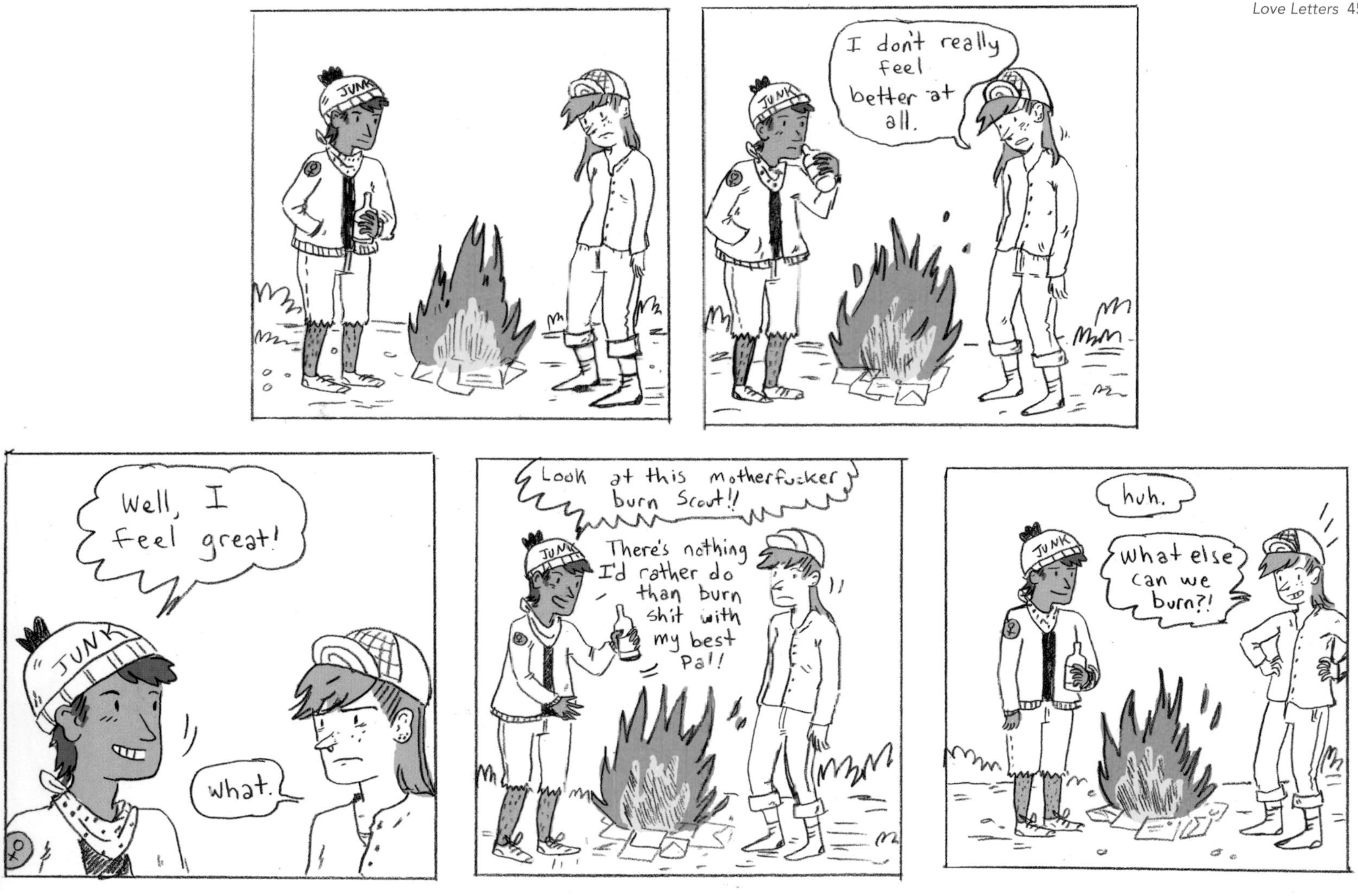
JUNK
I don't really feel better at all.
JUNK
Well, I feel great!
JUNK
what.
Look at this motherfucker burn Scout!!
JUNK
There's nothing I'd rather do than burn shit with my best Pal!
huh.
JUNK
What else can we burn?!

Swipe Right

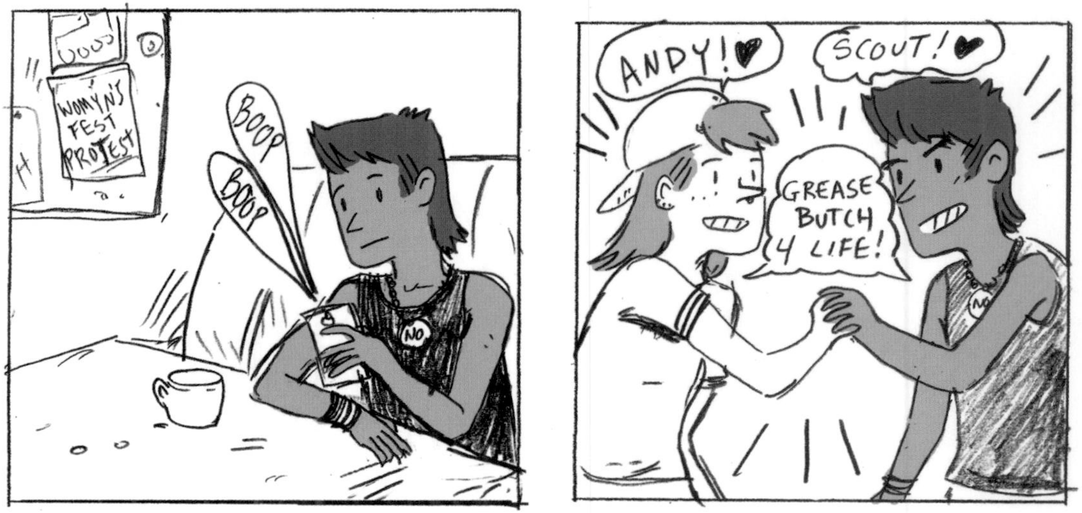
WOMYN'S FEST PROTEST
BOOP
BOOP
ANDY! ♥
SCOUT! ♥
GREASE BUTCH 4 LIFE!

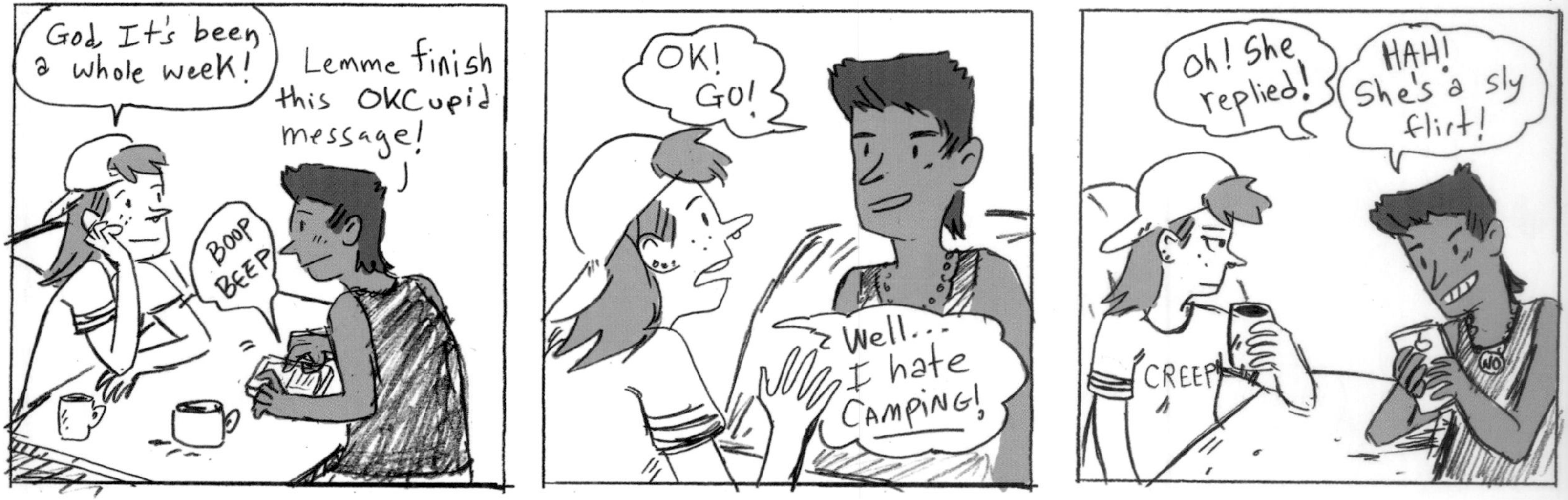
God, It's been a whole week!
Lemme finish this OKCupid message!
BOOP BEEP
OK! GO!
Well... I hate CAMPING!
Oh! She replied!
HAH! She's a sly flirt!
CREEP

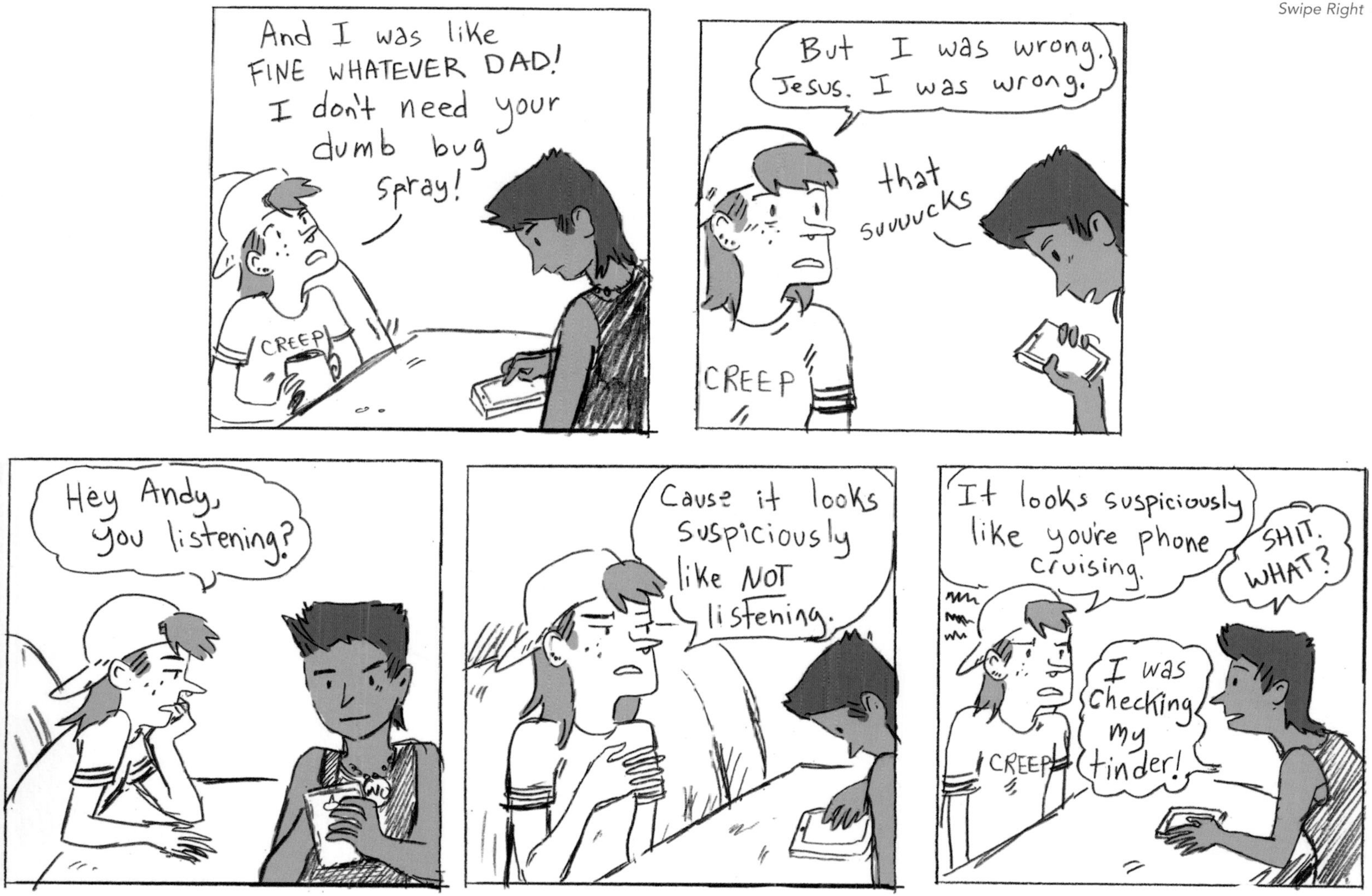
And I was like FINE WHATEVER DAD! I don't need your dumb bug spray!
CREEP
But I was wrong. Jesus. I was wrong.
that suuuucks
CREEP
Hey Andy, you listening?
Cause it looks suspiciously like NOT listening.
It looks suspiciously like you're phone cruising.
SHIT. WHAT?
I was checking my tinder!
CREEP

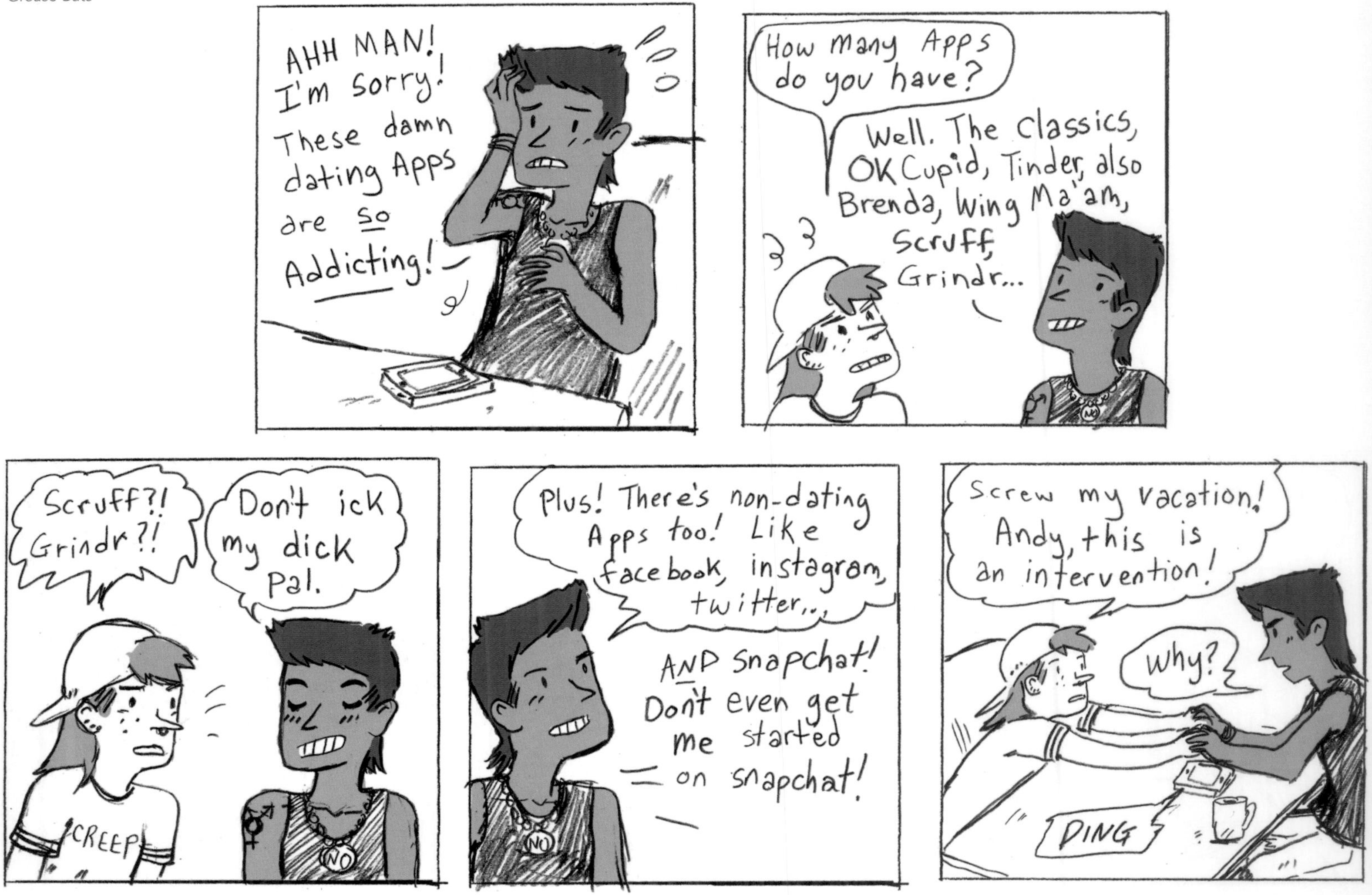
AHH MAN! I'm sorry! These damn dating Apps are so Addicting!
How many Apps do you have?
Well. The Classics, OK Cupid, Tinder, also Brenda, Wing Ma'am, Scruff, Grindr...
Scruff?! Grindr?!
Don't ick my dick Pal.
Plus! There's non-dating Apps too! Like facebook, instagram, twitter...
AND Snapchat! Don't even get me started on snapchat!
Screw my vacation! Andy, this is an intervention!
Why?
DING
CREEP
NO

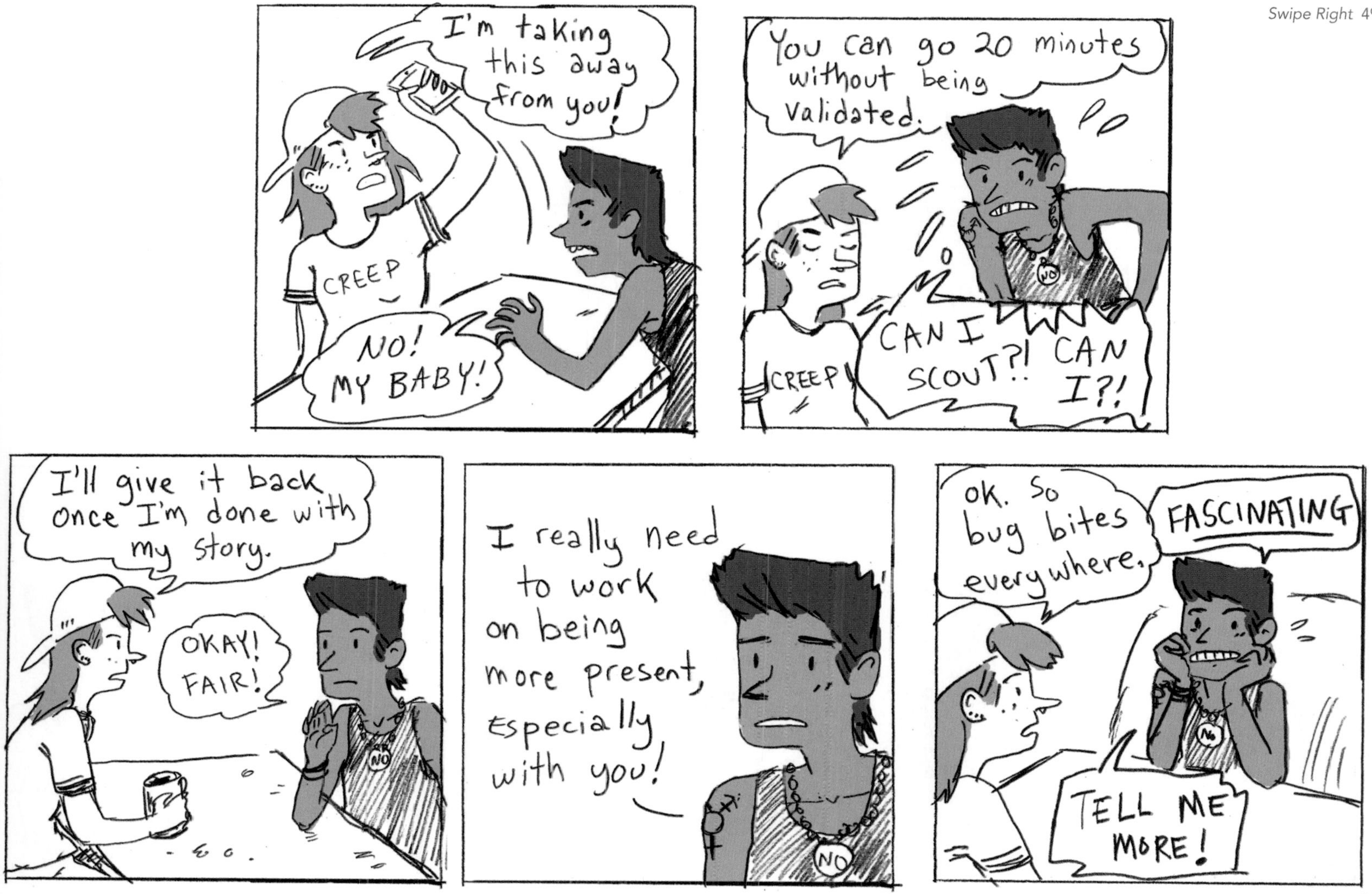
I'm taking this away from you!
NO! MY BABY!
You can go 20 minutes without being validated.
CREEP
CAN I SCOUT?! CAN I?!
CREEP
I'll give it back once I'm done with my story.
OKAY! FAIR!
NO
I really need to work on being more present, especially with you!
NO
ok. So bug bites everywhere.
FASCINATING
TELL ME MORE!

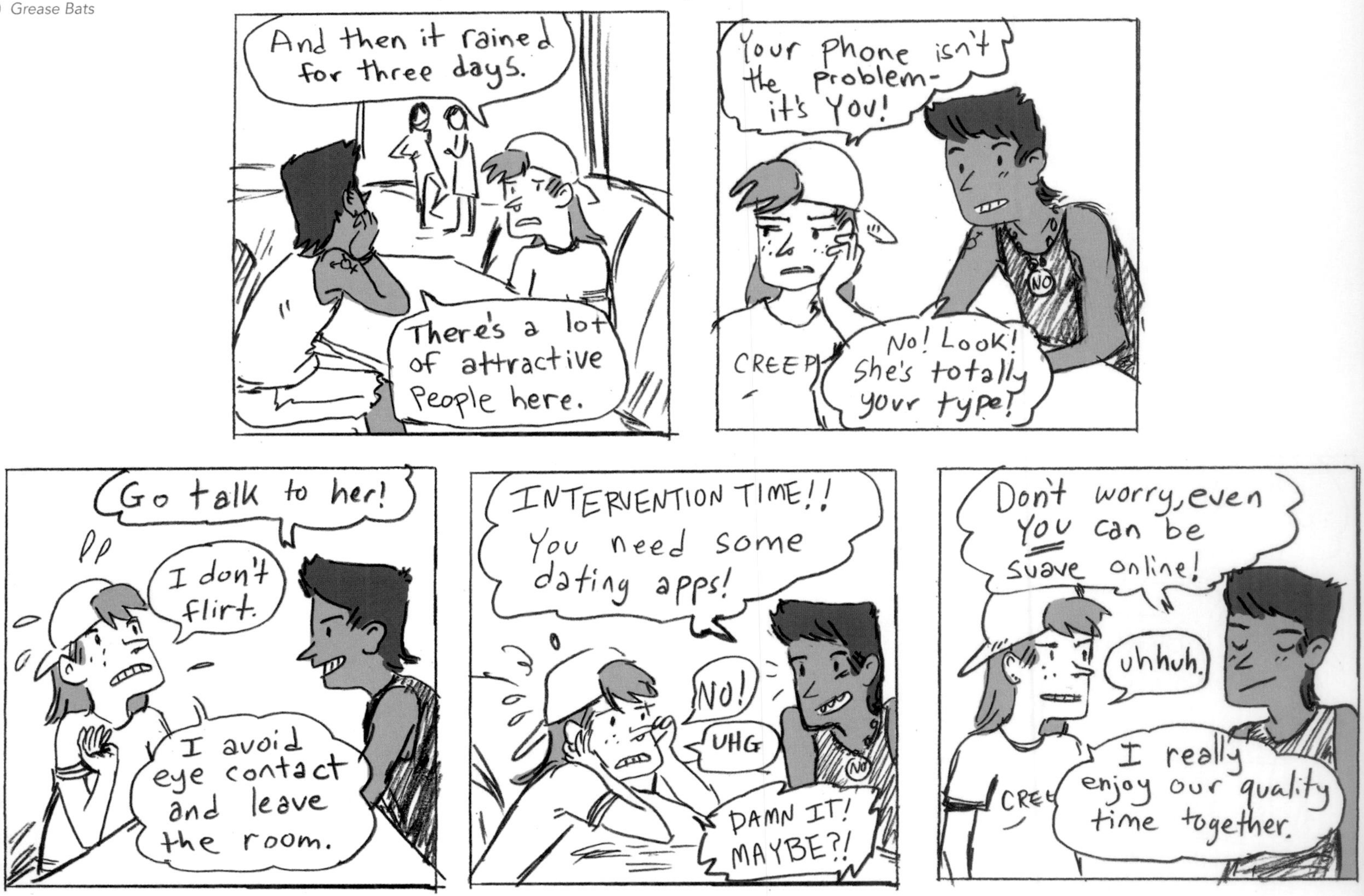
And then it rained for three days.
There's a lot of attractive people here.
Your phone isn't the problem- it's You!
CREEP
No! Look! She's totally your type!
Go talk to her!
I don't flirt.
I avoid eye contact and leave the room.
INTERVENTION TIME!! You need some dating apps!
NO!
UHG
DAMN IT! MAYBE?!
Don't worry, even YOU can be suave online!
uhhuh.
CRE
I really enjoy our quality time together.

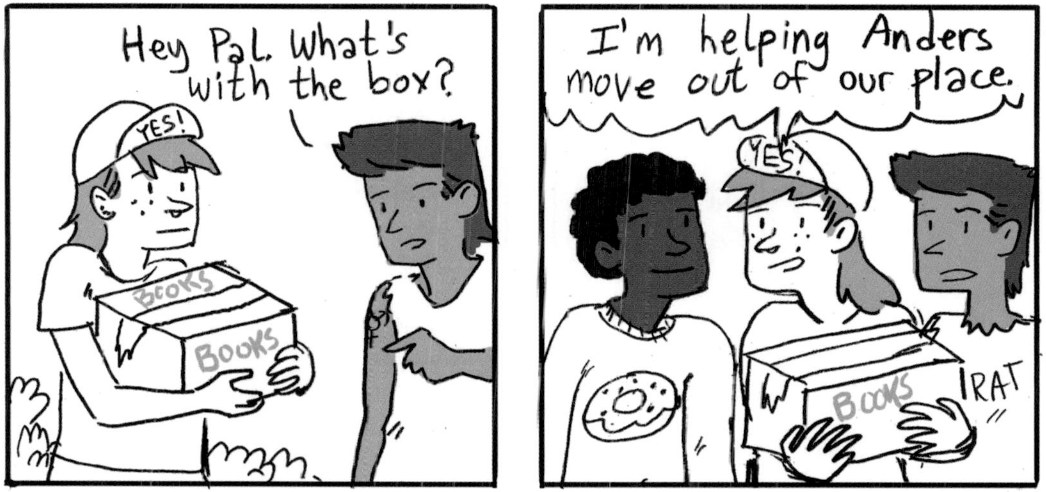
Hey Pal. What's with the box?
YES!
BOOKS
BOOKS
I'm helping Anders move out of our place.
YES!
BOOKS
BRAT

The Roommate

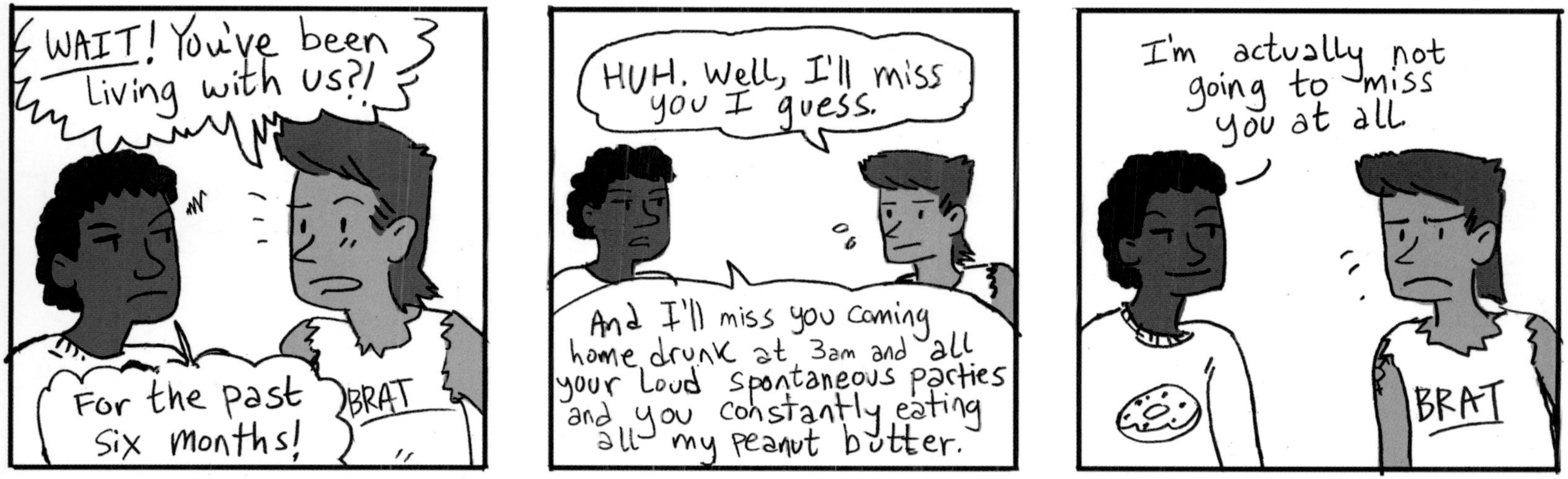
WAIT! You've been living with us?!
For the past six months!
BRAT
HUH. Well, I'll miss you I guess.
And I'll miss you coming home drunk at 3am and all your loud spontaneous parties and you constantly eating all my peanut butter.
I'm actually not going to miss you at all.
BRAT

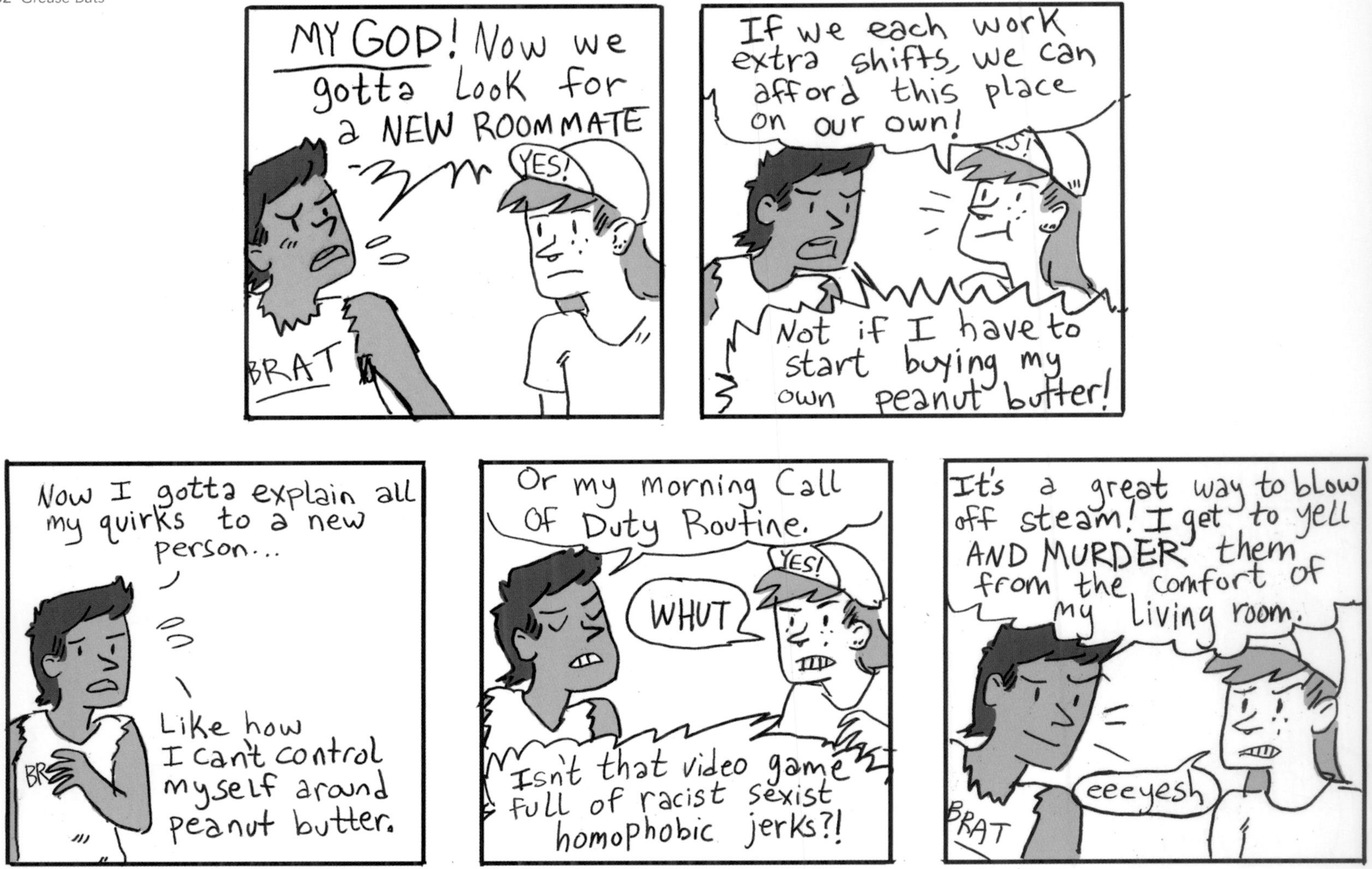
MY GOD! Now we gotta look for a NEW ROOMMATE
YES!
BRAT
If we each work extra shifts, we can afford this place on our own!
Not if I have to start buying my own peanut butter!
Now I gotta explain all my quirks to a new person...
Like how I can't control myself around peanut butter.
BR
Or my morning Call Of Duty Routine.
YES!
WHUT
Isn't that video game full of racist sexist homophobic jerks?!
It's a great way to blow off steam! I get to yell AND MURDER them from the comfort of my living room.
eeeyesh
BRAT

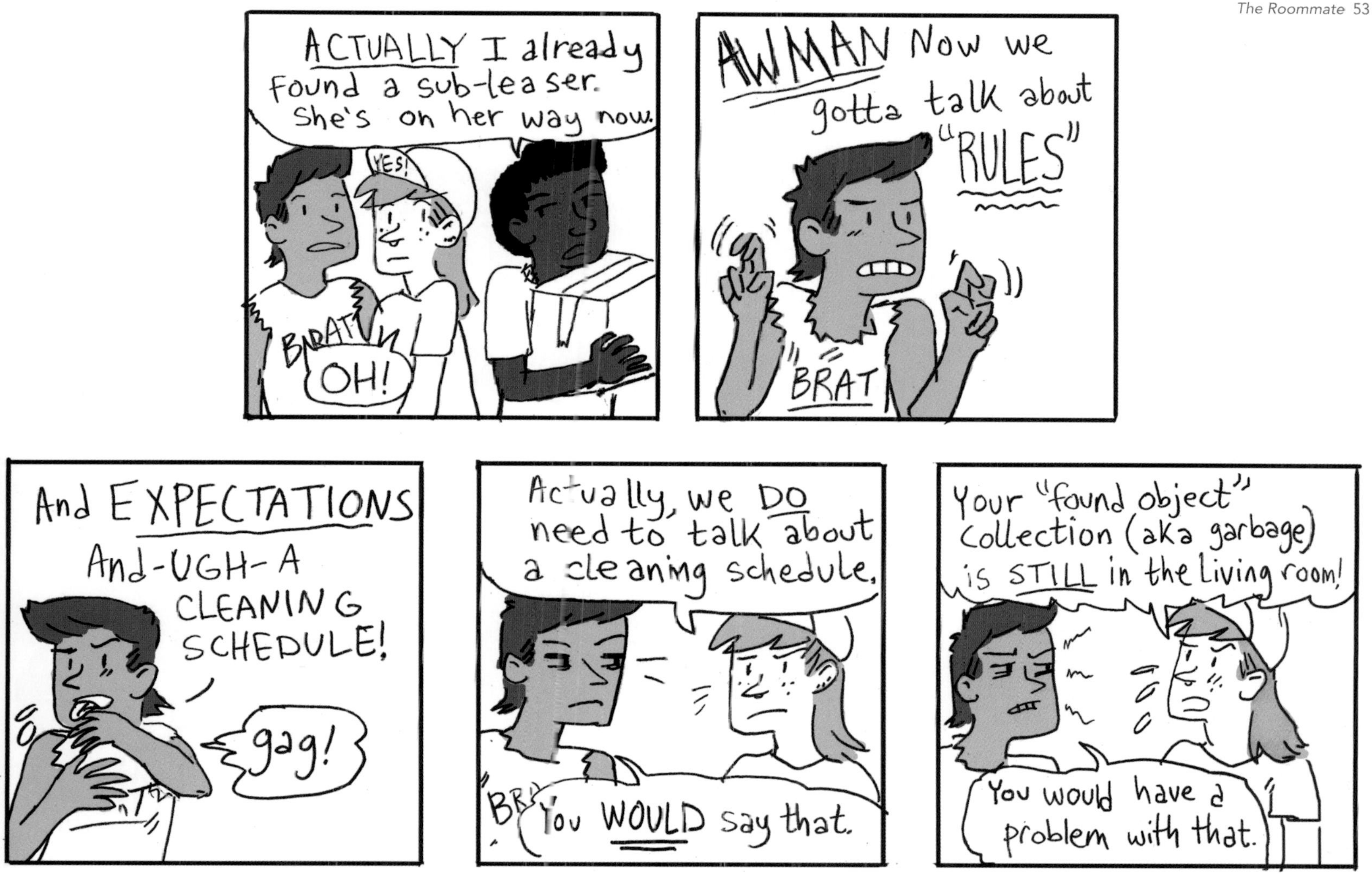
ACTUALLY I already found a sub-leaser. She's on her way now.
YES!
OH!
BRAT
AWMAN Now we gotta talk about "RULES"
BRAT
And EXPECTATIONS And-UGH-A CLEANING SCHEDULE!
gag!
Actually, we DO need to talk about a cleaning schedule.
You WOULD say that.
Your "found object" collection (aka garbage) is STILL in the living room!
You would have a problem with that.

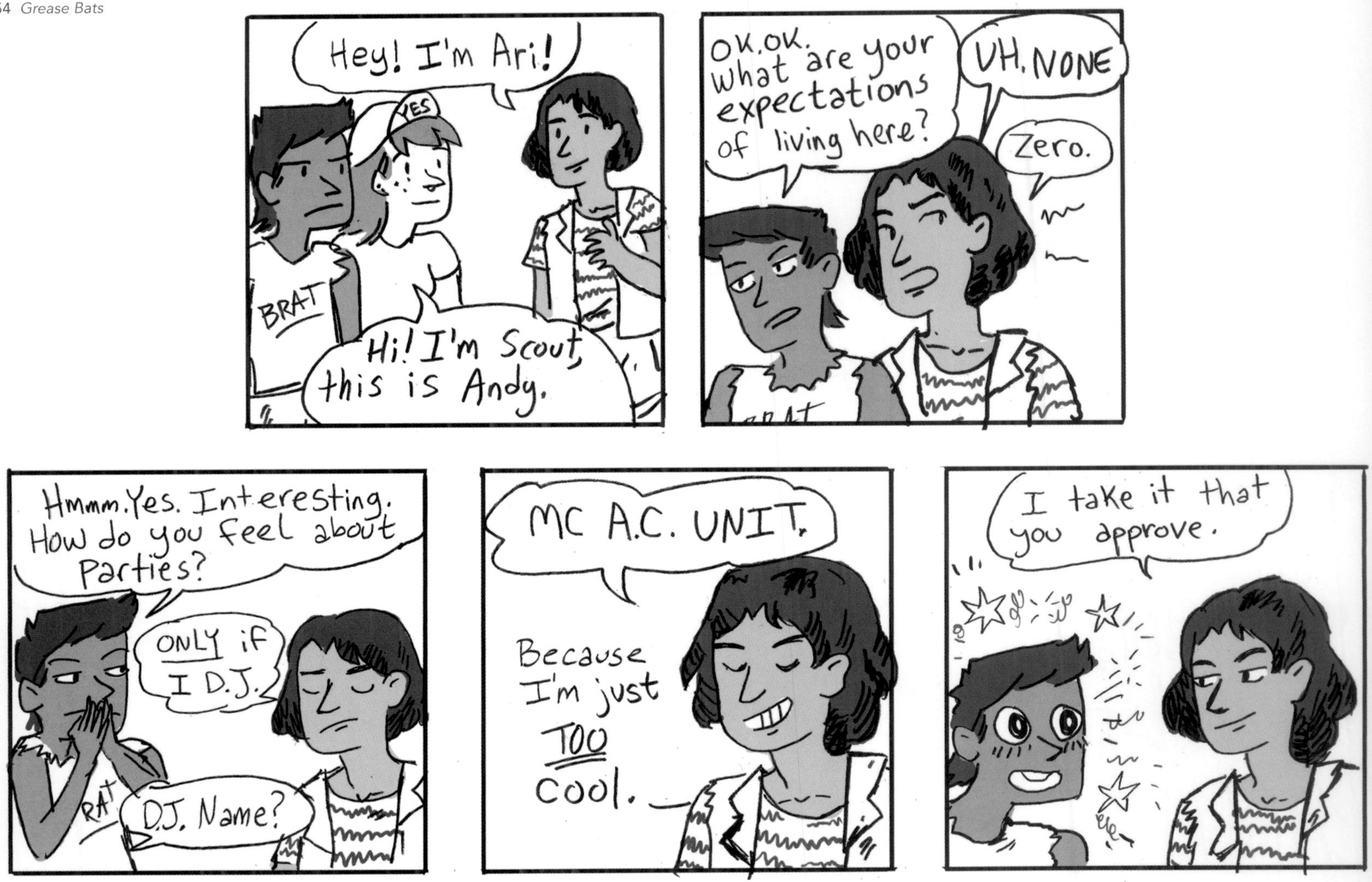
Hey! I'm Ari!
YES
BRAT
Hi! I'm Scout, this is Andy.
OK.OK. what are your expectations of living here?
UH. NONE
Zero.
Hmmm. Yes. Interesting. How do you feel about Parties?
ONLY if I D.J.
D.J. Name?
MC A.C. UNIT.
Because I'm just TOO cool.
I take it that you approve.

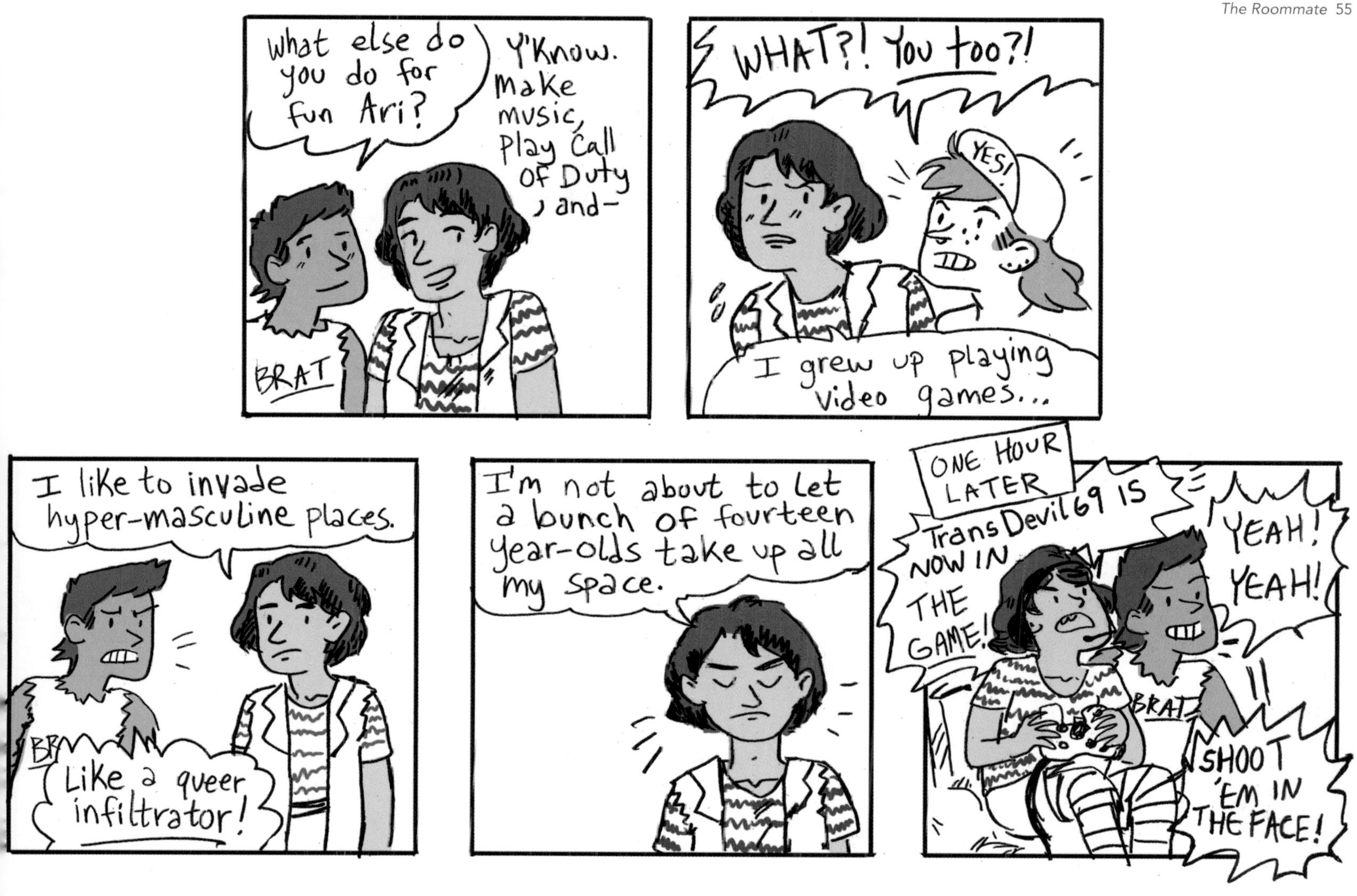
what else do you do for fun Ari?
Y'Know. Make music, Play Call Of Duty, and-
WHAT?! You too?!
YES!
I grew up playing video games...
I like to invade hyper-masculine places.
Like a queer infiltrator!
I'm not about to let a bunch of fourteen year-olds take up all my space.
ONE HOUR LATER
TransDevil69 IS NOW IN THE GAME!
YEAH! YEAH!
SHOOT 'EM IN THE FACE!

Inappropriate Crush

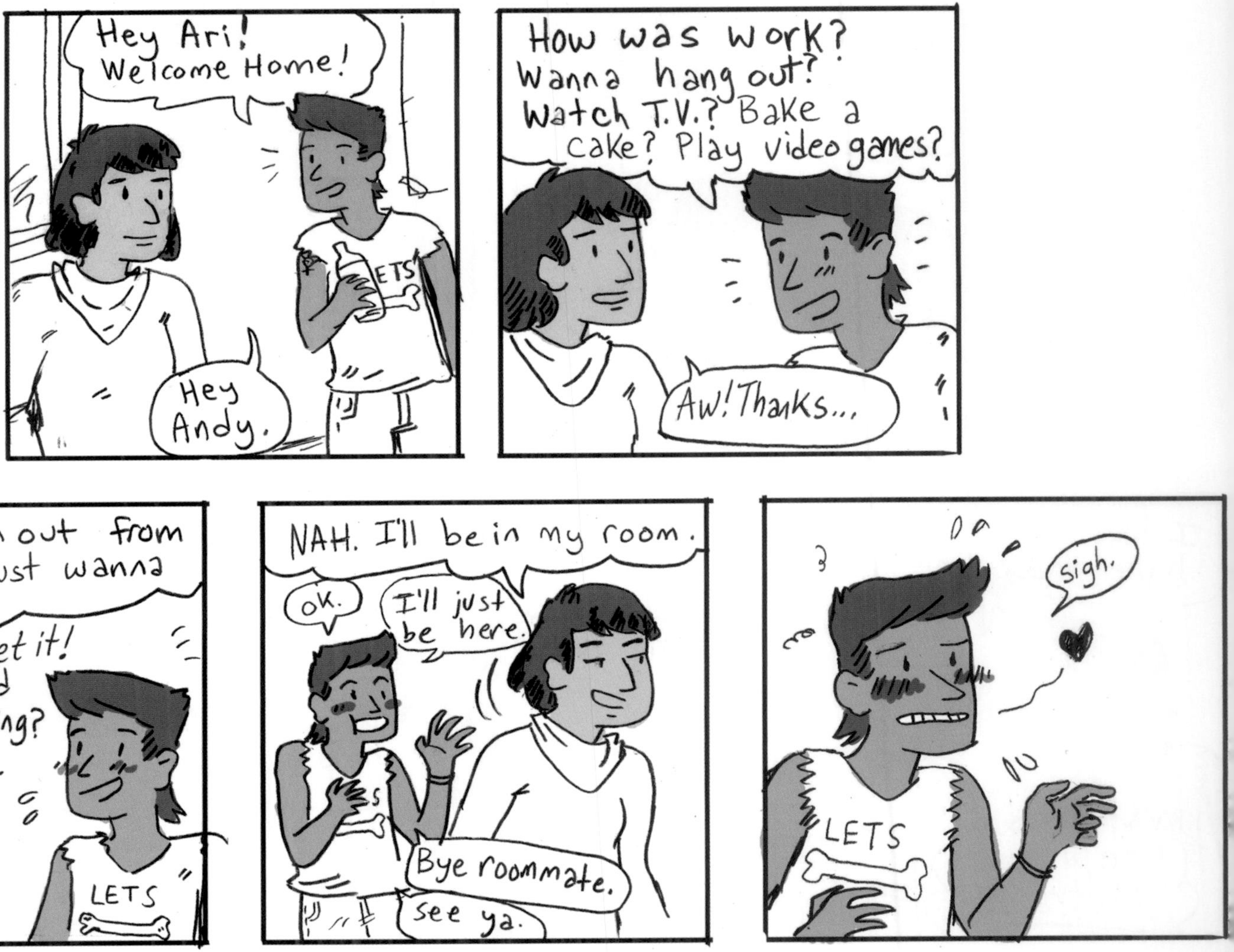
Hey Ari! Welcome Home!
Hey Andy.
How was work? Wanna hang out? Watch T.V.? Bake a cake? Play video games?
Aw! Thanks...
But I'm worn out from work and just wanna be alone.
I get it! Need anything?
NAH. I'll be in my room.
ok.
I'll just be here.
Bye roommate.
see ya.
LETS
sigh.

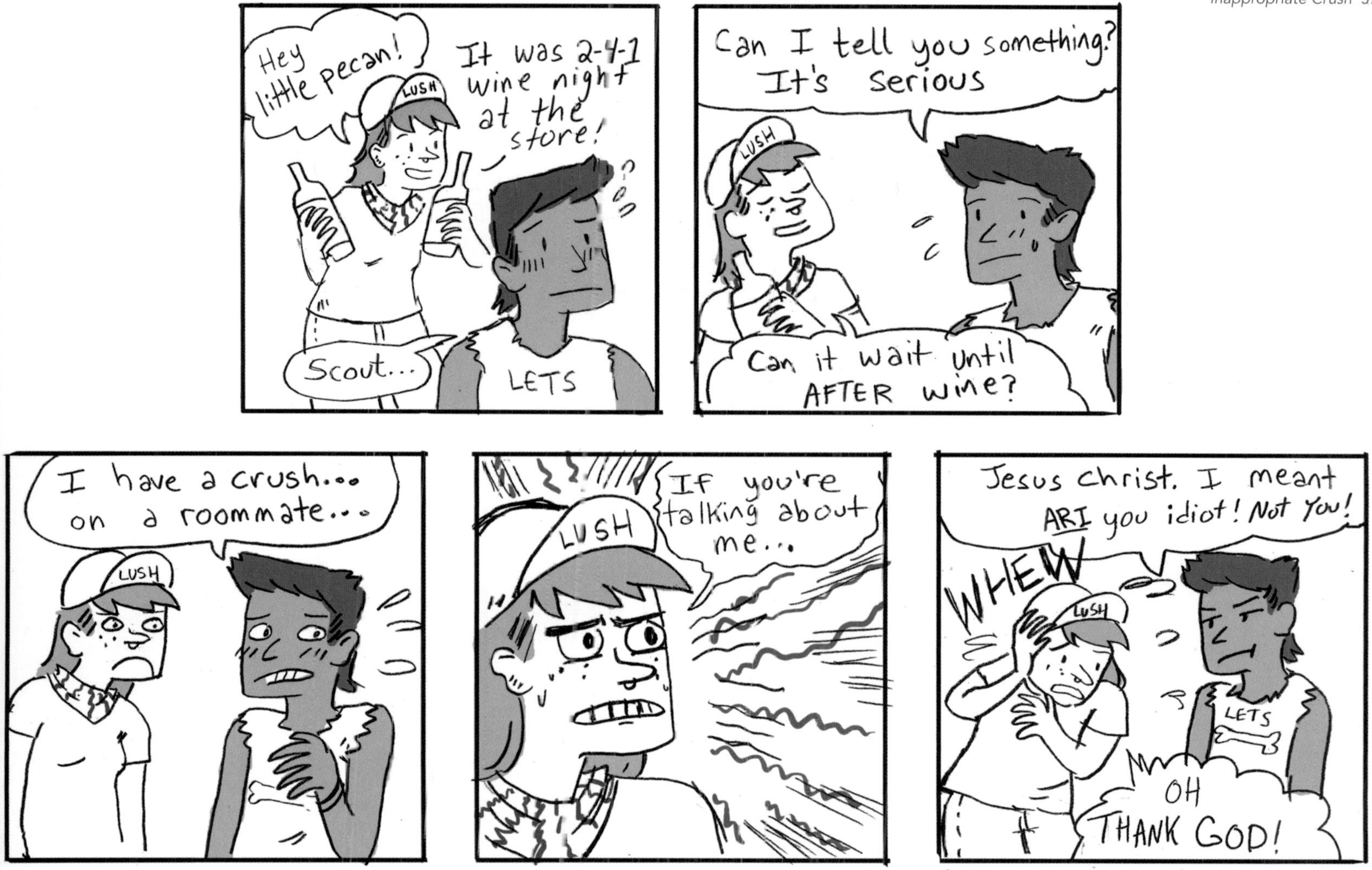
Hey little pecan!
It was 2-4-1 wine night at the store!
Scout...
LETS
Can I tell you something? It's serious
Can it wait until AFTER wine?
I have a crush... on a roommate...
If you're talking about me...
Jesus christ. I meant ARI you idiot! Not You!
WHEW
LETS
OH THANK GOD!

Panel 1: ANDY! You can't have a crush on someone who is paying us to live here.

Sure I can.

Panel 2: She's funny and cute and a super rad trans activist AND she hates Settlers of Catan as much as I do!

Panel 3: Not to mention she's sarcastic and witty and makes me feel like I'm speaking gibberish when we hang out.

Panel 4: And I haven't even mentioned that fanny pack she wears around.

ANDY! She's our roommate!

Panel 5: But were you listening about that fanny pack?

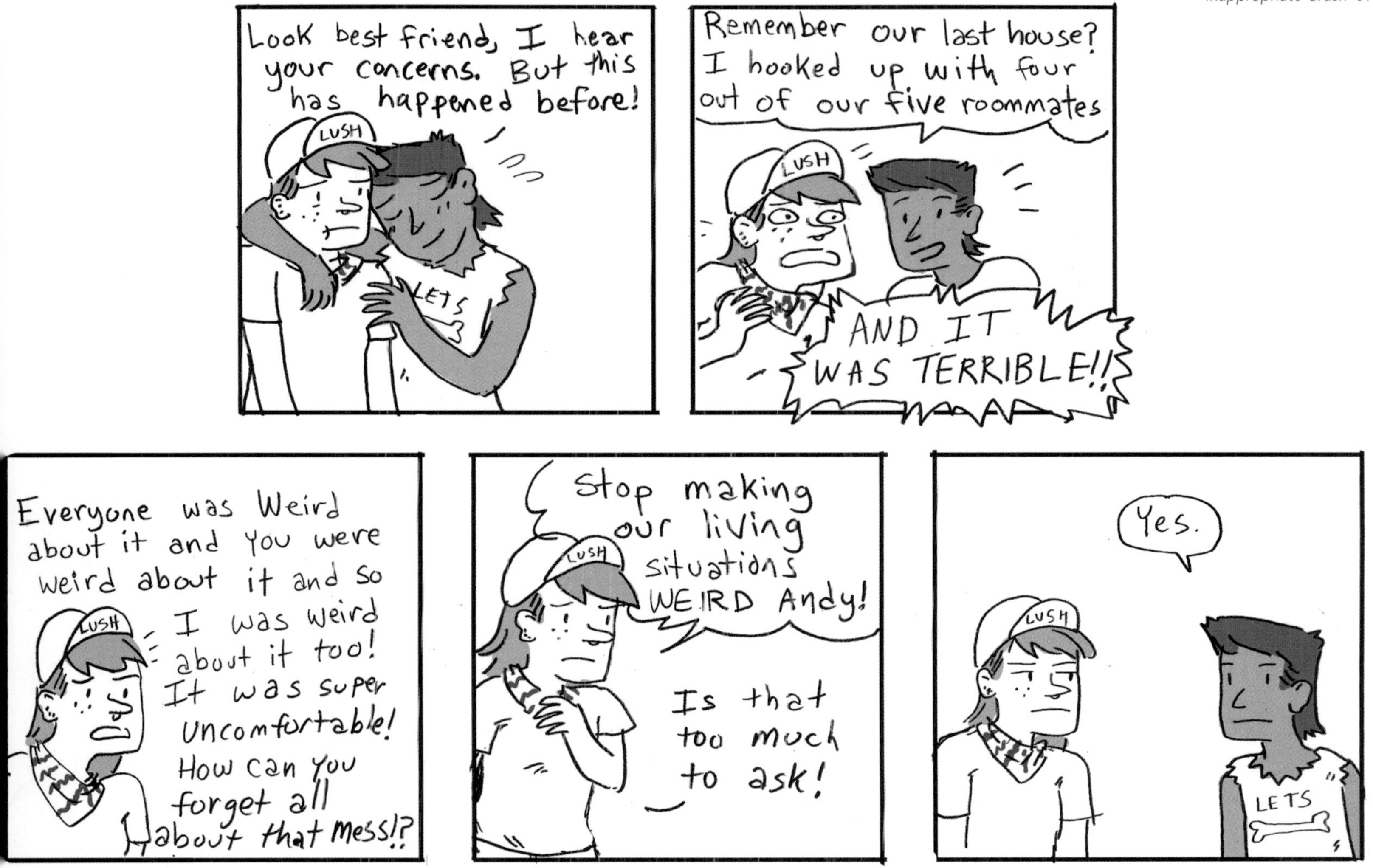
Look best friend, I hear your concerns. But this has happened before!
LUSH
LETS
Remember our last house? I hooked up with four out of our five roommates
LUSH
AND IT WAS TERRIBLE!!
Everyone was Weird about it and you were weird about it and so I was weird about it too! It was super uncomfortable! How can you forget all about that mess!?
LUSH
Stop making our living situations WEIRD Andy!
LUSH
Is that too much to ask!
Yes.
LUSH
LETS

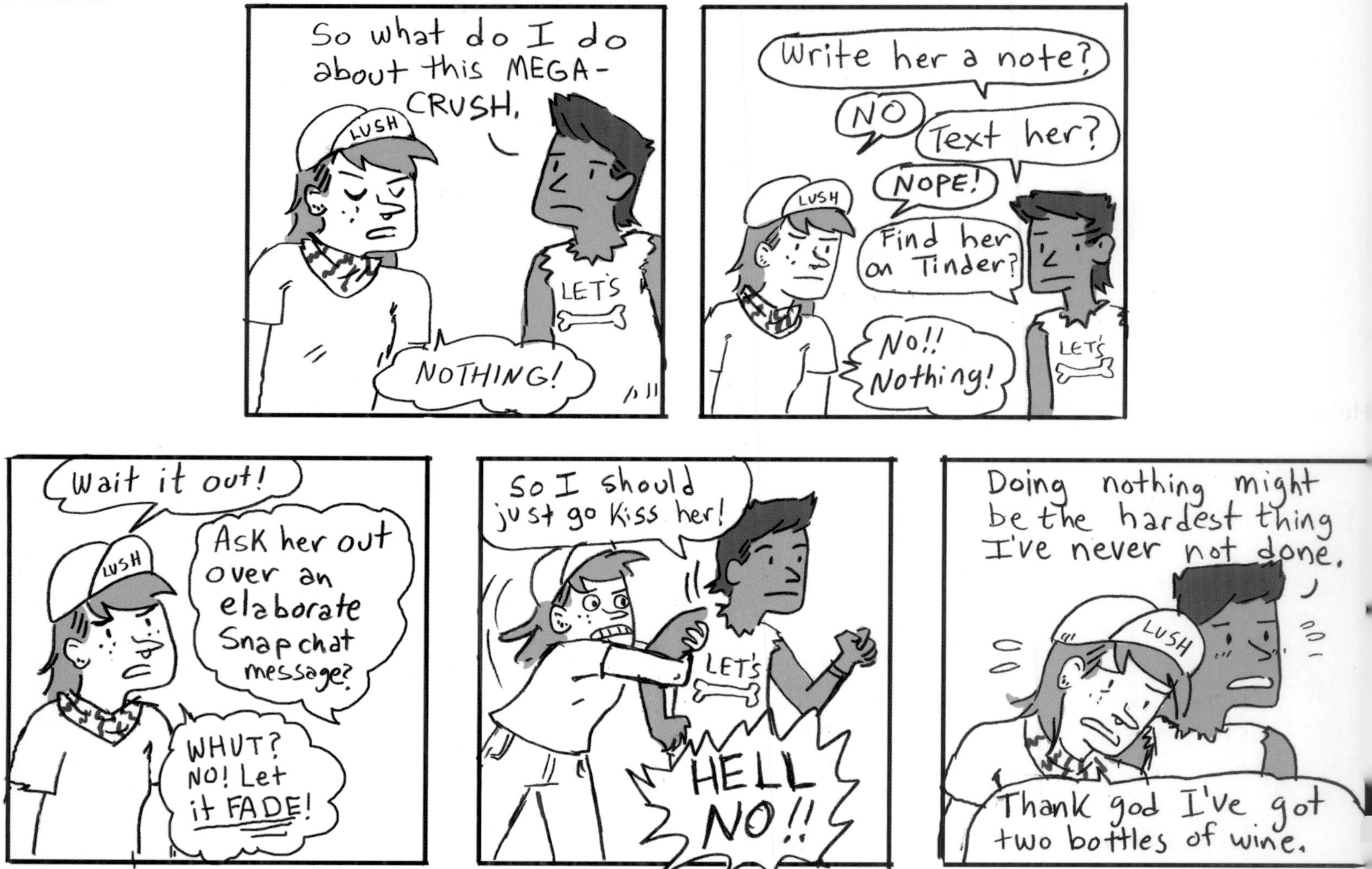

So what do I do about this MEGA-CRUSH.
LUSH
NOTHING!
LET'S
Write her a note?
NO
Text her?
NOPE!
Find her on Tinder?
No!! Nothing!
LUSH
LET'S
Wait it out!
Ask her out over an elaborate Snapchat message?
WHUT? NO! Let it FADE!
LUSH
So I should just go kiss her!
LET'S
HELL NO!!
Doing nothing might be the hardest thing I've never not done.
LUSH
Thank god I've got two bottles of wine.

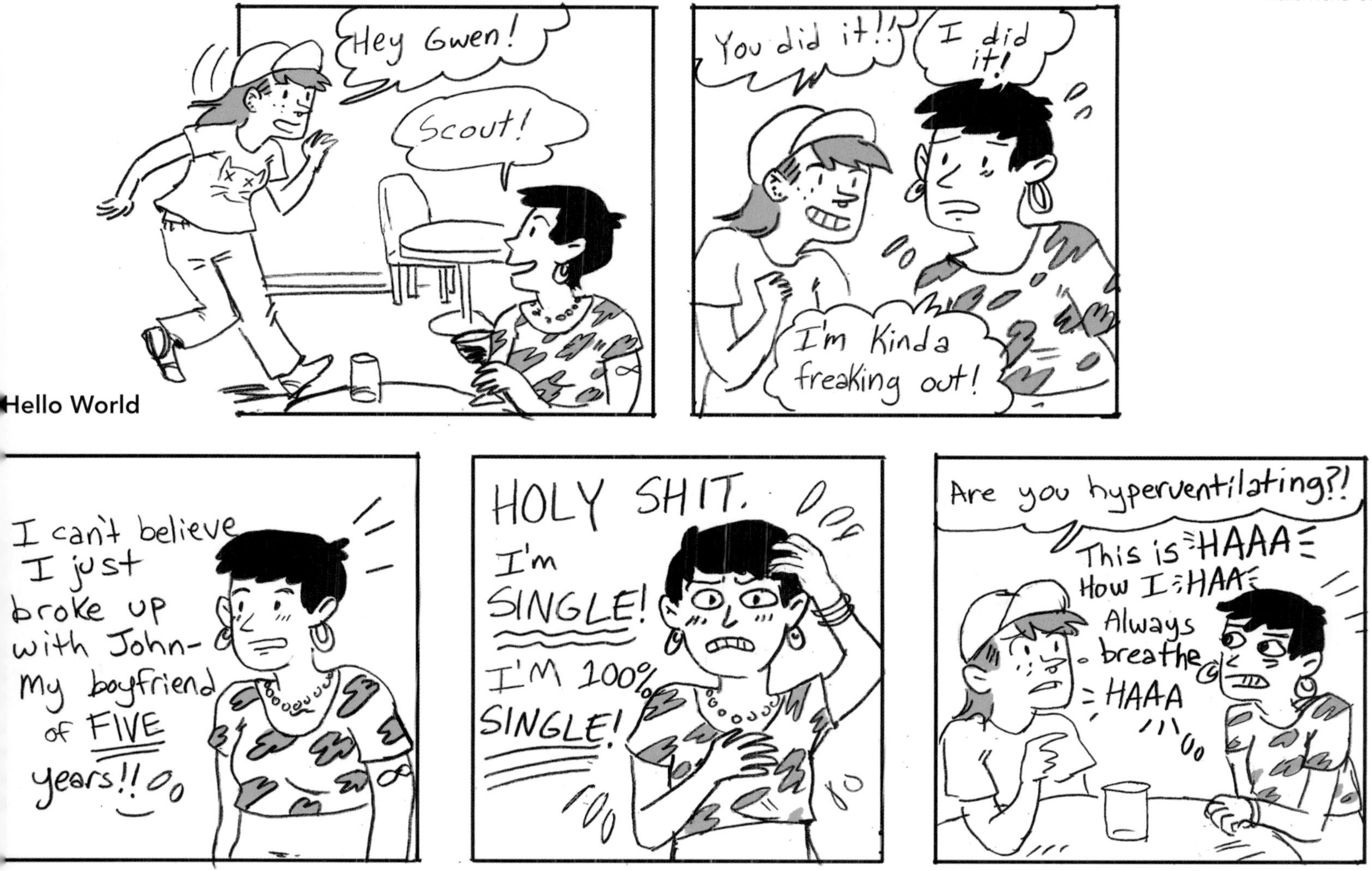
Hey Gwen!
Scout!
You did it!!
I did it!
I'm Kinda freaking out!
I can't believe I just broke up with John- my boyfriend of FIVE years!!
HOLY SHIT.
I'm SINGLE!
I'M 100% SINGLE!
Are you hyperventilating?!
This is HAAA
How I HAA
Always
breathe
HAAA

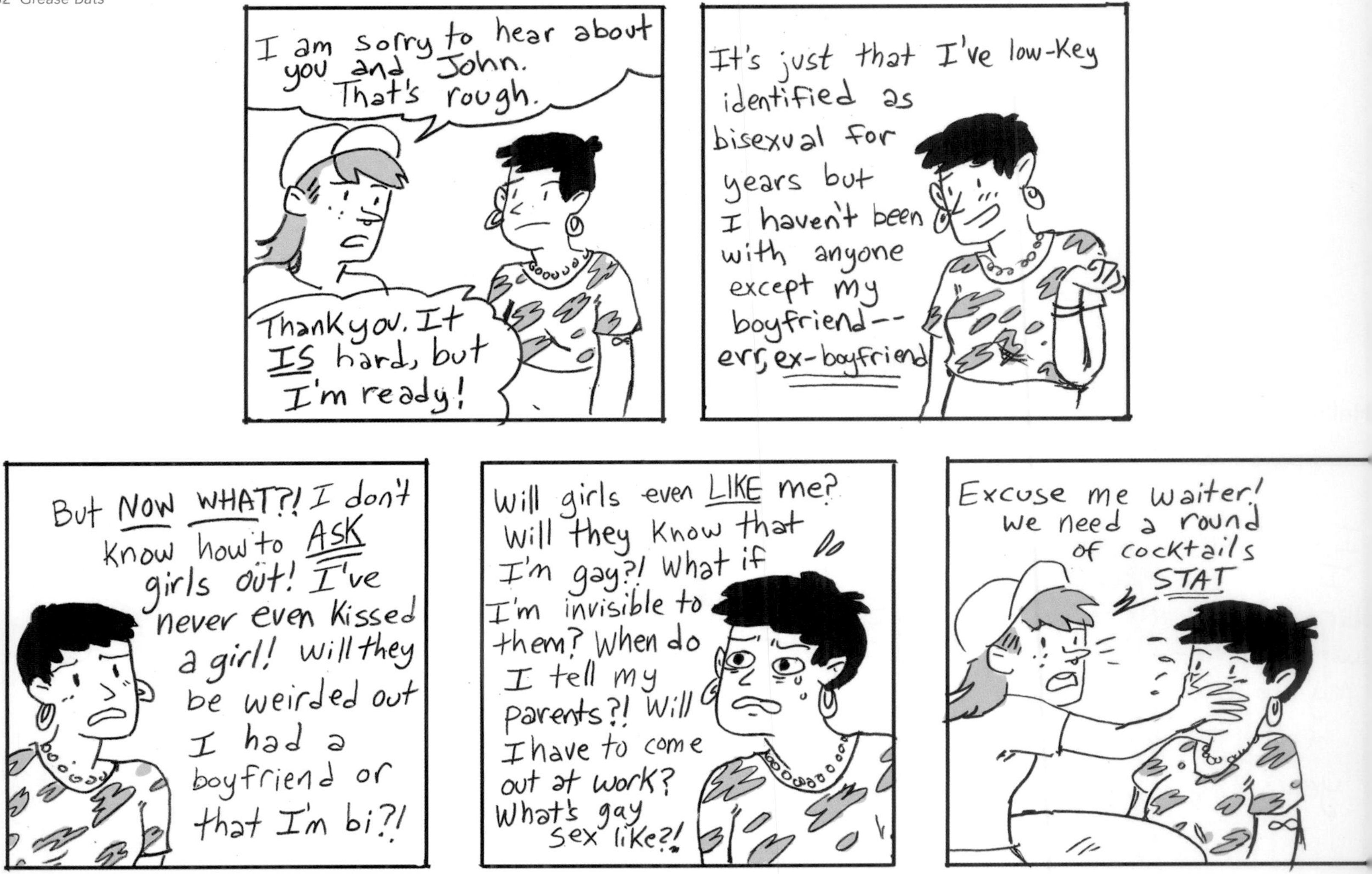
I am sorry to hear about you and John. That's rough.
Thank you. It IS hard, but I'm ready!
It's just that I've low-key identified as bisexual for years but I haven't been with anyone except my boyfriend-- err, ex-boyfriend
But NOW WHAT?! I don't know how to ASK girls out! I've never even kissed a girl! Will they be weirded out I had a boyfriend or that I'm bi?!
Will girls even LIKE me? Will they know that I'm gay?! What if I'm invisible to them? When do I tell my parents?! Will I have to come out at work? What's gay sex like?!
Excuse me waiter! We need a round of cocktails STAT

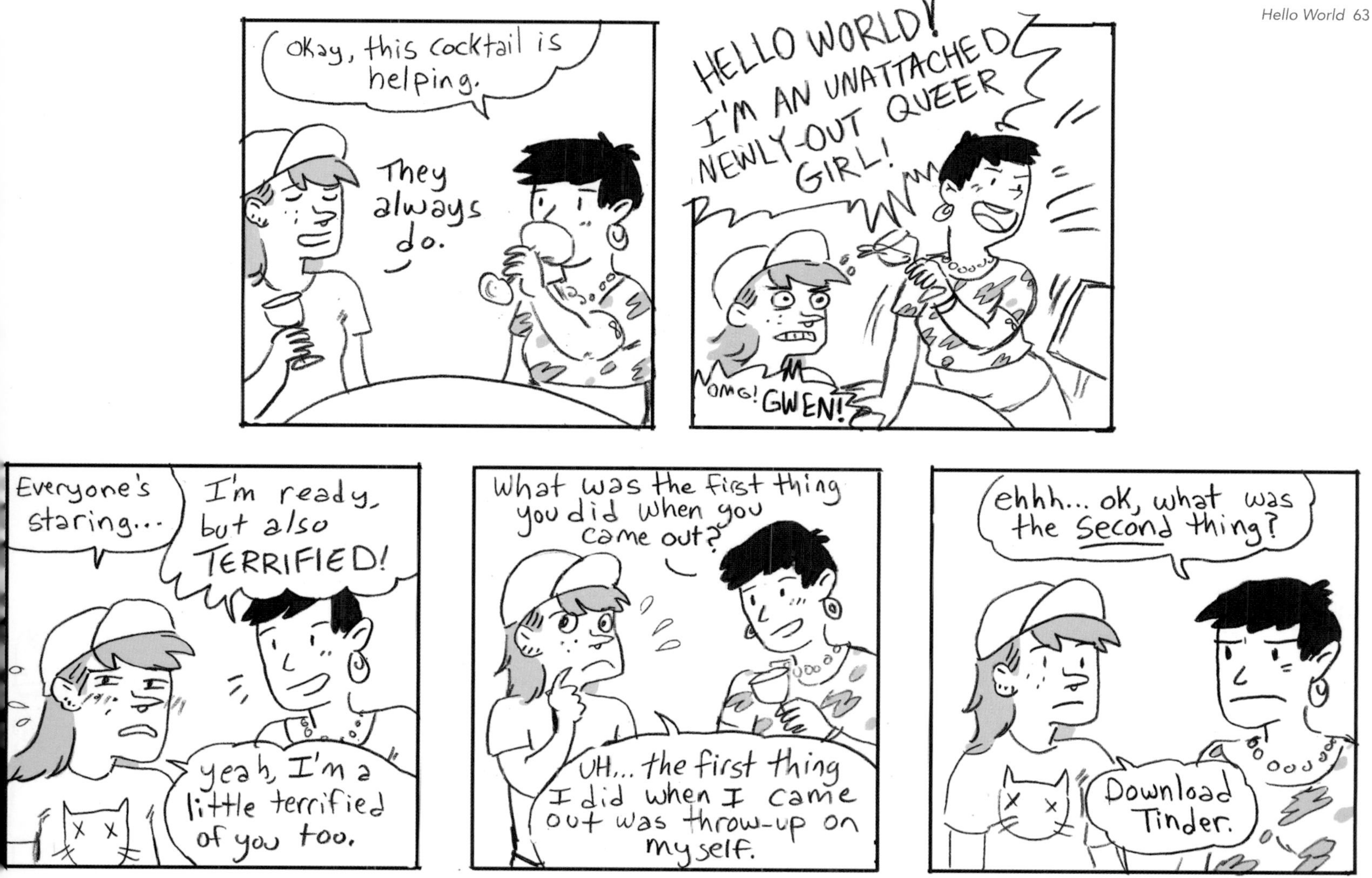
Okay, this cocktail is helping.
They always do.
HELLO WORLD! I'M AN UNATTACHED NEWLY-OUT QUEER GIRL!
OMG! GWEN!
Everyone's staring...
I'm ready, but also TERRIFIED!
yeah, I'm a little terrified of you too.
What was the first thing you did when you came out?
UH... the first thing I did when I came out was throw-up on myself.
ehhh... ok, what was the second thing?
Download Tinder.

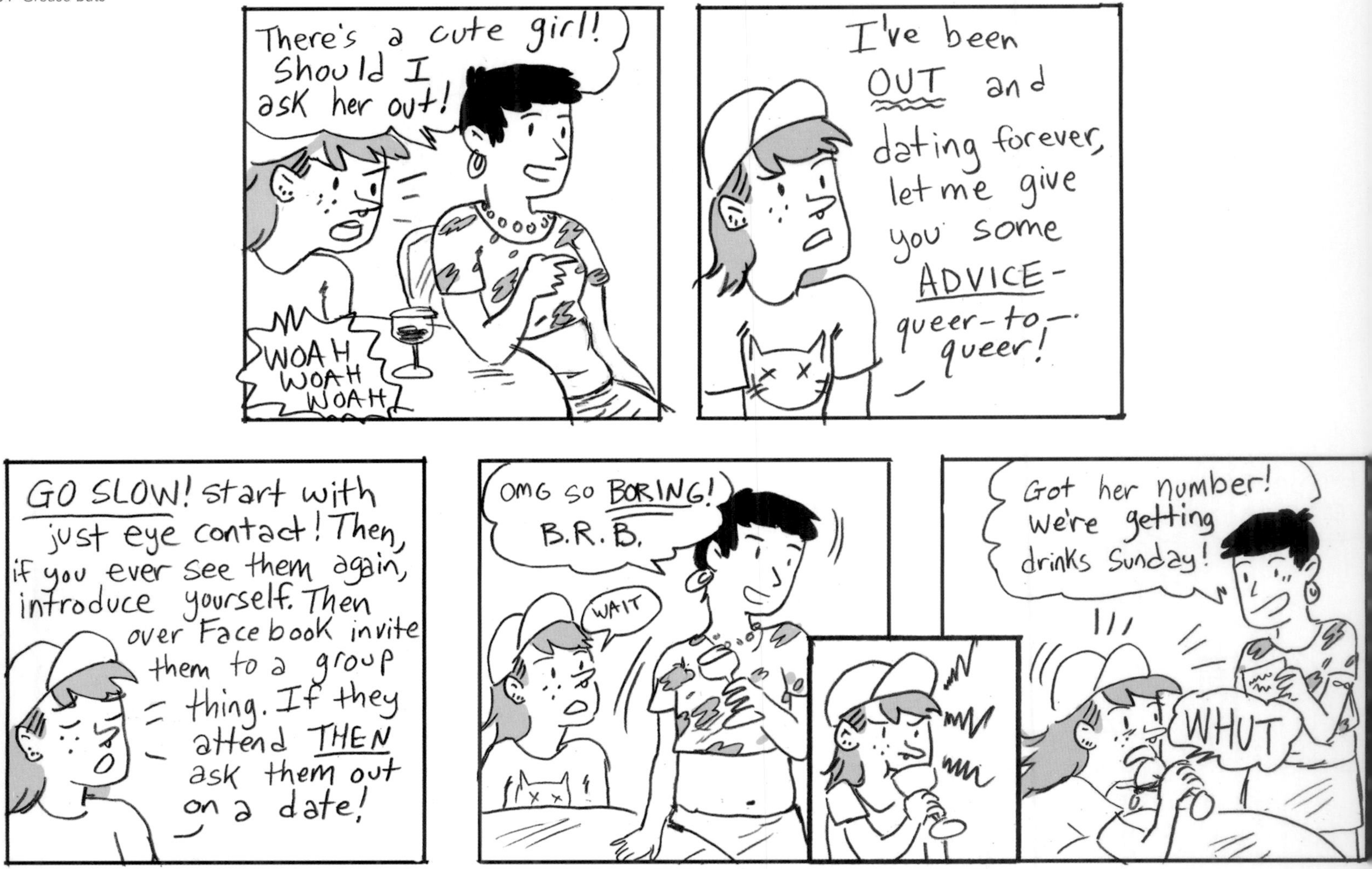
There's a cute girl! Should I ask her out!
WOAH WOAH WOAH
I've been OUT and dating forever, let me give you some ADVICE- queer-to-queer!
GO SLOW! start with just eye contact! Then, if you ever see them again, introduce yourself. Then over Facebook invite them to a group thing. If they attend THEN ask them out on a date!
OMG so BORING! B.R.B.
WAIT
Got her number! We're getting drinks Sunday!
WHUT

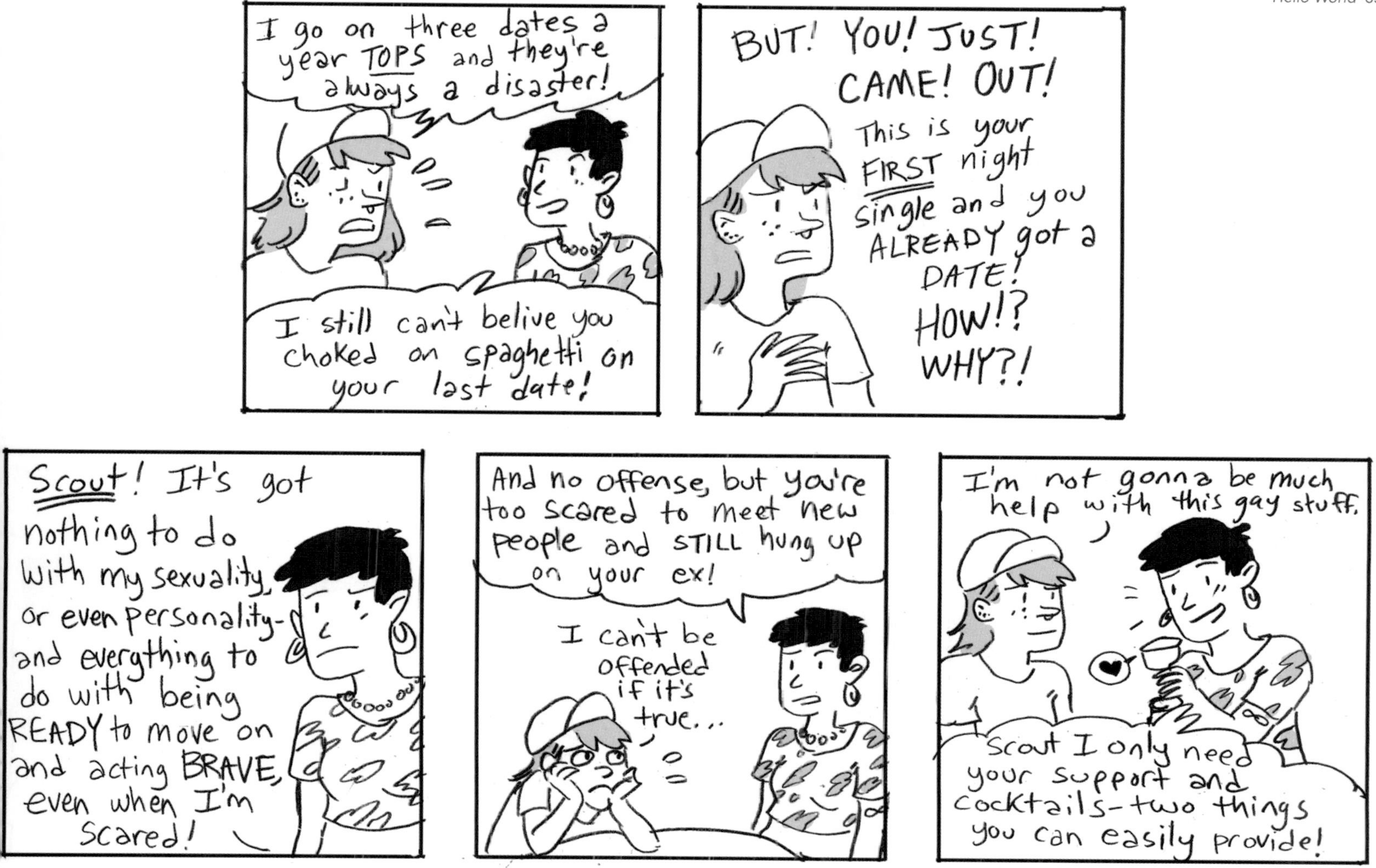
I go on three dates a year TOPS and they're always a disaster!
I still can't belive you choked on spaghetti on your last date!
BUT! YOU! JUST! CAME! OUT!
This is your FIRST night single and you ALREADY got a DATE! HOW!? WHY?!
Scout! It's got nothing to do with my sexuality, or even personality- and everything to do with being READY to move on and acting BRAVE, even when I'm scared!
And no offense, but you're too scared to meet new people and STILL hung up on your ex!
I can't be offended if it's true...
I'm not gonna be much help with this gay stuff.
Scout I only need your support and cocktails- two things you can easily provide!

Identity

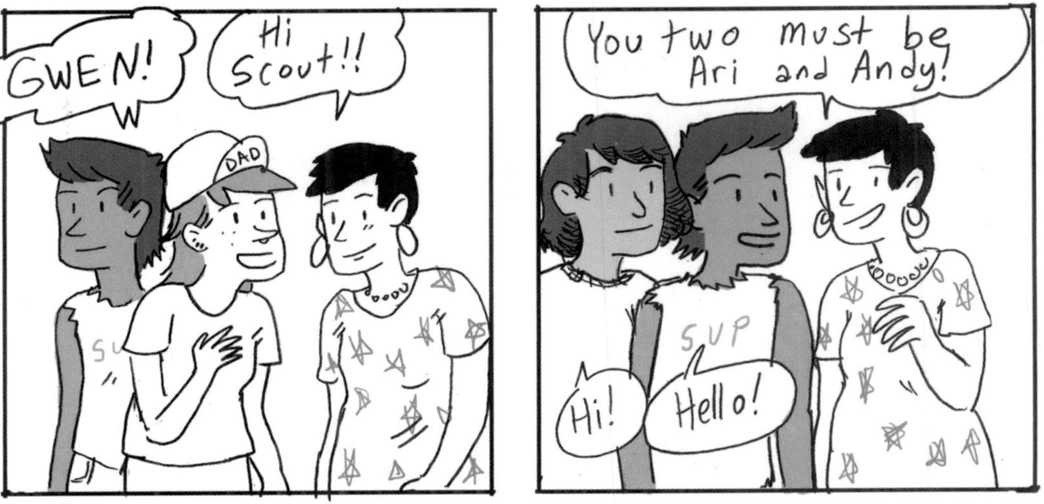
GWEN!
Hi Scout!!
You two must be Ari and Andy!
Hi!
Hello!

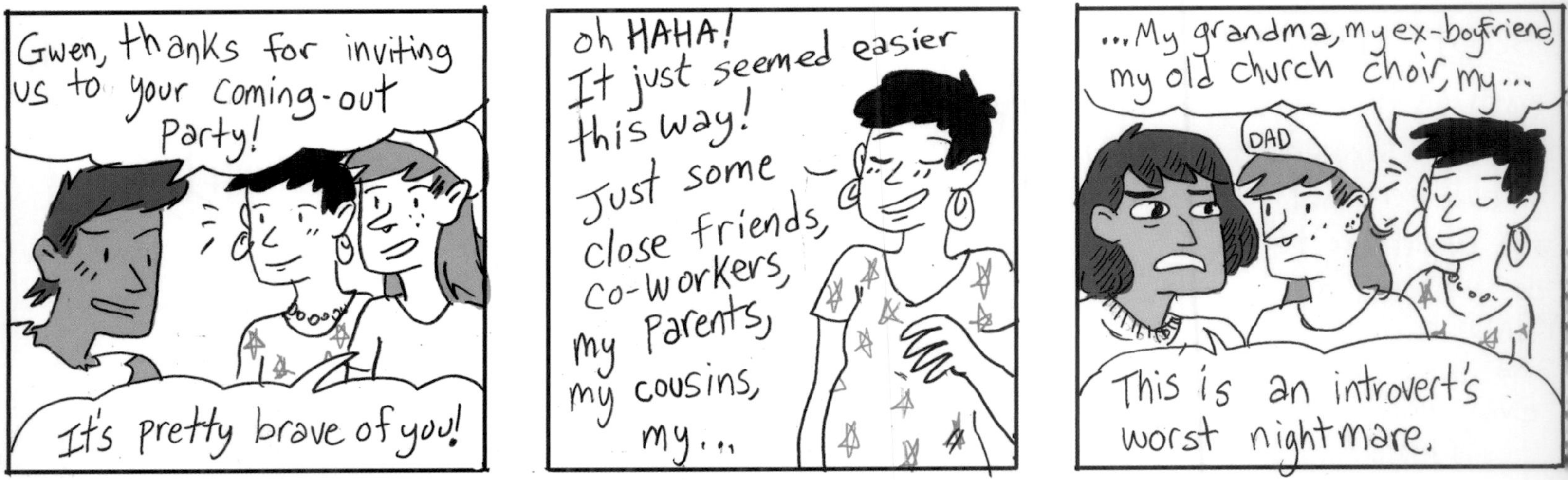
Gwen, thanks for inviting us to your coming-out Party!
It's pretty brave of you!
oh HAHA! It just seemed easier this way! Just some close friends, co-workers, my Parents, my cousins, my...
...My grandma, my ex-boyfriend, my old church choir, my...
This is an introvert's worst nightmare.

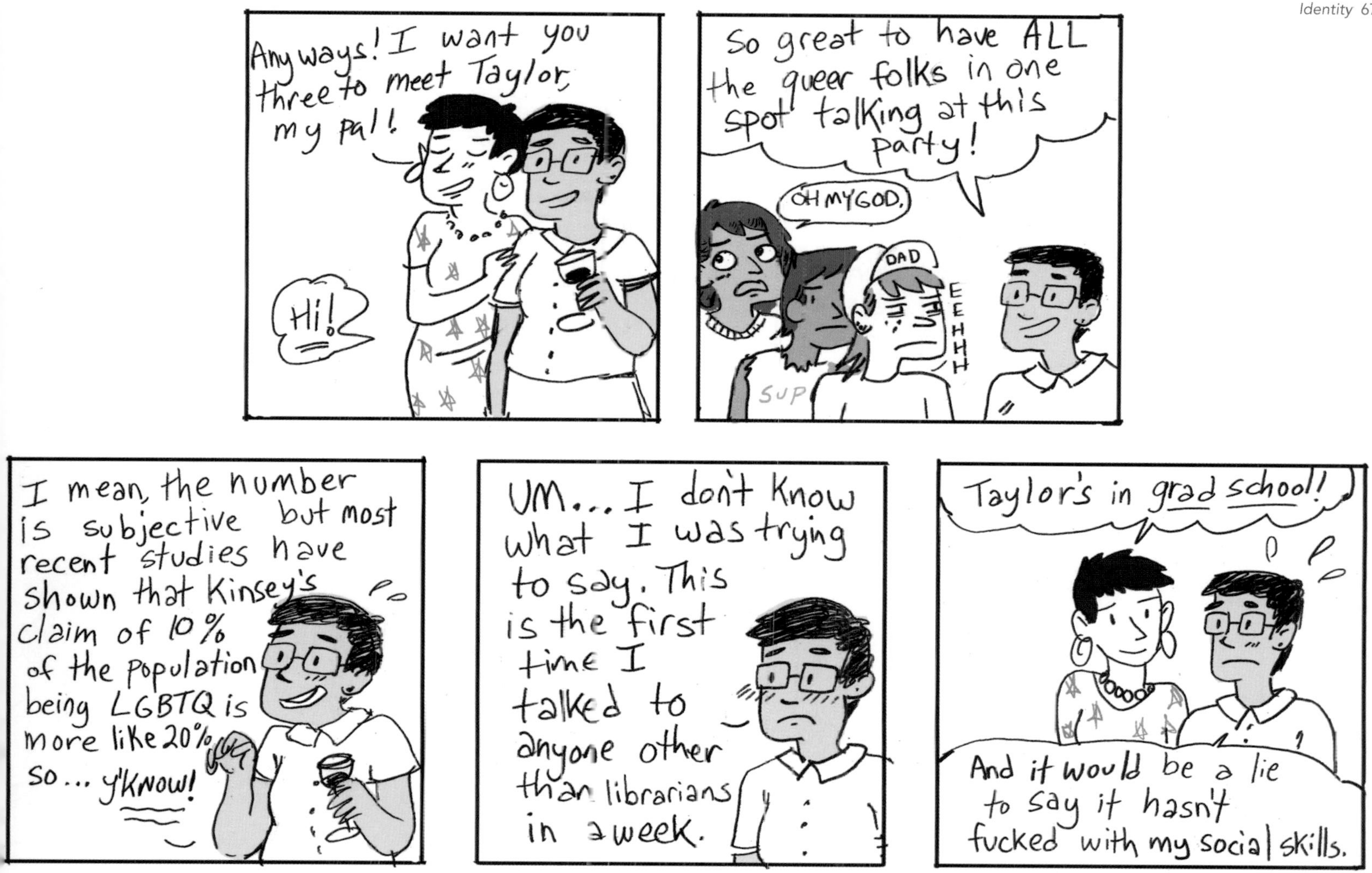
Anyways! I want you three to meet Taylor, my pal!
Hi!
So great to have ALL the queer folks in one spot talking at this party!
OH MY GOD.
DAD
SUP
EEHHHH
I mean, the number is subjective but most recent studies have shown that Kinsey's claim of 10% of the population being LGBTQ is more like 20% so... y'know!
UM... I don't know what I was trying to say. This is the first time I talked to anyone other than librarians in a week.
Taylor's in grad school!
And it would be a lie to say it hasn't fucked with my social skills.

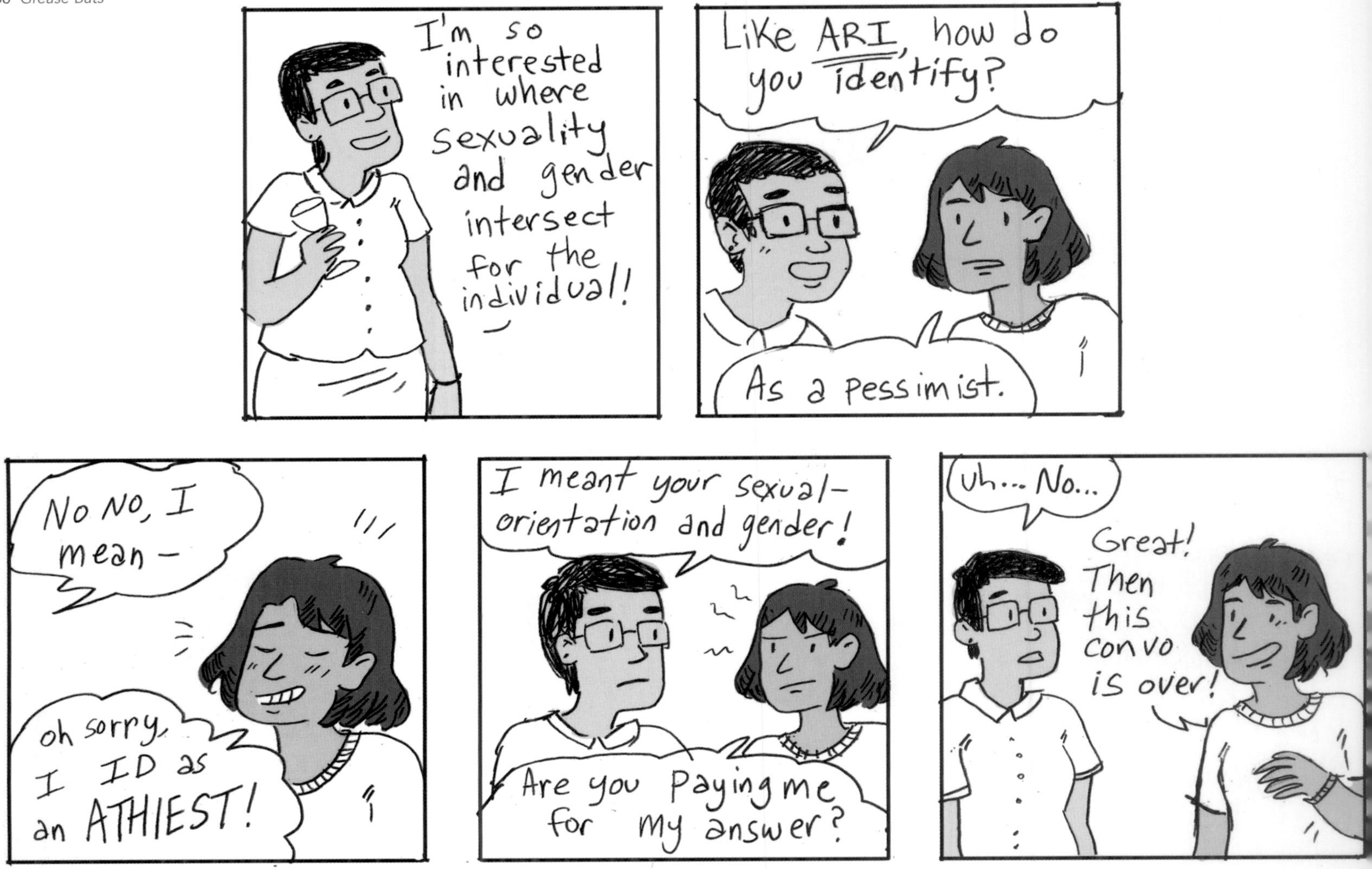
I'm so interested in where sexuality and gender intersect for the individual!
Like ARI, how do you identify?
As a pessimist.
No No, I mean –
oh sorry, I ID as an ATHIEST!
I meant your sexual-orientation and gender!
Are you Paying me for my answer?
uh... No...
Great! Then this convo is over!

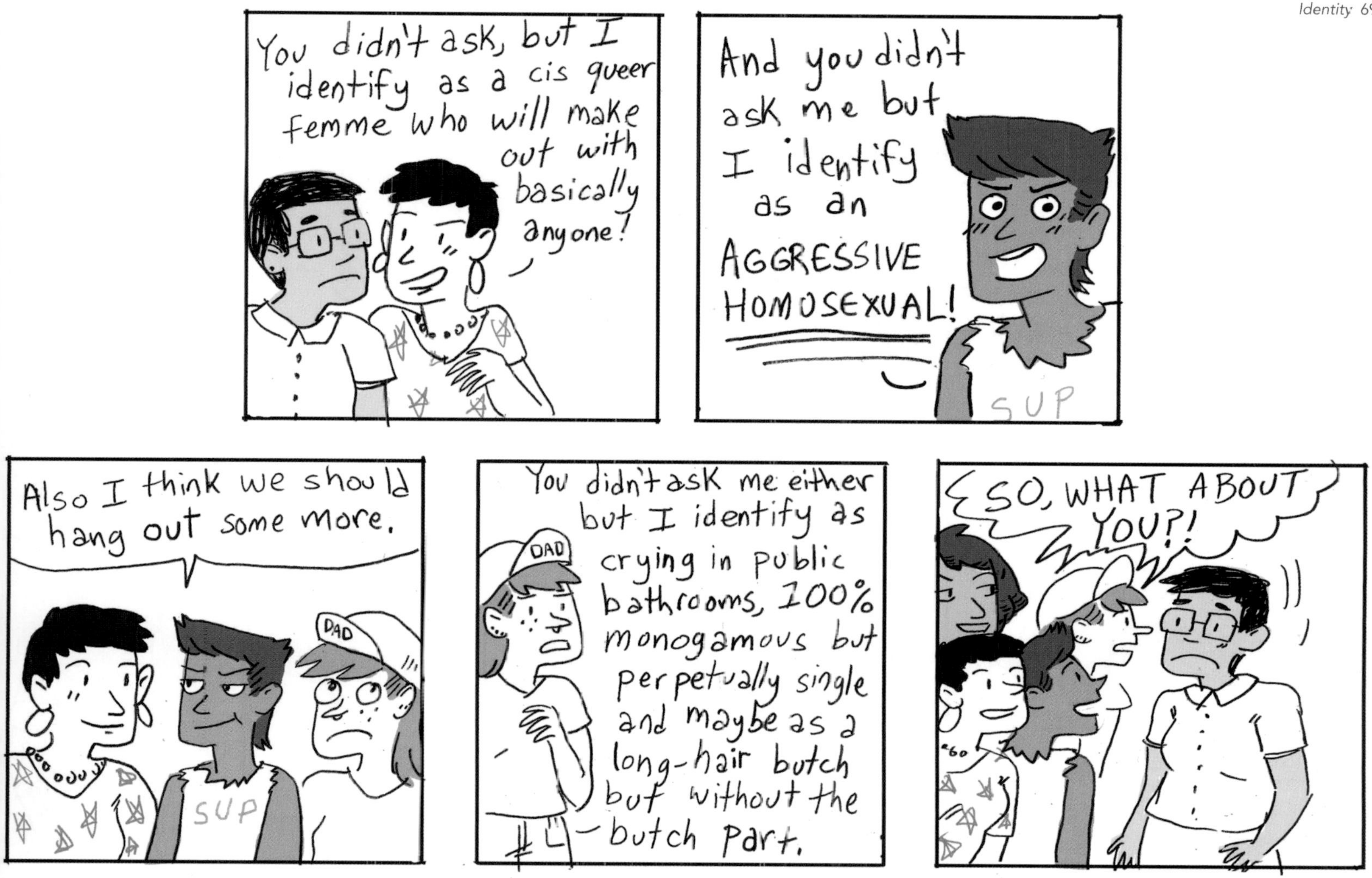

You didn't ask, but I identify as a cis queer femme who will make out with basically anyone!
And you didn't ask me but I identify as an AGGRESSIVE HOMOSEXUAL!
SUP
Also I think we should hang out some more.
DAD
SUP
DAD
You didn't ask me either but I identify as crying in public bathrooms, 100% monogamous but perpetually single and maybe as a long-hair butch but without the butch part.
SO, WHAT ABOUT YOU?!

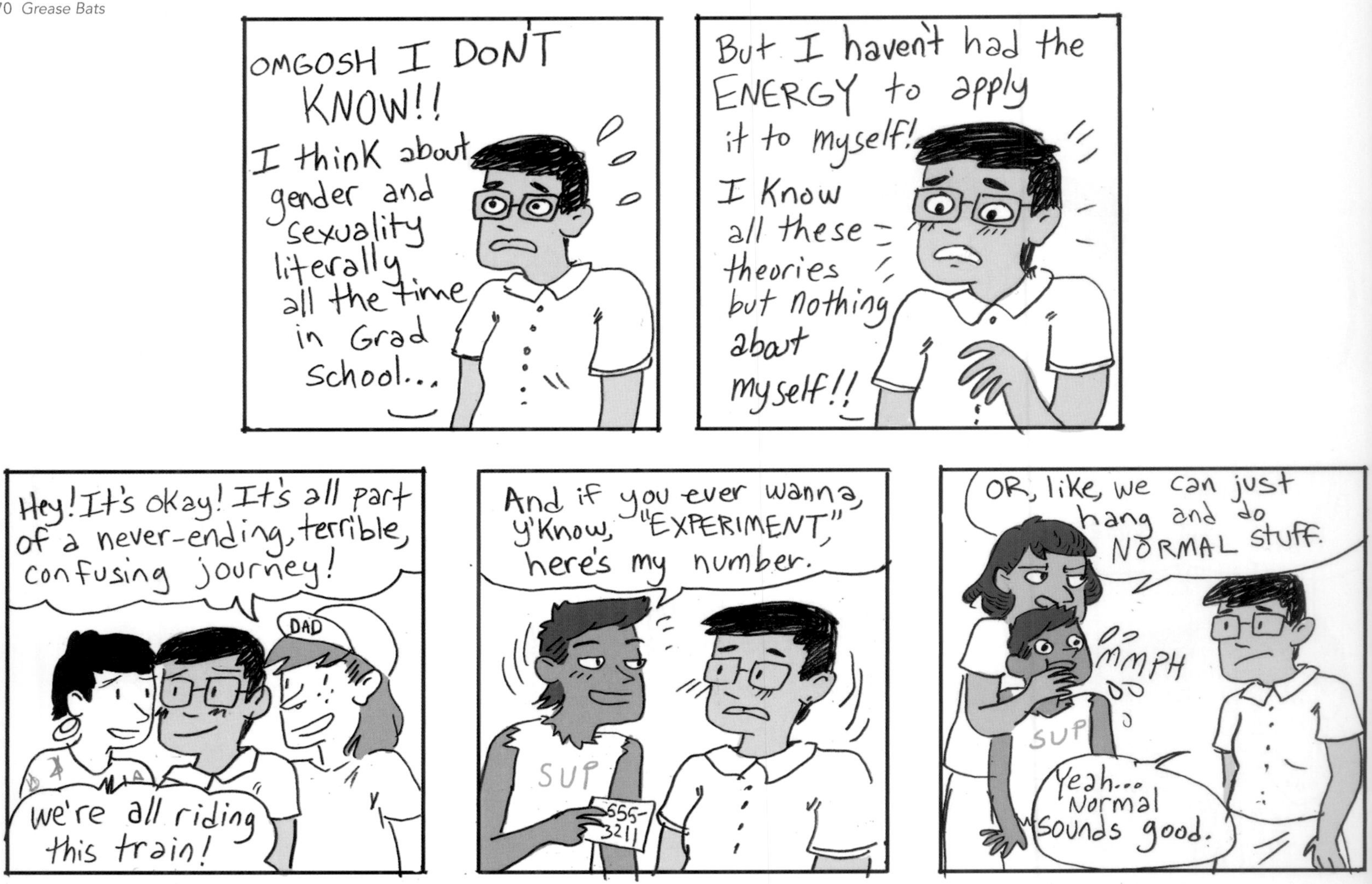
OMGOSH I DON'T KNOW!!
I think about gender and sexuality literally all the time in Grad school...
But I haven't had the ENERGY to apply it to myself!
I Know all these theories but nothing about myself!!
Hey! It's okay! It's all part of a never-ending, terrible, confusing journey!
DAD
we're all riding this train!
And if you ever wanna, y'Know, "EXPERIMENT," here's my number.
SUP
555-3211
OR, like, we can just hang and do NORMAL stuff.
MMPH
SUP
Yeah... Normal sounds good.

TAG YOURSELF

SCOUT

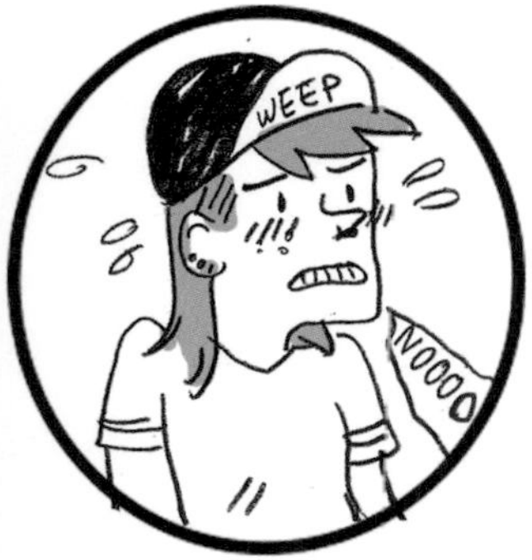
WEEP
NOOOO

- ~Covered in bike grease in a way she doesn't realize is sexy
- ~Feelings 24/7
- ~Can't handle her booze
- ~Loves burritos

TAYLOR

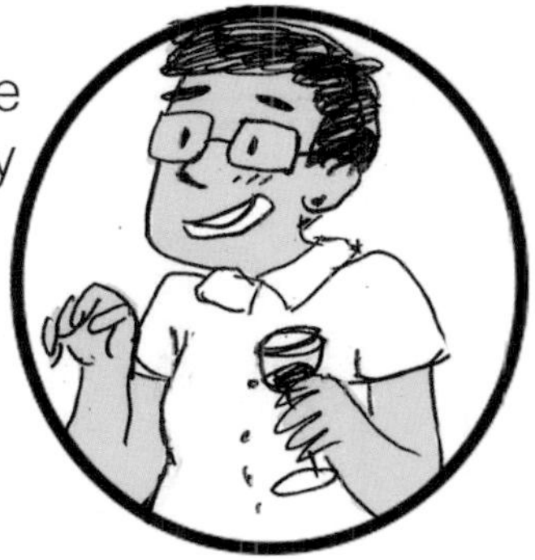

- ~Cannot turn off her analytical mind
- ~Looks @ ur bookshelf before looking @ u
- ~In grad school
- ~Awkward at parties

ARI

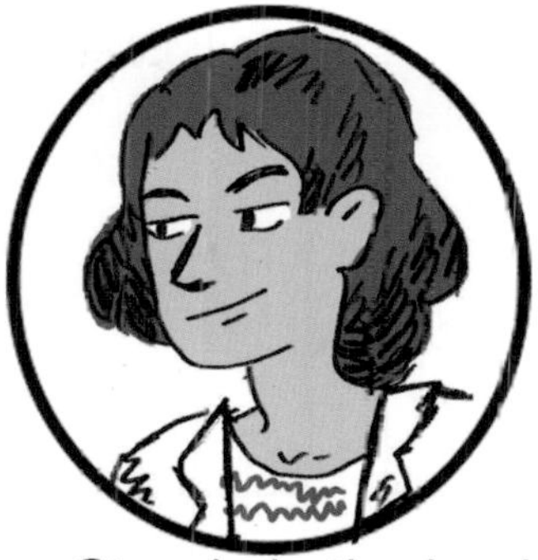

- ~Stands in the back at parties, quietly judging u
- ~More into brunch then beer pong
- ~Quietly sassy
- ~Loves being an introvert

GWEN

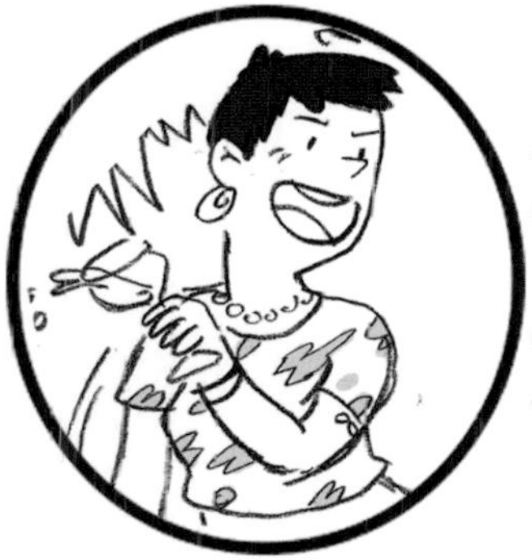

- ~Unironically drinks Cosmopolitans
- ~Will ruin u in a good way
- ~Knows how to accessorize
- ~Contagious enthusiasm

ANDY

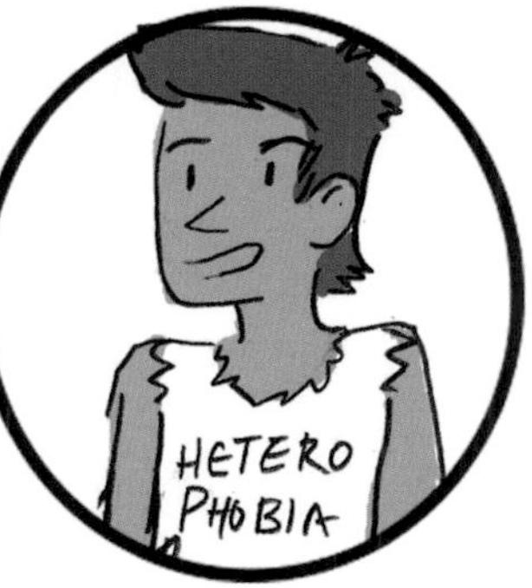
HETERO
PHOBIA

- ~Will crash a wedding
- ~Will hit on ur mom, ur neighbor, ur friend
- ~Stick-n-poke tattoos
- ~Not-so-secretly the most sensitive

SIR

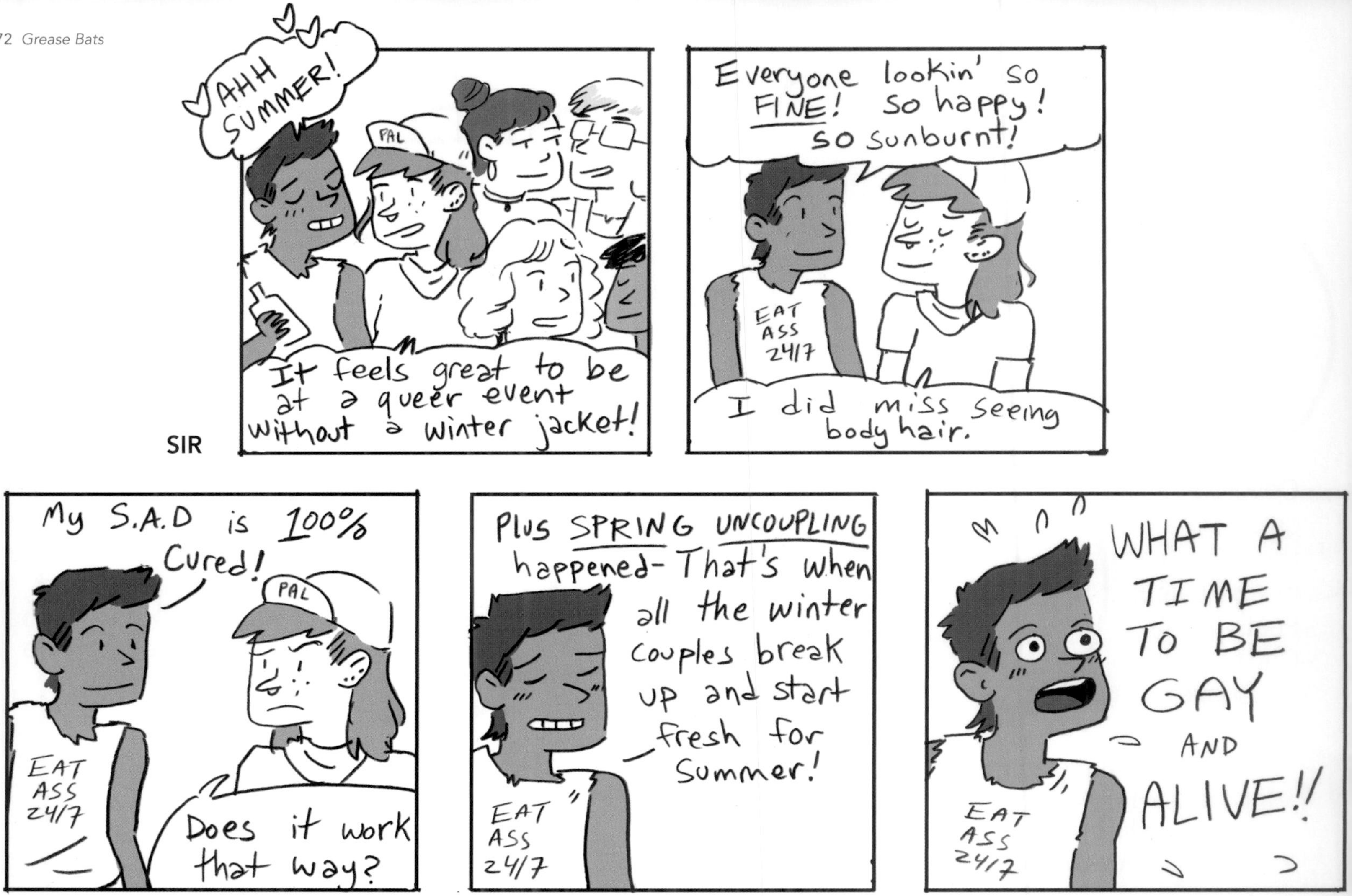
AHH SUMMER!
PAL
It feels great to be at a queer event without a winter jacket!
Everyone lookin' so FINE! so happy! so sunburnt!
I did miss seeing body hair.
EAT ASS 24/7
My S.A.D is 100% Cured!
PAL
Does it work that way?
Plus SPRING UNCOUPLING happened- That's when all the winter couples break up and start fresh for Summer!
WHAT A TIME TO BE GAY AND ALIVE!!

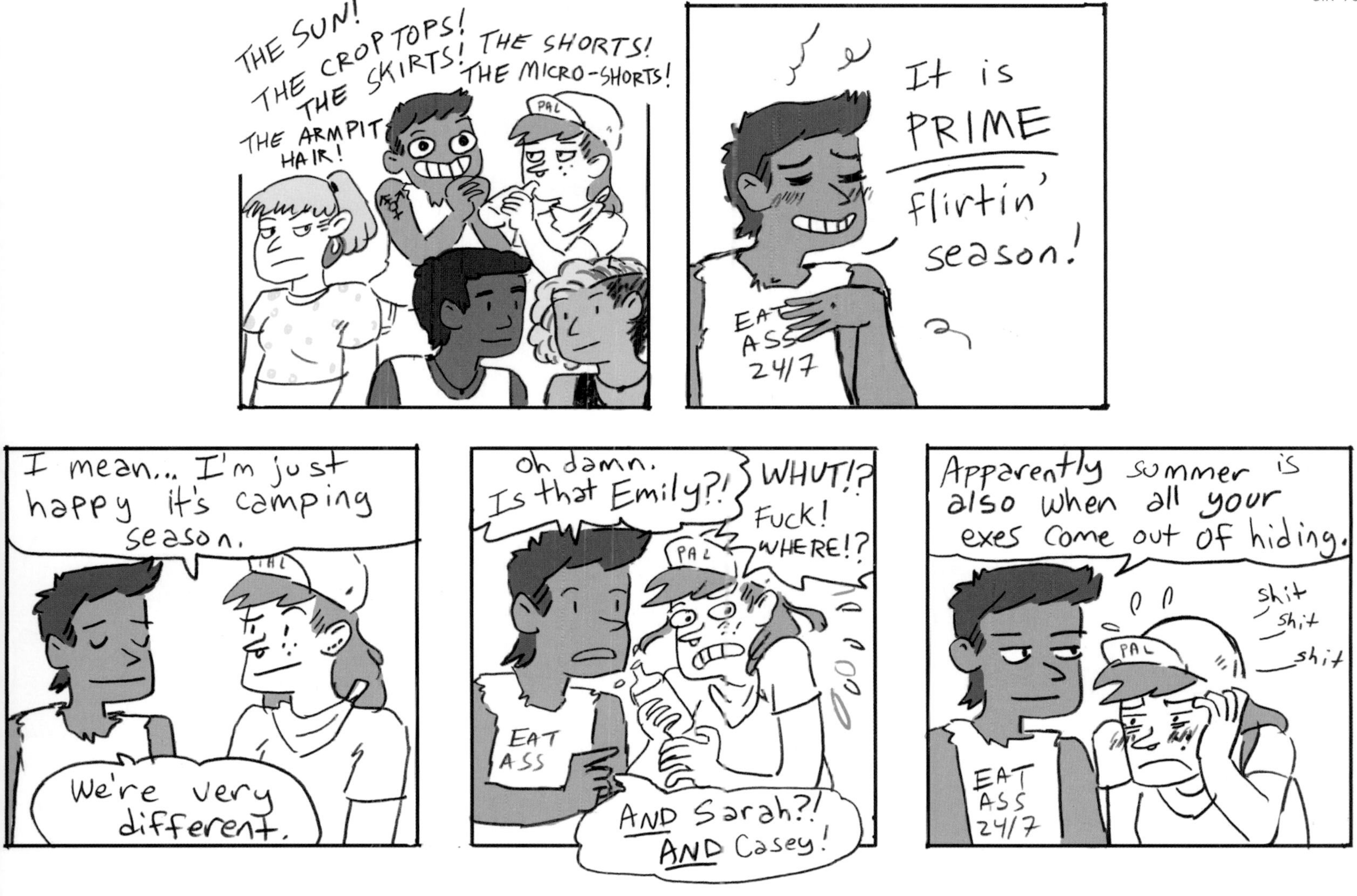
THE SUN!
THE CROP TOPS!
THE SKIRTS!
THE SHORTS!
THE MICRO-SHORTS!
THE ARMPIT HAIR!
PAL
It is PRIME flirtin' season!
EAT ASS 24/7
I mean... I'm just happy it's camping season.
PAL
We're very different.
oh damn. Is that Emily?!
WHUT!?
Fuck! WHERE!?
PAL
EAT ASS
AND Sarah?! AND Casey!
Apparently summer is also when all your exes come out of hiding.
shit
shit
shit
PAL
EAT ASS 24/7

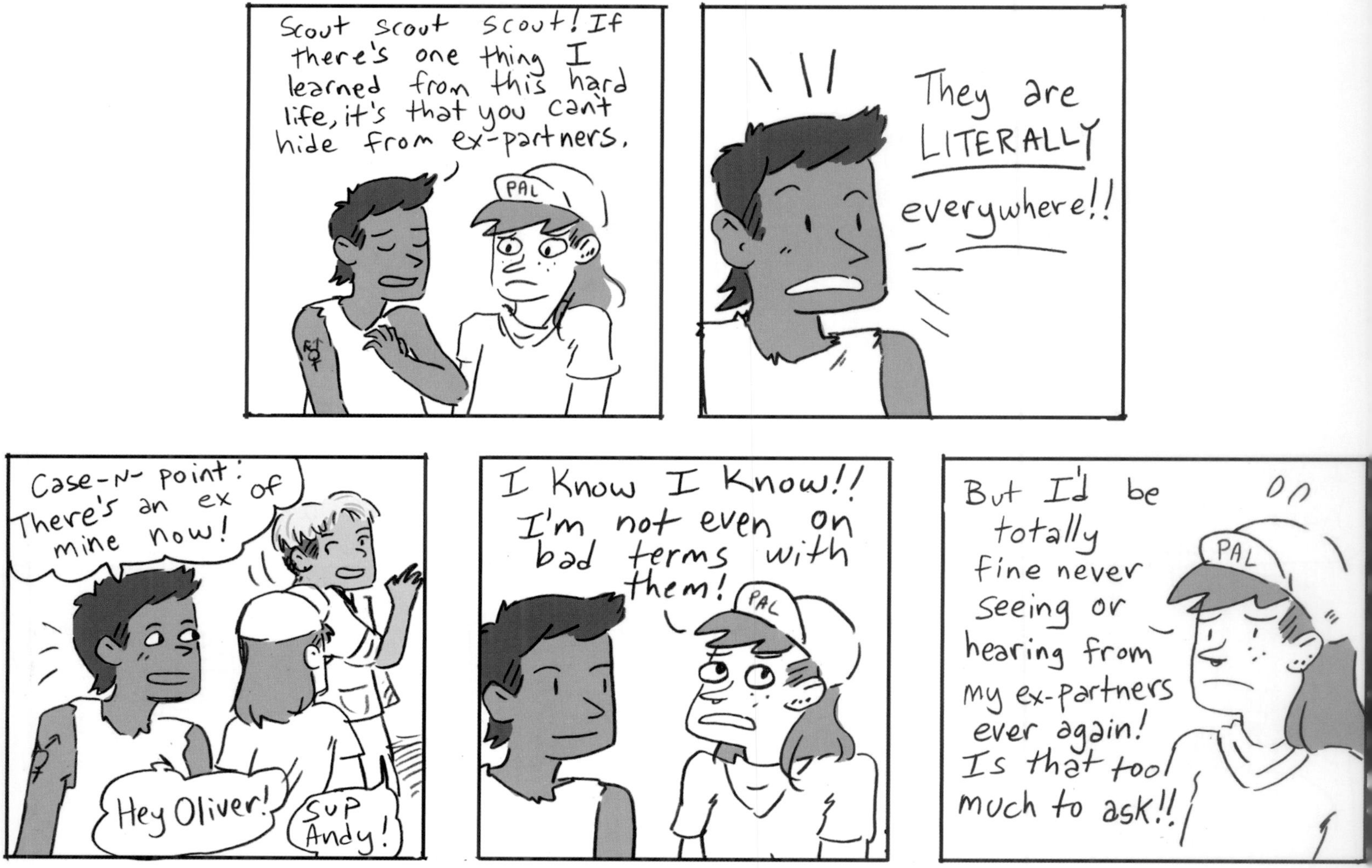
Scout scout scout! If there's one thing I learned from this hard life, it's that you can't hide from ex-partners.
They are LITERALLY everywhere!!
Case-N-point! There's an ex of mine now!
Hey Oliver!
Sup Andy!
I Know I Know!! I'm not even on bad terms with them!
But I'd be totally fine never seeing or hearing from my ex-partners ever again! Is that too much to ask!!
PAL

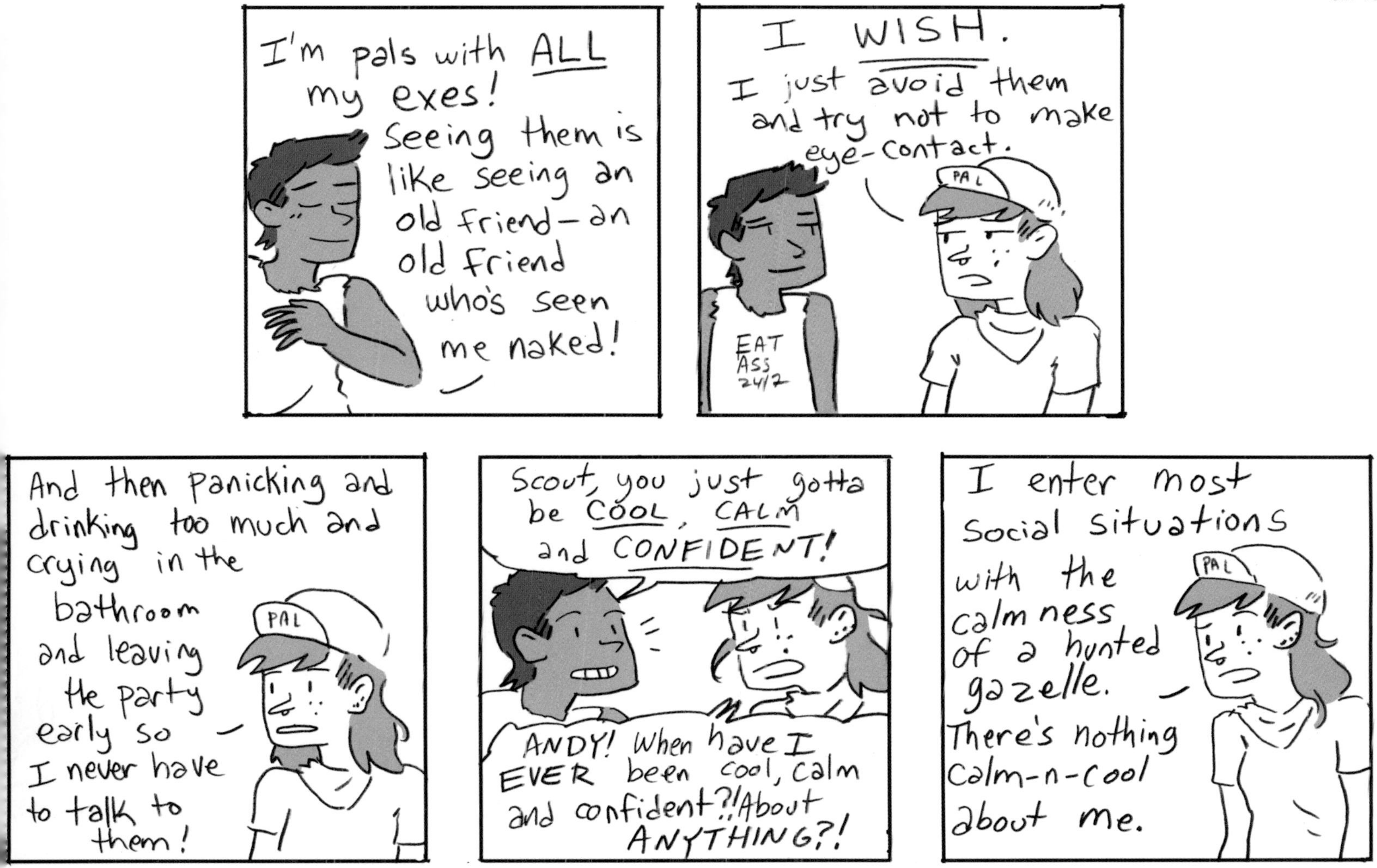
I'm pals with ALL my exes! Seeing them is like seeing an old friend—an old friend who's seen me naked!
I WISH.
I just avoid them and try not to make eye-contact.
EAT ASS 24/7
PAL
And then panicking and drinking too much and crying in the bathroom and leaving the party early so I never have to talk to them!
PAL
Scout, you just gotta be COOL, CALM and CONFIDENT!
ANDY! When have I EVER been cool, calm and confident?! About ANYTHING?!
I enter most social situations with the calmness of a hunted gazelle.
There's nothing calm-n-cool about me.
PAL

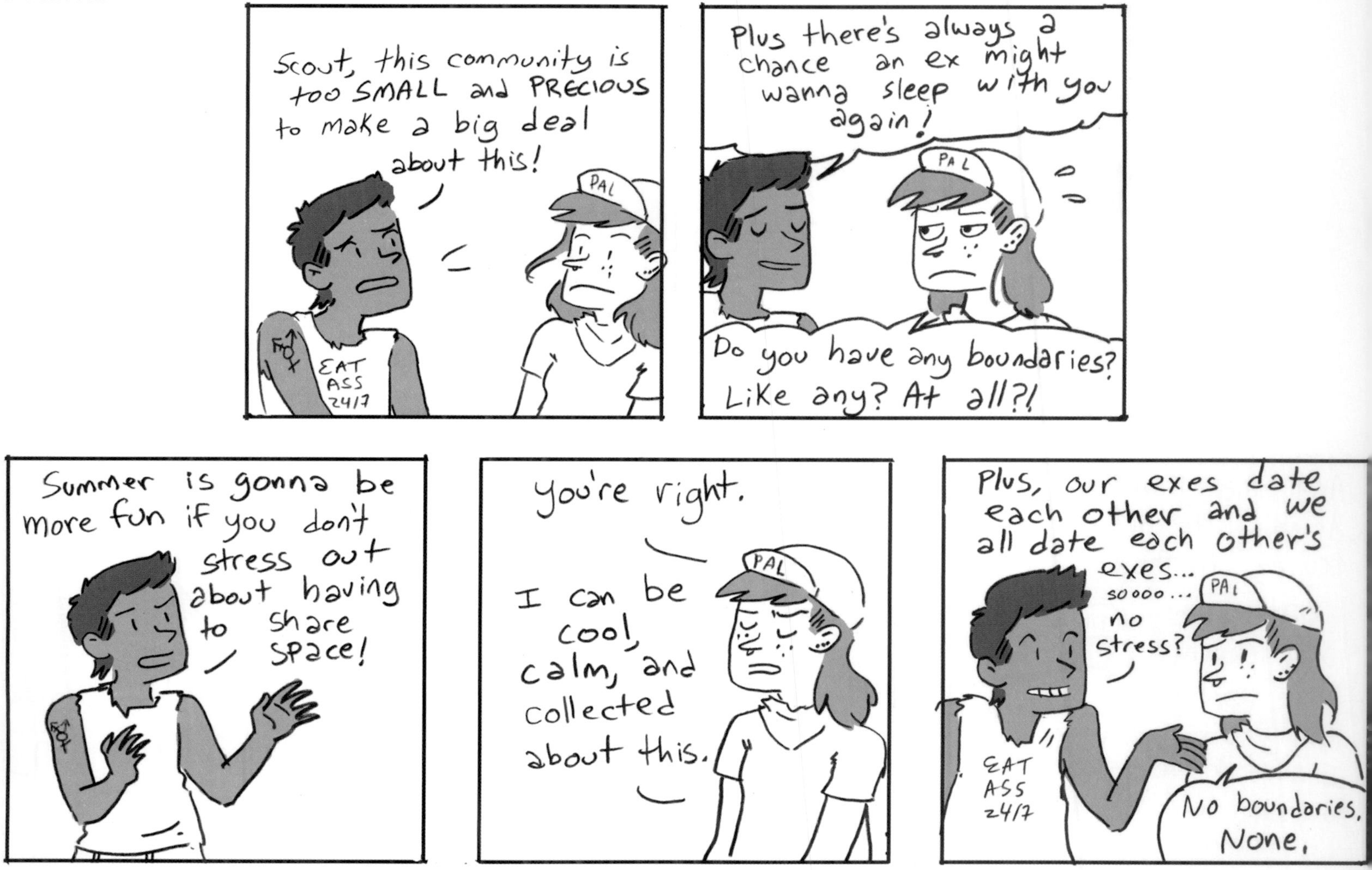
Scout, this community is too SMALL and PRECIOUS to make a big deal about this!
EAT ASS 24/7
Plus there's always a chance an ex might wanna sleep with you again!
PAL
Do you have any boundaries? Like any? At all?!
Summer is gonna be more fun if you don't stress out about having to share space!
You're right.
I can be cool, calm, and collected about this.
Plus, our exes date each other and we all date each other's exes... soooo... no stress?
No boundaries. None.

Summer Exes

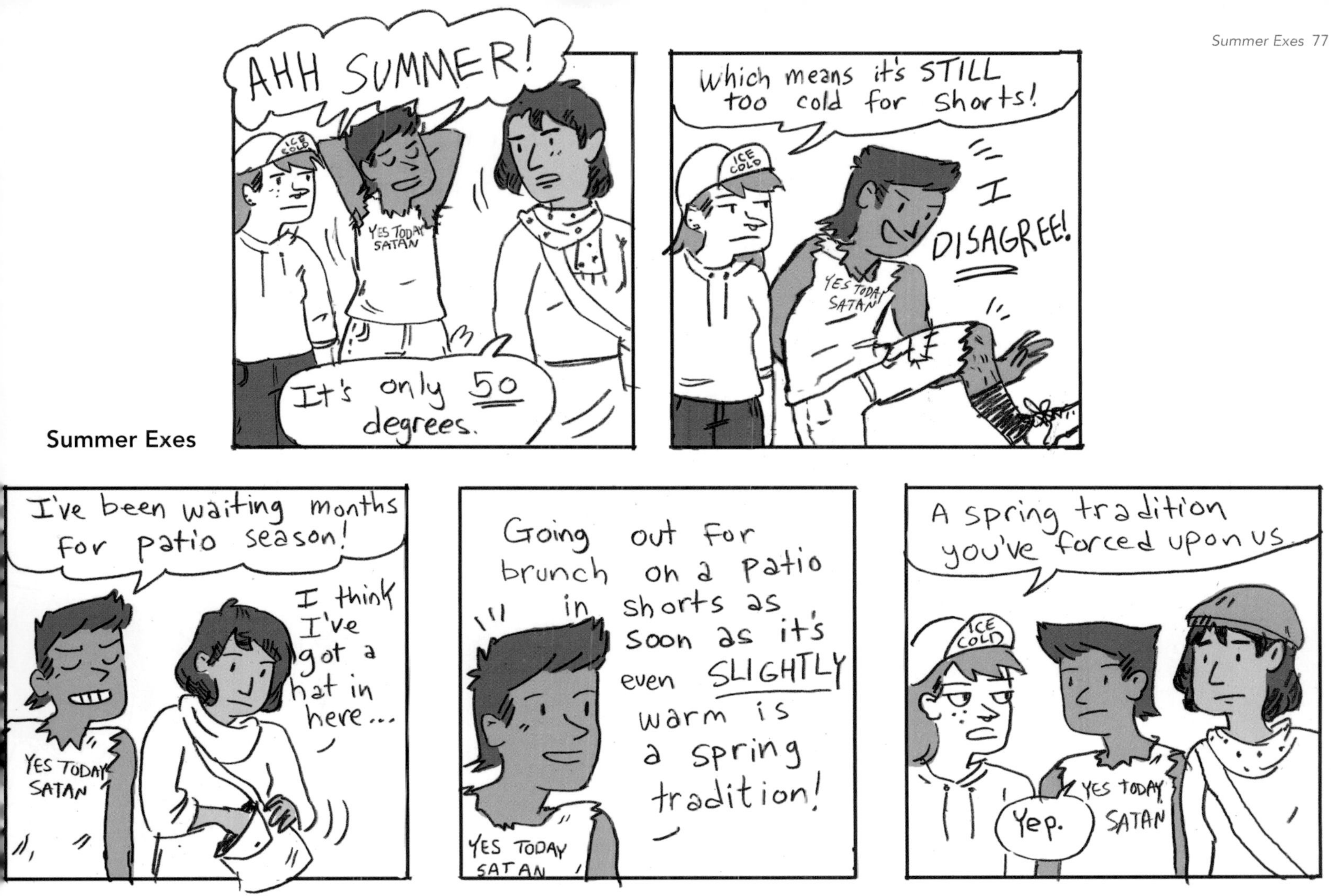
AHH SUMMER!
It's only 50 degrees.
Which means it's STILL too cold for shorts!
I DISAGREE!
YES TODAY SATAN
I've been waiting months for patio season!
I think I've got a hat in here...
Going out for brunch on a patio in shorts as soon as it's even SLIGHTLY warm is a spring tradition!
A spring tradition you've forced upon us.
Yep.
ICE COLD

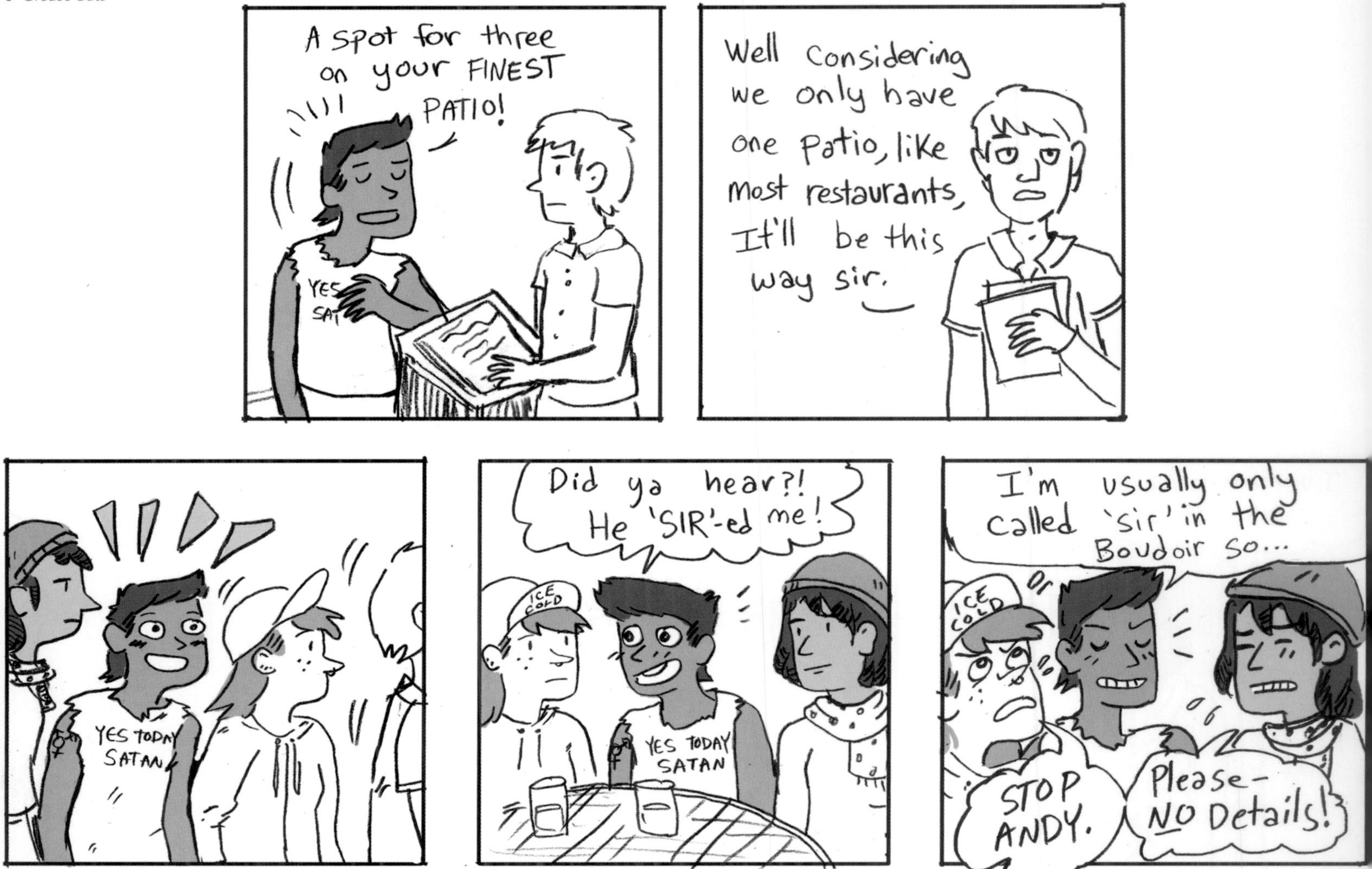
A spot for three on your FINEST PATIO!
YES SAT
Well considering we only have one Patio, like most restaurants, It'll be this way sir.
YES TODAY SATAN
Did ya hear?! He 'SIR'-ed me!
ICE COLD
YES TODAY SATAN
I'm usually only called 'sir' in the Boudoir so...
ICE COLD
STOP ANDY.
Please- NO Details!

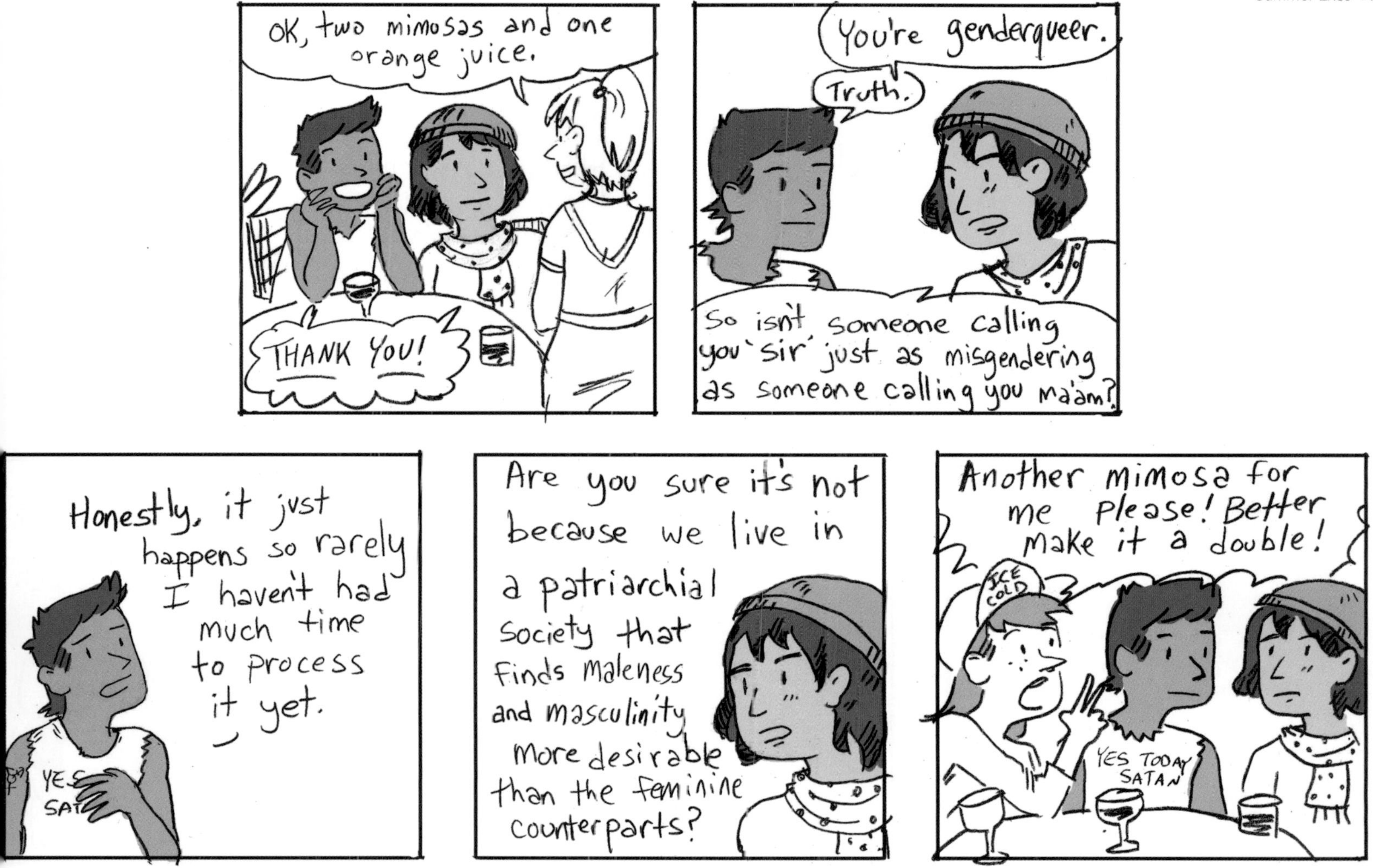
OK, two mimosas and one orange juice.
THANK YOU!
You're genderqueer.
Truth.
So isn't someone calling you 'sir' just as misgendering as someone calling you ma'am?
Honestly, it just happens so rarely I haven't had much time to process it yet.
Are you sure it's not because we live in a patriarchial society that finds maleness and masculinity more desirable than the feminine counterparts?
Another mimosa for me please! Better make it a double!
ICE COLD
YES TODAY SATAN

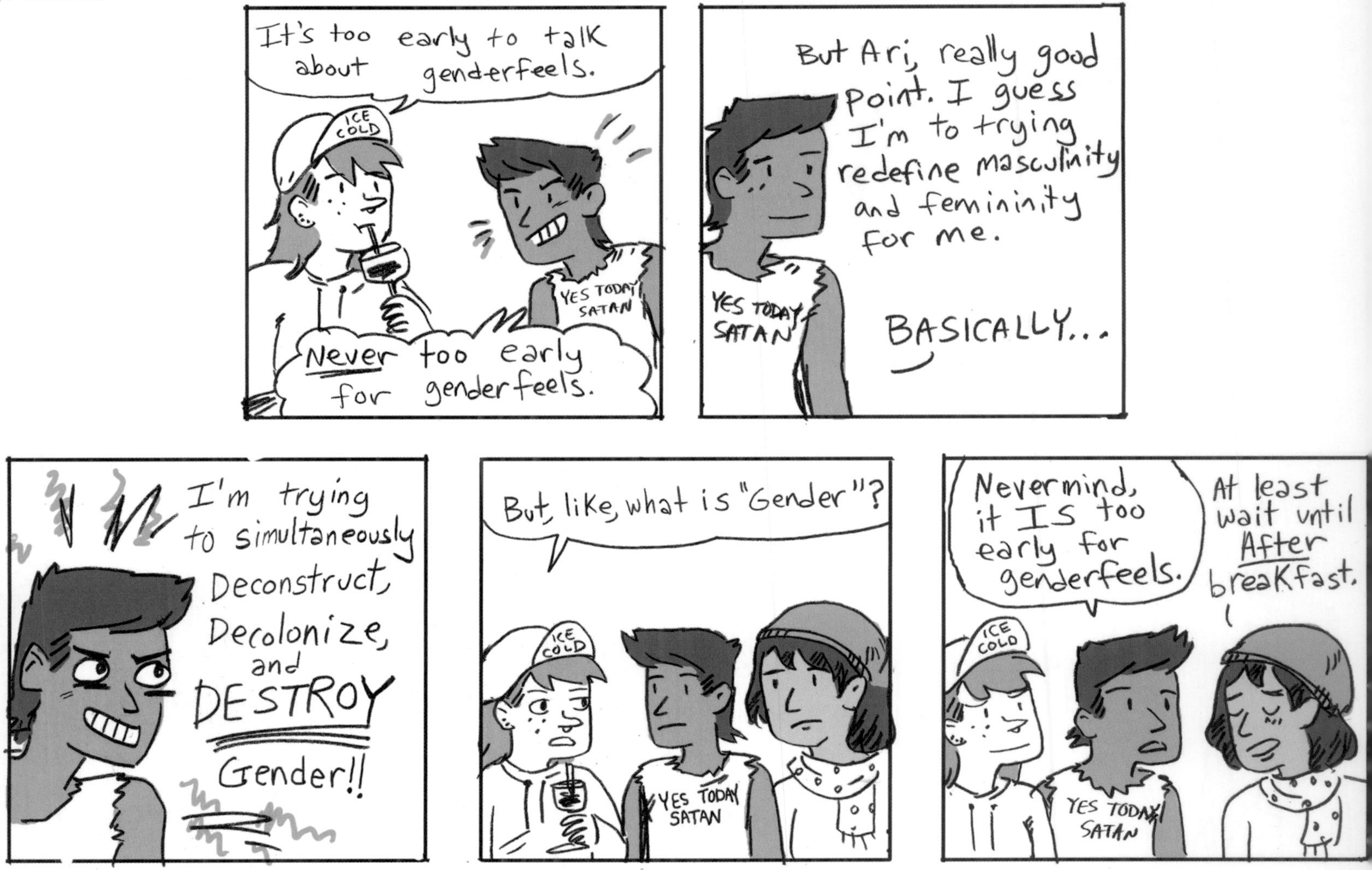
It's too early to talk about genderfeels.
ICE COLD
YES TODAY SATAN
Never too early for genderfeels.
YES TODAY SATAN
But Ari, really good point. I guess I'm to trying redefine masculinity and femininity for me.
BASICALLY...
I'm trying to simultaneously Deconstruct, Decolonize, and DESTROY Gender!!
But, like, what is "Gender"?
ICE COLD
YES TODAY SATAN
Nevermind, it IS too early for genderfeels.
At least wait until After breakfast.
ICE COLD
YES TODAY SATAN

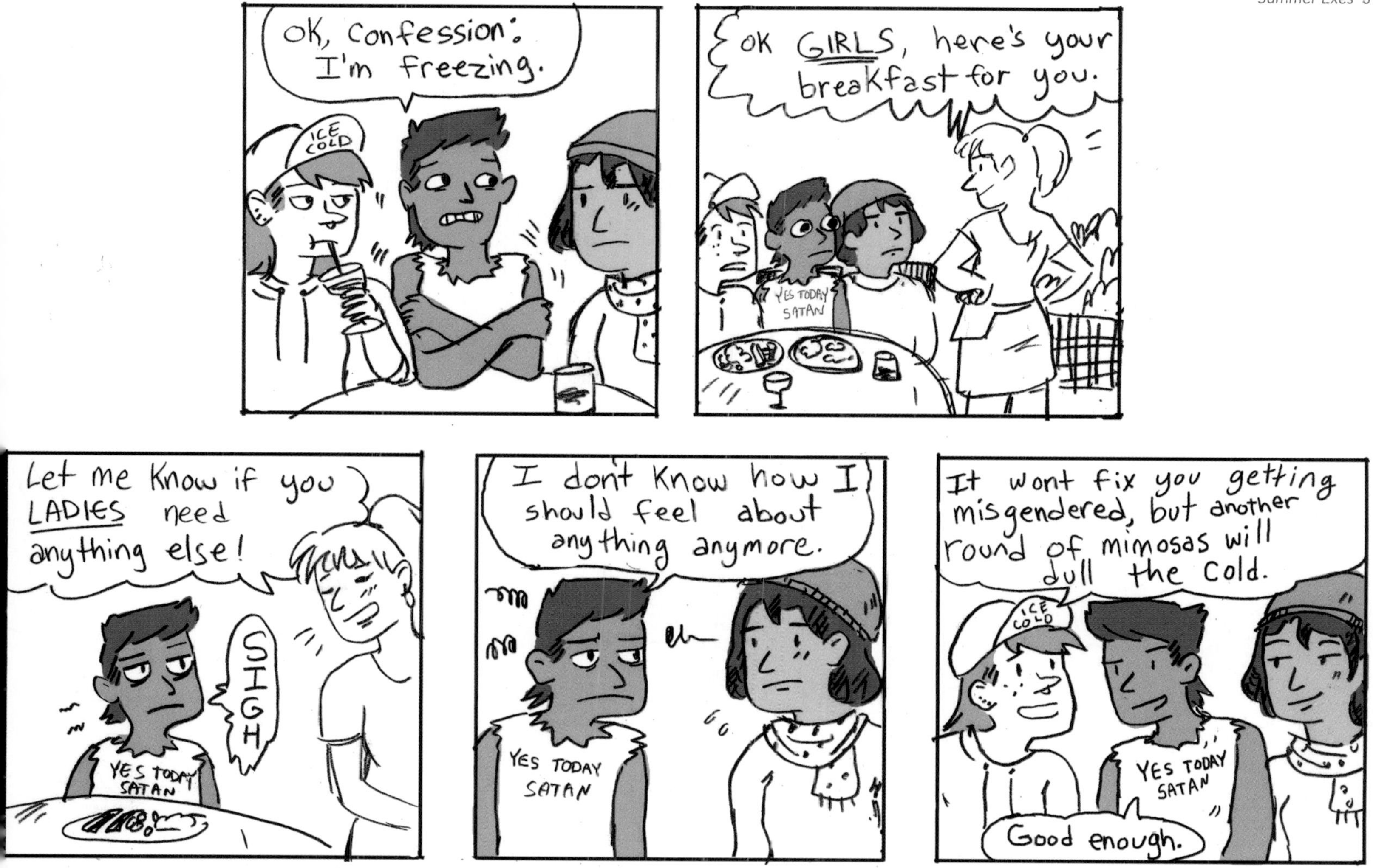
OK, confession: I'm freezing.
ICE COLD
OK GIRLS, here's your breakfast for you.
YES TODAY SATAN
Let me know if you LADIES need anything else!
SIGH
YES TODAY SATAN
I don't know how I should feel about anything anymore.
YES TODAY SATAN
It wont fix you getting misgendered, but another round of mimosas will dull the cold.
ICE COLD
YES TODAY SATAN
Good enough.

Rite of Passage

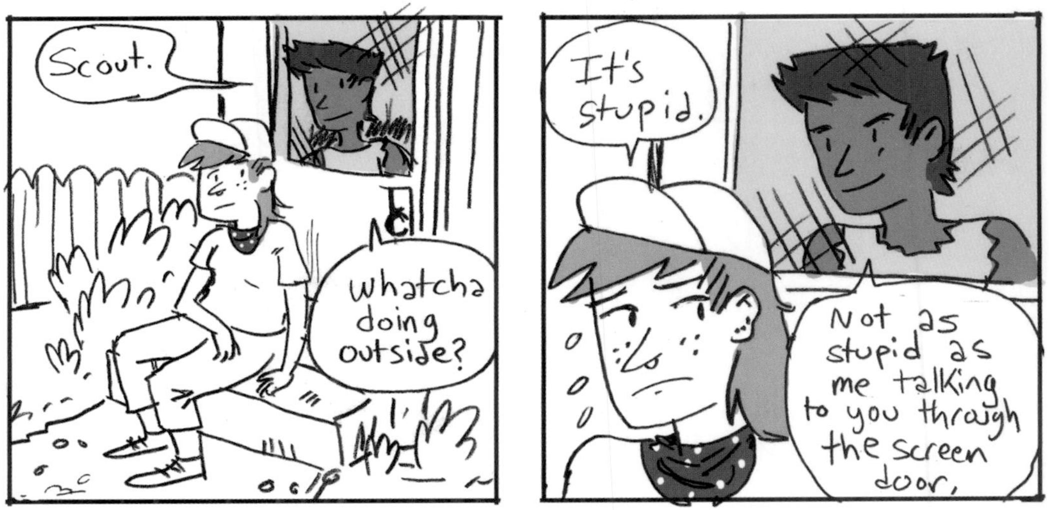
Scout.
whatcha doing outside?
It's stupid.
Not as stupid as me talking to you through the screen door,

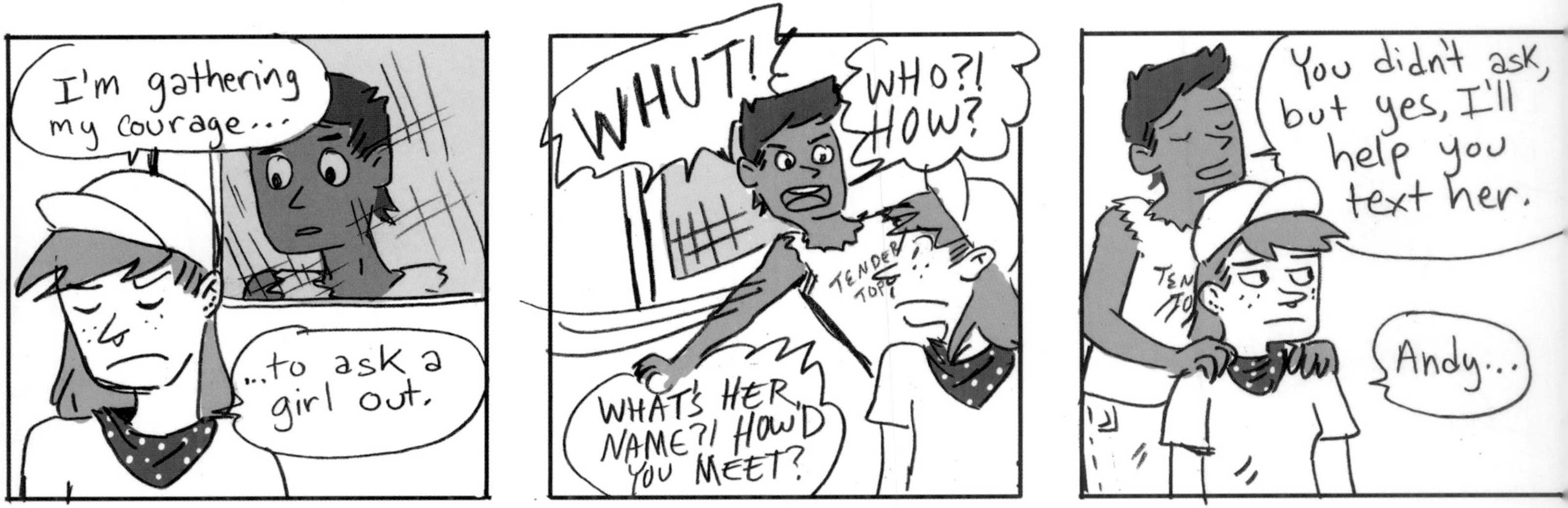
I'm gathering my courage...
...to ask a girl out.
WHUT!
WHO?! HOW?
WHAT'S HER NAME?! HOW'D YOU MEET?
You didn't ask, but yes, I'll help you text her.
Andy...

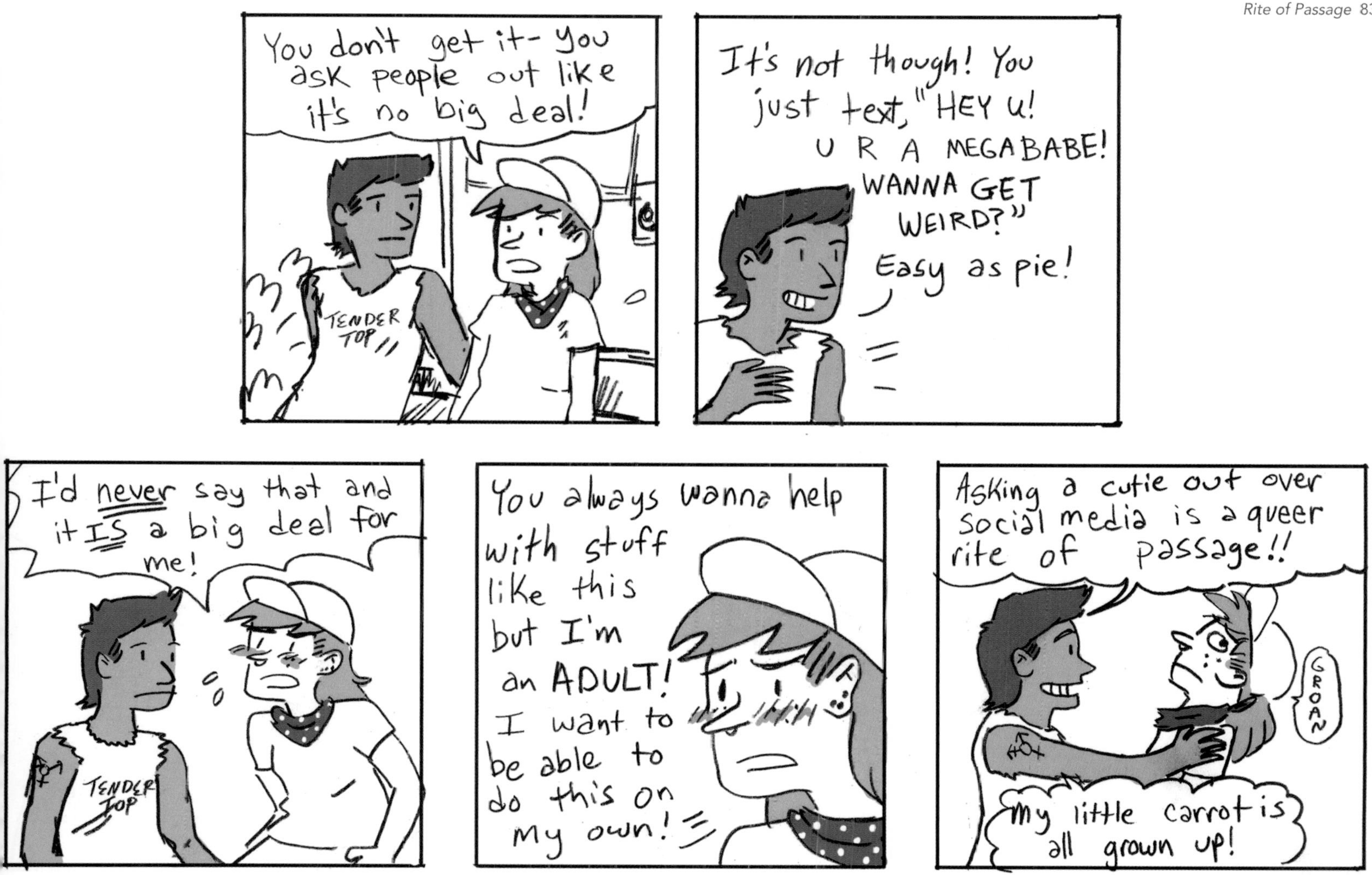
You don't get it- you ask people out like it's no big deal!
TENDER TOP
It's not though! You just text, "HEY U! U R A MEGABABE! WANNA GET WEIRD?"
Easy as pie!
I'd never say that and it IS a big deal for me!
TENDER TOP
You always wanna help with stuff like this but I'm an ADULT! I want to be able to do this on my own!
Asking a cutie out over social media is a queer rite of passage!!
GROAN
My little carrot is all grown up!

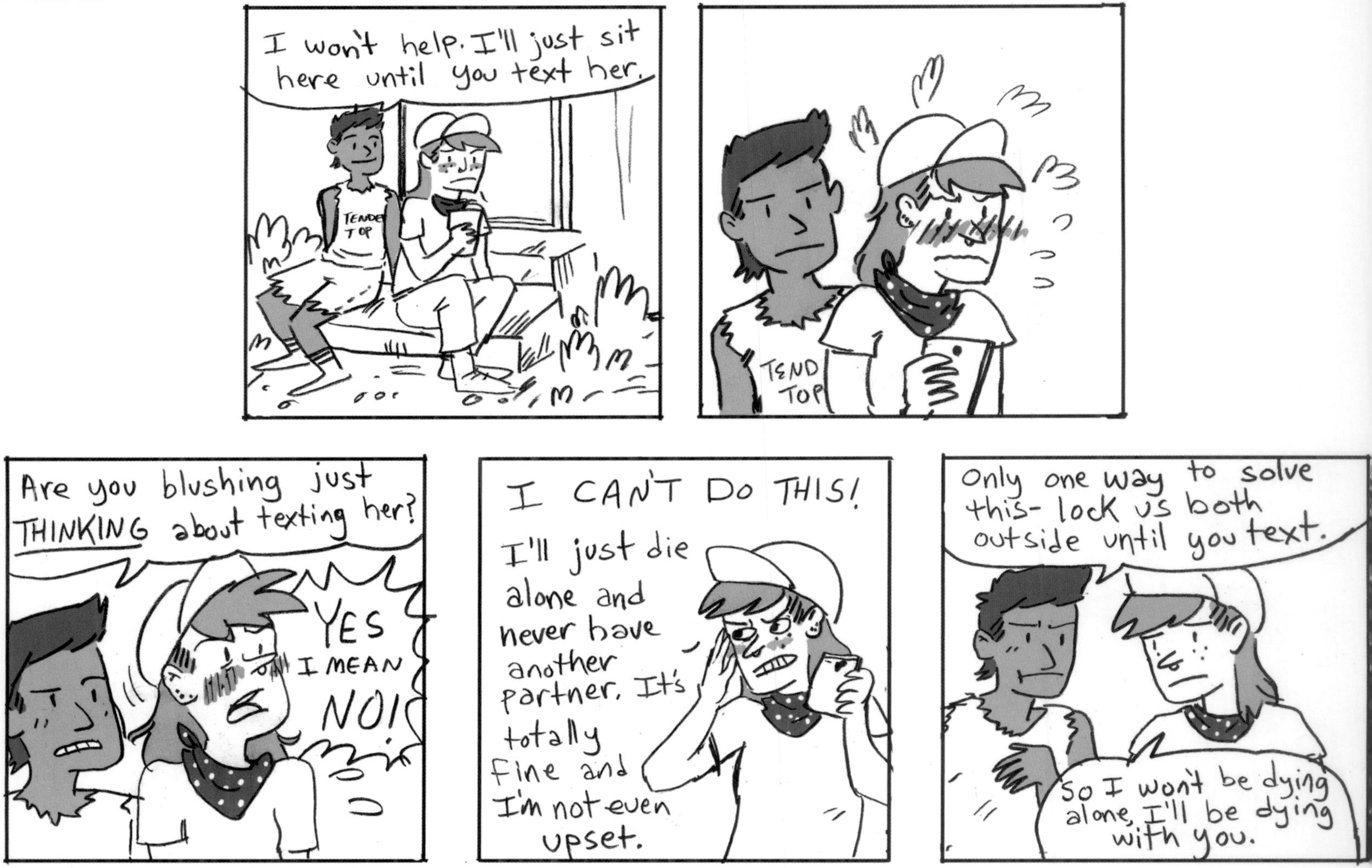
I won't help. I'll just sit here until you text her.
TENDER TOP
TEND TOP
Are you blushing just THINKING about texting her?
YES I MEAN NO!
I CAN'T DO THIS!
I'll just die alone and never have another partner. It's totally fine and I'm not even upset.
Only one way to solve this- lock us both outside until you text.
So I won't be dying alone, I'll be dying with you.

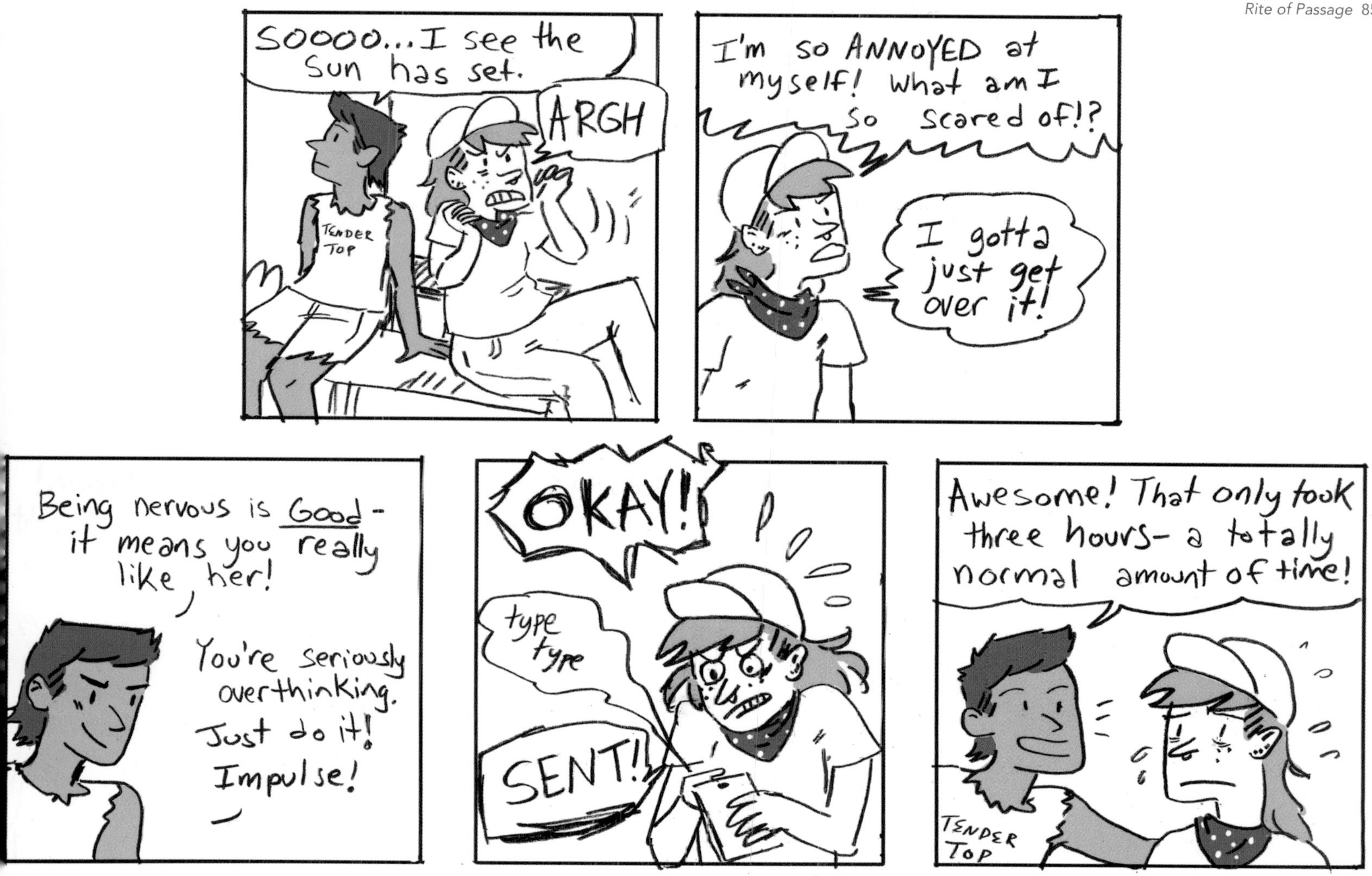
SOOOO... I see the Sun has set.
ARGH
TENDER TOP
I'm so ANNOYED at myself! What am I so scared of!?
I gotta just get over it!
Being nervous is Good - it means you really like her!
You're seriously overthinking. Just do it! Impulse!
OKAY!!
type type
SENT!
Awesome! That only took three hours - a totally normal amount of time!
TENDER TOP

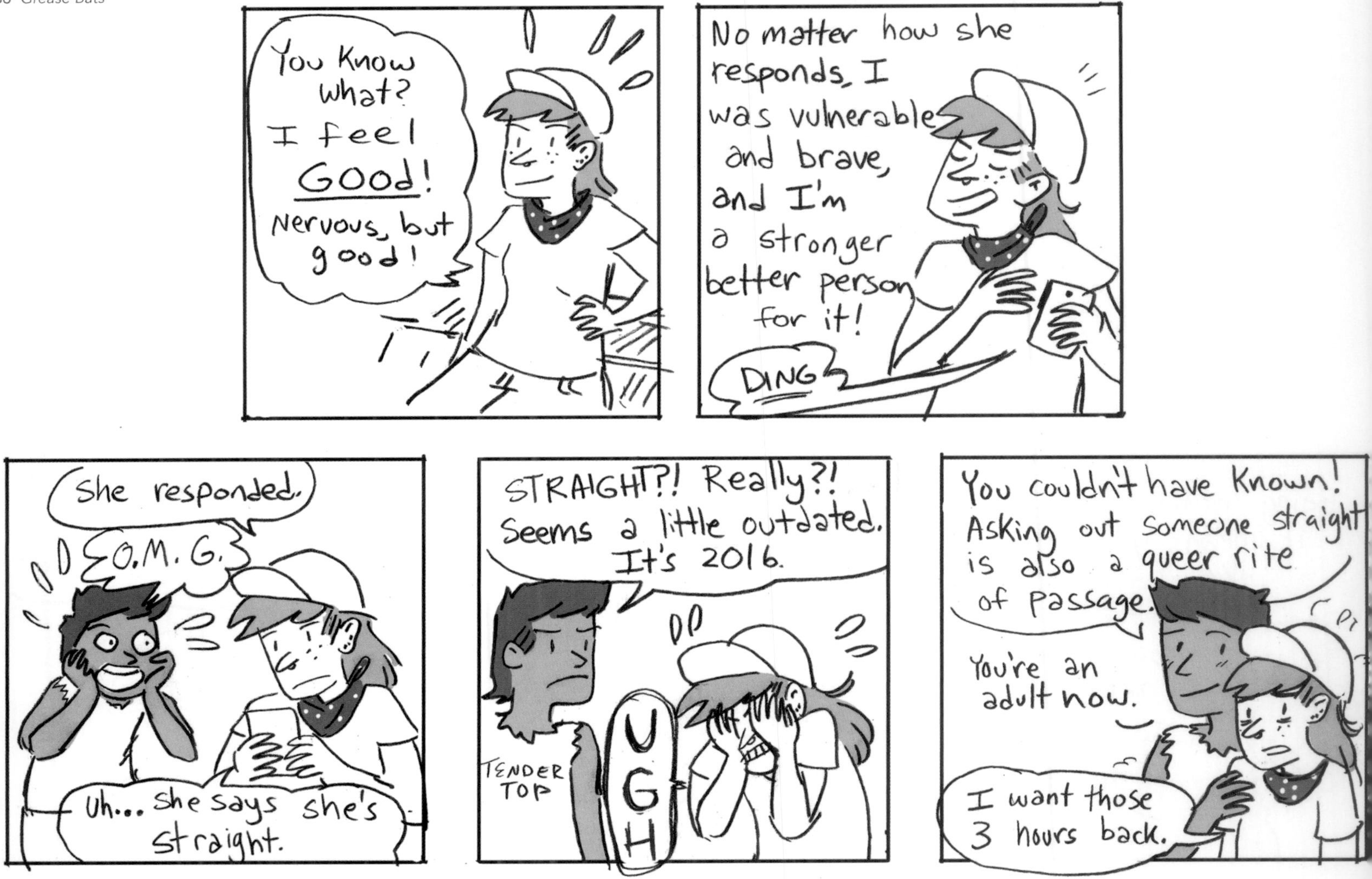
You Know what? I feel GOOD! Nervous, but good!
No matter how she responds, I was vulnerable and brave, and I'm a stronger better person for it!
DING
She responded.
O.M.G.
Uh... she says she's straight.
STRAIGHT?! Really?! Seems a little outdated. It's 2016.
TENDER TOP
UGH
You couldn't have Known! Asking out someone straight is also a queer rite of passage.
You're an adult now.
I want those 3 hours back.

XXL

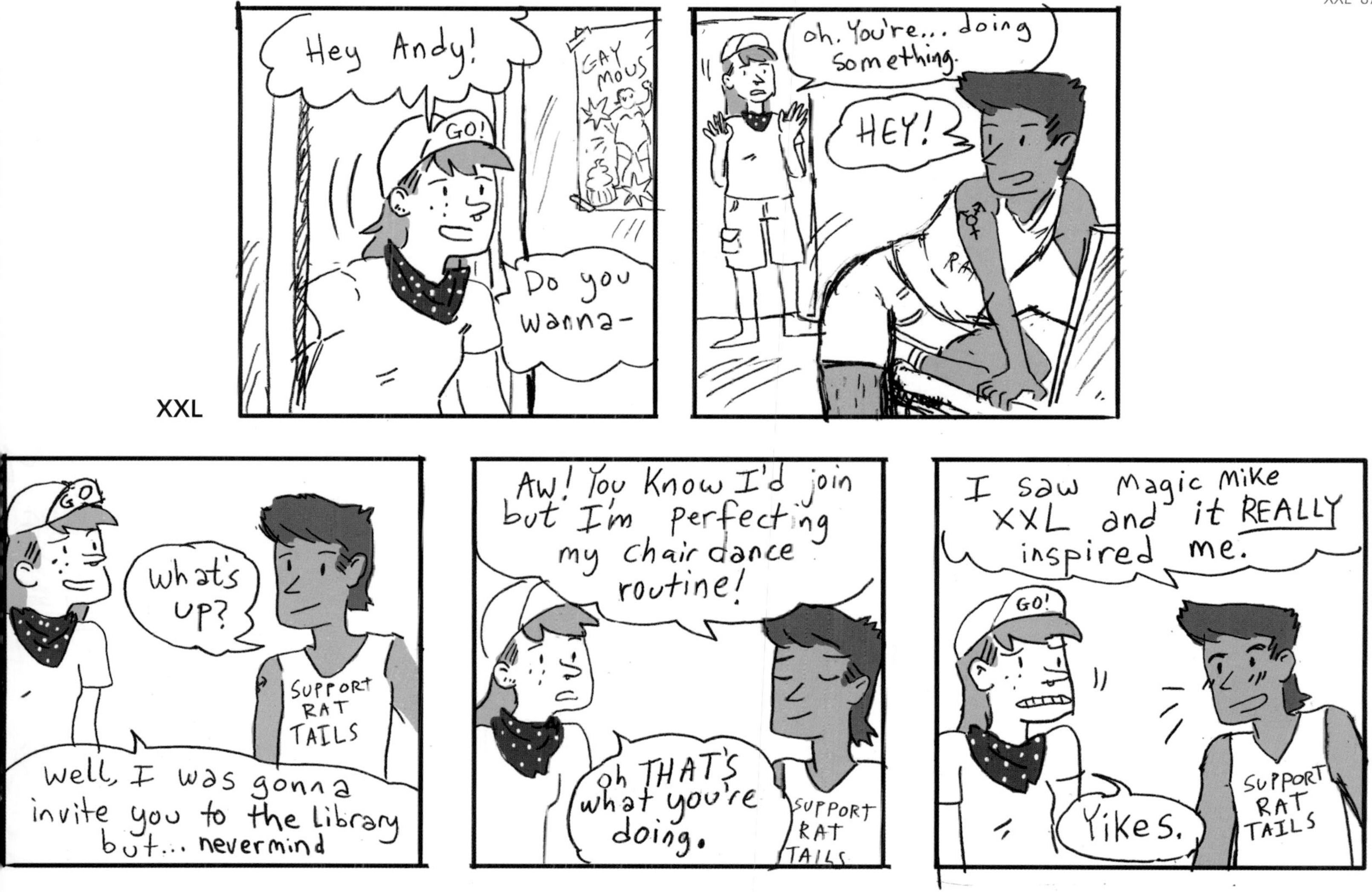
Hey Andy!
GO!
GAY MOUS
Do you wanna-
oh. You're... doing something.
HEY!
GO
what's up?
SUPPORT RAT TAILS
Well, I was gonna invite you to the library but... nevermind
Aw! You know I'd join but I'm perfecting my chair dance routine!
oh THAT'S what you're doing.
SUPPORT RAT TAILS
I saw Magic Mike XXL and it REALLY inspired me.
GO!
SUPPORT RAT TAILS
Yikes.

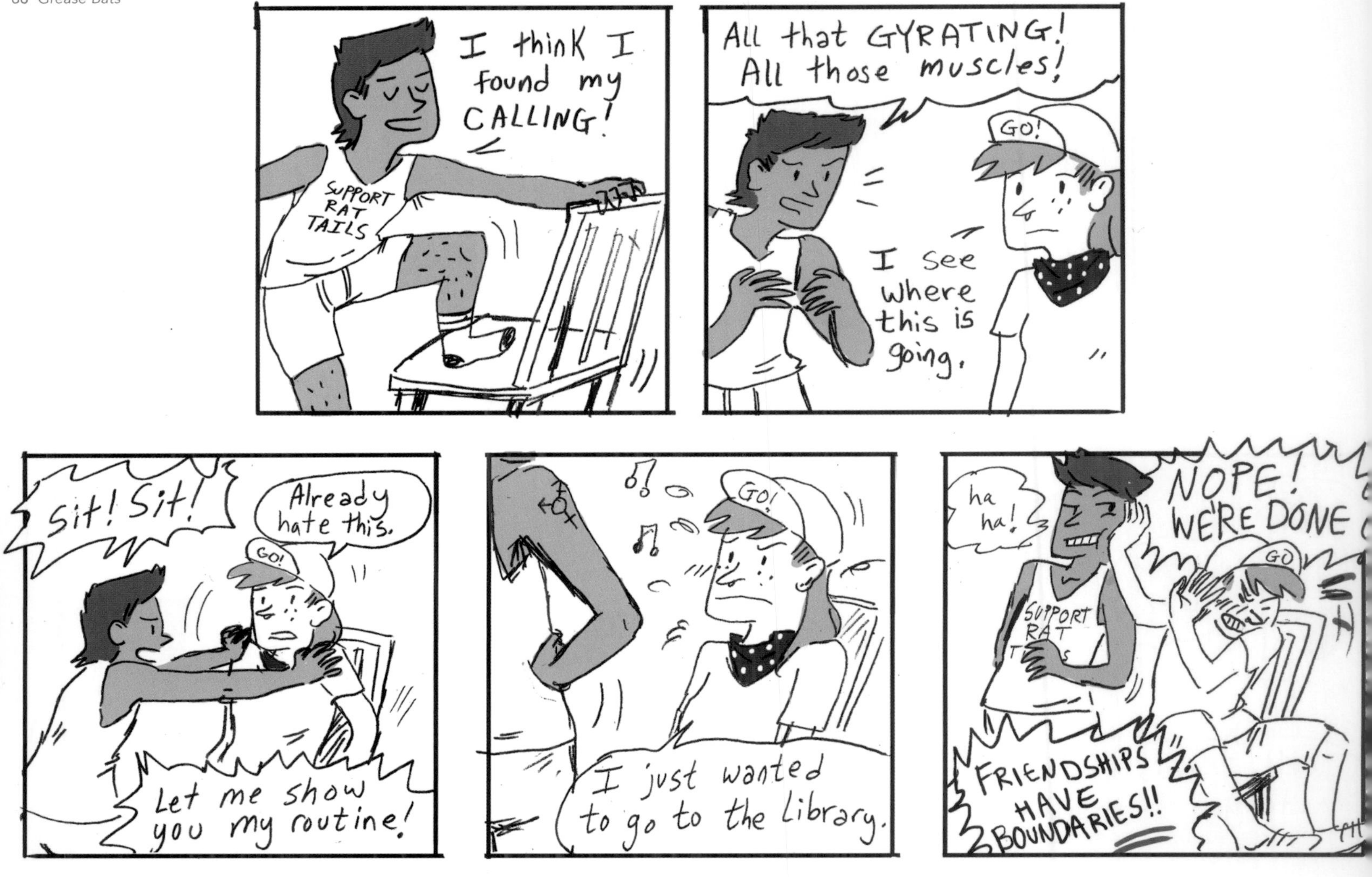
I think I found my CALLING!
SUPPORT RAT TAILS
All that GYRATING! All those muscles!
GO!
I see where this is going.
Sit! Sit!
Already hate this.
GO!
Let me show you my routine!
GO!
I just wanted to go to the library.
ha ha!
NOPE! WE'RE DONE
GO
SUPPORT RAT
FRIENDSHIPS HAVE BOUNDARIES!!

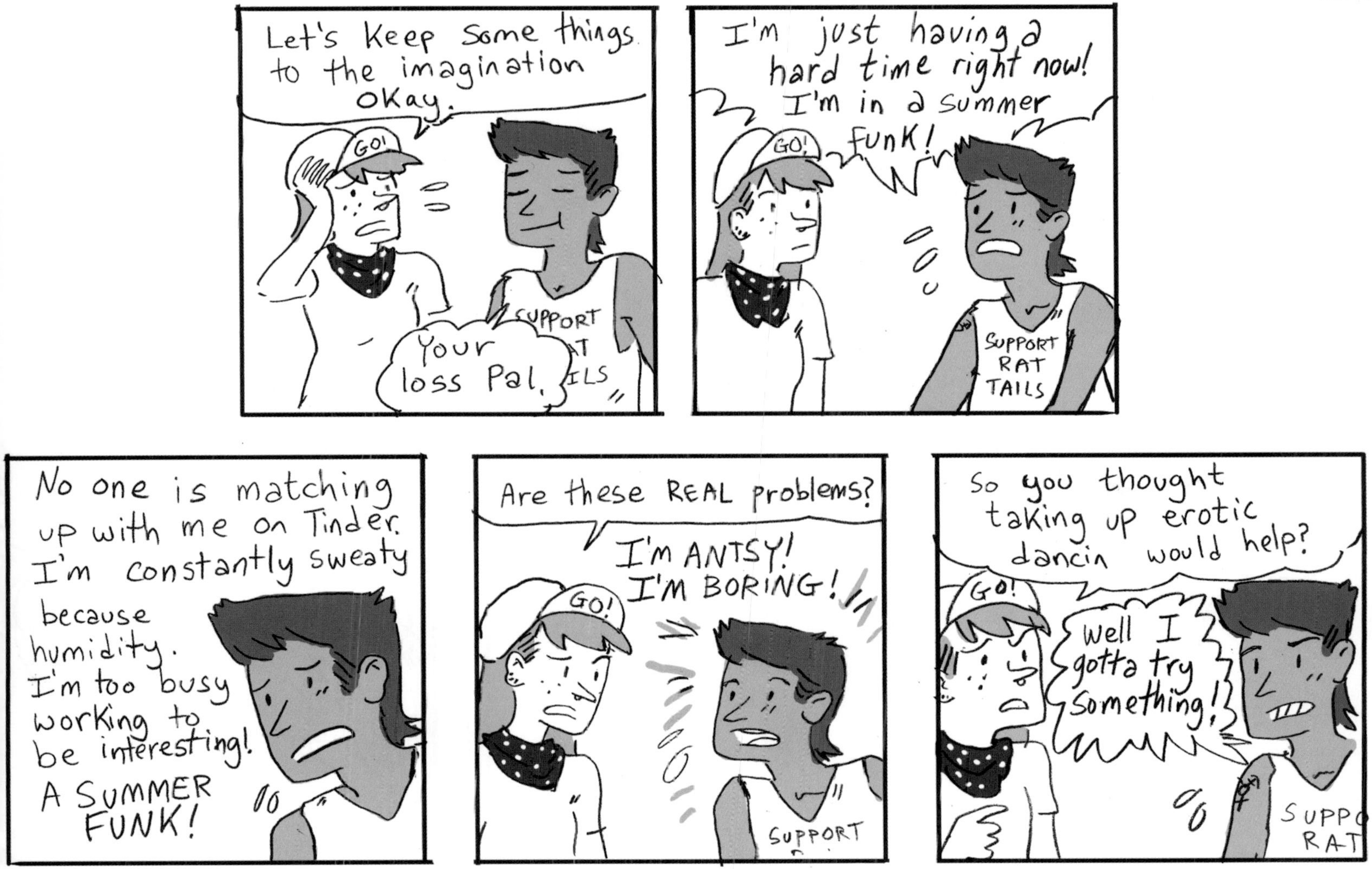
Let's Keep Some things to the imagination OKay.
Your loss Pal.
SUPPORT RAT TAILS
GO!
I'm just having a hard time right now! I'm in a summer FUNK!
SUPPORT RAT TAILS
GO!
No one is matching up with me on Tinder. I'm constantly sweaty because humidity. I'm too busy working to be interesting! A SUMMER FUNK!
Are these REAL problems?
I'M ANTSY! I'M BORING!
GO!
SUPPORT
So you thought taking up erotic dancin would help?
Well I gotta try Something!
GO!

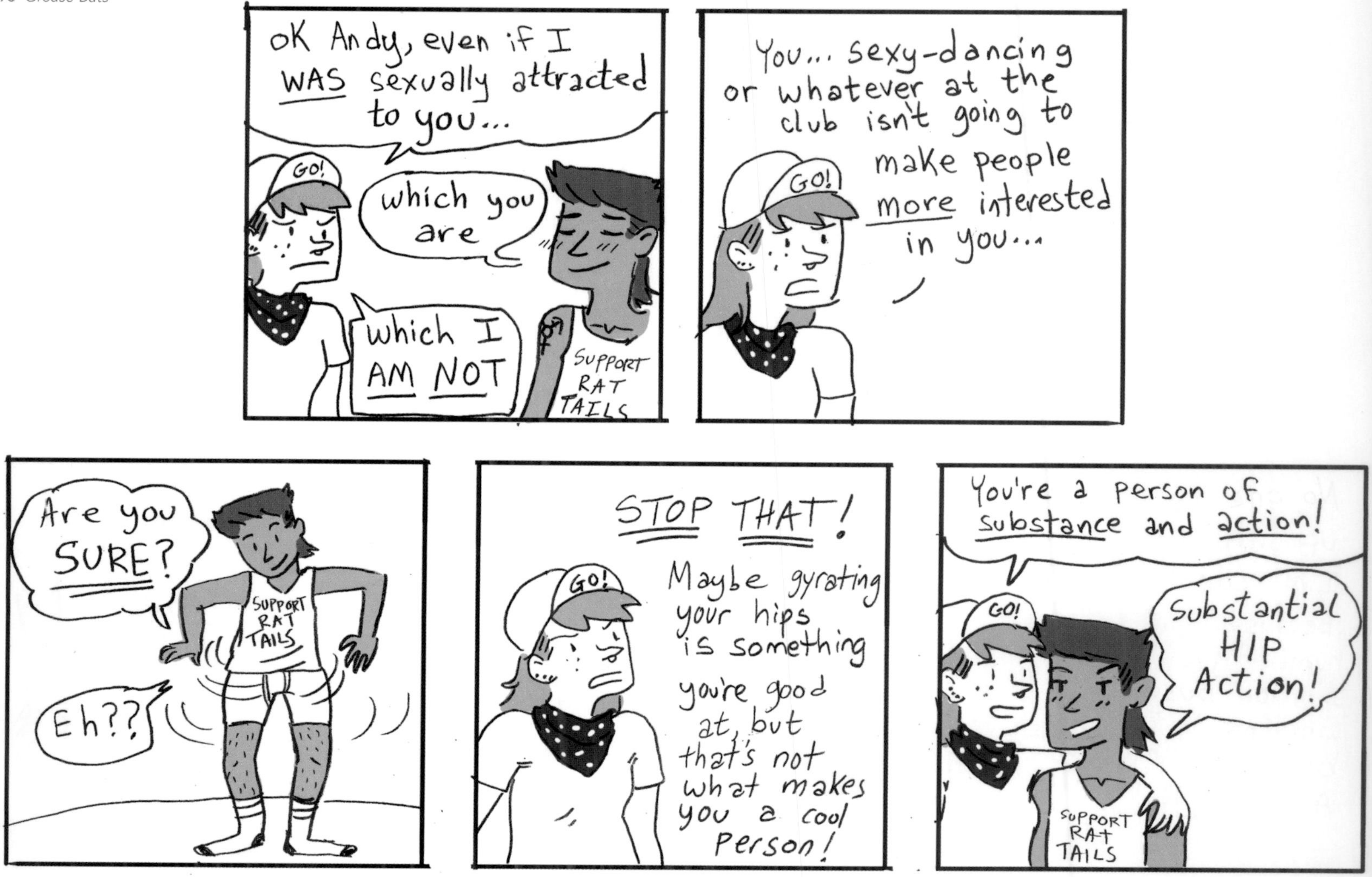
oK Andy, even if I WAS sexually attracted to you...
which you are
which I AM NOT
SUPPORT RAT TAILS
GO!
You... sexy-dancing or whatever at the club isn't going to make people more interested in you...
GO!
Are you SURE?
SUPPORT RAT TAILS
Eh??
STOP THAT!
Maybe gyrating your hips is something you're good at, but that's not what makes you a cool person!
GO!
You're a person of substance and action!
Substantial HIP Action!
GO!
SUPPORT RAT TAILS

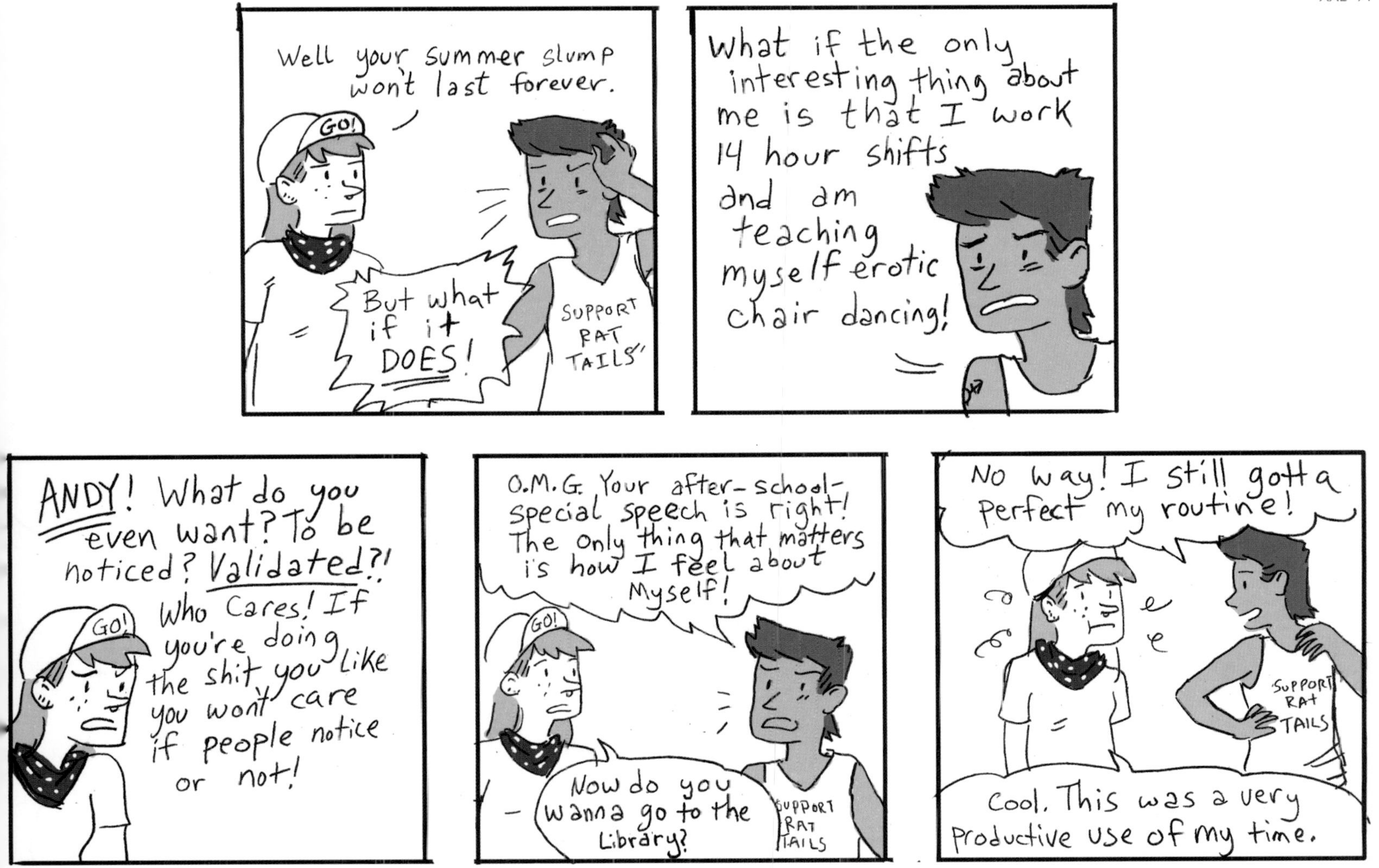
Well your summer slump won't last forever.
But what if it DOES!
SUPPORT RAT TAILS
What if the only interesting thing about me is that I work 14 hour shifts and am teaching myself erotic chair dancing!
ANDY! What do you even want? To be noticed? Validated?!
Who cares! If you're doing the shit you like you won't care if people notice or not!
O.M.G. Your after-school-special speech is right! The only thing that matters is how I feel about myself!
Now do you wanna go to the Library?
SUPPORT RAT TAILS
No way! I still gotta perfect my routine!
SUPPORT RAT TAILS
Cool. This was a very productive use of my time.

Suburb

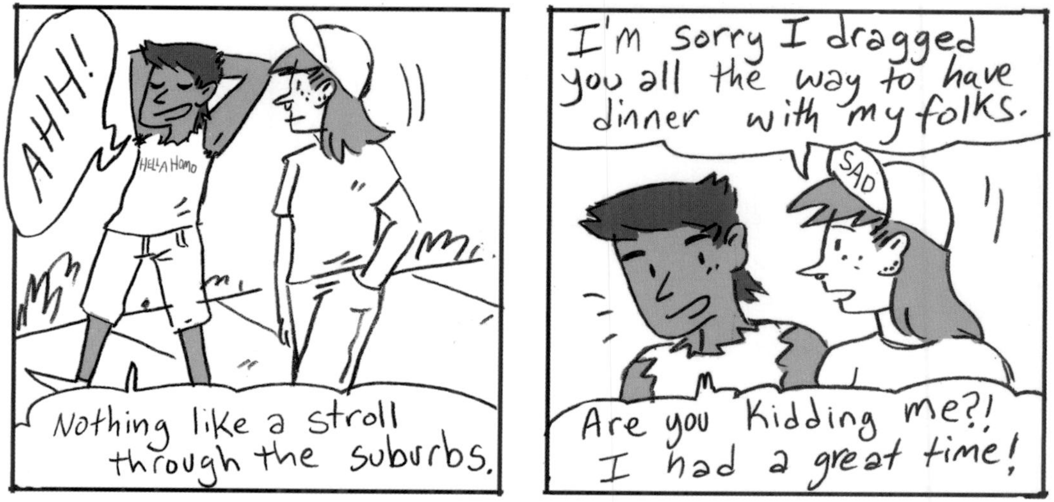
AHH!
HELLA HOMO
Nothing like a stroll through the suburbs.
I'm sorry I dragged you all the way to have dinner with my folks.
SAD
Are you kidding me?! I had a great time!

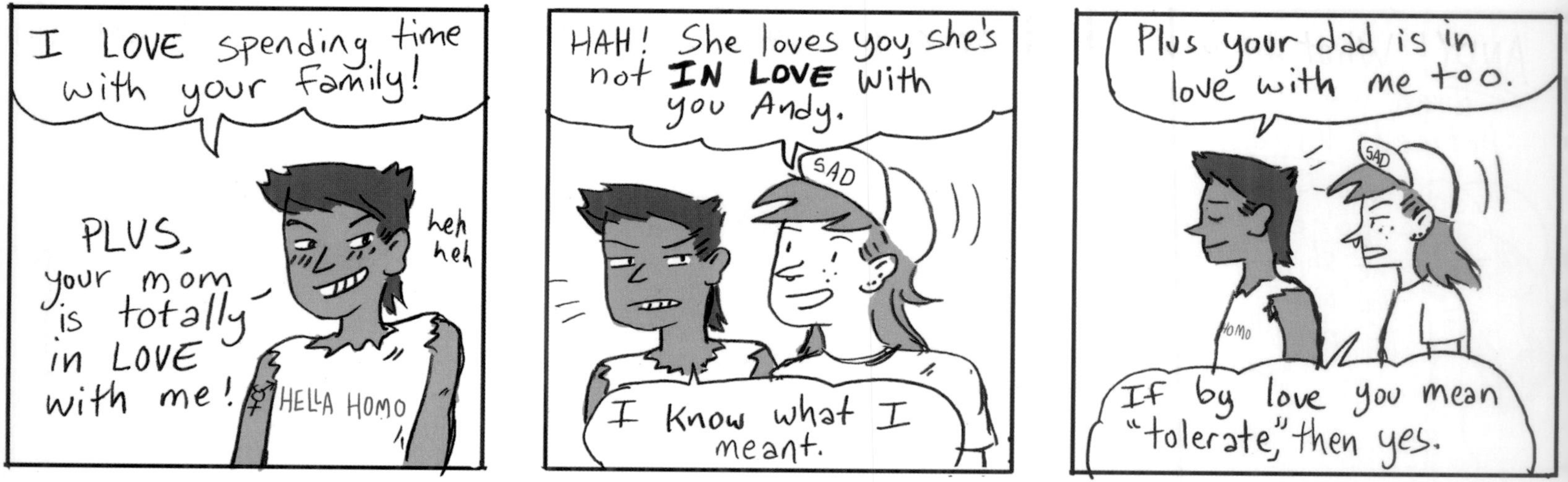
I LOVE spending time with your family!
PLUS, your mom is totally in LOVE with me!
heh heh
HELLA HOMO
HAH! She loves you, she's not **IN LOVE** with you Andy.
SAD
I know what I meant.
Plus your dad is in love with me too.
SAD
HOMO
If by love you mean "tolerate," then yes.

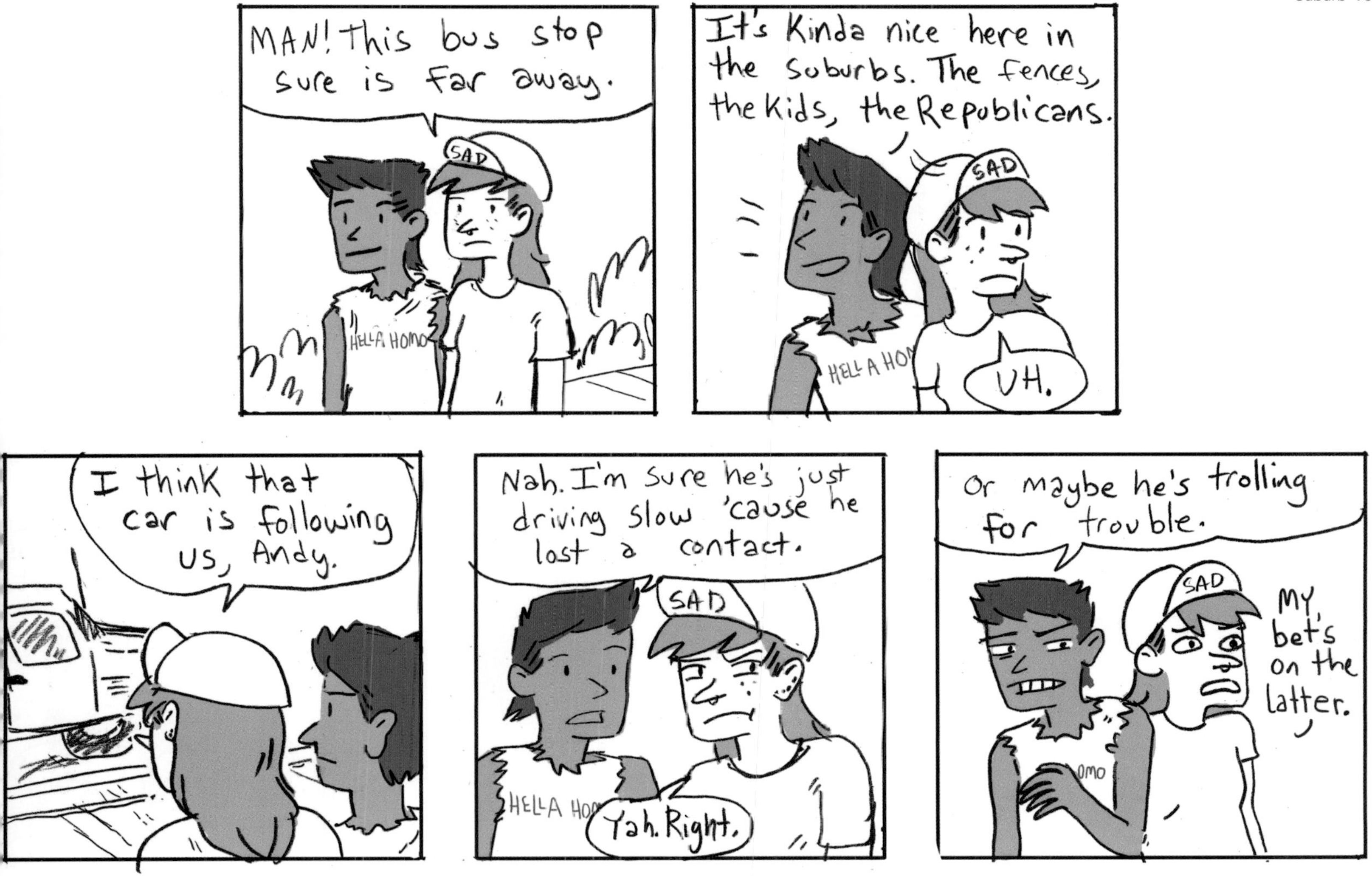
MAN! This bus stop sure is far away.
HELLA HOMO
SAD
It's kinda nice here in the suburbs. The fences, the kids, the Republicans.
UH.
I think that car is following us, Andy.
Nah. I'm sure he's just driving slow 'cause he lost a contact.
Yah. Right.
Or maybe he's trolling for trouble.
My bet's on the latter.

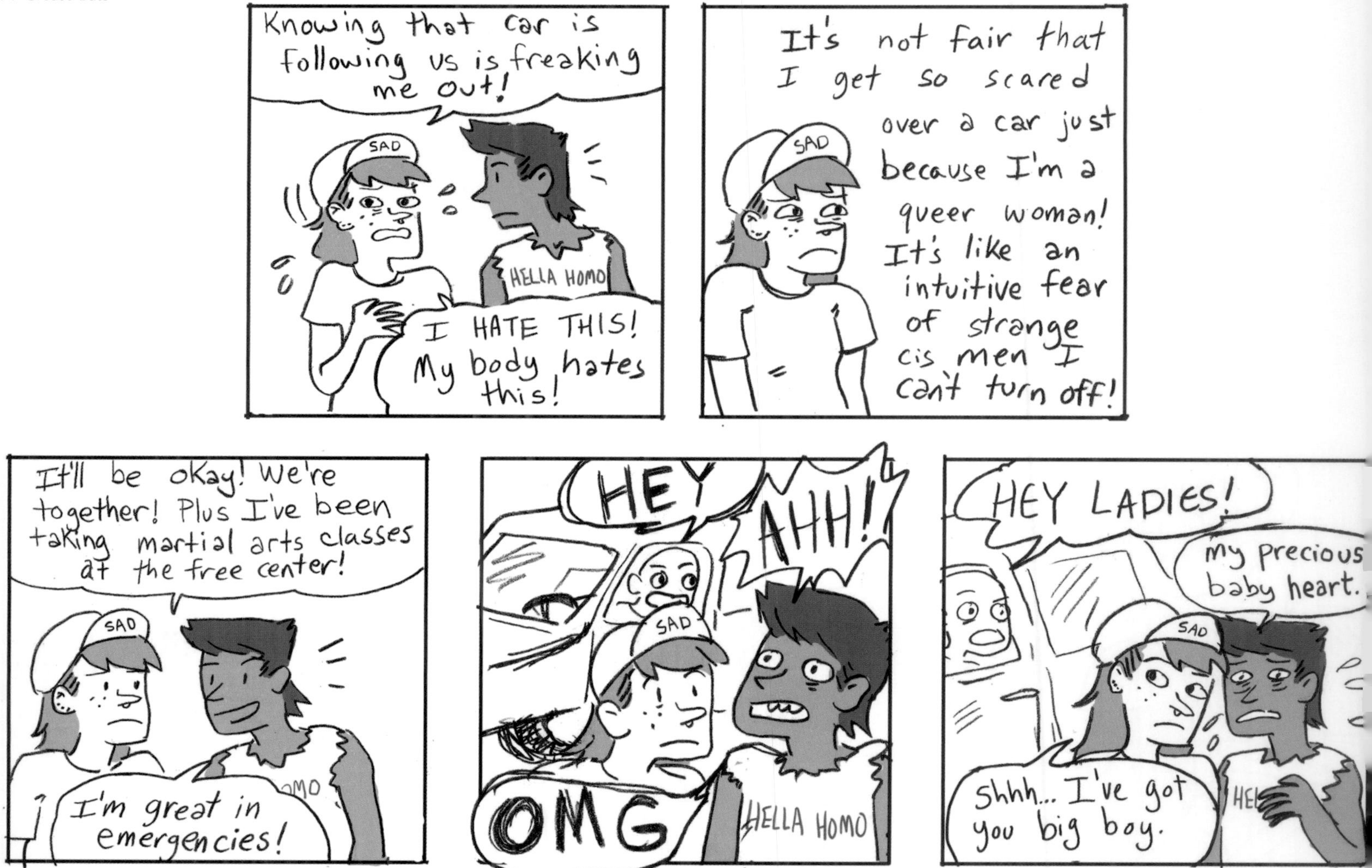
Knowing that car is following us is freaking me out!
SAD
HELLA HOMO
I HATE THIS! My body hates this!
It's not fair that I get so scared over a car just because I'm a queer woman! It's like an intuitive fear of strange cis men I can't turn off!
SAD
It'll be okay! We're together! Plus I've been taking martial arts classes at the free center!
SAD
I'm great in emergencies!
HEY
AHH!
SAD
OMG
HELLA HOMO
HEY LADIES!
my precious baby heart.
SAD
Shhh... I've got you big boy.

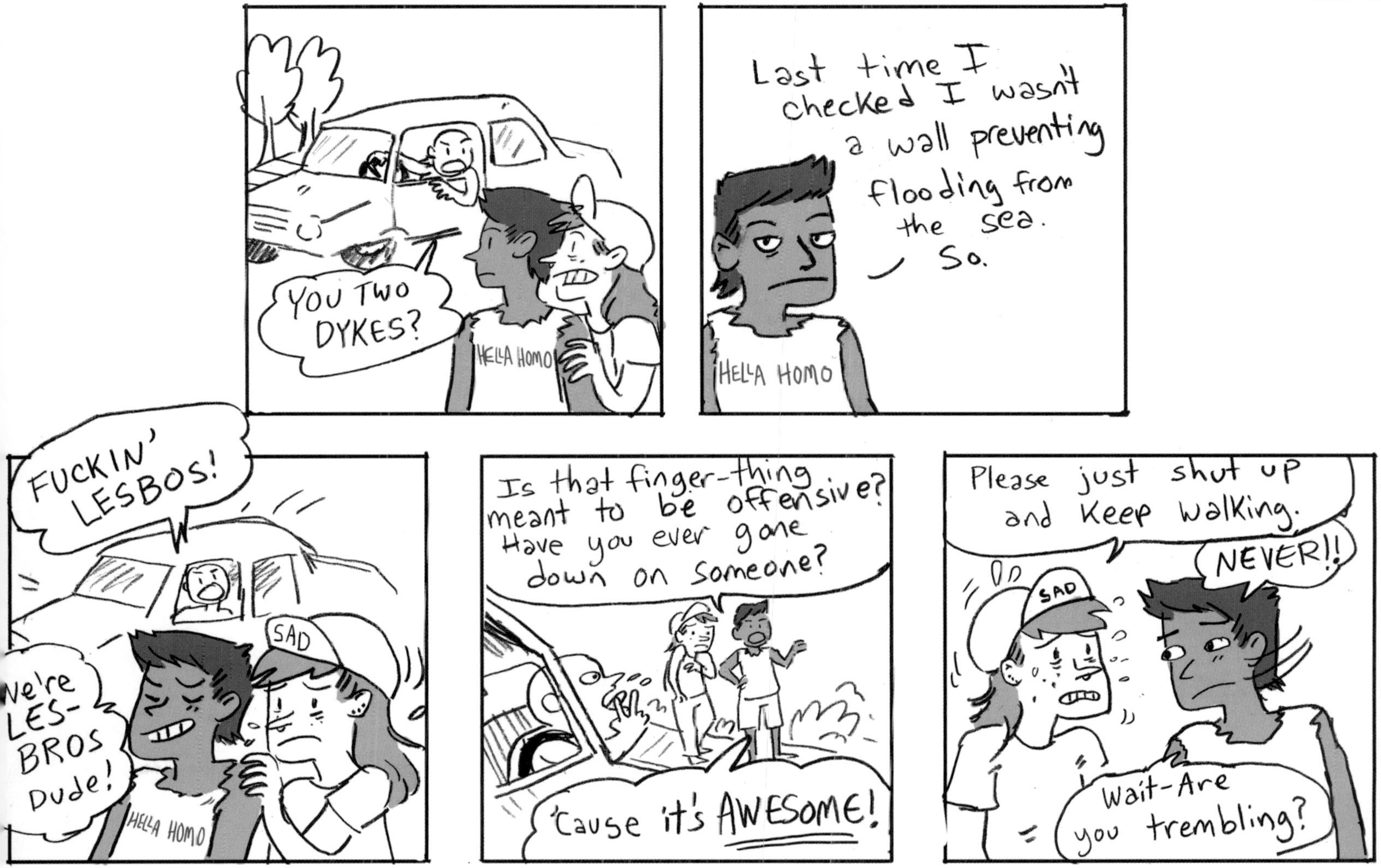
YOU TWO DYKES?
HELLA HOMO
Last time I checked I wasn't a wall preventing flooding from the sea. So.
HELLA HOMO
FUCKIN' LESBOS!
We're LES-BROS Dude!
HELLA HOMO
SAD
Is that finger-thing meant to be offensive? Have you ever gone down on someone?
'Cause it's AWESOME!
Please just shut up and keep walking.
NEVER!!
SAD
Wait-Are you trembling?

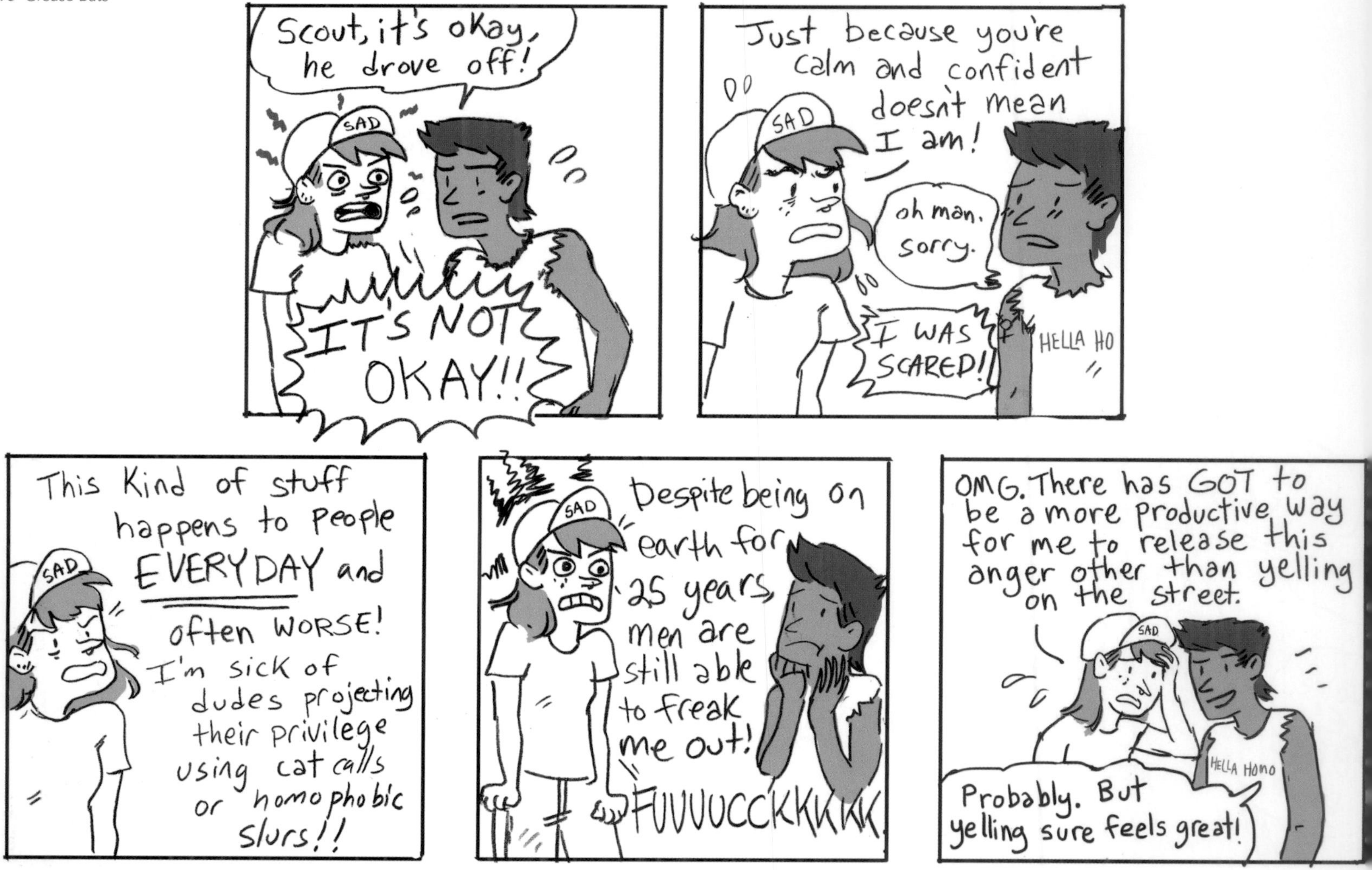
Scout, it's okay, he drove off!
SAD
IT'S NOT OKAY!!
Just because you're calm and confident doesn't mean I am!
SAD
oh man. sorry.
I WAS SCARED!
HELLA HO
This Kind of stuff happens to people EVERYDAY and often WORSE! I'm sick of dudes projecting their privilege using cat calls or homophobic slurs!!
SAD
SAD
Despite being on earth for 25 years, men are still able to freak me out!
FUUUUCCKKKKK
OMG. There has GOT to be a more productive way for me to release this anger other than yelling on the street.
SAD
HELLA HOMO
Probably. But yelling sure feels great!

Loose Morals

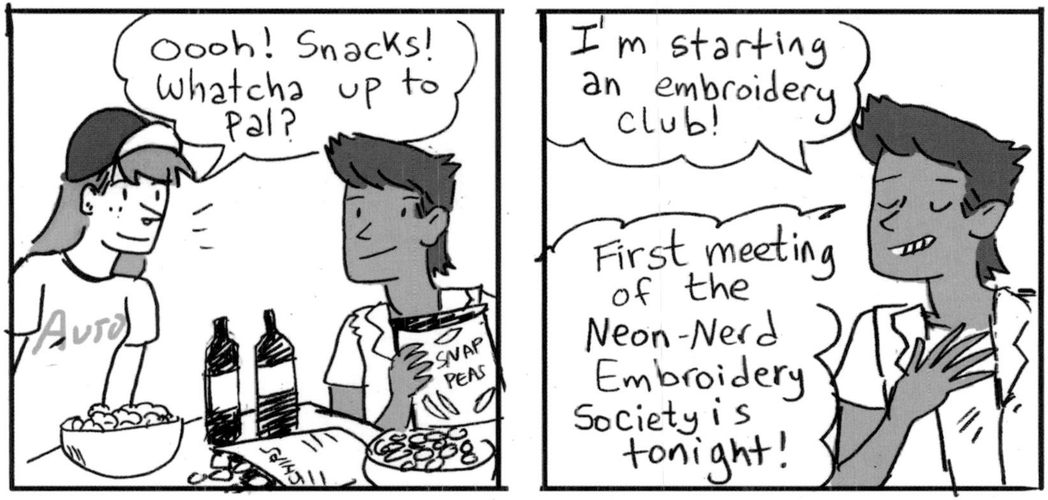
Oooh! Snacks! Whatcha up to pal?
AUTO
SNAP PEAS
I'm starting an embroidery club!
First meeting of the Neon-Nerd Embroidery Society is tonight!

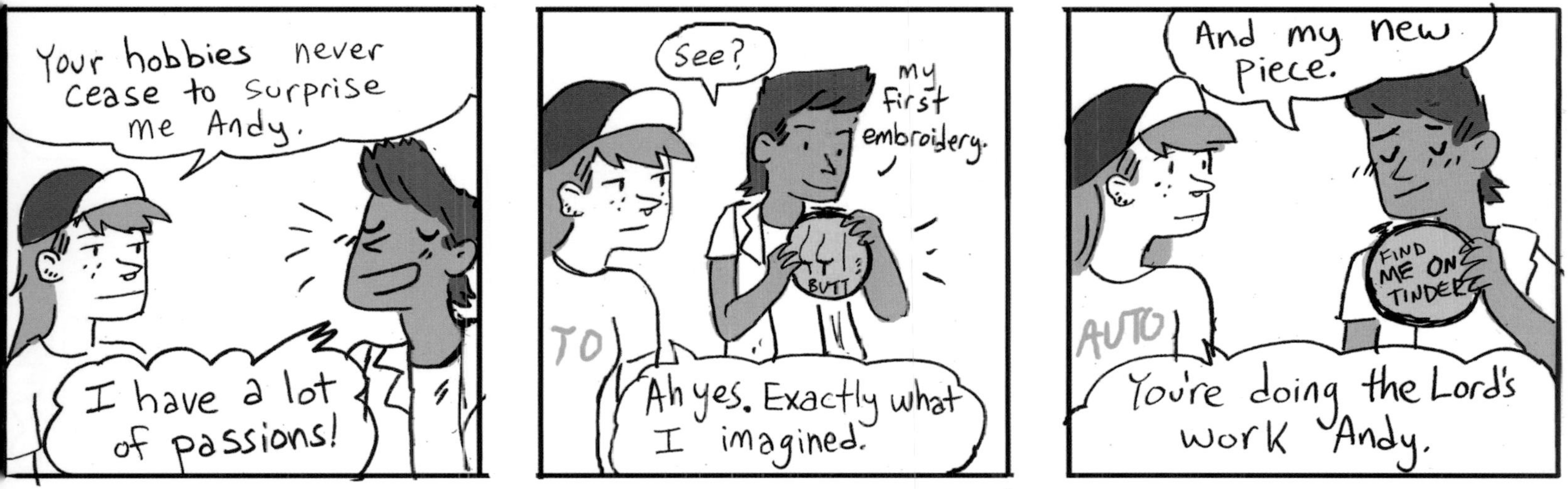
Your hobbies never cease to surprise me Andy.
I have a lot of passions!
See?
my first embroidery.
BUTT
TO
Ah yes. Exactly what I imagined.
And my new piece.
FIND ME ON TINDER
AUTO
You're doing the Lord's work Andy.

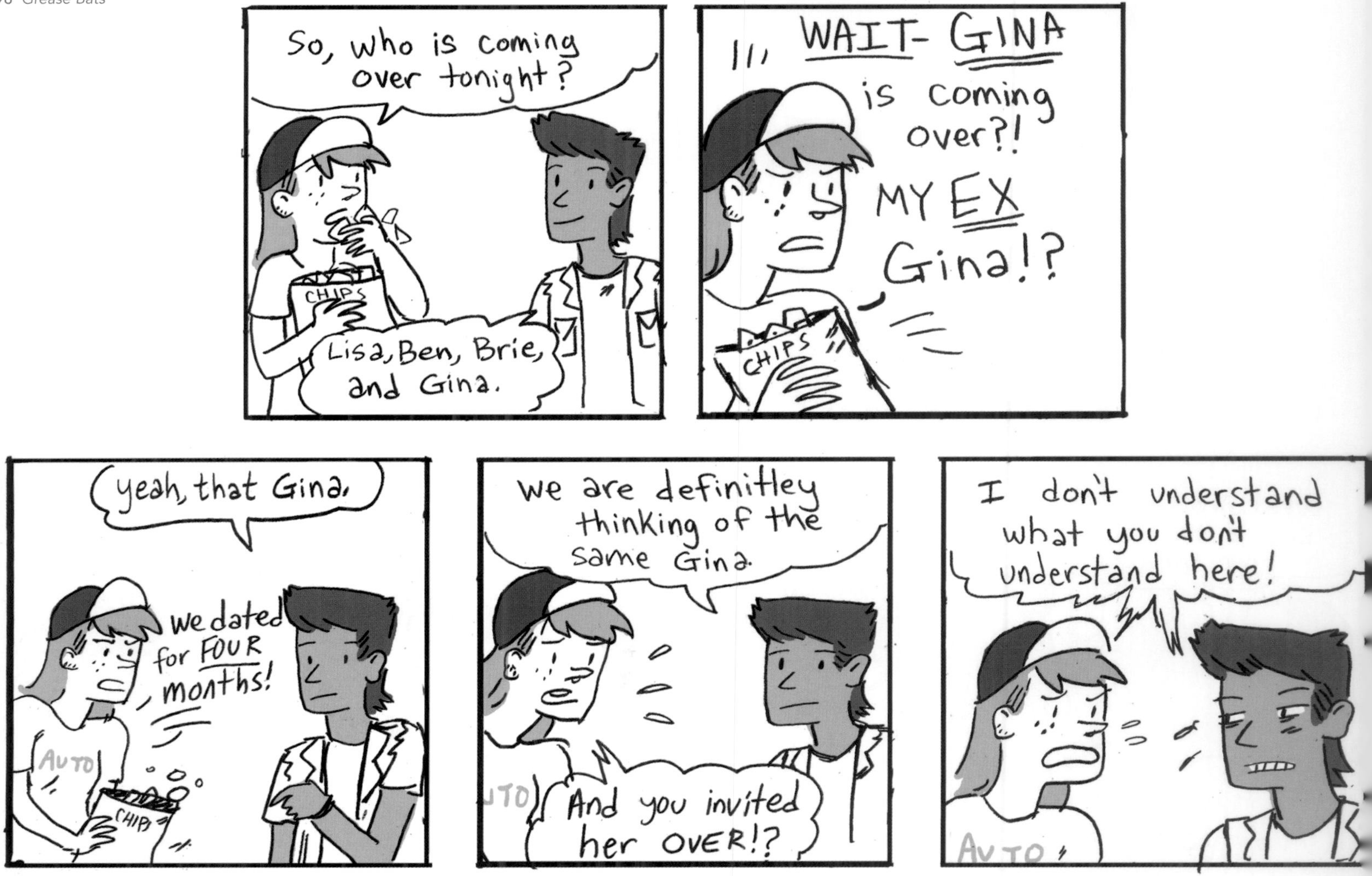
So, who is coming over tonight?
Lisa, Ben, Brie, and Gina.
WAIT- GINA is coming over?!
MY EX Gina!?
CHIPS
yeah, that Gina.
we dated for FOUR months!
AUTO
we are definitley thinking of the same Gina.
And you invited her OVER!?
I don't understand what you don't understand here!

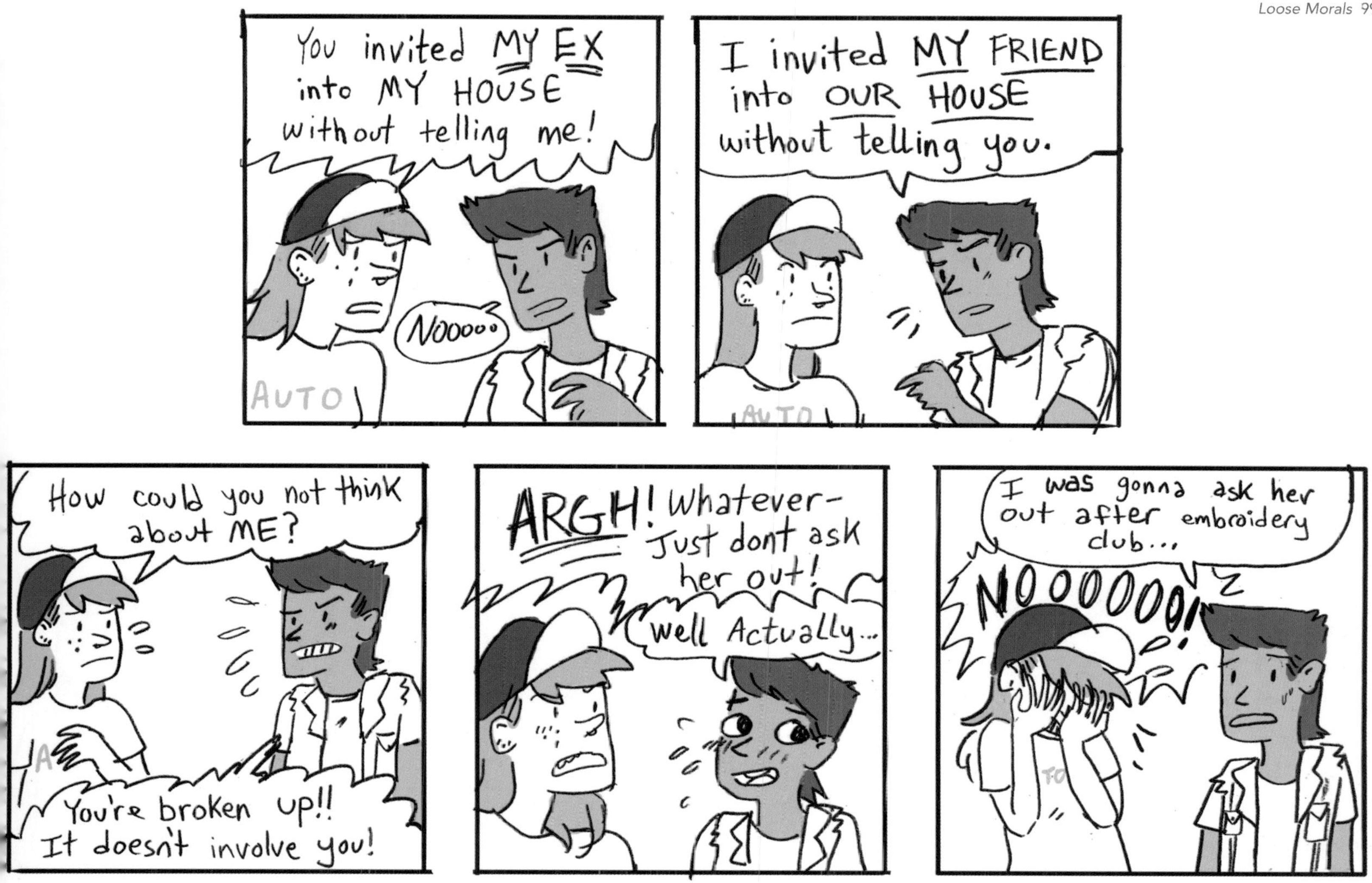
You invited MY EX into MY HOUSE without telling me!
Nooooo
AUTO
I invited MY FRIEND into OUR HOUSE without telling you.
How could you not think about ME?
You're broken up!! It doesn't involve you!
ARGH! Whatever- Just dont ask her out!
well Actually...
I was gonna ask her out after embroidery club...
NOOOOOO!

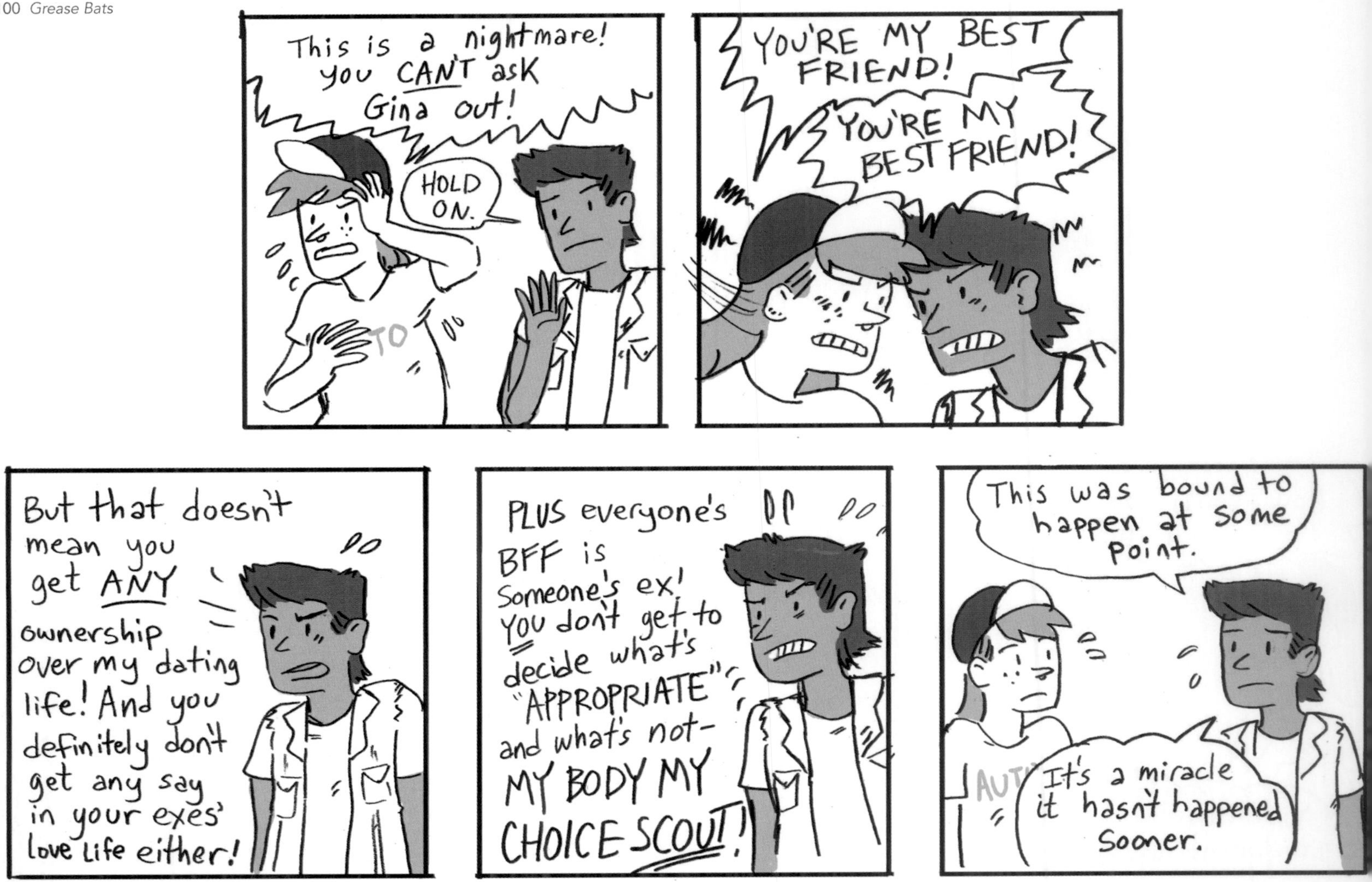

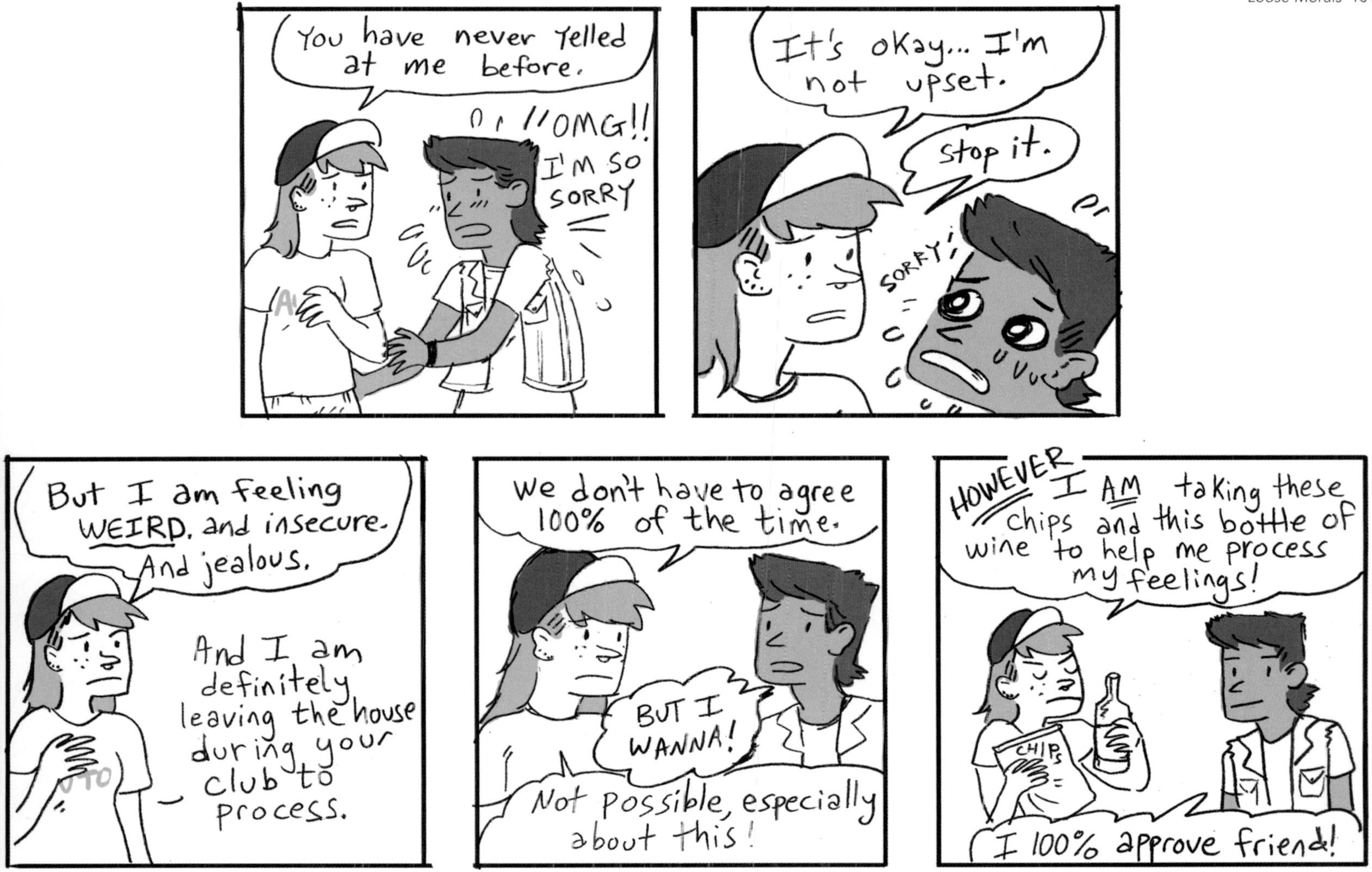
You have never yelled at me before.
OMG!! I'M SO SORRY
It's okay... I'm not upset.
Stop it.
SORRY
But I am feeling WEIRD. and insecure. And jealous.
And I am definitely leaving the house during your club to process.
We don't have to agree 100% of the time.
BUT I WANNA!
Not possible, especially about this!
HOWEVER I AM taking these chips and this bottle of wine to help me process my feelings!
CHIPS
I 100% approve friend!

Halloween Pressure

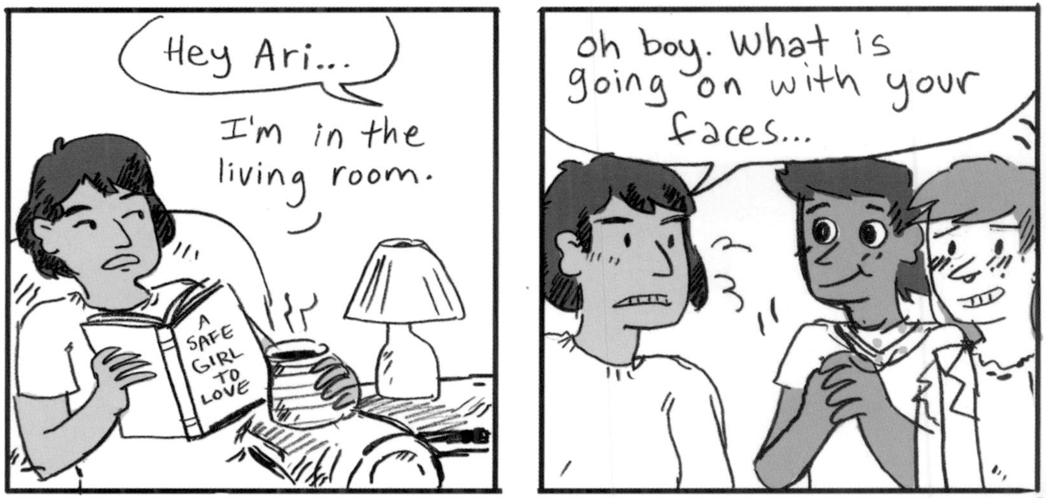
Hey Ari...
I'm in the living room.
A SAFE GIRL TO LOVE
oh boy. What is going on with your faces...

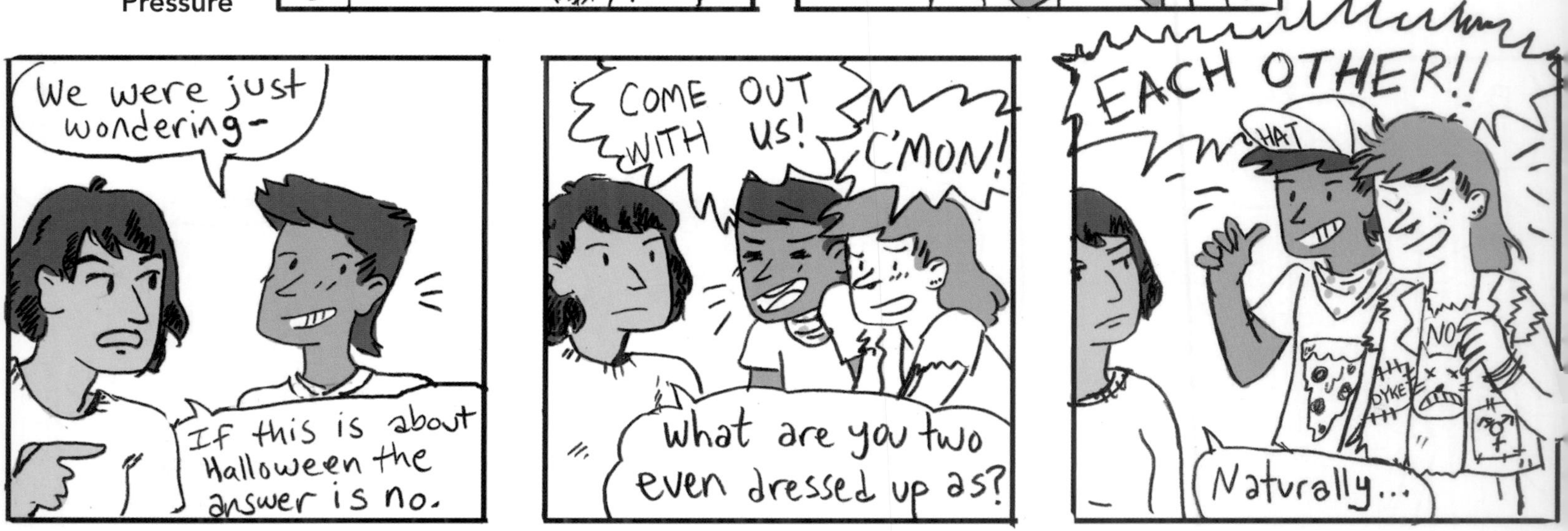
We were just wondering-
If this is about Halloween the answer is no.
COME OUT WITH US!
C'MON!
What are you two even dressed up as?
EACH OTHER!!
HAT
NO
DYKE
Naturally...

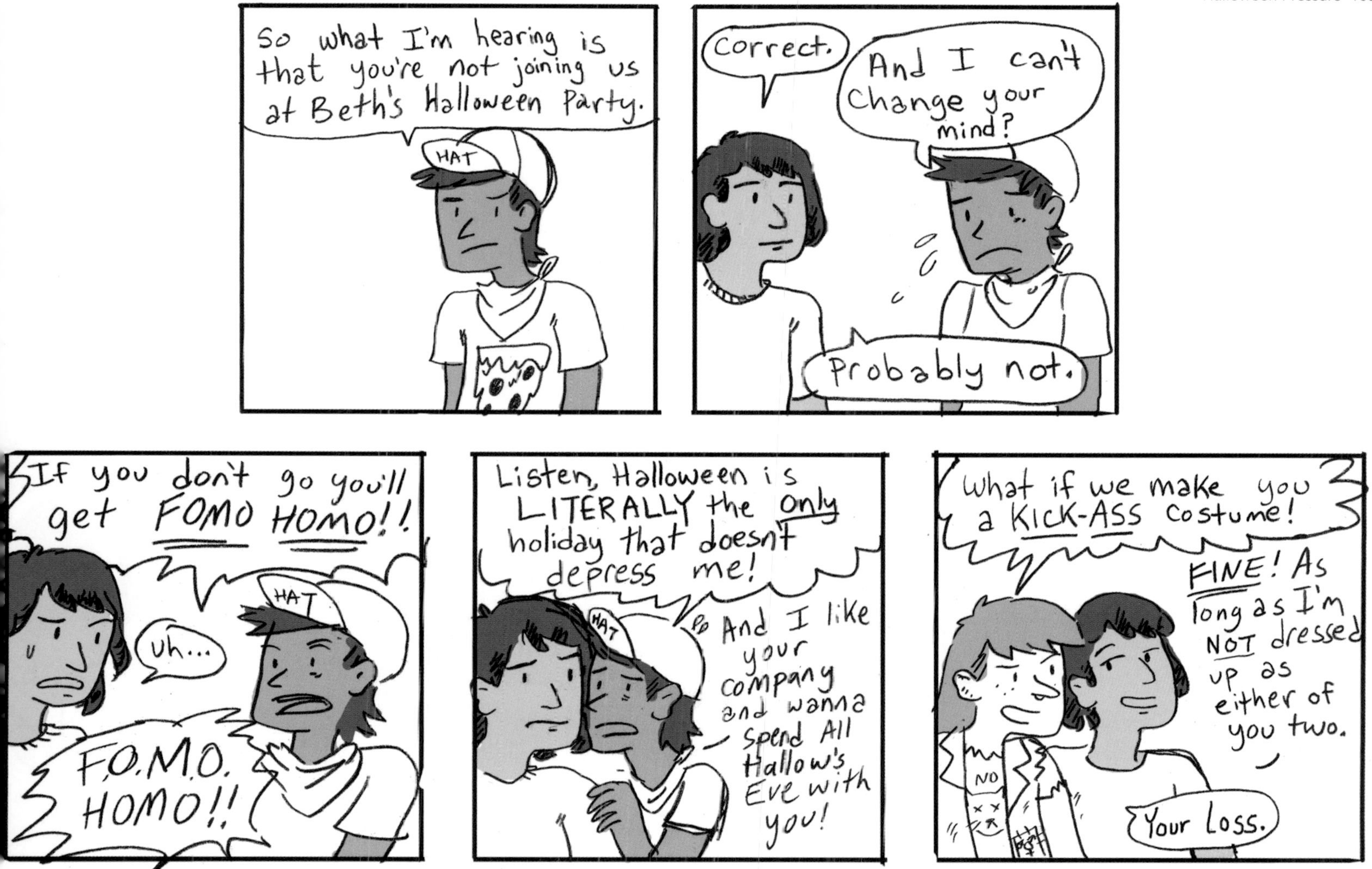
So what I'm hearing is that you're not joining us at Beth's Halloween Party.
Correct.
And I can't change your mind?
Probably not.
If you don't go you'll get FOMO HOMO!!
Uh...
F.O.M.O. HOMO!!
Listen, Halloween is LITERALLY the only holiday that doesn't depress me!
And I like your company and wanna spend All Hallow's Eve with you!
What if we make you a KICK-ASS costume!
FINE! As long as I'm NOT dressed up as either of you two.
Your loss.
HAT
NO

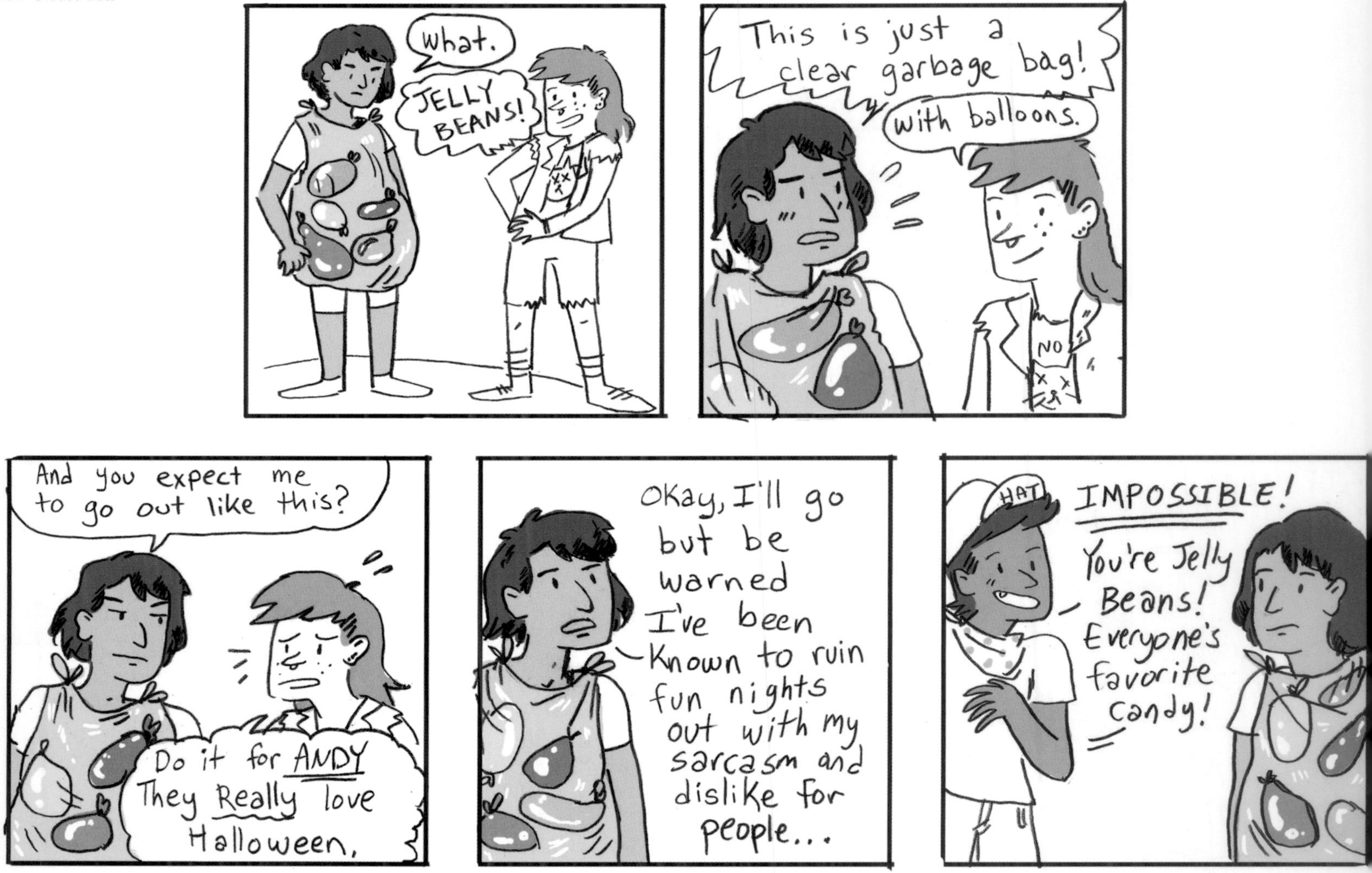
What.
JELLY BEANS!
This is just a clear garbage bag!
With balloons.
And you expect me to go out like this?
Do it for ANDY They Really love Halloween.
Okay, I'll go but be warned I've been Known to ruin fun nights out with my sarcasm and dislike for people...
HAT
IMPOSSIBLE!
You're Jelly Beans! Everyone's favorite candy!

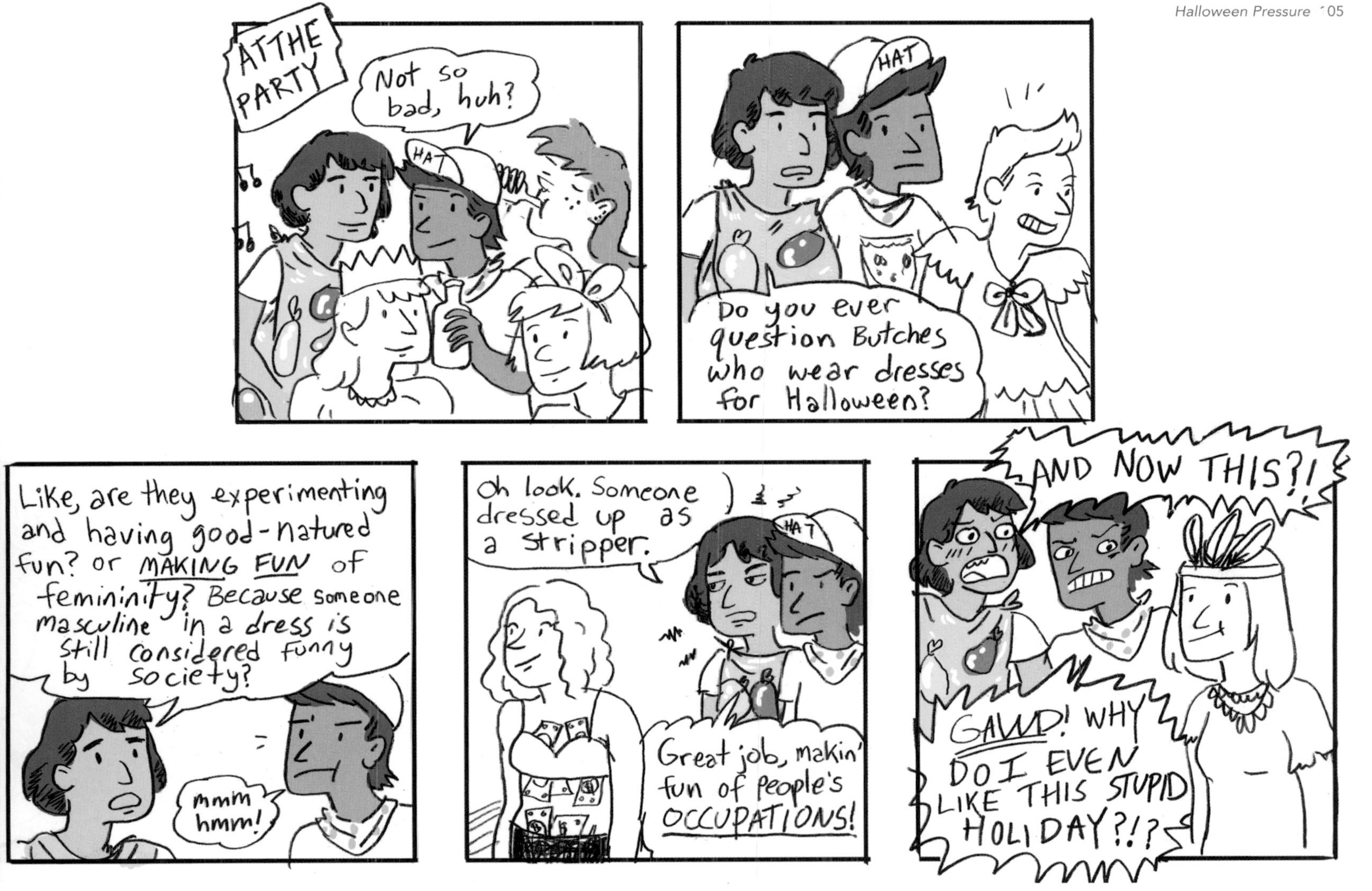
AT THE PARTY
Not so bad, huh?
HAT
HAT
Do you ever question Butches who wear dresses for Halloween?
Like, are they experimenting and having good-natured fun? or MAKING FUN of femininity? Because someone masculine in a dress is still considered funny by society?
mmm hmm!
Oh look. Someone dressed up as a stripper.
HAT
Great job, makin' fun of people's OCCUPATIONS!
AND NOW THIS?!
GAWD! WHY DO I EVEN LIKE THIS STUPID HOLIDAY?!?

Panel 1:
I'm sorry I ruined Halloween.

You didn't!

All those terrible and thoughtless costumes ruined Halloween!

Panel 2:
Halloween should be about being ok about being weird or different!

I'm sorry we pressured you into coming out tonight Ari...

HAT

Panel 3:
Actually I had fun!

I love hating people! Please respect me when I say no but I really enjoyed being out of my comfort zone!

Panel 4:
Also, if it makes you feel better, I usually always feel TOO weird and different so it was nice to be out and for once NOT feel that way!

Panel 5:
Aw!!

Plus you look real good in that trashbag!

HAT

I dunno if it's the sentimentality or all the candy corn I ate, but this is making me sick

Family

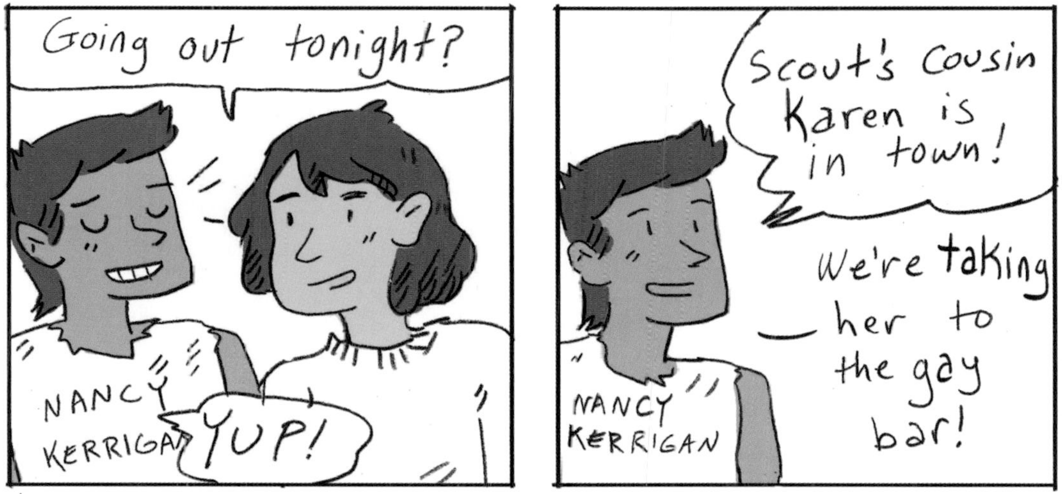
Going out tonight?
NANCY KERRIGAN
YUP!
Scout's Cousin Karen is in town!
We're taking her to the gay bar!
NANCY KERRIGAN

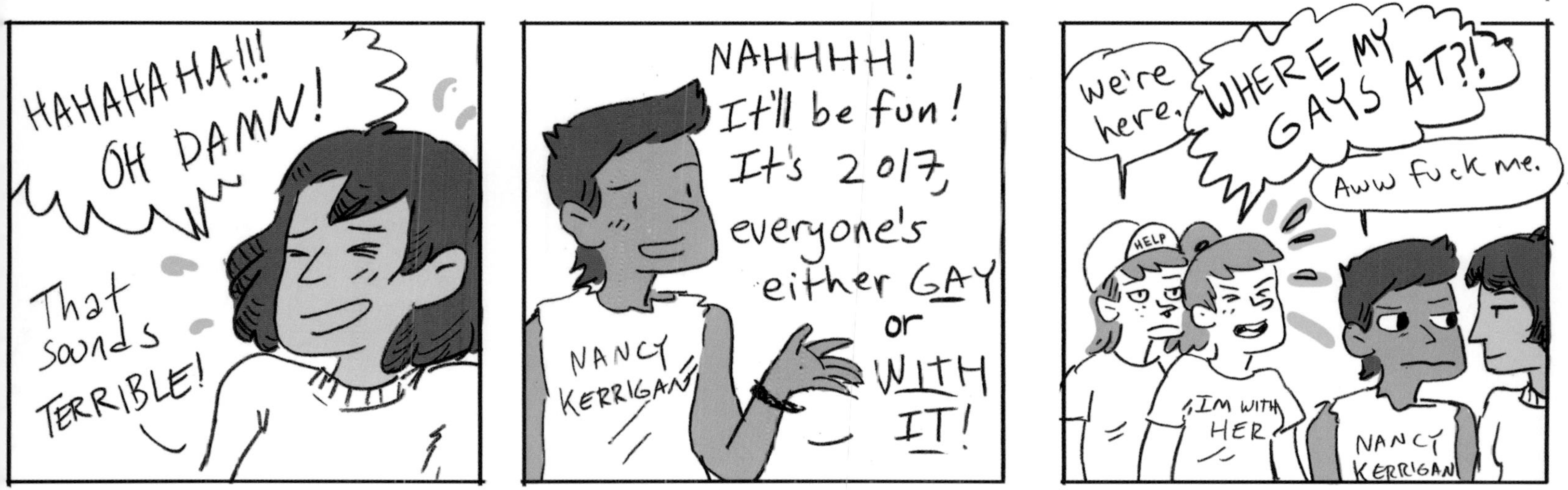
HAHAHAHA!!! OH DAMN!
That sounds TERRIBLE!
NAHHHH! It'll be fun! It's 2017, everyone's either GAY or WITH IT!
NANCY KERRIGAN
we're here.
WHERE MY GAYS AT?!
Aww fuck me.
HELP
IM WITH HER
NANCY KERRIGAN

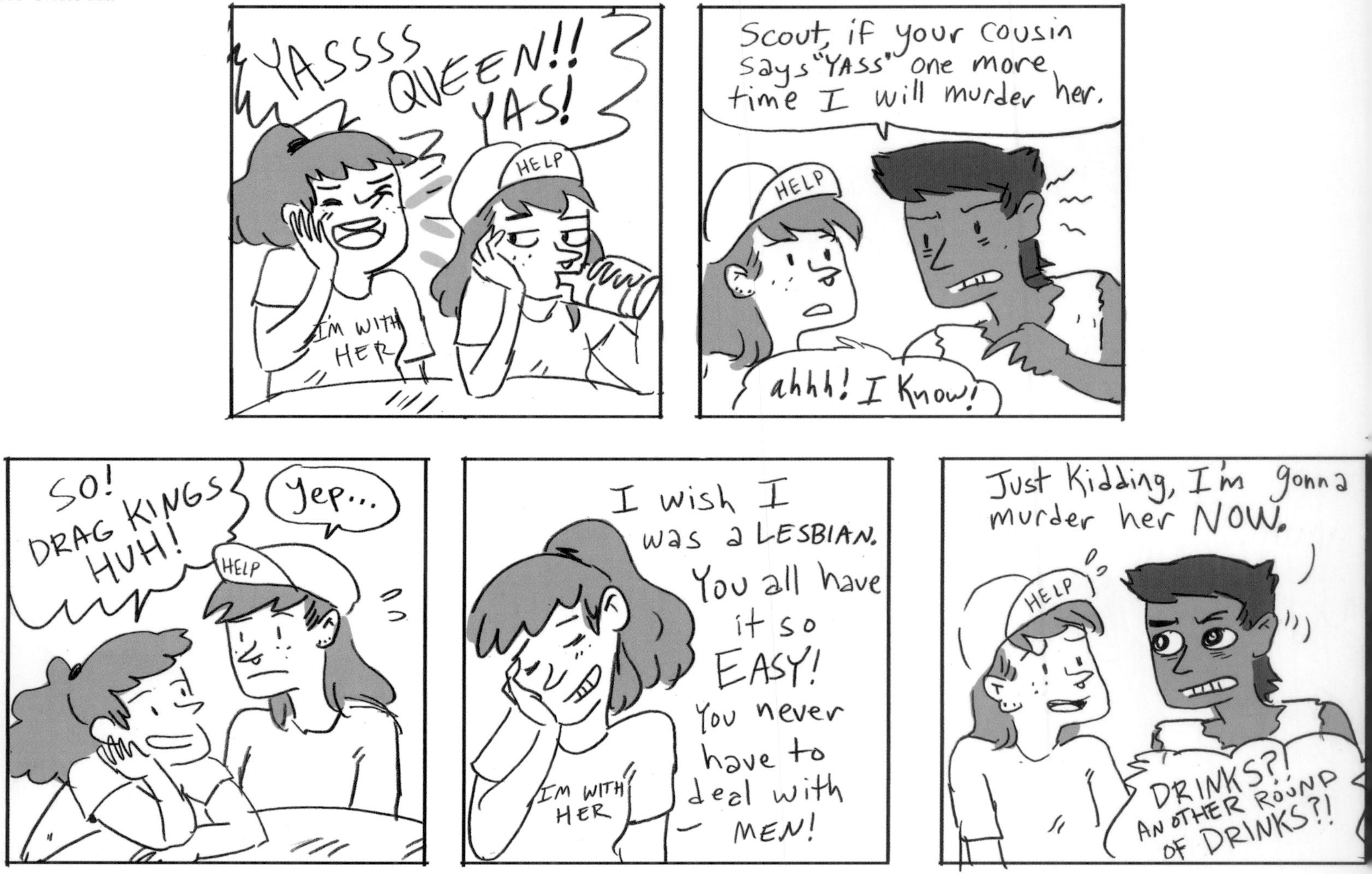
YASSSS QUEEN!! YAS!
HELP
I'M WITH HER
Scout, if your cousin says "YASS" one more time I will murder her.
HELP
ahhh! I Know!
SO! DRAG KINGS HUH!
Yep...
HELP
I wish I was a LESBIAN. You all have it so EASY! You never have to deal with MEN!
I'M WITH HER
Just Kidding, I'm gonna murder her NOW.
HELP
DRINKS?! ANOTHER ROUND OF DRINKS?!

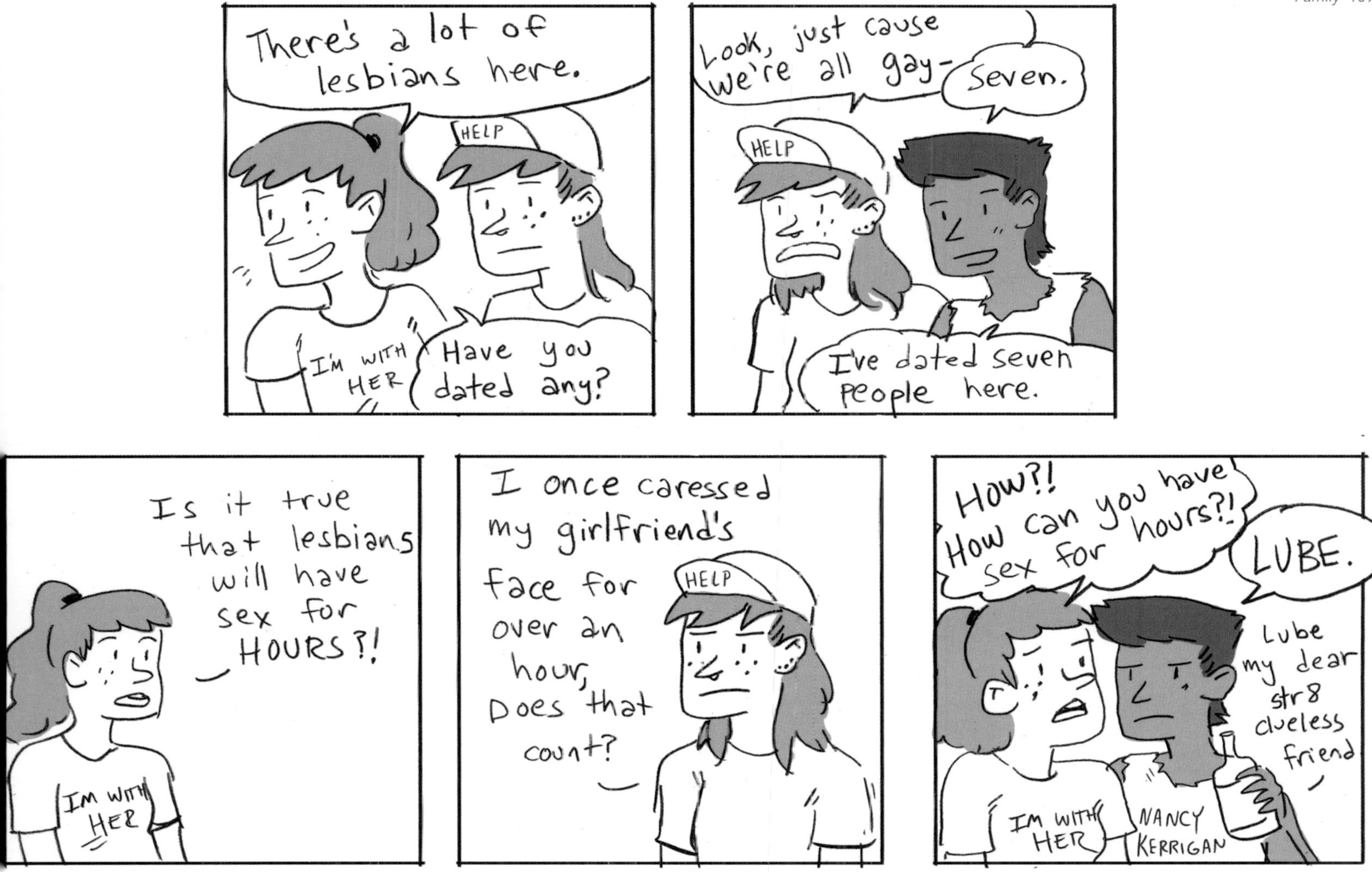
There's a lot of lesbians here.
I'M WITH HER
HELP
Have you dated any?
Look, just cause we're all gay-
Seven.
HELP
I've dated seven people here.
Is it true that lesbians will have sex for HOURS?!
IM WITH HER
I once caressed my girlfriend's face for over an hour, Does that count?
HELP
How?! How can you have sex for hours?!
LUBE.
Lube my dear str8 clueless friend
IM WITH HER
NANCY KERRIGAN

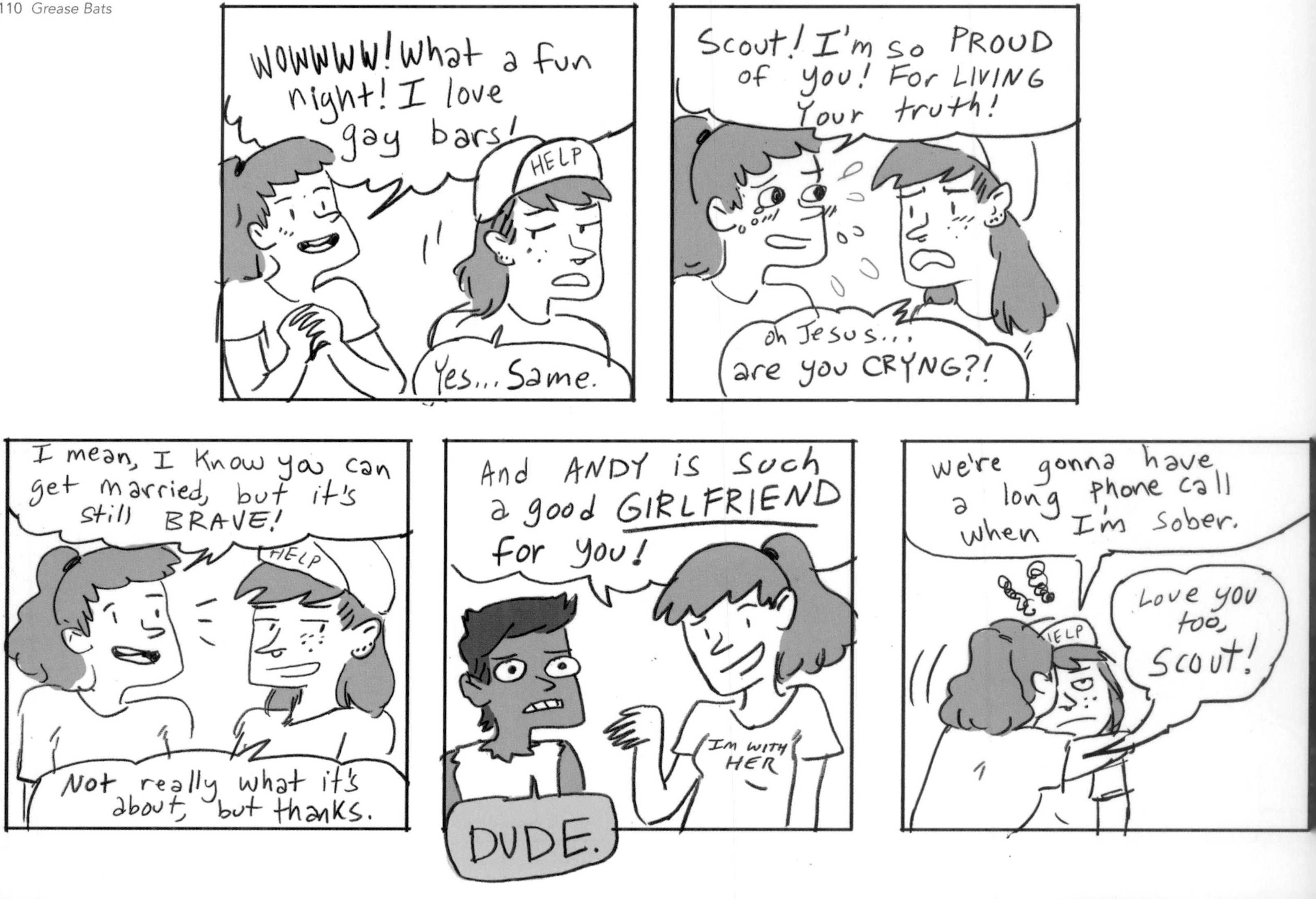
WOWWWW! What a fun night! I love gay bars!
HELP
Yes... Same.
Scout! I'm so PROUD of you! For LIVING Your truth!
oh Jesus... are you CRYNG?!
I mean, I know you can get married, but it's still BRAVE!
HELP
Not really what it's about, but thanks.
And ANDY is such a good GIRLFRIEND for you!
I'M WITH HER
DUDE.
We're gonna have a long phone call when I'm sober.
HELP
Love you too, Scout!

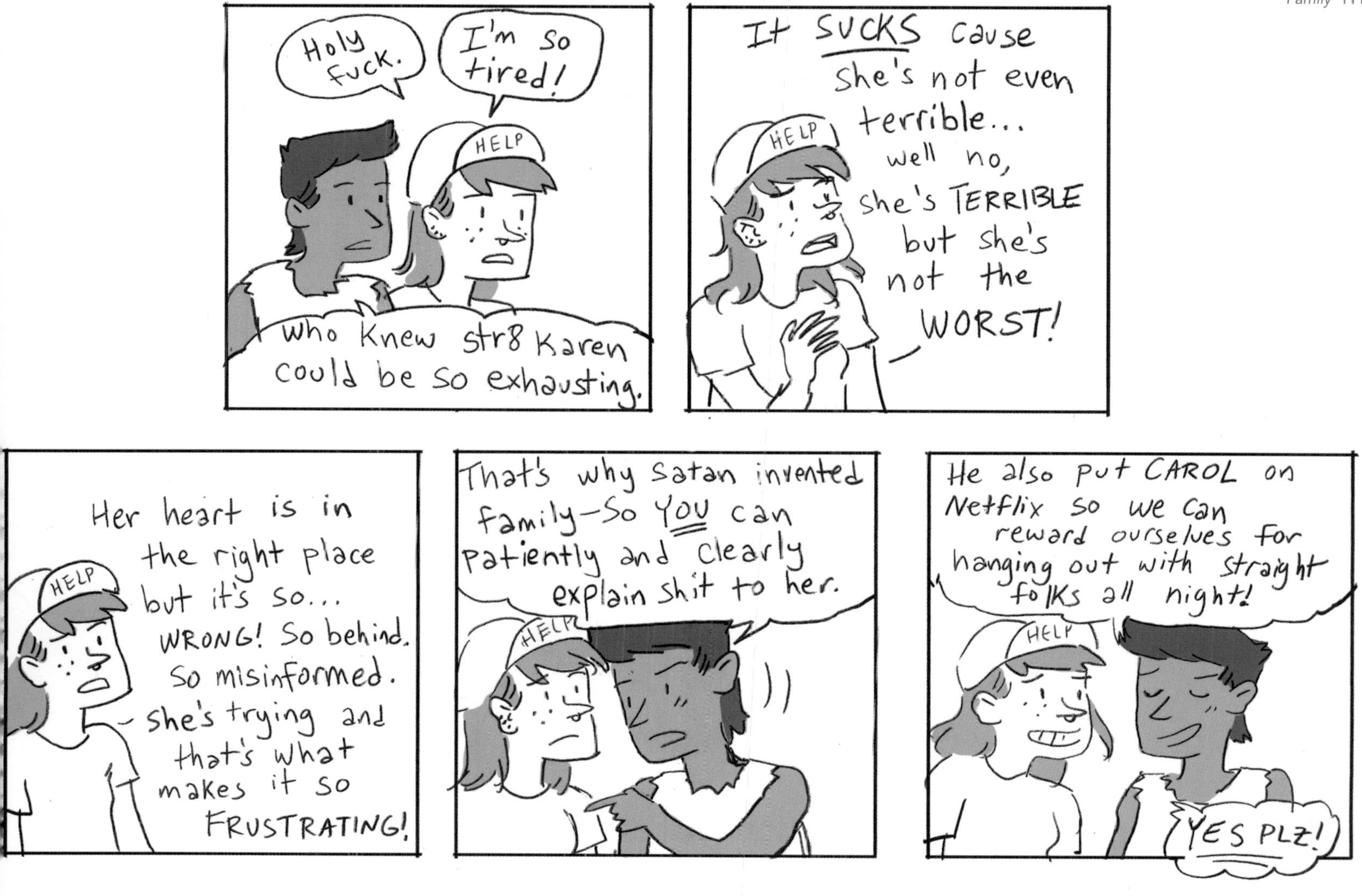
Holy fuck.
I'm so tired!
HELP
Who knew str8 Karen could be so exhausting.
It SUCKS cause she's not even terrible... well no, she's TERRIBLE but she's not the WORST!
HELP
Her heart is in the right place but it's so... WRONG! So behind. So misinformed. She's trying and that's what makes it so FRUSTRATING!
HELP
That's why satan invented family—So YOU can patiently and clearly explain shit to her.
HELP
He also put CAROL on Netflix so we can reward ourselves for hanging out with straight folks all night!
HELP
YES PLZ!

Friend4Friend

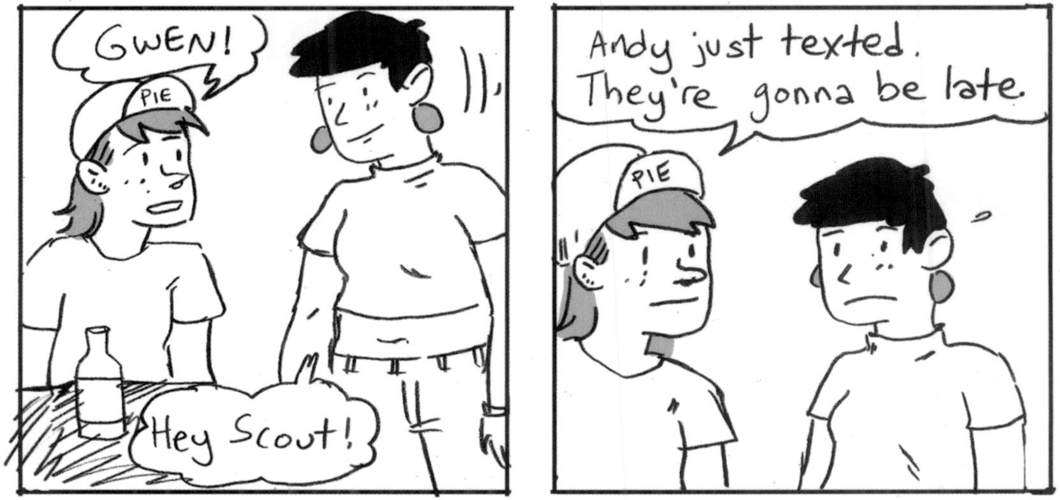
GWEN!
Hey Scout!
Andy just texted. They're gonna be late.

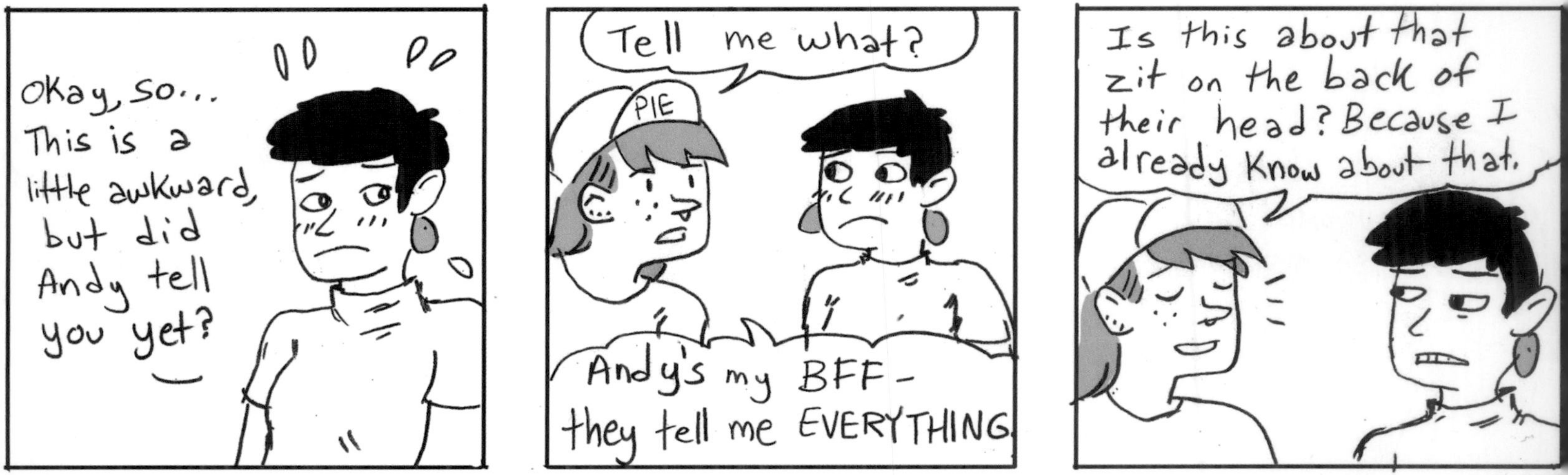
Okay, so... This is a little awkward, but did Andy tell you yet?
Tell me what?
Andy's my BFF - they tell me EVERYTHING.
Is this about that zit on the back of their head? Because I already know about that.

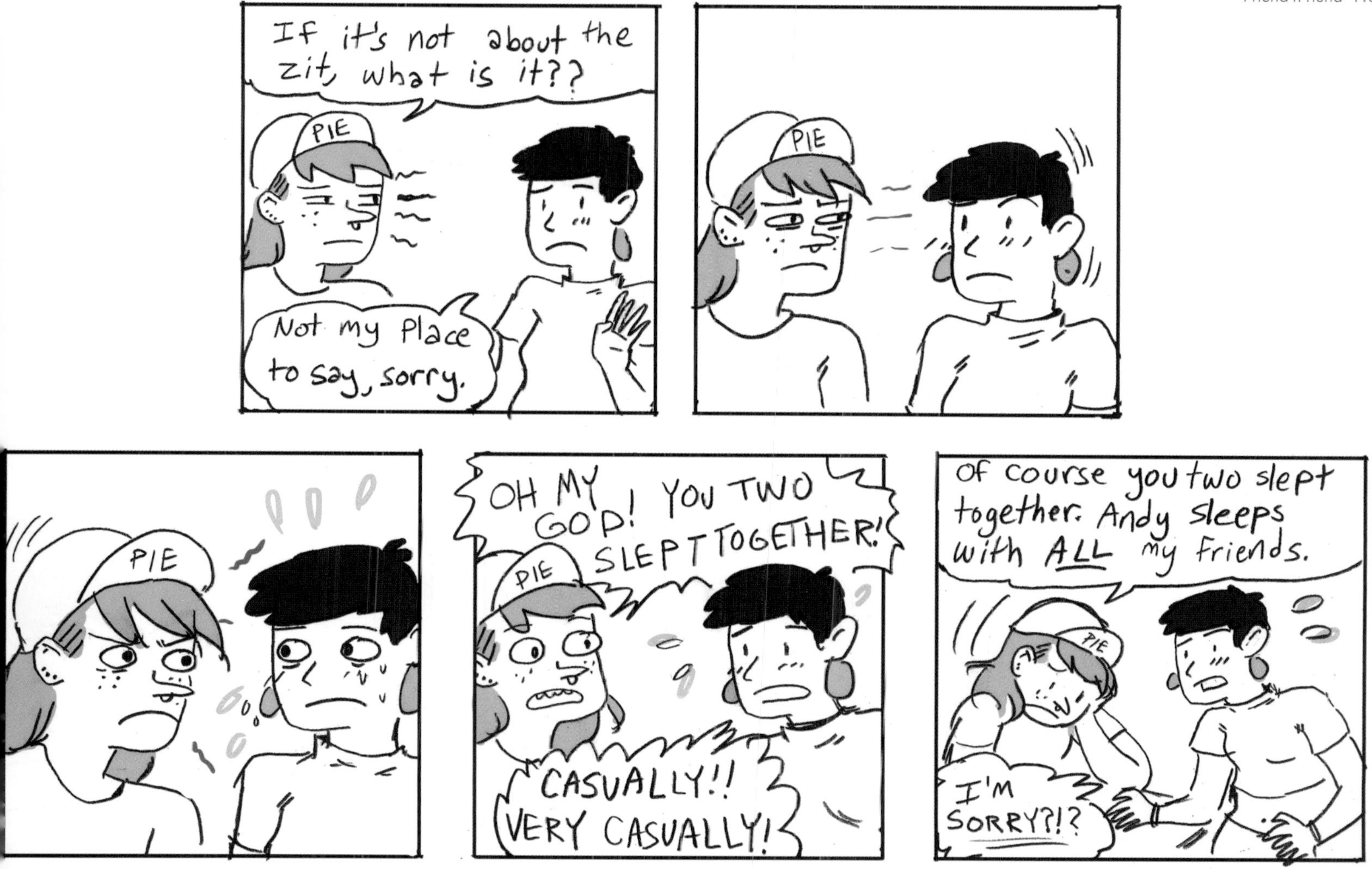
If it's not about the zit, what is it??
Not my Place to say, sorry.
PIE
PIE
PIE
OH MY GOD! YOU TWO SLEPT TOGETHER!
PIE
CASUALLY!! VERY CASUALLY!
Of course you two slept together. Andy sleeps with ALL my friends.
PIE
I'M SORRY?!?

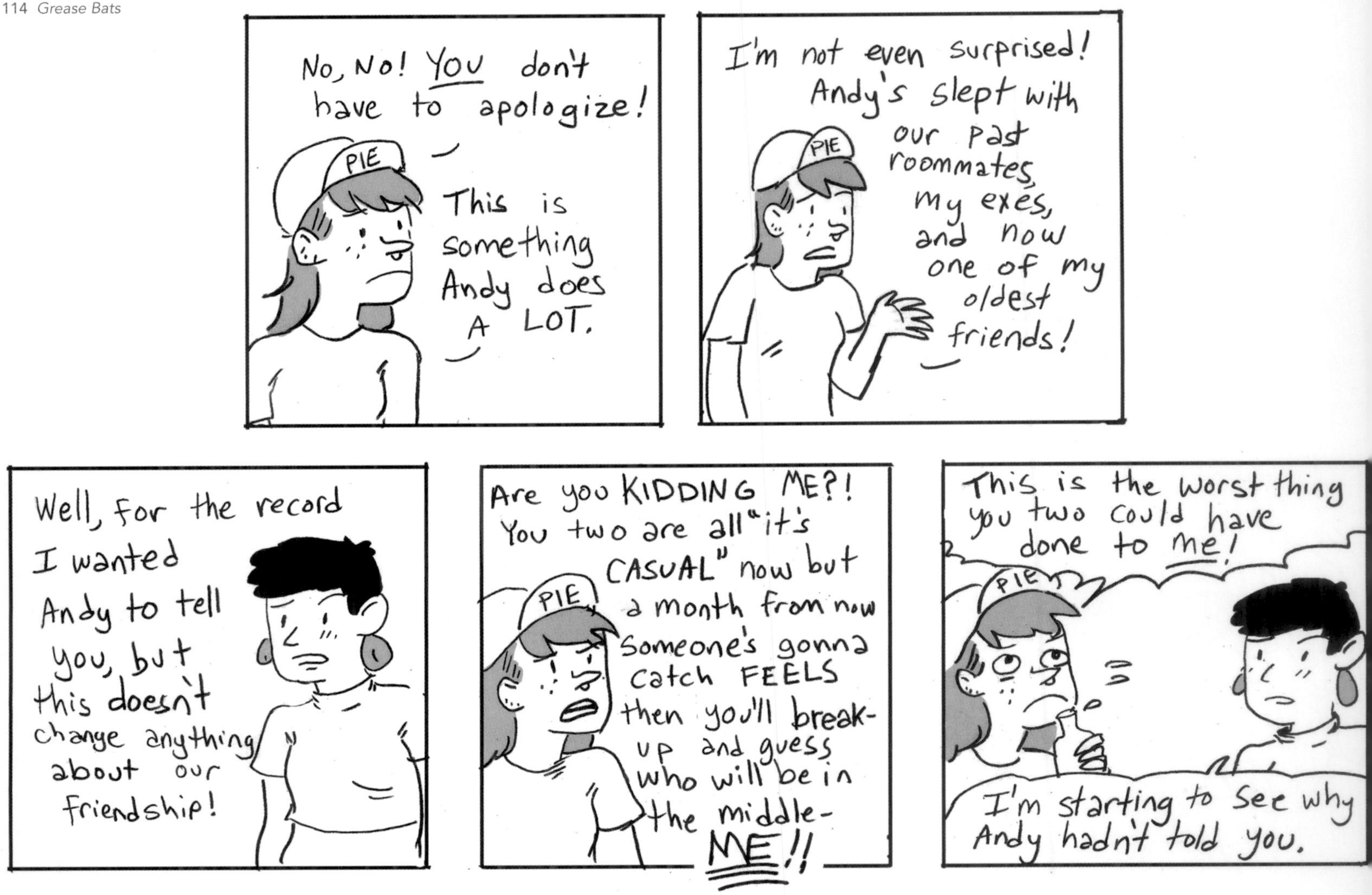
No, No! YOU don't have to apologize!
This is something Andy does A LOT.
I'm not even surprised! Andy's slept with our past roommates, my exes, and now one of my oldest friends!
Well, for the record I wanted Andy to tell you, but this doesn't change anything about our friendship!
Are you KIDDING ME?! You two are all "it's CASUAL" now but a month from now someone's gonna catch FEELS then you'll break-up and guess who will be in the middle- ME!!
PIE
This is the worst thing you two could have done to me!
I'm starting to see why Andy hadn't told you.

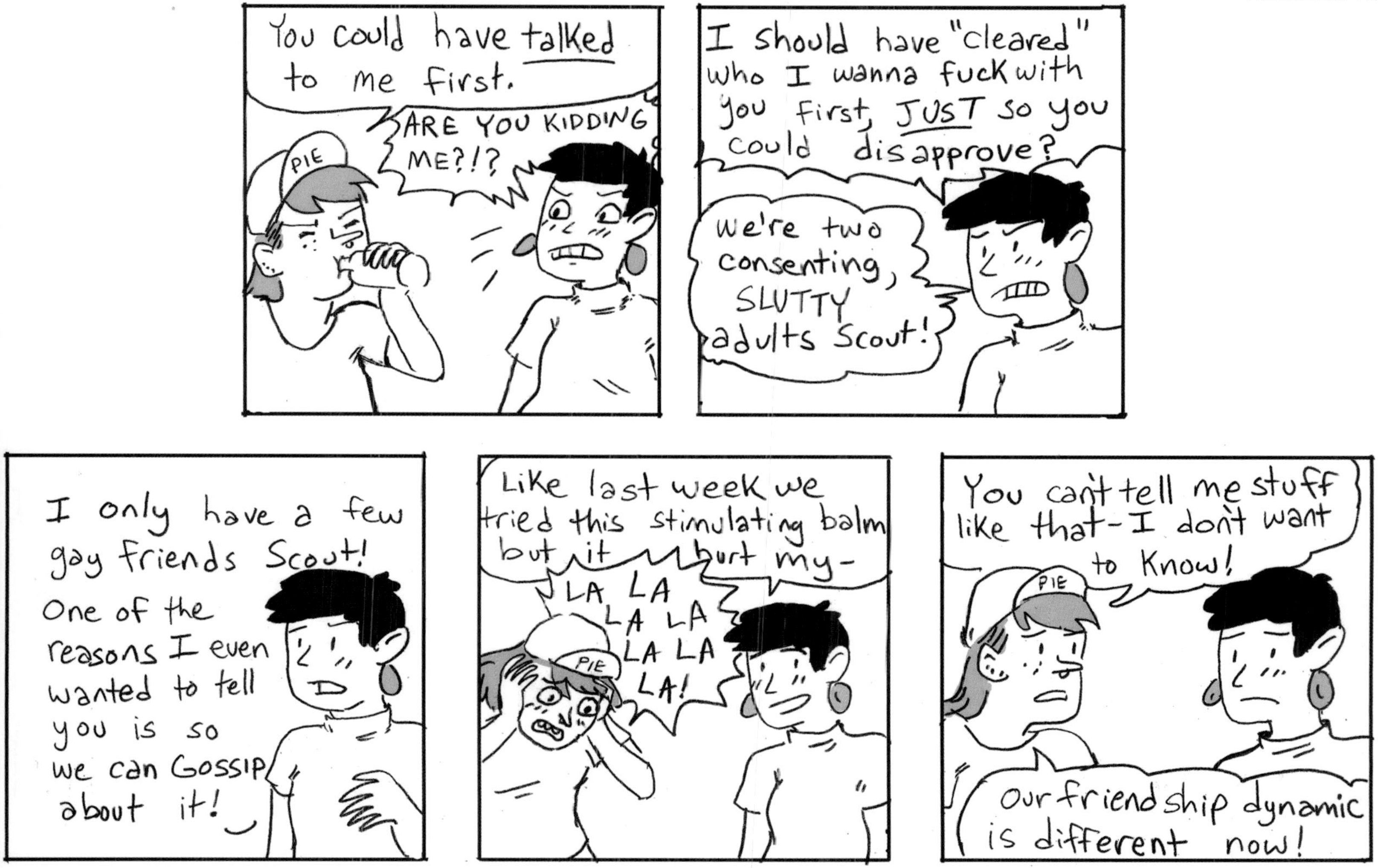
You could have talked to me first.
ARE YOU KIDDING ME?!?
I should have "cleared" who I wanna fuck with you first, JUST so you could disapprove?
We're two consenting, SLUTTY adults Scout!
I only have a few gay friends Scout!
One of the reasons I even wanted to tell you is so we can GOSSIP about it!
Like last week we tried this stimulating balm but it hurt my-
LA LA LA LA LA LA LA!
You can't tell me stuff like that- I don't want to know!
Our friendship dynamic is different now!
PIE

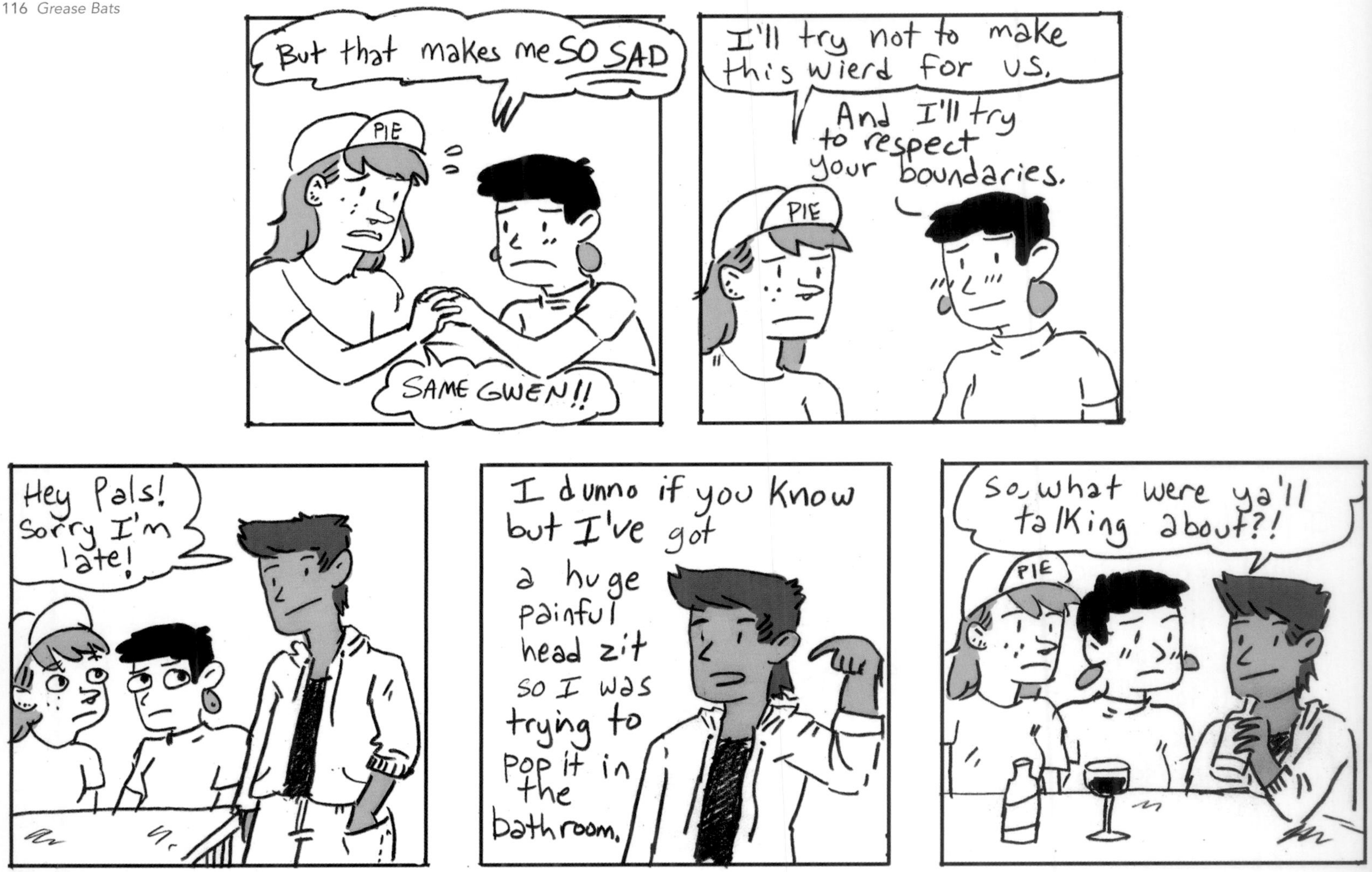
But that makes me SO SAD
SAME GWEN!!
I'll try not to make this wierd for us.
And I'll try to respect your boundaries.
Hey Pals! Sorry I'm late!
I dunno if you know but I've got
a huge painful head zit so I was trying to pop it in the bathroom.
So, what were ya'll talking about?!

The After Party

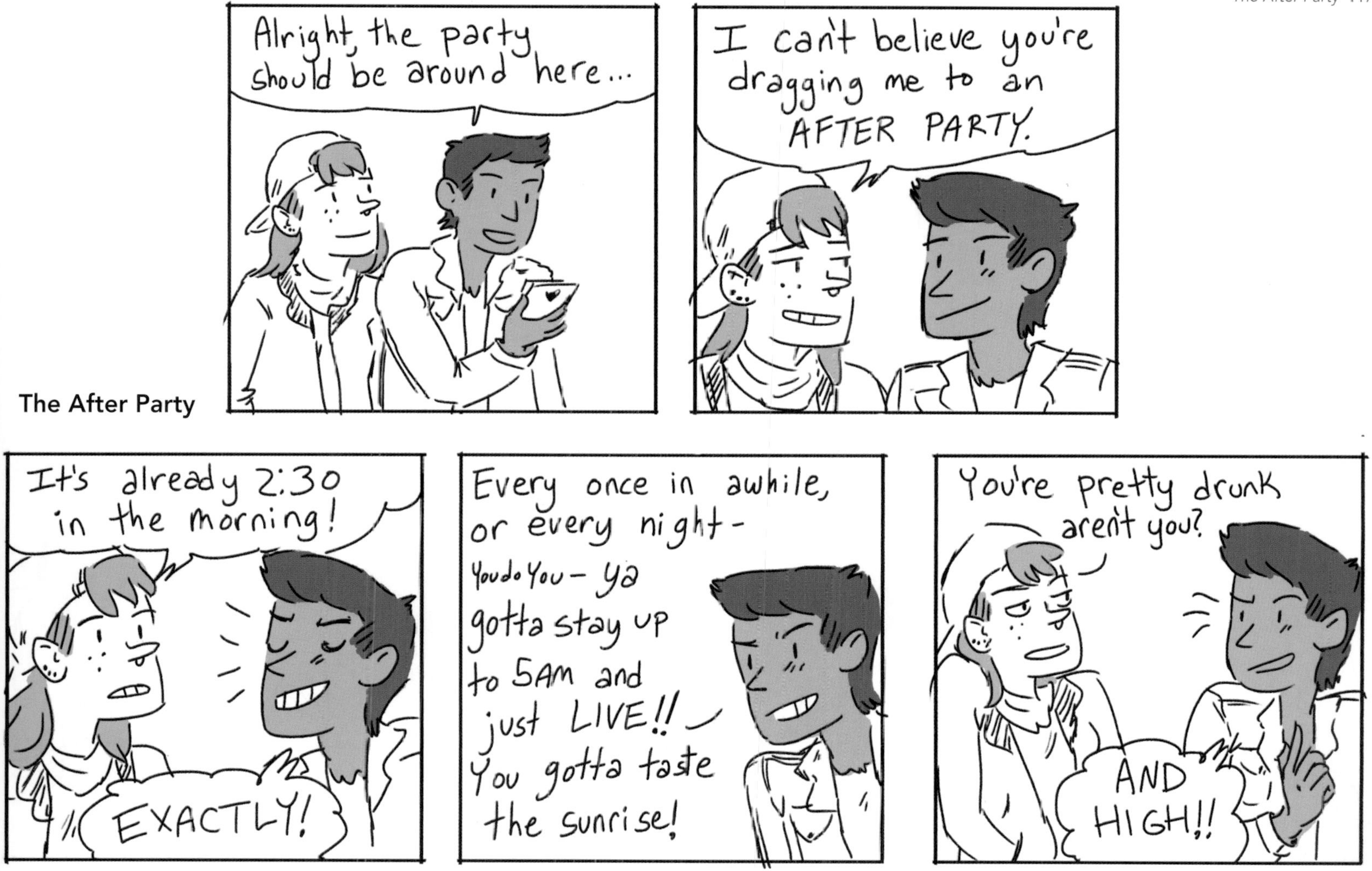
Alright, the party should be around here...
I can't believe you're dragging me to an AFTER PARTY.
It's already 2:30 in the morning!
EXACTLY!
Every once in awhile, or every night-
You do You - ya gotta stay up to 5AM and just LIVE!! You gotta taste the sunrise!
You're pretty drunk aren't you?
AND HIGH!!

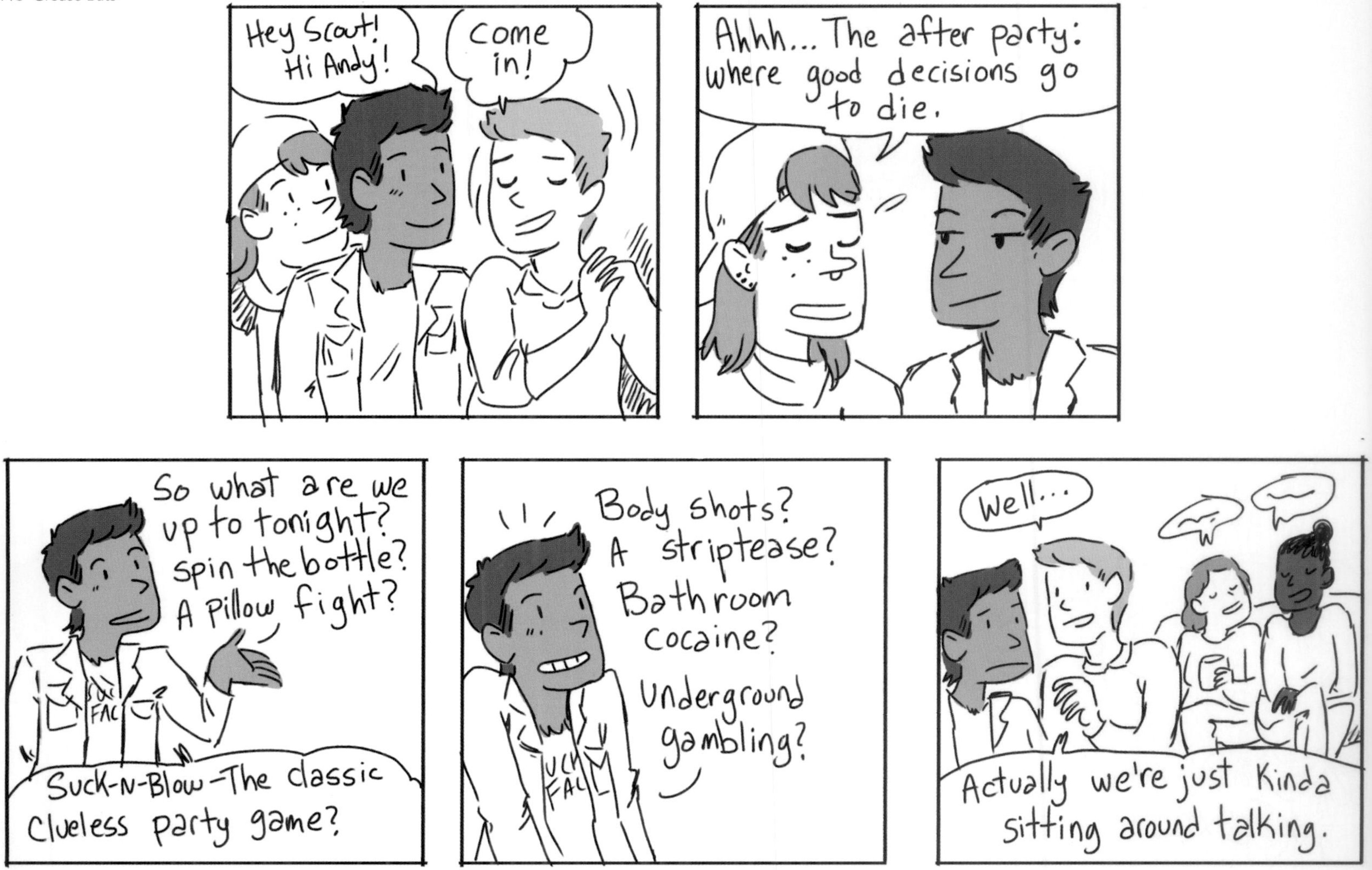
Hey Scout! Hi Andy!
Come in!
Ahhh... The after party: where good decisions go to die.
So what are we up to tonight? Spin the bottle? A pillow fight?
Suck-N-Blow–The classic Clueless party game?
Body shots? A striptease? Bathroom cocaine?
Underground gambling?
Well...
Actually we're just kinda sitting around talking.

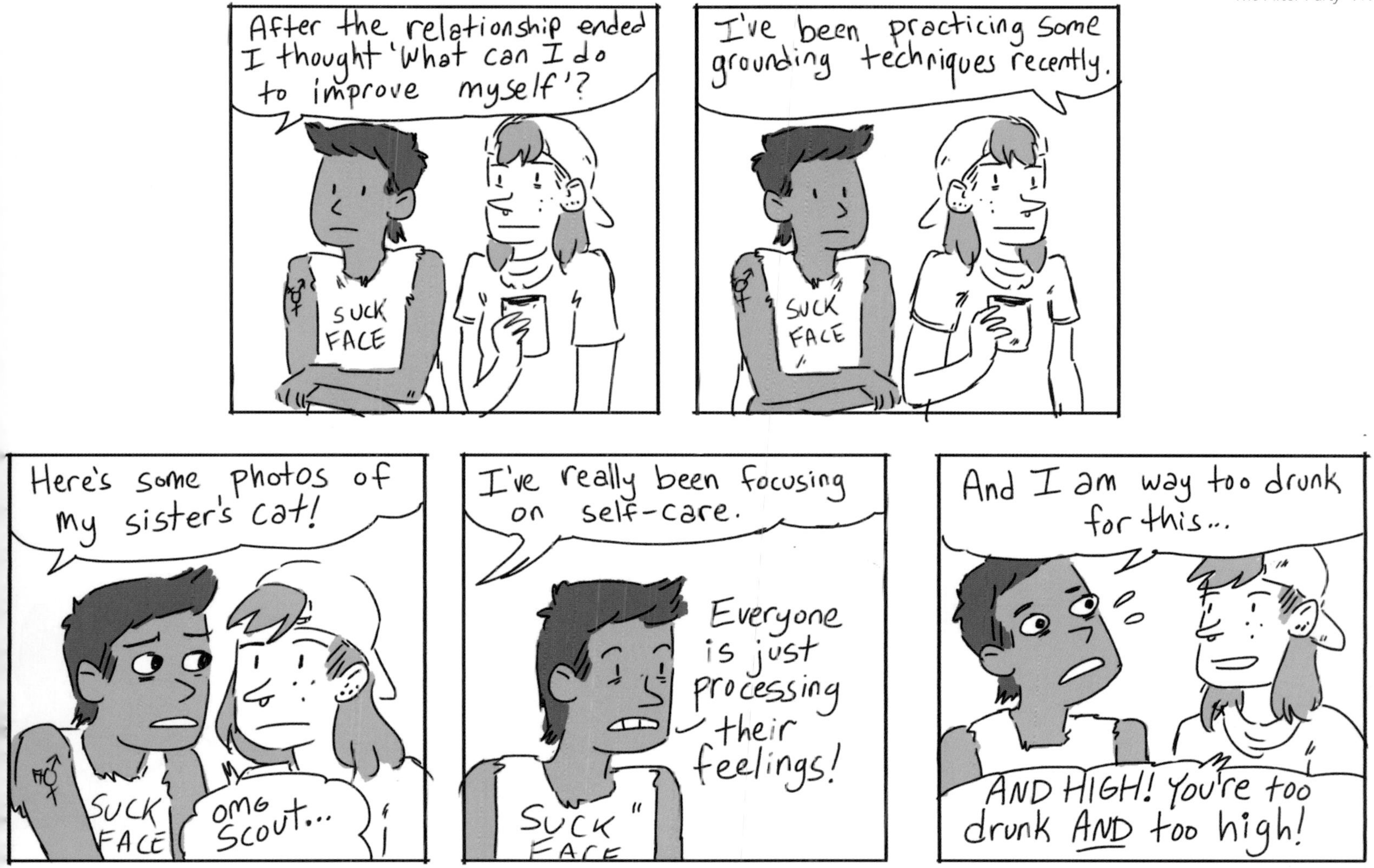
After the relationship ended I thought 'What can I do to improve myself'?
I've been practicing some grounding techniques recently.
Here's some photos of my sister's cat!
OMG Scout...
I've really been focusing on self-care.
Everyone is just processing their feelings!
And I am way too drunk for this...
AND HIGH! You're too drunk AND too high!

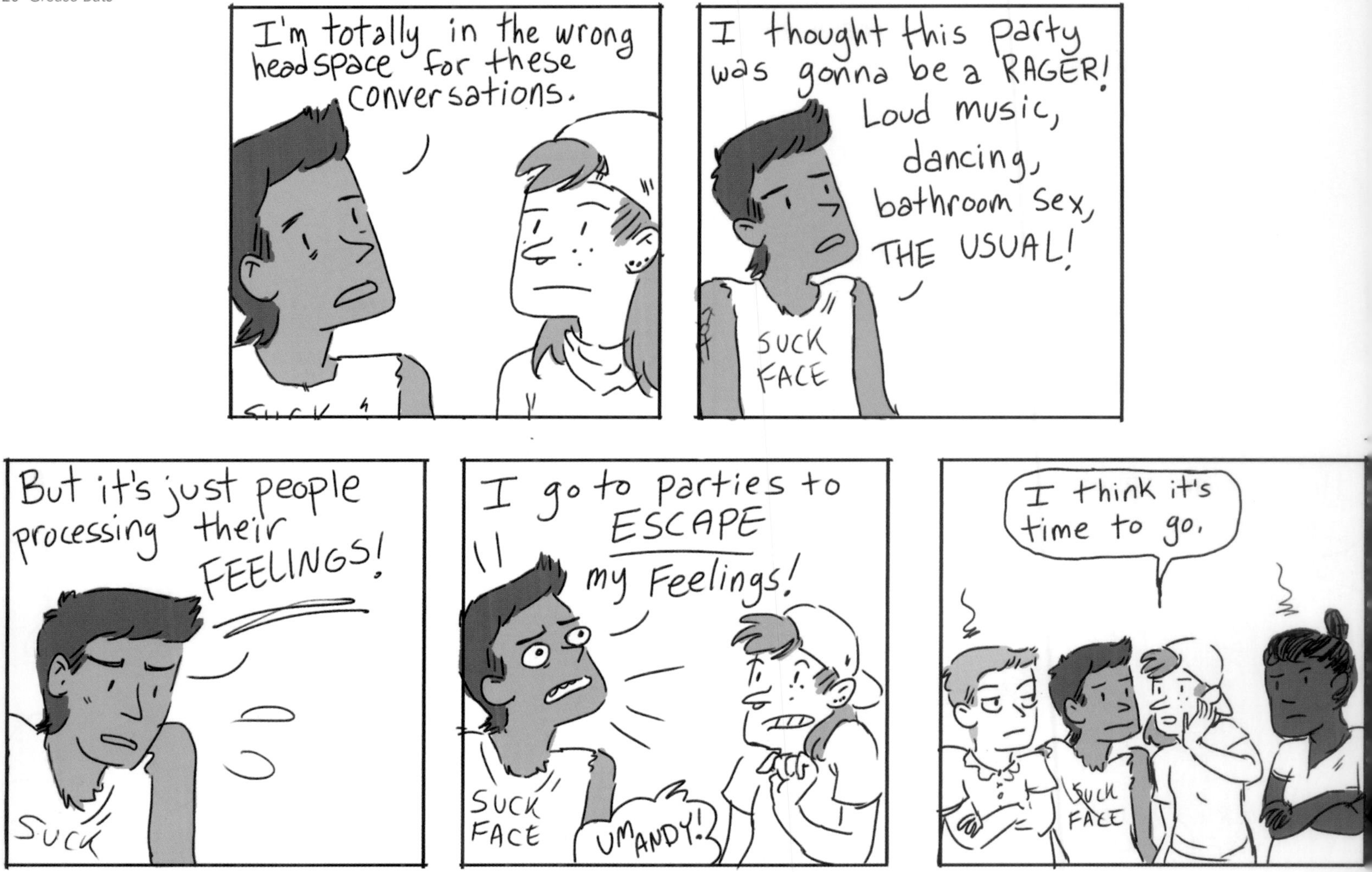
I'm totally in the wrong headspace for these conversations.
I thought this party was gonna be a RAGER! Loud music, dancing, bathroom sex, THE USUAL!
SUCK FACE
But it's just people processing their FEELINGS!
SUCK
I go to parties to ESCAPE my Feelings!
SUCK FACE
UMANDY!
I think it's time to go.
SUCK FACE

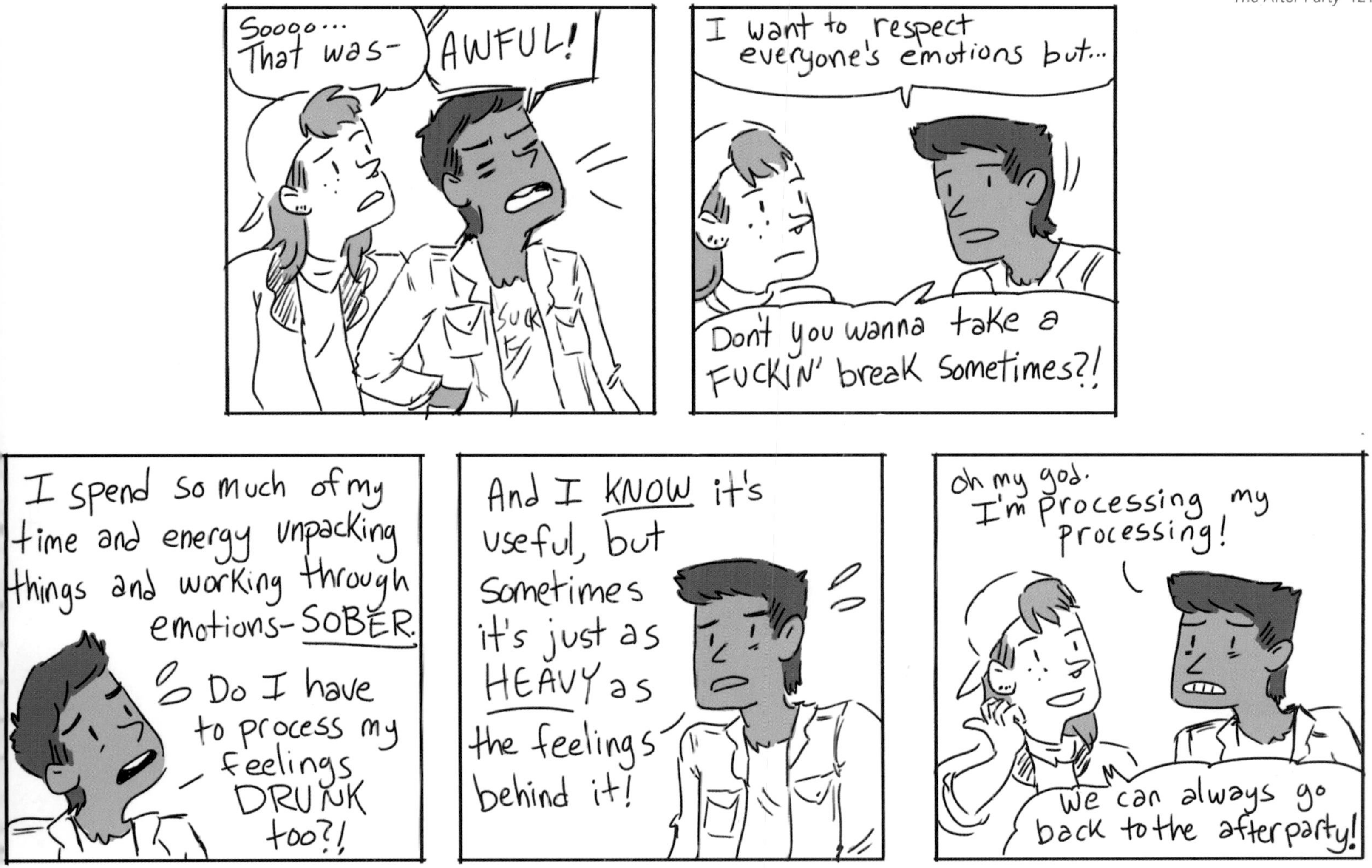
Soooo... That was-
AWFUL!
I want to respect everyone's emotions but...
Don't you wanna take a FUCKIN' break sometimes?!
I spend so much of my time and energy unpacking things and working through emotions- SOBER.
Do I have to process my feelings DRUNK too?!
And I KNOW it's useful, but sometimes it's just as HEAVY as the feelings behind it!
Oh my god. I'm processing my processing!
We can always go back to the afterparty!

Holigay Obligations

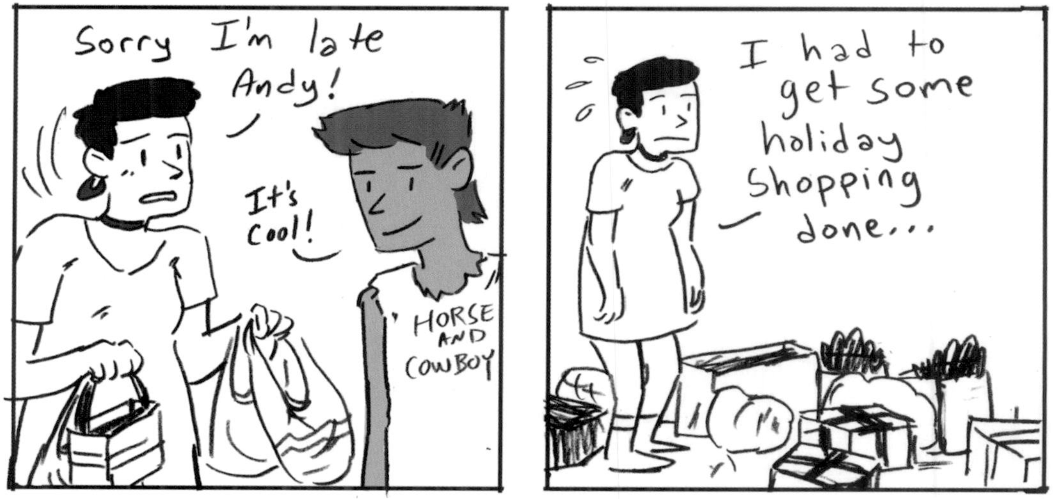
Sorry I'm late Andy!
It's cool!
HORSE AND COWBOY
I had to get some holiday shopping done...

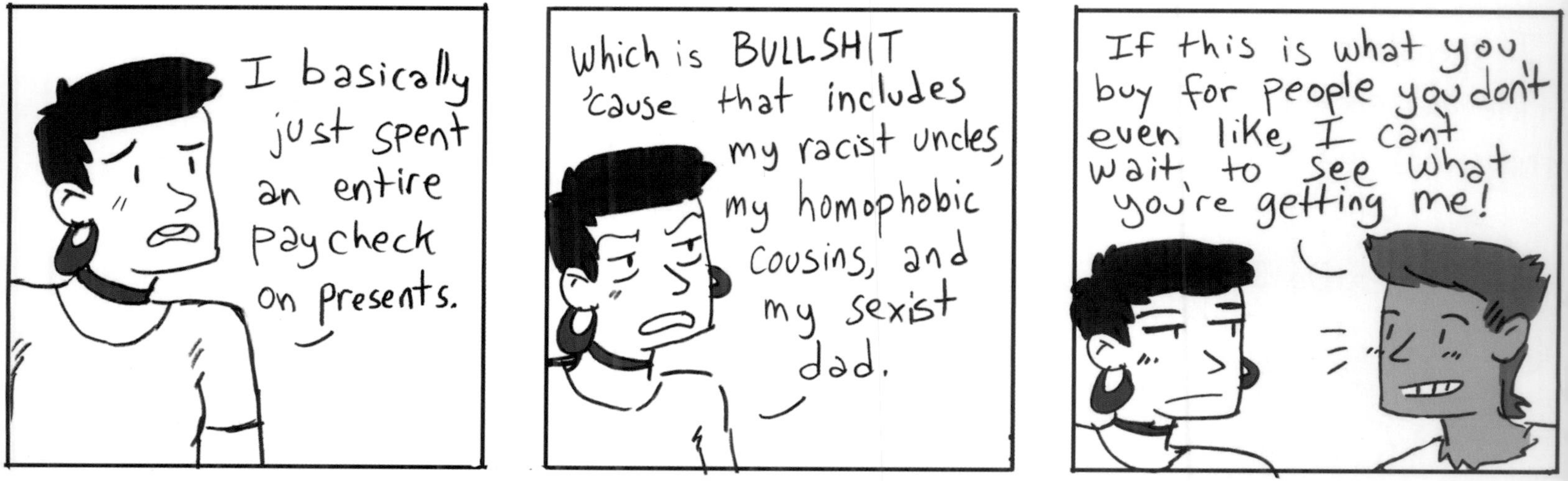
I basically just spent an entire paycheck on presents.
Which is BULLSHIT 'cause that includes my racist uncles, my homophobic cousins, and my sexist dad.
If this is what you buy for people you don't even like, I can't wait to see what you're getting me!

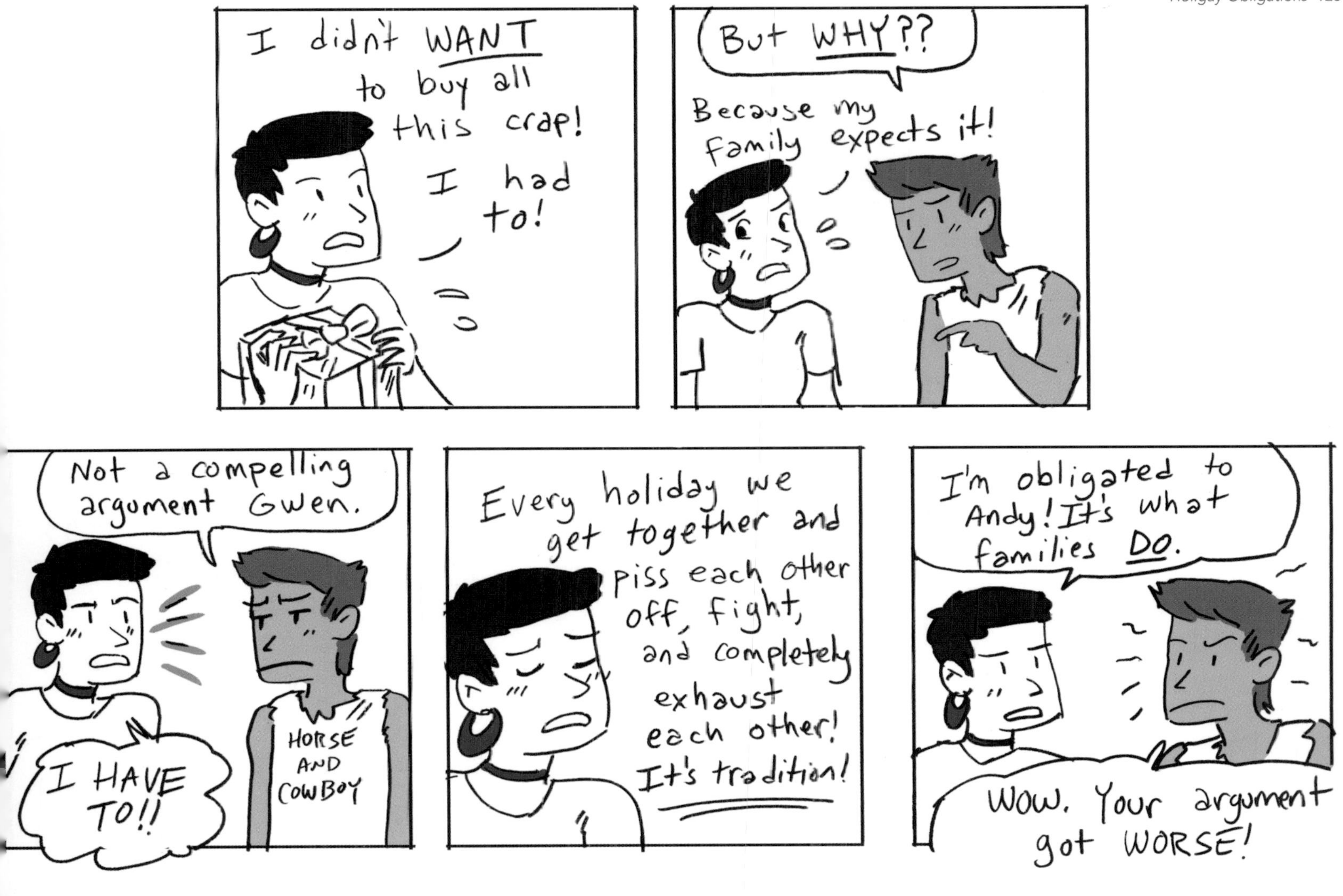
I didn't WANT to buy all this crap!
I had to!
But WHY??
Because my family expects it!
Not a compelling argument Gwen.
I HAVE TO!!
HORSE AND COWBOY
Every holiday we get together and piss each other off, fight, and completely exhaust each other! It's tradition!
I'm obligated to Andy! It's what families DO.
WOW. Your argument got WORSE!

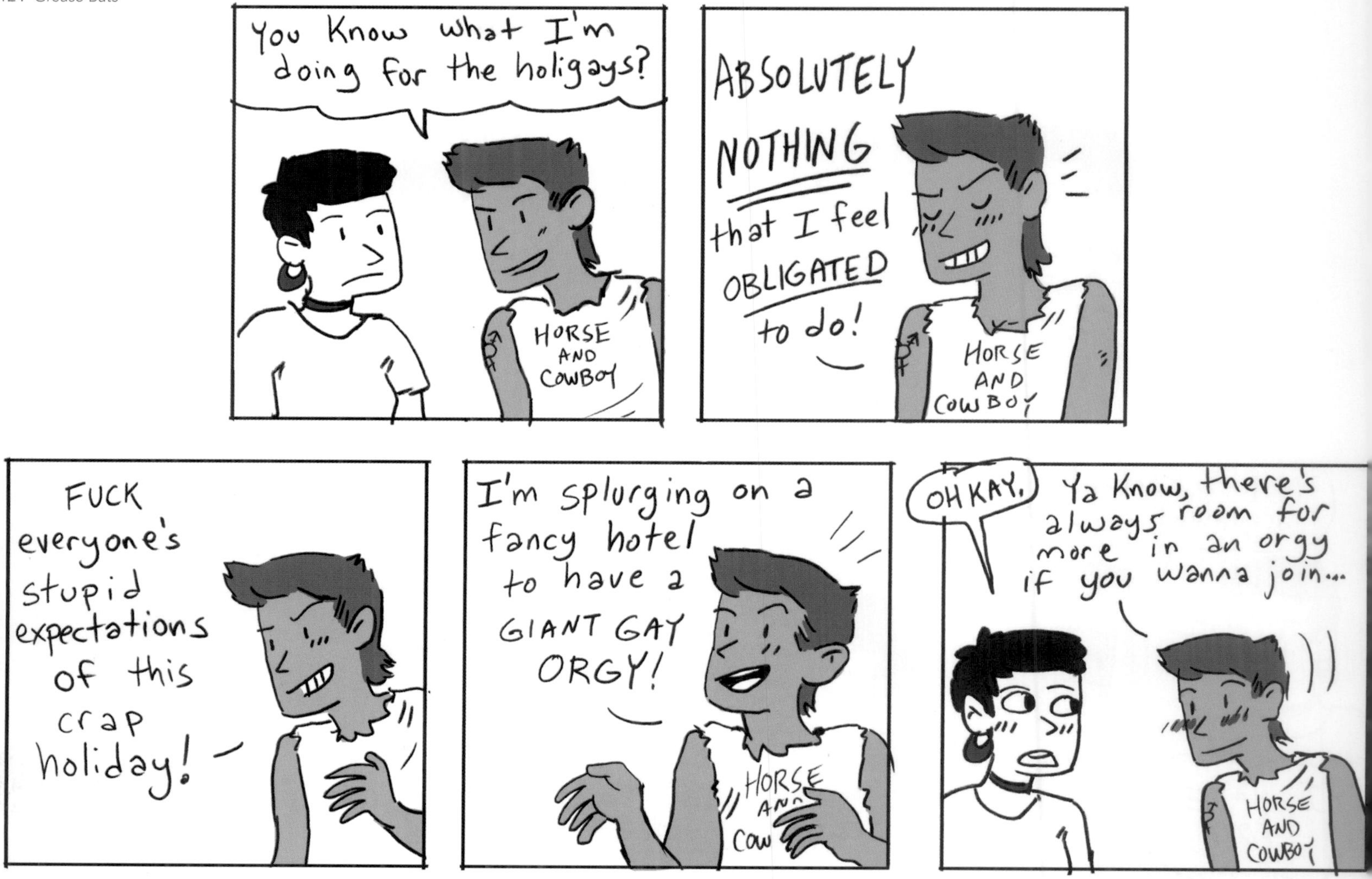
You Know what I'm doing for the holigays?
ABSOLUTELY NOTHING that I feel OBLIGATED to do!
HORSE AND COWBOY
FUCK everyone's stupid expectations of this crap holiday!
I'm splurging on a fancy hotel to have a GIANT GAY ORGY!
OHKAY.
Ya Know, there's always room for more in an orgy if you wanna join...
HORSE AND COWBOY

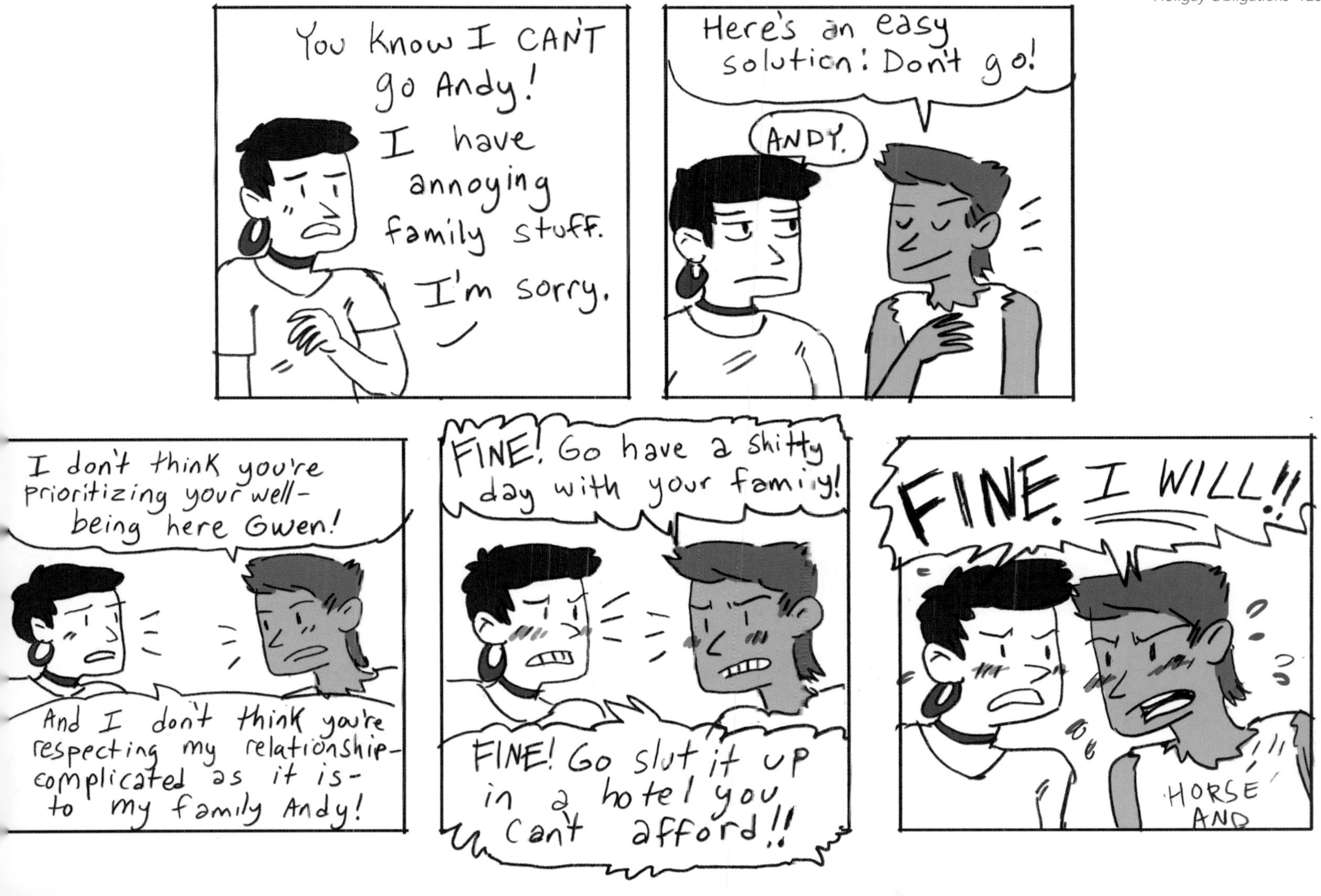
You know I CAN'T go Andy! I have annoying family stuff. I'm sorry.
Here's an easy solution: Don't go!
ANDY.
I don't think you're prioritizing your well-being here Gwen!
And I don't think you're respecting my relationship- complicated as it is- to my family Andy!
FINE! Go have a shitty day with your family!
FINE! Go slut it up in a hotel you can't afford!!
FINE. I WILL!!
HORSE AND

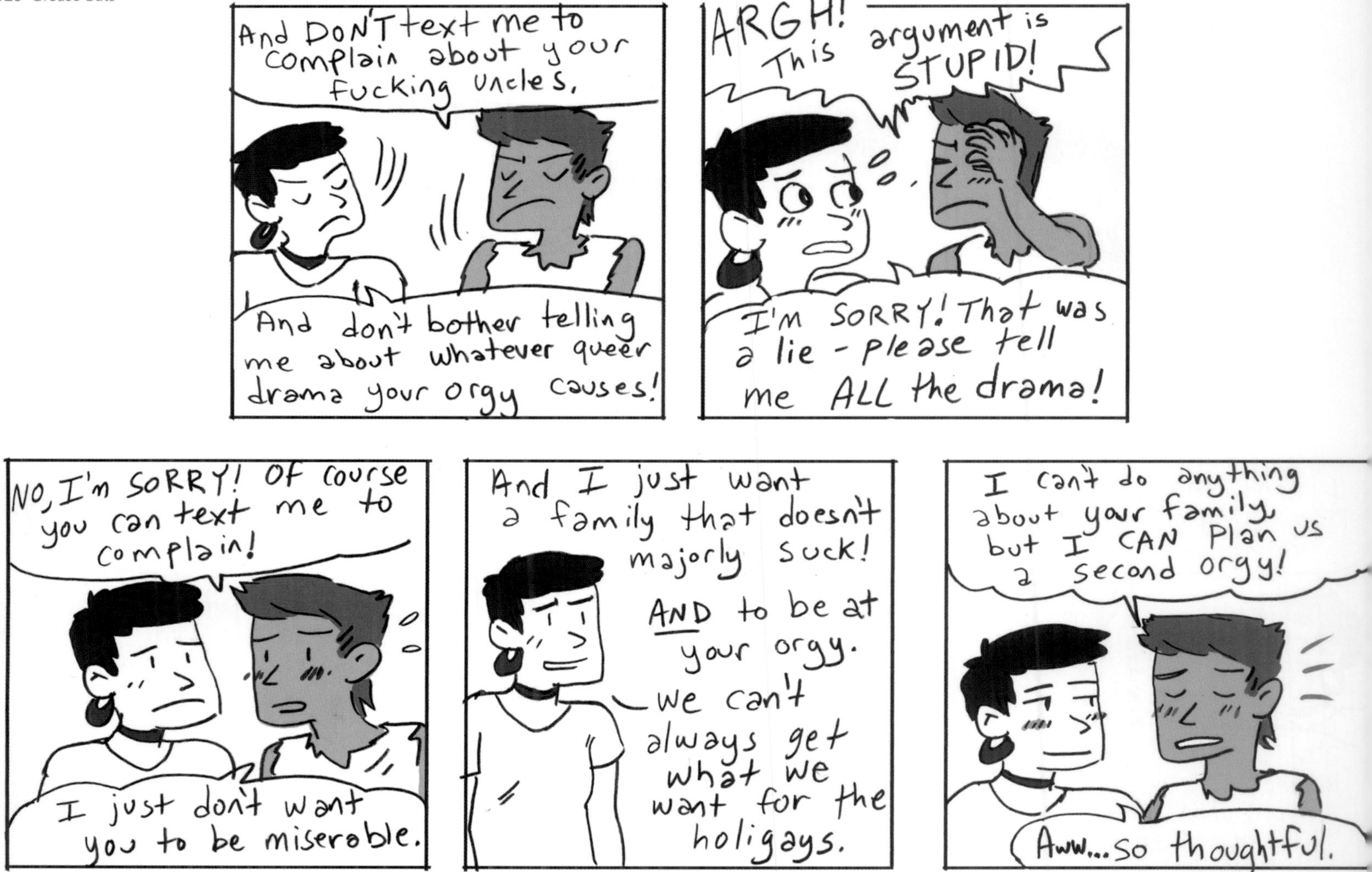
And DON'T text me to complain about your fucking uncles.
And don't bother telling me about whatever queer drama your orgy causes!
ARGH! This argument is STUPID!
I'M SORRY! That was a lie - please tell me ALL the drama!
NO, I'm SORRY! Of course you can text me to complain!
I just don't want you to be miserable.
And I just want a family that doesn't majorly suck!
AND to be at your orgy.
We can't always get what we want for the holigays.
I can't do anything about your family, but I CAN plan us a second orgy!
Aww... so thoughtful.

Tired

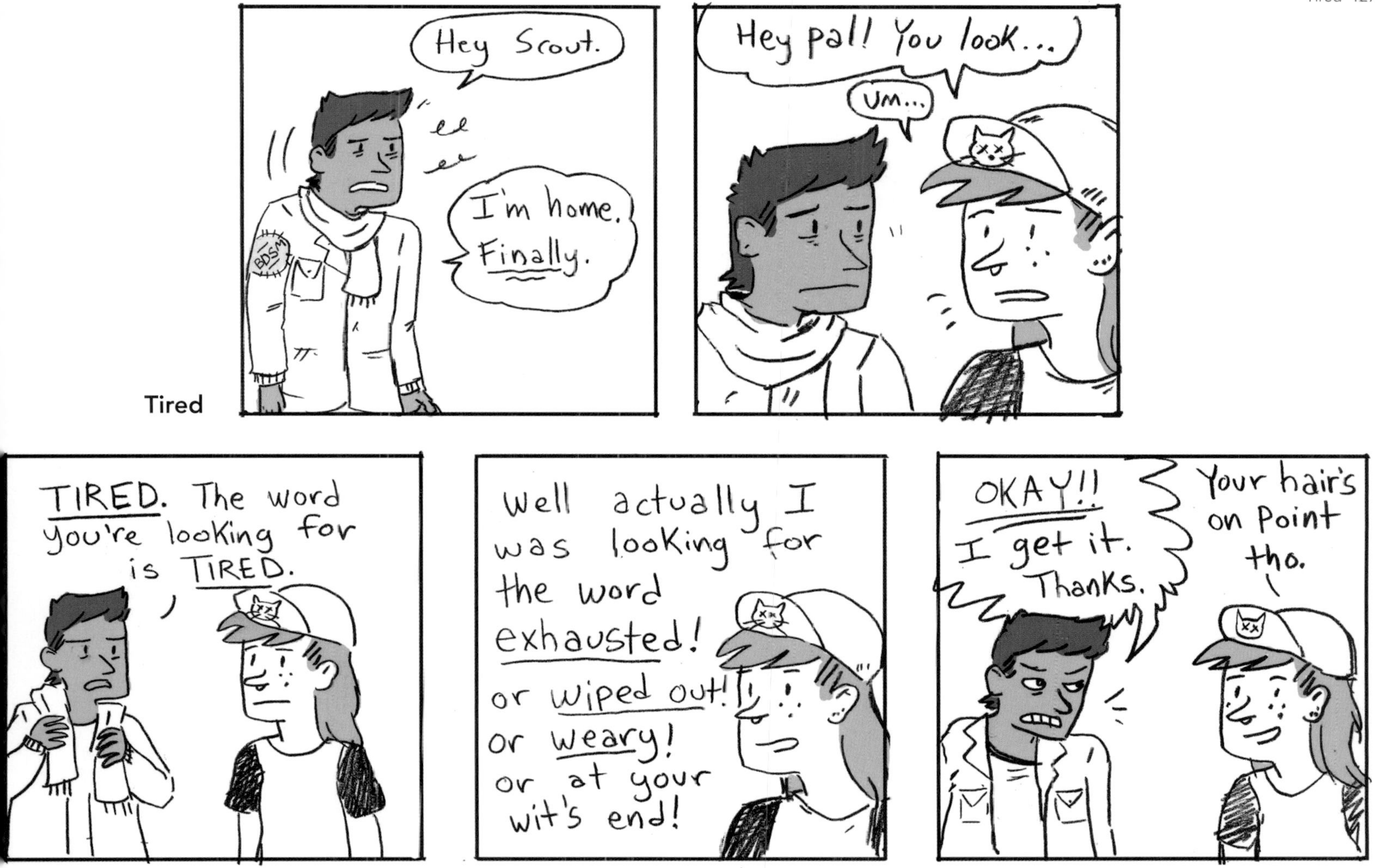
Hey Scout.
I'm home. Finally.
BDSM
Hey pal! You look...
Um...
TIRED. The word you're looking for is TIRED.
Well actually I was looking for the word exhausted! or wiped out! or weary! or at your wit's end!
OKAY!! I get it. Thanks.
Your hair's on Point tho.

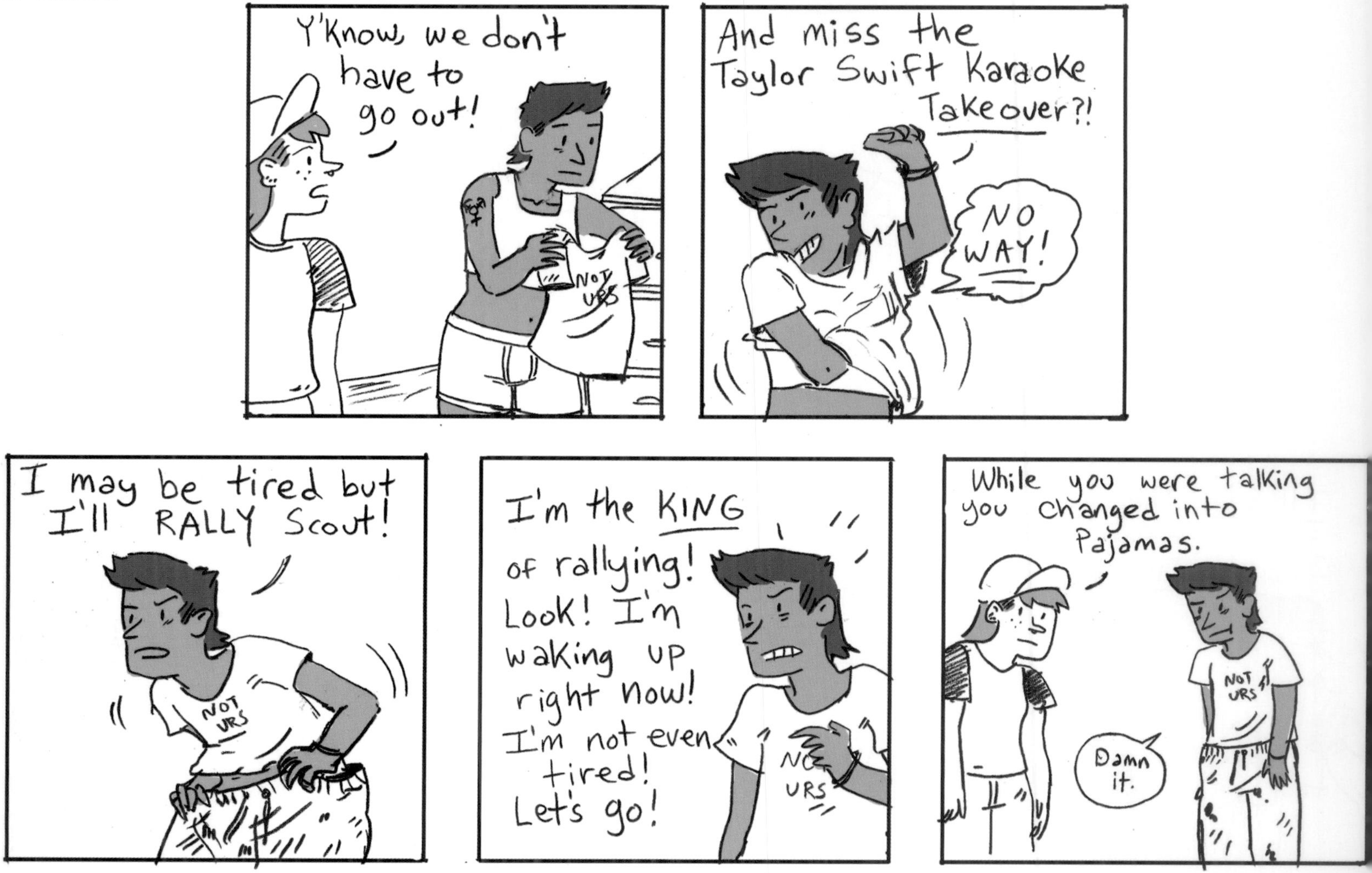
Y'Know, we don't have to go out!
NOT URS
And miss the Taylor Swift Karaoke Takeover?!
NO WAY!
I may be tired but I'll RALLY Scout!
NOT URS
I'm the KING of rallying! Look! I'm waking up right now! I'm not even tired! Let's go!
URS
While you were talking you changed into Pajamas.
NOT URS
Damn it.

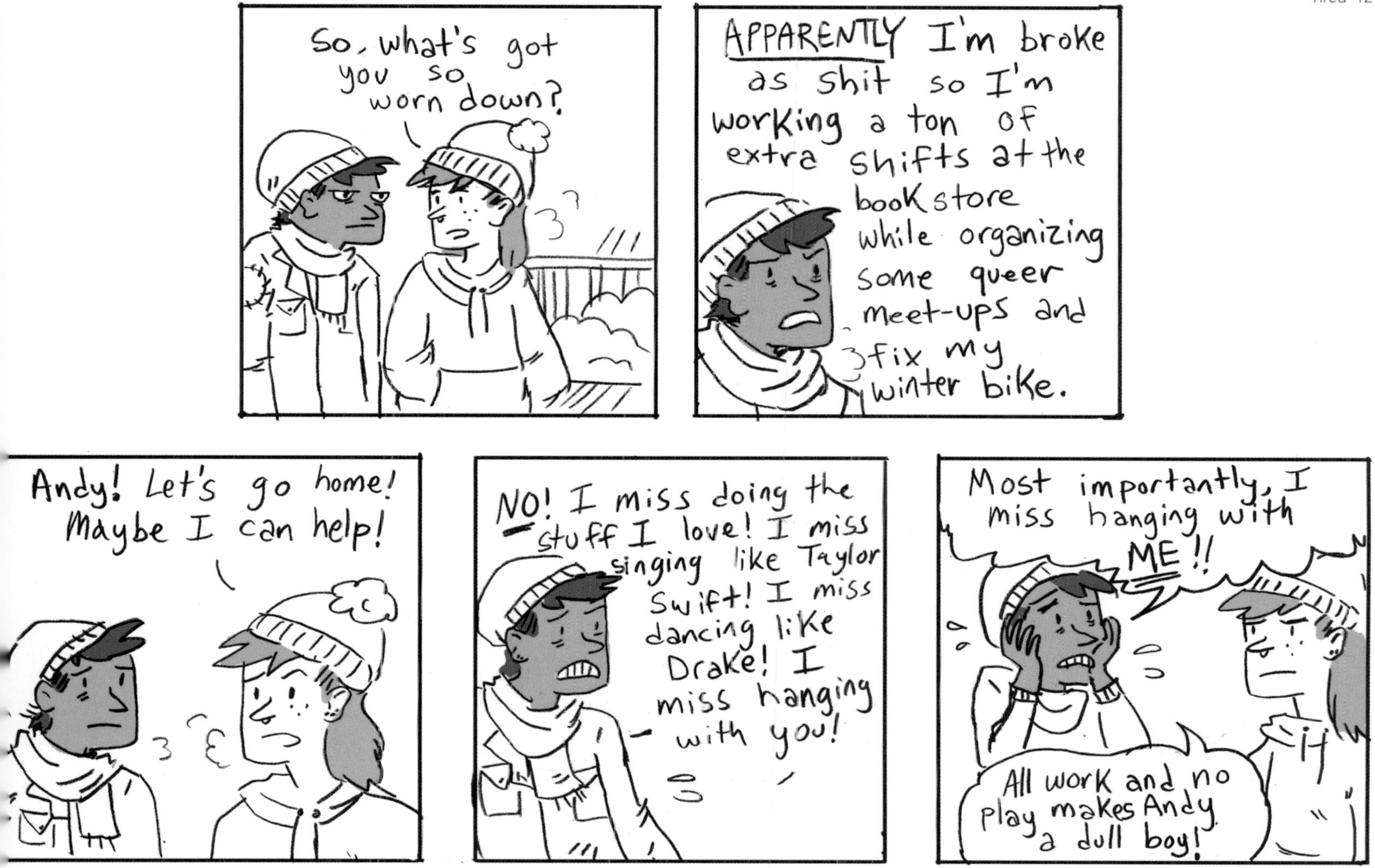
So, what's got you so worn down?
APPARENTLY I'm broke as shit so I'm working a ton of extra shifts at the bookstore while organizing some queer meet-ups and fix my winter bike.
Andy! Let's go home! Maybe I can help!
NO! I miss doing the stuff I love! I miss singing like Taylor Swift! I miss dancing like Drake! I miss hanging with you!
Most importantly, I miss hanging with ME!!
All work and no play makes Andy a dull boy!

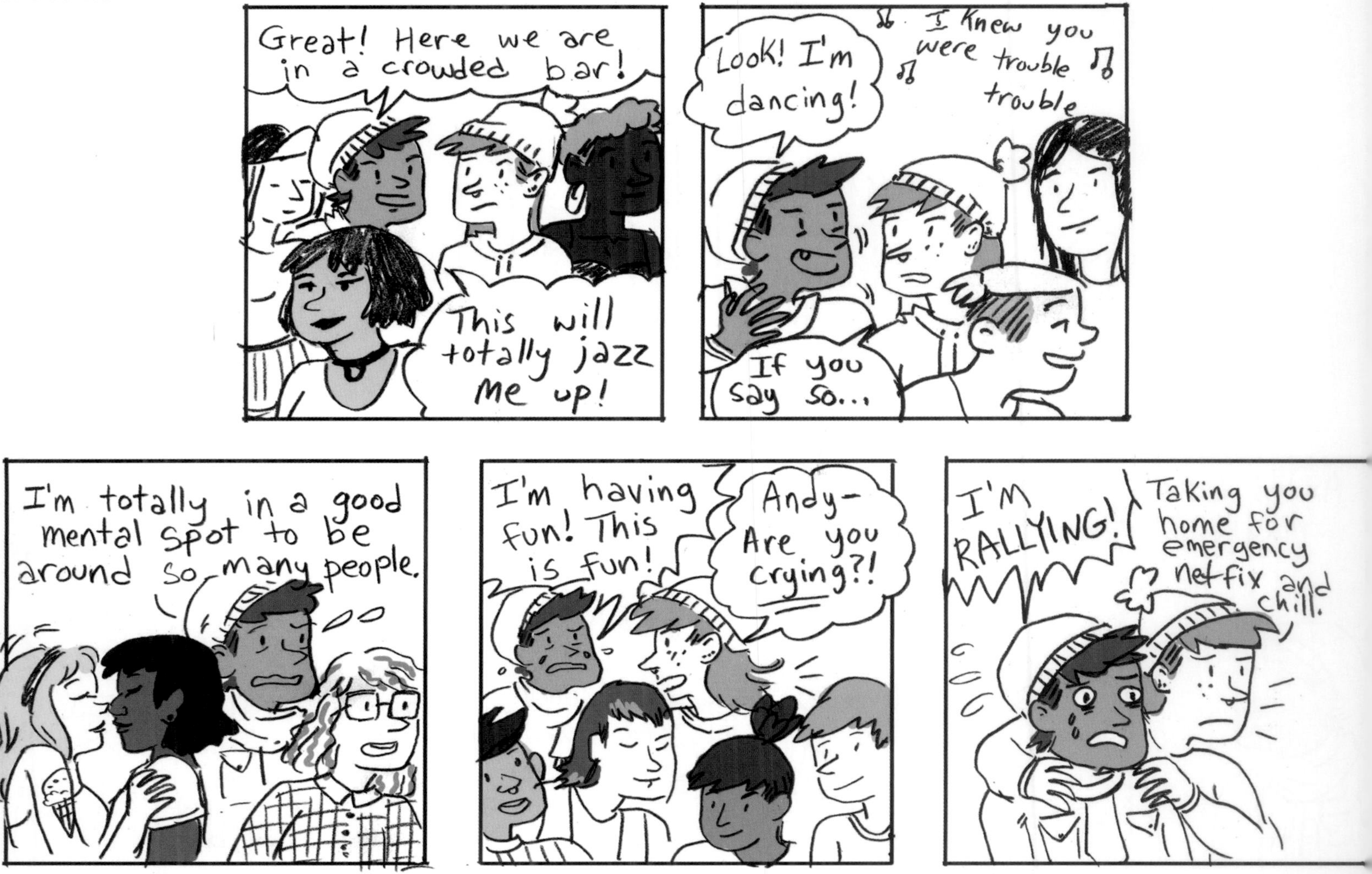
Great! Here we are in a crowded bar!
This will totally jazz me up!
Look! I'm dancing!
I knew you were trouble trouble
If you say so...
I'm totally in a good mental spot to be around so many people.
I'm having fun! This is fun!
Andy- Are you crying?!
I'M RALLYING!
Taking you home for emergency netfix and chill.

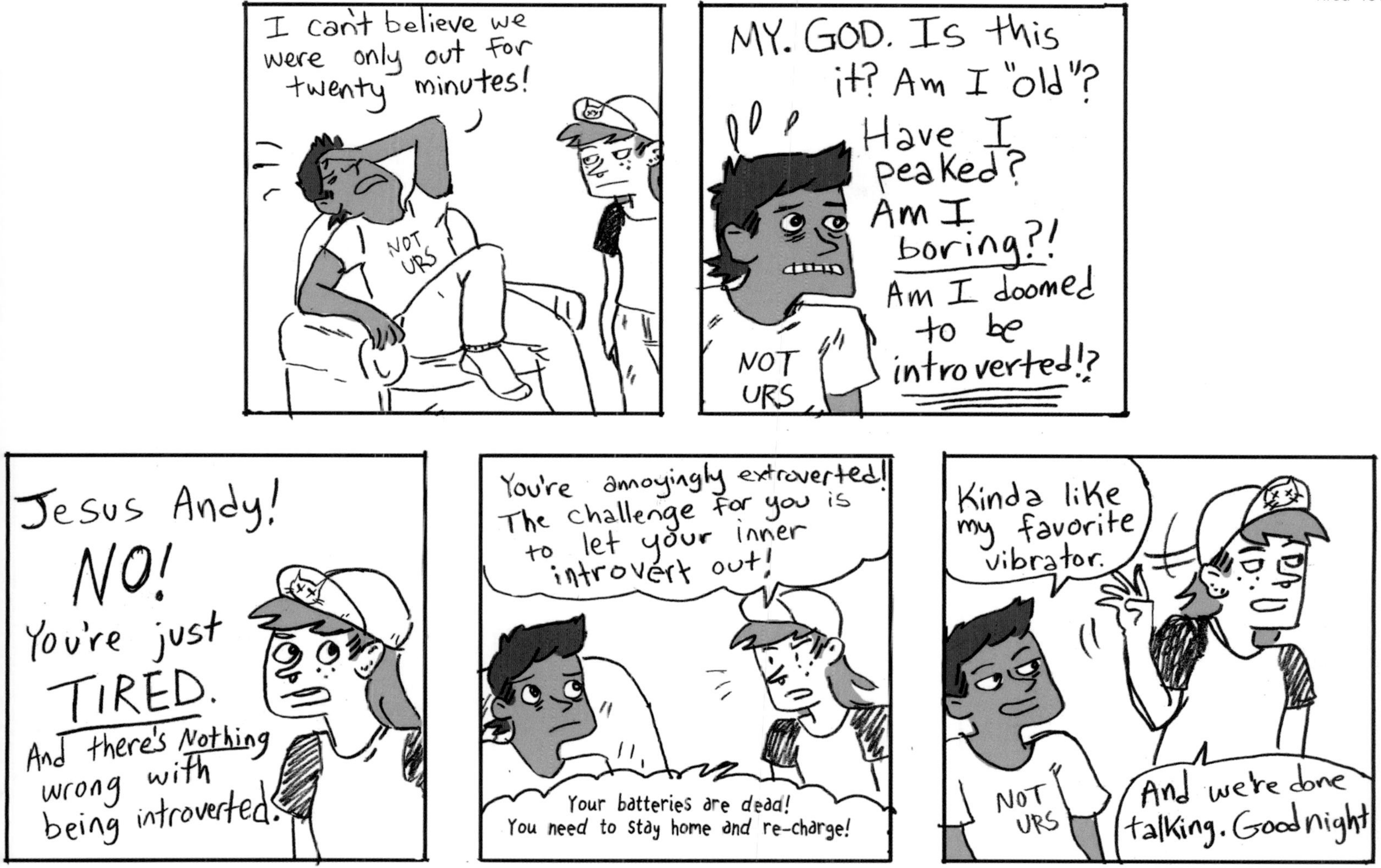
I can't believe we were only out for twenty minutes!
NOT URS
MY. GOD. Is this it? Am I "old"? Have I peaked? Am I boring?! Am I doomed to be introverted!?
NOT URS
Jesus Andy! NO! You're just TIRED. And there's Nothing wrong with being introverted.
You're annoyingly extroverted! The challenge for you is to let your inner introvert out!
Your batteries are dead! You need to stay home and re-charge!
Kinda like my favorite vibrator.
NOT URS
And we're done talking. Goodnight

Don't Cancel Your Sex Date

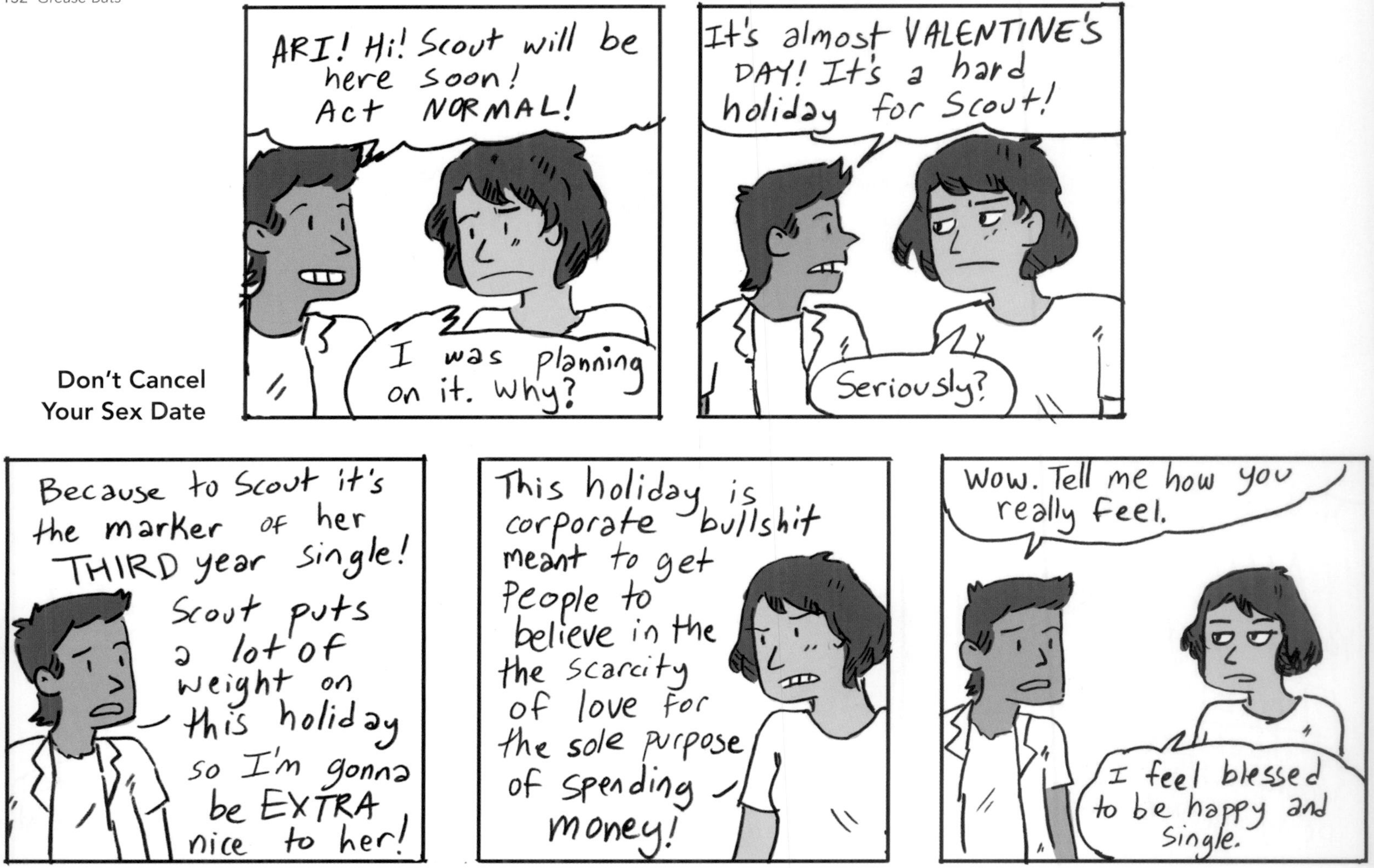
ARI! Hi! Scout will be here soon! Act NORMAL!
I was planning on it. Why?
It's almost VALENTINE'S DAY! It's a hard holiday for Scout!
Seriously?
Because to Scout it's the marker of her THIRD year single!
Scout puts a lot of weight on this holiday so I'm gonna be EXTRA nice to her!
This holiday is corporate bullshit meant to get people to believe in the the scarcity of love for the sole purpose of spending money!
Wow. Tell me how you really feel.
I feel blessed to be happy and single.

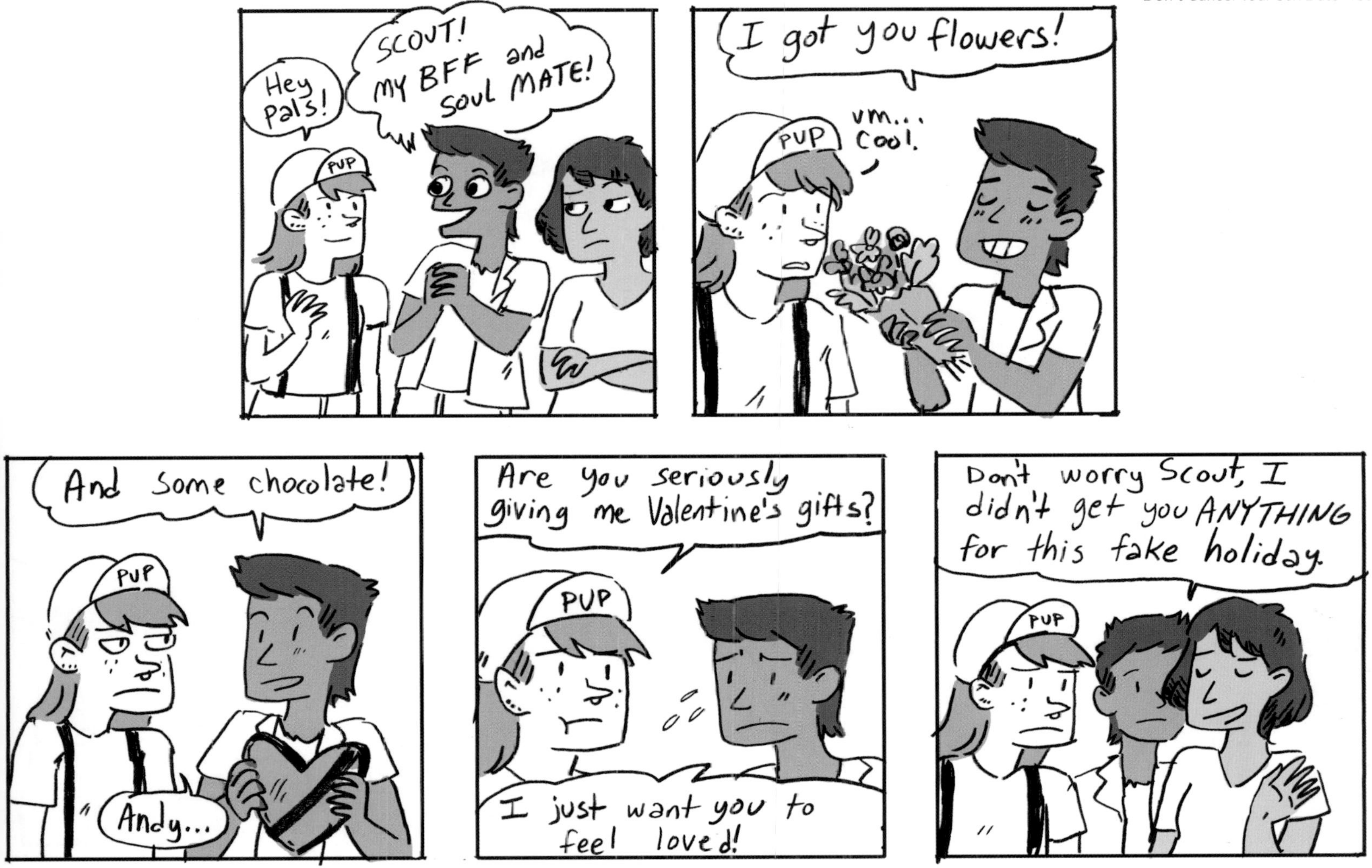
Hey pals!
SCOUT! MY BFF and SOUL MATE!
I got you flowers!
um... cool.
And some chocolate!
Andy...
Are you seriously giving me Valentine's gifts?
I just want you to feel loved!
Don't worry Scout, I didn't get you ANYTHING for this fake holiday.

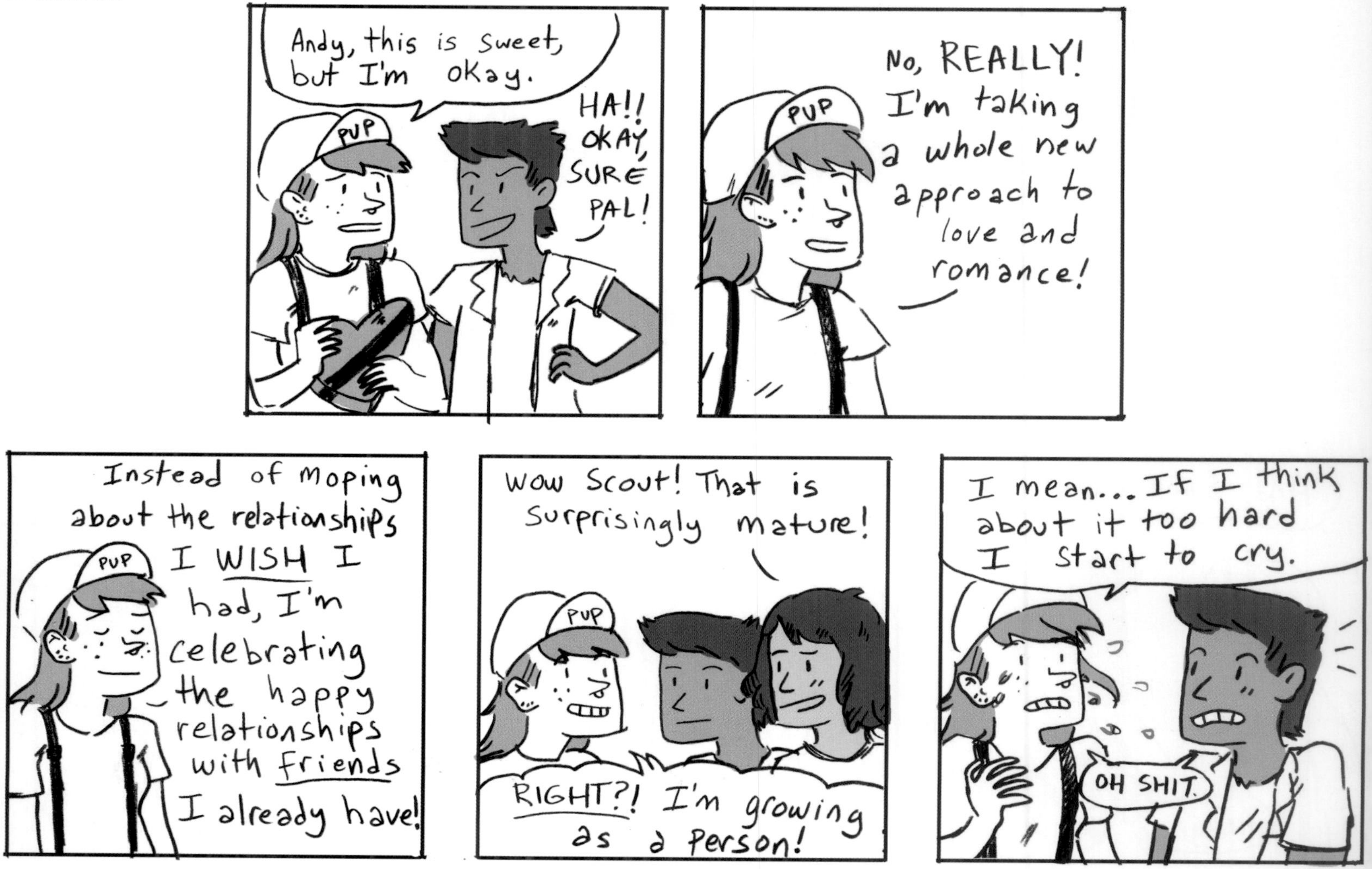

Andy, this is sweet, but I'm okay.
HA!! OKAY, SURE PAL!
No, REALLY! I'm taking a whole new approach to love and romance!
Instead of moping about the relationships I WISH I had, I'm celebrating the happy relationships with friends I already have!
Wow Scout! That is surprisingly mature!
RIGHT?! I'm growing as a person!
I mean... If I think about it too hard I start to cry.
OH SHIT.

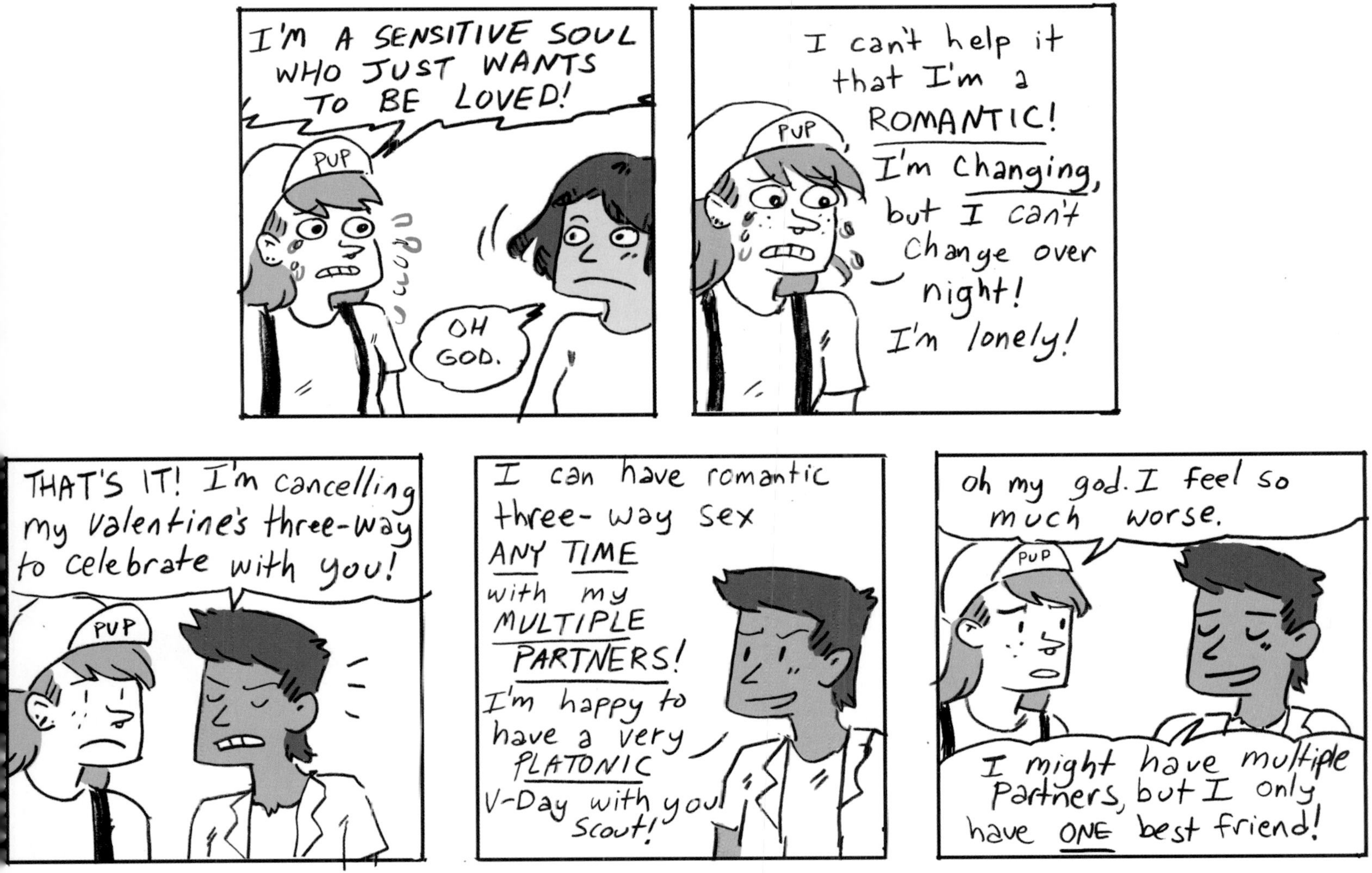
I'M A SENSITIVE SOUL WHO JUST WANTS TO BE LOVED!
OH GOD.
I can't help it that I'm a ROMANTIC! I'm changing, but I can't change over night! I'm lonely!
THAT'S IT! I'm cancelling my Valentine's three-way to celebrate with you!
I can have romantic three-way sex ANY TIME with my MULTIPLE PARTNERS! I'm happy to have a very PLATONIC V-Day with you! Scout!
oh my god. I feel so much worse.
I might have multiple Partners, but I only have ONE best friend!

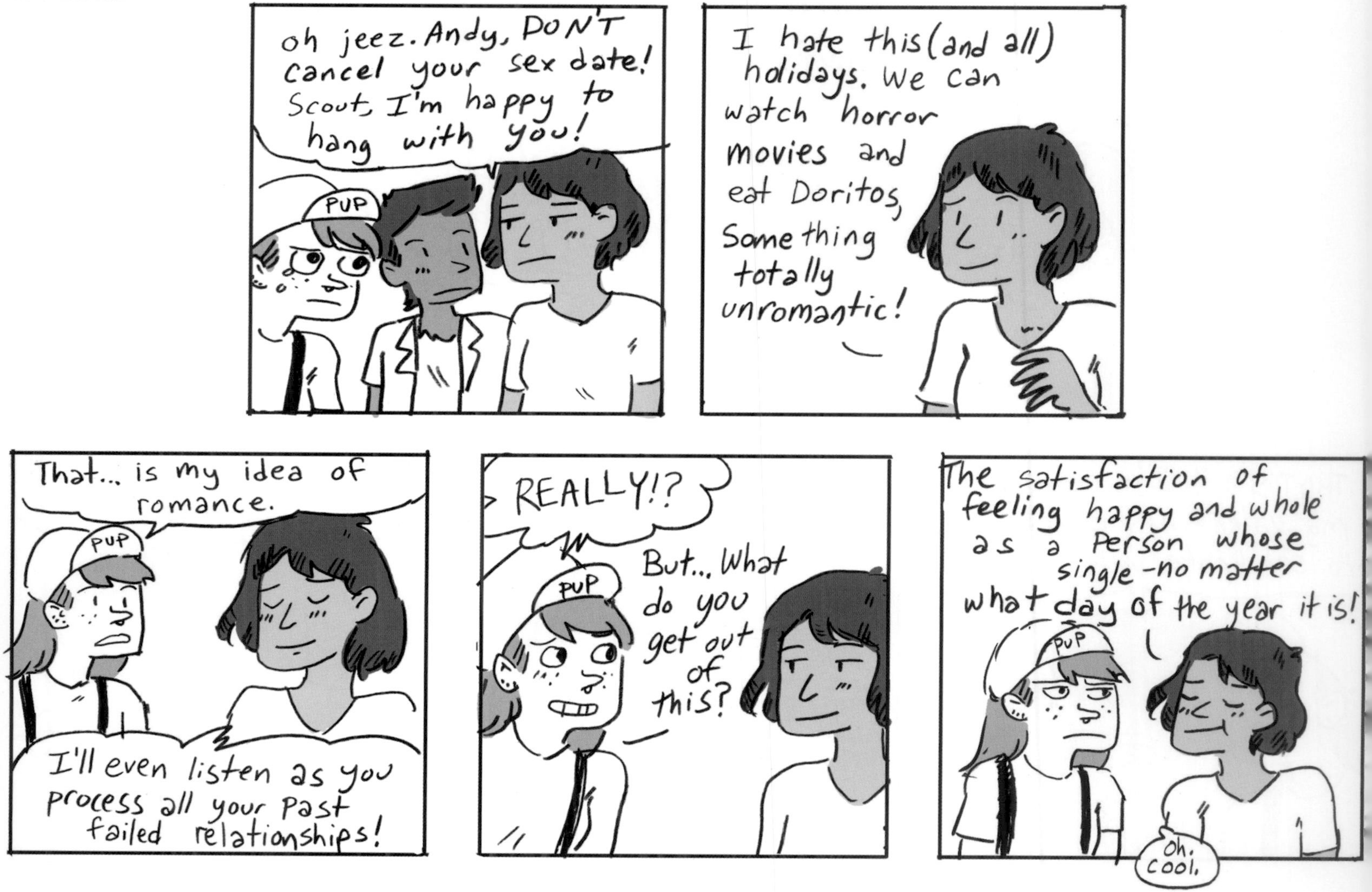
oh jeez. Andy, DON'T cancel your sex date! Scout, I'm happy to hang with you!
I hate this (and all) holidays. We can watch horror movies and eat Doritos, Some thing totally unromantic!
That... is my idea of romance.
I'll even listen as you process all your past failed relationships!
REALLY!?
But... What do you get out of this?
The satisfaction of feeling happy and whole as a person whose single-no matter what day of the year it is!
Oh. cool.

Top, Bottom, or Switch?

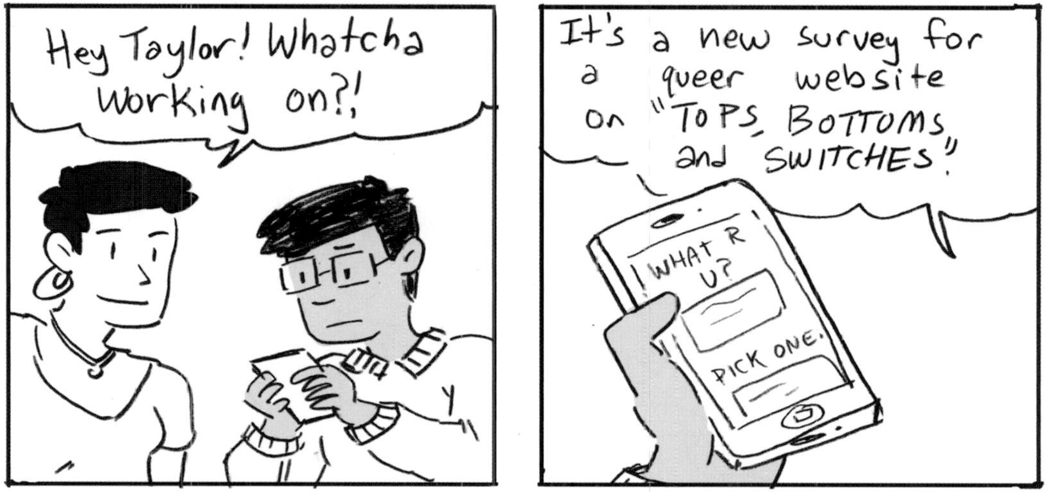
Hey Taylor! Whatcha working on?!
It's a new survey for a queer website on "TOPS, BOTTOMS, and SWITCHES"!
WHAT R U?
PICK ONE.

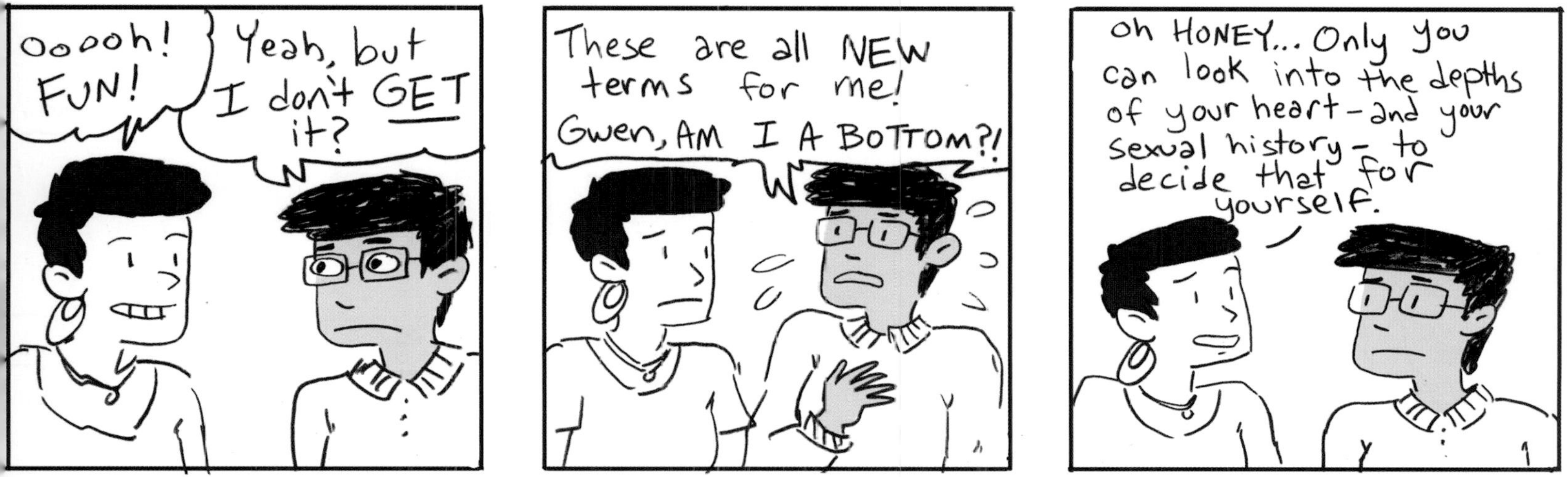
Ooooh! FUN!
Yeah, but I don't GET it?
These are all NEW terms for me! Gwen, AM I A BOTTOM?!
Oh HONEY... Only you can look into the depths of your heart—and your sexual history—to decide that for yourself.

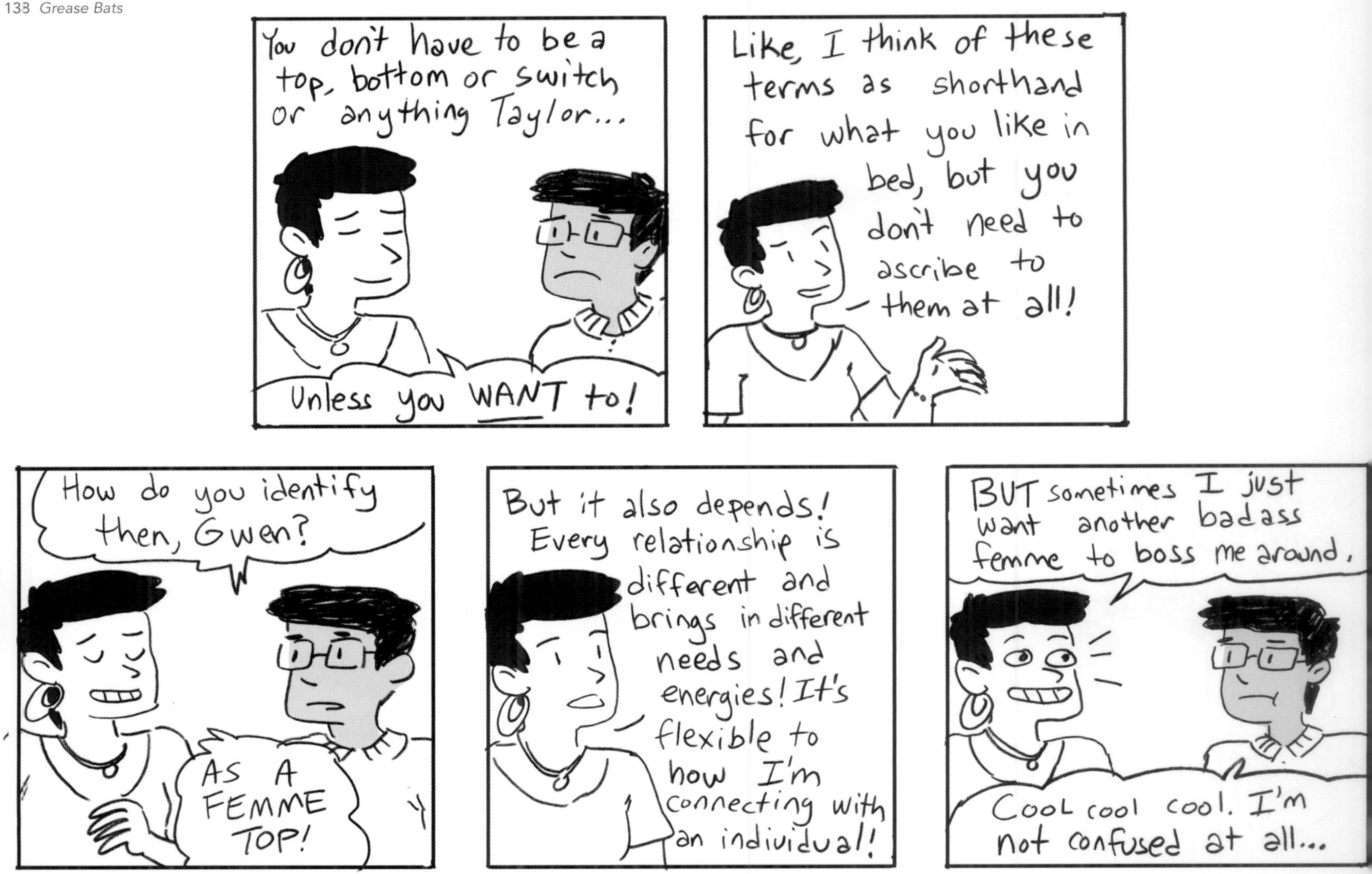
You don't have to be a top, bottom or switch or anything Taylor...
Unless you WANT to!
Like, I think of these terms as shorthand for what you like in bed, but you don't need to ascribe to them at all!
How do you identify then, Gwen?
AS A FEMME TOP!
But it also depends! Every relationship is different and brings in different needs and energies! It's flexible to how I'm connecting with an individual!
BUT sometimes I just want another badass femme to boss me around.
Cool cool cool. I'm not confused at all...

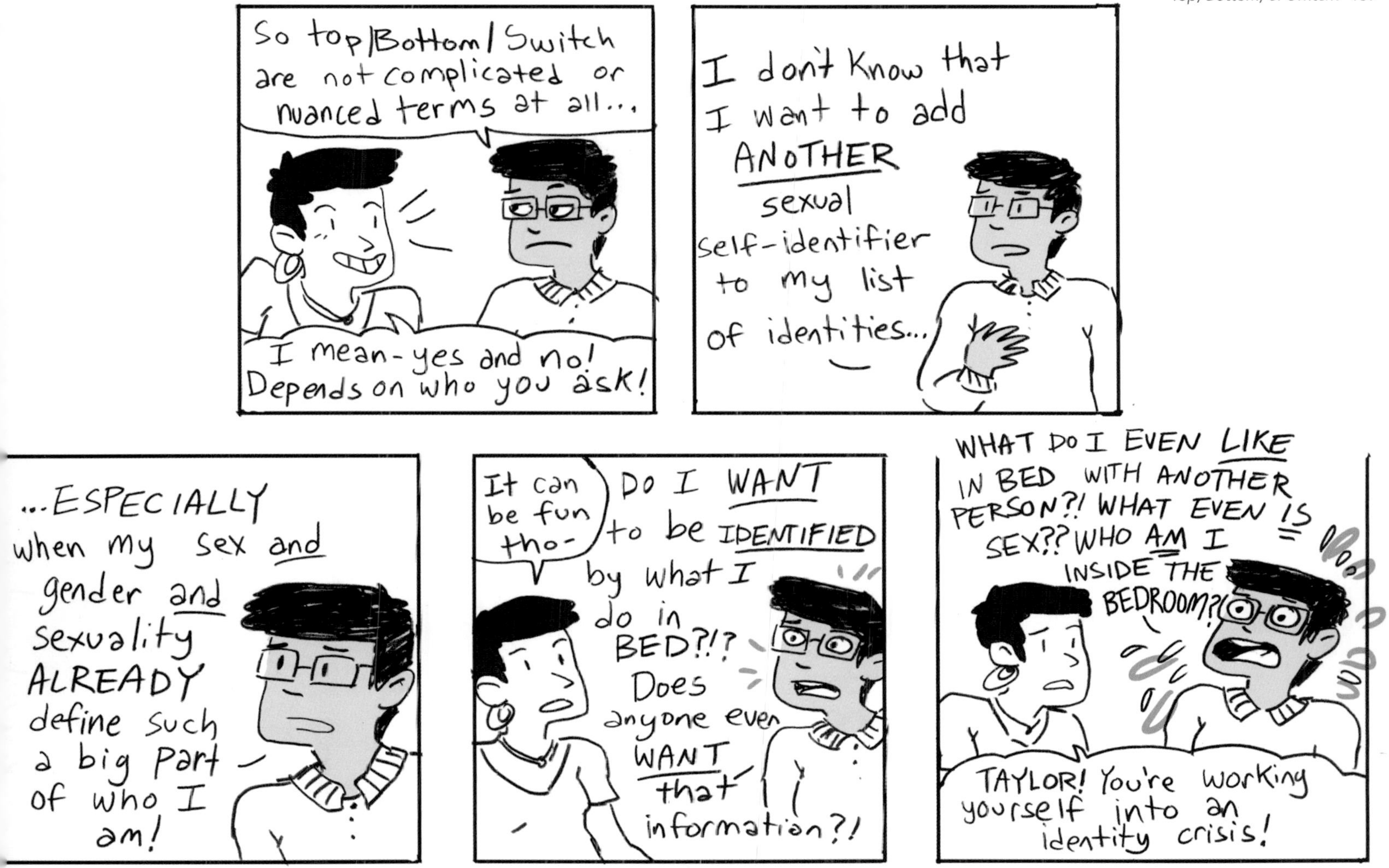
So top/Bottom/Switch are not complicated or nuanced terms at all...
I mean-yes and no! Depends on who you ask!
I don't Know that I want to add ANOTHER sexual self-identifier to my list of identities...
...ESPECIALLY when my sex and gender and sexuality ALREADY define such a big Part of who I am!
It can be fun tho-
DO I WANT to be IDENTIFIED by what I do in BED?!? Does anyone even WANT that information?!
WHAT DO I EVEN LIKE IN BED WITH ANOTHER PERSON?! WHAT EVEN IS SEX?? WHO AM I INSIDE THE BEDROOM?!
TAYLOR! You're working yourself into an identity crisis!

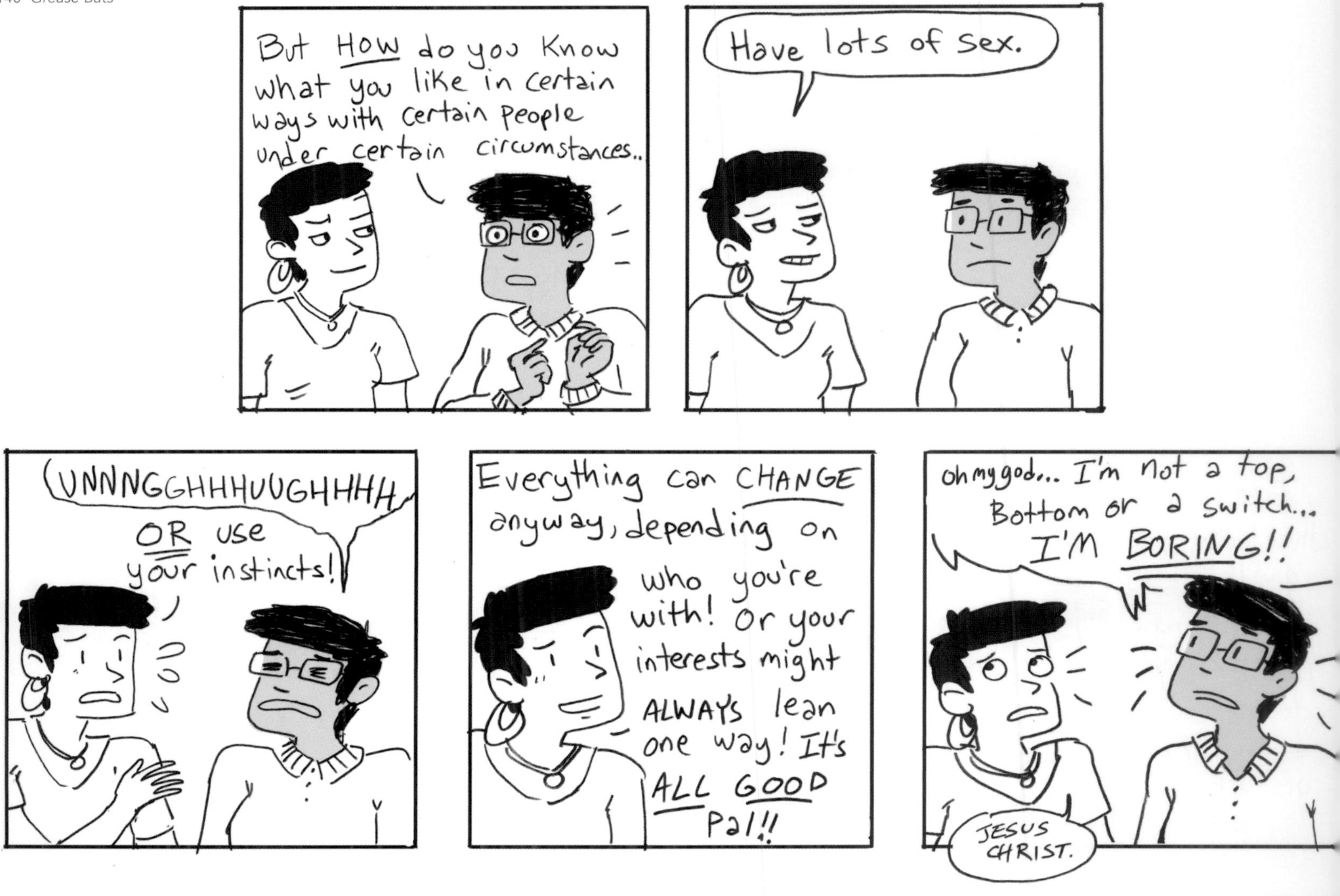

But HOW do you Know what you like in certain ways with certain people under certain circumstances..
Have lots of sex.
(UNNNGGHHHUUGHHHH
OR use your instincts!
Everything can CHANGE anyway, depending on who you're with! Or your interests might ALWAYS lean one way! It's ALL GOOD Pal!!
ohmygod... I'm not a top, Bottom or a switch... I'M BORING!!
JESUS CHRIST.

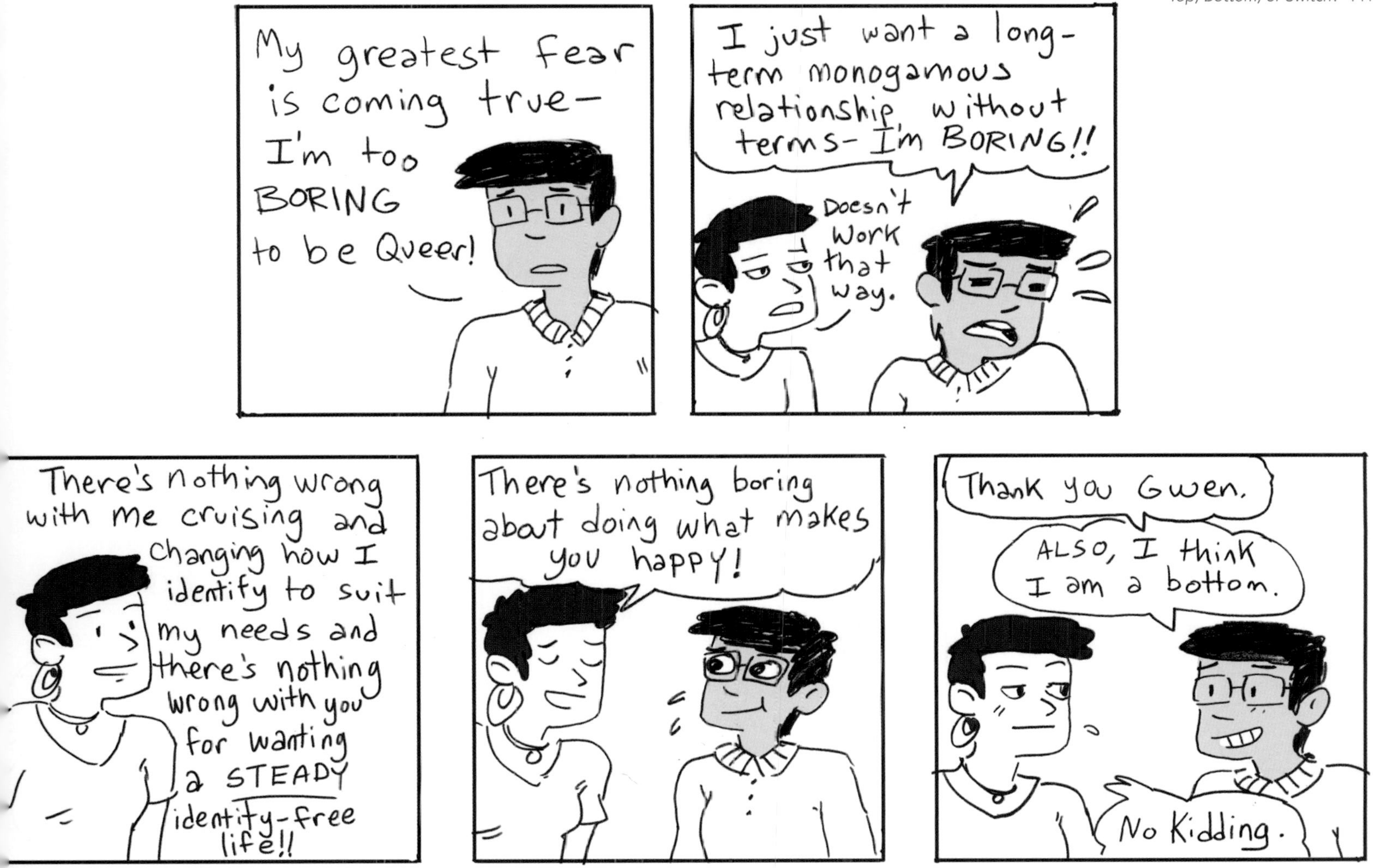
My greatest fear is coming true- I'm too BORING to be Queer!
I just want a long-term monogamous relationship without terms- I'm BORING!!
Doesn't work that way.
There's nothing wrong with me cruising and changing how I identify to suit my needs and there's nothing wrong with you for wanting a STEADY identity-free life!!
There's nothing boring about doing what makes you happy!
Thank you Gwen.
ALSO, I think I am a bottom.
No Kidding.

Coping

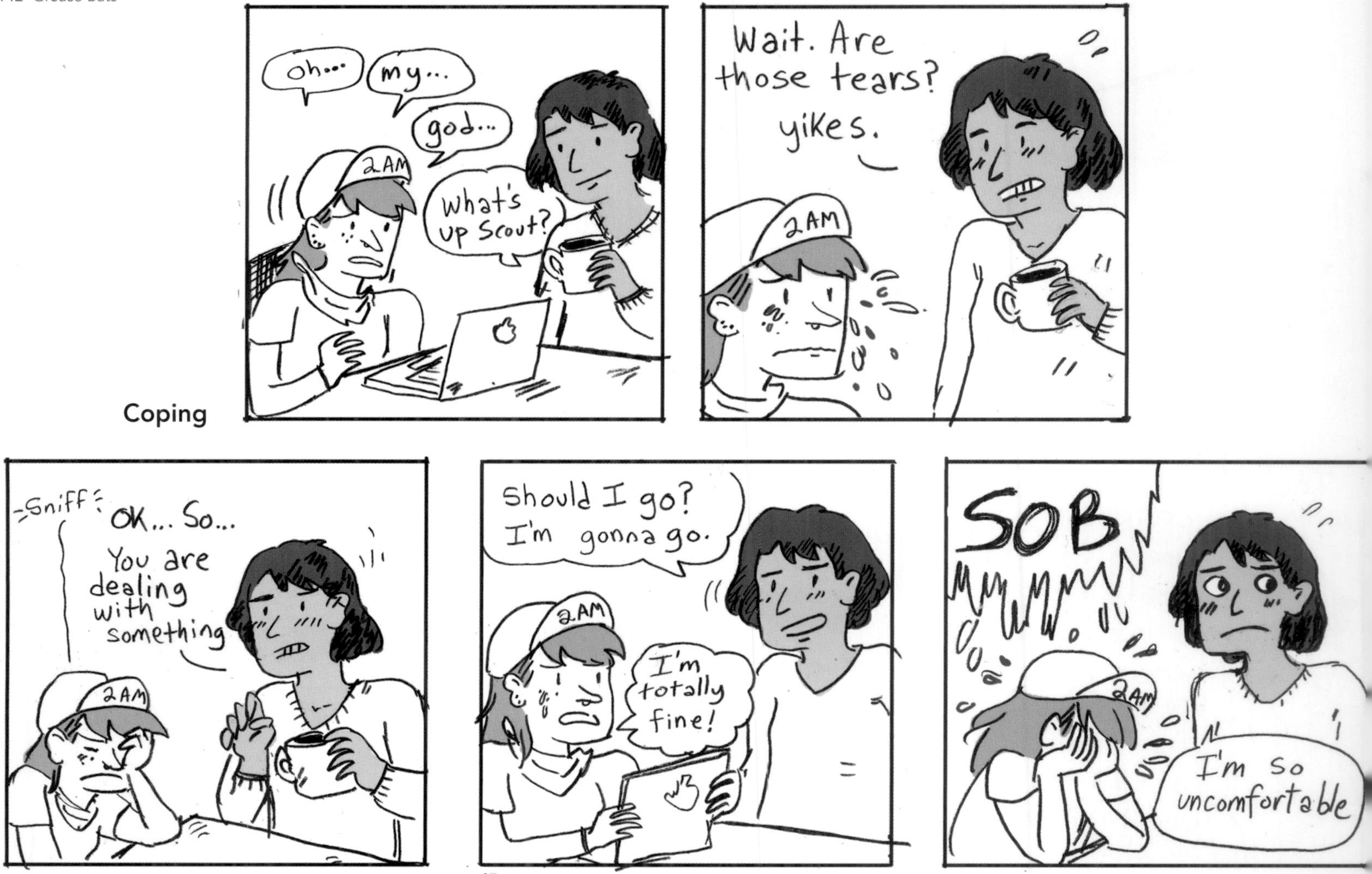

oh...
my...
god...
What's up Scout?
Wait. Are those tears?
yikes.
Sniff
OK... So...
You are dealing with something
Should I go? I'm gonna go.
I'm totally fine!
SOB
I'm so uncomfortable

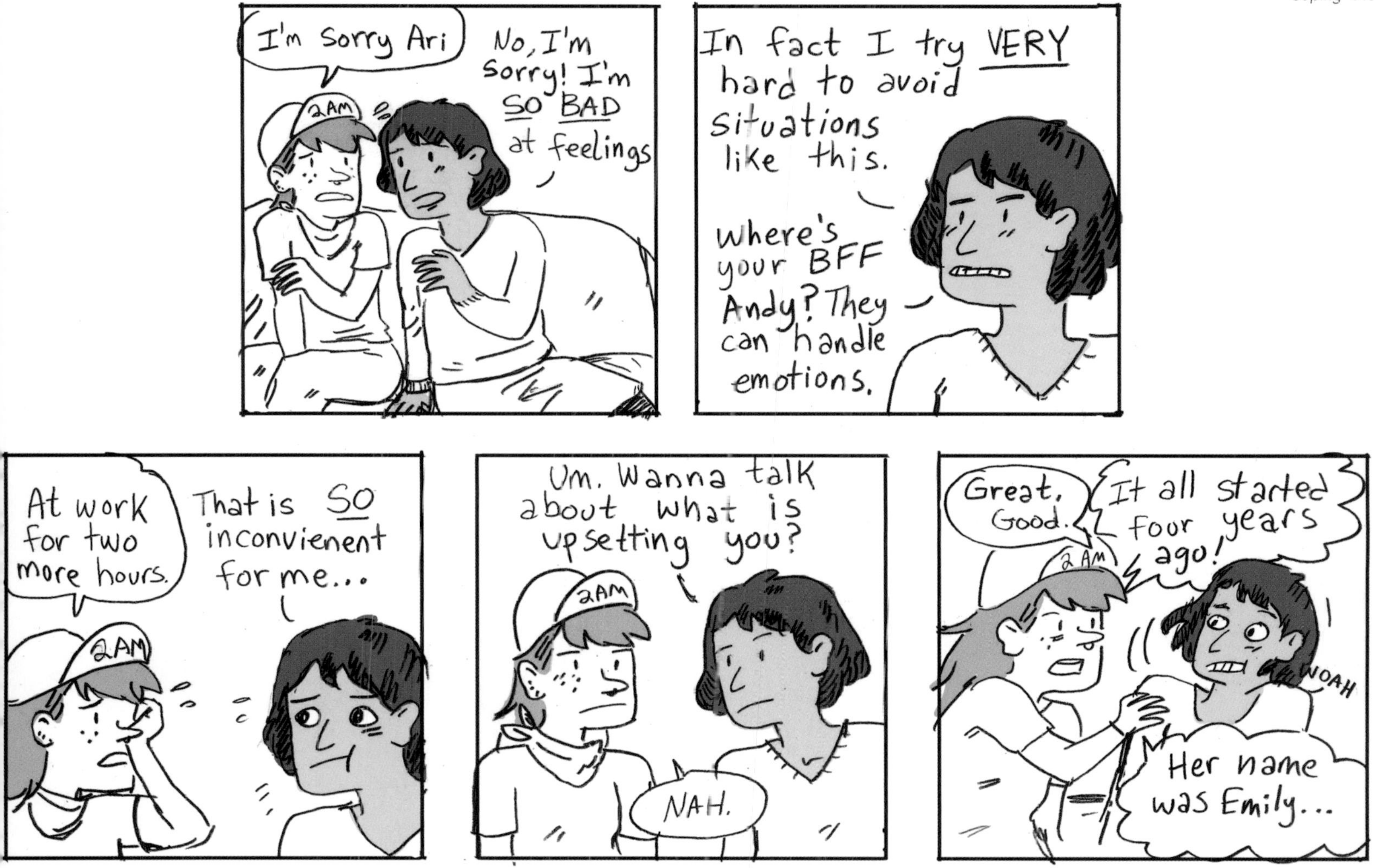
I'm sorry Ari
No, I'm sorry! I'm SO BAD at feelings
2AM
In fact I try VERY hard to avoid situations like this.
Where's your BFF Andy? They can handle emotions.
At work for two more hours.
That is SO inconvient for me...
2AM
Um. Wanna talk about what is upsetting you?
2AM
NAH.
Great. Good.
It all started four years ago!
2AM
WOAH
Her name was Emily...

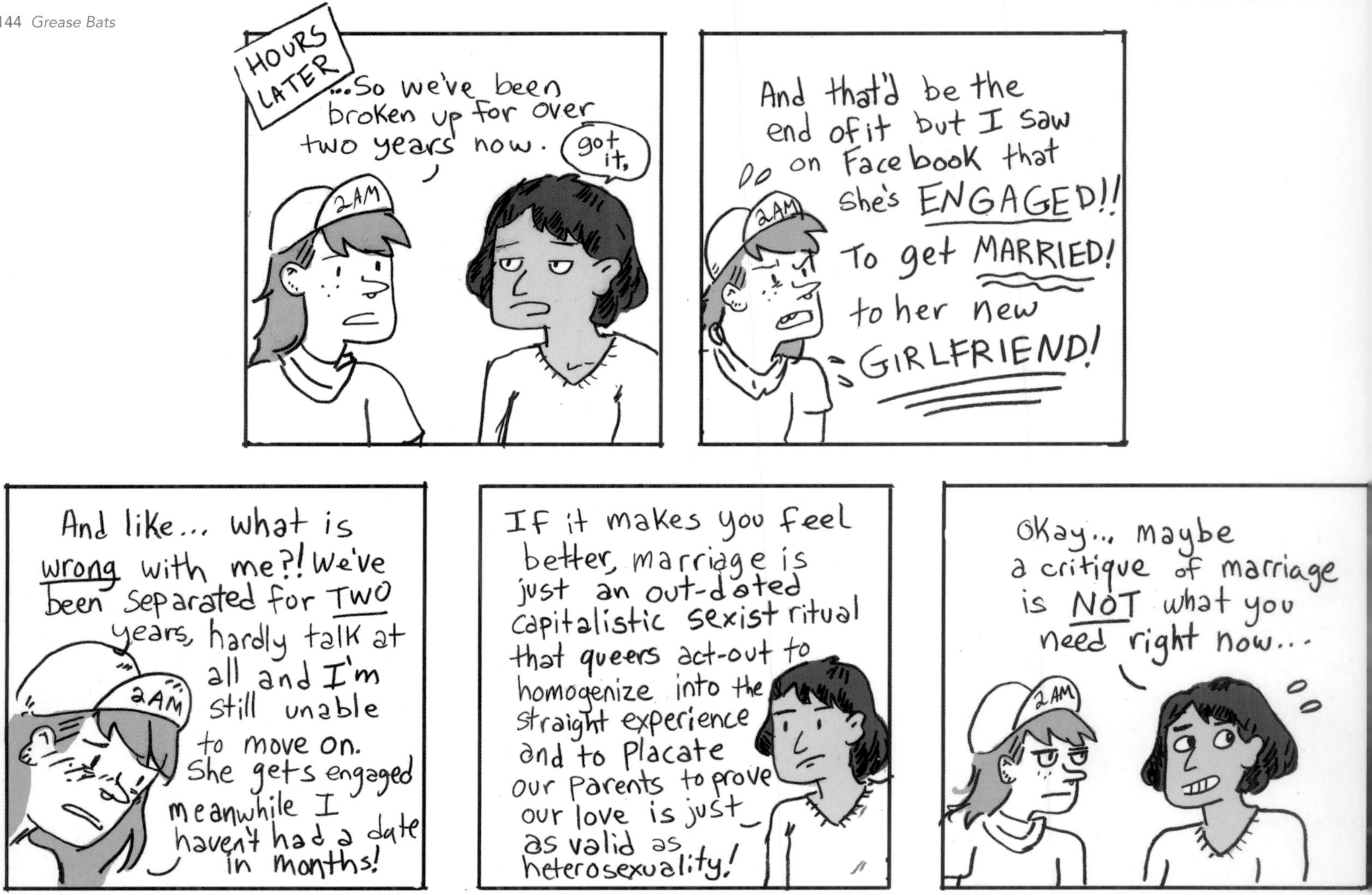
HOURS LATER
...So we've been broken up for over two years now.
got it,
And that'd be the end of it but I saw on Facebook that she's ENGAGED!! To get MARRIED! to her new GIRLFRIEND!
2AM
And like... what is wrong with me?! We've been separated for TWO years, hardly talk at all and I'm still unable to move on. She gets engaged meanwhile I haven't had a date in months!
If it makes you feel better, marriage is just an out-dated capitalistic sexist ritual that queers act-out to homogenize into the straight experience and to Placate our Parents to prove our love is just as valid as heterosexuality!
Okay... maybe a critique of marriage is NOT what you need right now...

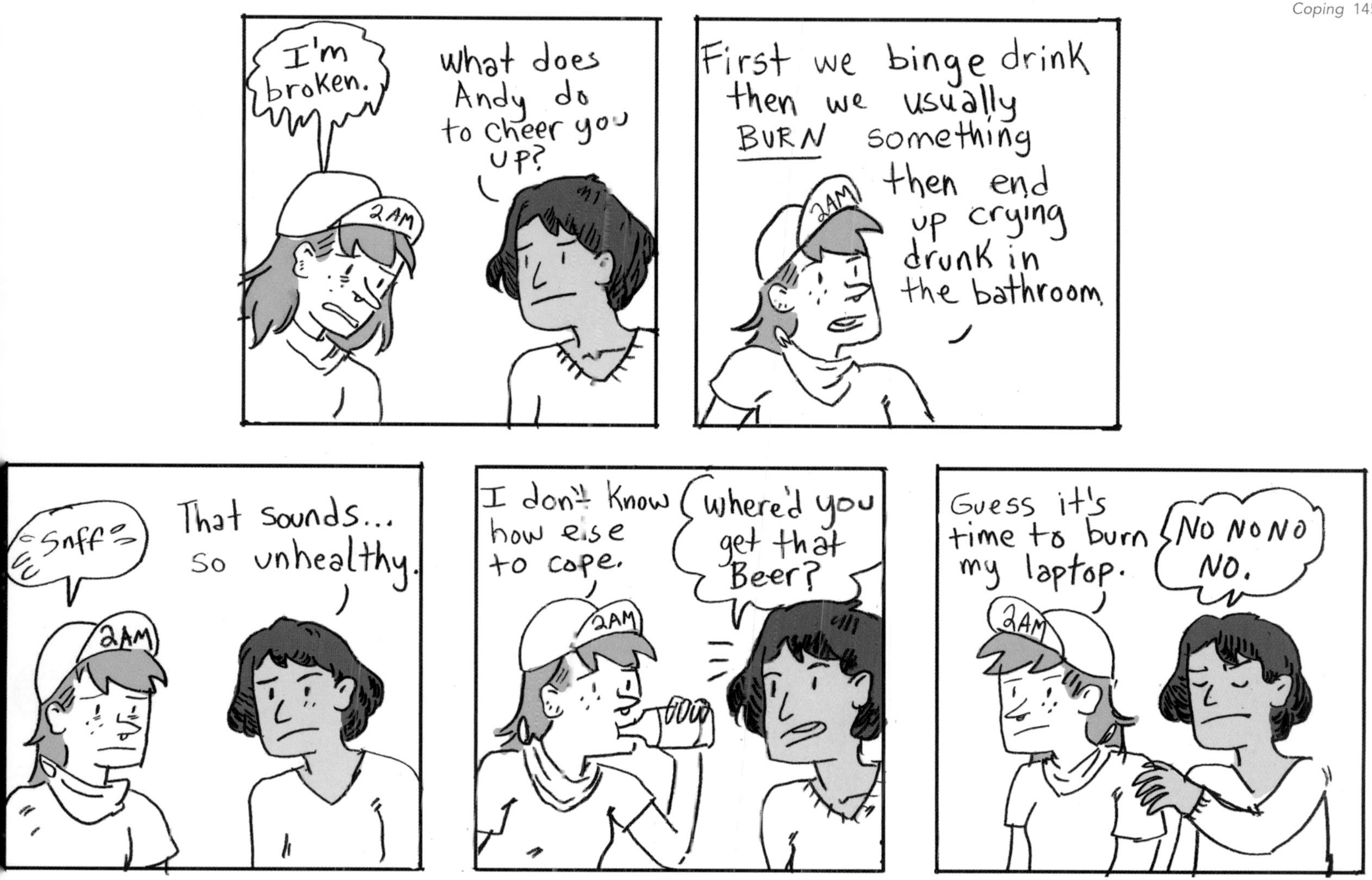
I'm broken.
What does Andy do to cheer you up?
First we binge drink then we usually BURN something
then end up crying drunk in the bathroom.
Snff
That sounds... so unhealthy.
I don't know how else to cope.
Where'd you get that Beer?
Guess it's time to burn my laptop.
NO NO NO NO.

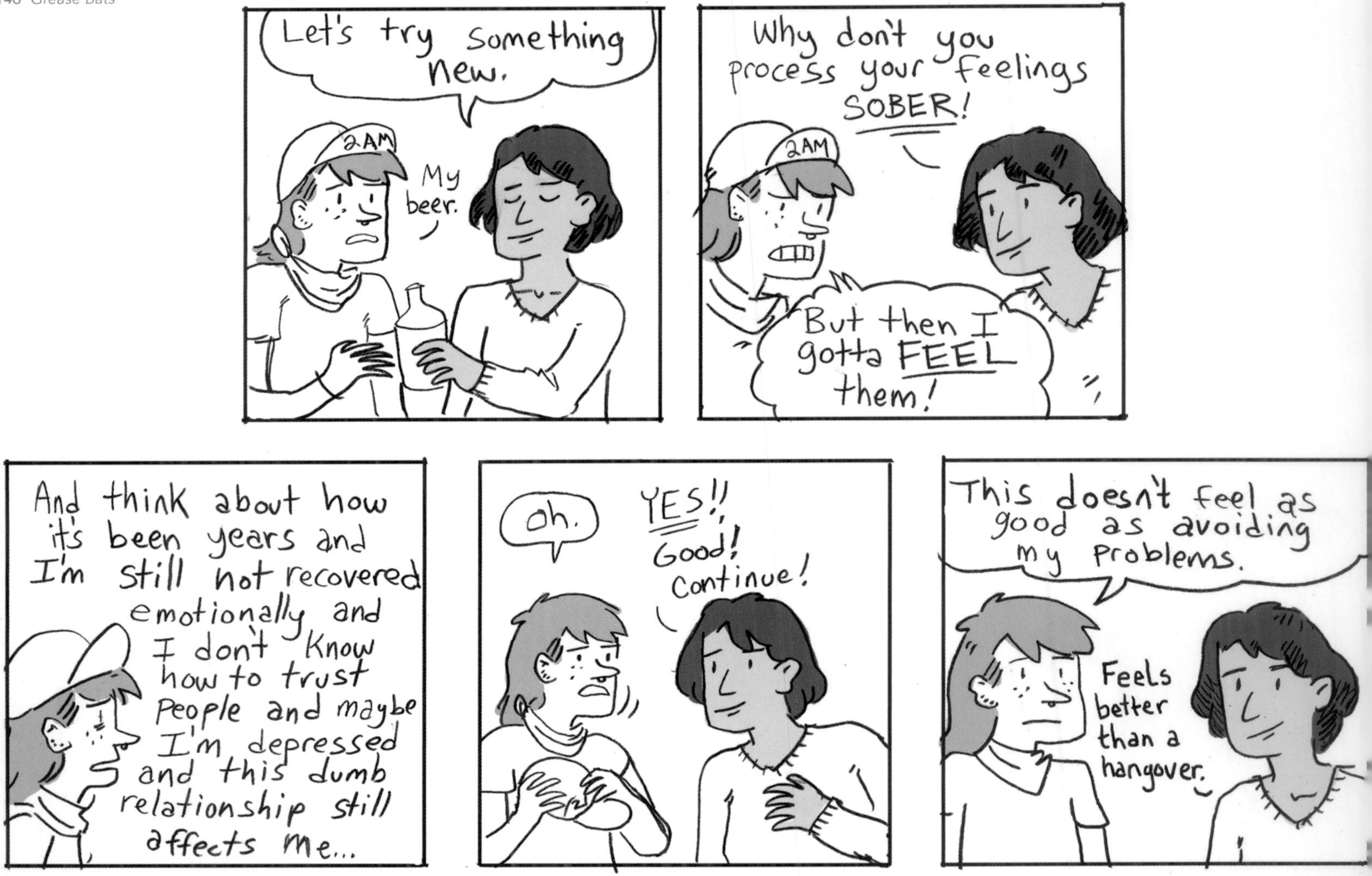
Let's try something new.
My beer.
Why don't you process your feelings SOBER!
But then I gotta FEEL them!
And think about how it's been years and I'm still not recovered emotionally and I don't know how to trust people and maybe I'm depressed and this dumb relationship still affects me...
Oh.
YES!! Good! Continue!
This doesn't feel as good as avoiding my problems.
Feels better than a hangover.

Gold Star Slut

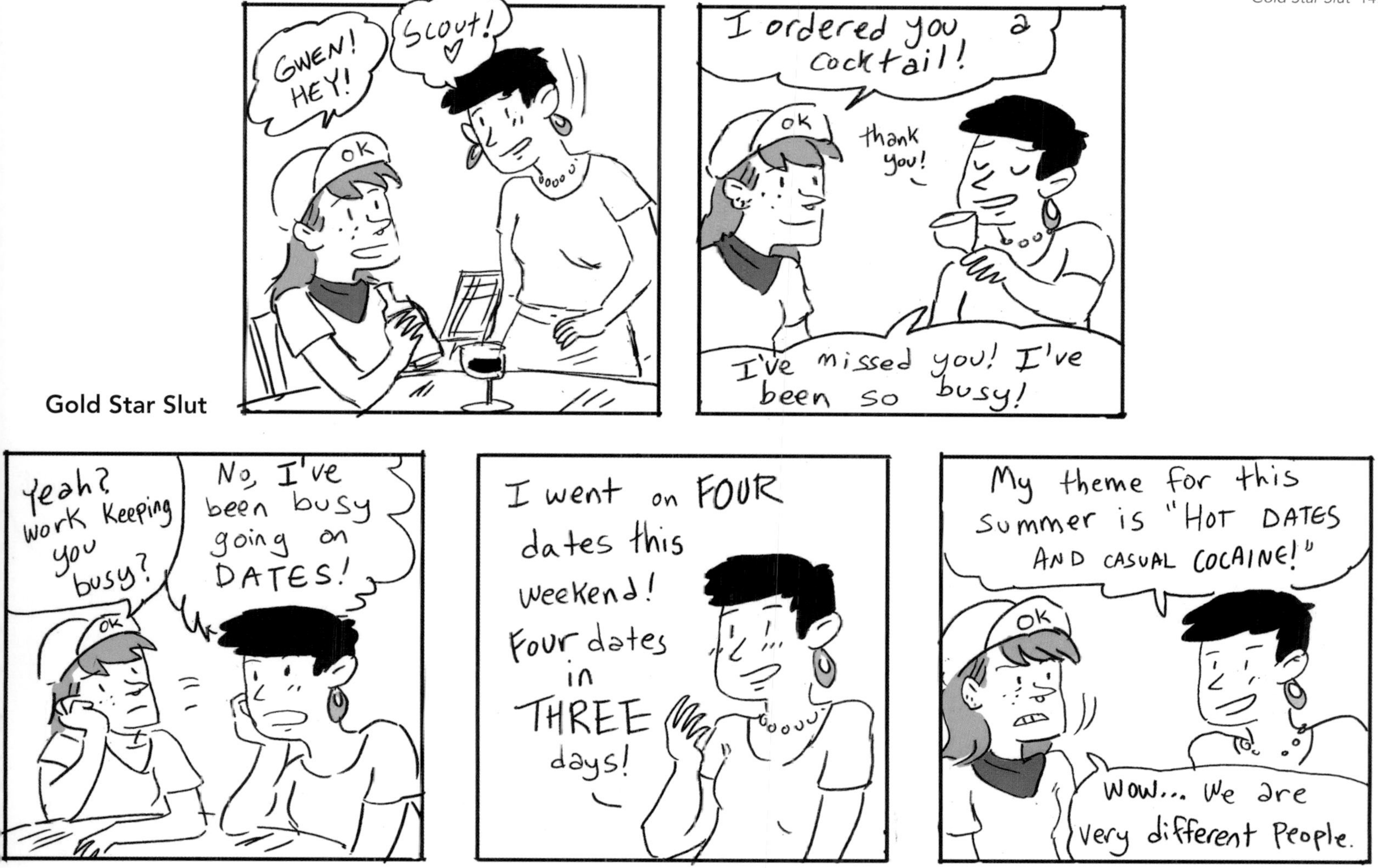
GWEN! HEY!
Scout! ♡
I ordered you a cocktail!
thank you!
I've missed you! I've been so busy!
Yeah? work keeping you busy?
No, I've been busy going on DATES!
I went on FOUR dates this weekend! Four dates in THREE days!
My theme for this summer is "HOT DATES AND CASUAL COCAINE!"
WOW... We are very different People.

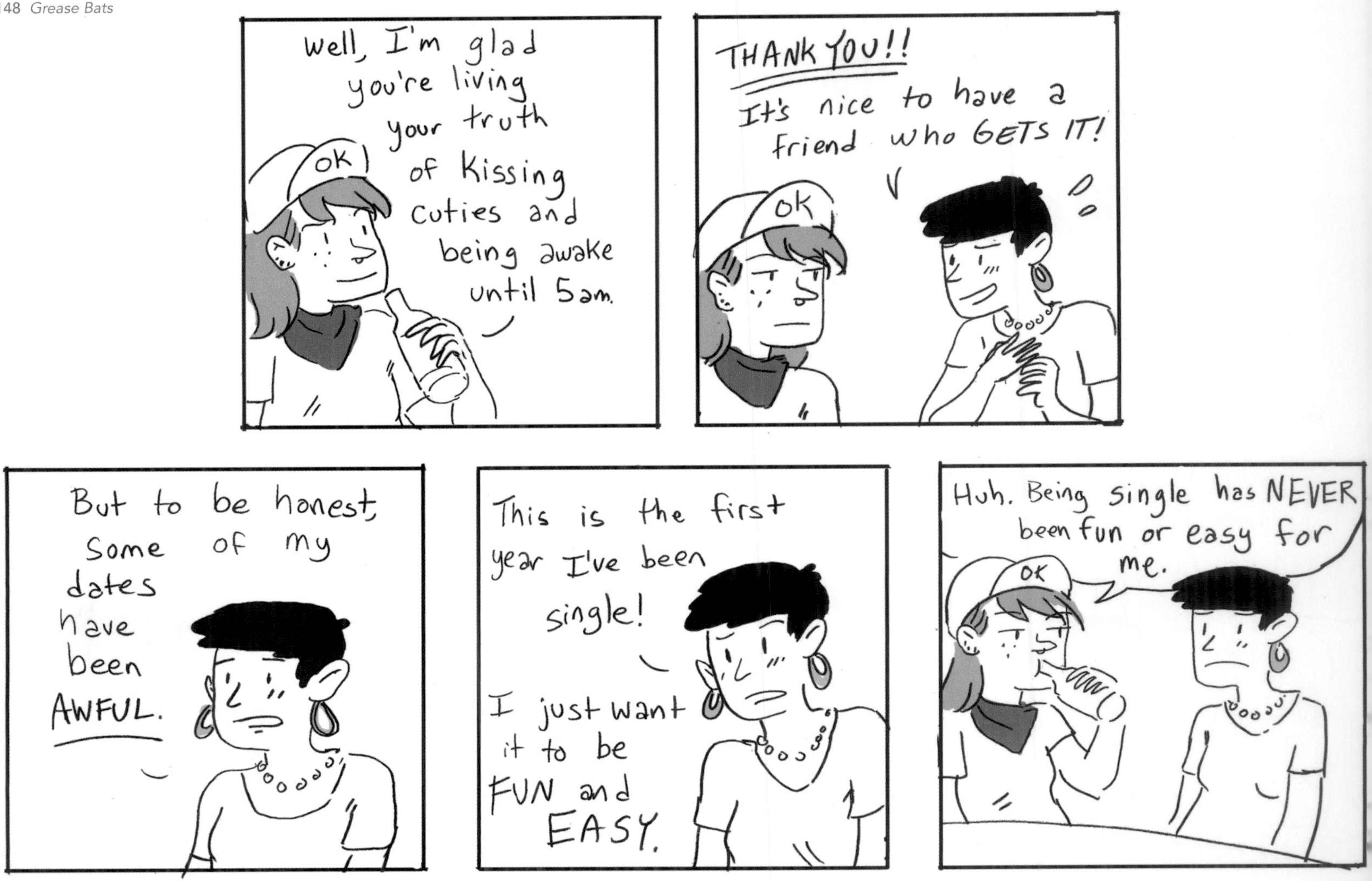
Well, I'm glad you're living your truth of kissing cuties and being awake until 5am.
OK
THANK YOU!!
It's nice to have a friend who GETS IT!
OK
But to be honest, some of my dates have been AWFUL.
This is the first year I've been single!
I just want it to be FUN and EASY.
Huh. Being single has NEVER been fun or easy for me.
OK

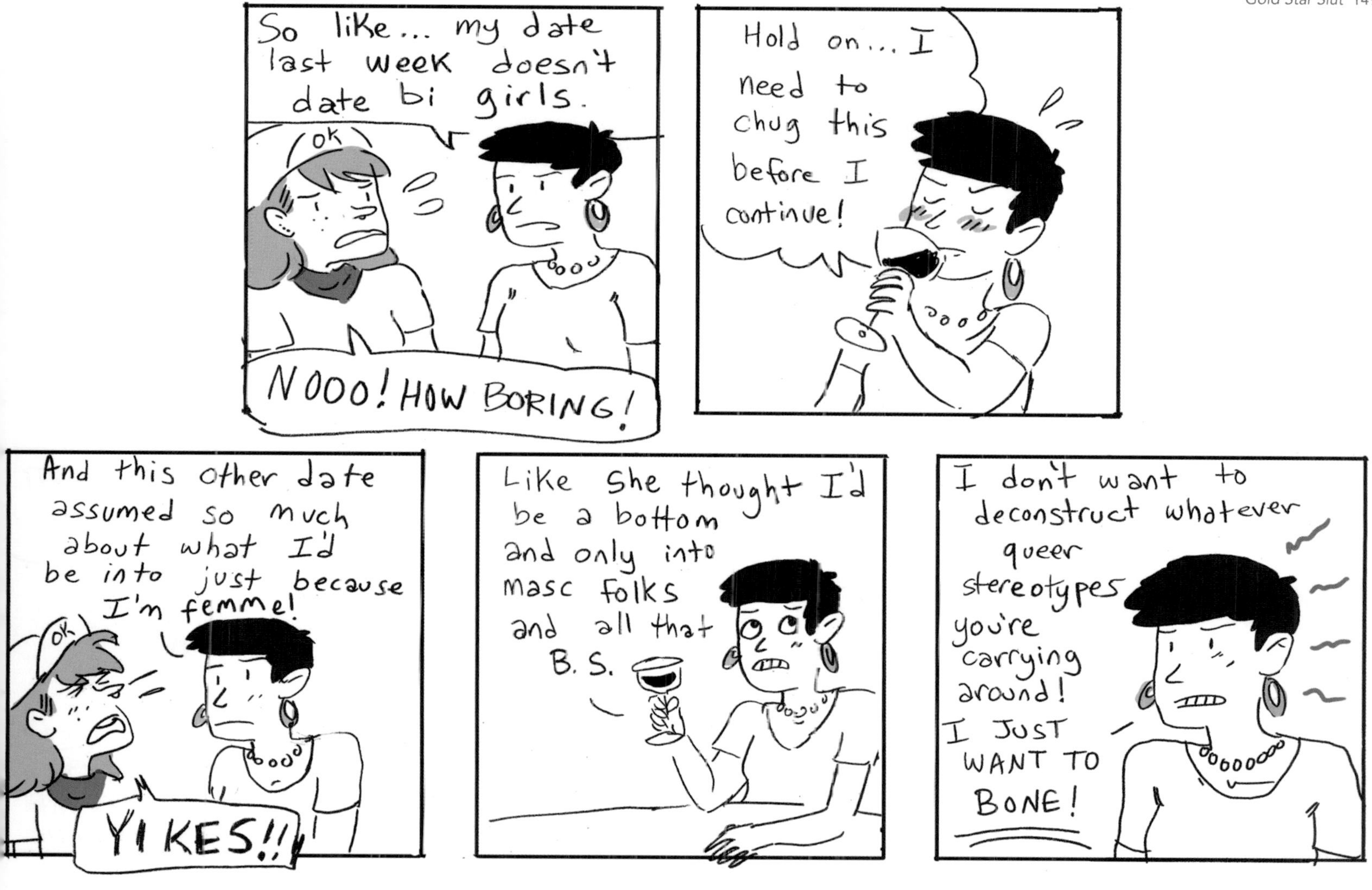
So like... my date last week doesn't date bi girls.
OK
NOOO! HOW BORING!
Hold on... I need to chug this before I continue!
And this other date assumed so much about what I'd be into just because I'm femme!
OK
YIKES!!
Like she thought I'd be a bottom and only into masc folks and all that B.S.
I don't want to deconstruct whatever queer stereotypes you're carrying around!
I JUST WANT TO BONE!

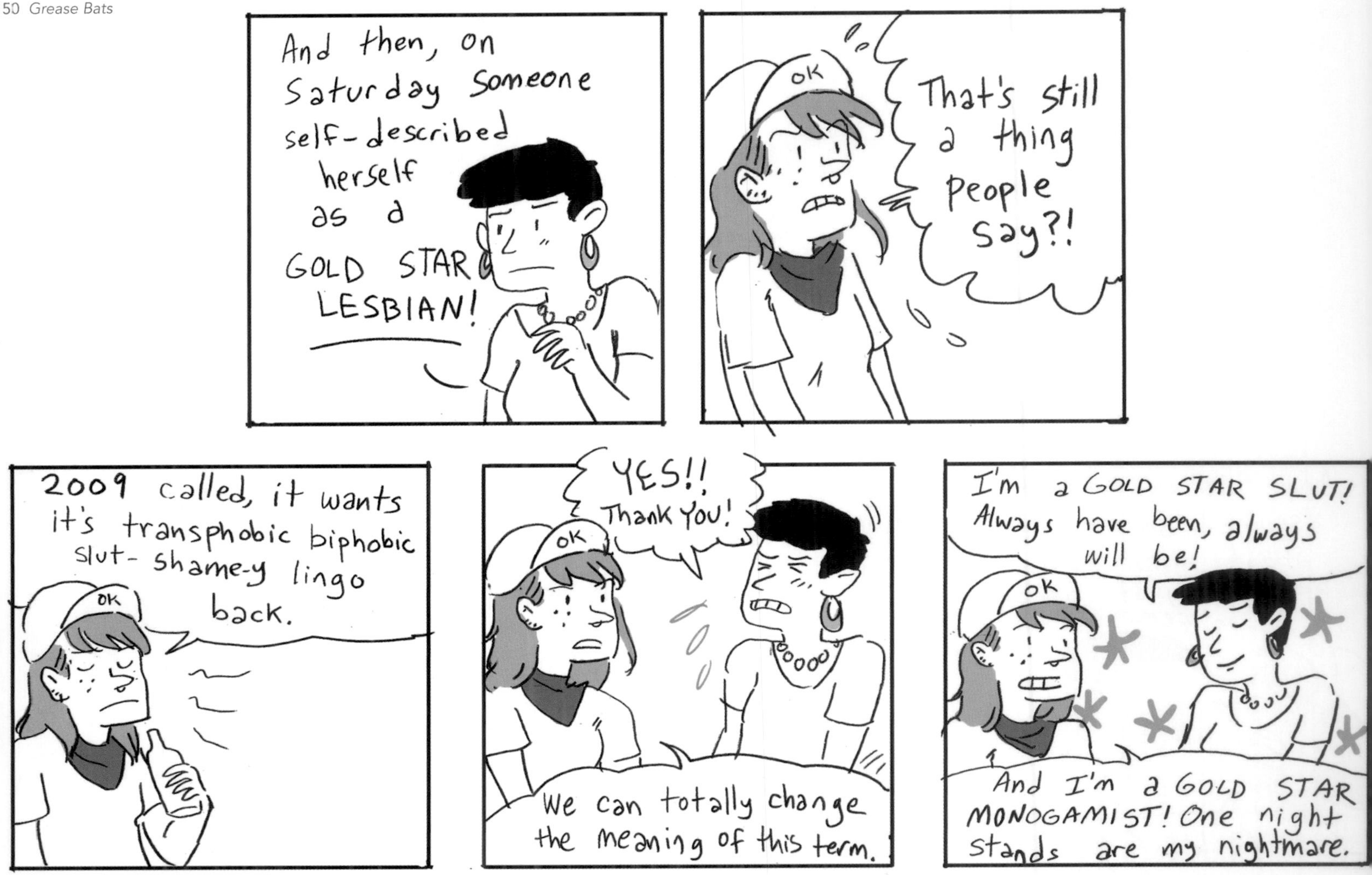
And then, on Saturday someone self-described herself as a GOLD STAR LESBIAN!
That's still a thing people say?!
2009 called, it wants it's transphobic biphobic slut-shame-y lingo back.
YES!! Thank You!
We can totally change the meaning of this term.
I'm a GOLD STAR SLUT! Always have been, always will be!
And I'm a GOLD STAR MONOGAMIST! One night stands are my nightmare.

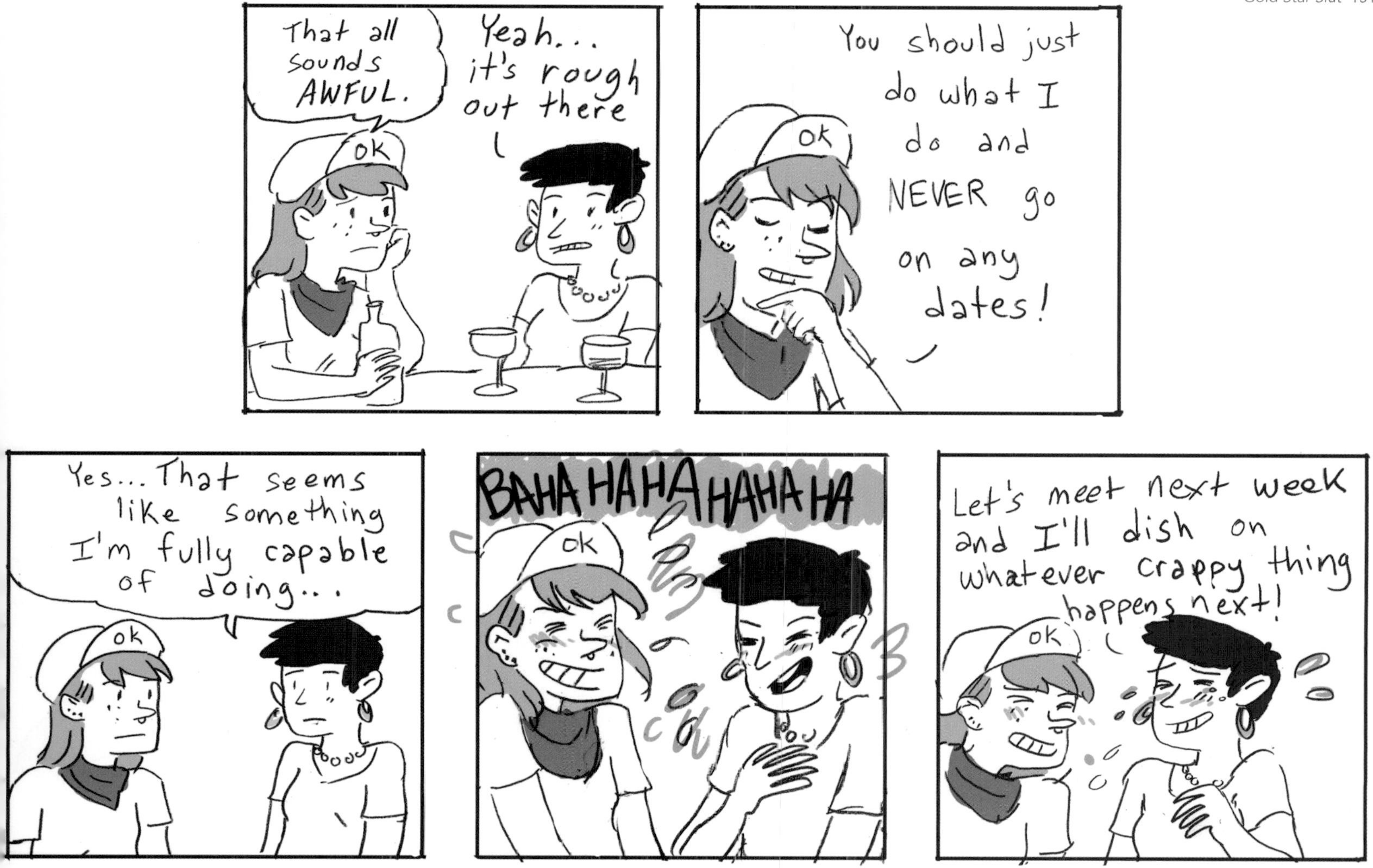
That all sounds AWFUL.
Yeah... it's rough out there
You should just do what I do and NEVER go on any dates!
Yes... That seems like something I'm fully capable of doing...
BAHA HAHA HAHA HA
Let's meet next week and I'll dish on whatever crappy thing happens next!

The Ex

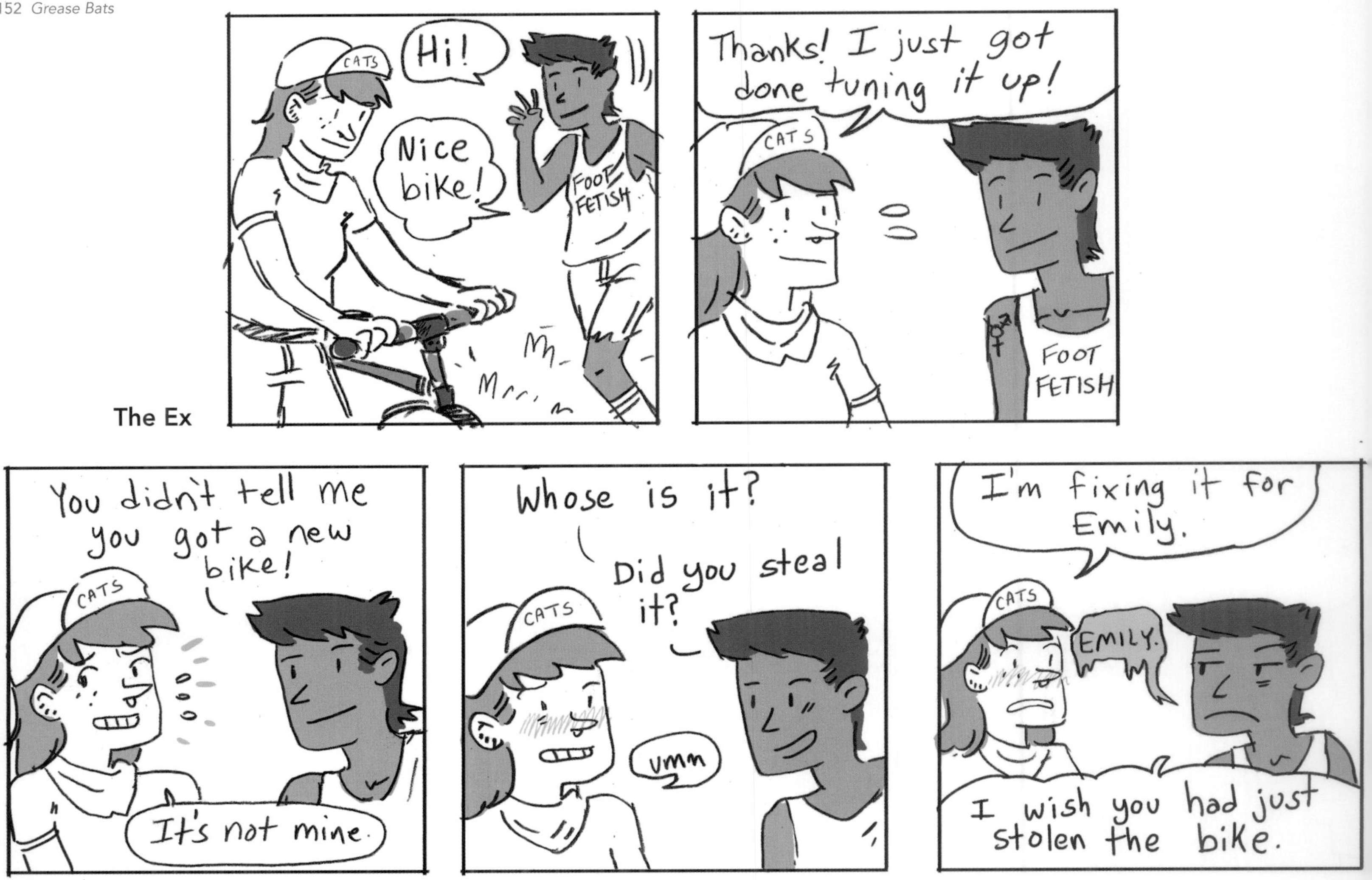
CATS
Hi!
Nice bike!
FOOT FETISH
Thanks! I just got done tuning it up!
CATS
FOOT FETISH
You didn't tell me you got a new bike!
CATS
It's not mine.
Whose is it?
Did you steal it?
CATS
umm
I'm fixing it for Emily.
CATS
EMILY.
I wish you had just stolen the bike.

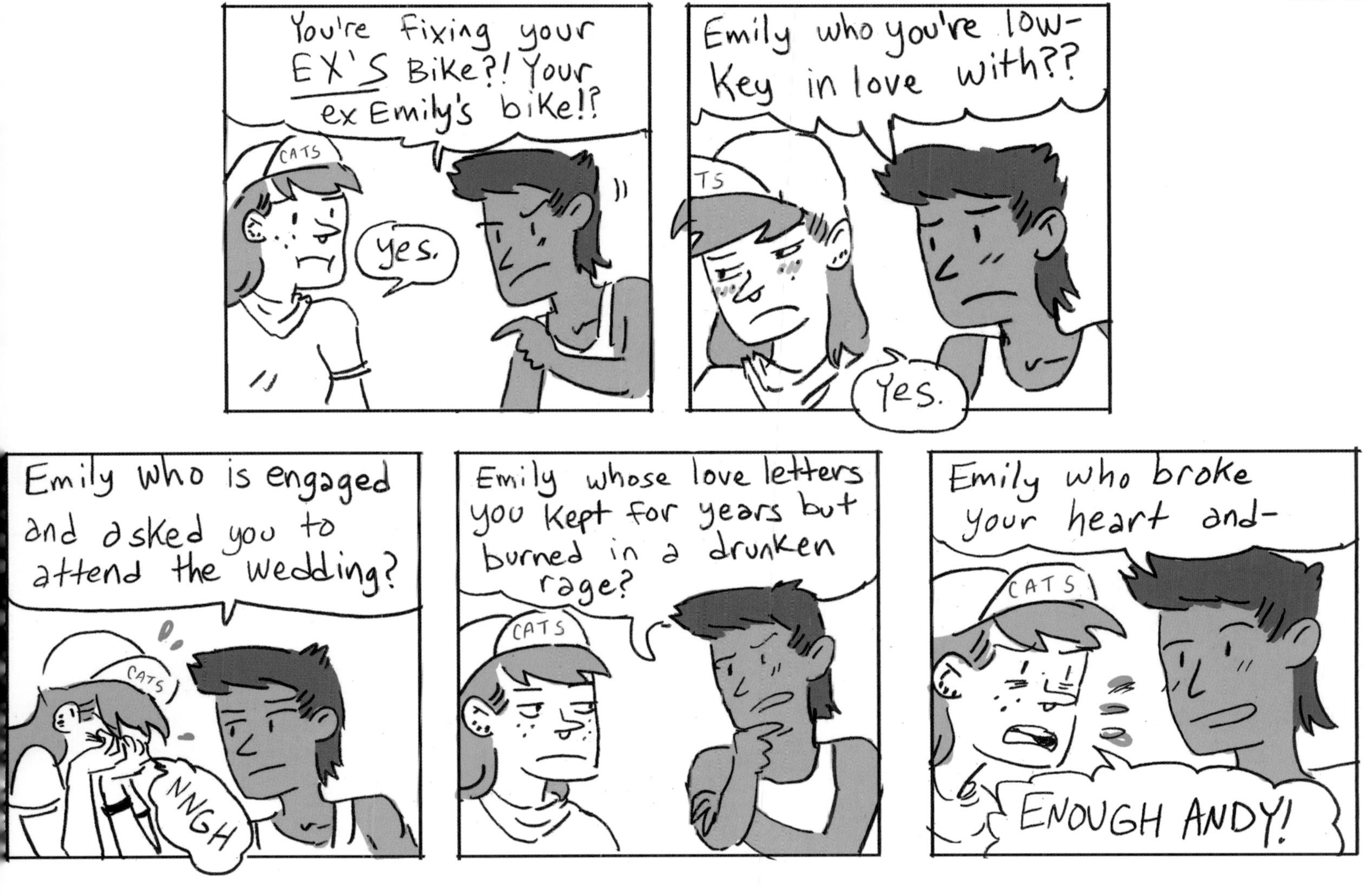
You're fixing your EX'S Bike?! Your ex Emily's bike!?
CATS
yes.
Emily who you're low-key in love with??
TS
Yes.
Emily who is engaged and asked you to attend the wedding?
CATS
NNGH
Emily whose love letters you kept for years but burned in a drunken rage?
CATS
Emily who broke your heart and-
CATS
ENOUGH ANDY!

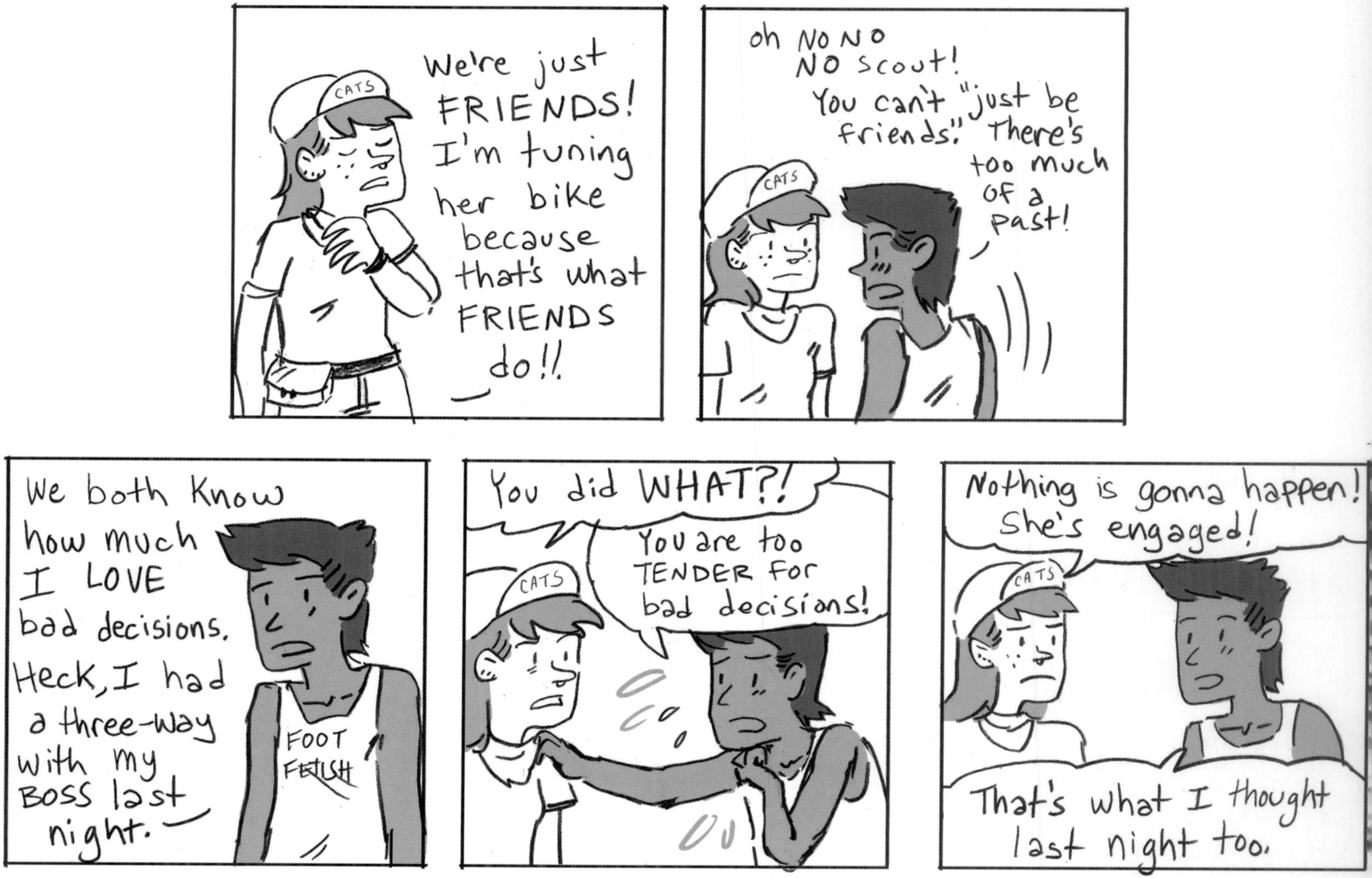
We're just FRIENDS! I'm tuning her bike because that's what FRIENDS do!!
oh NO NO NO Scout! You can't "just be friends." There's too much of a past!
We both Know how much I LOVE bad decisions. Heck, I had a three-way with my BOSS last night.
FOOT FETISH
You did WHAT?!
You are too TENDER for bad decisions!
Nothing is gonna happen! She's engaged!
That's what I thought last night too.

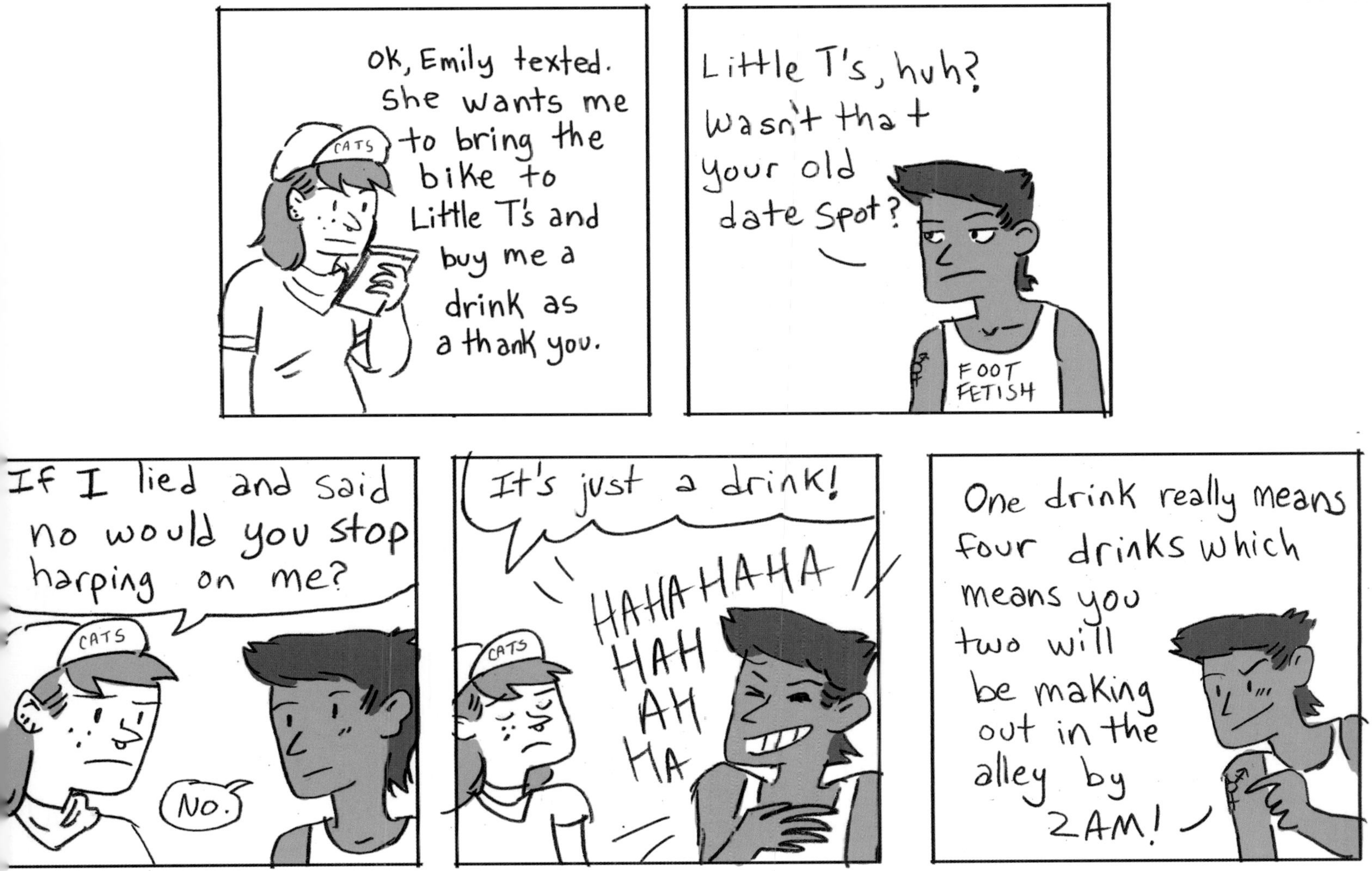
OK, Emily texted. She wants me to bring the bike to Little T's and buy me a drink as a thank you.
CATS
Little T's, huh? Wasn't that your old date spot?
FOOT FETISH
If I lied and said no would you stop harping on me?
CATS
No.
It's just a drink!
HAHAHAHA HAH AH HA
CATS
One drink really means four drinks which means you two will be making out in the alley by 2AM!

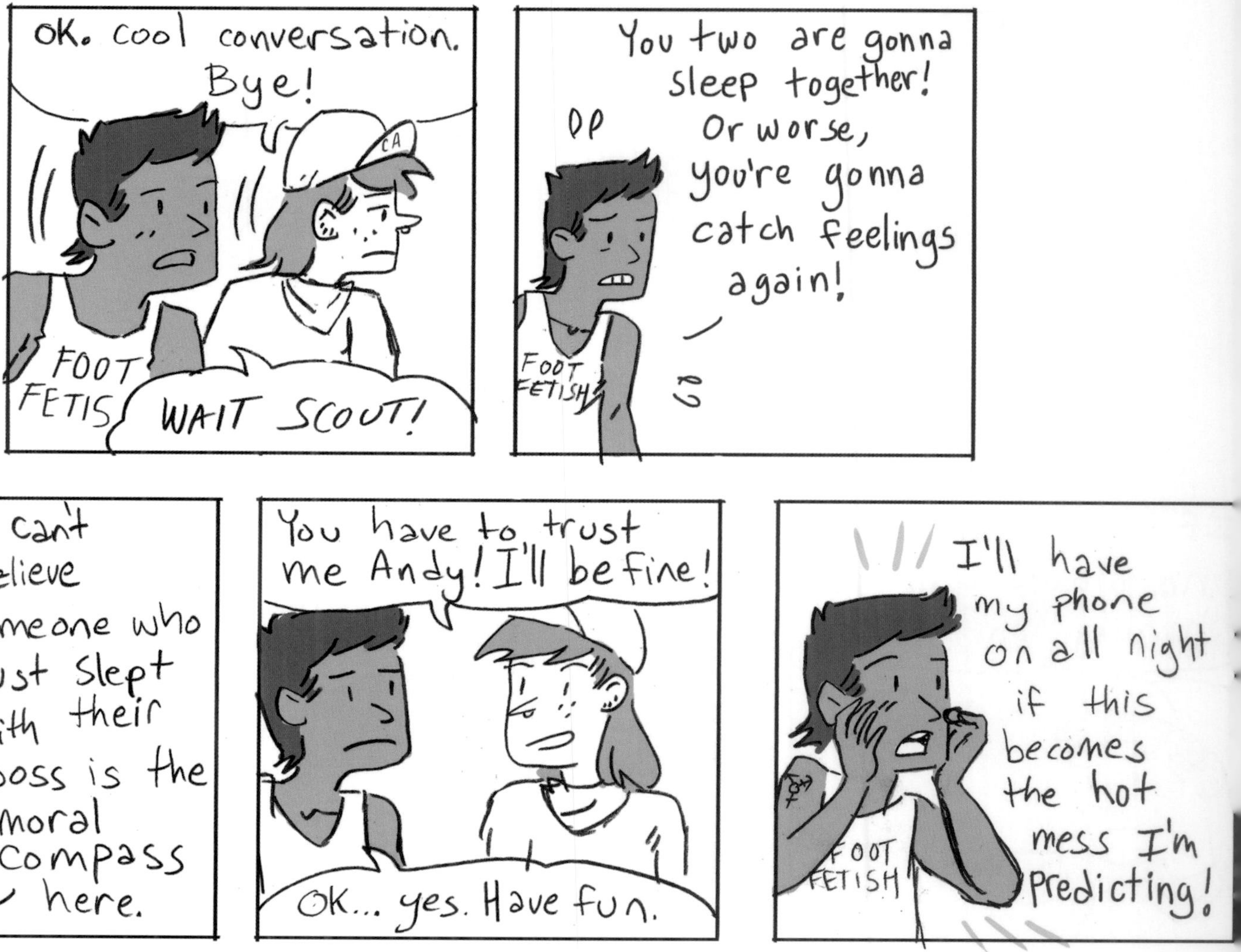
OK. cool conversation. Bye!
FOOT FETIS
WAIT SCOUT!
DP
You two are gonna sleep together! Or worse, you're gonna catch feelings again!
FOOT FETISH
I can't believe someone who just slept with their boss is the moral compass here.
FOOT FETISH
You have to trust me Andy! I'll be fine!
OK... yes. Have fun.
I'll have my phone on all night if this becomes the hot mess I'm predicting!
FOOT FETISH

Pride Hangover

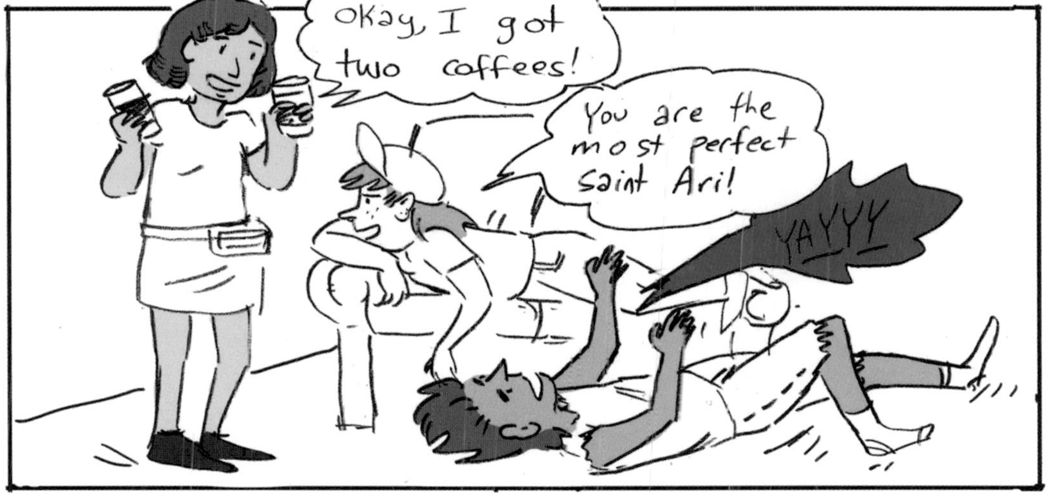
Okay, I got two coffees!
You are the most perfect saint Ari!
YAYYY

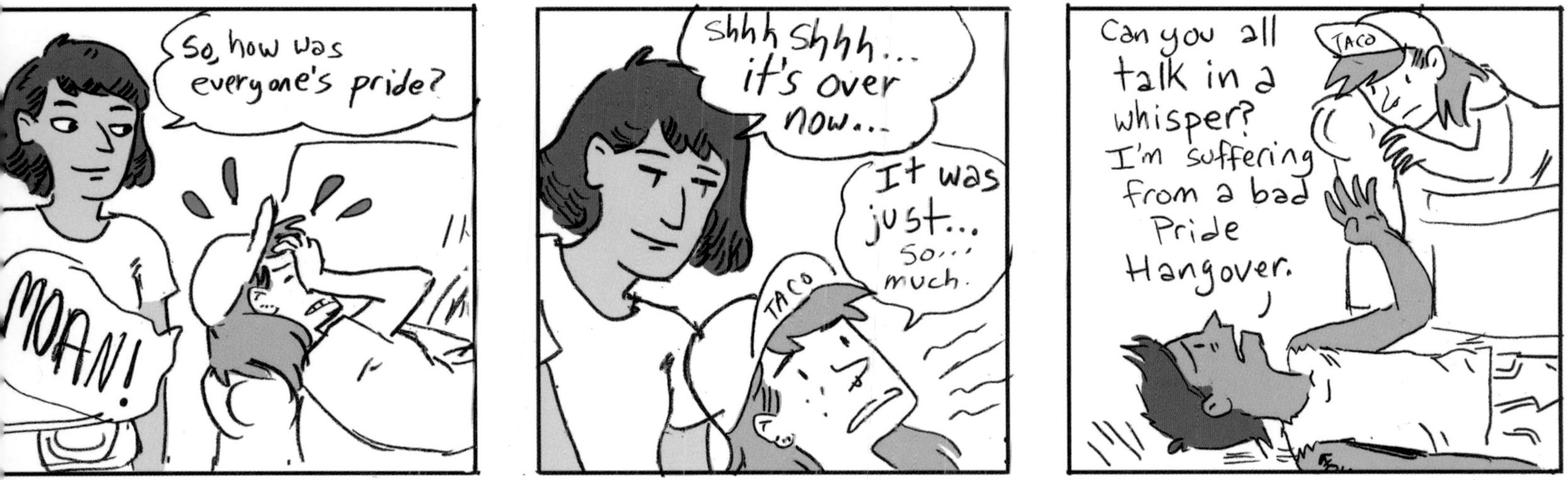
So, how was everyone's pride?
MOAN!
Shhh Shhh... it's over now...
It was just... so... much.
TACO
Can you all talk in a whisper? I'm suffering from a bad Pride Hangover.
TACO

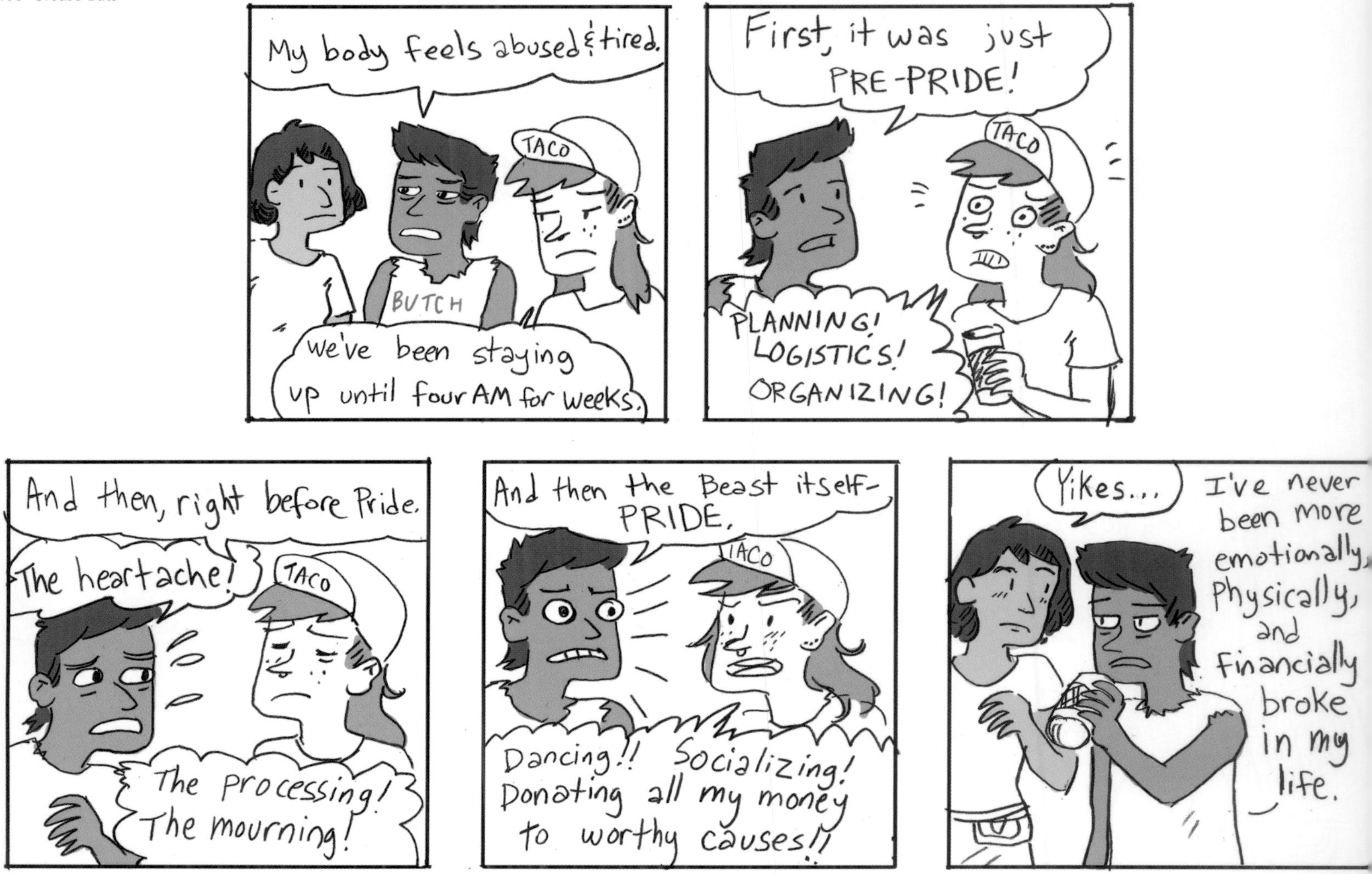
My body feels abused & tired.
BUTCH
We've been staying up until four AM for weeks.
TACO
First, it was just PRE-PRIDE!
TACO
PLANNING! LOGISTICS! ORGANIZING!
And then, right before Pride.
The heartache!
TACO
The processing! The mourning!
And then the Beast itself- PRIDE.
TACO
Dancing!! Socializing! Donating all my money to worthy causes!!
Yikes...
I've never been more emotionally, Physically, and Financially broke in my life.

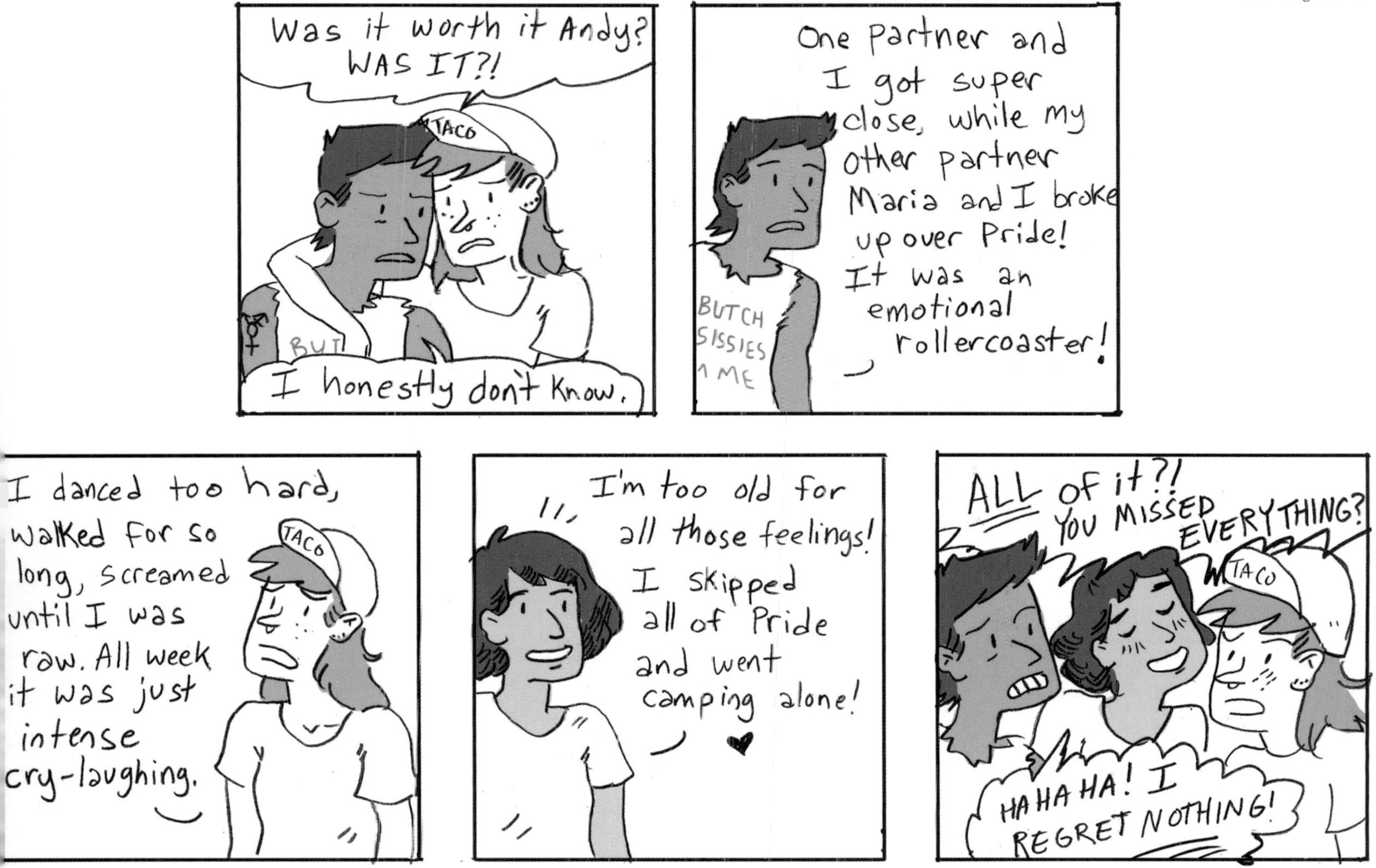
Was it worth it Andy? WAS IT?!
BUTCH SISSIES ♡ ME
I honestly don't Know.
One partner and I got super close, while my other partner Maria and I broke up over Pride! It was an emotional rollercoaster!
BUTCH SISSIES ♡ ME
I danced too hard, walked for so long, screamed until I was raw. All week it was just intense cry-laughing.
I'm too old for all those feelings! I skipped all of Pride and went camping alone! ♥
ALL of it?! YOU MISSED EVERYTHING?
HAHAHA! I REGRET NOTHING!

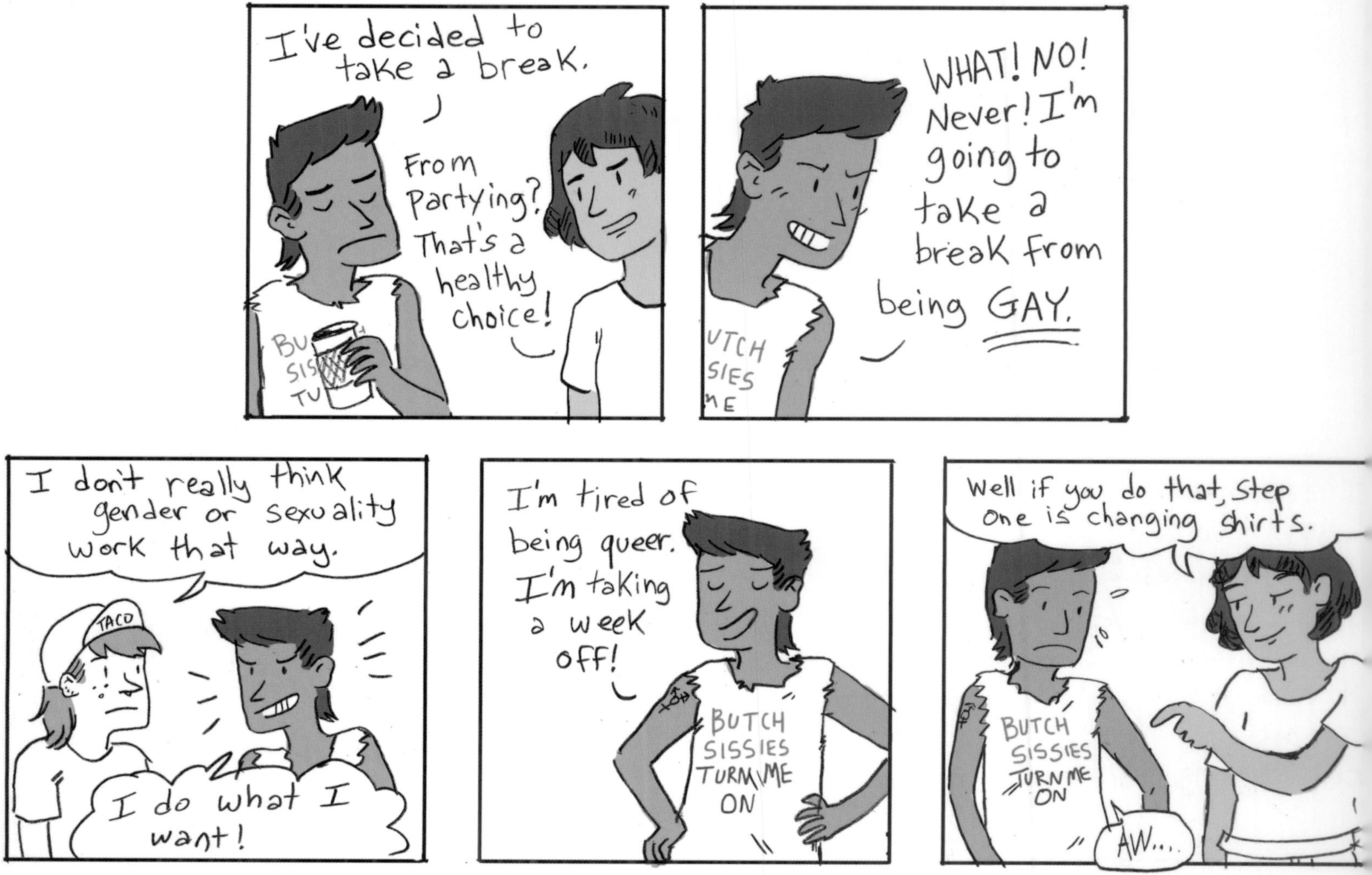
I've decided to take a break.
From partying? That's a healthy choice!
BUTCH SISSIES TU
WHAT! NO! Never! I'm going to take a break from being GAY.
UTCH SIES
I don't really think gender or sexuality work that way.
TACO
I do what I want!
I'm tired of being queer. I'm taking a week off!
BUTCH SISSIES TURN ME ON
Well if you do that, step one is changing shirts.
BUTCH SISSIES TURN ME ON
AW...

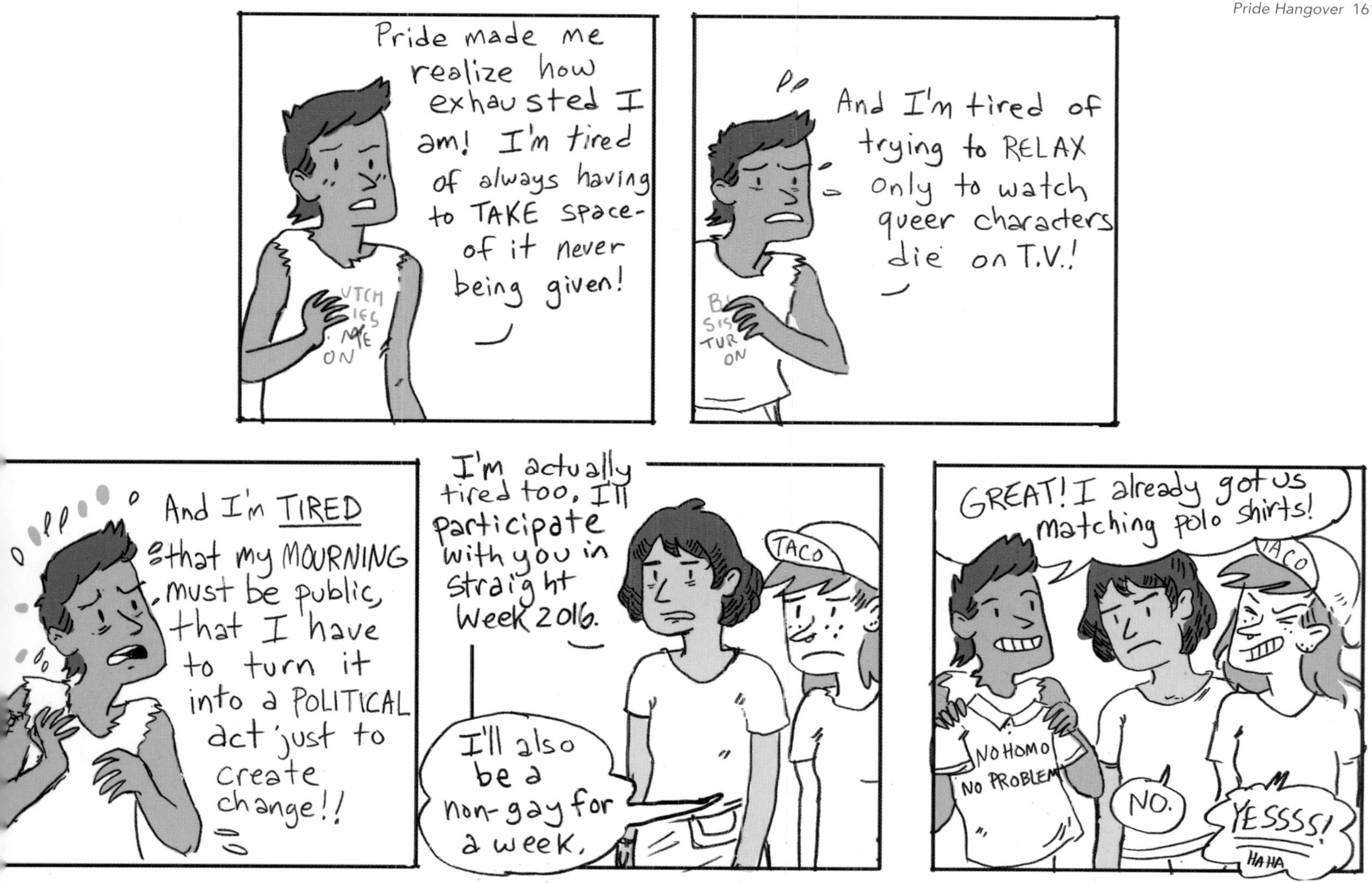
Pride made me realize how exhausted I am! I'm tired of always having to TAKE space- of it never being given!
And I'm tired of trying to RELAX only to watch queer characters die on T.V.!
And I'm TIRED that my MOURNING must be public, that I have to turn it into a POLITICAL act just to create change!!
I'm actually tired too. I'll participate with you in straight week 2016.
I'll also be a non-gay for a week.
TACO
GREAT! I already got us matching polo shirts!
TACO
NO HOMO NO PROBLEM
NO.
YESSSS!
HAHA

The Cheater

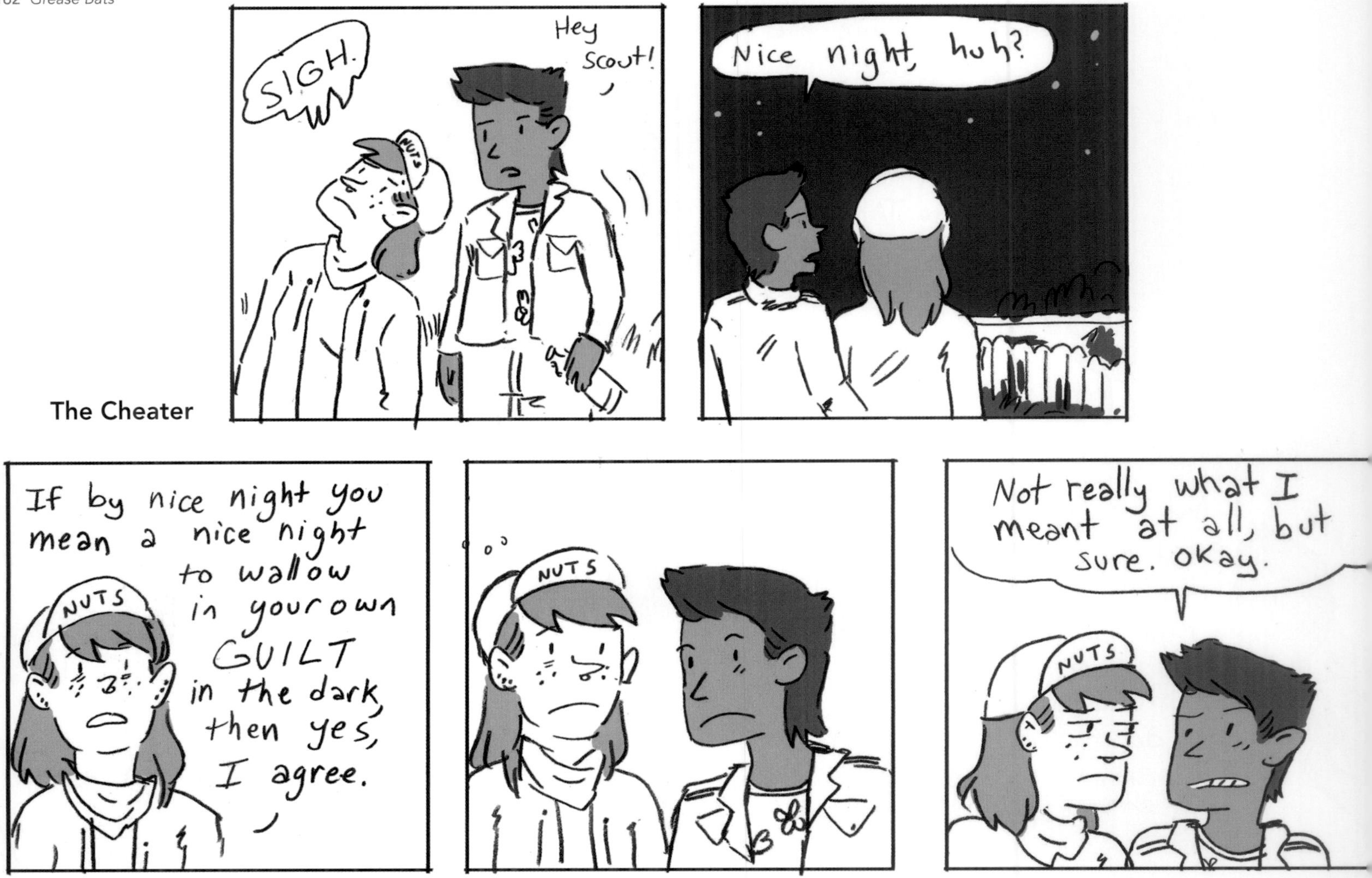
SIGH.
Hey Scout!
NUTS
Nice night, huh?
If by nice night you mean a nice night to wallow in your own GUILT in the dark, then yes, I agree.
NUTS
NUTS
Not really what I meant at all, but sure. okay.
NUTS

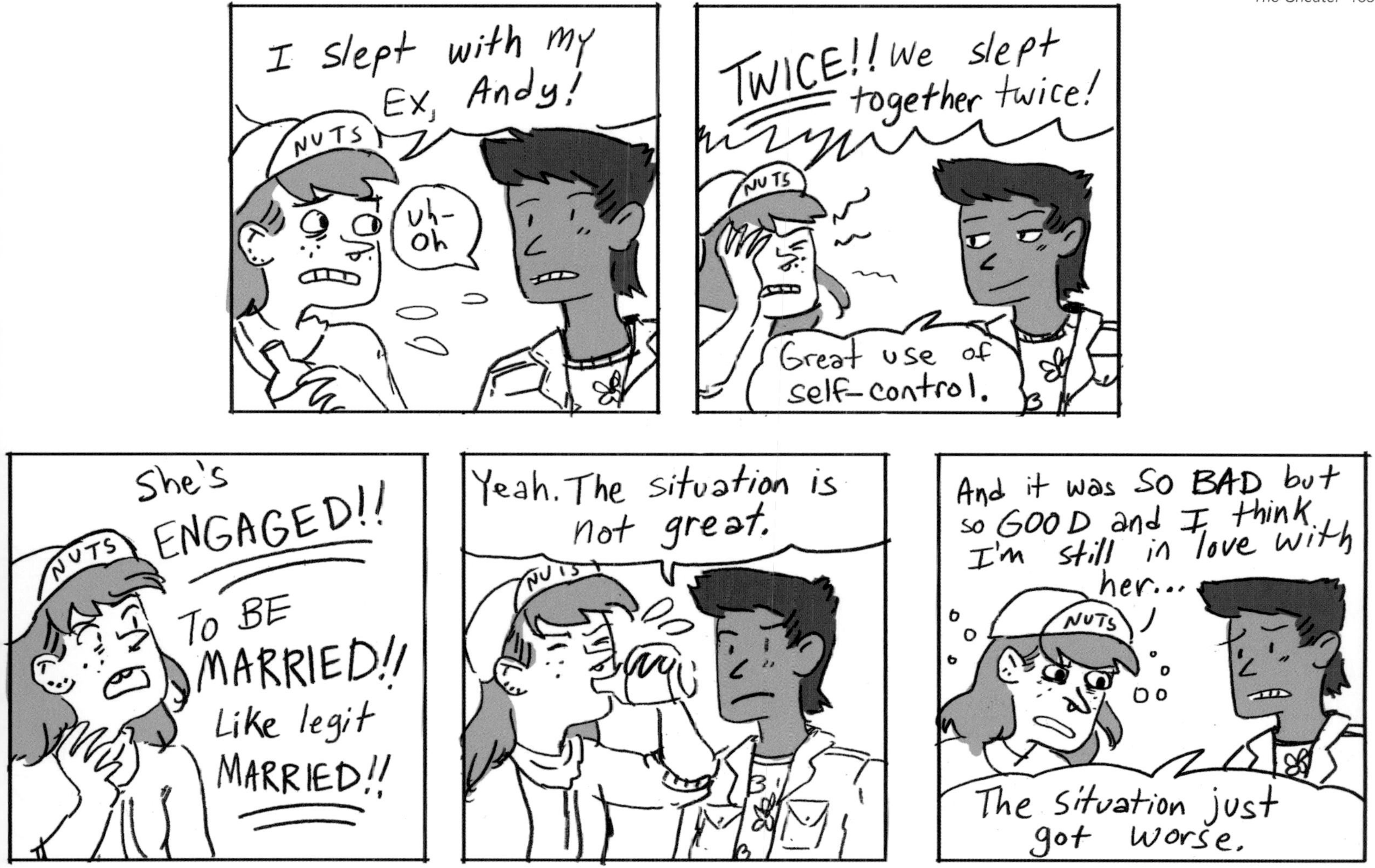
I slept with my Ex, Andy!
Uh-Oh
TWICE!! We slept together twice!
Great use of self-control.
She's ENGAGED!!
To BE MARRIED!! Like legit MARRIED!!
Yeah. The situation is not great.
And it was SO BAD but so GOOD and I think I'm still in love with her...
The situation just got worse.

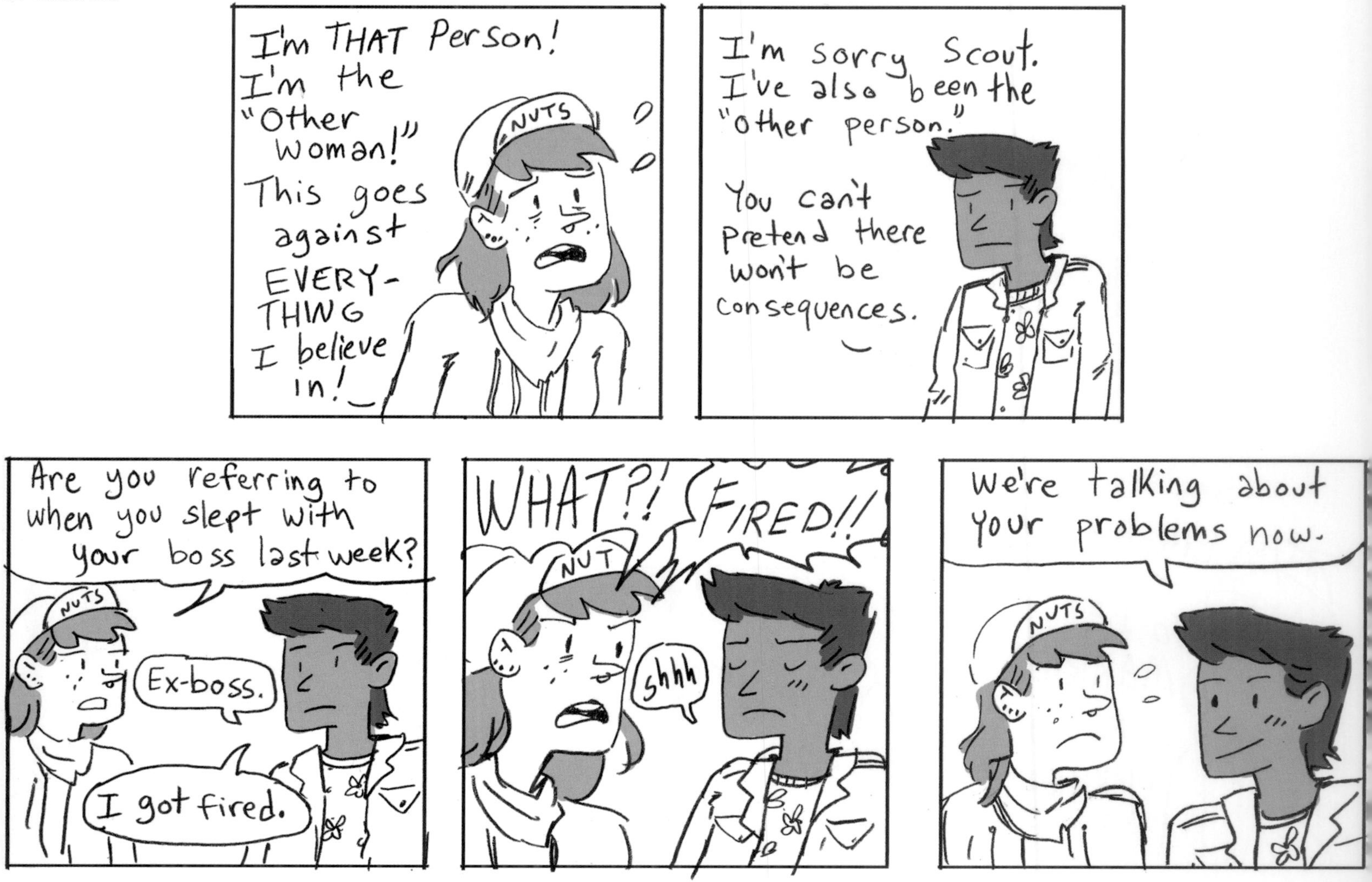
I'm THAT Person! I'm the "Other woman!" This goes against EVERYTHING I believe in!
NUTS
I'm sorry Scout. I've also been the "other person."
You can't pretend there won't be consequences.
Are you referring to when you slept with your boss last week?
NUTS
Ex-boss.
I got fired.
WHAT?!
FIRED!!
NUT
shhh
We're talking about your problems now.
NUTS

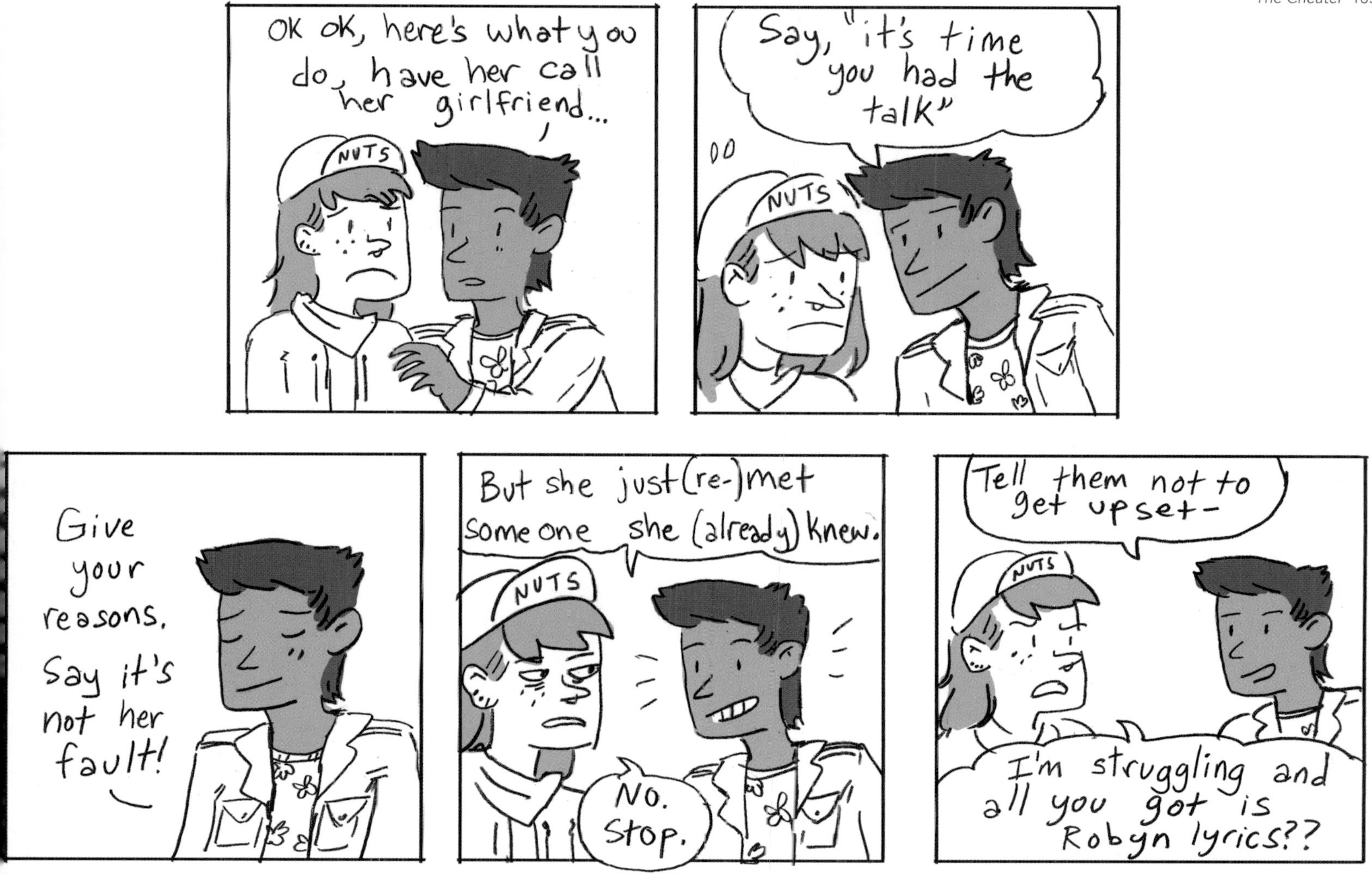
OK OK, here's what you do, have her call her girlfriend...
Say, "it's time you had the talk"
Give your reasons.
Say it's not her fault!
But she just (re-) met someone she (already) knew.
No. Stop.
Tell them not to get upset-
I'm struggling and all you got is Robyn lyrics??

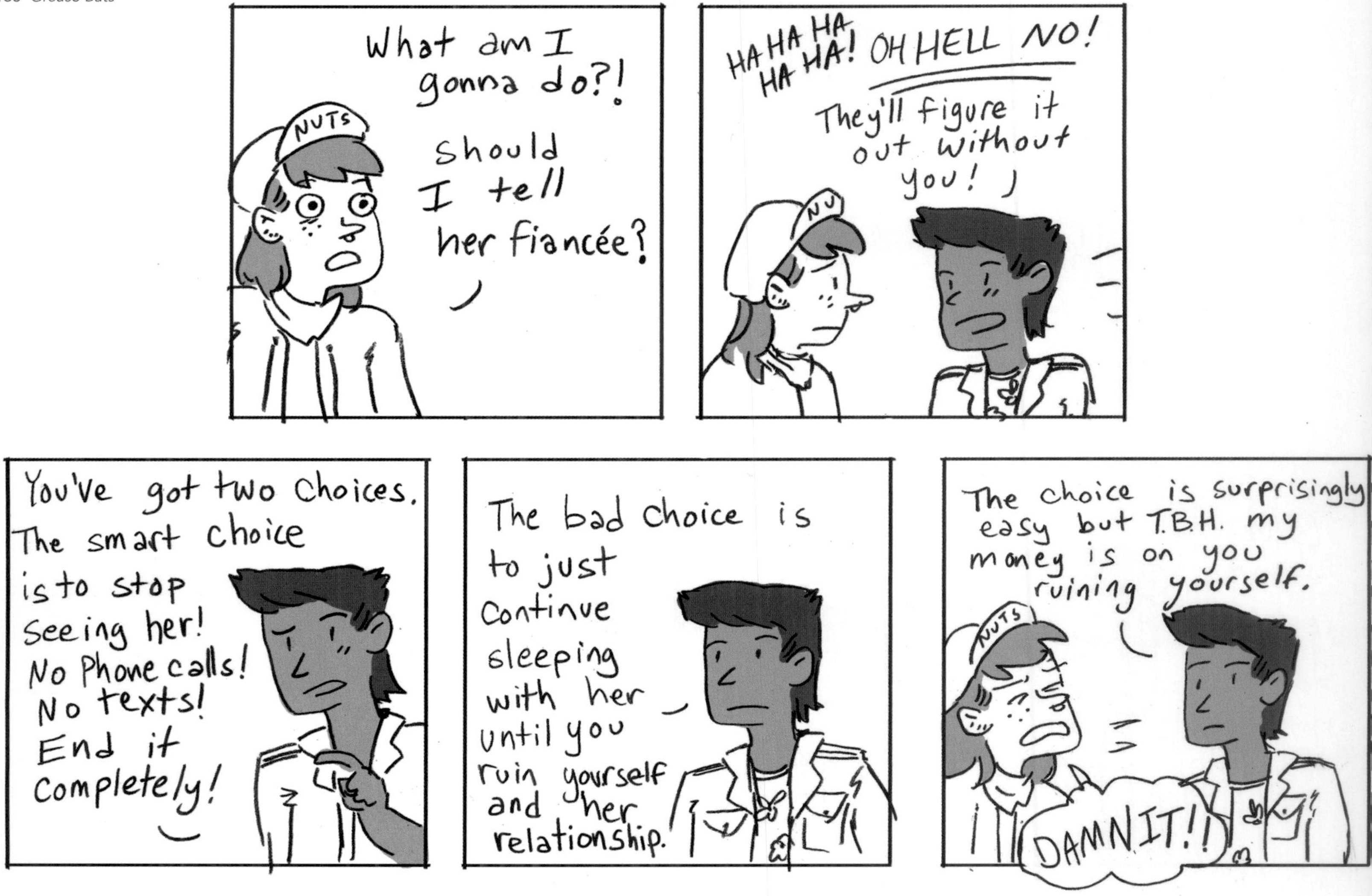
NUTS
What am I gonna do?!
Should I tell her fiancée?
HA HA HA HA HA HA! OH HELL NO!
They'll figure it out without you!
NU
You've got two choices. The smart choice is to stop seeing her! No phone calls! No texts! End it completely!
The bad choice is to just continue sleeping with her until you ruin yourself and her relationship.
The choice is surprisingly easy but T.B.H. my money is on you ruining yourself.
NUTS
DAMN IT!!

Trump

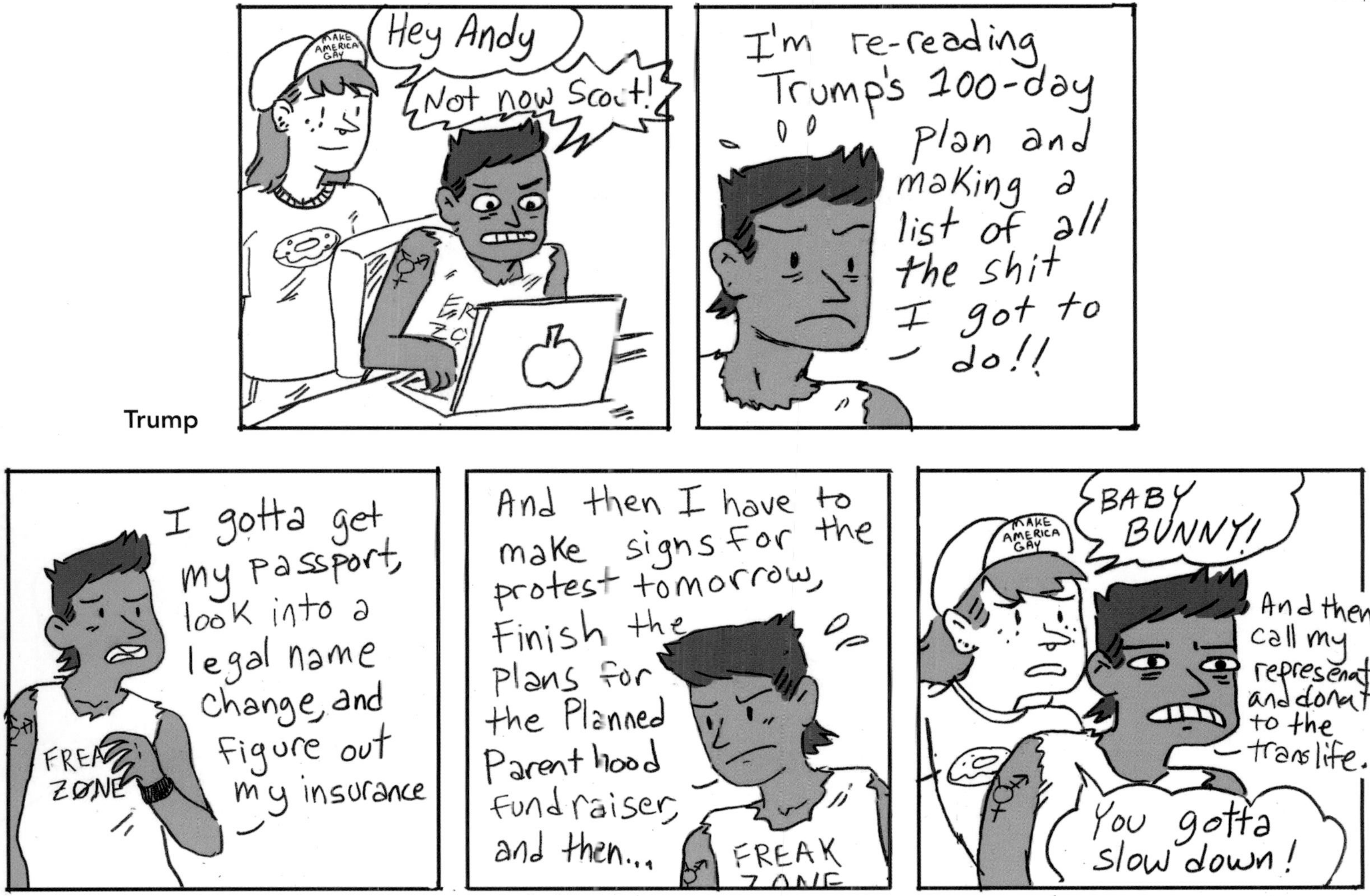
MAKE AMERICA GAY
Hey Andy
Not now Scout!
I'm re-reading Trump's 100-day plan and making a list of all the shit I got to do!!
I gotta get my passport, look into a legal name change, and figure out my insurance
FREAK ZONE
And then I have to make signs for the protest tomorrow, Finish the plans for the Planned Parenthood fundraiser, and then...
FREAK
MAKE AMERICA GAY
BABY BUNNY!
And then call my represenatives and donate to the trans life...
You gotta slow down!

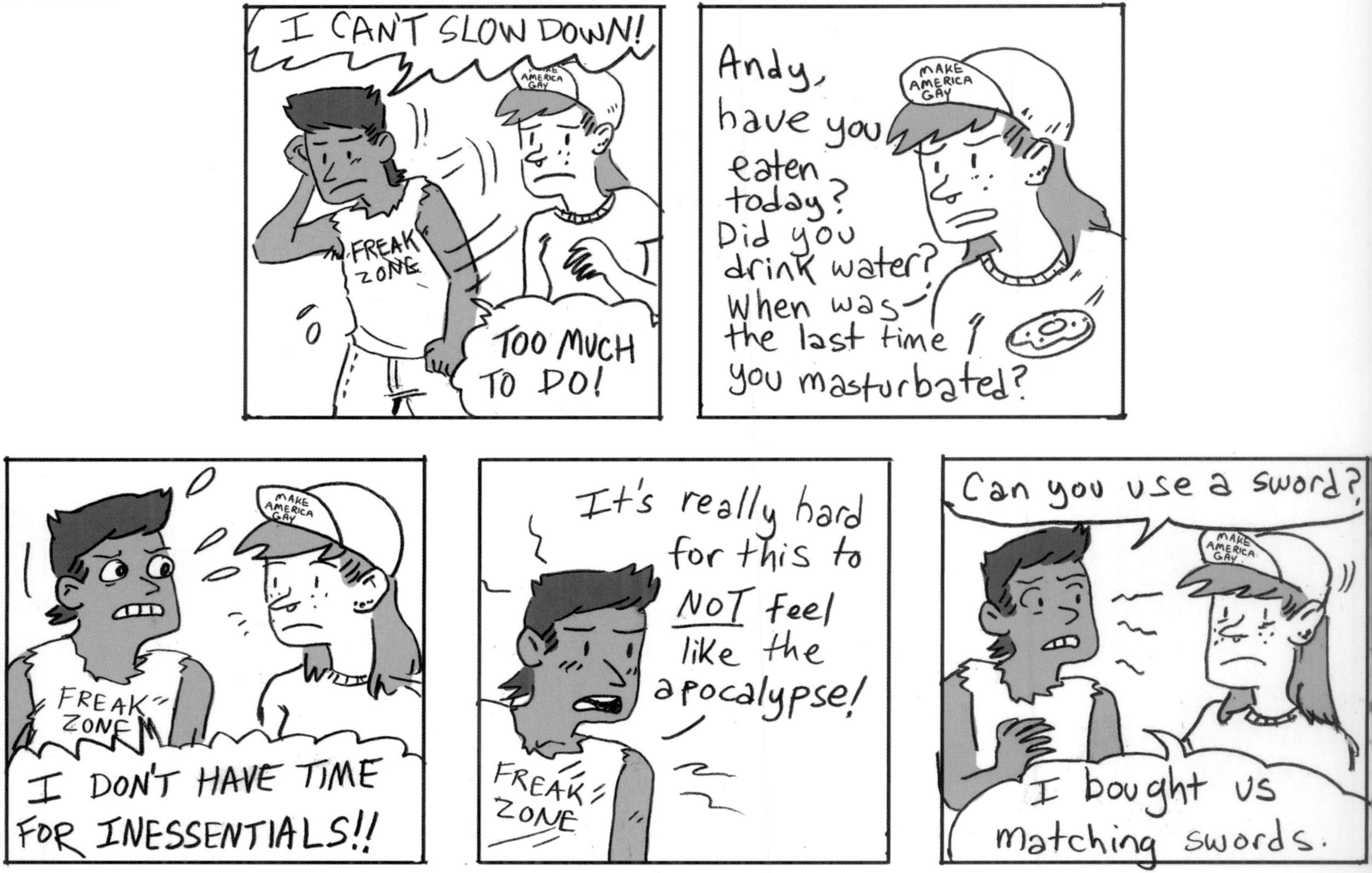
I CAN'T SLOW DOWN!
MAKE AMERICA GAY
FREAK ZONE
TOO MUCH TO DO!
MAKE AMERICA GAY
Andy, have you eaten today? Did you drink water? When was the last time you masturbated?
MAKE AMERICA GAY
FREAK ZONE
I DON'T HAVE TIME FOR INESSENTIALS!!
It's really hard for this to NOT feel like the apocalypse!
FREAK ZONE
Can you use a sword?
MAKE AMERICA GAY
I bought us matching swords.

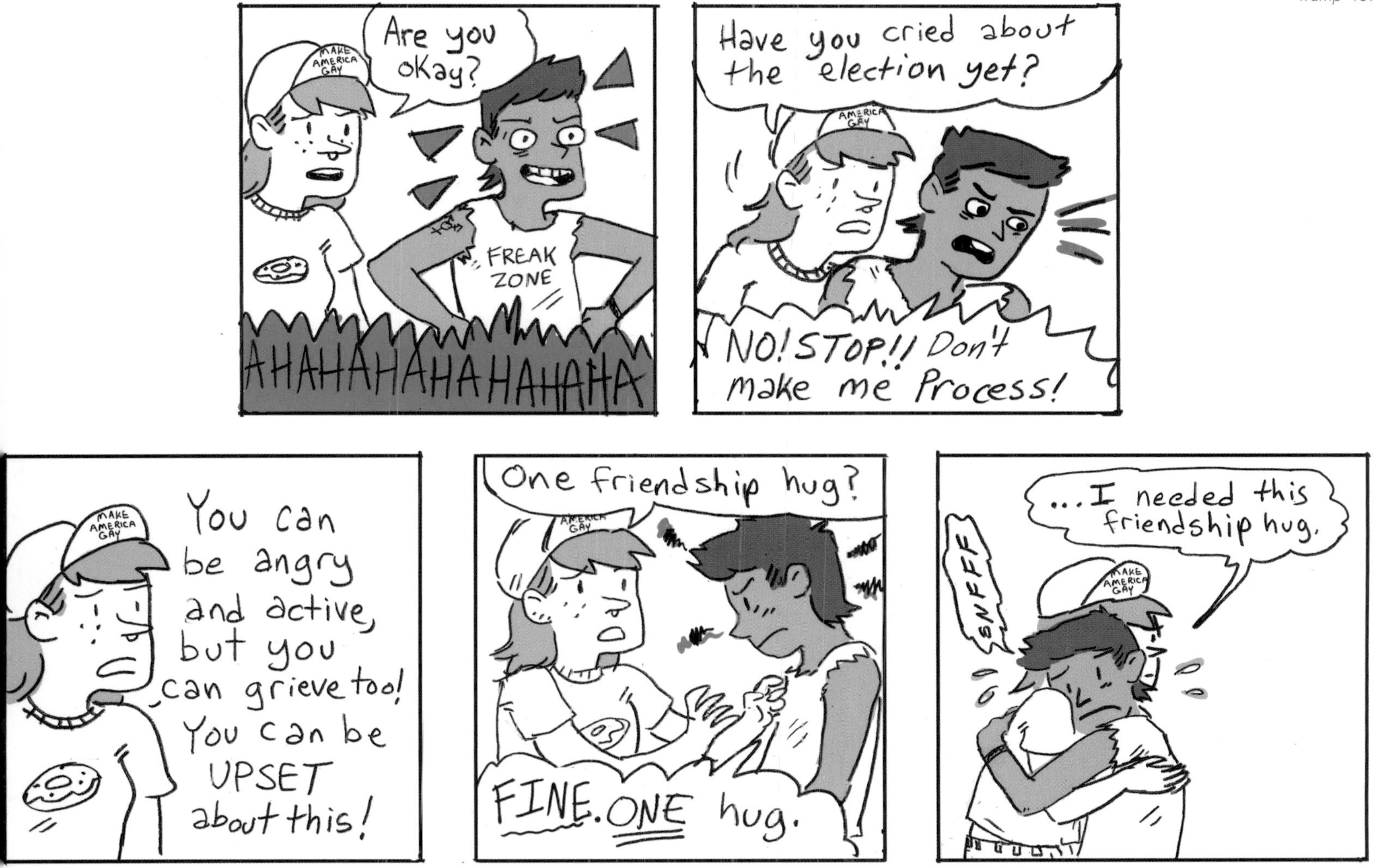
MAKE AMERICA GAY
Are you oKay?
FREAK ZONE
AHAHAHAHAHAHAHAHA
Have you cried about the election yet?
AMERICA GAY
NO! STOP!! Don't make me Process!
MAKE AMERICA GAY
You can be angry and active, but you can grieve too! You can be UPSET about this!
One friendship hug?
AMERICA GAY
FINE. ONE hug.
...I needed this friendship hug.
SNFFF
MAKE AMERICA GAY

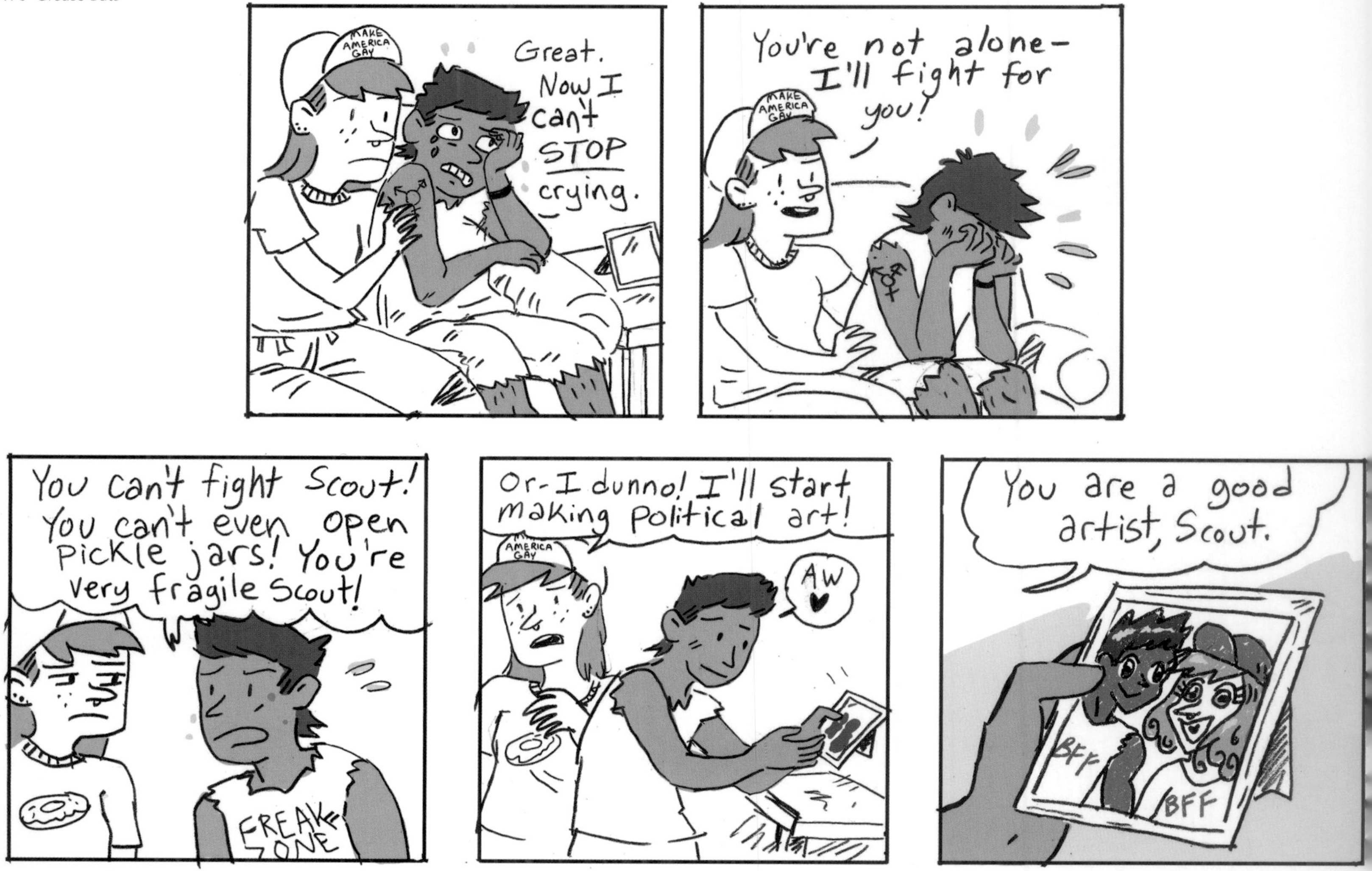
MAKE AMERICA GAY
Great. Now I can't STOP crying.
You're not alone- I'll fight for you!
MAKE AMERICA GAY
You can't fight Scout! You can't even open pickle jars! You're very fragile Scout!
FREAK ZONE
Or- I dunno! I'll start making political art!
AMERICA GAY
AW ♥
You are a good artist, Scout.
BFF
BFF

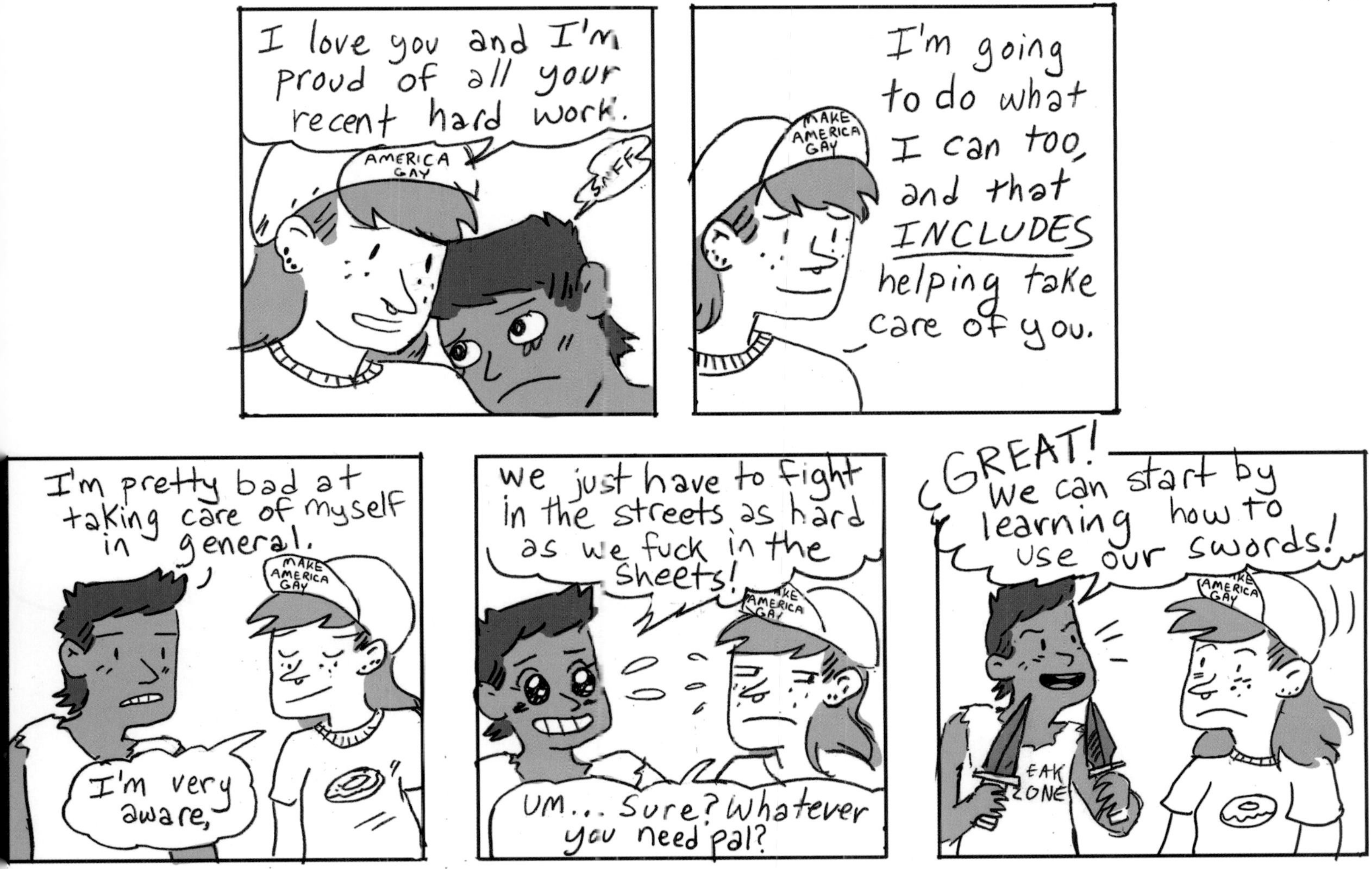
I love you and I'm proud of all your recent hard work.
AMERICA GAY
SNIFF
I'm going to do what I can too, and that INCLUDES helping take care of you.
MAKE AMERICA GAY
I'm pretty bad at taking care of myself in general.
MAKE AMERICA GAY
I'm very aware,
We just have to fight in the streets as hard as we fuck in the sheets!
MAKE AMERICA GAY
Um... Sure? Whatever you need pal?
GREAT! We can start by learning how to use our swords!
MAKE AMERICA GAY
EAK ZONE

The Protest

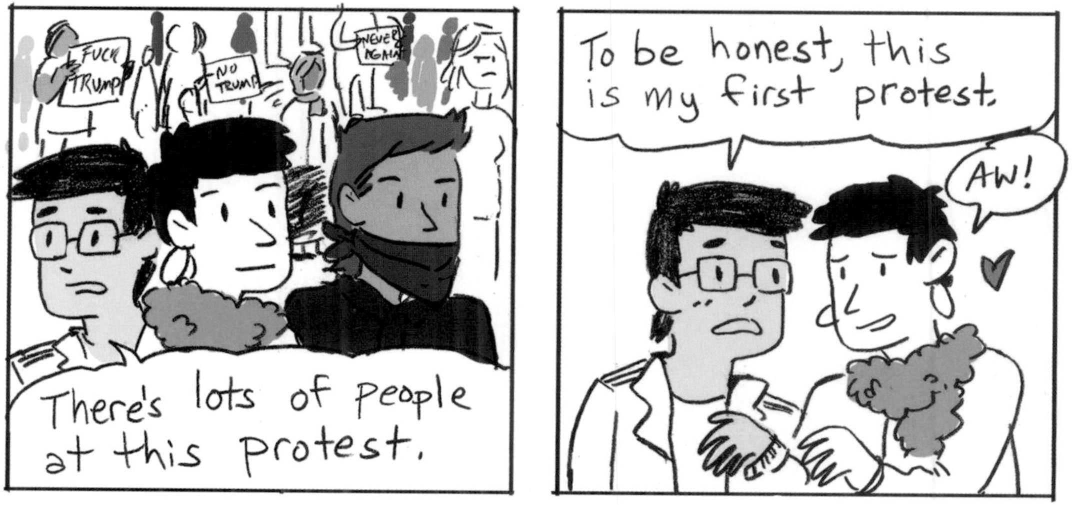
FUCK TRUMP
NO TRUMP
NEVER AGAIN
There's lots of people at this protest.
To be honest, this is my first protest.
AW!

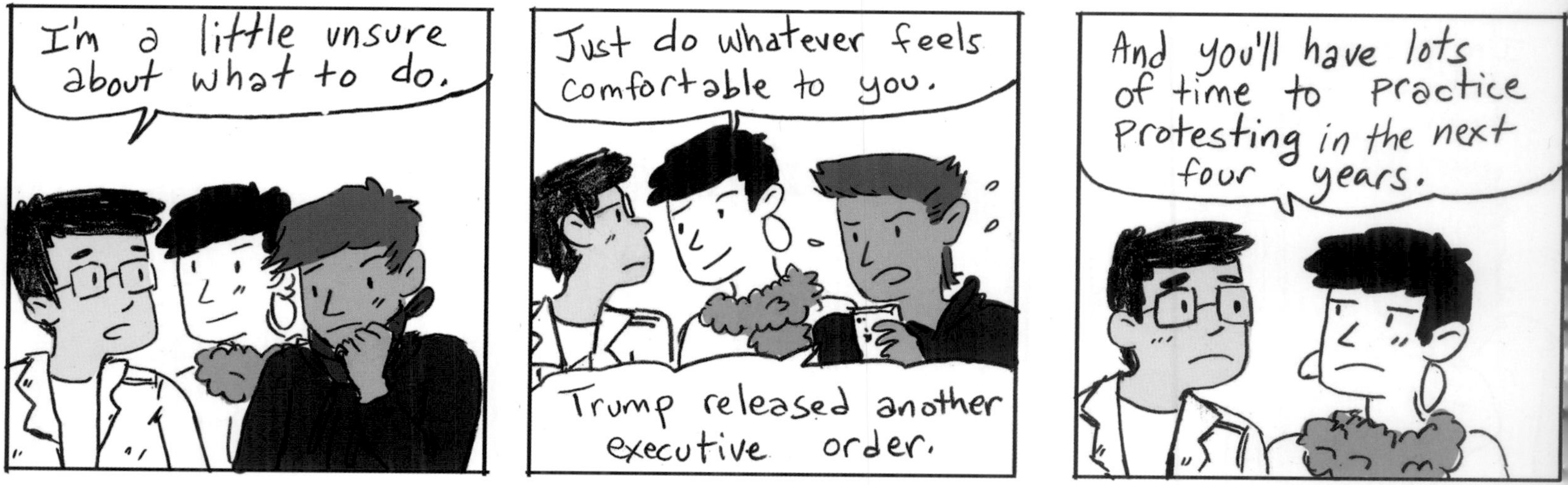
I'm a little unsure about what to do.
Just do whatever feels comfortable to you.
Trump released another executive order.
And you'll have lots of time to practice protesting in the next four years.

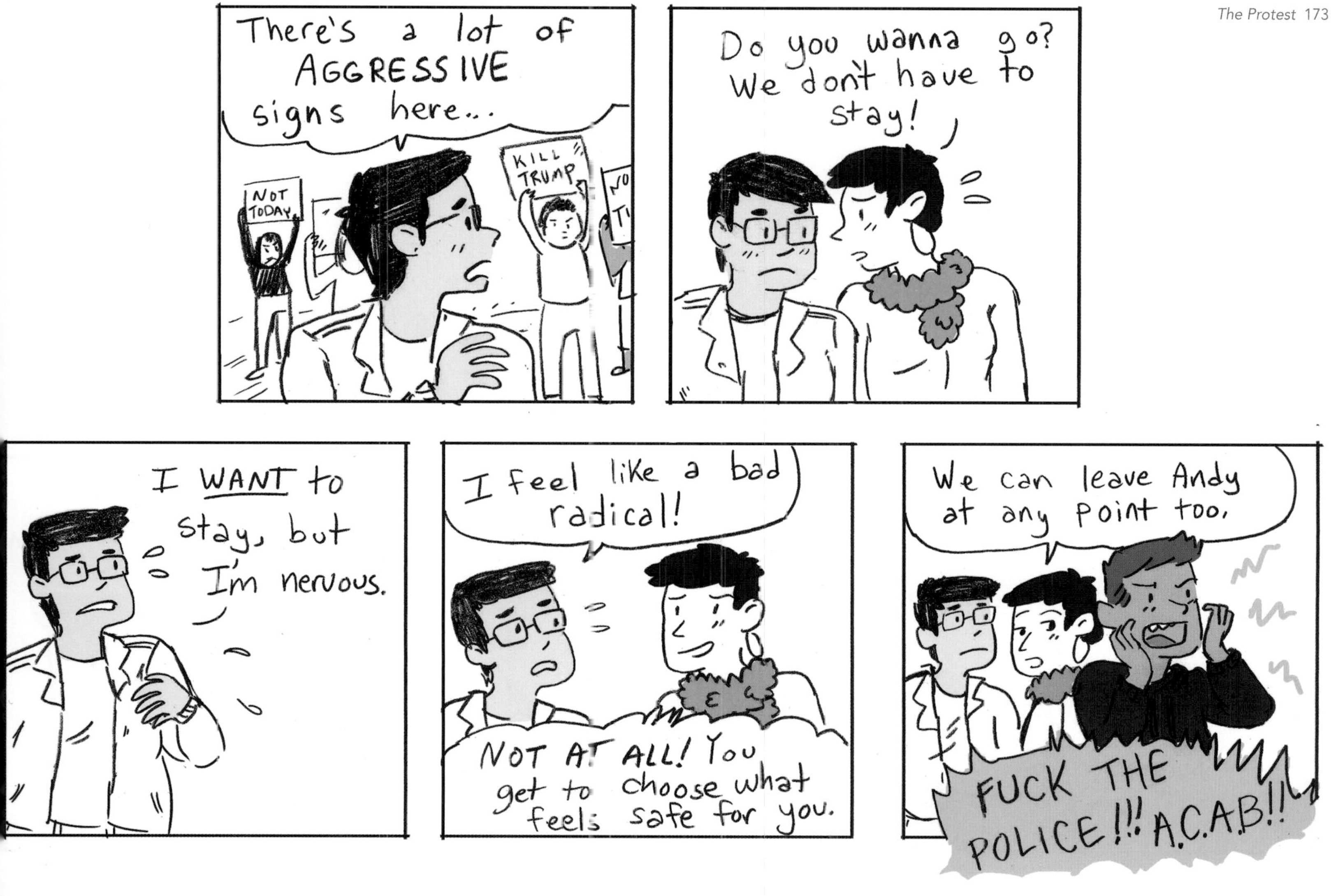
There's a lot of AGGRESSIVE signs here...
NOT TODAY
KILL TRUMP
Do you wanna go? We don't have to stay!
I WANT to stay, but I'm nervous.
I feel like a bad radical!
NOT AT ALL! You get to choose what feels safe for you.
We can leave Andy at any point too.
FUCK THE POLICE!!! A.C.A.B!!

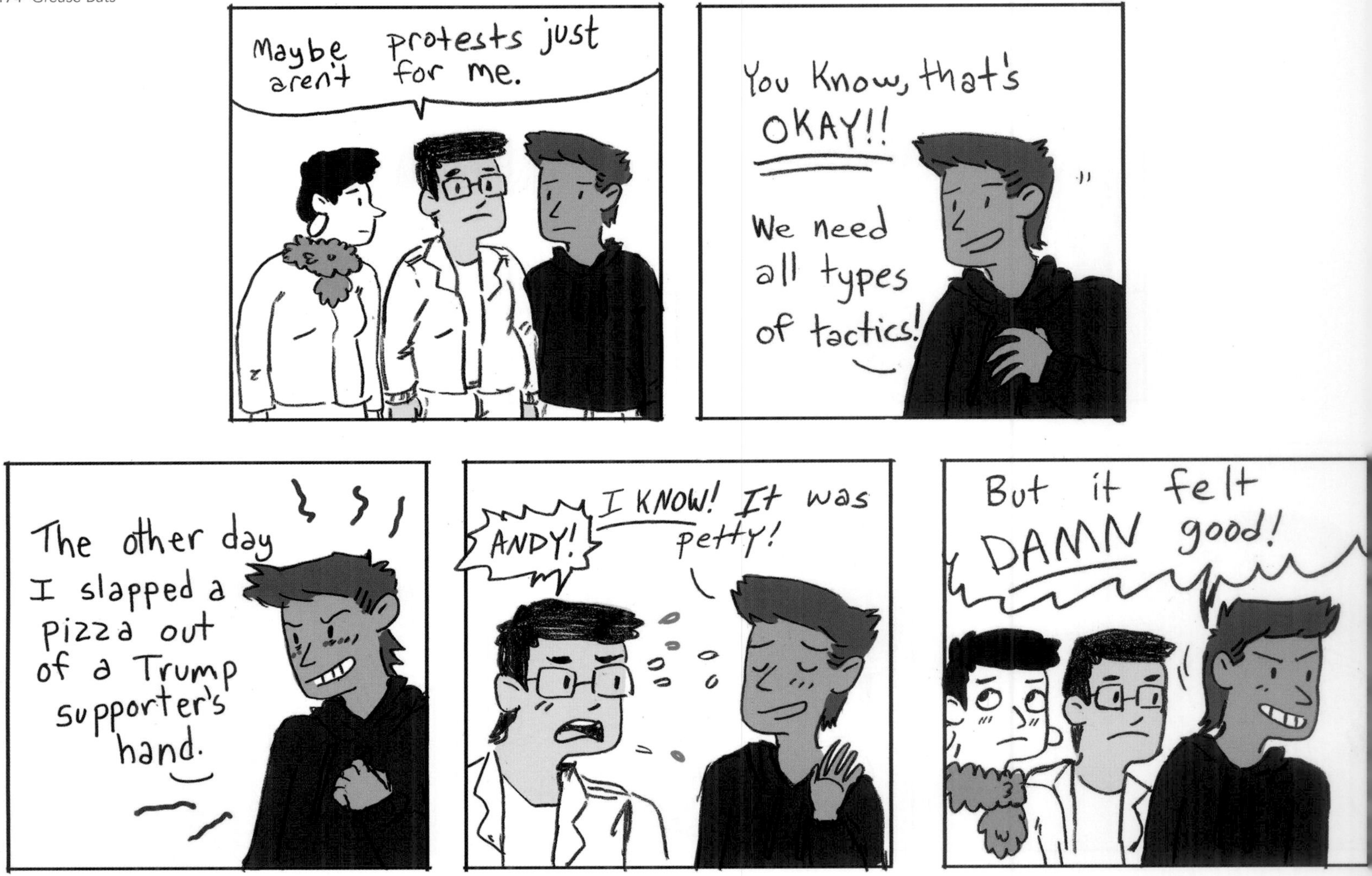
Maybe protests just aren't for me.
You know, that's OKAY!!
We need all types of tactics!
The other day I slapped a pizza out of a Trump supporter's hand.
ANDY!
I KNOW! It was petty!
But it felt DAMN good!

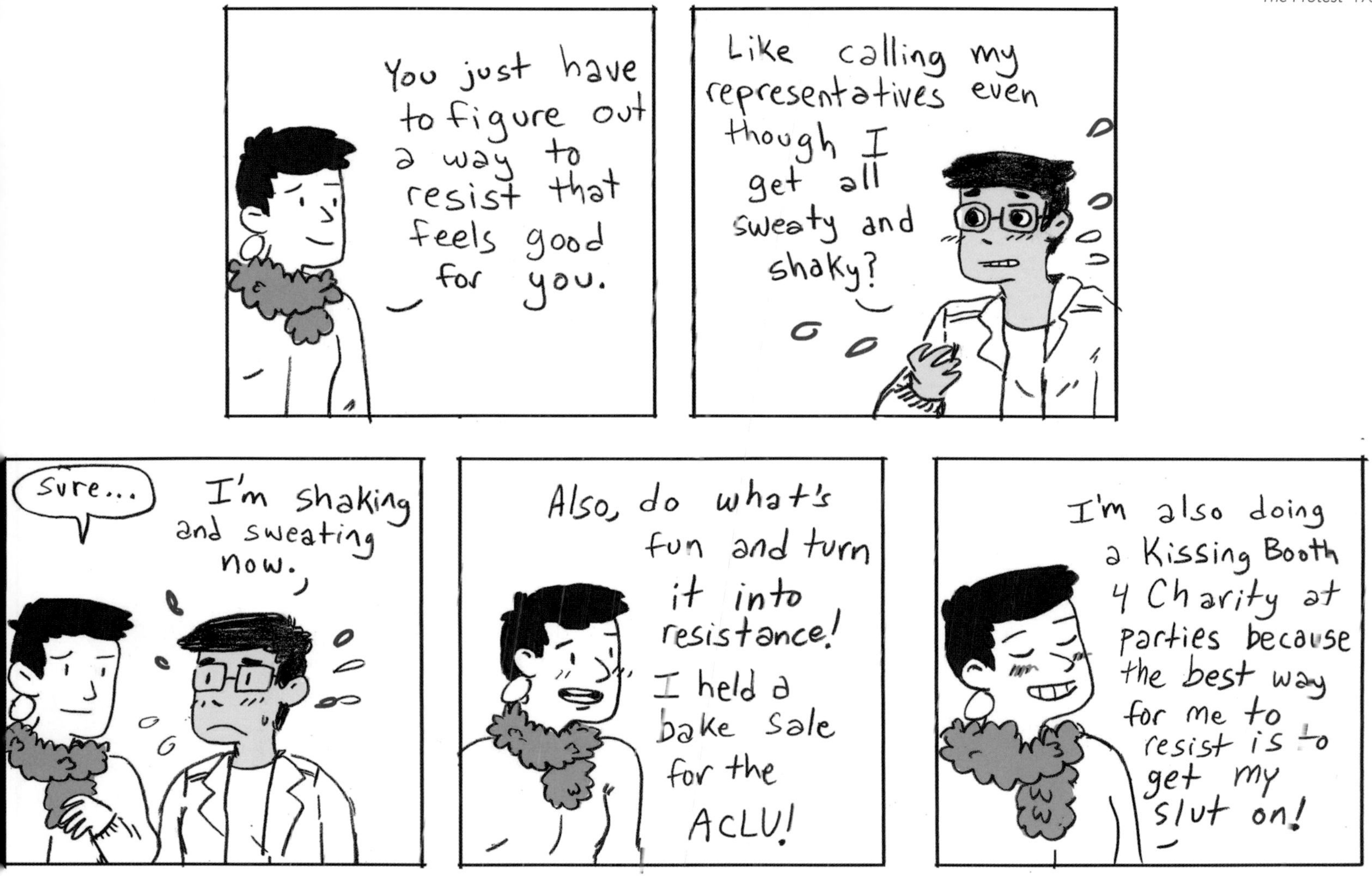
You just have to figure out a way to resist that feels good for you.
Like calling my representatives even though I get all sweaty and shaky?
Sure...
I'm shaking and sweating now.
Also, do what's fun and turn it into resistance! I held a bake sale for the ACLU!
I'm also doing a Kissing Booth 4 Charity at parties because the best way for me to resist is to get my slut on!

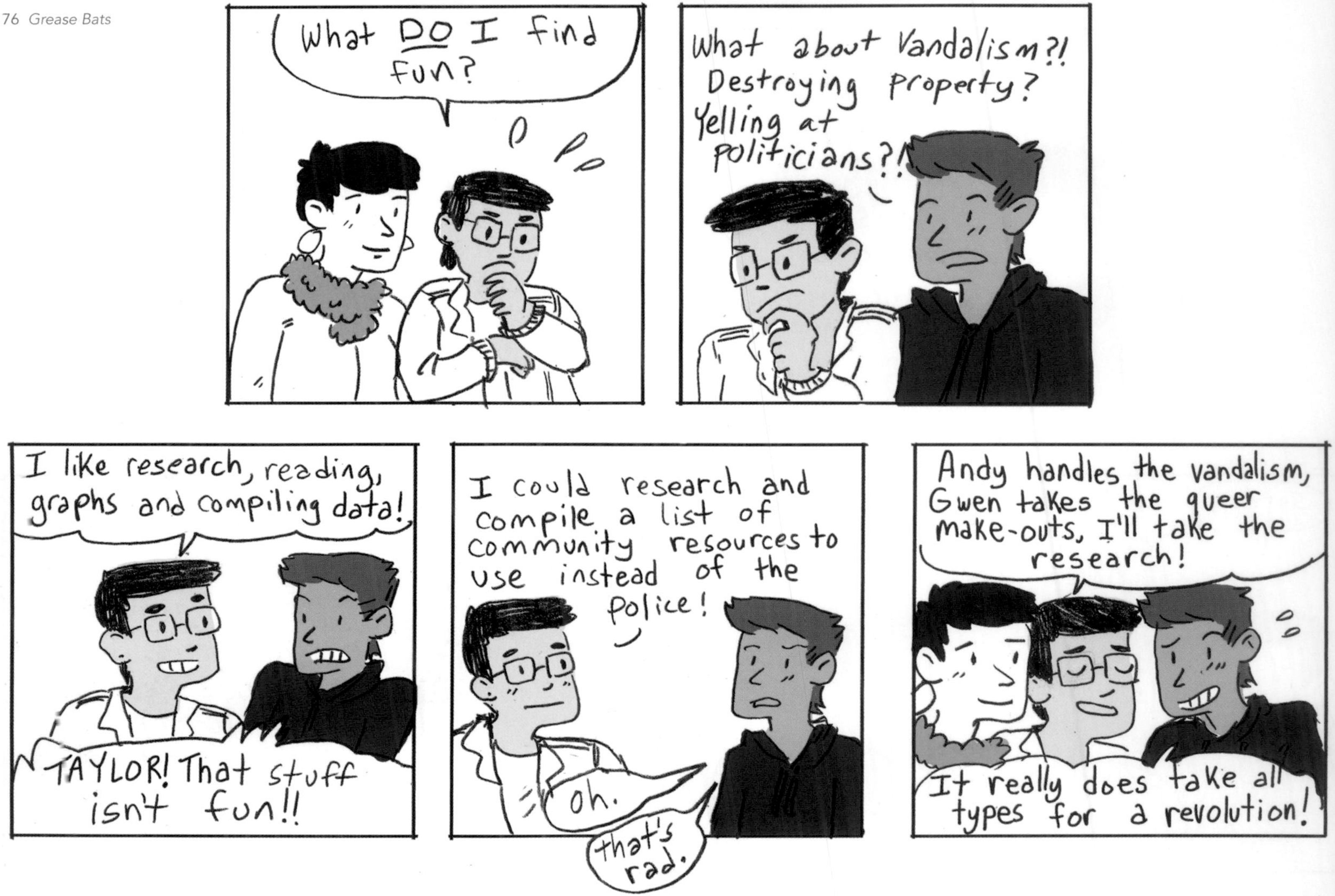
What DO I find fun?
What about Vandalism?! Destroying property? Yelling at politicians?!
I like research, reading, graphs and compiling data!
TAYLOR! That stuff isn't fun!!
I could research and compile a list of community resources to use instead of the police!
oh.
that's rad.
Andy handles the vandalism, Gwen takes the queer make-outs, I'll take the research!
It really does take all types for a revolution!

Feeling the
Gender Feels

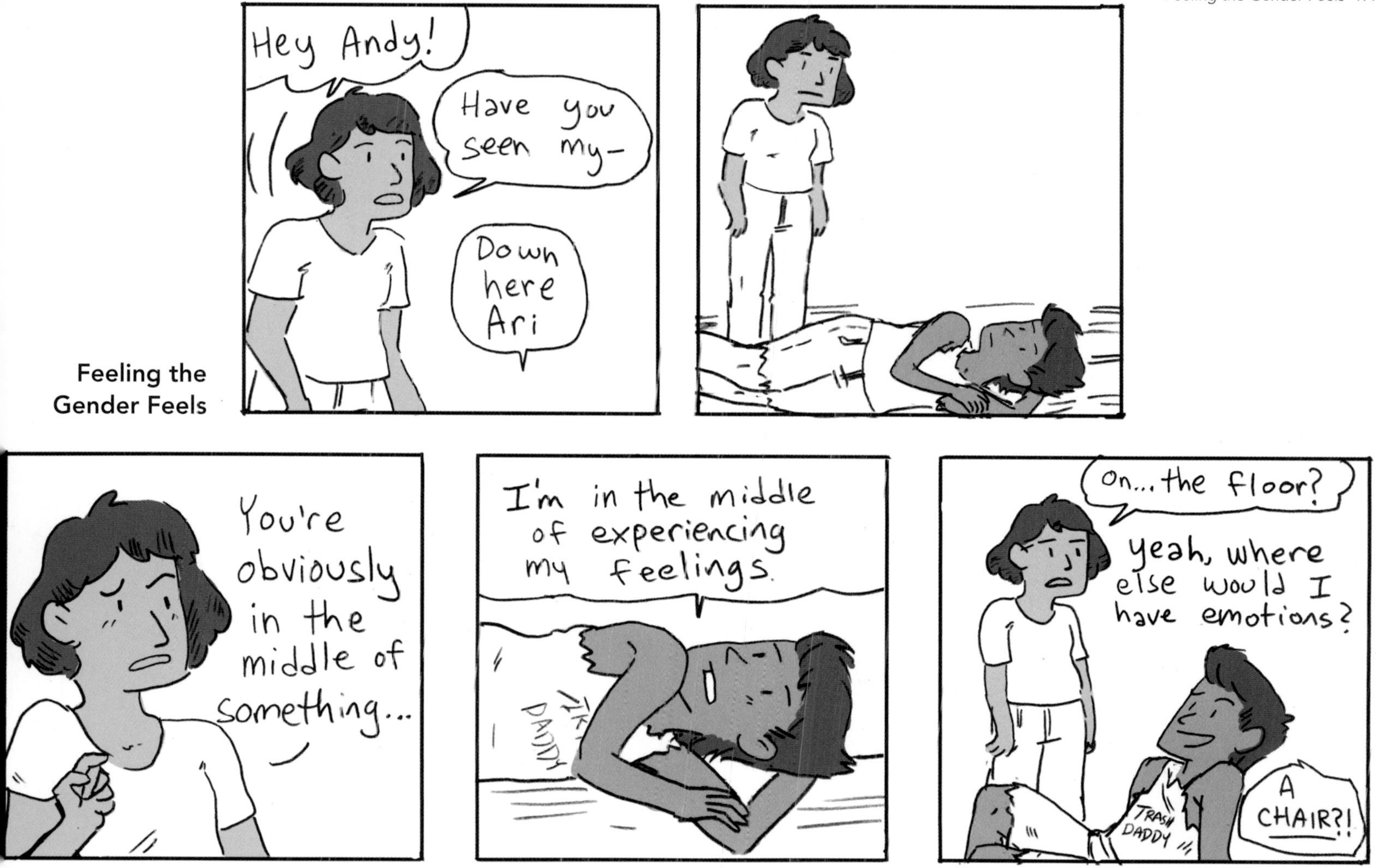
Hey Andy!
Have you seen my-
Down here Ari
You're obviously in the middle of something...
I'm in the middle of experiencing my feelings.
On... the floor?
yeah, where else would I have emotions?
A CHAIR?!
TRASH DADDY

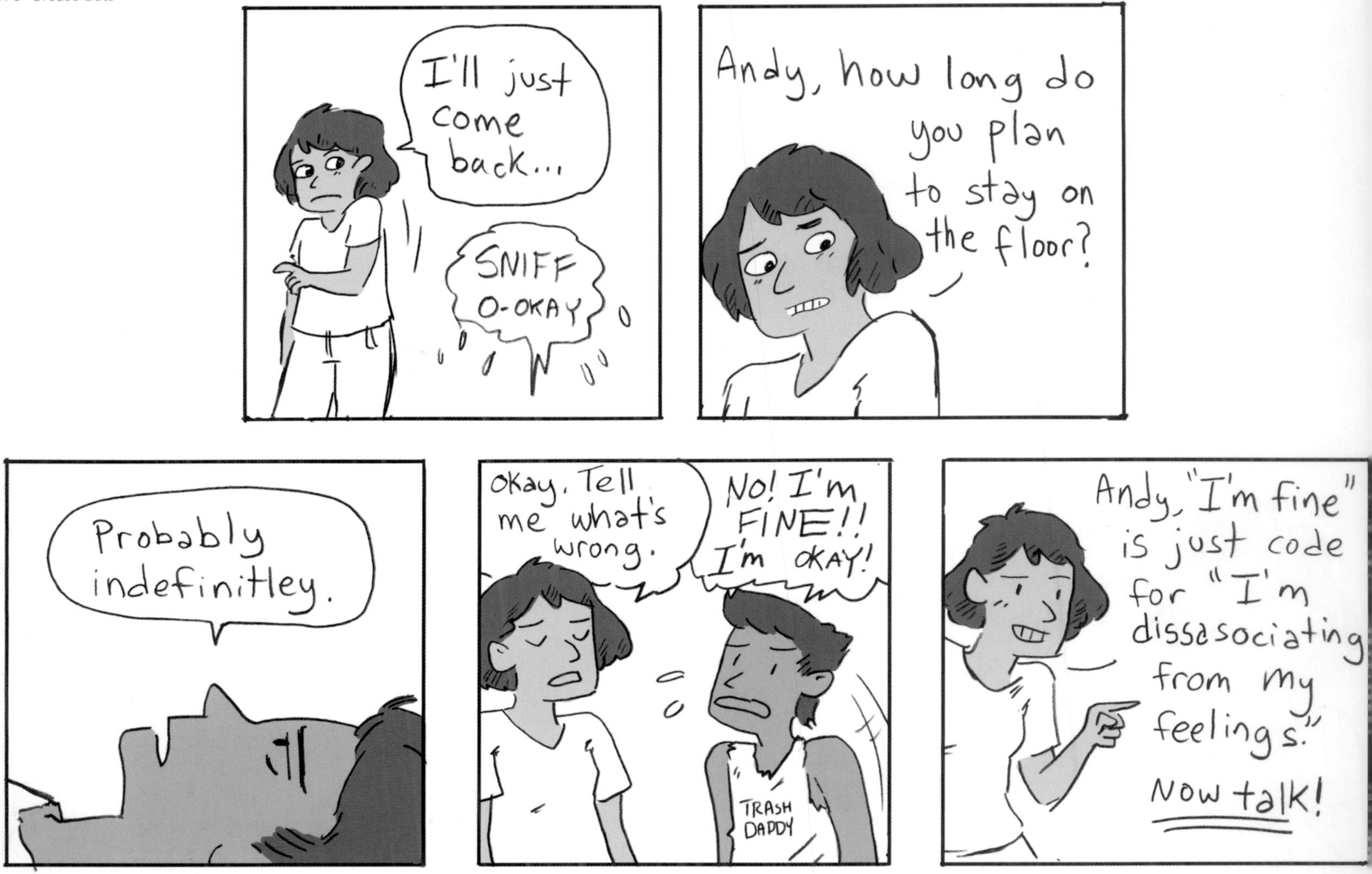
I'll just come back...
SNIFF O-OKAY
Andy, how long do you plan to stay on the floor?
Probably indefinitley.
Okay. Tell me what's wrong.
No! I'm FINE!! I'm OKAY!
TRASH DADDY
Andy, "I'm fine" is just code for "I'm dissasociating from my feelings."
Now talk!

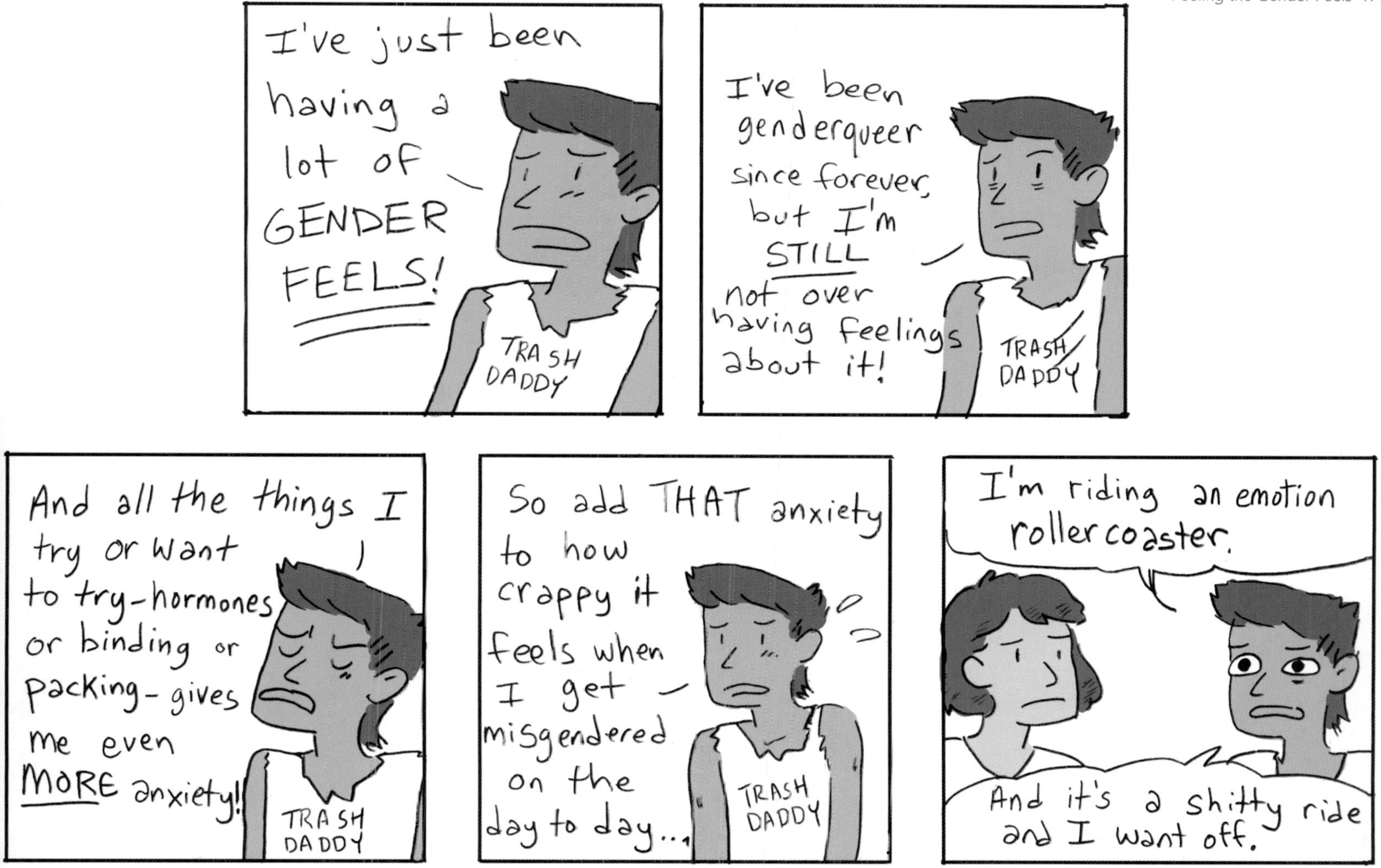
I've just been having a lot of GENDER FEELS!
TRASH DADDY
I've been genderqueer since forever, but I'm STILL not over having feelings about it!
TRASH DADDY
And all the things I try or want to try-hormones or binding or packing- gives me even MORE anxiety!
TRASH DADDY
So add THAT anxiety to how crappy it feels when I get misgendered on the day to day...
TRASH DADDY
I'm riding an emotion rollercoaster.
And it's a shitty ride and I want off.

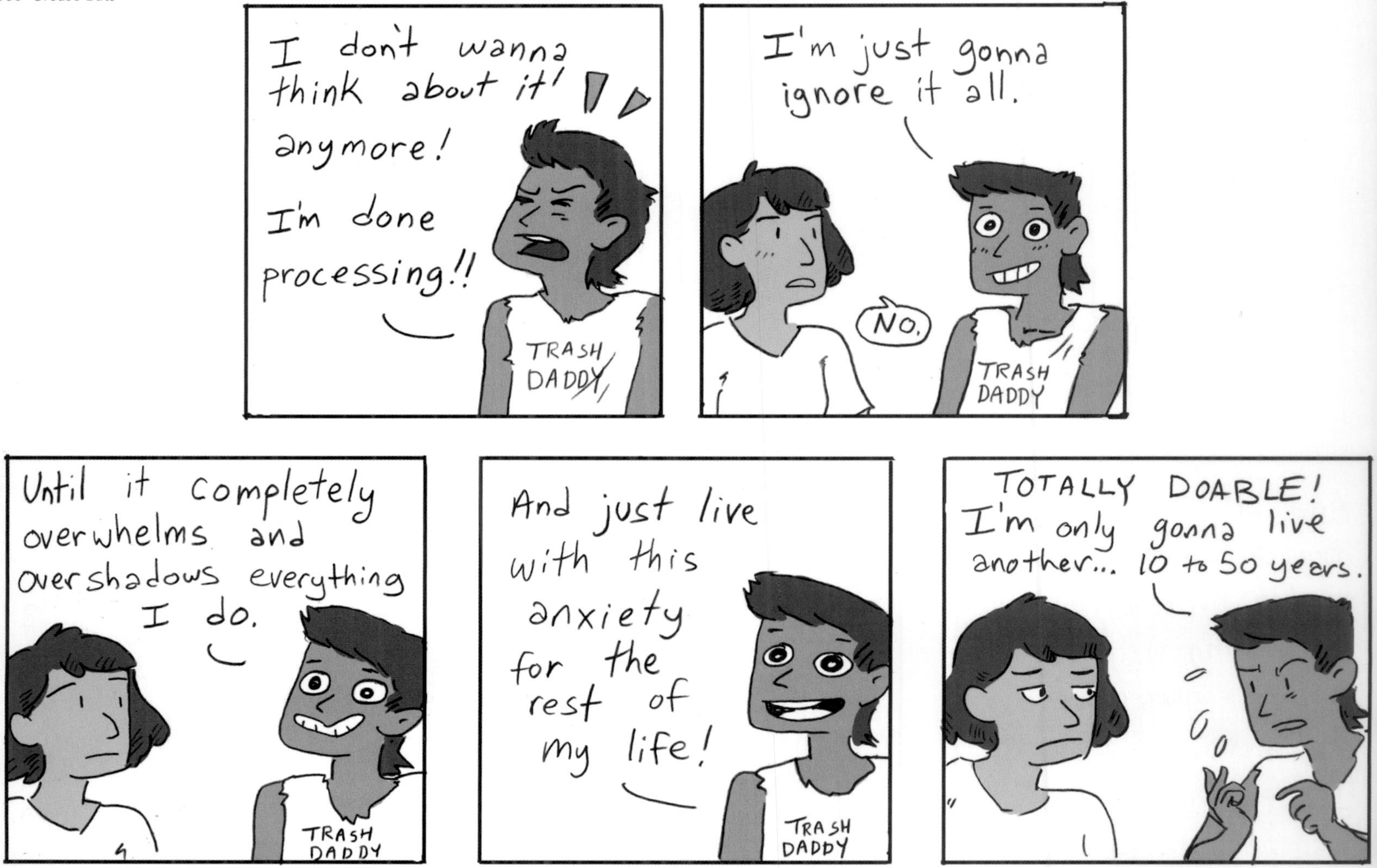
I don't wanna think about it anymore!
I'm done processing!!
TRASH DADDY
I'm just gonna ignore it all.
NO.
TRASH DADDY
Until it completely overwhelms and overshadows everything I do.
TRASH DADDY
And just live with this anxiety for the rest of my life!
TRASH DADDY
TOTALLY DOABLE! I'm only gonna live another... 10 to 50 years.

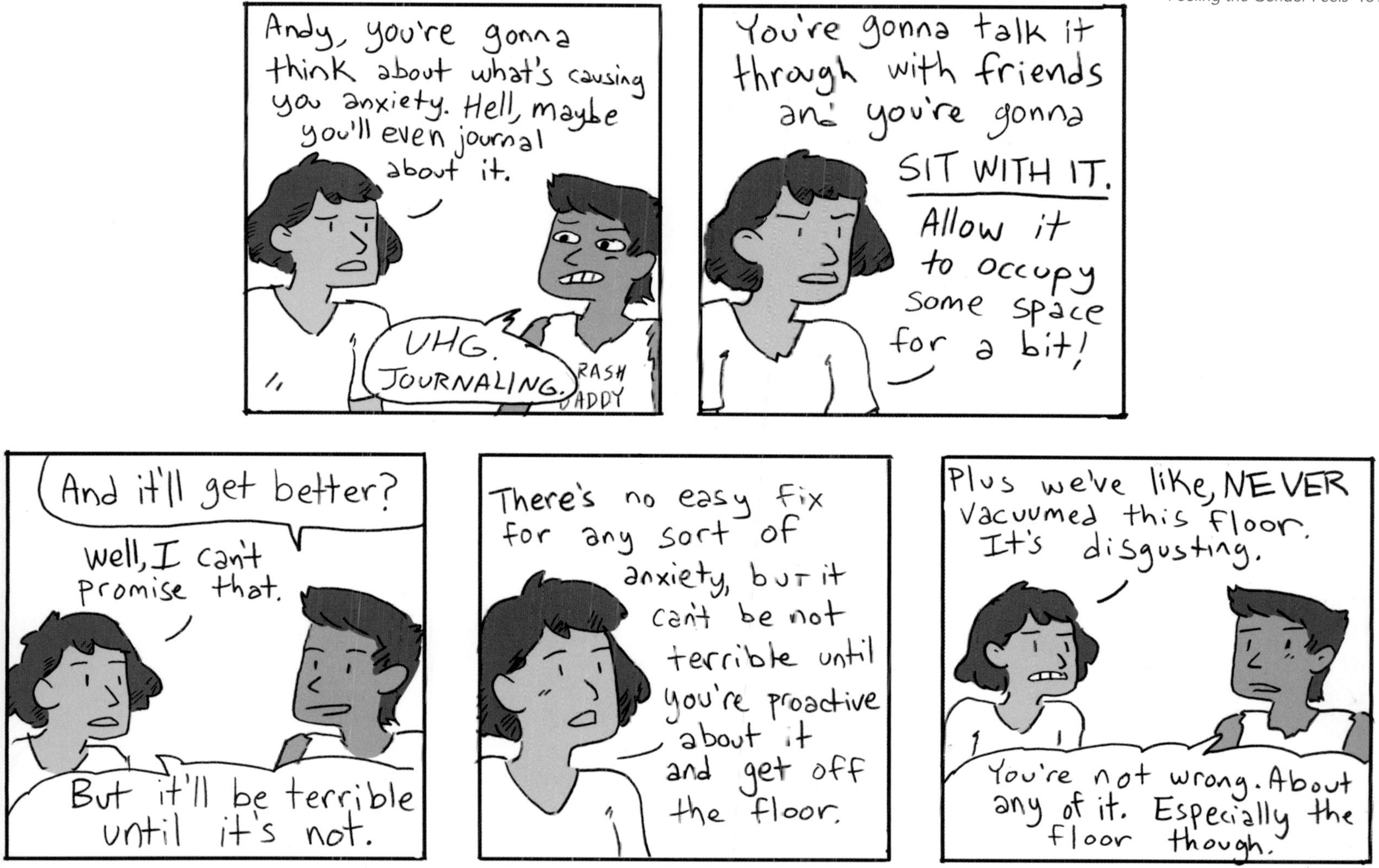
Andy, you're gonna think about what's causing you anxiety. Hell, maybe you'll even journal about it.
UHG. JOURNALING.
RASH DADDY
You're gonna talk it through with friends and you're gonna SIT WITH IT. Allow it to occupy some space for a bit!
And it'll get better?
Well, I can't promise that.
But it'll be terrible until it's not.
There's no easy fix for any sort of anxiety, but it can't be not terrible until you're proactive about it and get off the floor.
Plus we've like, NEVER vacuumed this floor. It's disgusting.
You're not wrong. About any of it. Especially the floor though.

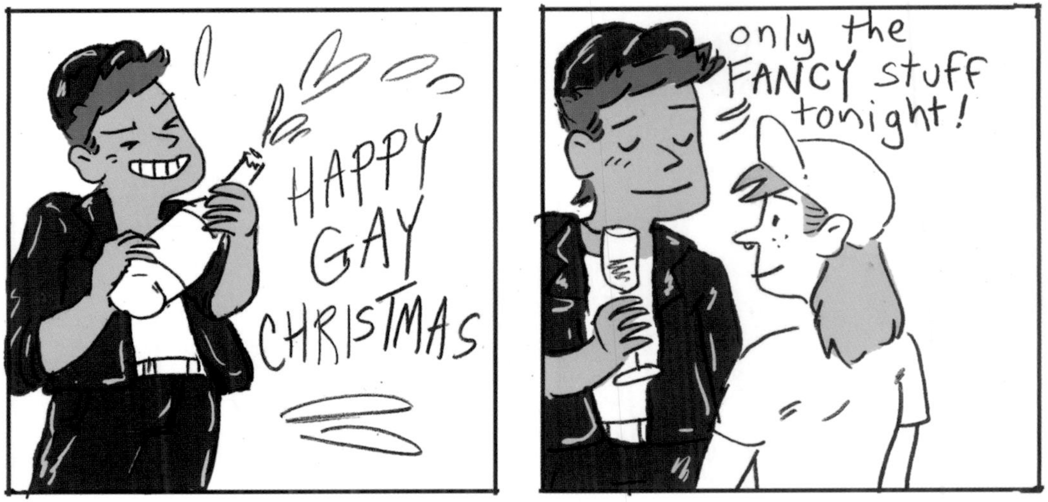
HAPPY GAY CHRISTMAS
only the FANCY stuff tonight!

Pre-Halloween

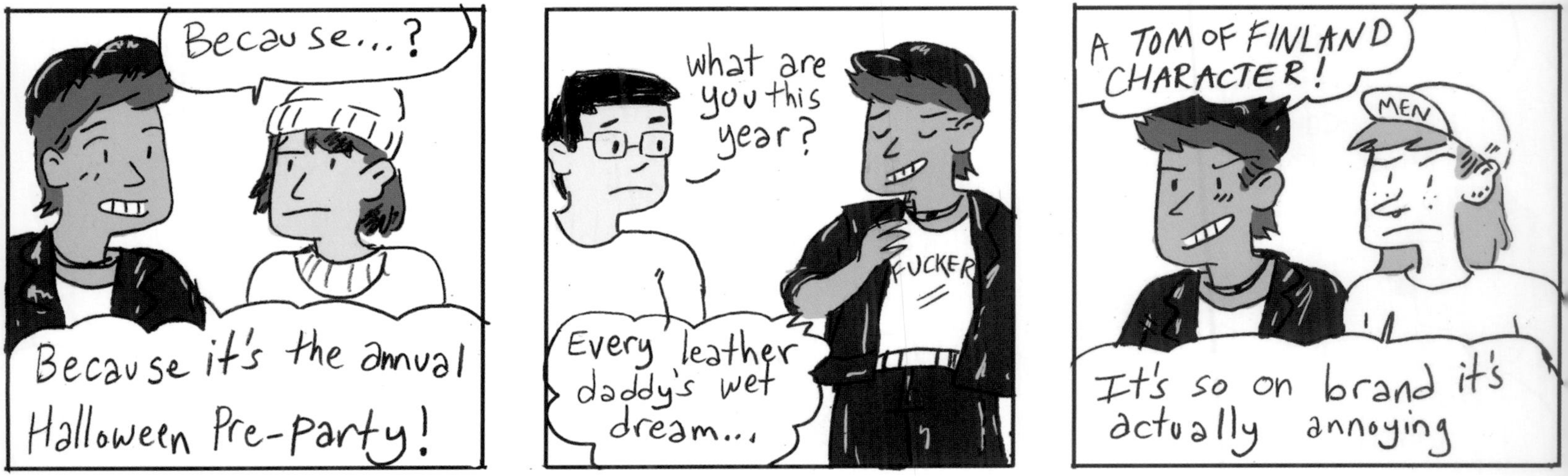
Because...?
Because it's the annual Halloween Pre-Party!
what are you this year?
Every leather daddy's wet dream...
FUCKER
A TOM OF FINLAND CHARACTER!
MEN
It's so on brand it's actually annoying

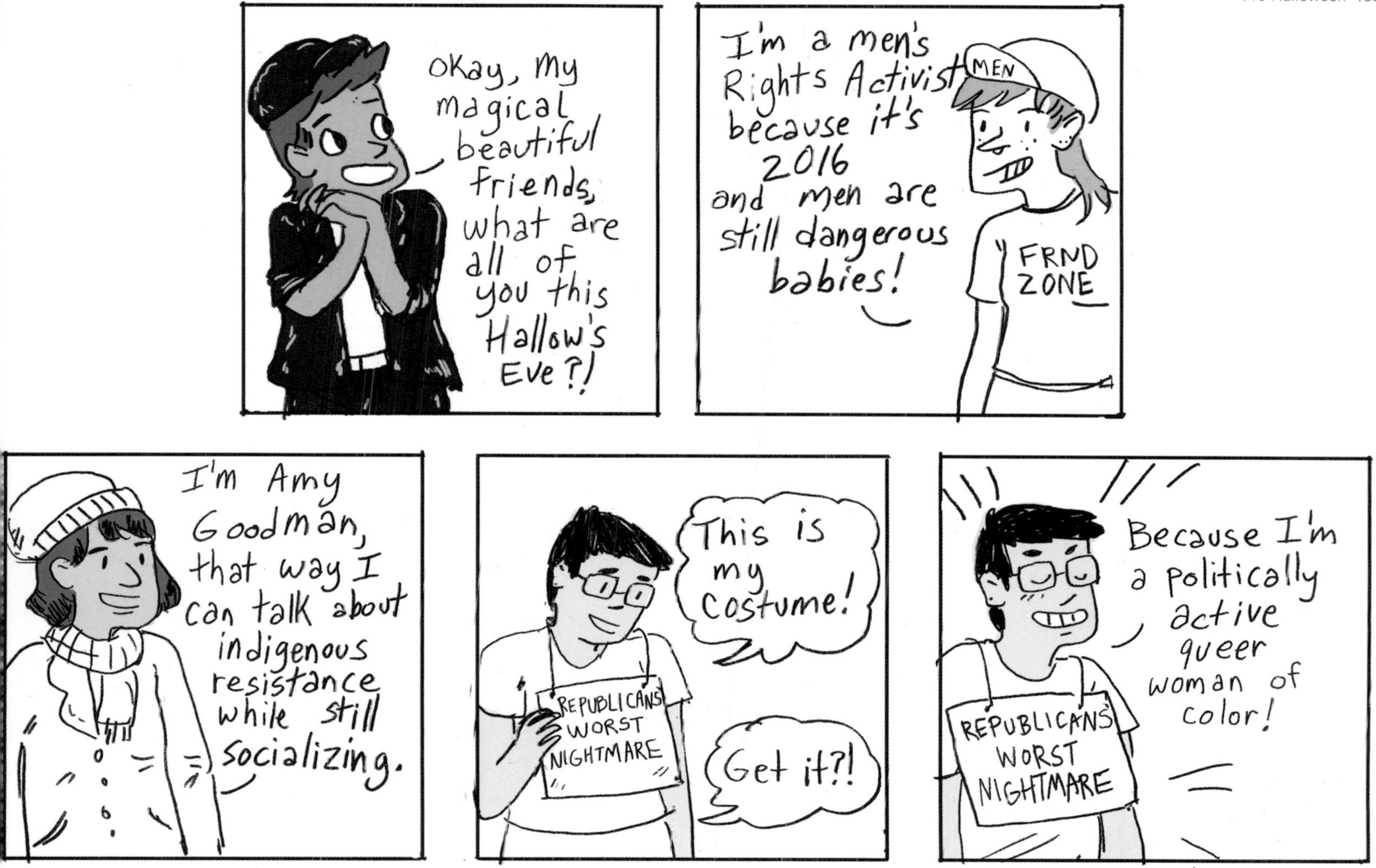

Okay, my magical beautiful friends, what are all of you this Hallow's Eve?!
I'm a men's Rights Activist because it's 2016 and men are still dangerous babies!
MEN
FRND ZONE
I'm Amy Goodman, that way I can talk about indigenous resistance while still socializing.
This is my costume!
REPUBLICANS WORST NIGHTMARE
Get it?!
Because I'm a politically active queer woman of color!
REPUBLICANS WORST NIGHTMARE

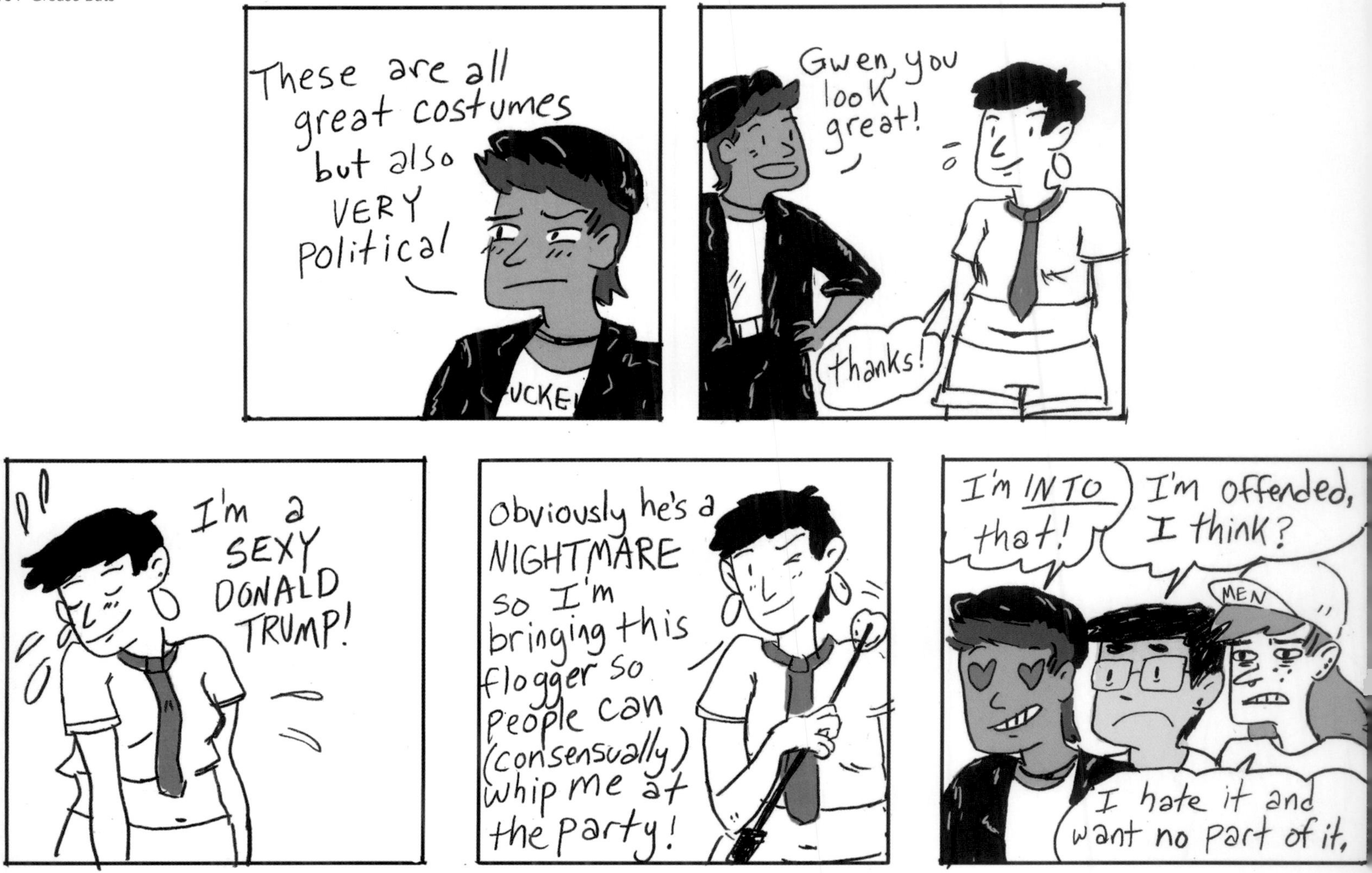
These are all great costumes but also VERY political
UCKE
Gwen, you look great!
thanks!
I'm a SEXY DONALD TRUMP!
Obviously he's a NIGHTMARE so I'm bringing this flogger so people can (consensually) whip me at the party!
I'm INTO that!
I'm offended, I think?
MEN
I hate it and want no part of it,

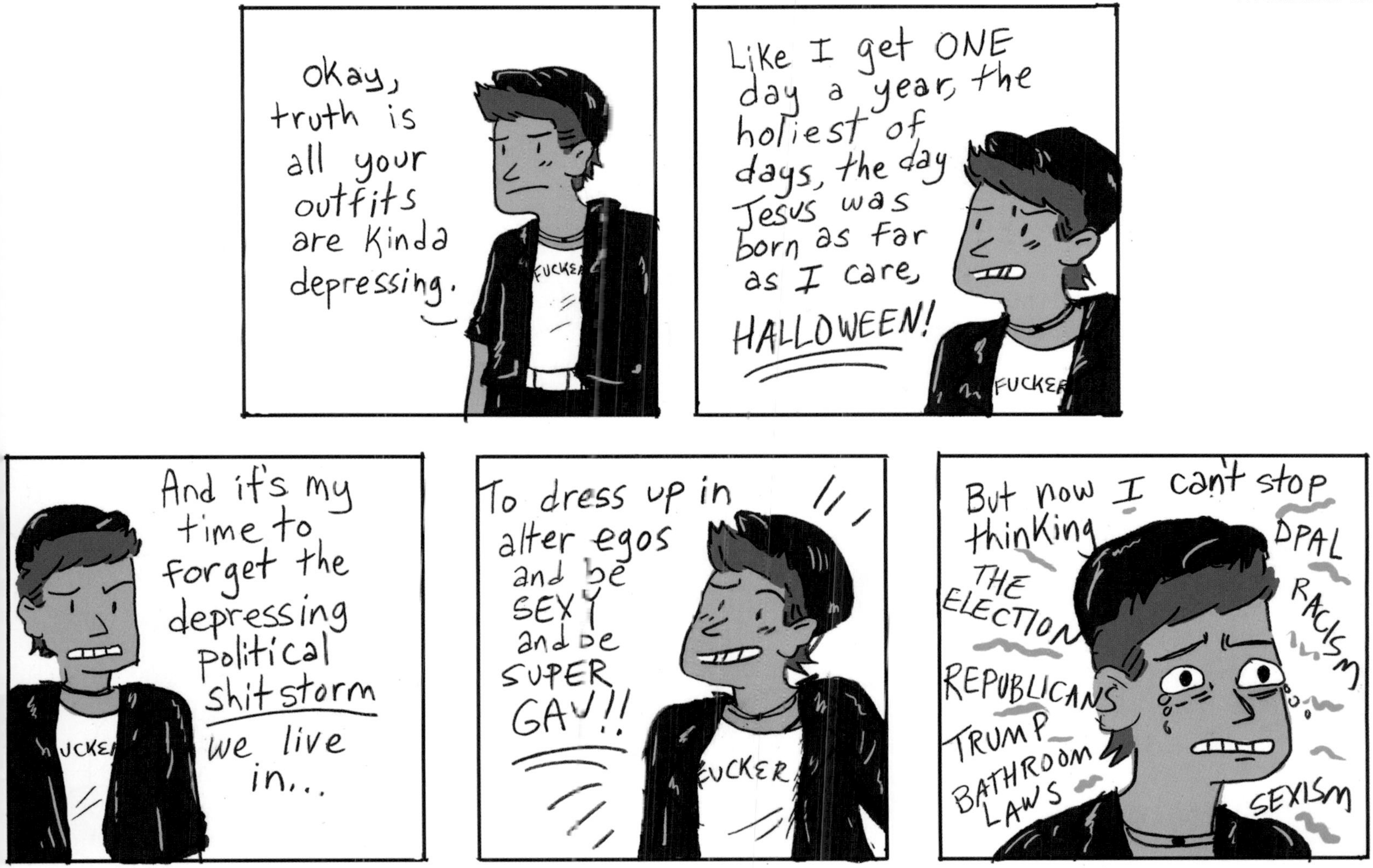

Okay, truth is all your outfits are kinda depressing.
FUCKER
Like I get ONE day a year, the holiest of days, the day Jesus was born as far as I care, HALLOWEEN!
FUCKER
And it's my time to forget the depressing political shitstorm we live in...
UCKER
To dress up in alter egos and be SEXY and be SUPER GAY!!
FUCKER
But now I can't stop thinking
DPAL
THE ELECTION
RACISM
REPUBLICANS
TRUMP
BATHROOM LAWS
SEXISM

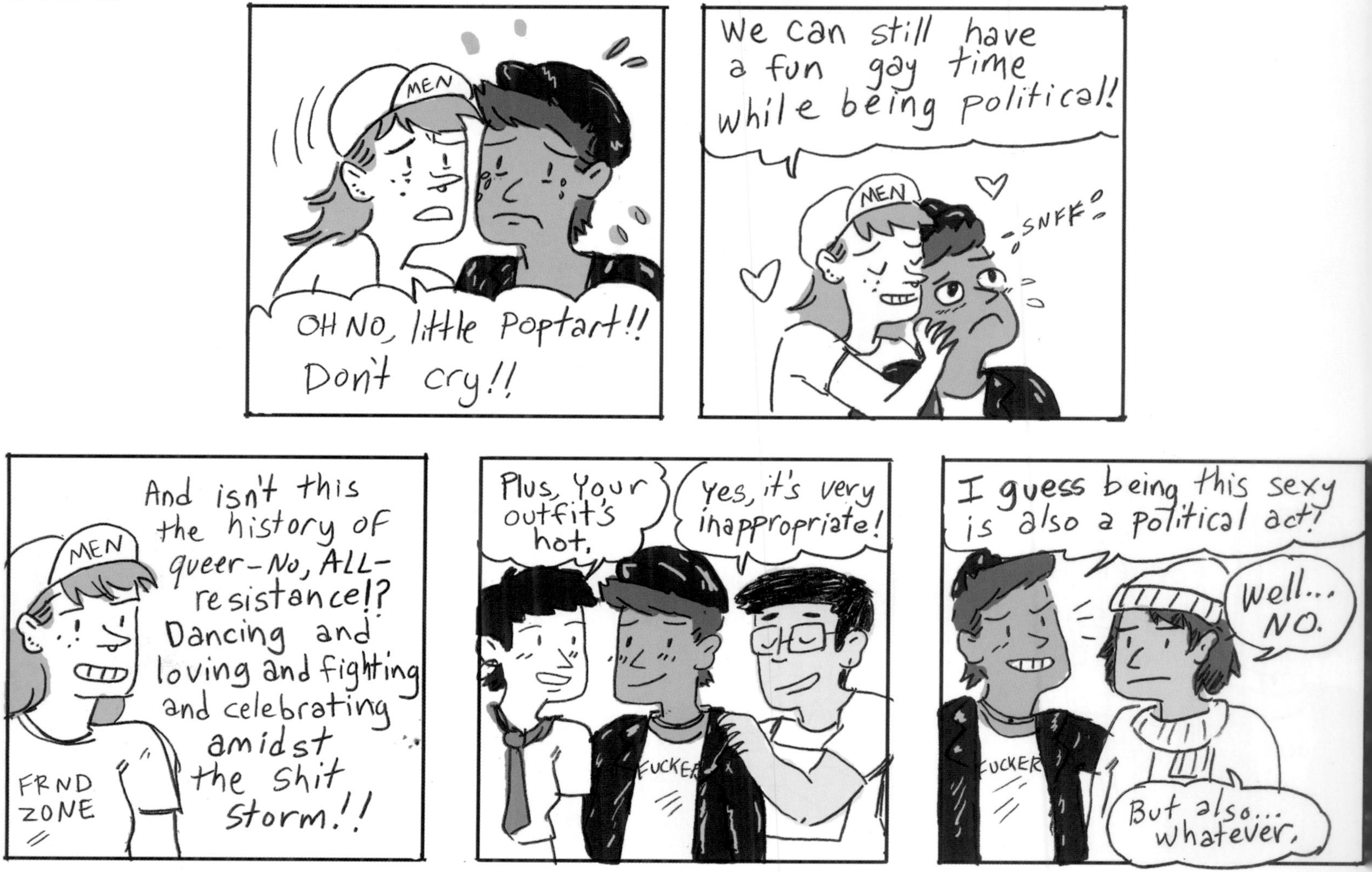
MEN
OH NO, little Poptart!! Don't cry!!
We can still have a fun gay time while being political!
MEN
SNFF
MEN
And isn't this the history of queer-No, ALL-resistance!? Dancing and loving and fighting and celebrating amidst the shit storm!!
FRND ZONE
Plus, your outfit's hot.
Yes, it's very inappropriate!
FUCKER
I guess being this sexy is also a political act!
Well... NO.
FUCKER
But also... whatever.

Astrology is Real and Powerful

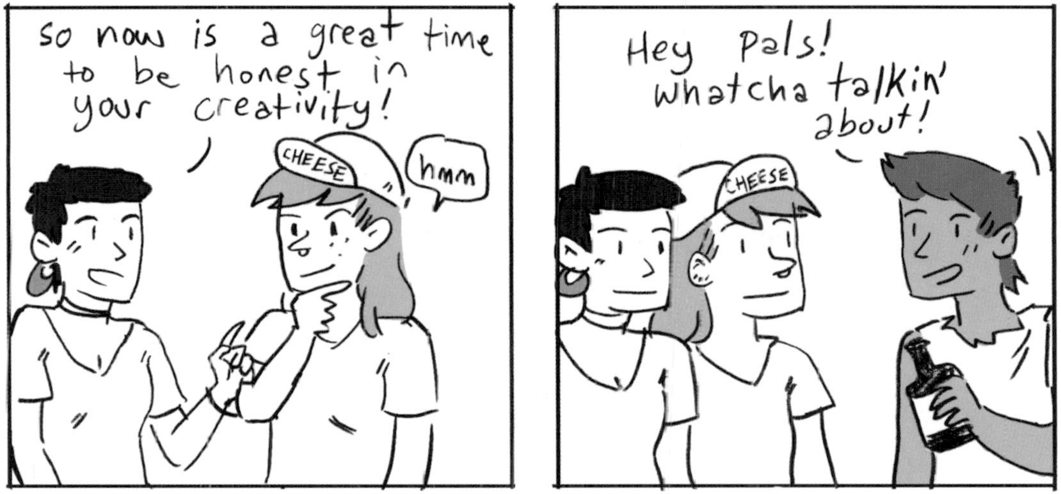
so now is a great time to be honest in your creativity!
hmm
Hey Pals! whatcha talkin' about!
CHEESE

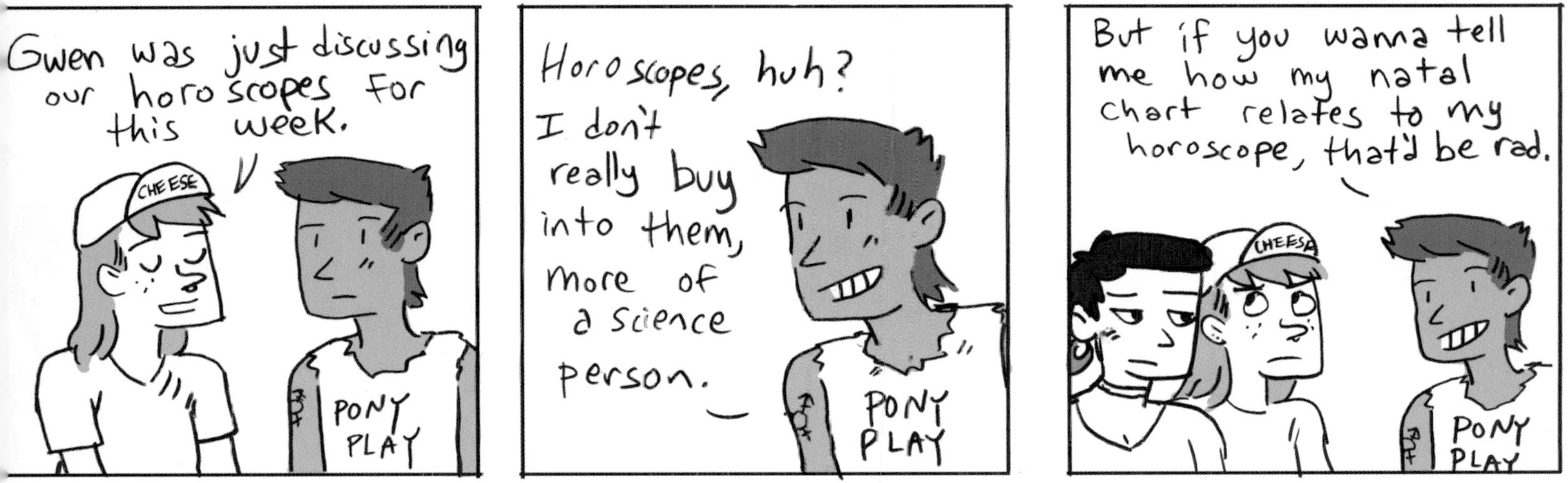
Gwen was just discussing our horoscopes for this week.
Horoscopes, huh? I don't really buy into them, more of a science person.
But if you wanna tell me how my natal chart relates to my horoscope, that'd be rad.
CHEESE
PONY PLAY

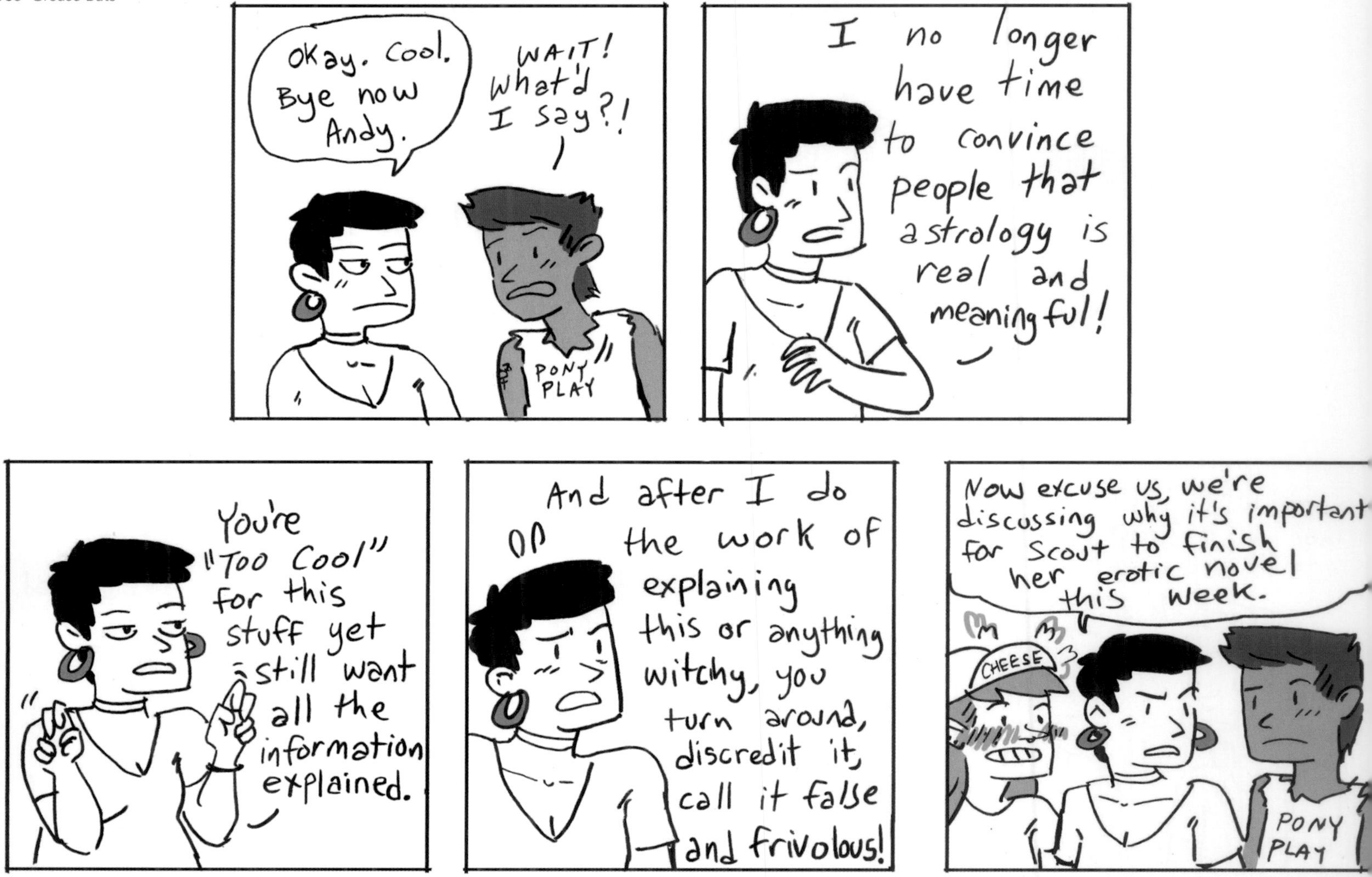
Okay. Cool. Bye now Andy.
WAIT! What'd I say?!
PONY PLAY
I no longer have time to convince people that astrology is real and meaningful!
You're "Too Cool" for this stuff yet still want all the information explained.
And after I do the work of explaining this or anything witchy, you turn around, discredit it, call it false and frivolous!
Now excuse us, we're discussing why it's important for Scout to finish her erotic novel this week.
CHEESE
PONY PLAY

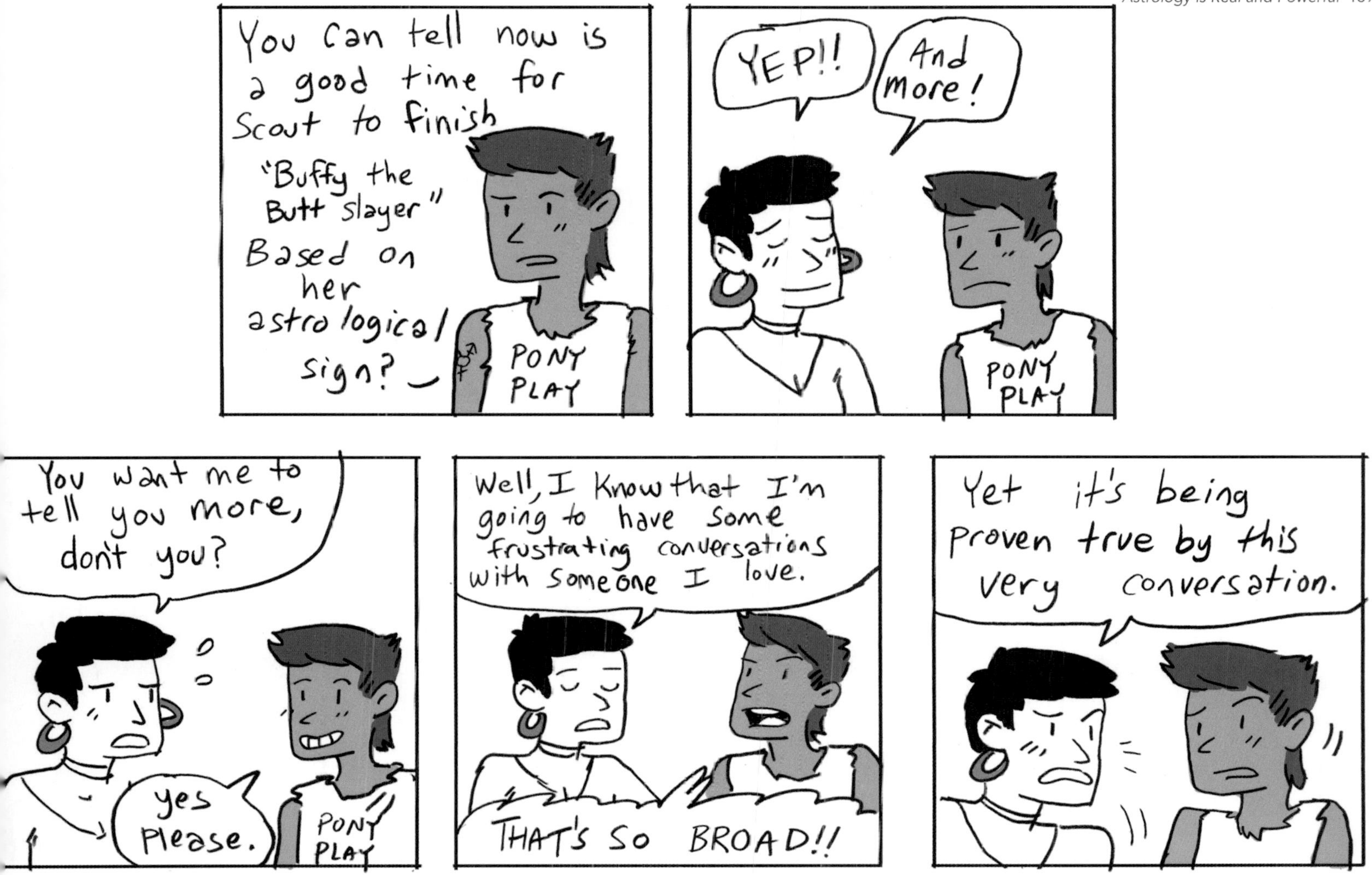
You can tell now is a good time for Scout to finish "Buffy the Butt slayer" Based on her astrological sign?
PONY PLAY
YEP!!
And more!
PONY PLAY
You want me to tell you more, don't you?
yes Please.
PONY PLAY
Well, I Know that I'm going to have some frustrating conversations with someone I love.
THAT'S SO BROAD!!
Yet it's being proven true by this very conversation.

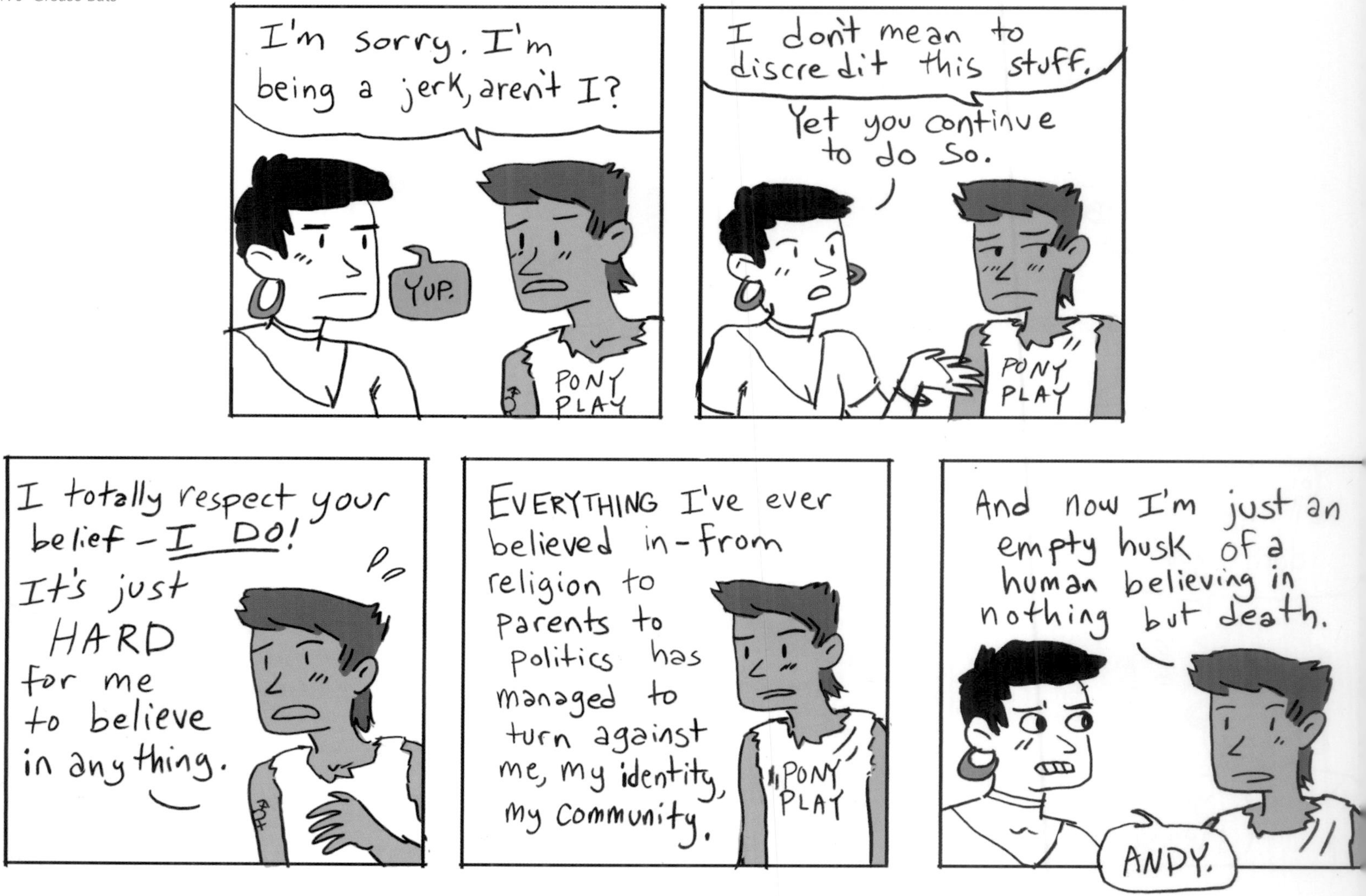
I'm sorry. I'm being a jerk, aren't I?
YUP.
PONY PLAY
I don't mean to discredit this stuff.
Yet you continue to do so.
PONY PLAY
I totally respect your belief - I DO! It's just HARD for me to believe in anything.
EVERYTHING I've ever believed in - from religion to parents to politics has managed to turn against me, my identity, my community.
PONY PLAY
And now I'm just an empty husk of a human believing in nothing but death.
ANDY.

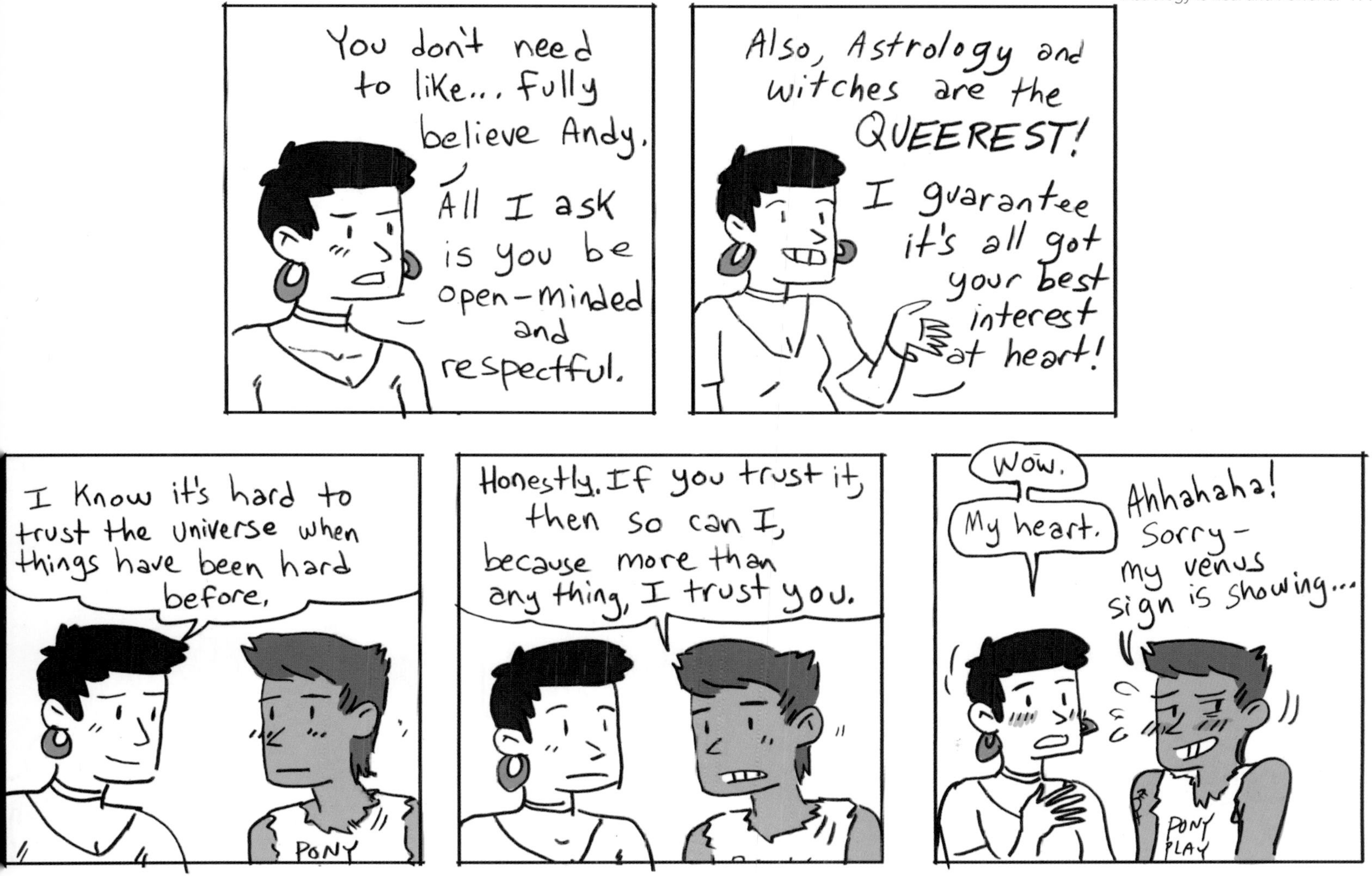
You don't need to like... fully believe Andy.
All I ask is you be open-minded and respectful.
Also, Astrology and witches are the QUEEREST!
I guarantee it's all got your best interest at heart!
I Know it's hard to trust the universe when things have been hard before,
PONY
Honestly. If you trust it, then so can I, because more than any thing, I trust you.
Wow.
My heart.
Ahhahaha! Sorry - my venus sign is showing...
PONY PLAY

Eat a Carrot

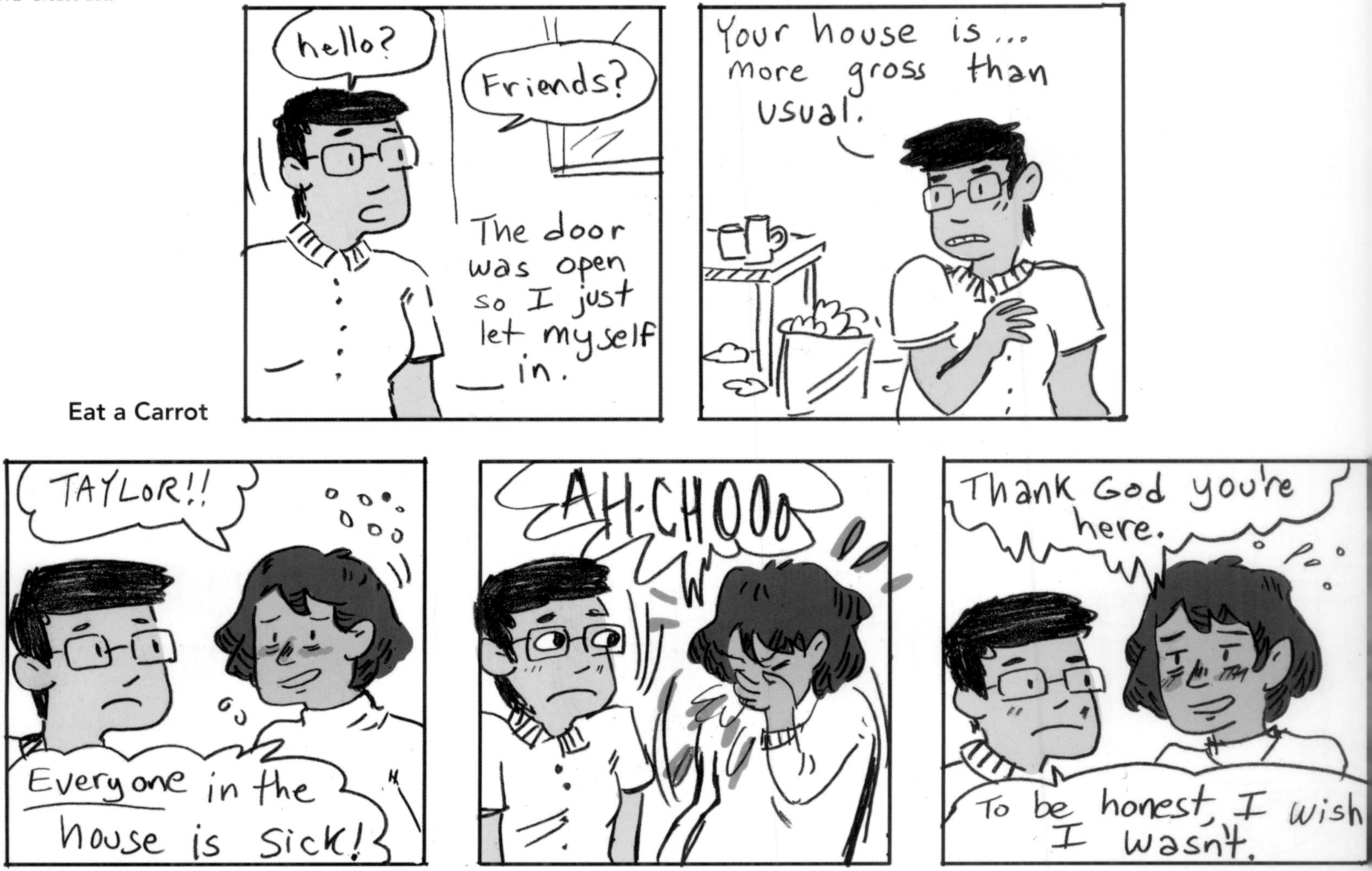
hello?
Friends?
The door was open so I just let myself in.
Your house is... more gross than usual.
TAYLOR!!
Everyone in the house is sick!
AH-CHOOO
Thank God you're here.
To be honest, I wish I wasn't.

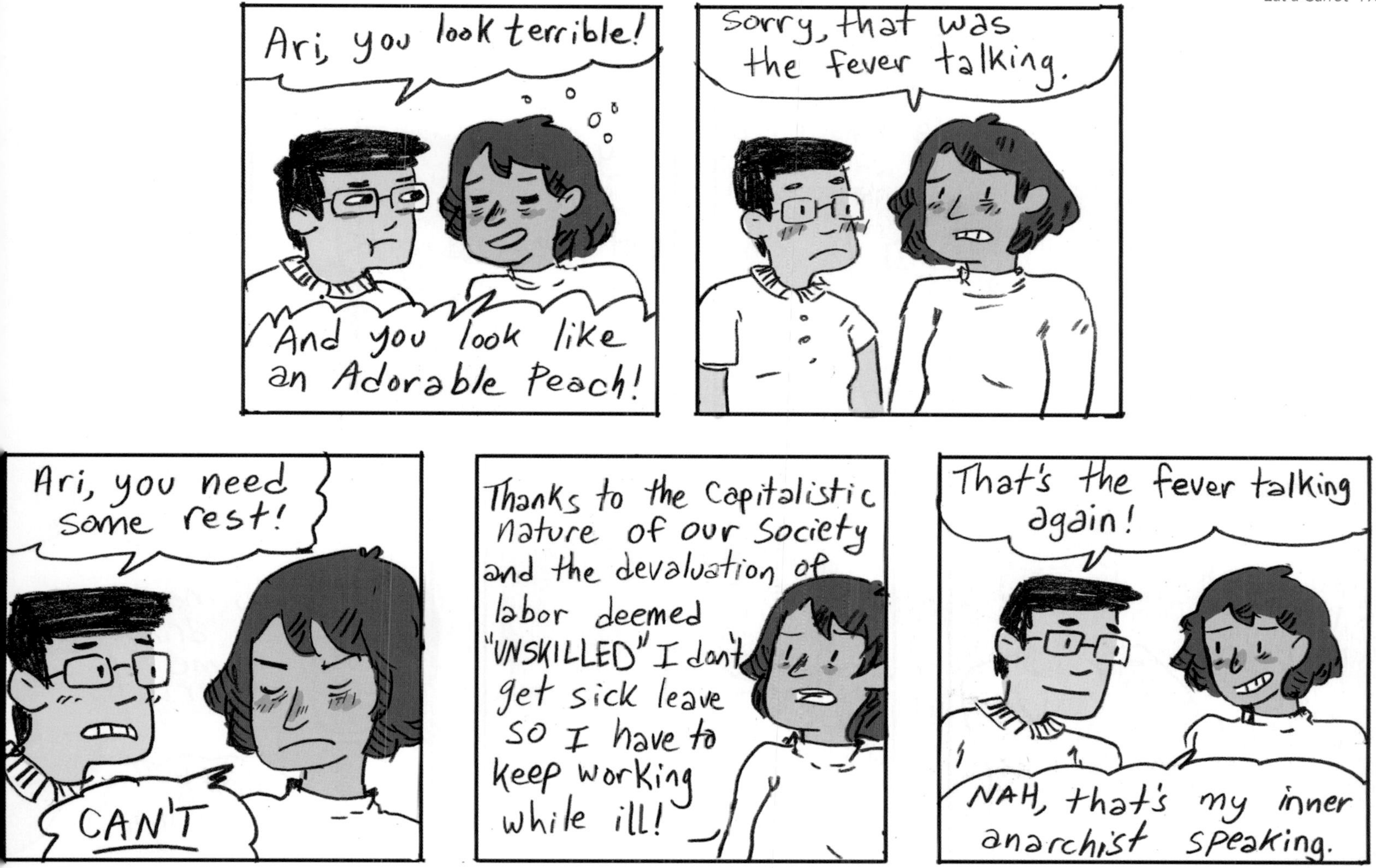
Ari, you look terrible!
And you look like an Adorable Peach!
Sorry, that was the fever talking.
Ari, you need some rest!
CAN'T
Thanks to the capitalistic nature of our society and the devaluation of labor deemed "UNSKILLED" I don't get sick leave so I have to keep working while ill!
That's the fever talking again!
NAH, that's my inner anarchist speaking.

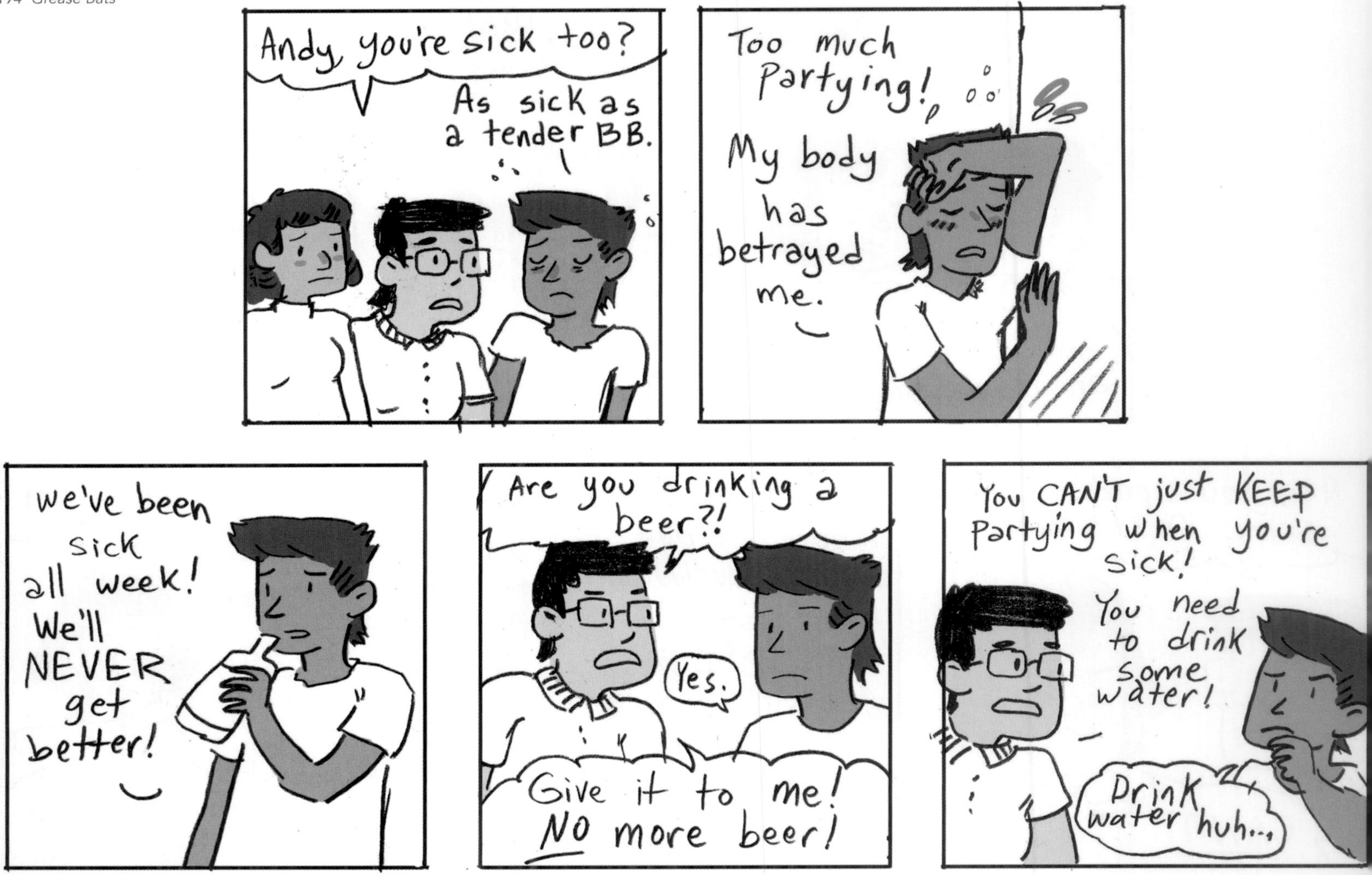

Andy, you're sick too?
As sick as a tender BB.
Too much Partying!
My body has betrayed me.
we've been sick all week! We'll NEVER get better!
Are you drinking a beer?!
Yes.
Give it to me! NO more beer!
You CAN'T just KEEP Partying when you're sick!
You need to drink some water!
Drink water huh...

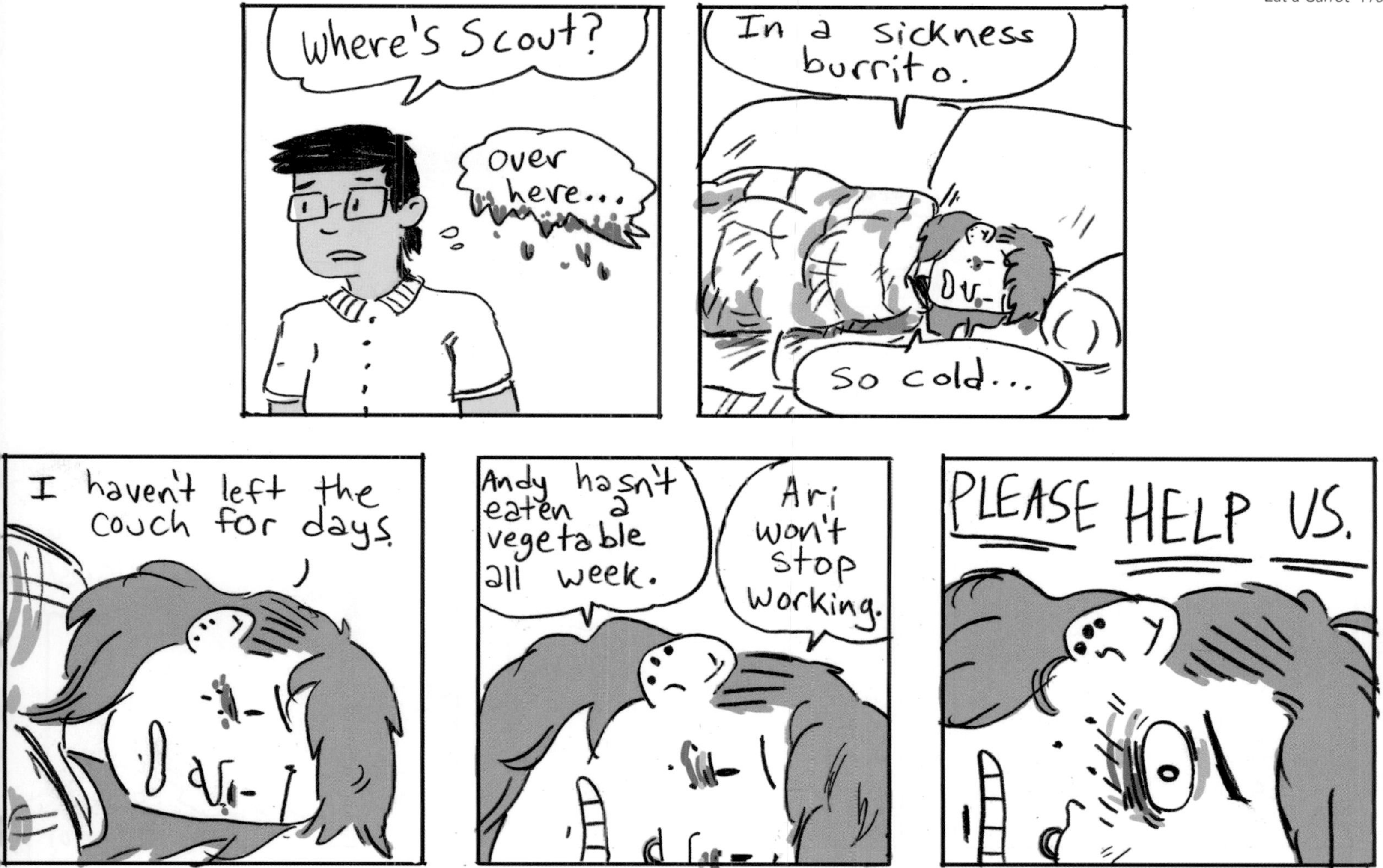
Where's Scout?
Over here...
In a sickness burrito.
So cold...
I haven't left the couch for days.
Andy hasn't eaten a vegetable all week.
Ari won't stop working.
PLEASE HELP US.

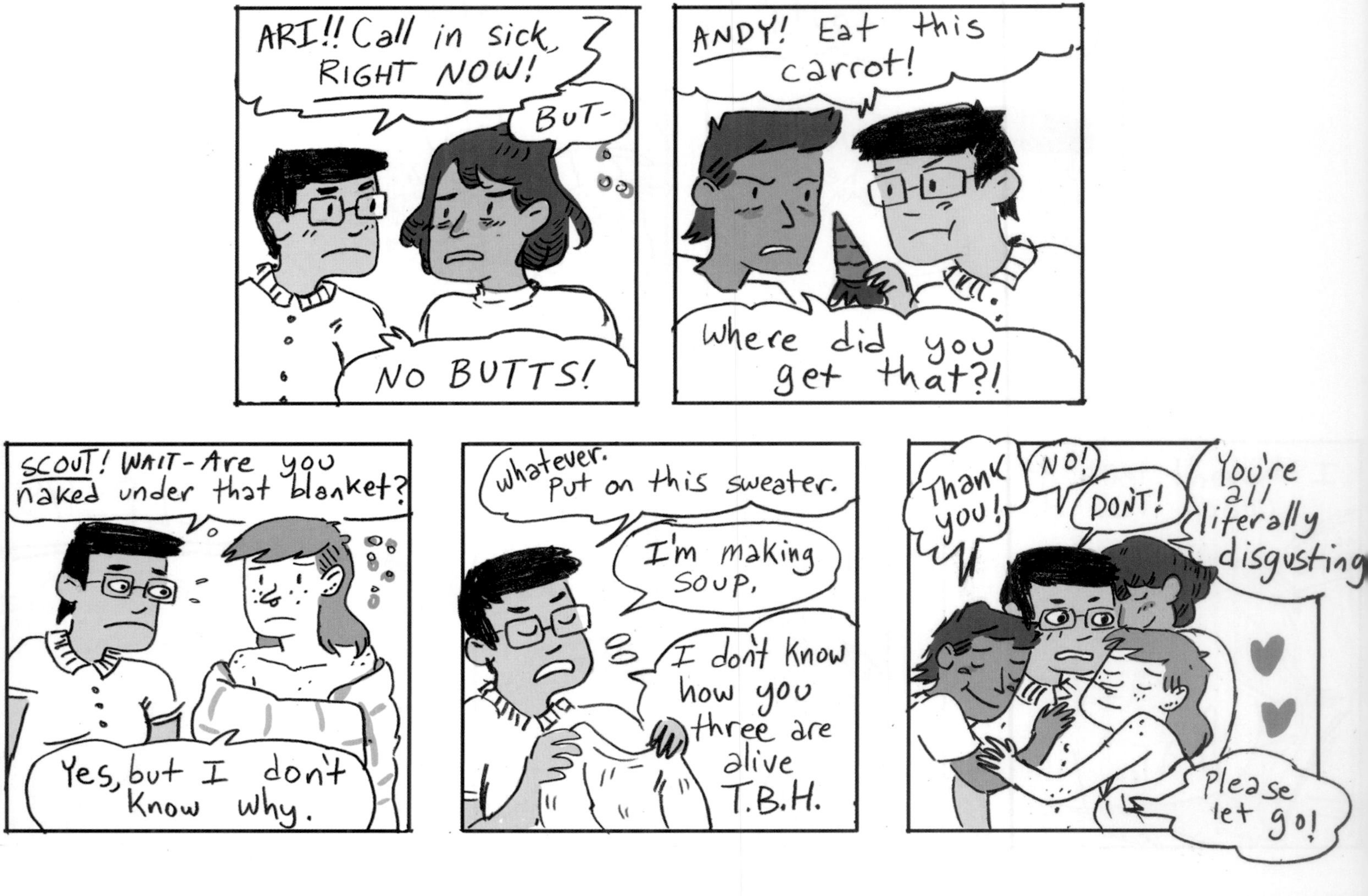
ARI!! Call in sick, RIGHT NOW!
BUT-
NO BUTTS!
ANDY! Eat this carrot!
Where did you get that?!
SCOUT! WAIT- Are you naked under that blanket?
Yes, but I don't know why.
whatever. Put on this sweater.
I'm making soup.
I don't know how you three are alive T.B.H.
Thank you!
NO!
DONT!
You're all literally disgusting
Please let go!

Trivia

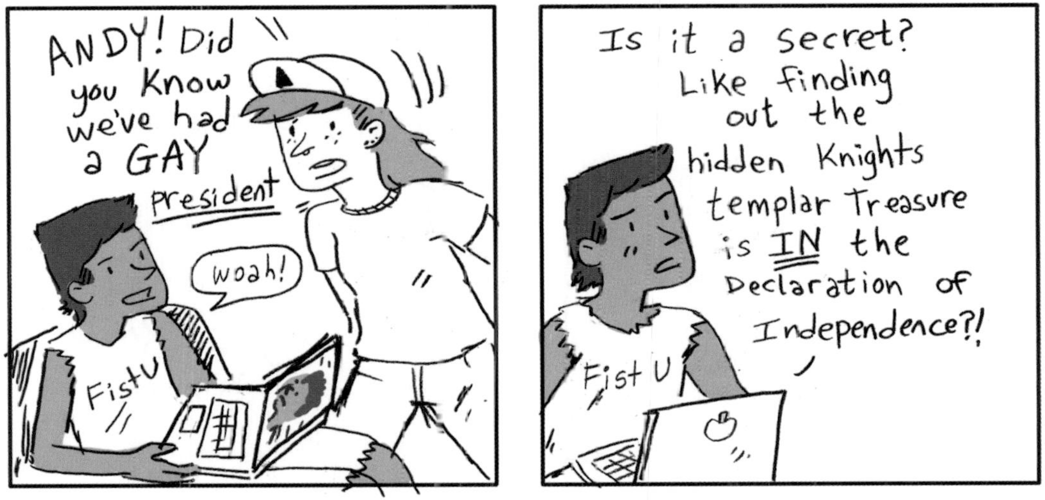
ANDY! Did you Know we've had a GAY president
woah!
Is it a secret? Like finding out the hidden Knights templar Treasure is IN the Declaration of Independence?!
Fist U

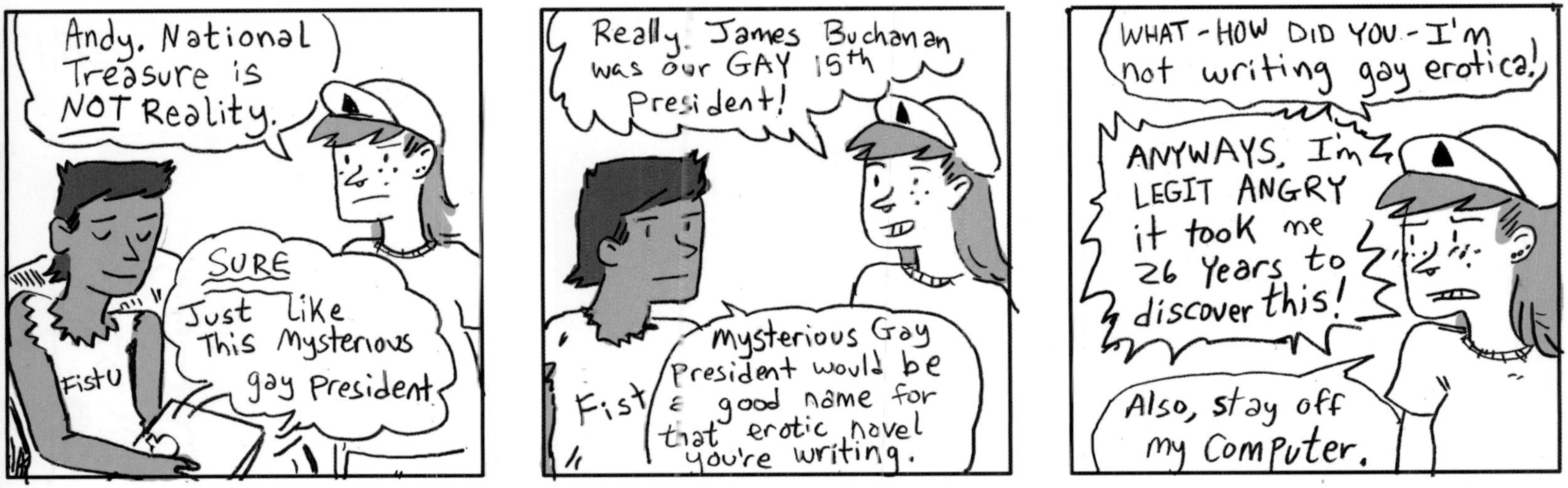
Andy. National Treasure is NOT Reality.
SURE Just like This Mysterious gay President
FistU
Really. James Buchanan was our GAY 15th President!
Mysterious Gay President would be a good name for that erotic novel you're writing.
WHAT - HOW DID YOU - I'm not writing gay erotica!
ANYWAYS, I'm LEGIT ANGRY it took me 26 Years to discover this!
Also, stay off my Computer.

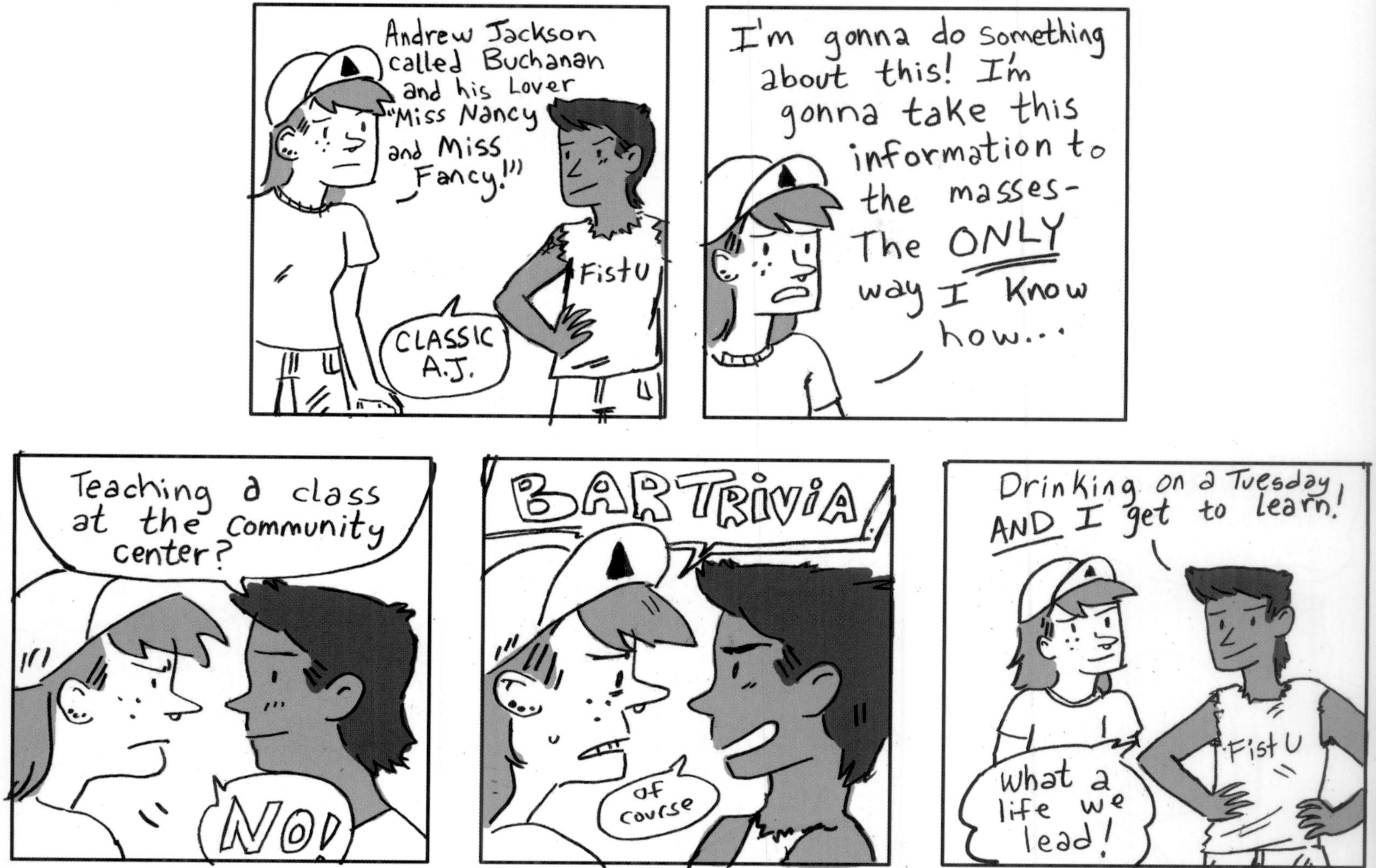
Andrew Jackson called Buchanan and his Lover "Miss Nancy and Miss Fancy!"
FistU
CLASSIC A.J.
I'm gonna do something about this! I'm gonna take this information to the masses- The ONLY way I Know how...
Teaching a class at the community center?
NO!
BARTRIVIA
Of course
Drinking on a Tuesday, AND I get to learn!
What a life we lead!
FistU

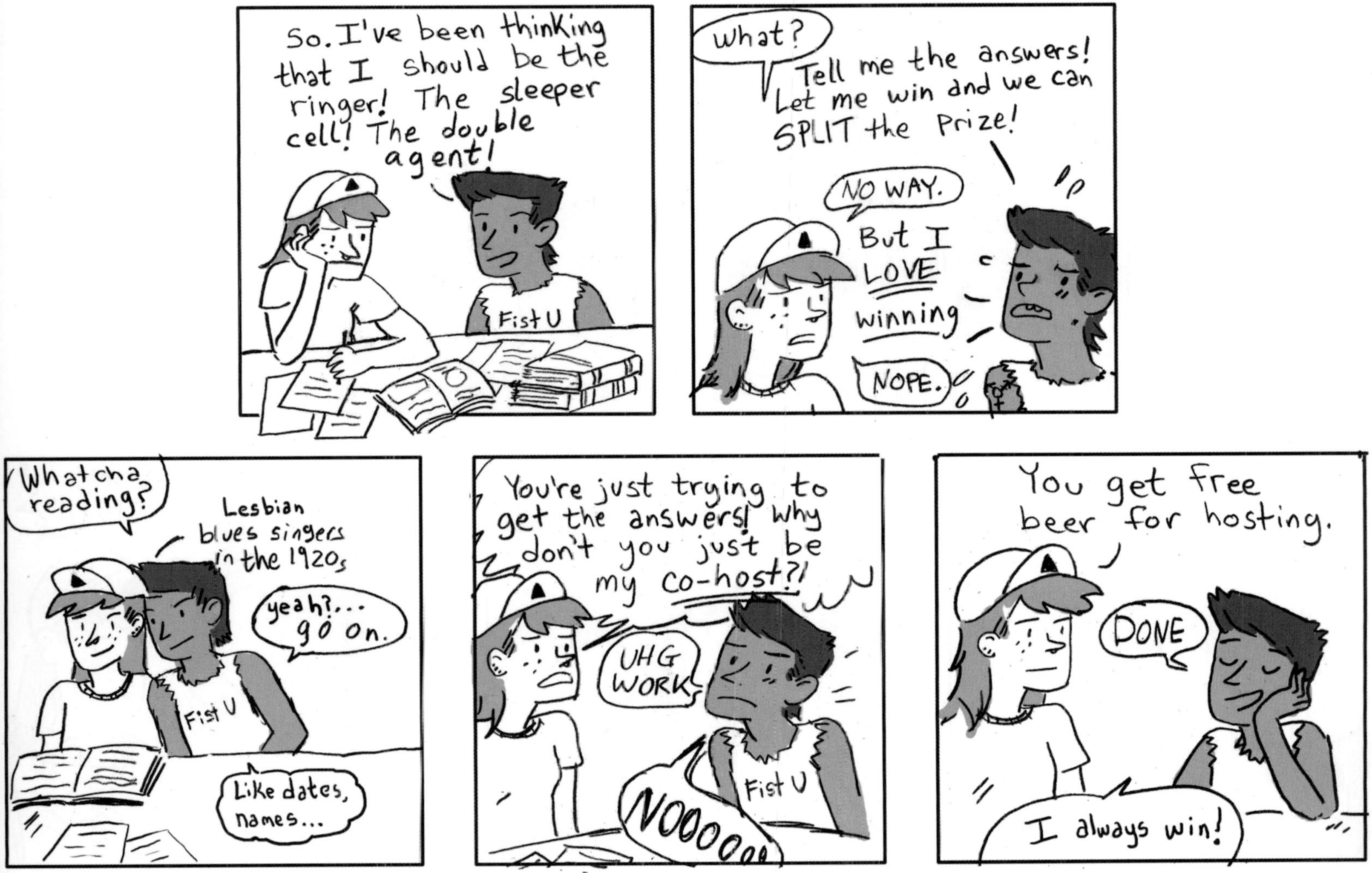
So. I've been thinking that I should be the ringer! The sleeper cell! The double agent!
Fist U
what?
Tell me the answers! Let me win and we can SPLIT the prize!
NO WAY.
But I LOVE winning
NOPE.
Whatcha reading?
Lesbian blues singers in the 1920s
yeah?... go on.
Fist U
Like dates, names...
You're just trying to get the answers! Why don't you just be my co-host?!
UHG WORK
Fist U
NOOOOooo
You get free beer for hosting.
DONE
I always win!

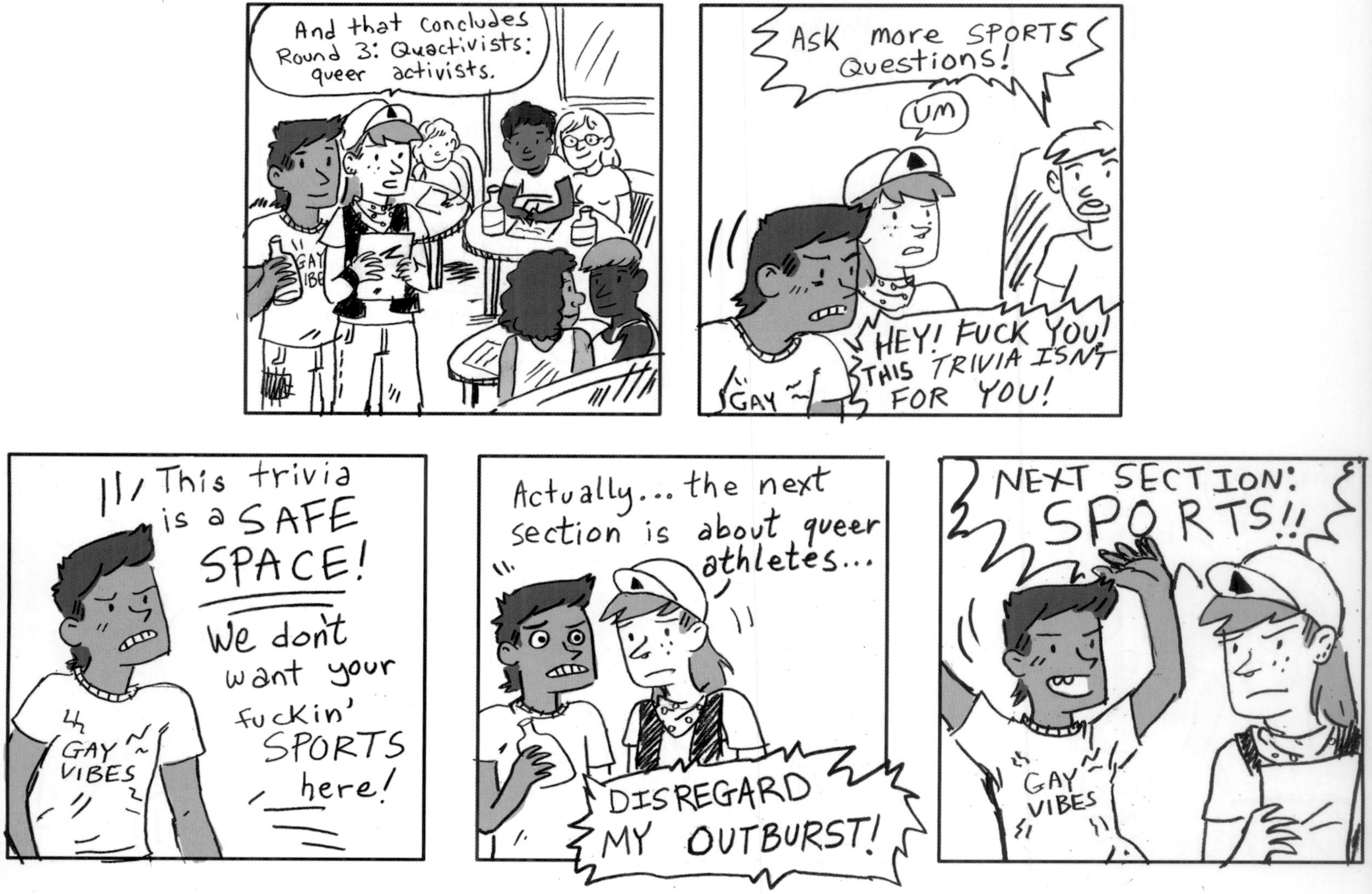

And that concludes Round 3: Quactivists: queer activists.
GAY VIBES
Ask more SPORTS Questions!
UM
HEY! FUCK YOU! THIS TRIVIA ISN'T FOR YOU!
GAY
This trivia is a SAFE SPACE!
We don't want your fuckin' SPORTS here!
GAY VIBES
Actually... the next section is about queer athletes...
DISREGARD MY OUTBURST!
NEXT SECTION: SPORTS!!
GAY VIBES

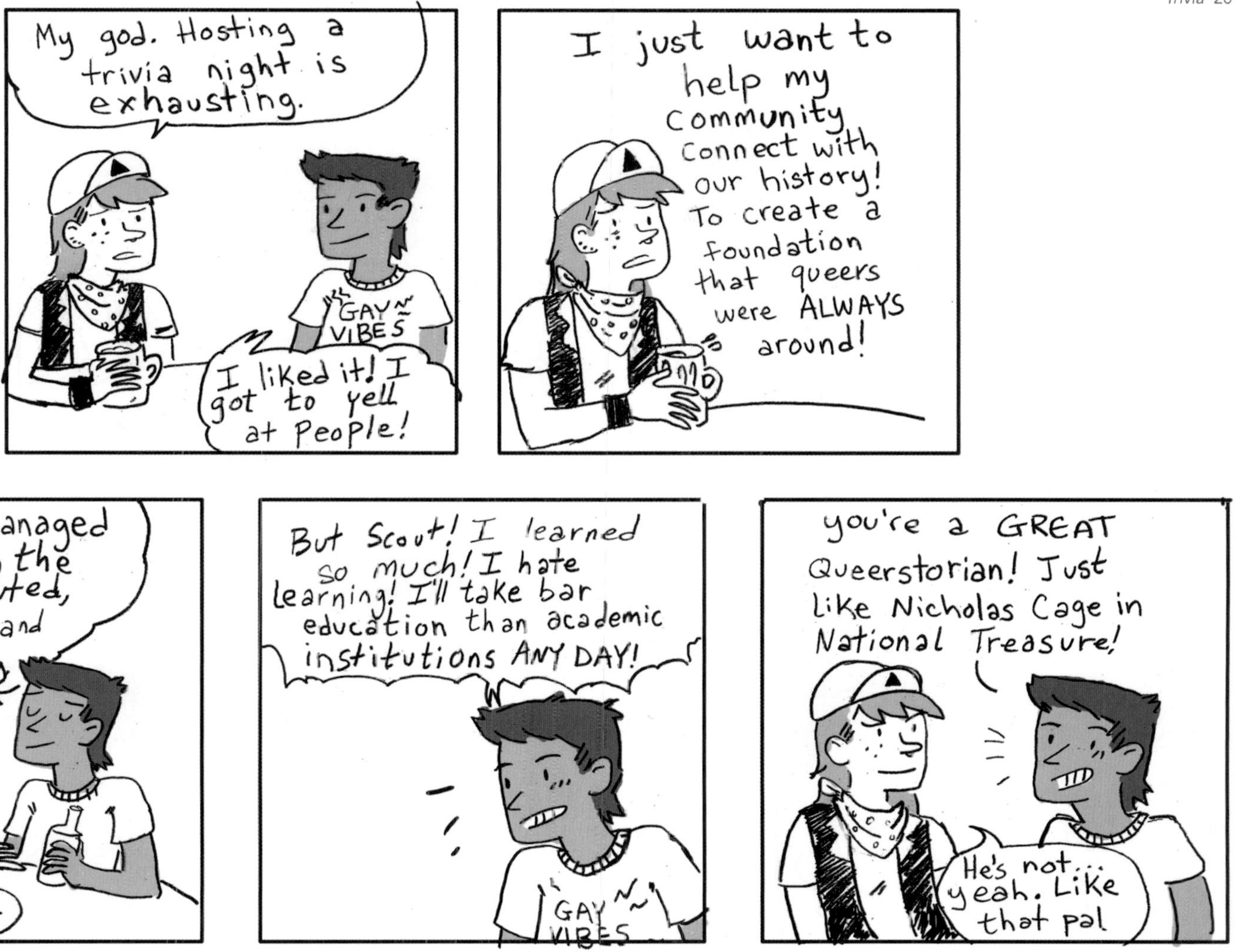
My god. Hosting a trivia night is exhausting.
I liked it! I got to yell at People!
I just want to help my community connect with our history! To create a foundation that queers were ALWAYS around!
And you managed to do it in the most convoluted, work-intensive and roundabout way.
Uhg.
But Scout! I learned so much! I hate learning! I'll take bar education than academic institutions ANY DAY!
You're a GREAT Queerstorian! Just Like Nicholas Cage in National Treasure!
He's not... yeah. Like that pal
GAY VIBES

Donut Worry About Tinder

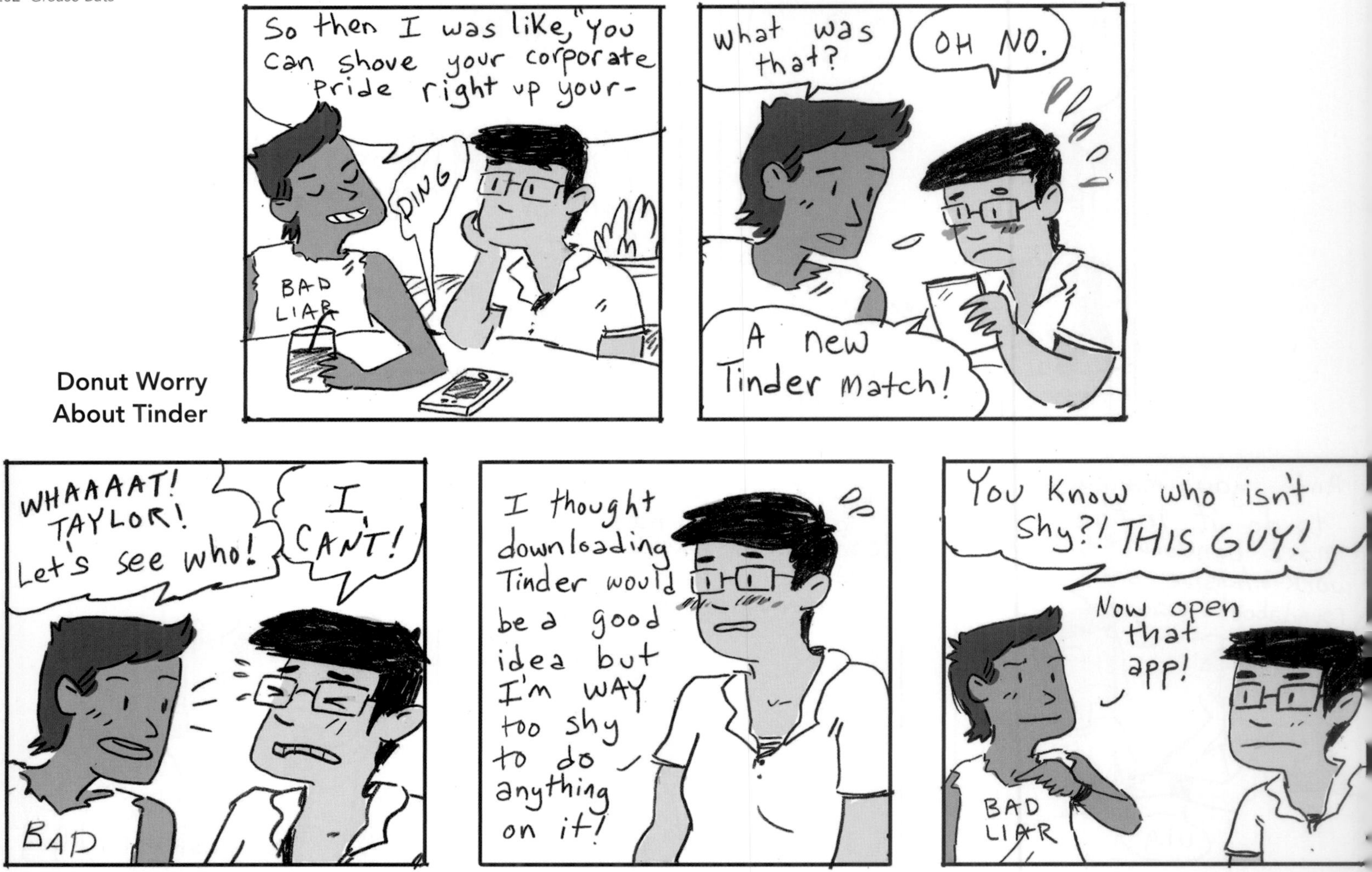
So then I was like, "You can shove your corporate pride right up your-
DING
BAD LIAR
What was that?
OH NO.
A new Tinder match!
WHAAAAT! TAYLOR! Let's see who!
I CAN'T!
BAD
I thought downloading Tinder would be a good idea but I'm WAY too shy to do anything on it!
You know who isn't shy?! THIS GUY!
Now open that app!
BAD LIAR

Panel 1: Here! You can take a peek at my profile first.

Panel 2: "Genderqueer leather daddy-in-training looking for a mommi, a boi or a brat. Open to other butch-sissies. I like hunkbabes, homosensuous hook-ups and NSFW Snaps. Rose emoji. Rose emoji. Rose emoji."

Panel 3: Andy, this is gibberish. Queers have their own language. Now let's see yours!

BAD LIAR

Panel 4: TAYLOR ·LESS THAN A MILE· I'M IN GRAD SCHOOL.

Panel 5: "I'm in grad school"?? THAT'S IT?! WHAT?! I AM in grad school!

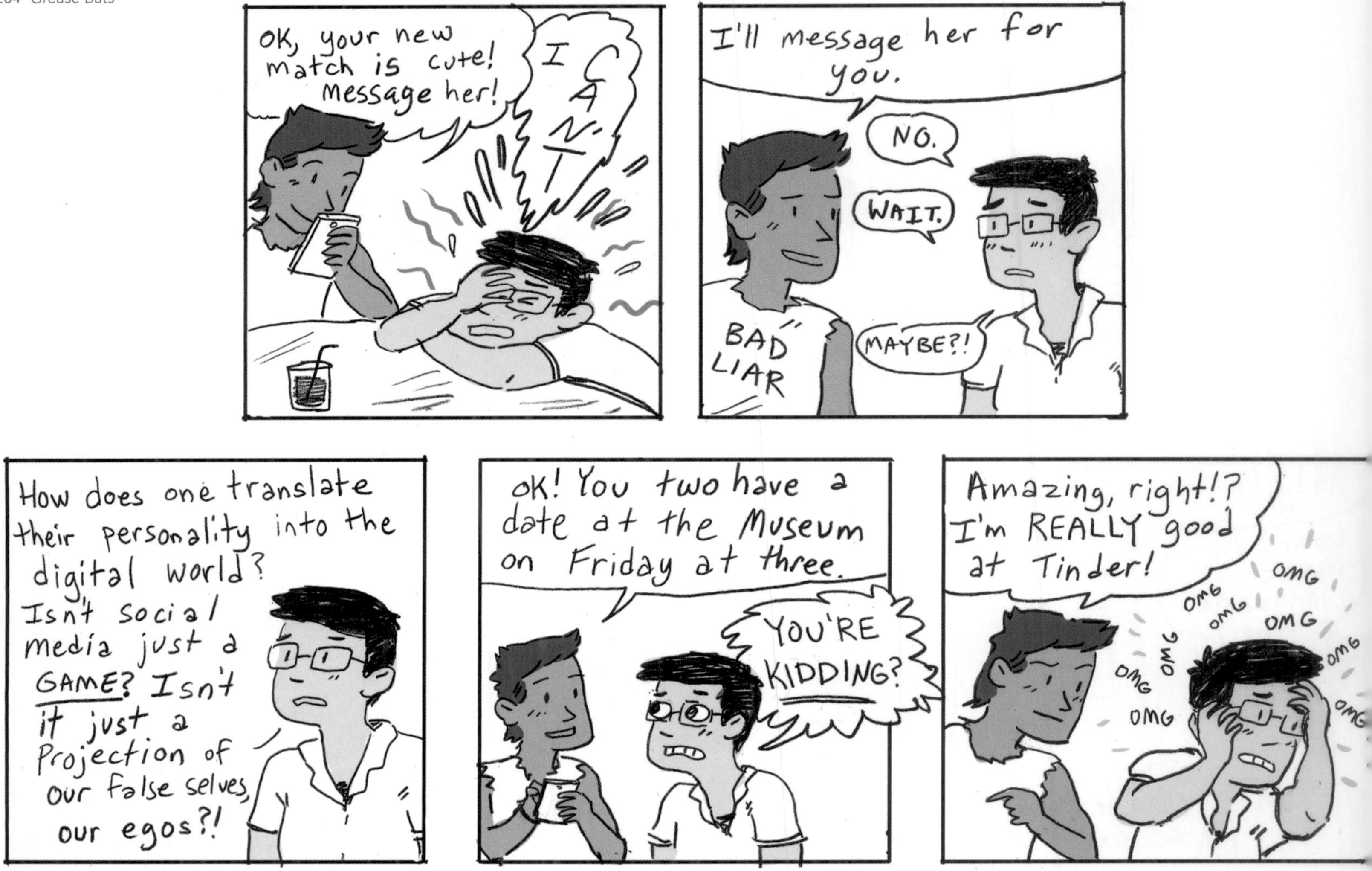
OK, your new match is cute! message her!
I CAN'T
I'll message her for you.
NO.
WAIT.
MAYBE?!
BAD LIAR
How does one translate their personality into the digital world? Isn't social media just a GAME? Isn't it just a projection of our false selves, our egos?!
OK! You two have a date at the Museum on Friday at three.
YOU'RE KIDDING?
Amazing, right!? I'm REALLY good at Tinder!
OMG OMG OMG OMG OMG OMG OMG OMG OMG OMG

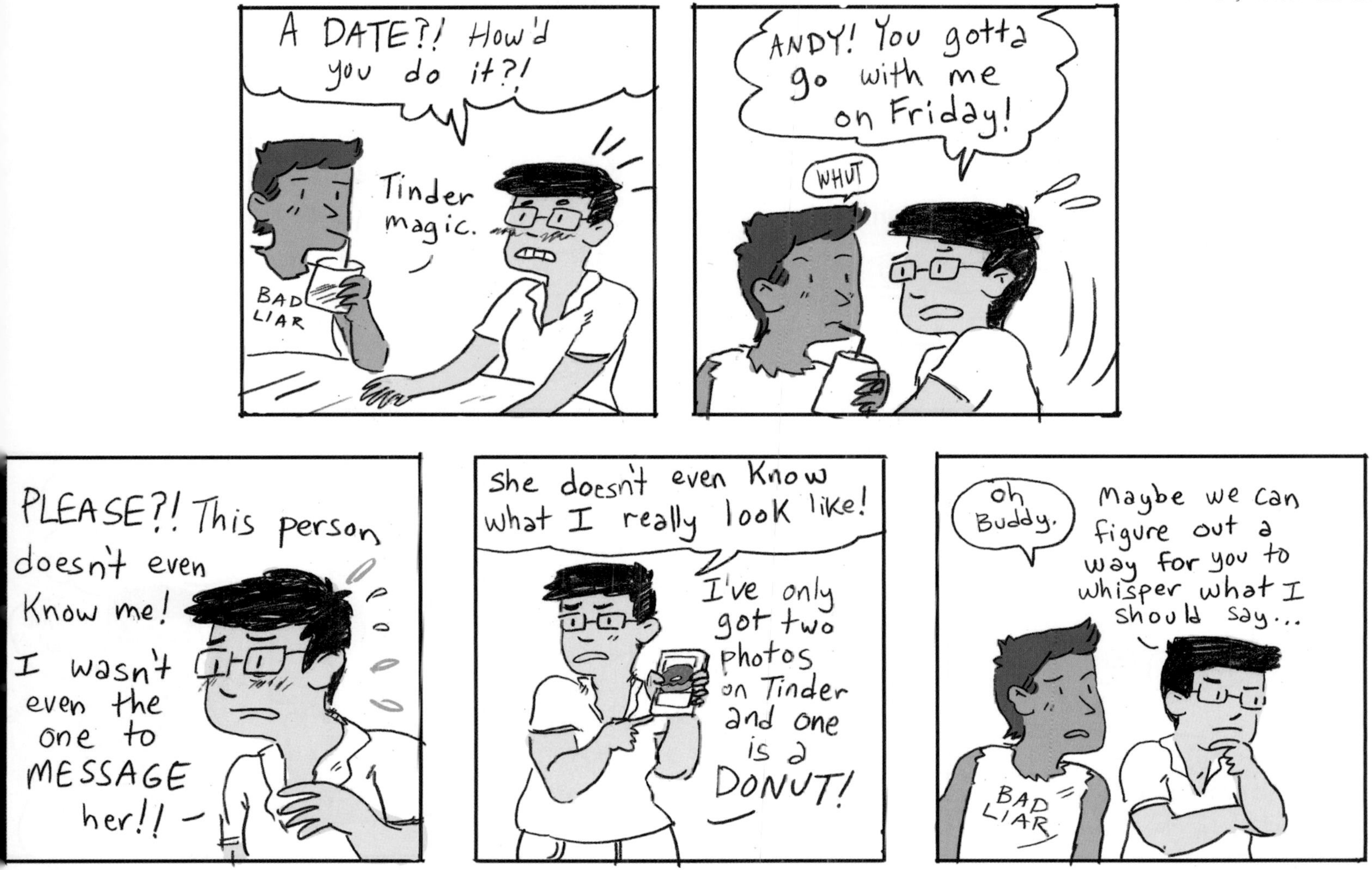
A DATE?! How'd you do it?!
Tinder magic.
BAD LIAR
ANDY! You gotta go with me on Friday!
WHUT
PLEASE?! This person doesn't even know me!
I wasn't even the one to MESSAGE her!!
She doesn't even know what I really look like!
I've only got two photos on Tinder and one is a DONUT!
Oh Buddy.
Maybe we can figure out a way for you to whisper what I should say...
BAD LIAR

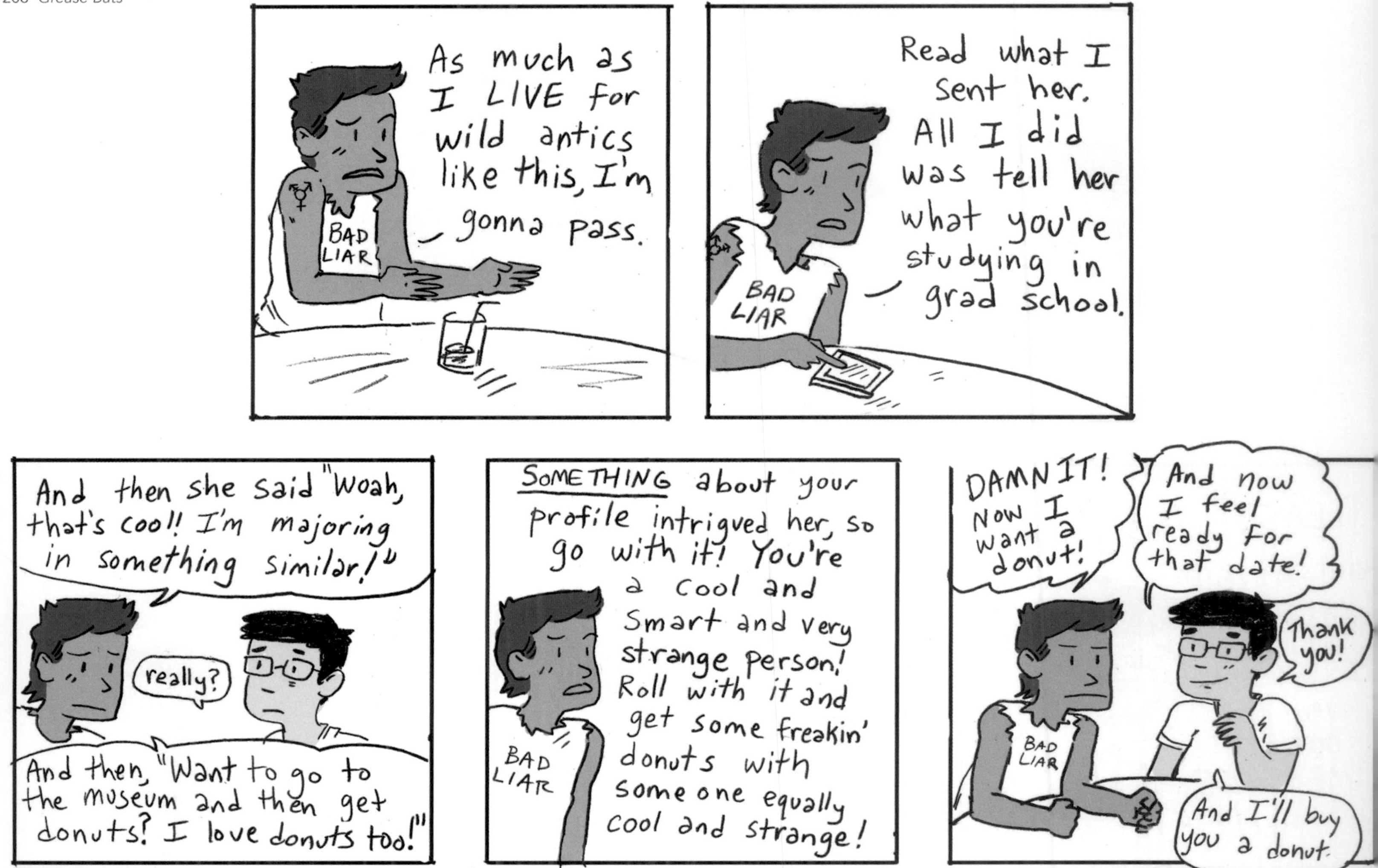
As much as I LIVE for wild antics like this, I'm gonna pass.
Read what I sent her. All I did was tell her what you're studying in grad school.
BAD LIAR
And then she said "Woah, that's cool! I'm majoring in something similar!"
really?
And then, "Want to go to the museum and then get donuts? I love donuts too!"
SOMETHING about your profile intrigued her, so go with it! You're a cool and smart and very strange person! Roll with it and get some freakin' donuts with someone equally cool and strange!
DAMNIT! Now I want a donut!
And now I feel ready for that date!
Thank you!
And I'll buy you a donut.

Homophobic Inheritance

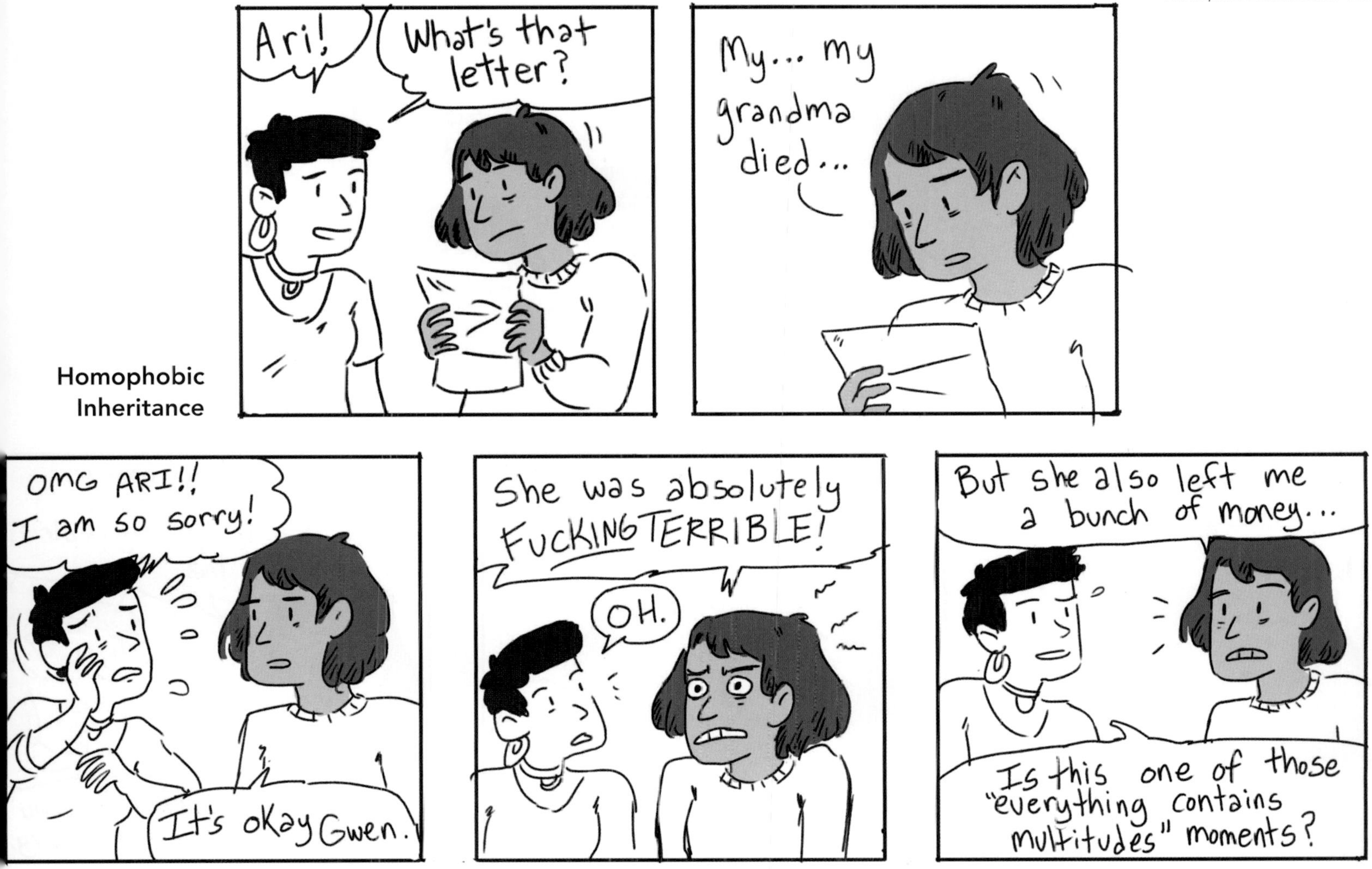
Ari!
What's that letter?
My... my grandma died...
OMG ARI!! I am so sorry!
It's okay Gwen.
She was absolutely FUCKING TERRIBLE!
OH.
But she also left me a bunch of money...
Is this one of those "everything contains multitudes" moments?

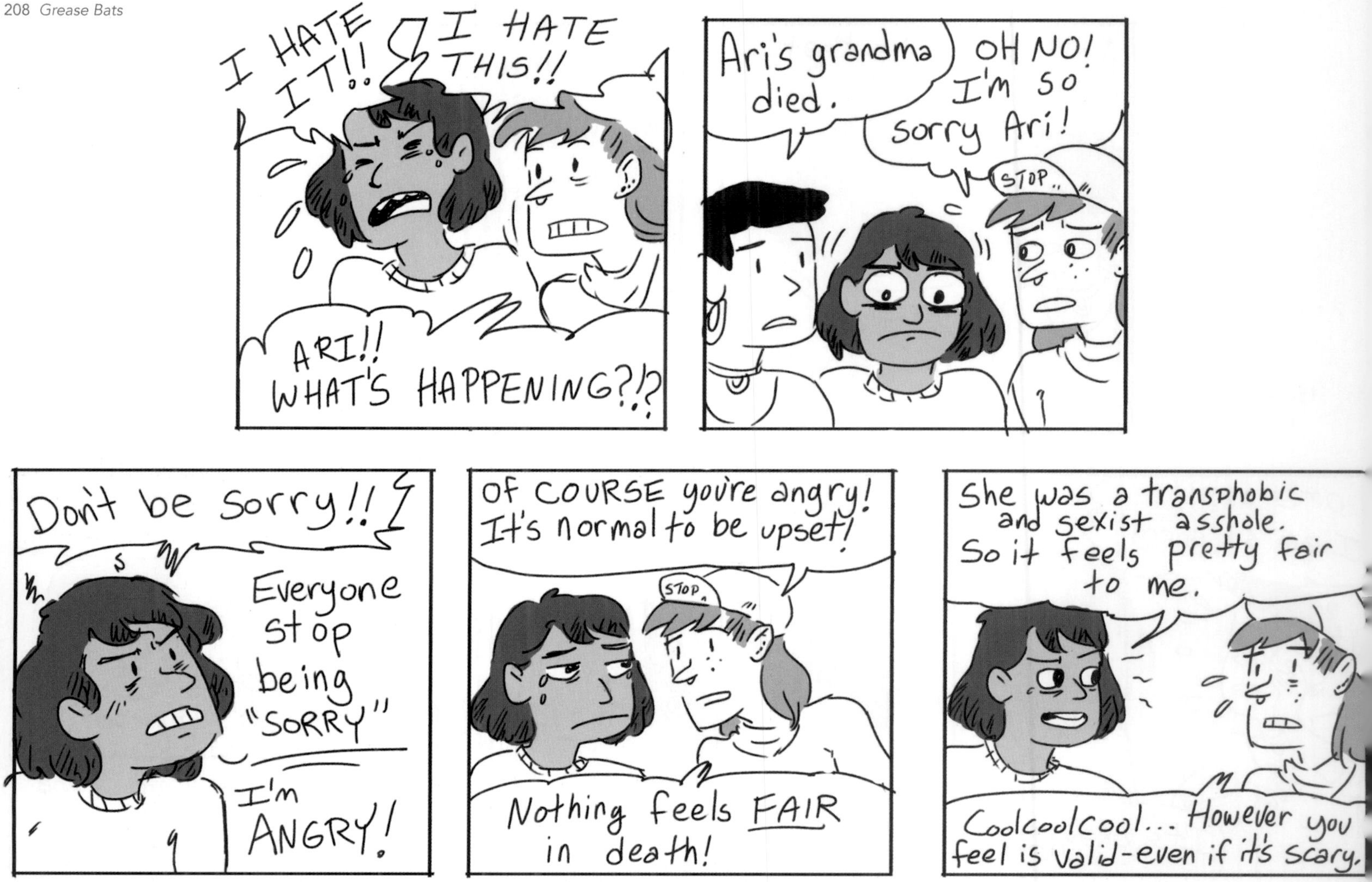
I HATE IT!!
I HATE THIS!!
ARI!! WHAT'S HAPPENING?!?
Ari's grandma died.
OH NO! I'm so sorry Ari!
STOP..
Don't be sorry!!
Everyone stop being "SORRY"
I'm ANGRY!
OF COURSE you're angry! It's normal to be upset!
STOP..
Nothing feels FAIR in death!
She was a transphobic and sexist asshole. So it feels pretty fair to me.
Coolcoolcool... However you feel is valid-even if it's scary.

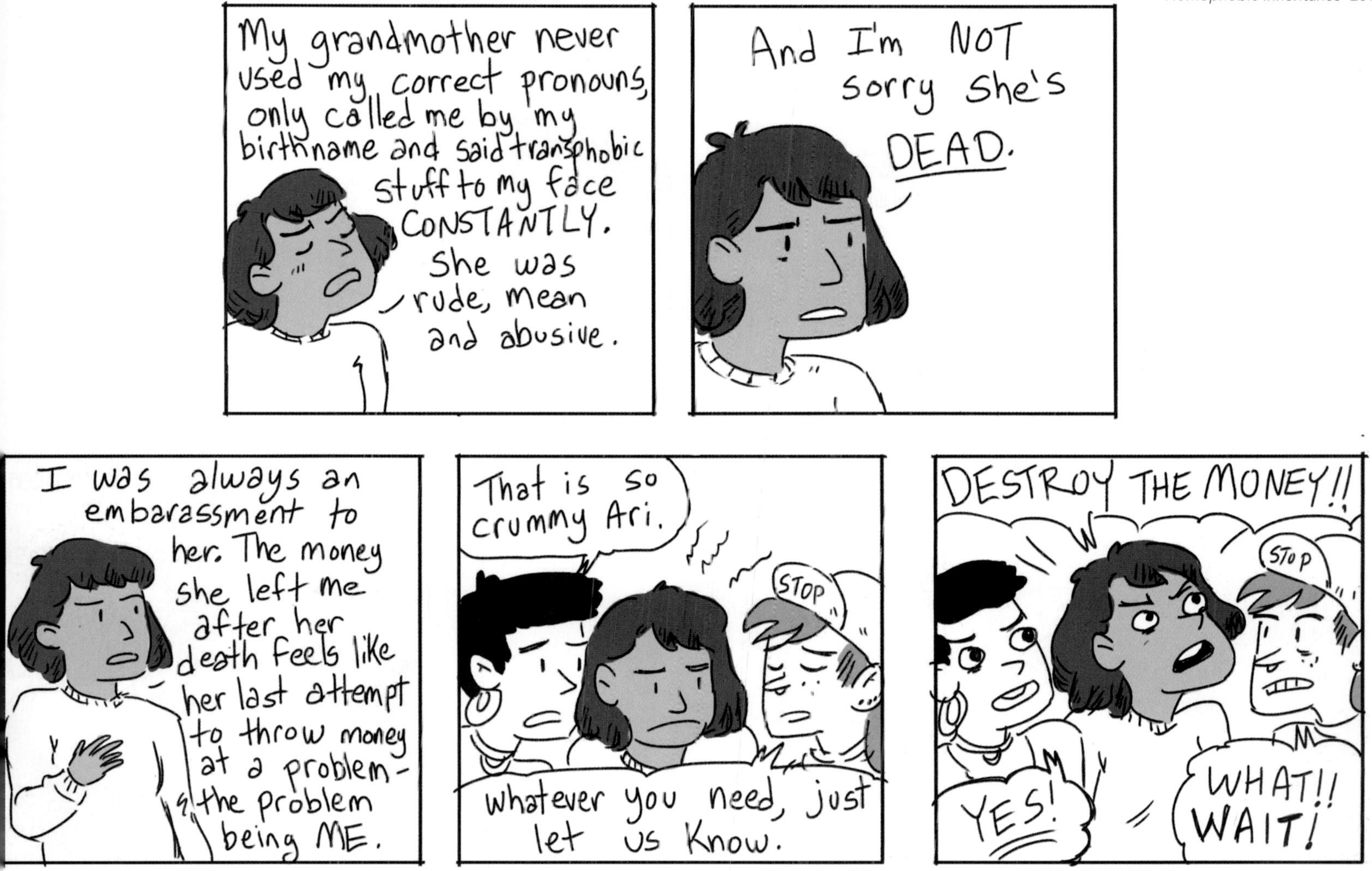
My grandmother never used my correct pronouns, only called me by my birthname and said transphobic stuff to my face CONSTANTLY. She was rude, mean and abusive.
And I'm NOT sorry she's DEAD.
I was always an embarassment to her. The money she left me after her death feels like her last attempt to throw money at a problem - the problem being ME.
That is so crummy Ari.
STOP
whatever you need, just let us know.
DESTROY THE MONEY!!
STOP
YES!
WHAT!! WAIT!

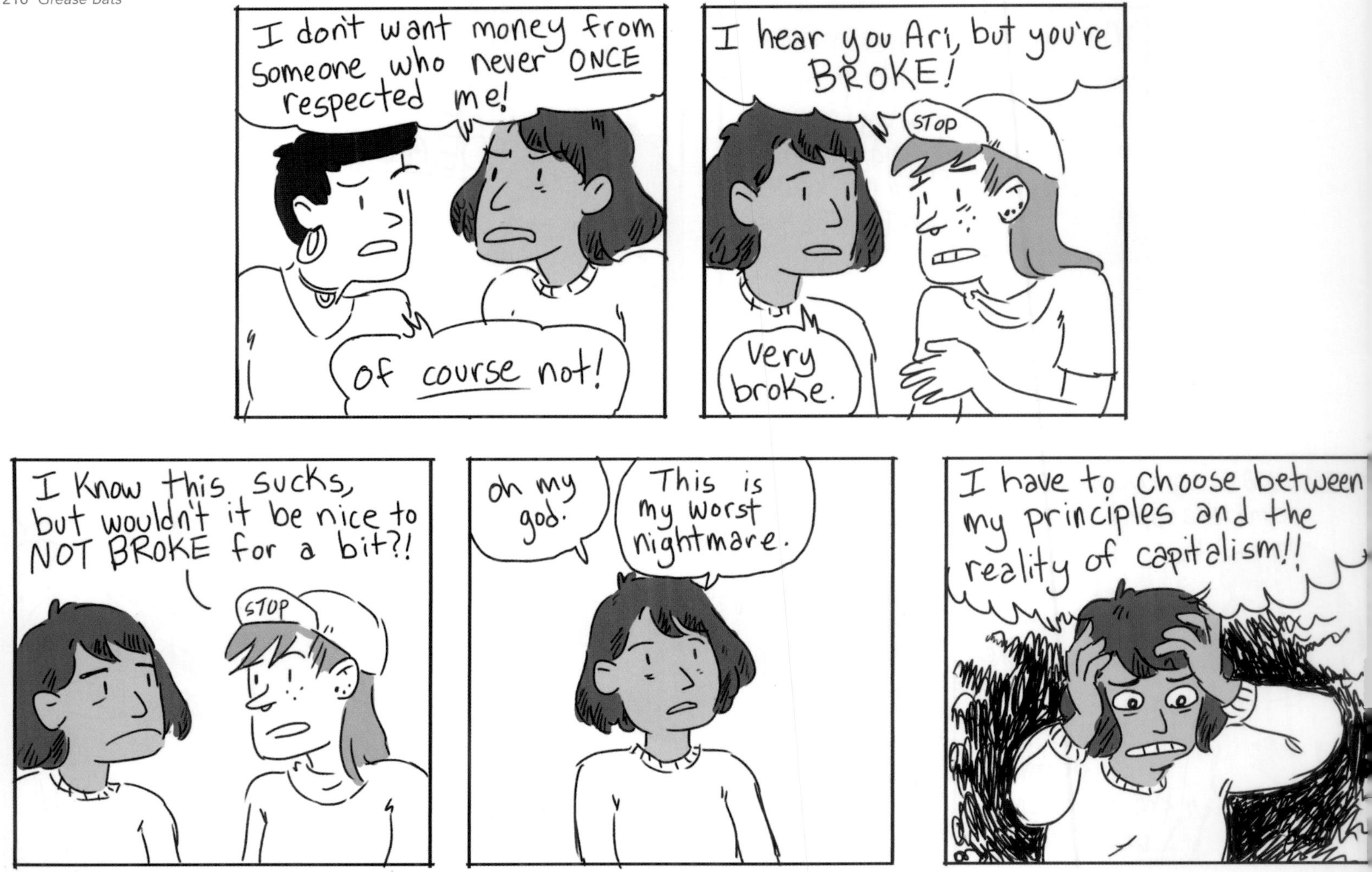
I don't want money from someone who never ONCE respected me!
of course not!
I hear you Ari, but you're BROKE!
Very broke.
STOP
I Know this sucks, but wouldn't it be nice to NOT BROKE for a bit?!
STOP
oh my god.
This is my worst nightmare.
I have to choose between my principles and the reality of capitalism!!

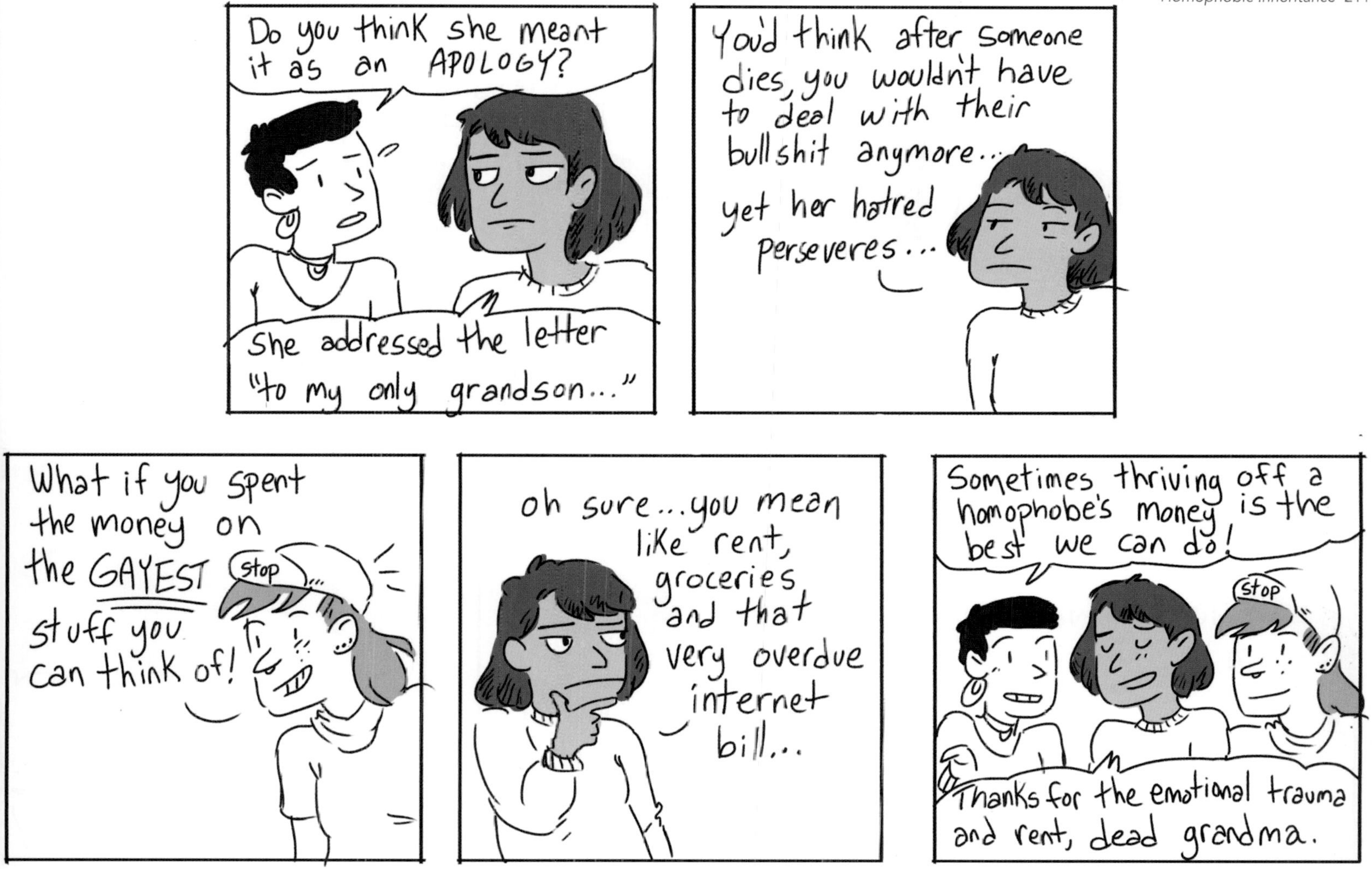
Do you think she meant it as an APOLOGY?
She addressed the letter "to my only grandson..."
You'd think after someone dies, you wouldn't have to deal with their bullshit anymore...
yet her hatred perseveres...
What if you spent the money on the GAYEST stuff you can think of!
STOP
oh sure...you mean like rent, groceries and that very overdue internet bill...
Sometimes thriving off a homophobe's money is the best we can do!
STOP
Thanks for the emotional trauma and rent, dead grandma.

New Relationship Energy

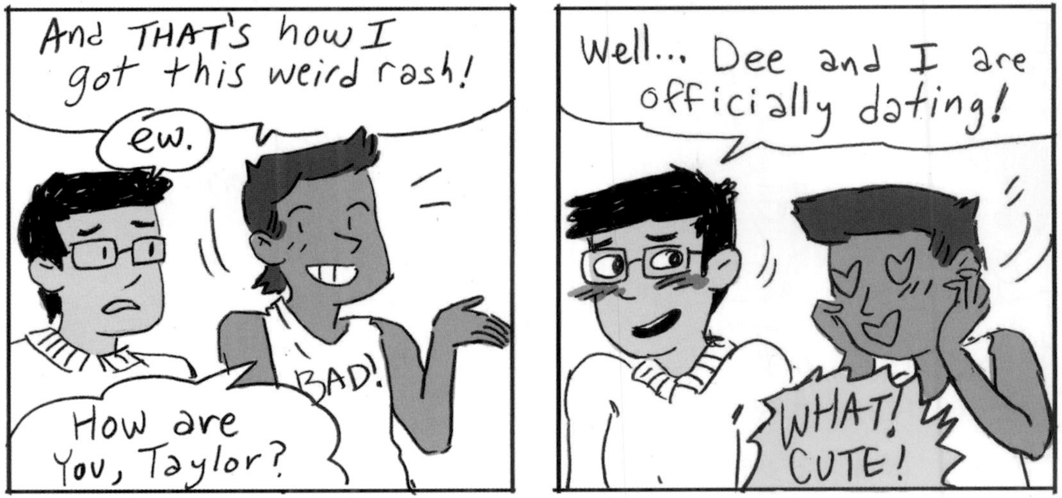

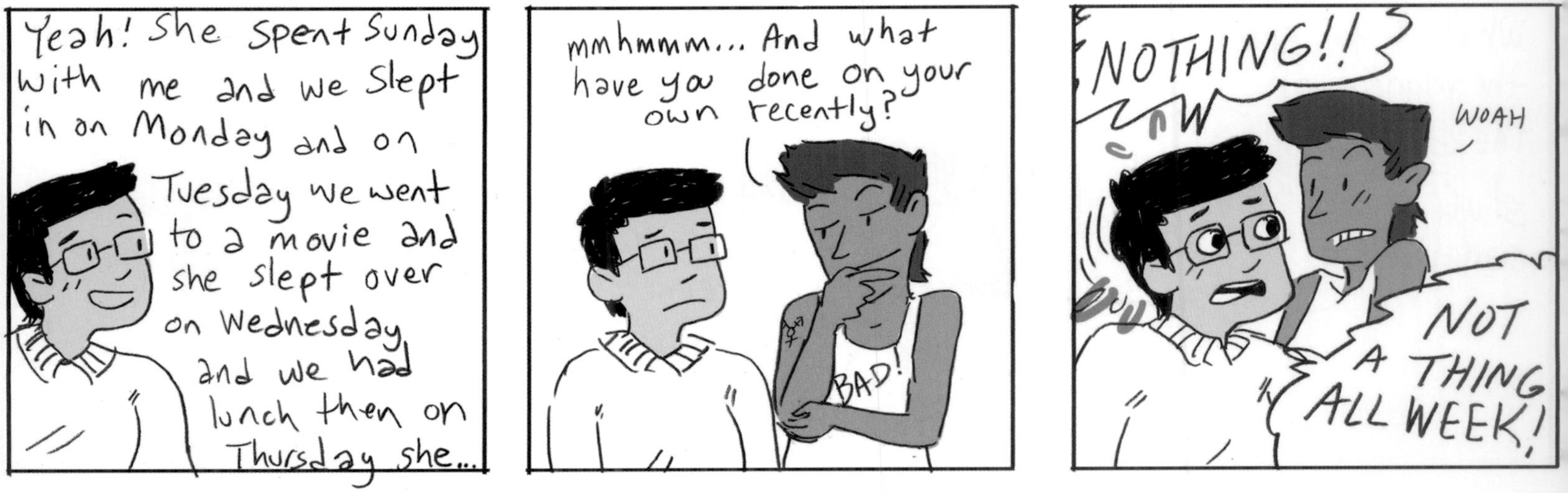

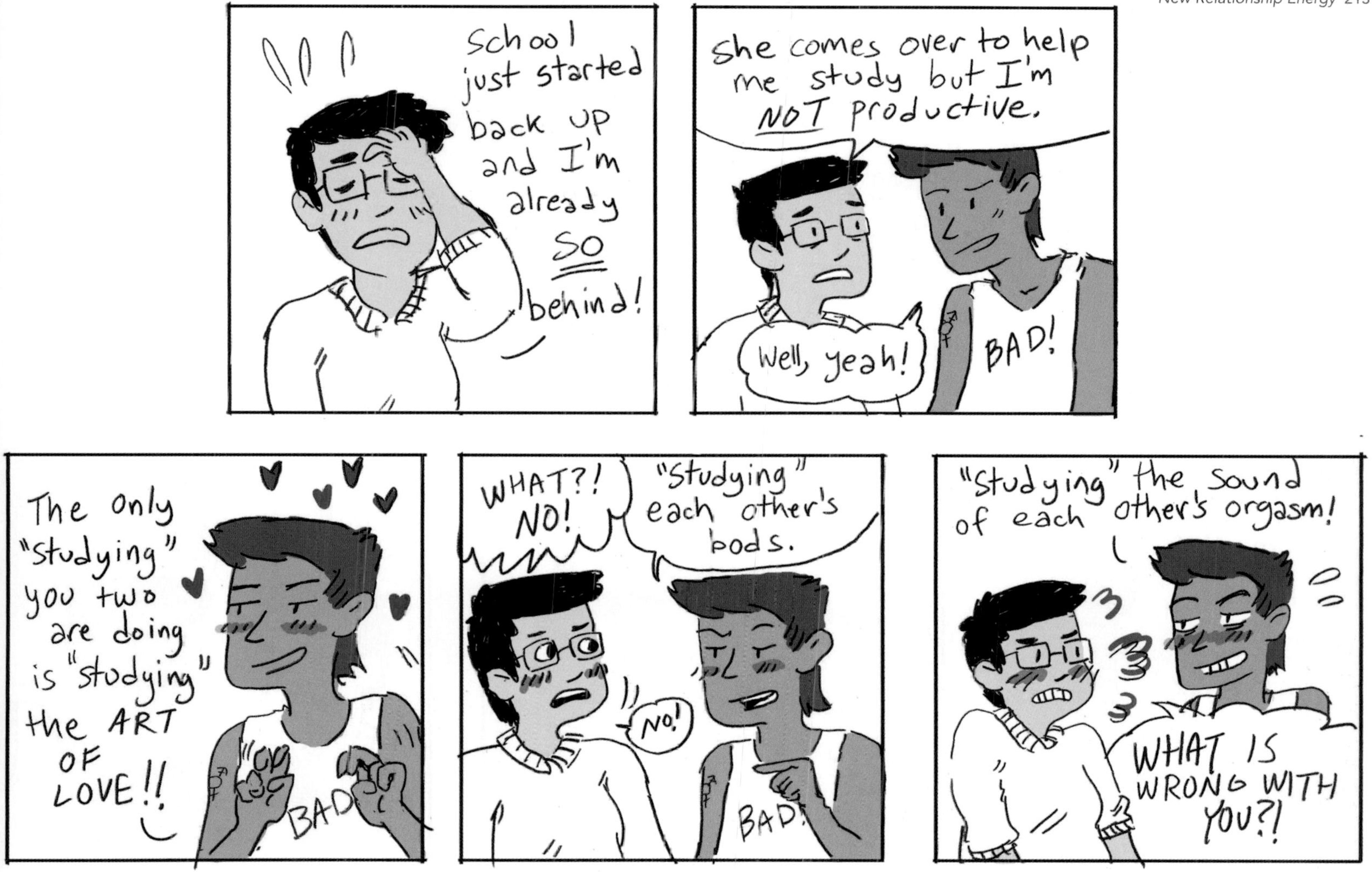
School just started back up and I'm already SO behind!
She comes over to help me study but I'm NOT productive.
Well, yeah!
BAD!
The only "studying" you two are doing is "studying" the ART OF LOVE!!
BAD
WHAT?! NO!
"studying" each other's bods.
NO!
BAD
"Studying" the sound of each other's orgasm!
WHAT IS WRONG WITH YOU?!

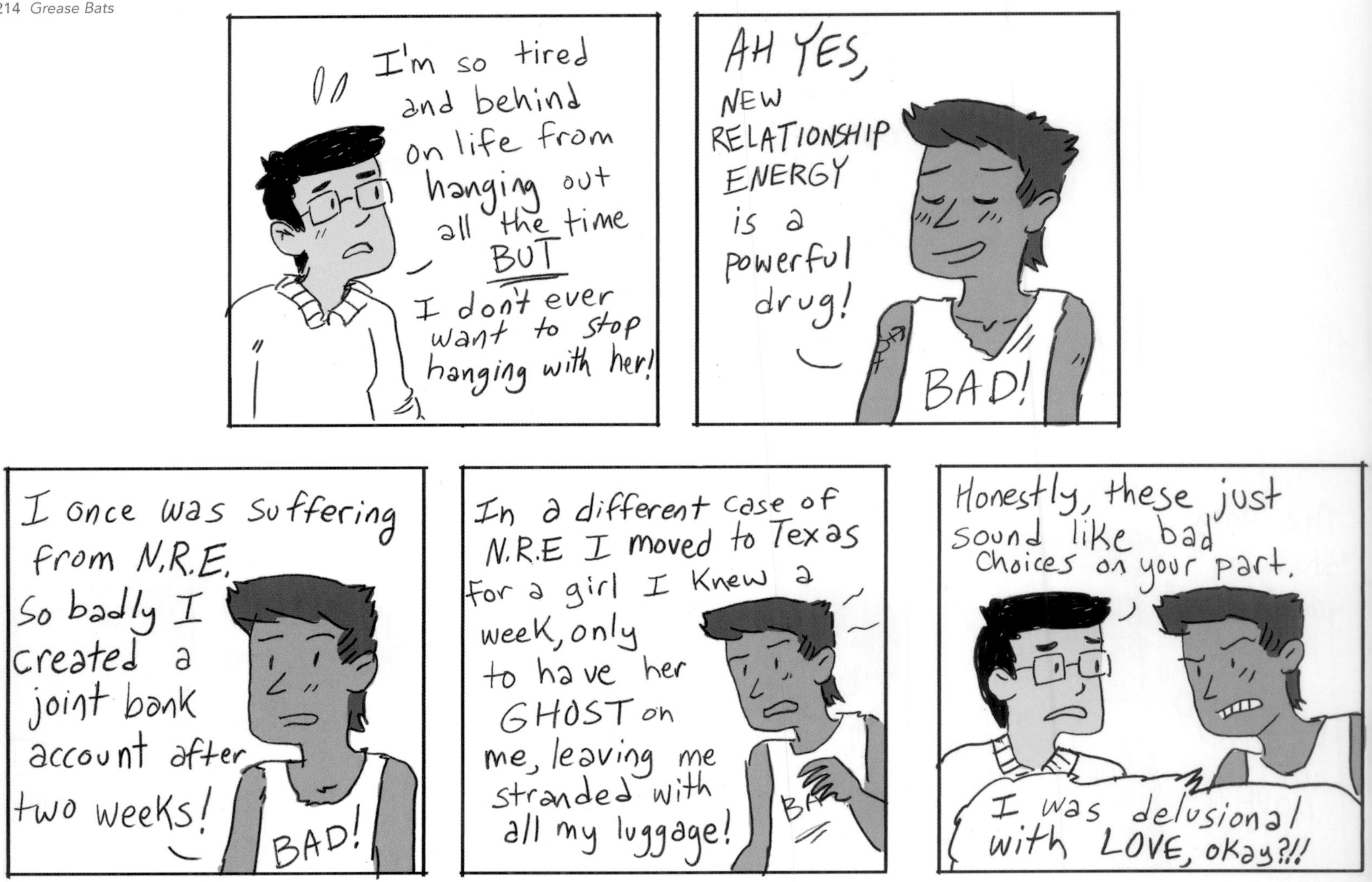
I'm so tired and behind on life from hanging out all the time BUT I don't ever want to stop hanging with her!
AH YES, NEW RELATIONSHIP ENERGY is a powerful drug!
BAD!
I once was suffering from N.R.E. So badly I created a joint bank account after two weeks!
BAD!
In a different case of N.R.E I moved to Texas for a girl I Knew a week, only to have her GHOST on me, leaving me stranded with all my luggage!
Honestly, these just sound like bad choices on your part.
I was delusional with LOVE, okay?!!

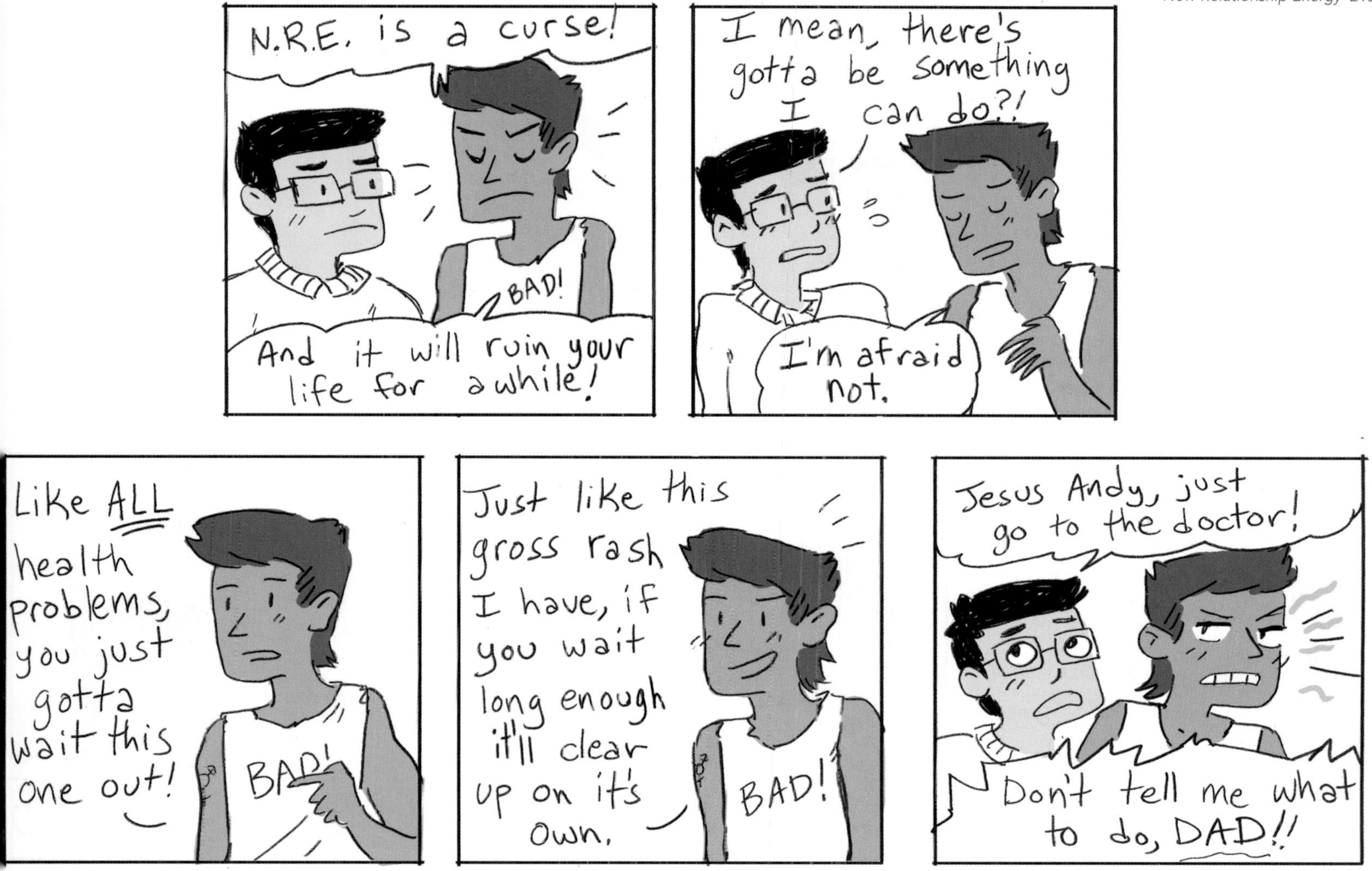
N.R.E. is a curse!
And it will ruin your life for awhile!
BAD!
I mean, there's gotta be something I can do?!
I'm afraid not.
Like ALL health problems, you just gotta wait this one out!
BAD!
Just like this gross rash I have, if you wait long enough it'll clear up on it's own.
BAD!
Jesus Andy, just go to the doctor!
Don't tell me what to do, DAD!!

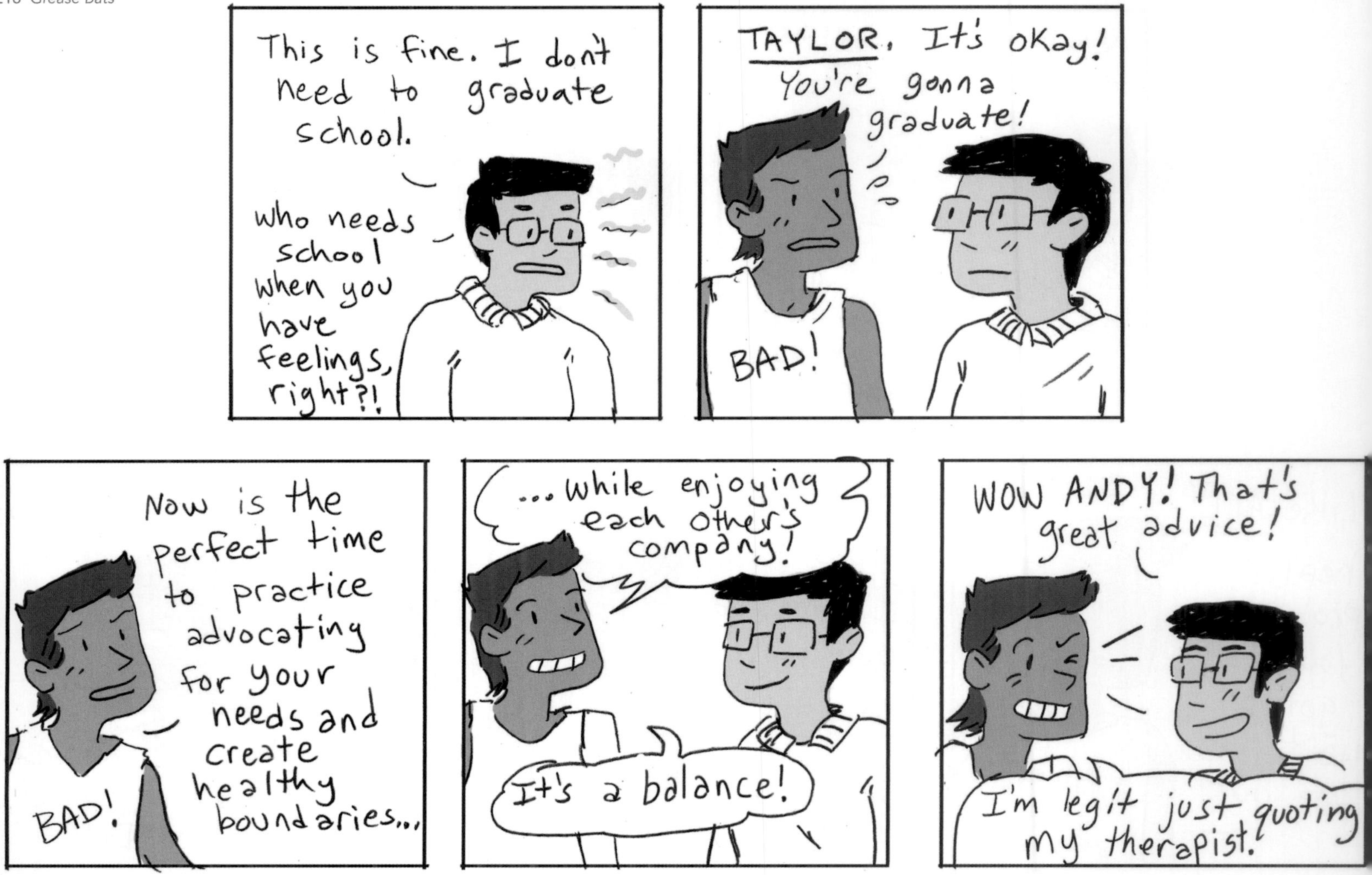
This is fine. I don't need to graduate school.
who needs school when you have feelings, right?!
TAYLOR. It's okay! You're gonna graduate!
BAD!
Now is the perfect time to practice advocating for your needs and create healthy boundaries...
BAD!
...while enjoying each other's company!
It's a balance!
WOW ANDY! That's great advice!
I'm legit just quoting my therapist.

Grab Yer Pumpkins

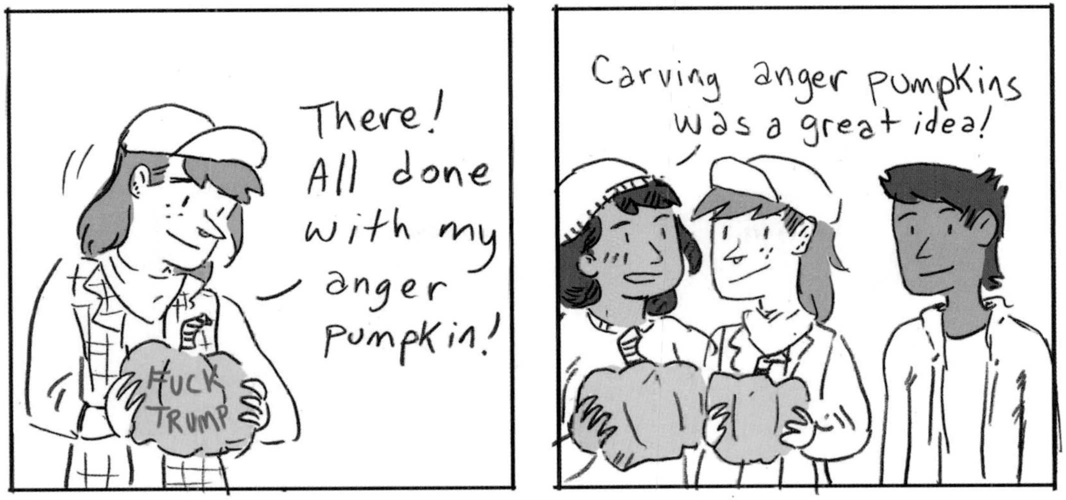

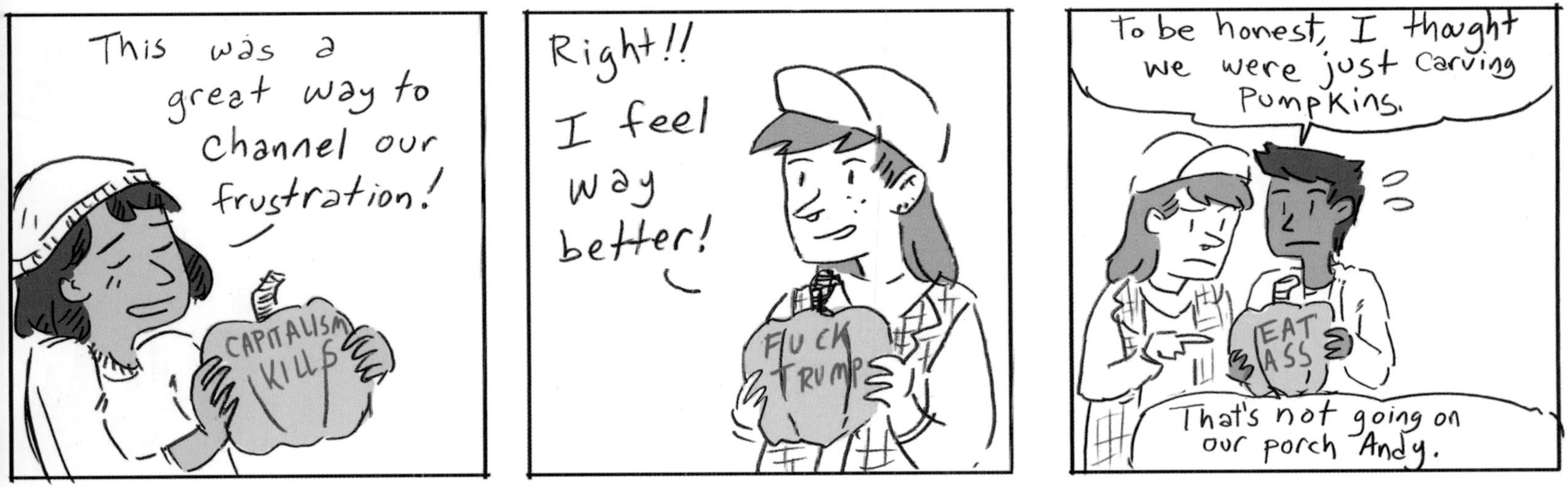

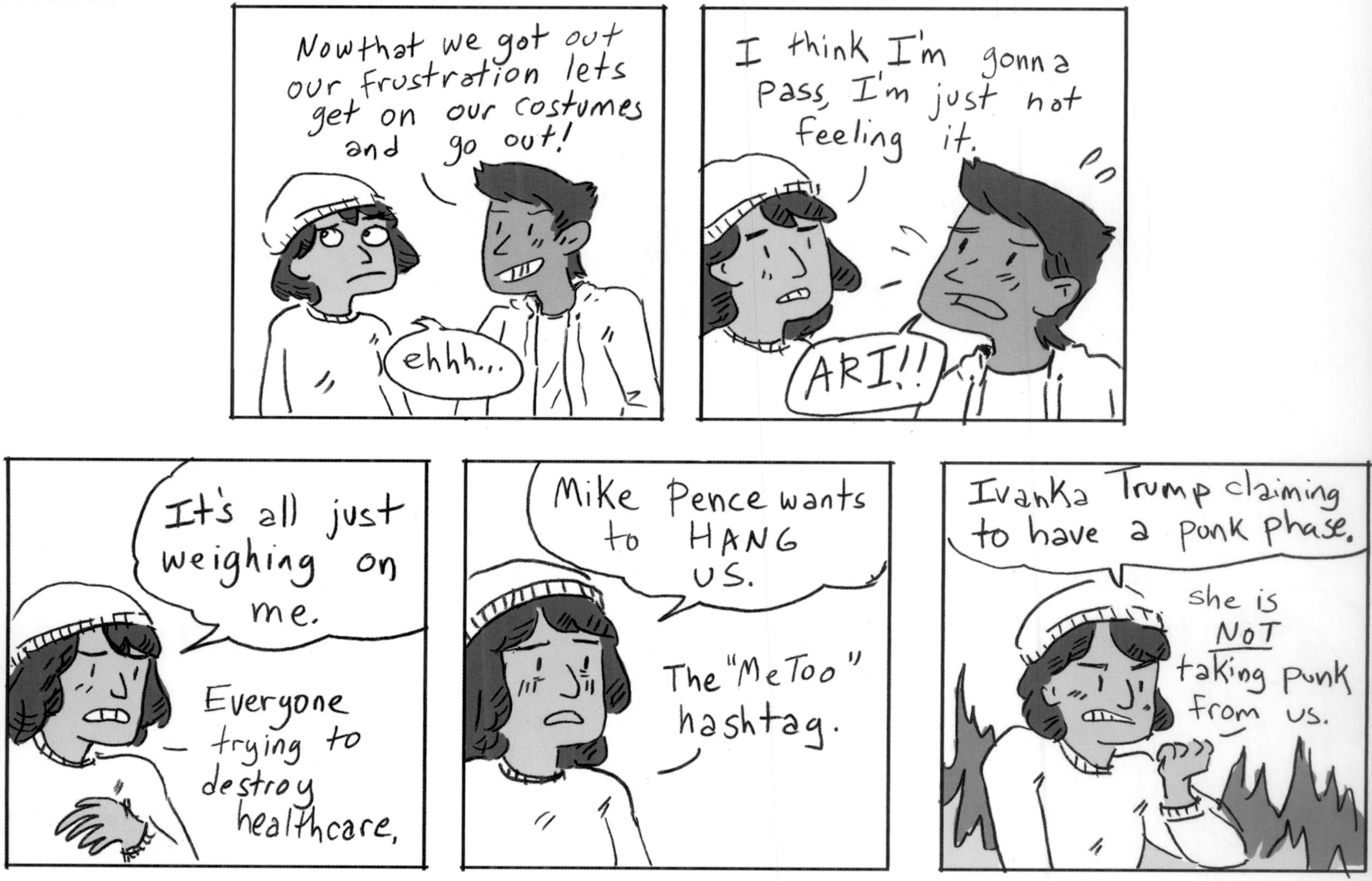
Now that we got out our frustration lets get on our costumes and go out!
ehhh...
I think I'm gonna pass, I'm just not feeling it.
ARI!!
It's all just weighing on me.
Everyone trying to destroy healthcare,
Mike Pence wants to HANG US.
The "MeToo" hashtag.
Ivanka Trump claiming to have a punk phase.
she is NOT taking punk from us.

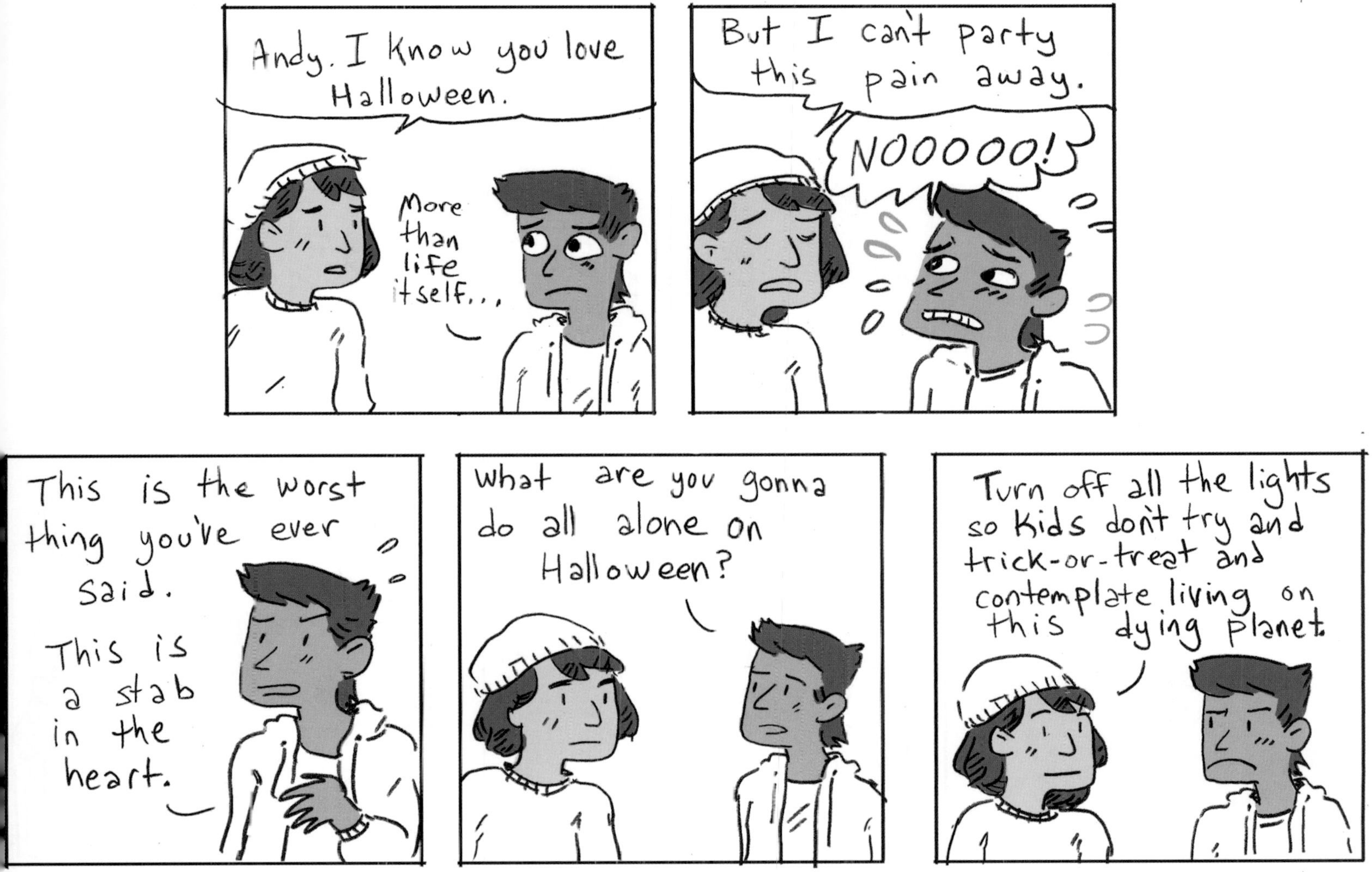
Andy. I know you love Halloween.
More than life itself...
But I can't party this pain away.
NOOOOO!
This is the worst thing you've ever said.
This is a stab in the heart.
What are you gonna do all alone on Halloween?
Turn off all the lights so kids don't try and trick-or-treat and contemplate living on this dying planet.

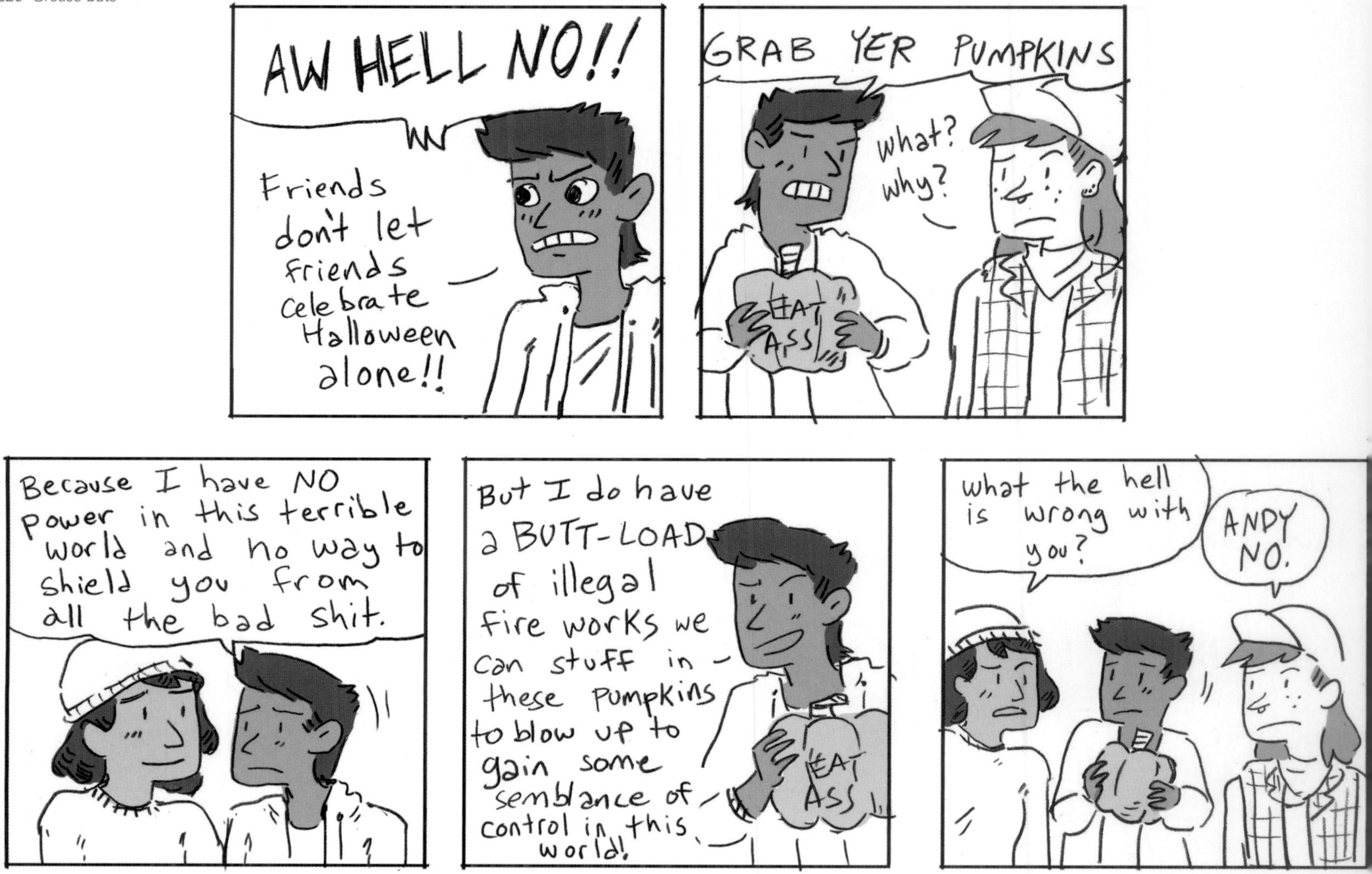
AW HELL NO!!
Friends don't let friends celebrate Halloween alone!!
GRAB YER PUMPKINS
what? why?
EAT ASS
Because I have NO power in this terrible world and no way to shield you from all the bad shit.
But I do have a BUTT-LOAD of illegal fire works we can stuff in these pumpkins to blow up to gain some semblance of control in this world!
EAT ASS
what the hell is wrong with you?
ANDY NO.

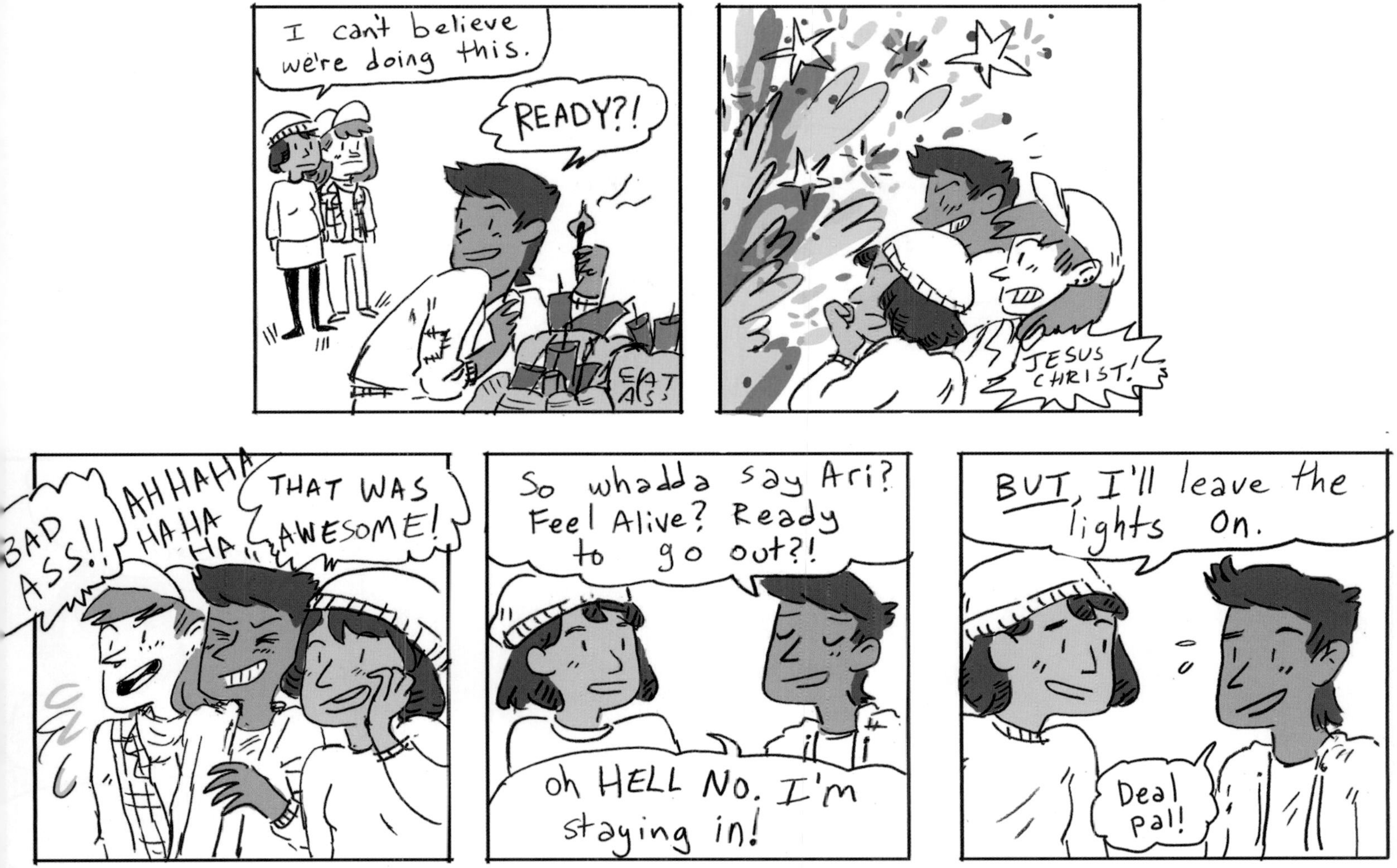
I can't believe we're doing this.
READY?!
JESUS CHRIST!
BAD ASS!!
AHHAHA HAHA HA
THAT WAS AWESOME!
So whadda say Ari? Feel Alive? Ready to go out?!
oh HELL NO. I'm staying in!
BUT, I'll leave the lights on.
Deal pal!

New Friends

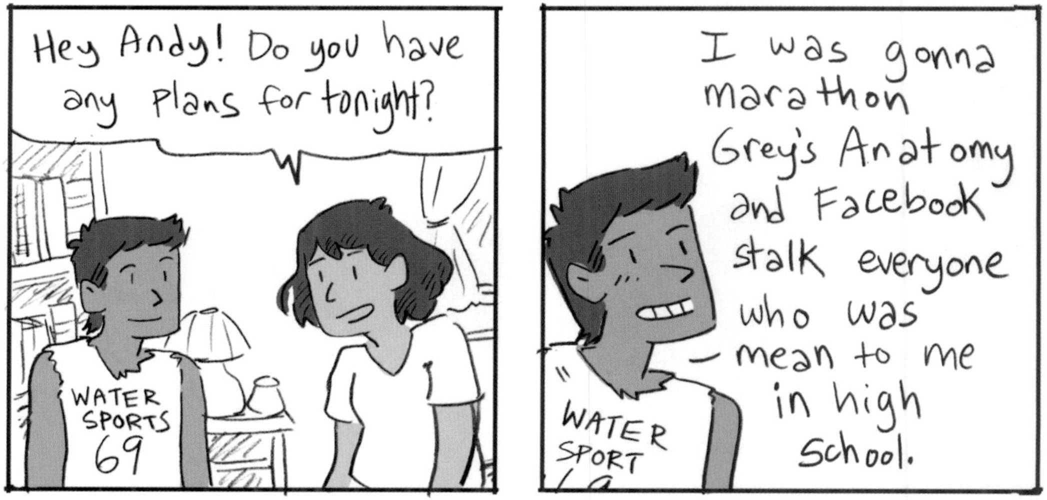
Hey Andy! Do you have any plans for tonight?
WATER SPORTS 69
I was gonna marathon Grey's Anatomy and Facebook stalk everyone who was mean to me in high school.
WATER SPORT

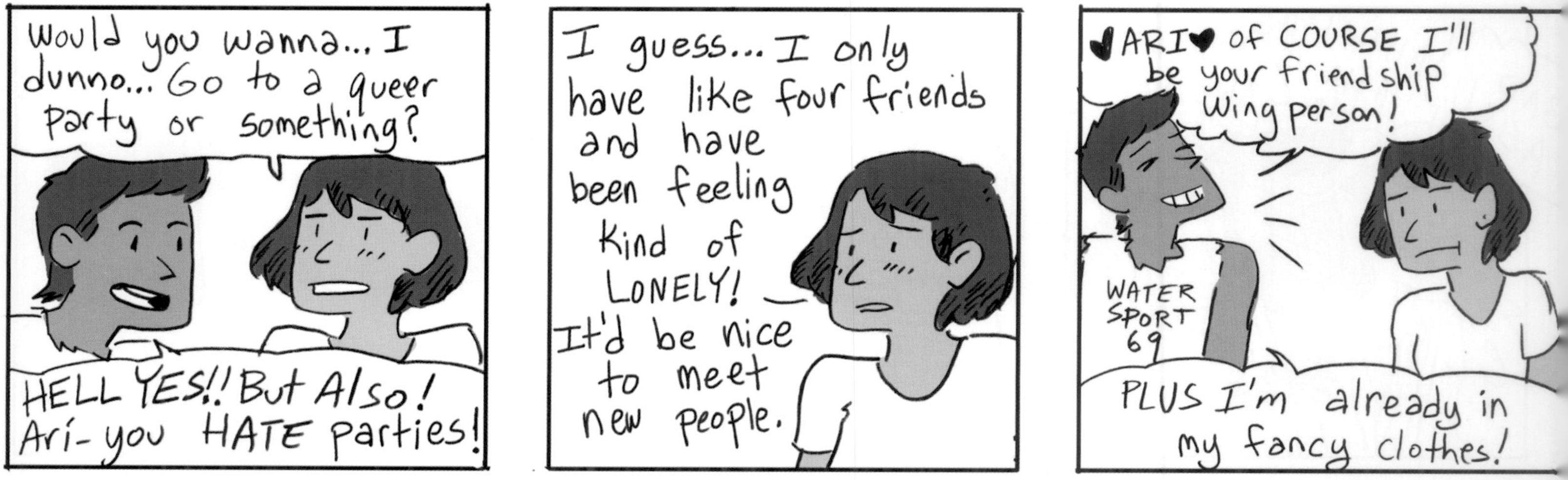
Would you wanna... I dunno... Go to a queer party or something?
HELL YES!! But Also! Ari- you HATE parties!
I guess... I only have like four friends and have been feeling kind of LONELY! It'd be nice to meet new people.
ARI of COURSE I'll be your friendship wing person!
WATER SPORT 69
PLUS I'm already in my fancy clothes!

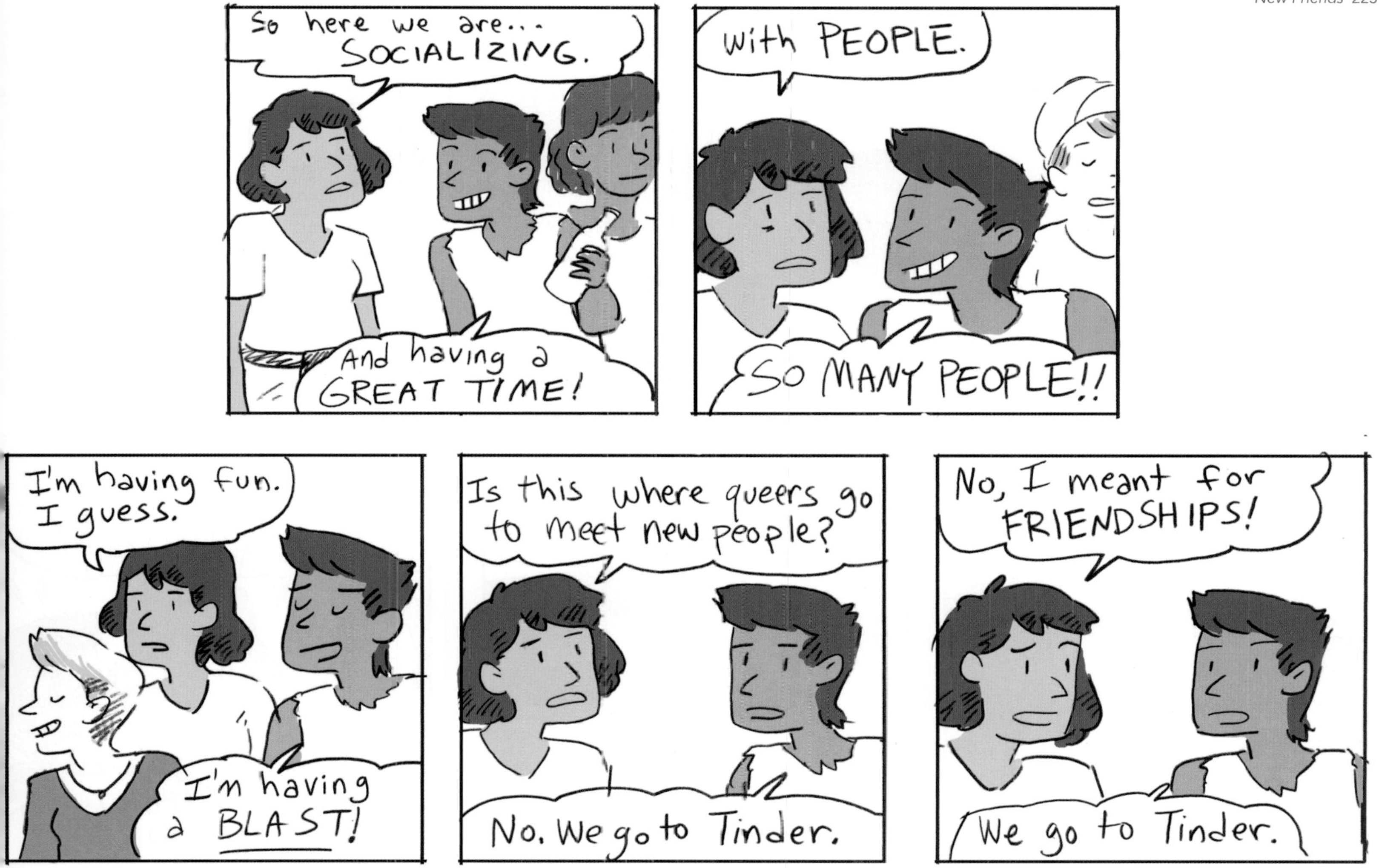
So here we are... SOCIALIZING.
And having a GREAT TIME!
with PEOPLE.
SO MANY PEOPLE!!
I'm having fun. I guess.
I'm having a BLAST!
Is this where queers go to meet new people?
No. We go to Tinder.
No, I meant for FRIENDSHIPS!
We go to Tinder.

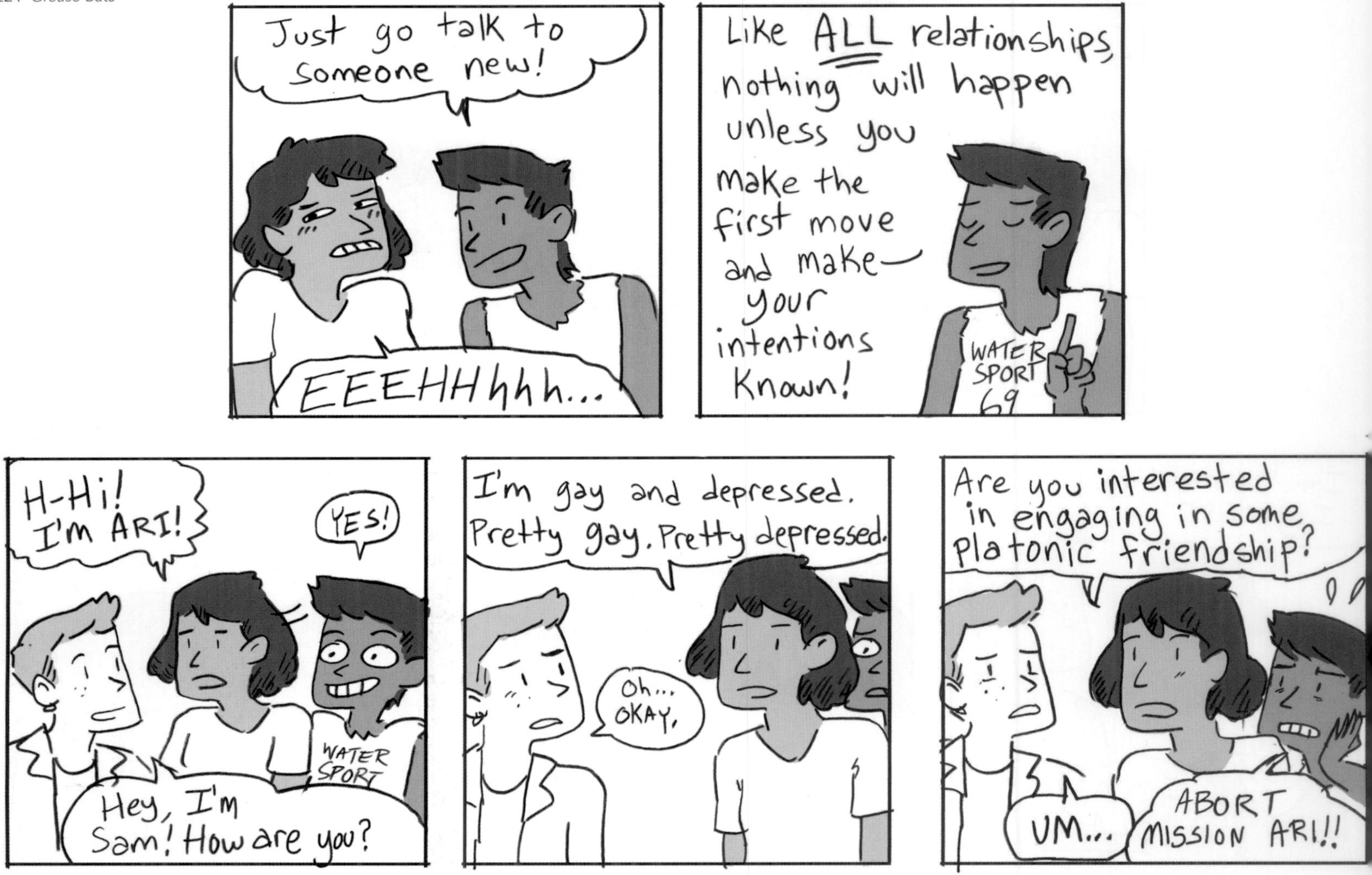
Just go talk to someone new!
EEEHHhhh...
Like ALL relationships, nothing will happen unless you make the first move and make— your intentions Known!
WATER SPORT 69
H-Hi! I'm ARI!
YES!
Hey, I'm Sam! How are you?
WATER SPORT
I'm gay and depressed. Pretty gay. Pretty depressed.
Oh... OKAY,
Are you interested in engaging in some platonic friendship?
UM...
ABORT MISSION ARI!!

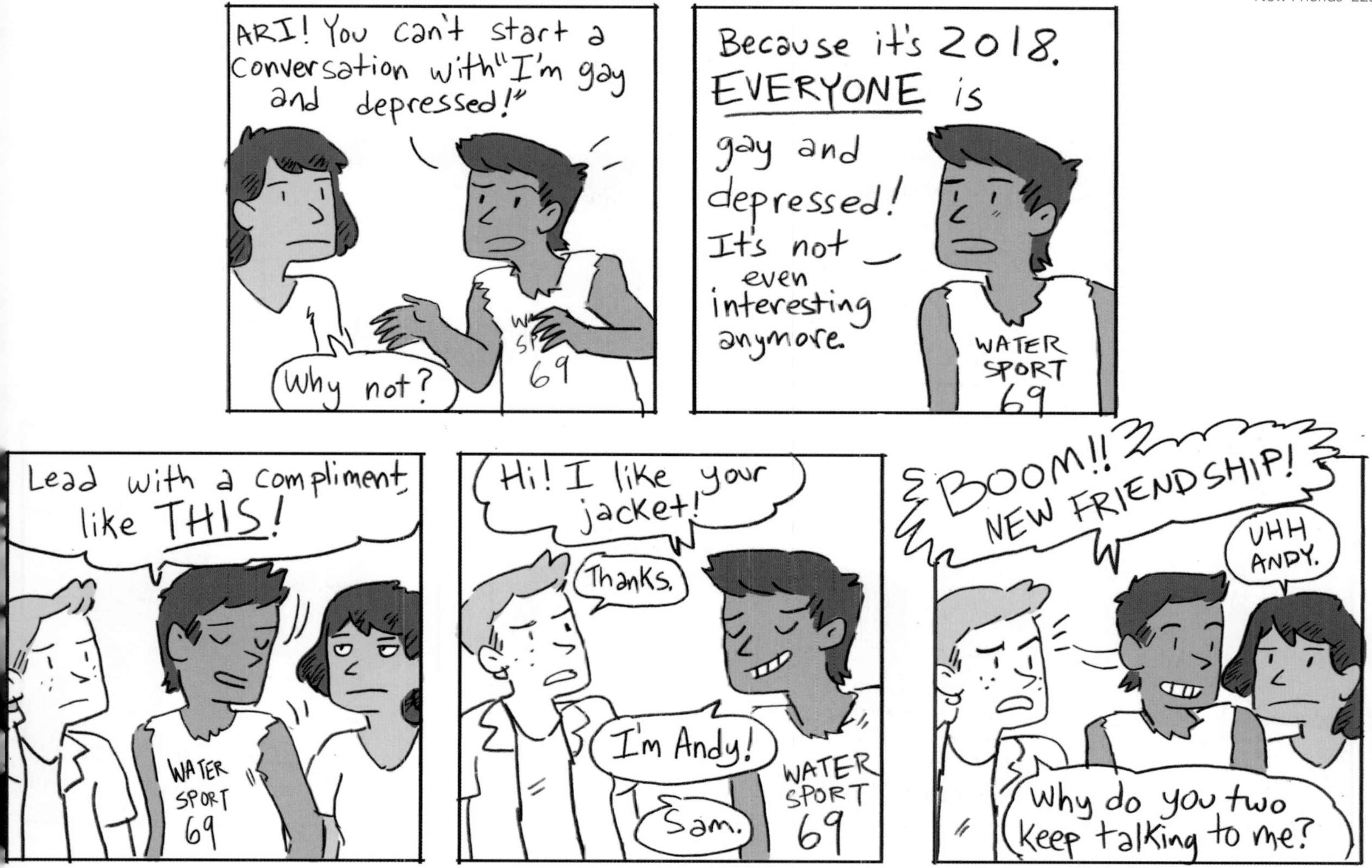
ARI! You can't start a conversation with "I'm gay and depressed!"
Why not?
WATER SPORT 69
Because it's 2018. EVERYONE is gay and depressed! It's not even interesting anymore.
WATER SPORT 69
Lead with a compliment like THIS!
WATER SPORT 69
Hi! I like your jacket!
Thanks.
I'm Andy!
Sam.
WATER SPORT 69
BOOM!! NEW FRIENDSHIP!
UHH ANDY.
Why do you two keep talking to me?

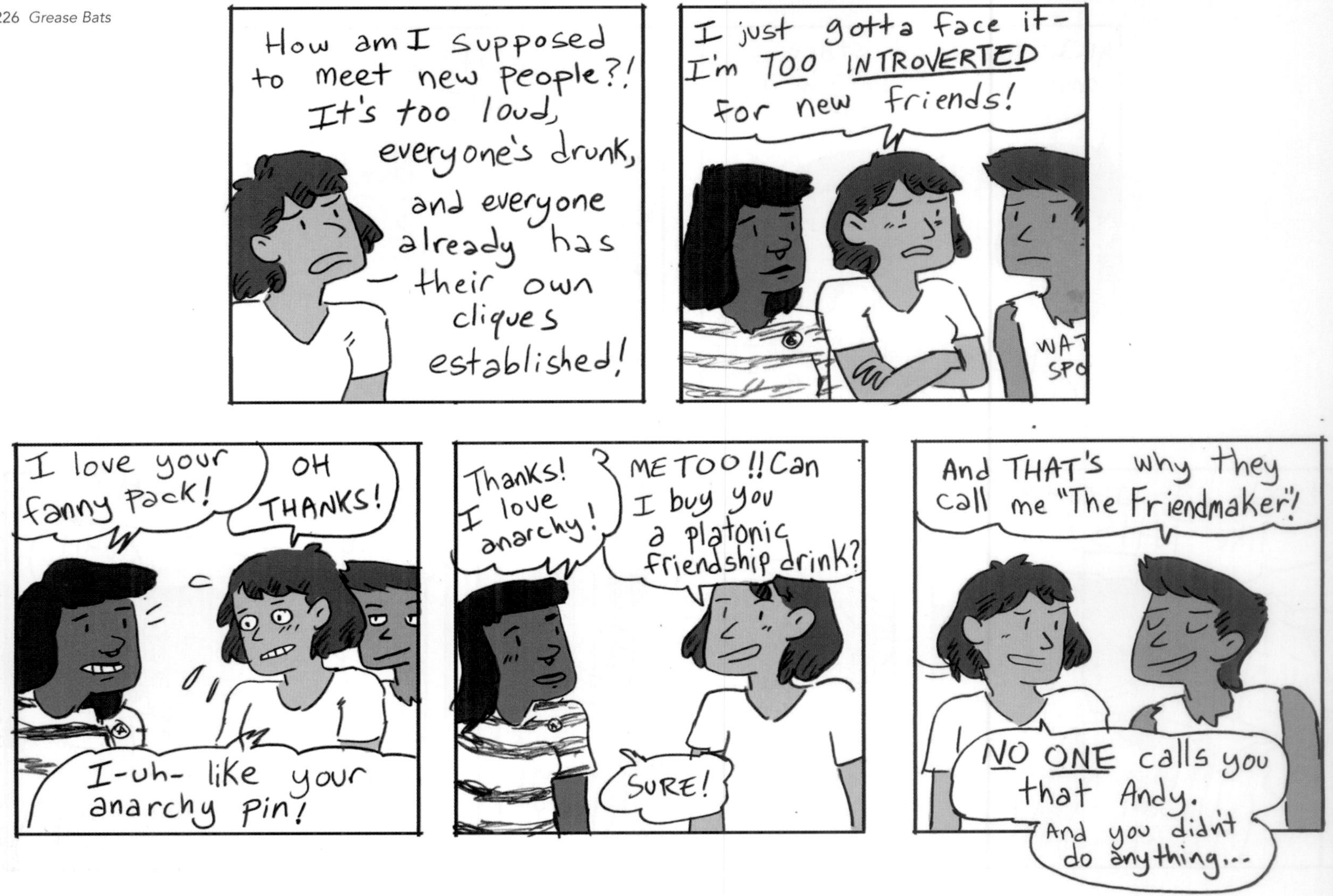
How am I supposed to meet new people?! It's too loud, everyone's drunk, and everyone already has their own cliques established!
I just gotta face it- I'm TOO INTROVERTED for new friends!
I love your fanny pack!
OH THANKS!
I-uh- like your anarchy pin!
Thanks! I love anarchy!
ME TOO!! Can I buy you a platonic friendship drink?
SURE!
And THAT'S why they call me "The Friendmaker"!
NO ONE calls you that Andy.
And you didn't do anything...

Heartbroken

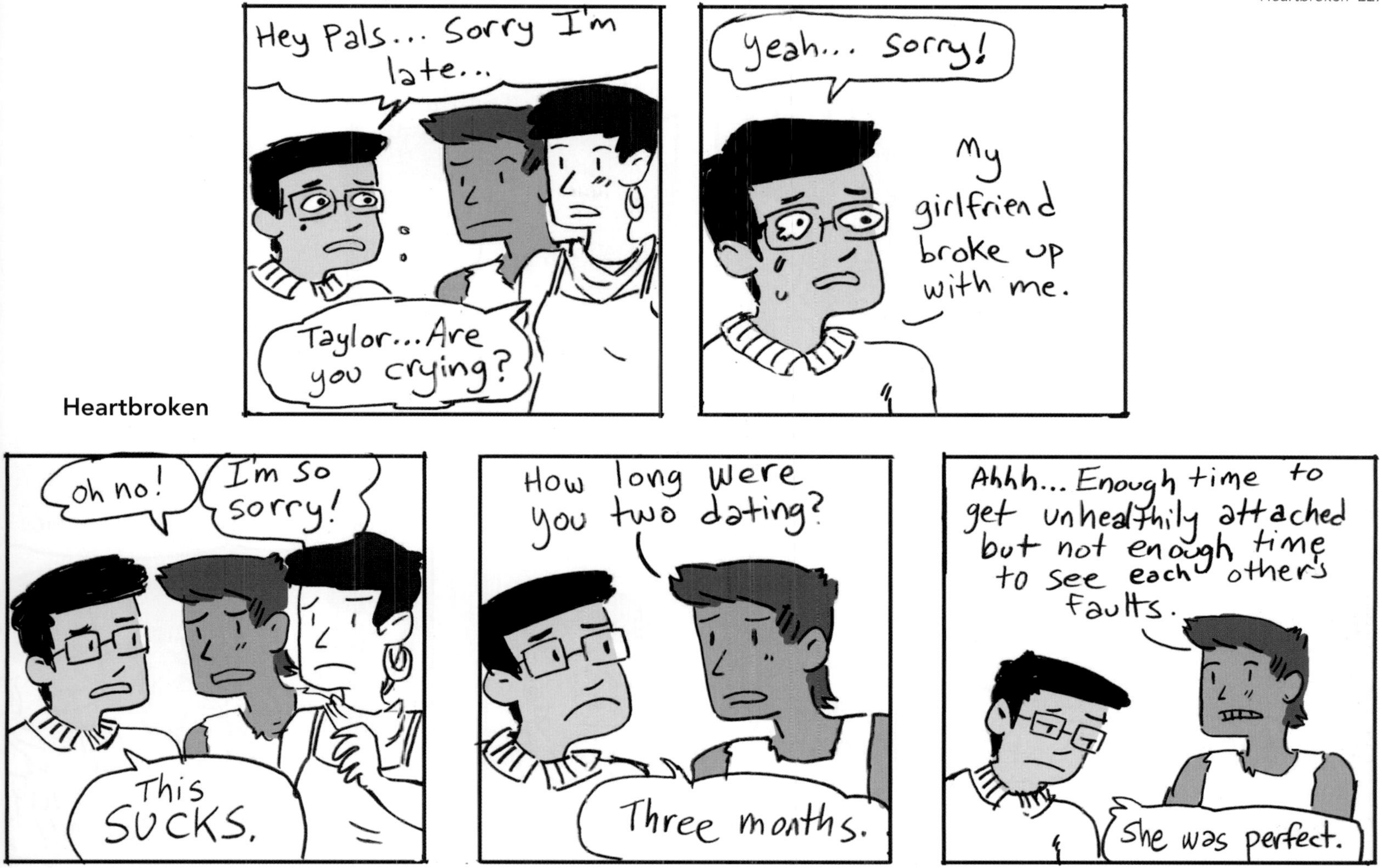
Hey Pals... Sorry I'm late...
Taylor...Are you crying?
yeah... sorry!
My girlfriend broke up with me.
oh no!
I'm so sorry!
This SUCKS.
How long were you two dating?
Three months.
Ahhh... Enough time to get unhealthily attached but not enough time to see each other's faults.
She was perfect.

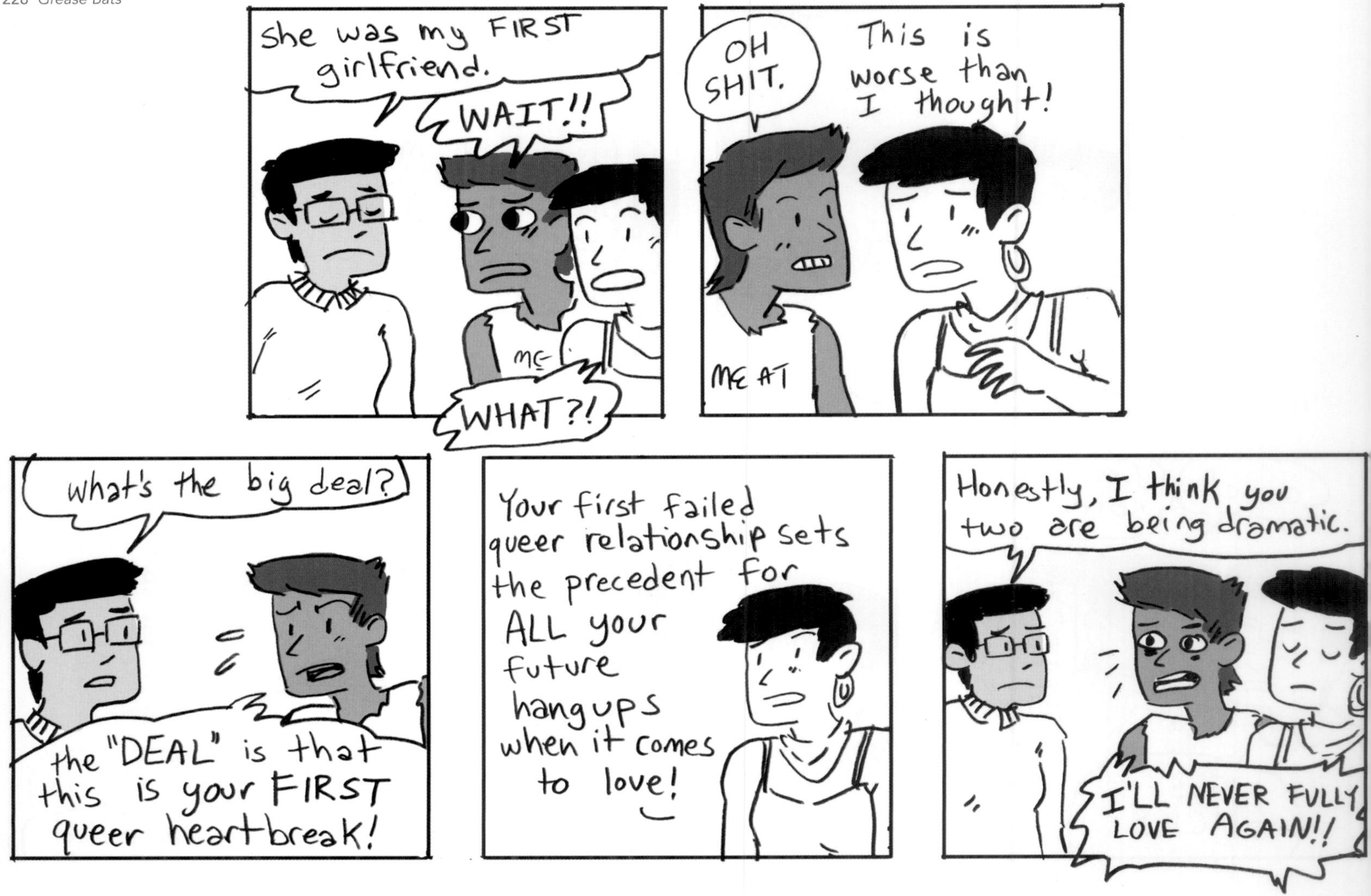
She was my FIRST girlfriend.
WAIT!!
WHAT?!
ME
OH SHIT.
This is worse than I thought!
ME AT
what's the big deal?
the "DEAL" is that this is your FIRST queer heartbreak!
Your first failed queer relationship sets the precedent for ALL your future hangups when it comes to love!
Honestly, I think you two are being dramatic.
I'LL NEVER FULLY LOVE AGAIN!!

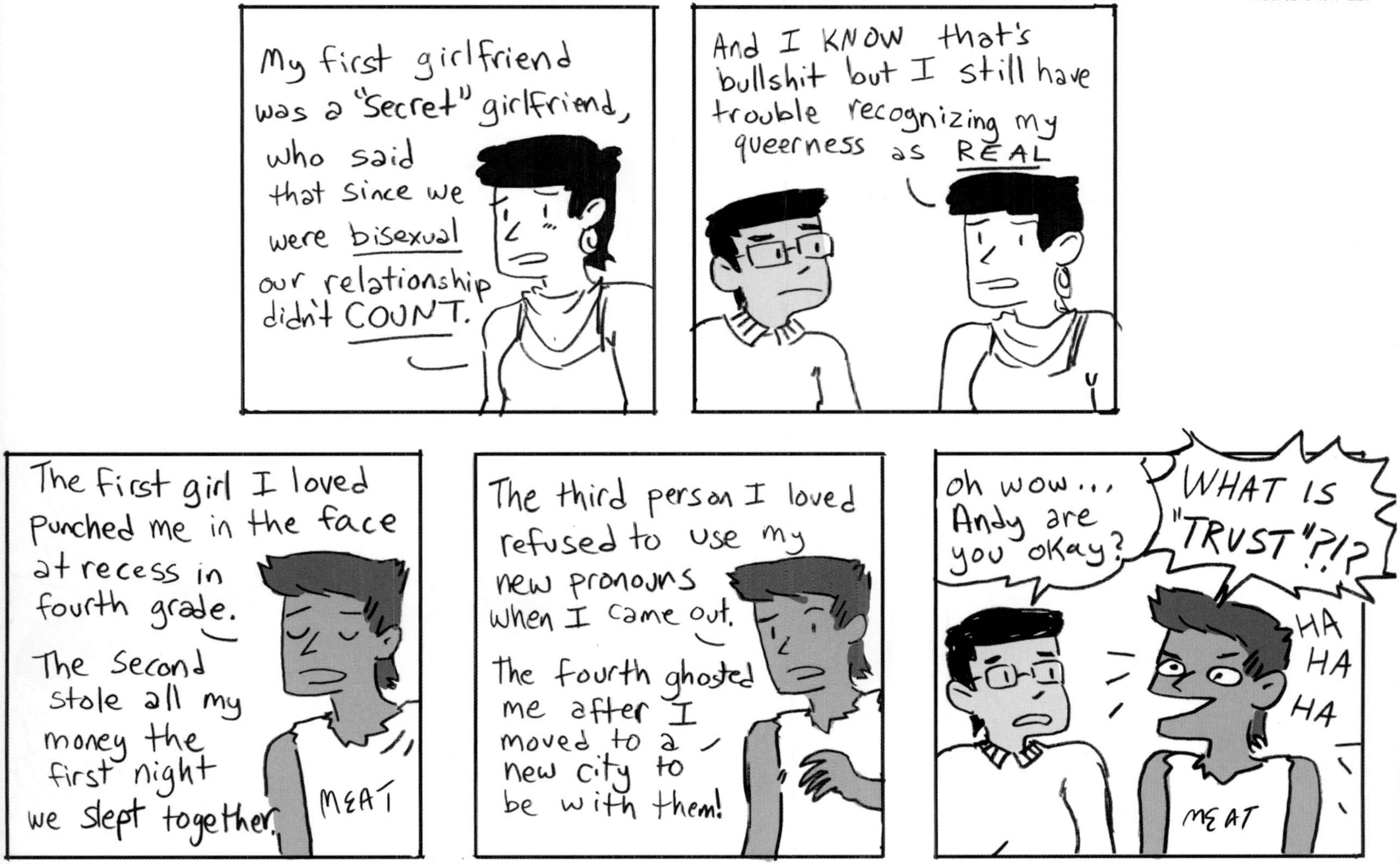
My first girlfriend was a "secret" girlfriend, who said that since we were bisexual our relationship didn't COUNT.
And I KNOW that's bullshit but I still have trouble recognizing my queerness as REAL
The first girl I loved punched me in the face at recess in fourth grade.
The second stole all my money the first night we slept together.
MEAT
The third person I loved refused to use my new pronouns when I came out.
The fourth ghosted me after I moved to a new city to be with them!
oh wow... Andy are you okay?
WHAT IS "TRUST"?!?
HA HA HA
MEAT

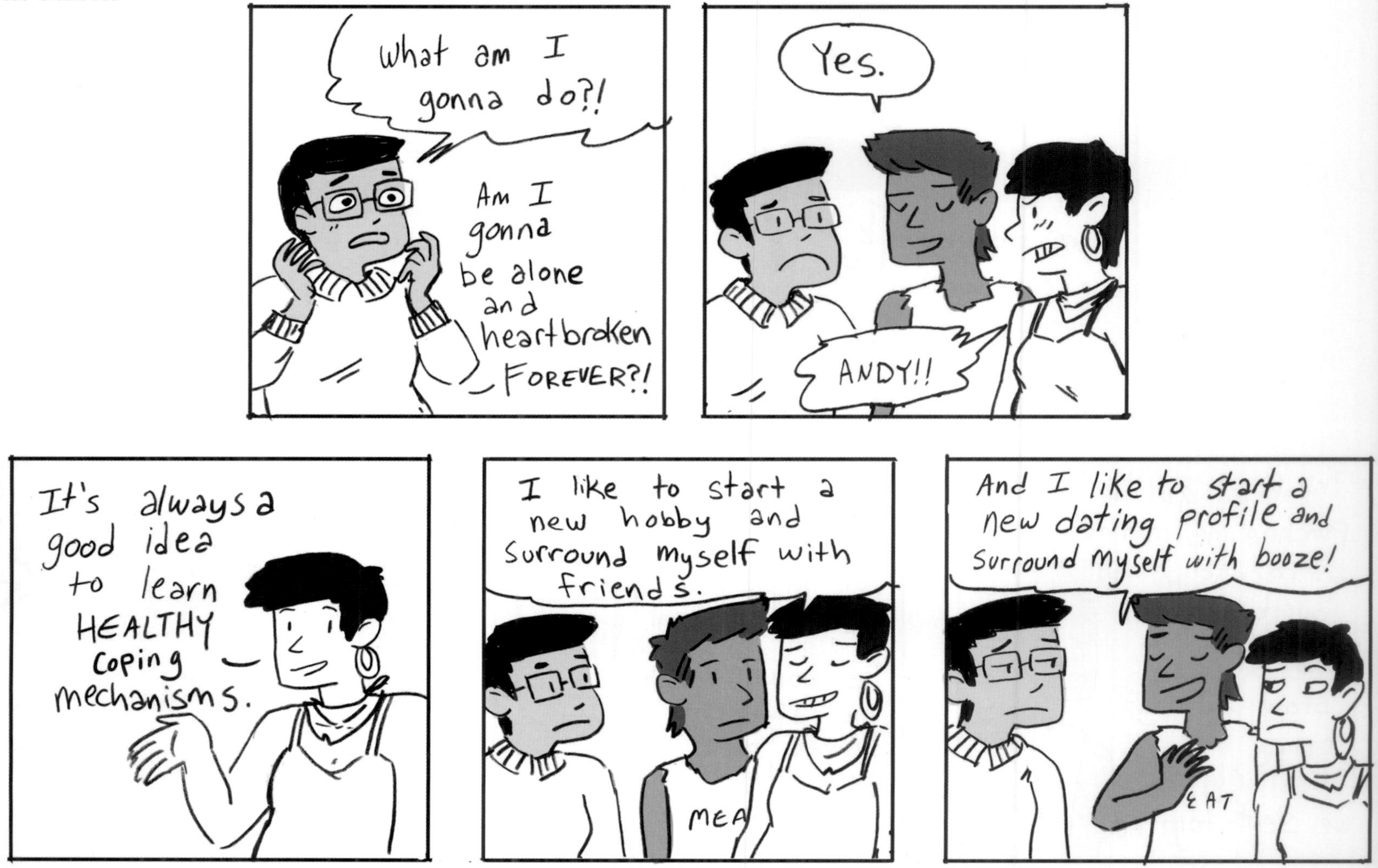
What am I gonna do?!
Am I gonna be alone and heartbroken FOREVER?!
Yes.
ANDY!!
It's always a good idea to learn HEALTHY coping mechanisms.
I like to start a new hobby and surround myself with friends.
MEA
And I like to start a new dating profile and surround myself with booze!
EAT

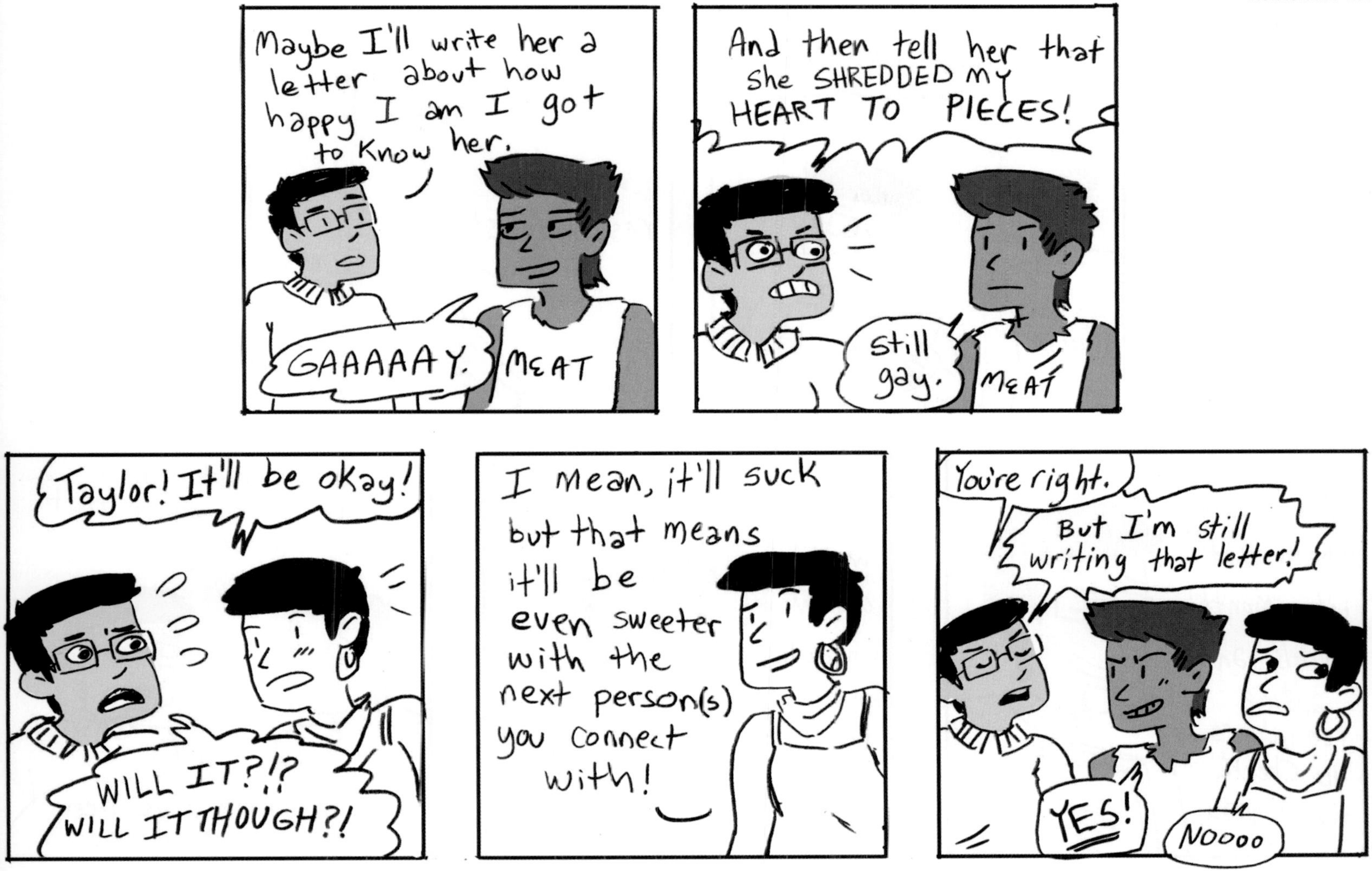
Maybe I'll write her a letter about how happy I am I got to know her.
GAAAAAY.
MEAT
And then tell her that she SHREDDED MY HEART TO PIECES!
Still gay.
MEAT
Taylor! It'll be okay!
WILL IT?!? WILL IT THOUGH?!
I mean, it'll suck but that means it'll be even sweeter with the next person(s) you connect with!
You're right.
But I'm still writing that letter!
YES!
NOOOO

New Years Resolutions

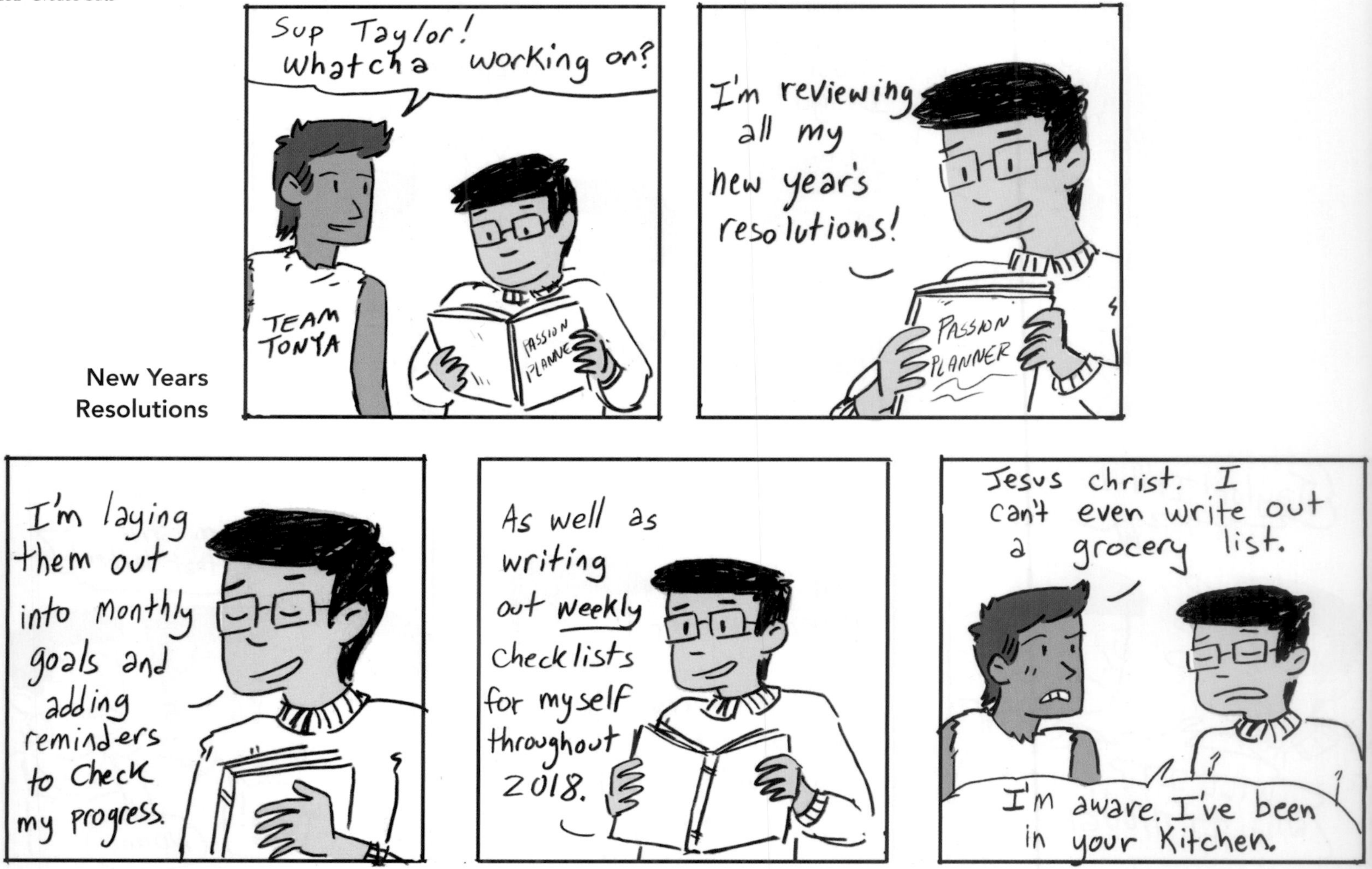

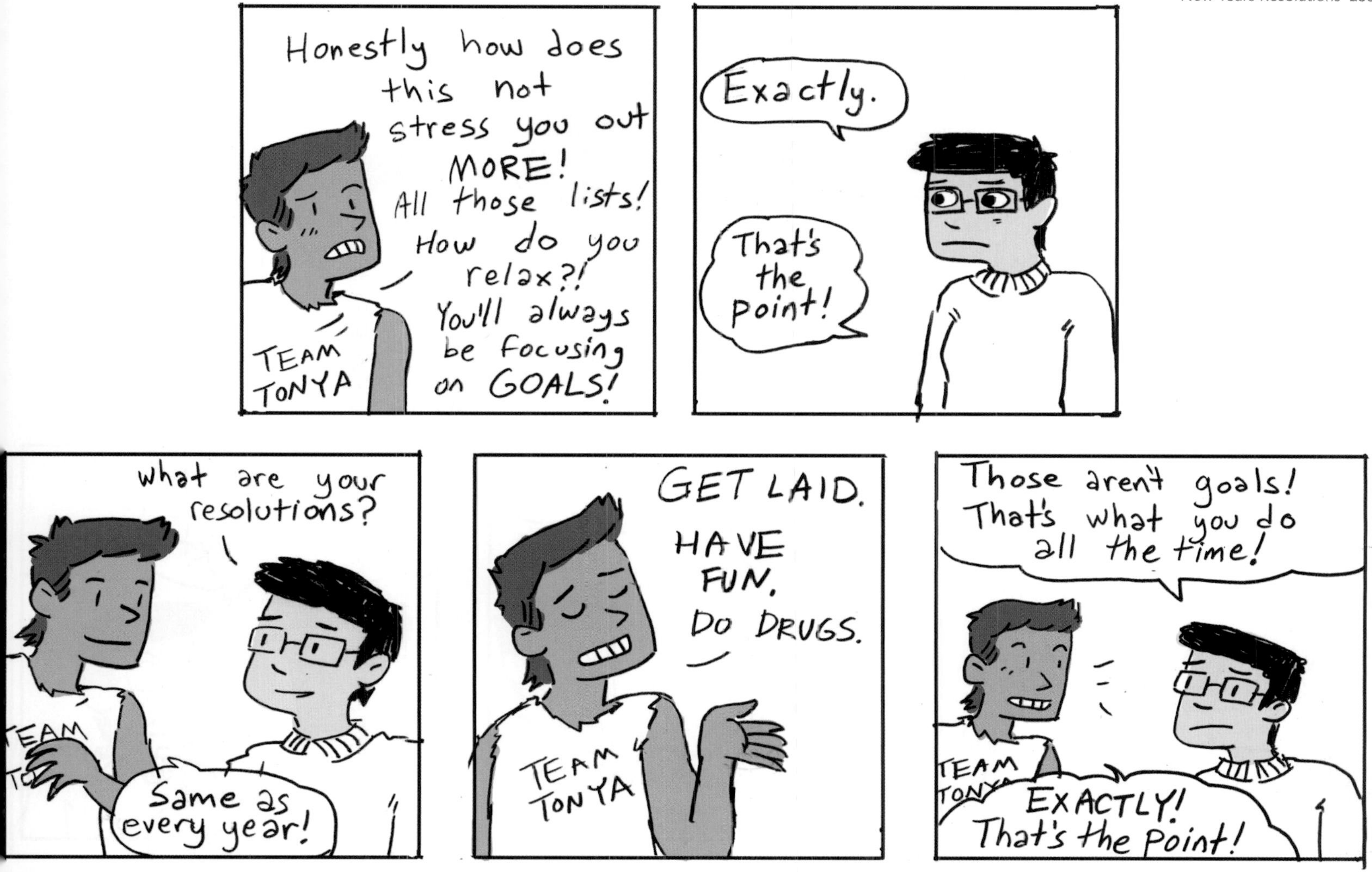
Honestly how does this not stress you out MORE! All those lists! How do you relax?! You'll always be focusing on GOALS!
TEAM TONYA
Exactly.
That's the point!
what are your resolutions?
TEAM TO
Same as every year!
GET LAID.
HAVE FUN.
DO DRUGS.
TEAM TONYA
Those aren't goals! That's what you do all the time!
TEAM TONYA
EXACTLY! That's the point!

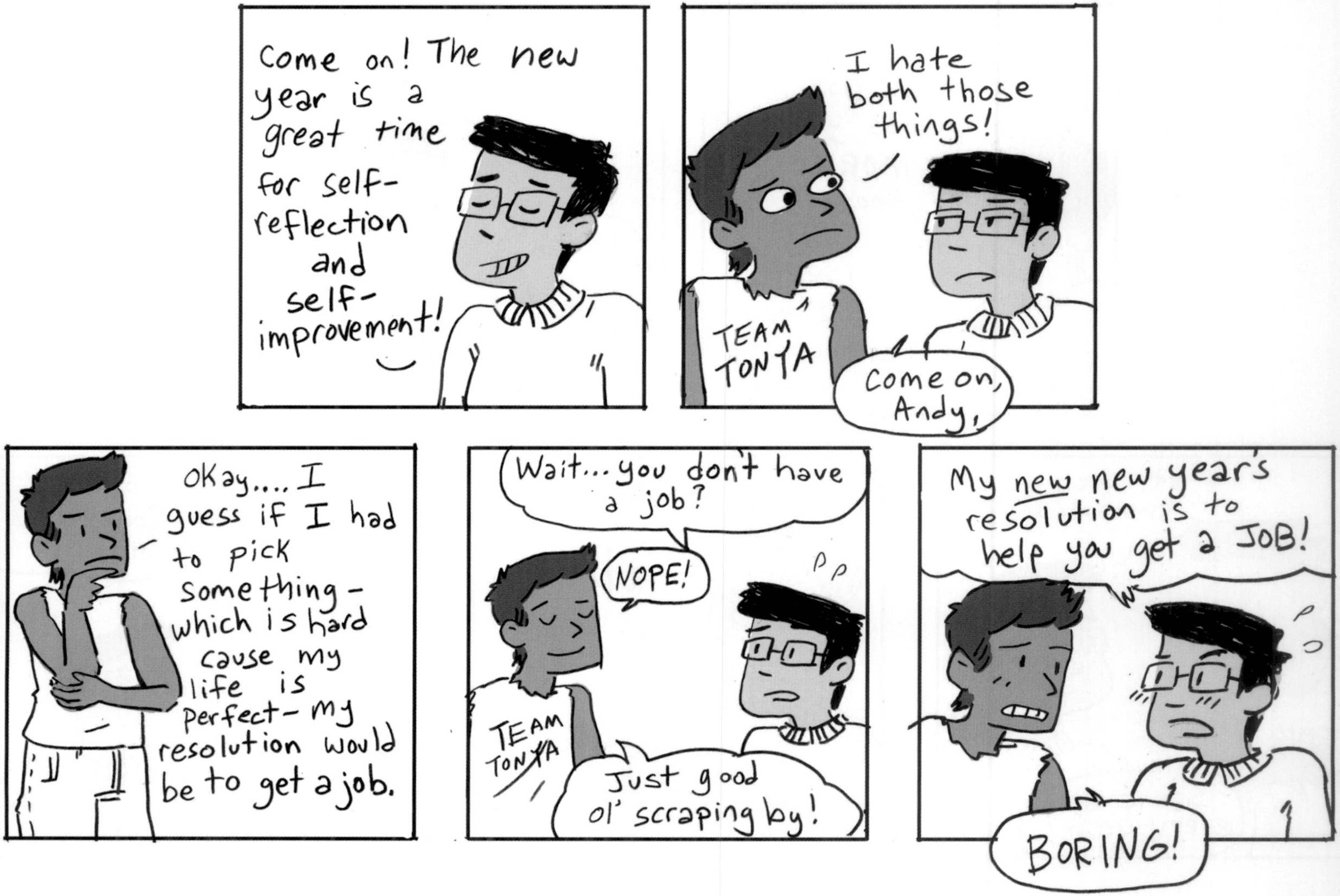
Come on! The new year is a great time for self-reflection and self-improvement!
I hate both those things!
Come on, Andy,
Okay.... I guess if I had to pick something - which is hard cause my life is perfect - my resolution would be to get a job.
Wait... you don't have a job?
NOPE!
Just good ol' scraping by!
TEAM TONYA
My new new year's resolution is to help you get a JOB!
BORING!

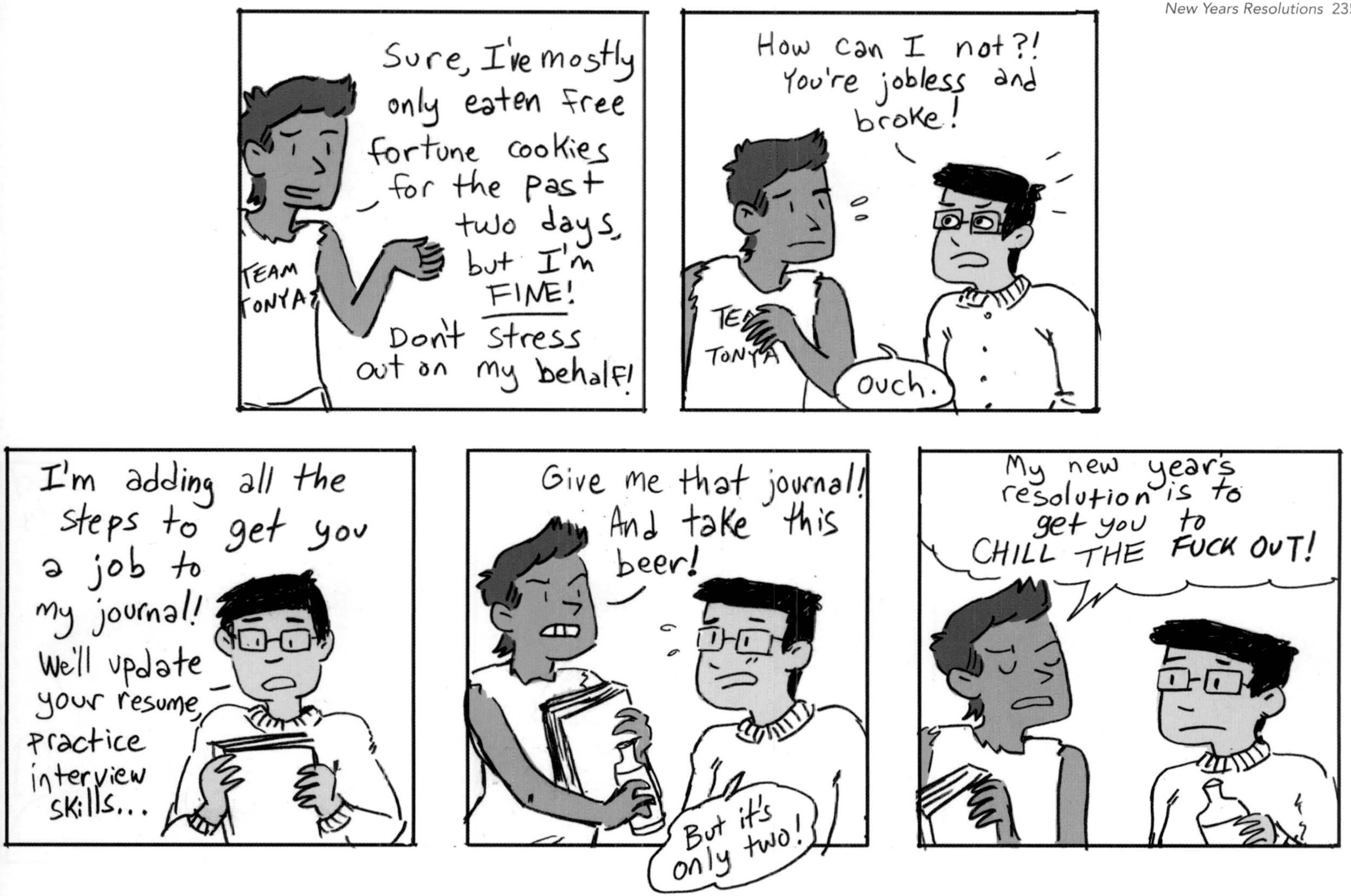
Sure, I've mostly only eaten free fortune cookies for the past two days, but I'm FINE! Don't stress out on my behalf!
TEAM TONYA
How can I not?! You're jobless and broke!
TEAM TONYA
Ouch.
I'm adding all the steps to get you a job to my journal! We'll update your resume, practice interview skills...
Give me that journal! And take this beer!
But it's only two!
My new year's resolution is to get you to CHILL THE FUCK OUT!

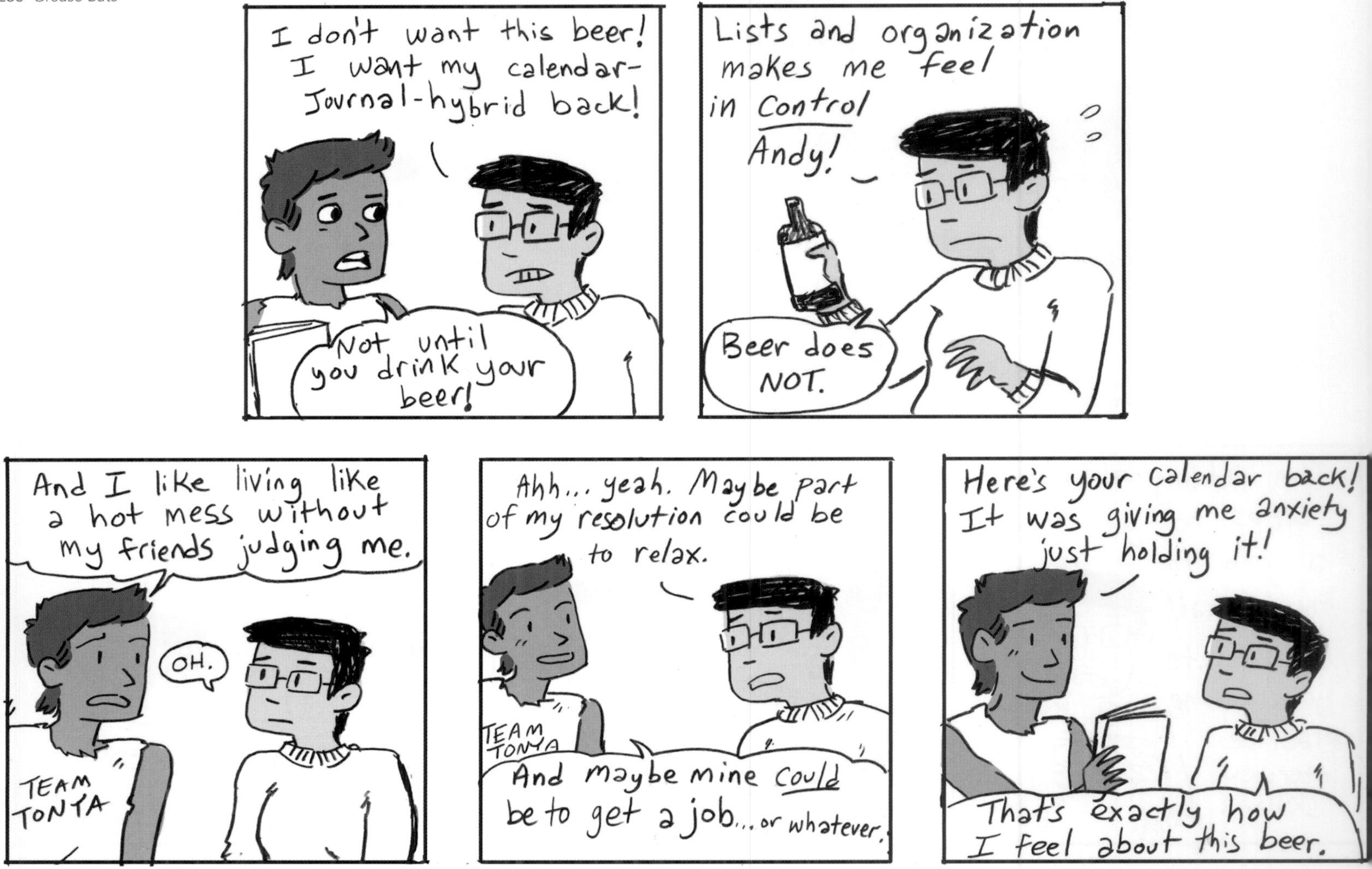
I don't want this beer! I want my calendar-Journal-hybrid back!
Not until you drink your beer!
Lists and organization makes me feel in Control Andy!
Beer does NOT.
And I like living like a hot mess without my friends judging me.
OH.
TEAM TONYA
Ahh... yeah. Maybe part of my resolution could be to relax.
TEAM TONYA
And maybe mine Could be to get a job... or whatever.
Here's your calendar back! It was giving me anxiety just holding it!
That's exactly how I feel about this beer.

Not My Jam

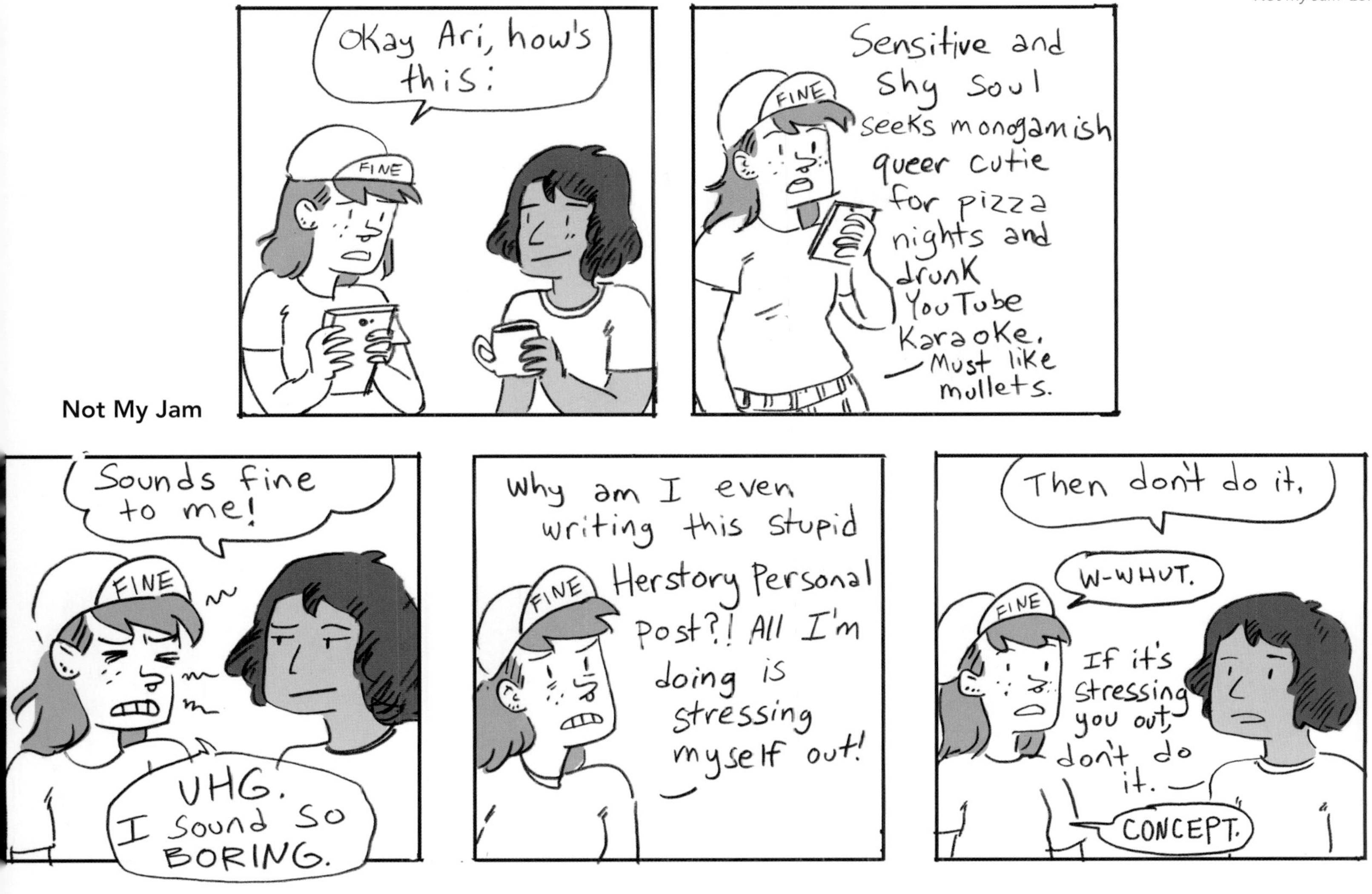
OKay Ari, how's this:
FINE
Sensitive and Shy Soul seeks monogamish queer cutie for pizza nights and drunk YouTube Karaoke. Must like mullets.
Sounds fine to me!
UHG. I sound so BORING.
Why am I even writing this stupid Herstory Personal Post?! All I'm doing is stressing myself out!
Then don't do it.
W-WHUT.
If it's stressing you out, don't do it.
"CONCEPT."

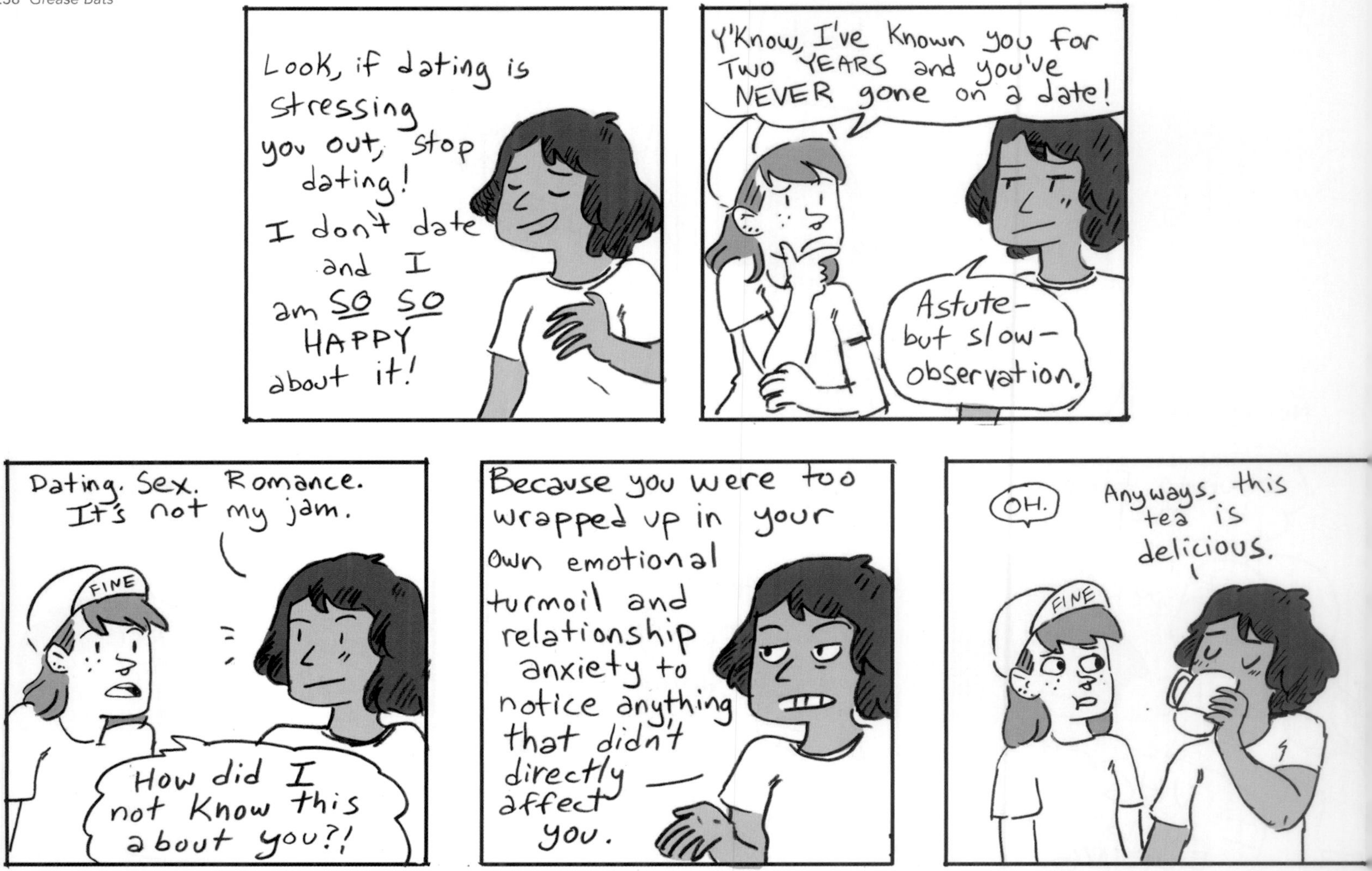
Look, if dating is stressing you out, stop dating! I don't date and I am SO SO HAPPY about it!
Y'Know, I've Known you for TWO YEARS and you've NEVER gone on a date!
Astute-but slow-observation.
Dating. Sex. Romance. It's not my jam.
How did I not Know this about you?!
Because you were too wrapped up in your own emotional turmoil and relationship anxiety to notice anything that didn't directly affect you.
OH.
Anyways, this tea is delicious.
FINE

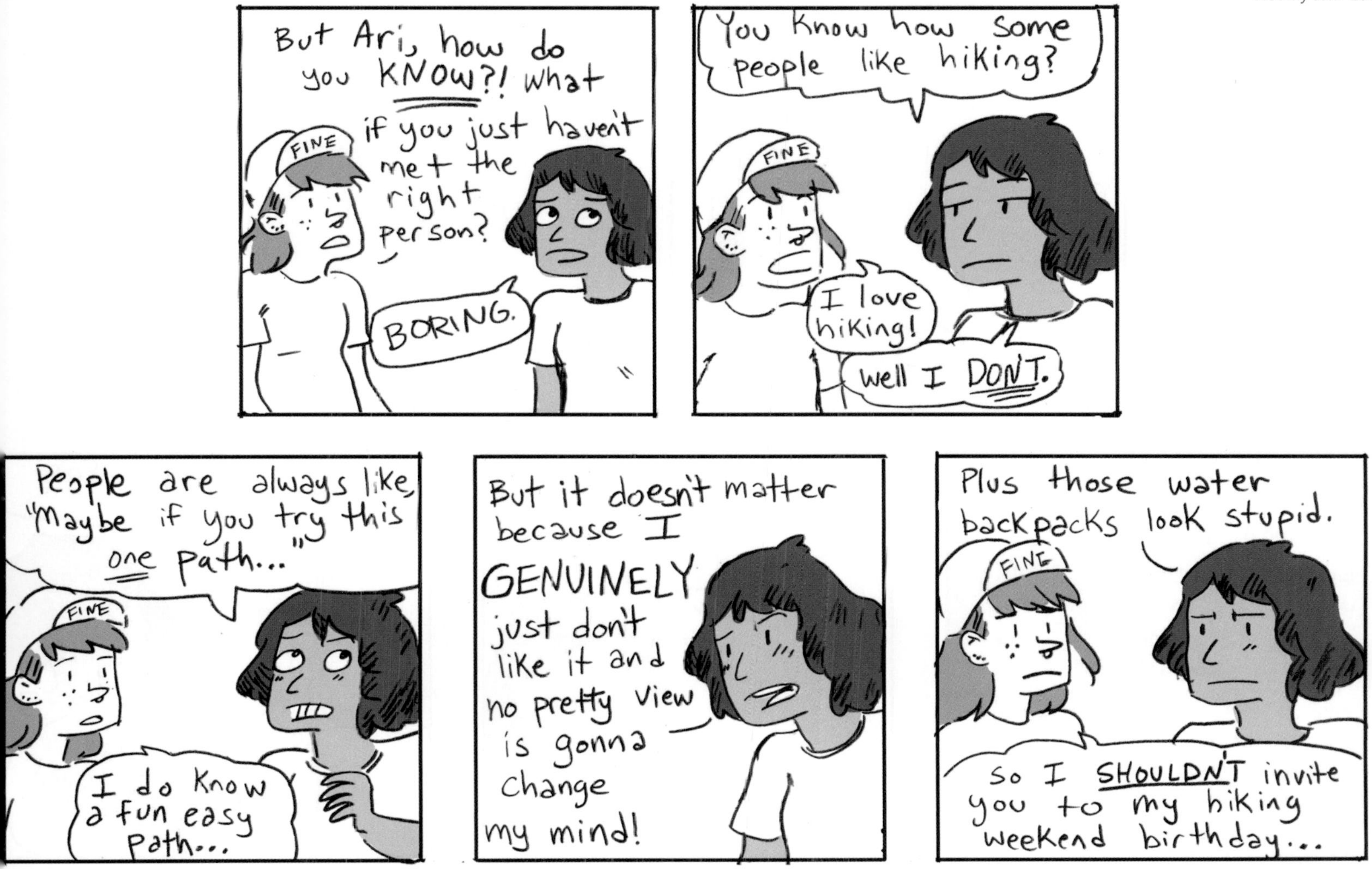
But Ari, how do you KNOW?! what if you just haven't met the right person?
BORING.
You know how some people like hiking?
I love hiking!
well I DON'T.
People are always like, "Maybe if you try this one path..."
I do know a fun easy path...
But it doesn't matter because I GENUINELY just don't like it and no pretty view is gonna change my mind!
Plus those water backpacks look stupid.
So I SHOULDN'T invite you to my hiking weekend birthday...

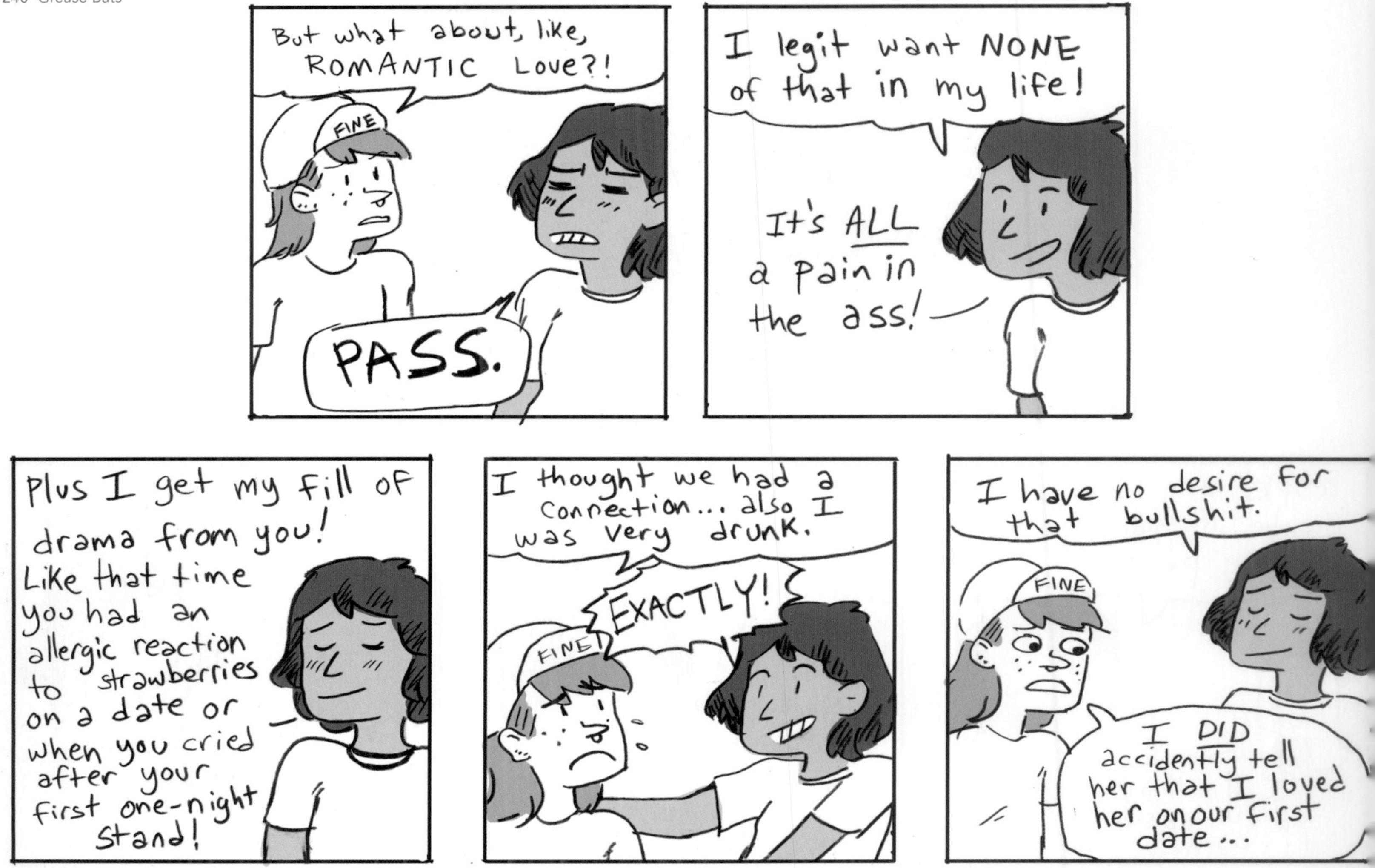
But what about, like, ROMANTIC LOVE?!
FINE
PASS.
I legit want NONE of that in my life!
It's ALL a pain in the ass!
Plus I get my fill of drama from you!
Like that time you had an allergic reaction to strawberries on a date or when you cried after your first one-night stand!
I thought we had a connection... also I was very drunk.
FINE
EXACTLY!
I have no desire for that bullshit.
FINE
I DID accidently tell her that I loved her on our first date...

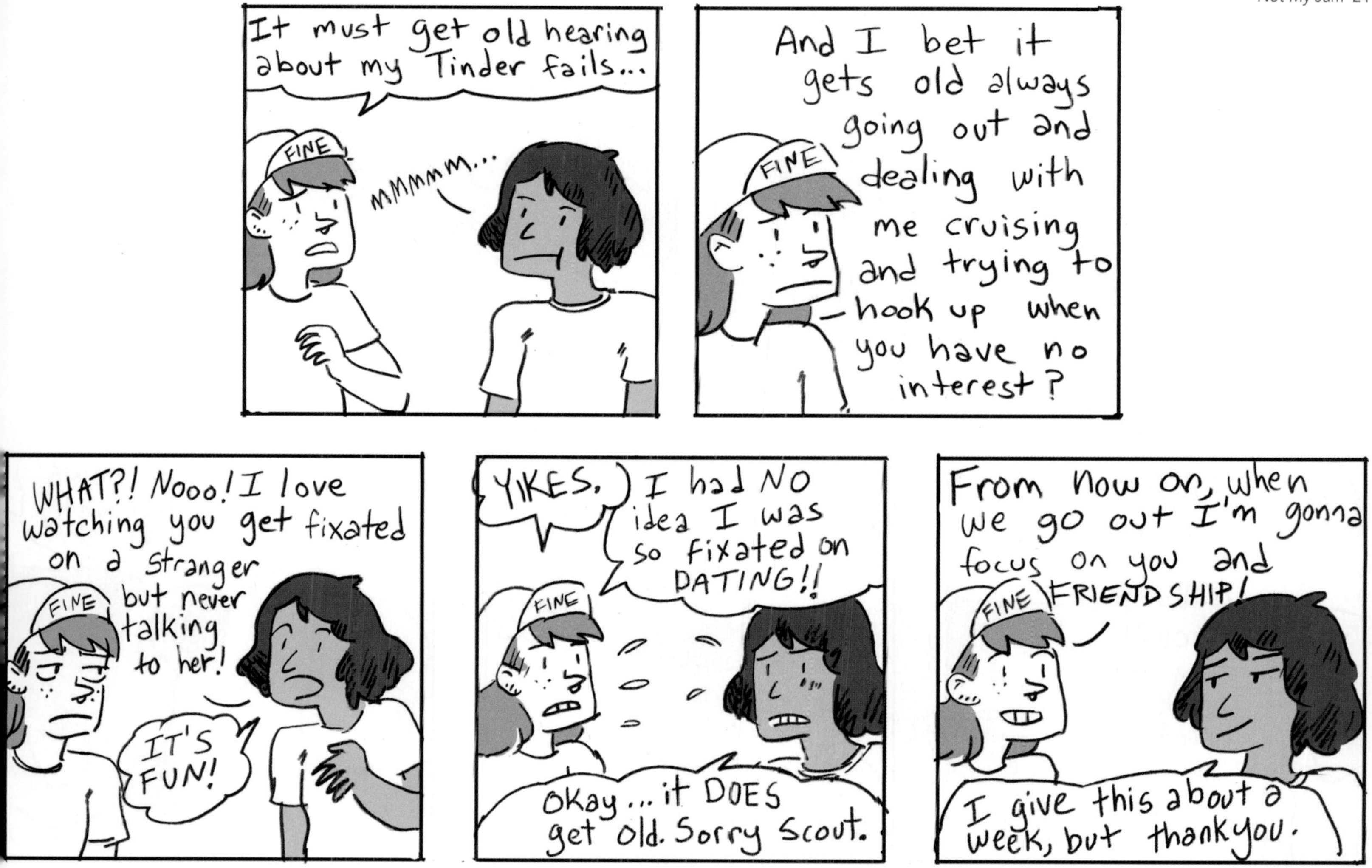
It must get old hearing about my Tinder fails...
MMMMM...
And I bet it gets old always going out and dealing with me cruising and trying to hook up when you have no interest?
WHAT?! Nooo! I love watching you get fixated on a stranger but never talking to her!
IT'S FUN!
YIKES.
I had NO idea I was so fixated on DATING!!
Okay ... it DOES get old. Sorry Scout.
From now on, when we go out I'm gonna focus on you and FRIENDSHIP!
I give this about a week, but thank you.
FINE

Garage Sale

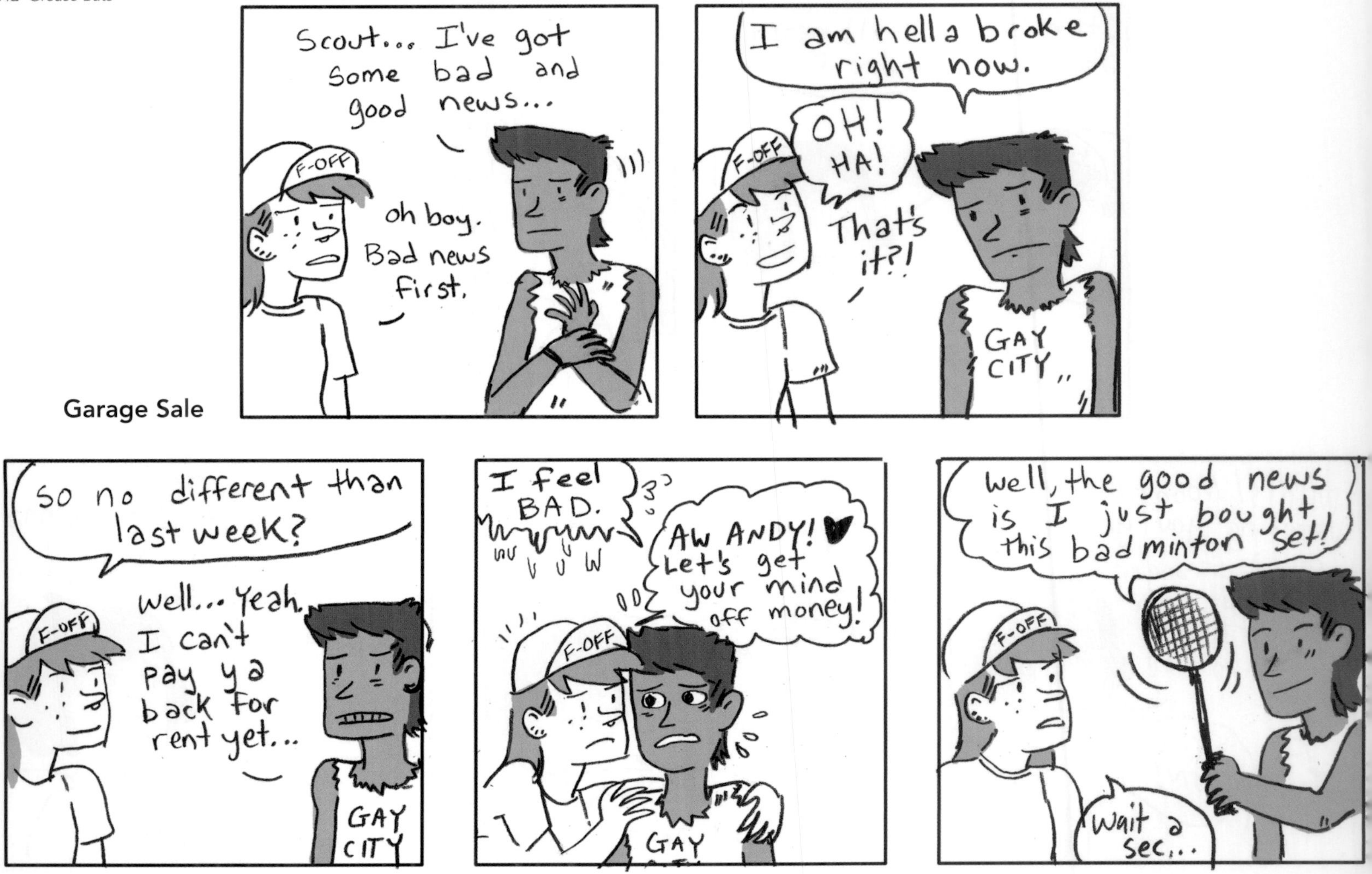
Scout... I've got some bad and good news...
oh boy. Bad news first.
F-OFF
I am hella broke right now.
OH! HA!
That's it?!
F-OFF
GAY CITY
so no different than last week?
well... Yeah. I can't pay ya back for rent yet...
F-OFF
GAY CITY
I feel BAD.
AW ANDY! Let's get your mind off money!
F-OFF
GAY
well, the good news is I just bought this badminton set!
wait a sec...
F-OFF

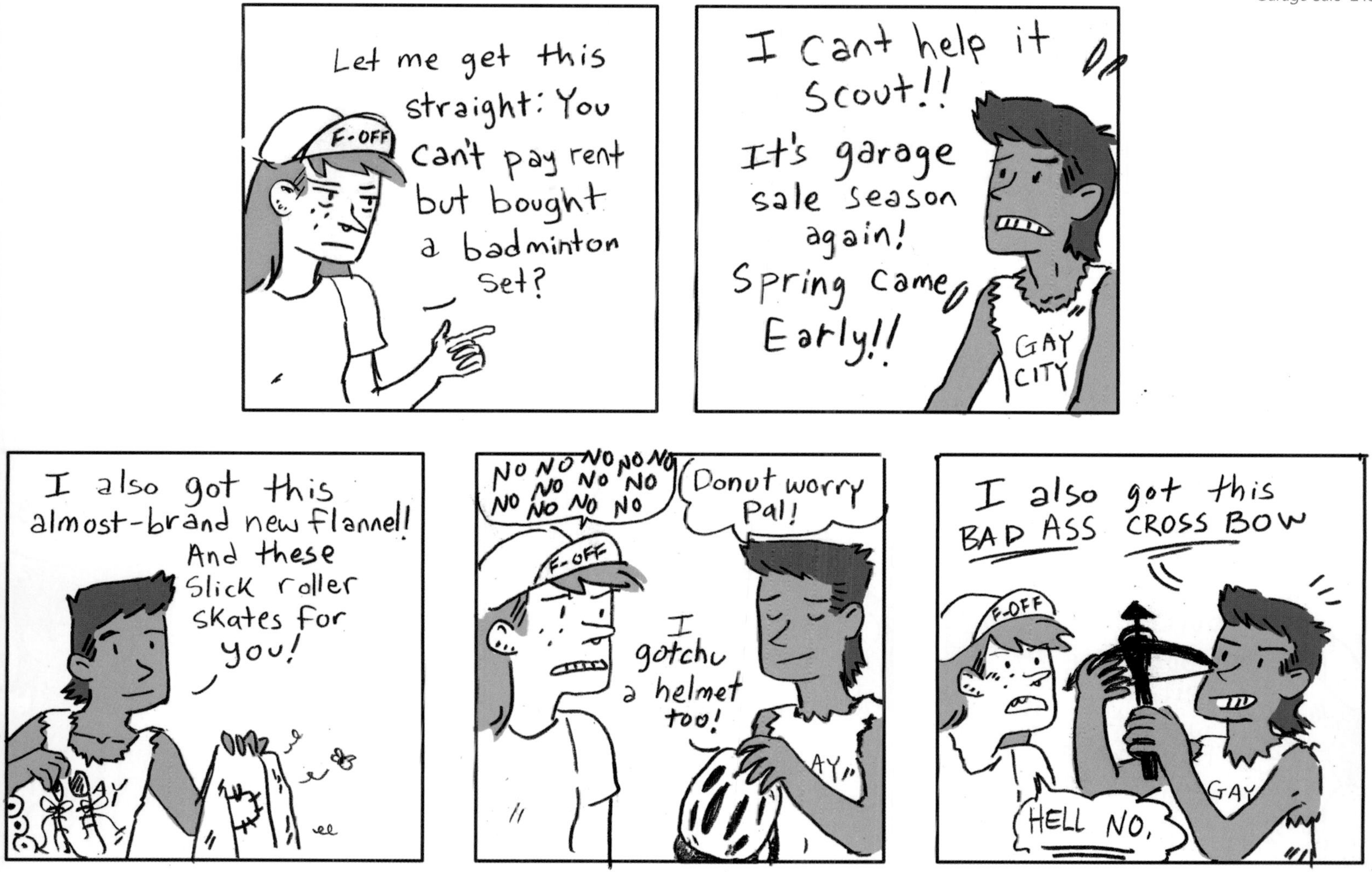
Let me get this straight: You can't pay rent but bought a badminton set?
F-OFF
I cant help it Scout!! It's garage sale season again! Spring came Early!!
GAY CITY
I also got this almost-brand new flannel! And these slick roller skates for you!
NO NO NO NO NO NO NO NO NO NO NO NO NO
Donut worry Pal!
I gotchu a helmet too!
I also got this BAD ASS CROSS BOW
HELL NO.

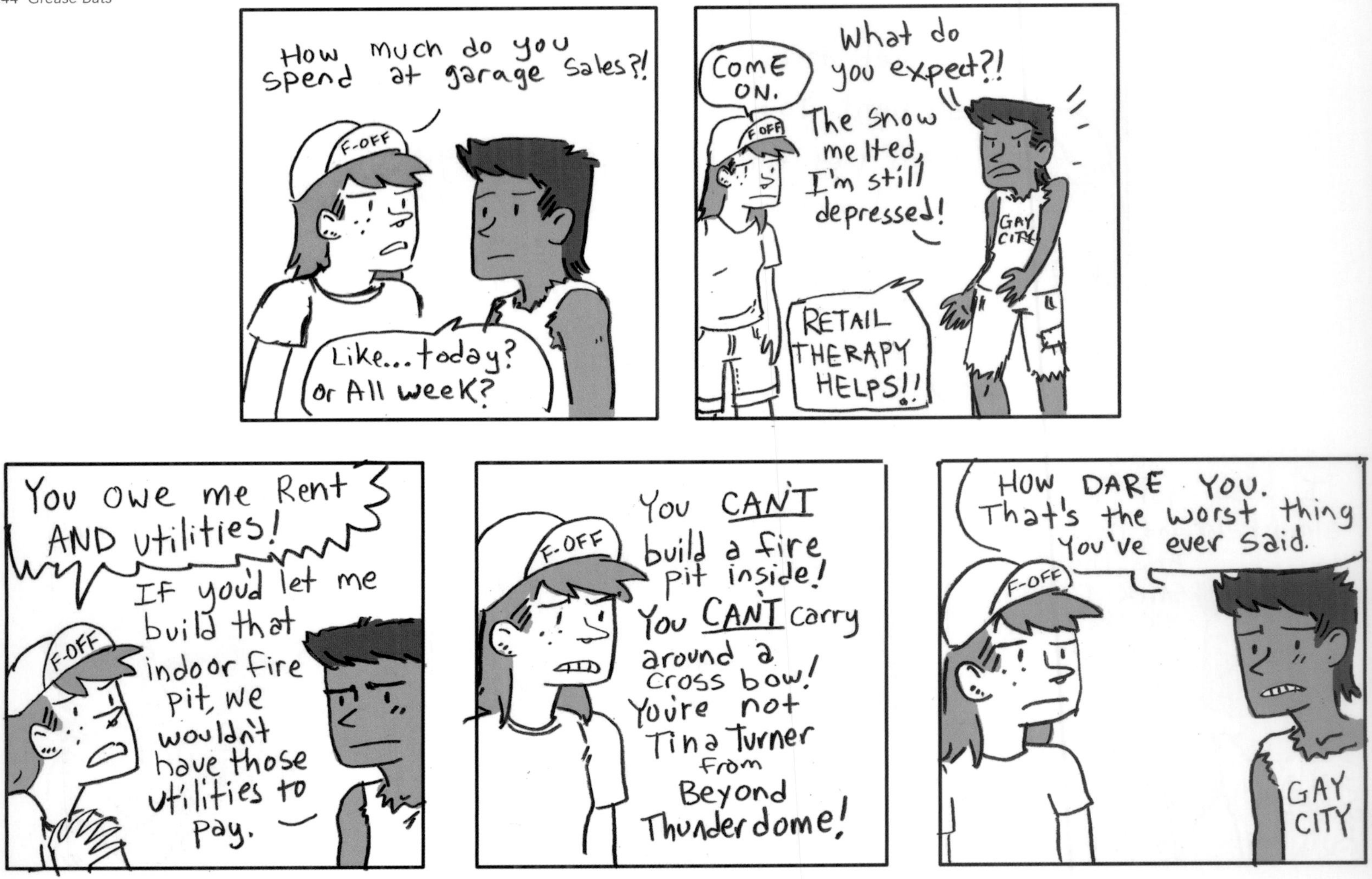
How much do you spend at garage sales?!
Like... today? or All week?
COME ON.
What do you expect?!
The snow melted, I'm still depressed!
RETAIL THERAPY HELPS!!
GAY CITY
You owe me Rent AND utilities!
If you'd let me build that indoor fire pit, we wouldn't have those utilities to pay.
You CAN'T build a fire pit inside! You CAN'T carry around a cross bow! You're not Tina Turner from Beyond Thunderdome!
HOW DARE YOU. That's the worst thing you've ever said.
GAY CITY

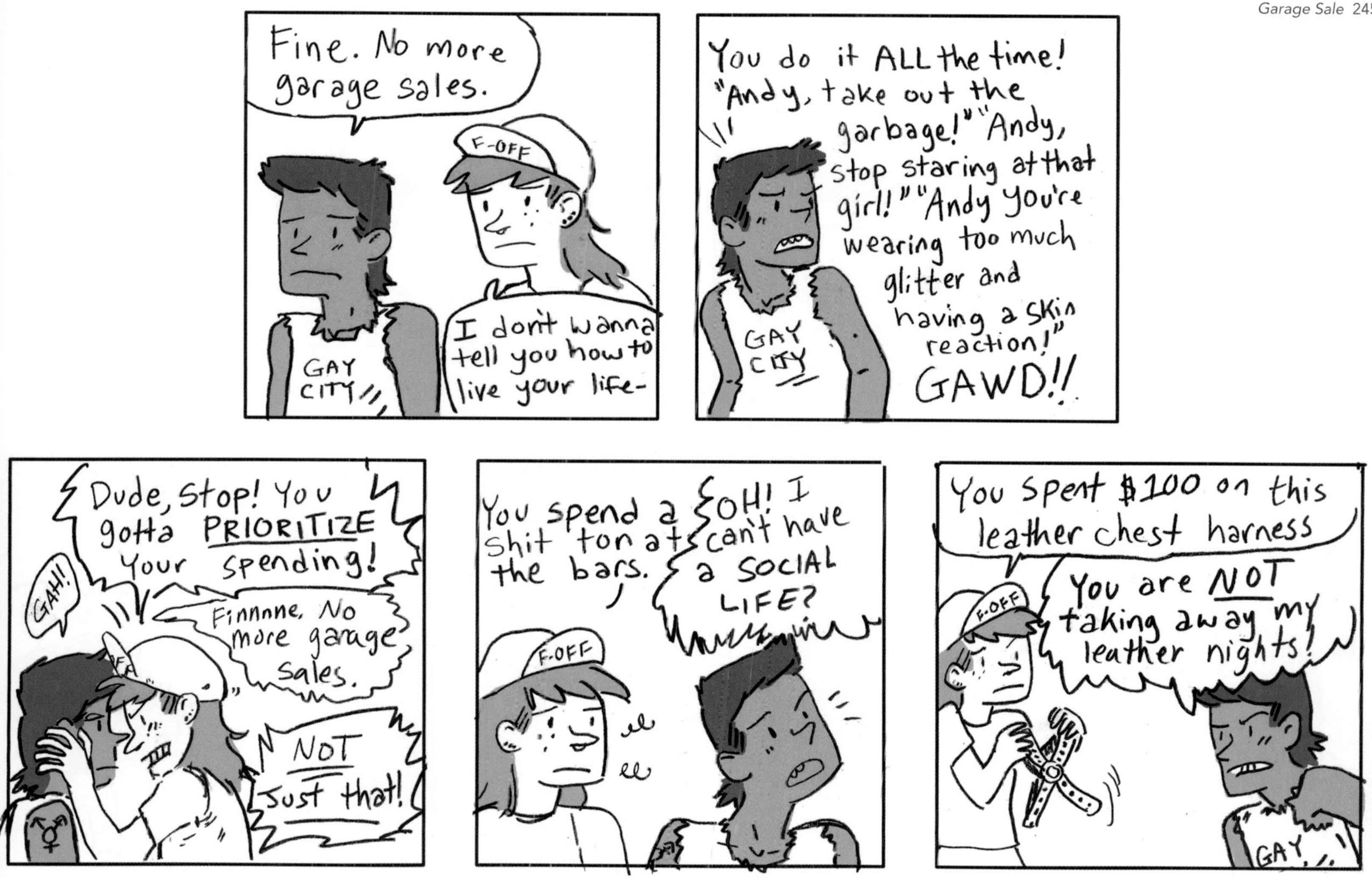

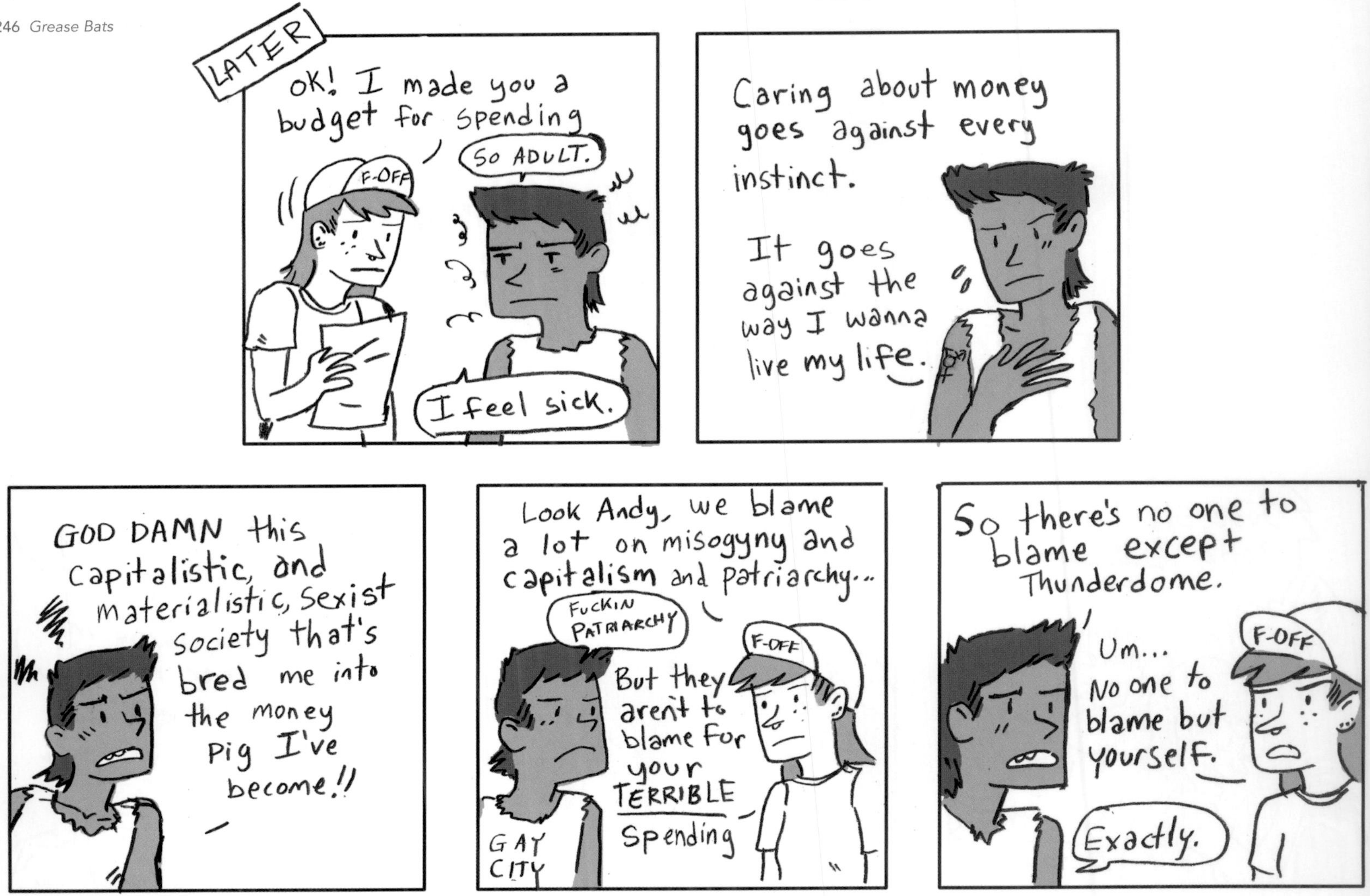
LATER
OK! I made you a budget for spending
SO ADULT.
I feel sick.
Caring about money goes against every instinct.
It goes against the way I wanna live my life.
GOD DAMN this capitalistic, and materialistic, sexist society that's bred me into the money pig I've become!!
Look Andy, we blame a lot on misogyny and capitalism and patriarchy...
FUCKIN PATRIARCHY
F-OFF
But they aren't to blame for your TERRIBLE spending
GAY CITY
So there's no one to blame except Thunderdome.
F-OFF
Um... No one to blame but yourself.
Exactly.

Homosexual Imposter

Panel 1: Taylor - Can I complain for a second? / Of course!

Panel 2: So I was in a bar with some new friends and we started talking about our past sexual experiences... / Maybe I don't want to hear this...

Panel 3: And although this year has been the WILDEST, WETTEST, MOST EXPERIMENTAL year of my life...

Panel 4: Everyone else had queer stories from when they were young - and I have none! And, I dunno, I suddenly felt...

Panel 5: NOT QUEER ENOUGH!! / Every gay's nightmare!

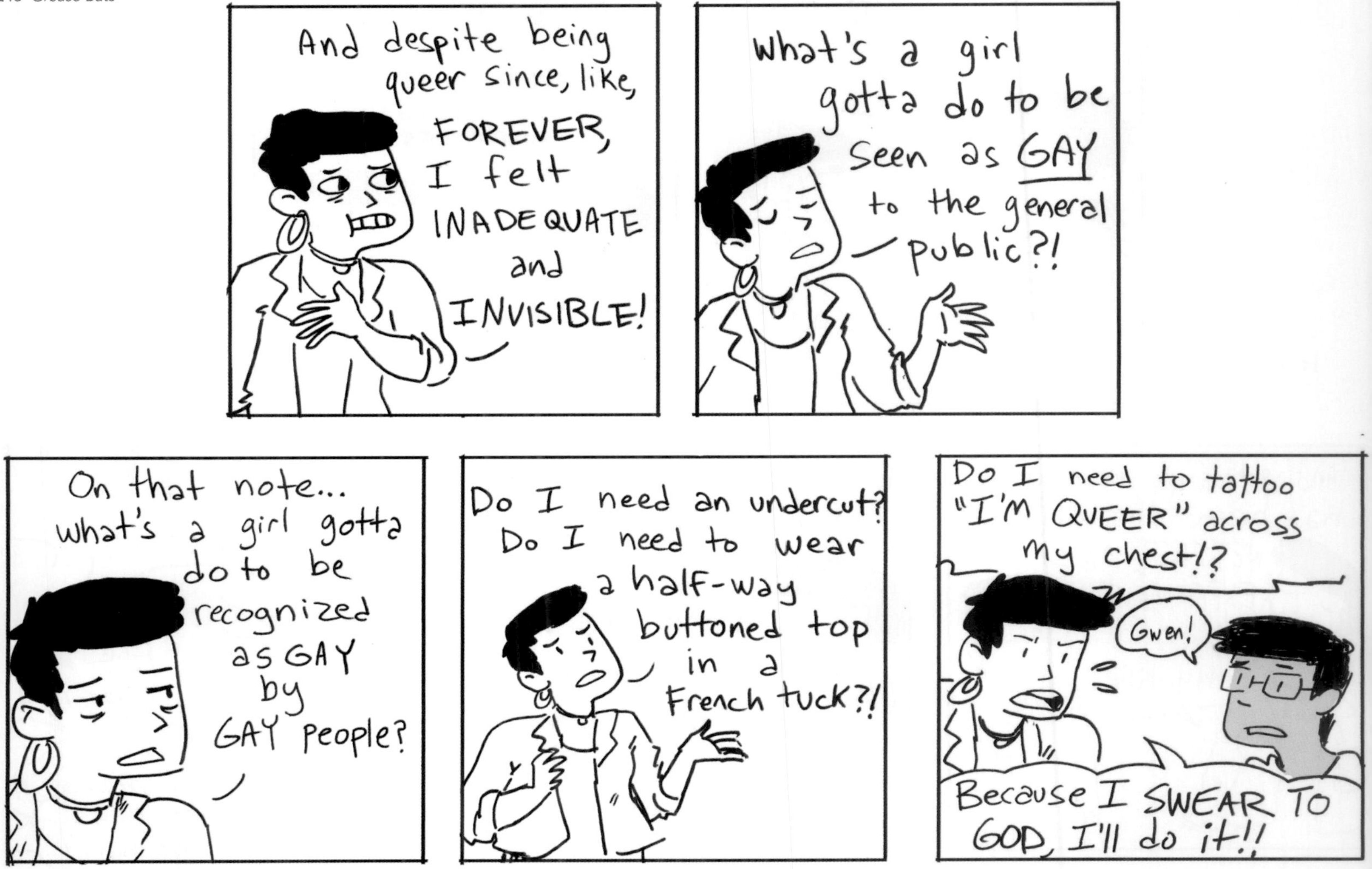
And despite being queer since, like, FOREVER, I felt INADEQUATE and INVISIBLE!
What's a girl gotta do to be seen as GAY to the general public?!
On that note... what's a girl gotta do to be recognized as GAY by GAY people?
Do I need an undercut? Do I need to wear a half-way buttoned top in a French tuck?!
Do I need to tattoo "I'M QUEER" across my chest!?
Gwen!
Because I SWEAR TO GOD, I'll do it!!

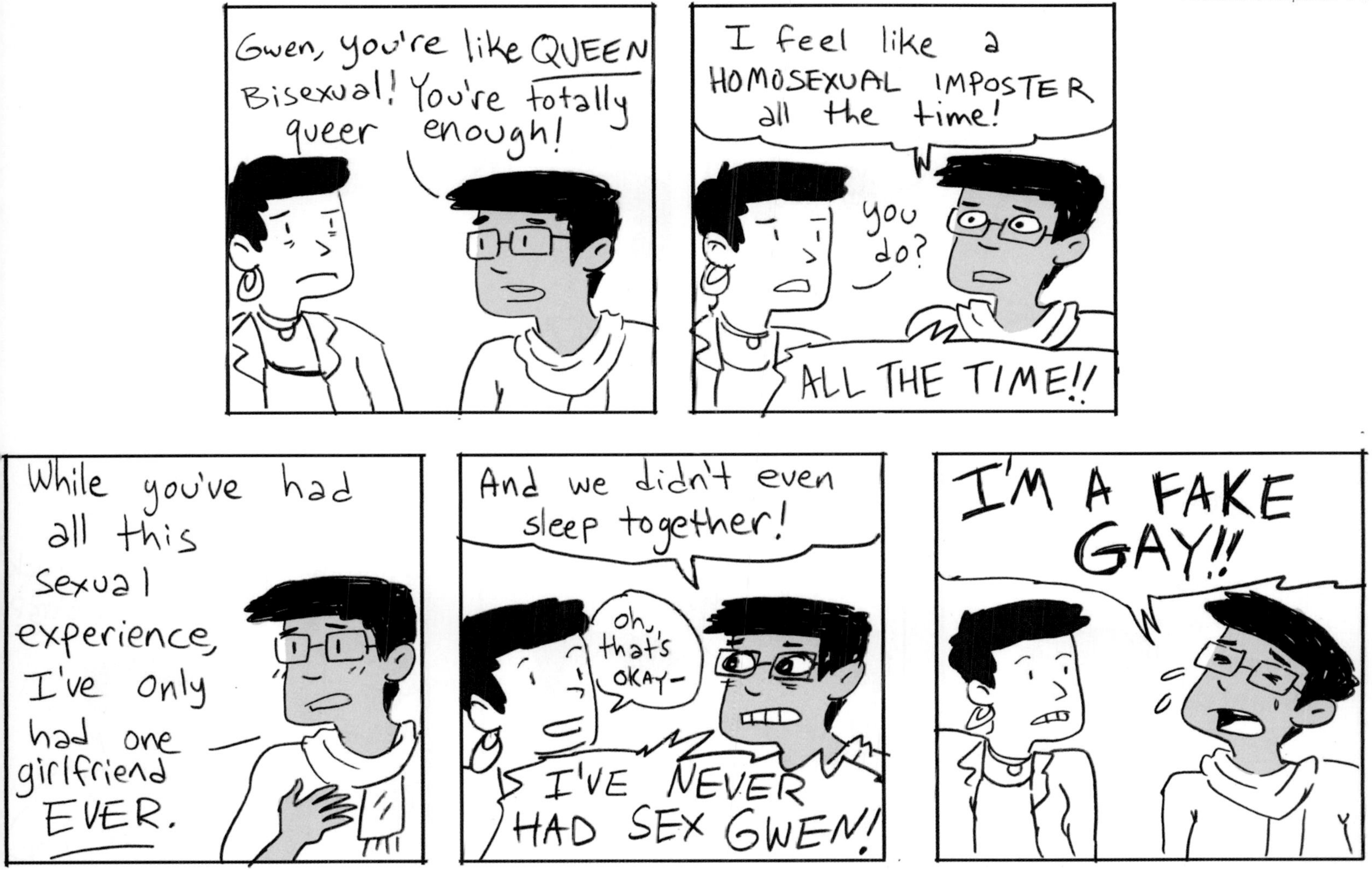
Gwen, you're like QUEEN Bisexual! You're totally queer enough!
I feel like a HOMOSEXUAL IMPOSTER all the time!
you do?
ALL THE TIME!!
While you've had all this sexual experience, I've only had one girlfriend EVER.
And we didn't even sleep together!
oh, that's OKAY-
I'VE NEVER HAD SEX GWEN!
I'M A FAKE GAY!!

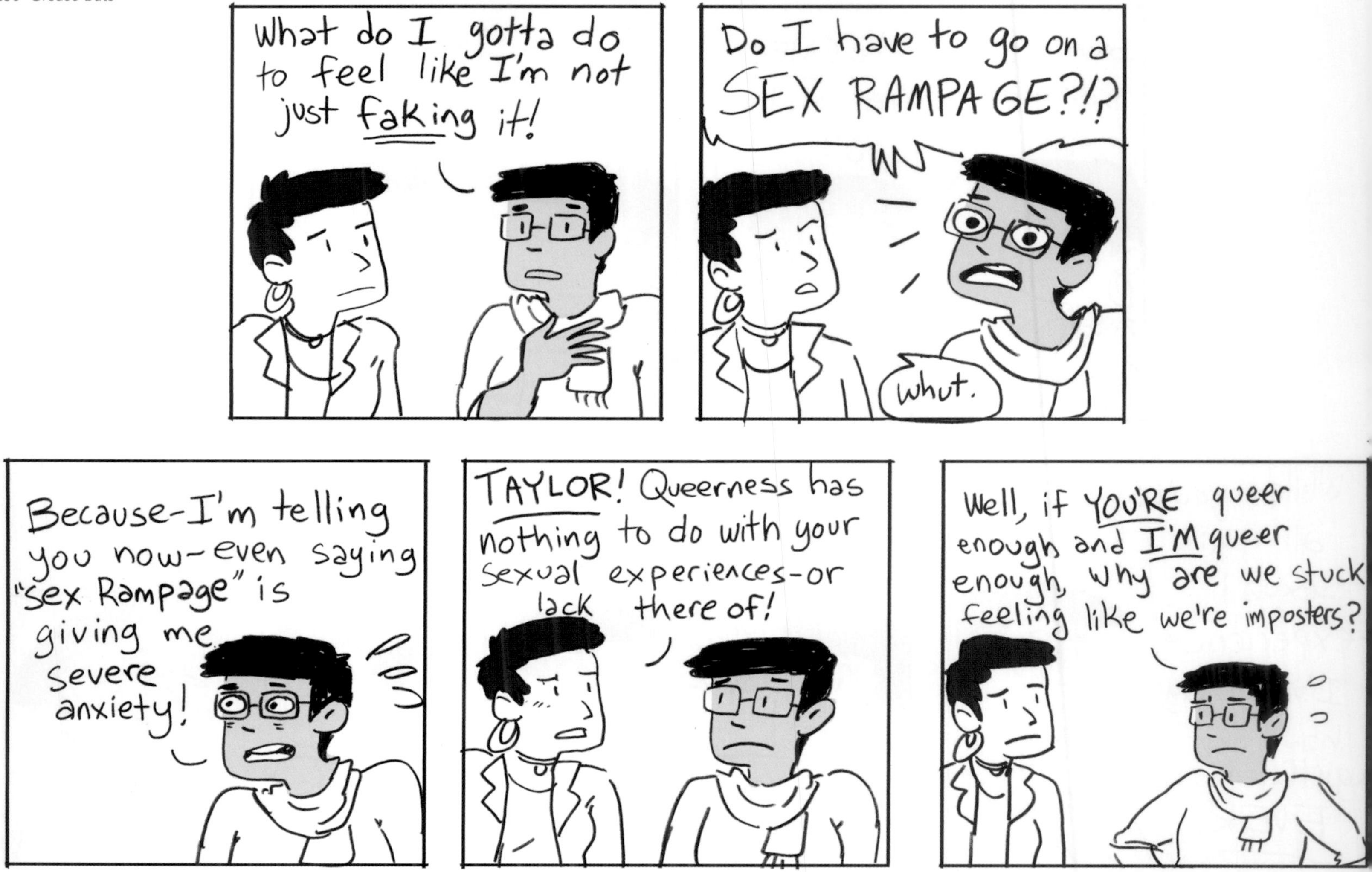
What do I gotta do to feel like I'm not just faking it!
Do I have to go on a SEX RAMPAGE?!?
whut.
Because-I'm telling you now-even saying "sex Rampage" is giving me severe anxiety!
TAYLOR! Queerness has nothing to do with your sexual experiences-or lack there of!
Well, if YOU'RE queer enough and I'M queer enough, why are we stuck feeling like we're imposters?

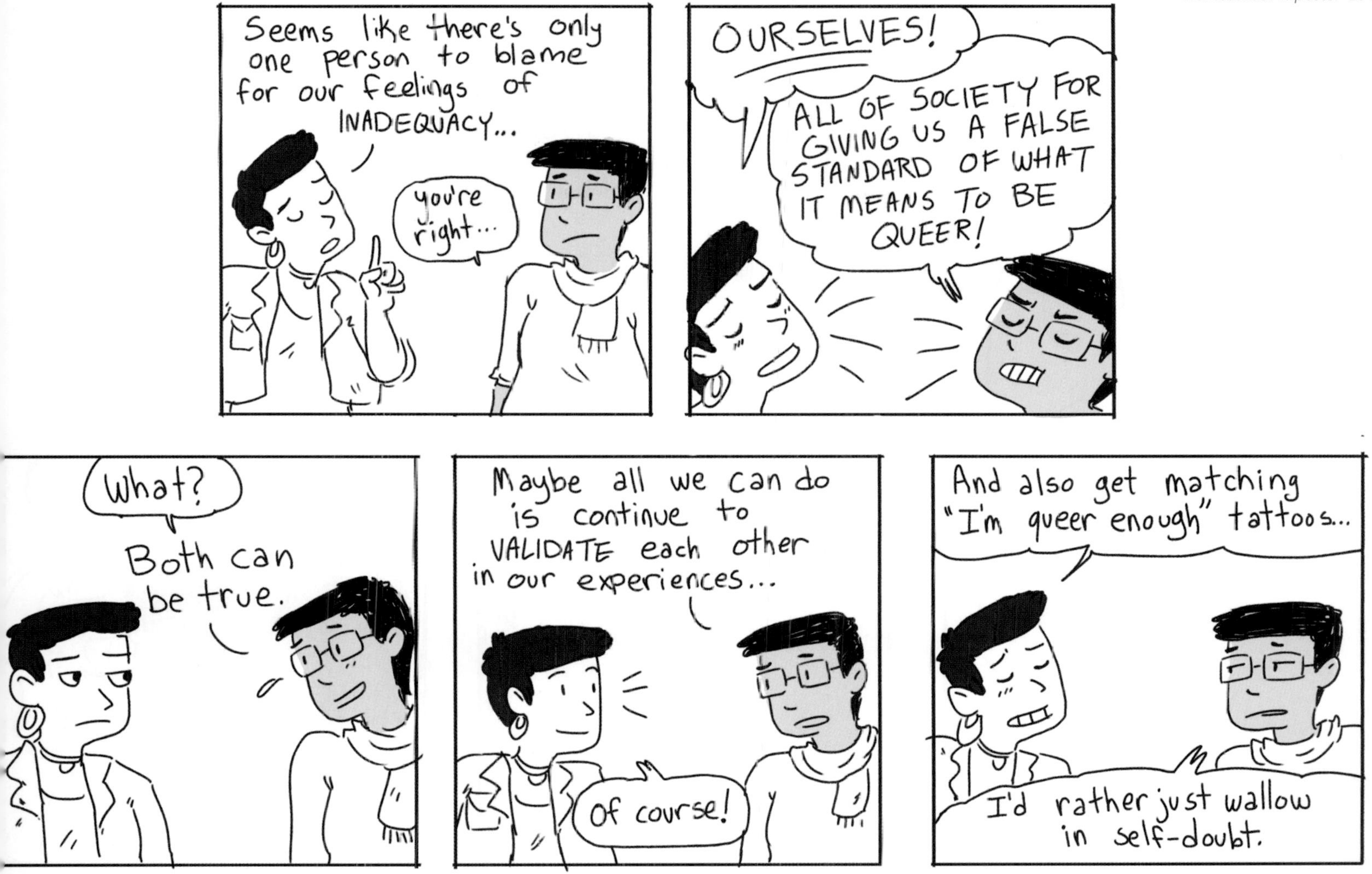
Seems like there's only one person to blame for our feelings of INADEQUACY...
you're right...
OURSELVES!
ALL OF SOCIETY FOR GIVING US A FALSE STANDARD OF WHAT IT MEANS TO BE QUEER!
What?
Both can be true.
Maybe all we can do is continue to VALIDATE each other in our experiences...
Of course!
And also get matching "I'm queer enough" tattoos...
I'd rather just wallow in self-doubt.

The Concert

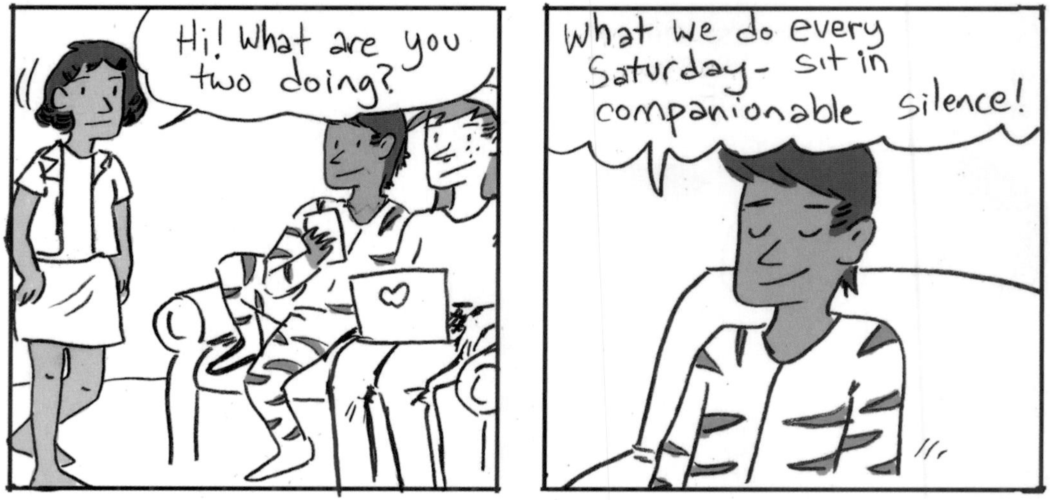
Hi! What are you two doing?
What we do every Saturday- sit in companionable silence!

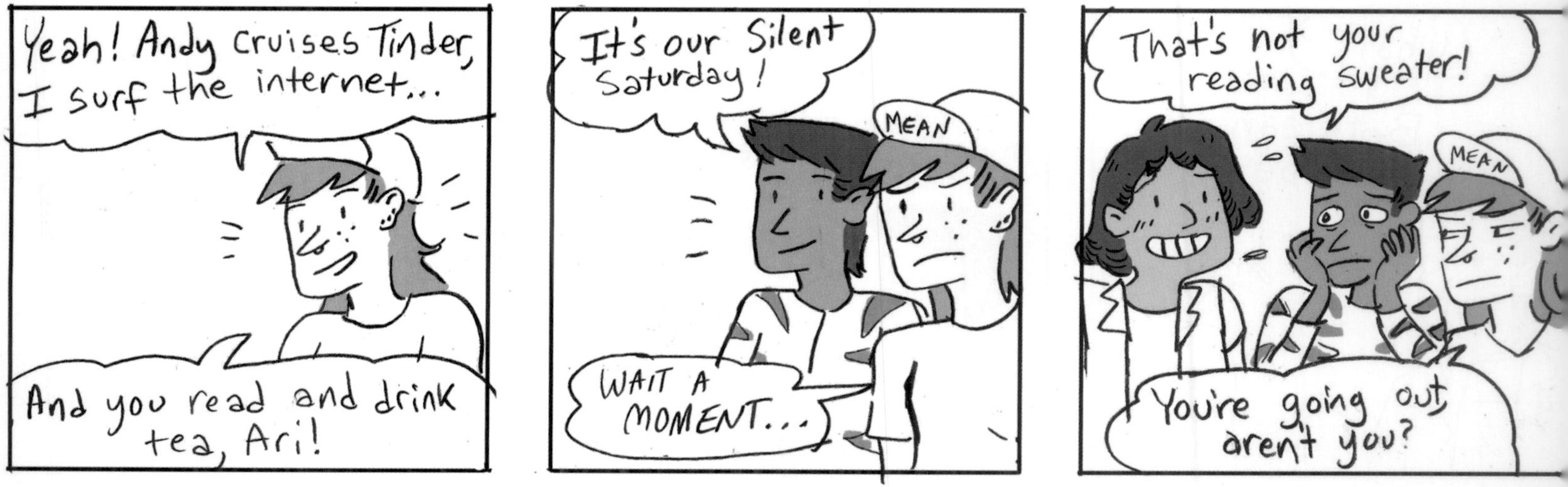
Yeah! Andy cruises Tinder, I surf the internet...
And you read and drink tea, Ari!
It's our Silent Saturday!
MEAN
WAIT A MOMENT...
That's not your reading sweater!
MEAN
You're going out, aren't you?

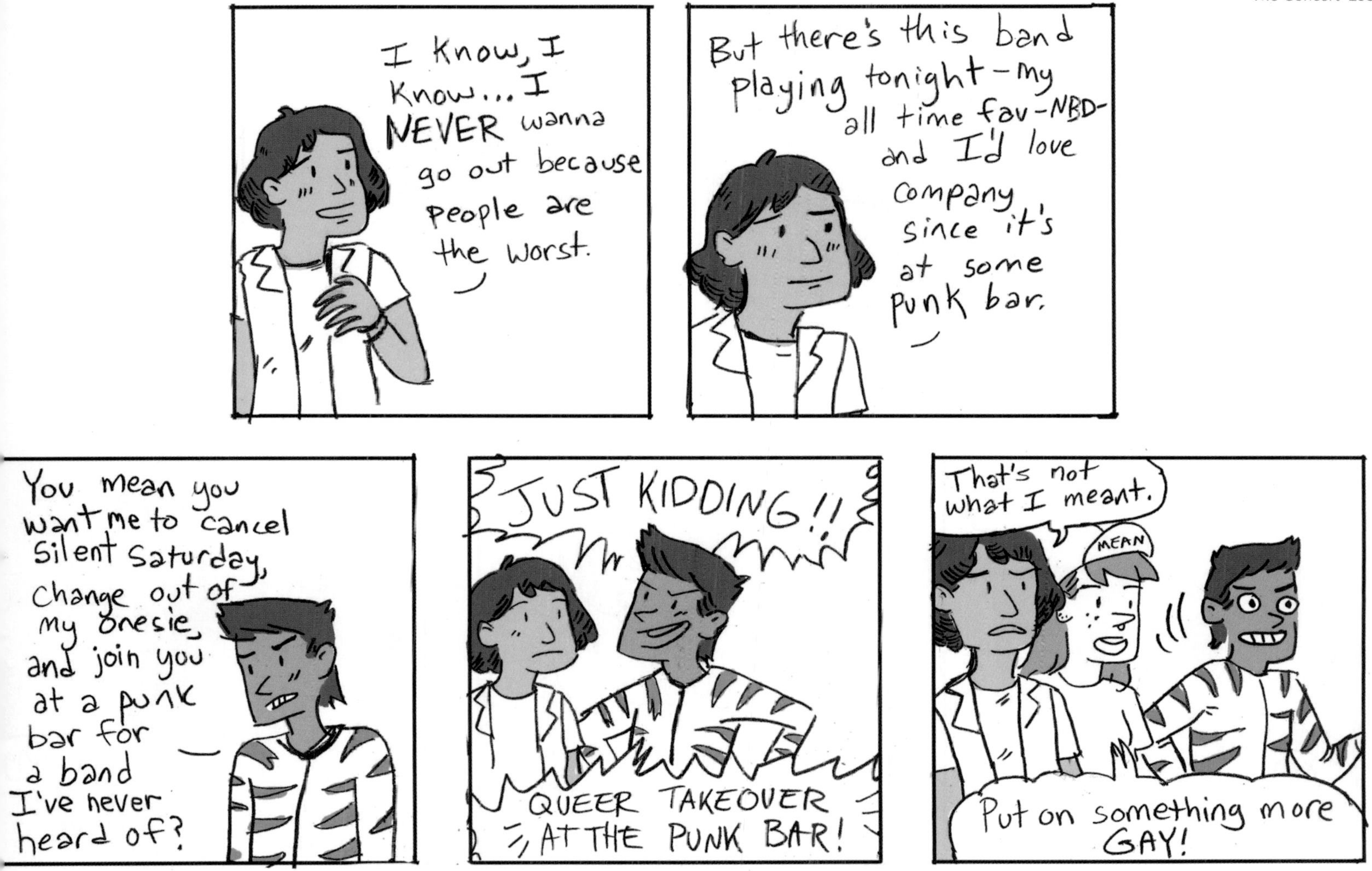
I know, I know... I NEVER wanna go out because people are the worst.
But there's this band playing tonight—my all time fav—NBD—and I'd love company since it's at some punk bar.
You mean you want me to cancel Silent Saturday, change out of my onesie, and join you at a punk bar for a band I've never heard of?
JUST KIDDING!!
QUEER TAKEOVER AT THE PUNK BAR!
That's not what I meant.
MEAN
Put on something more GAY!

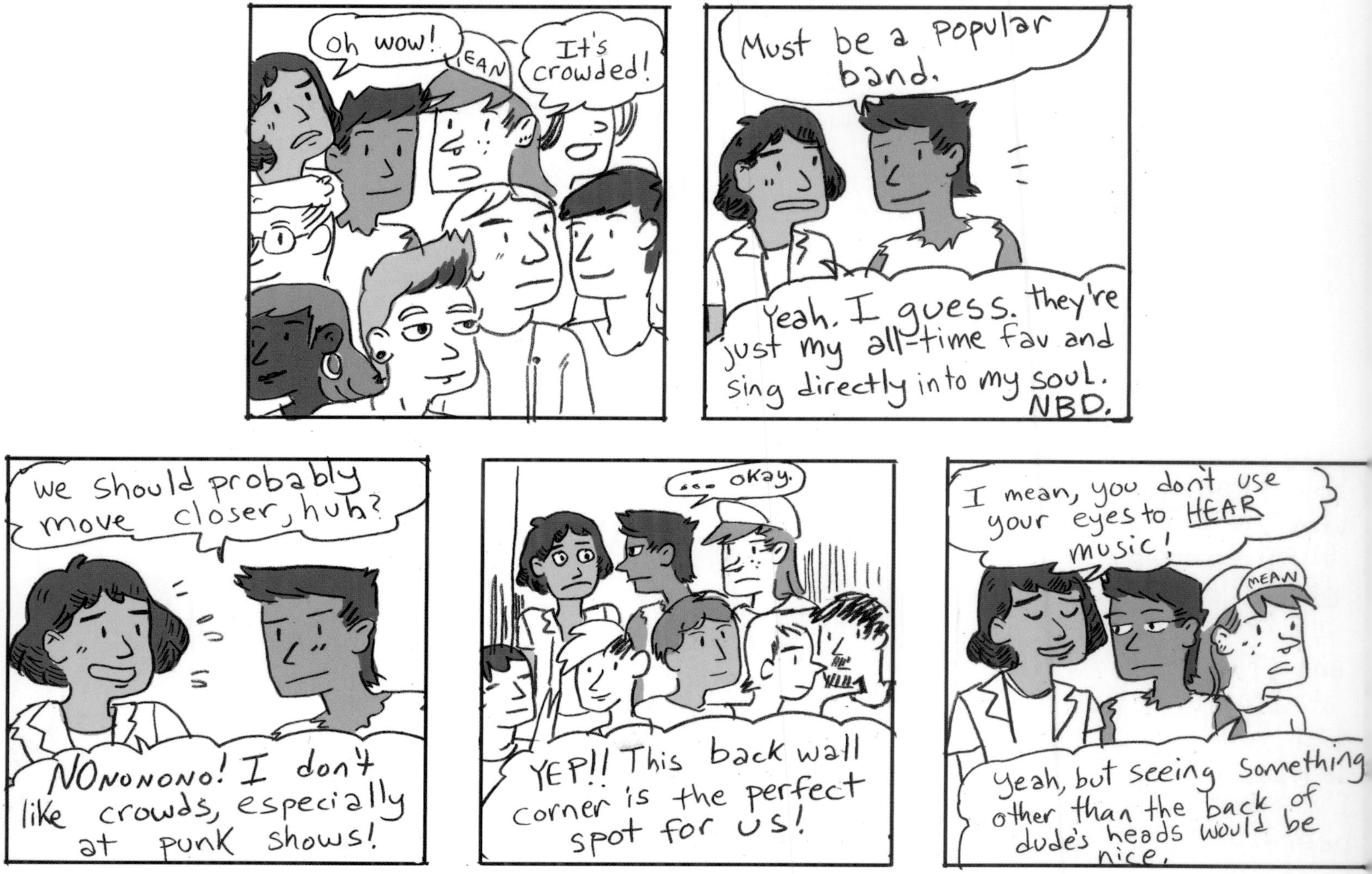

Oh wow!
It's crowded!
Must be a popular band.
Yeah. I guess. they're just my all-time fav and sing directly into my soul. NBD.
we should probably move closer, huh?
NOnonono! I don't like crowds, especially at punk shows!
... okay.
YEP!! This back wall corner is the perfect spot for us!
I mean, you don't use your eyes to HEAR music!
MEAN
Yeah, but seeing something other than the back of dude's heads would be nice.

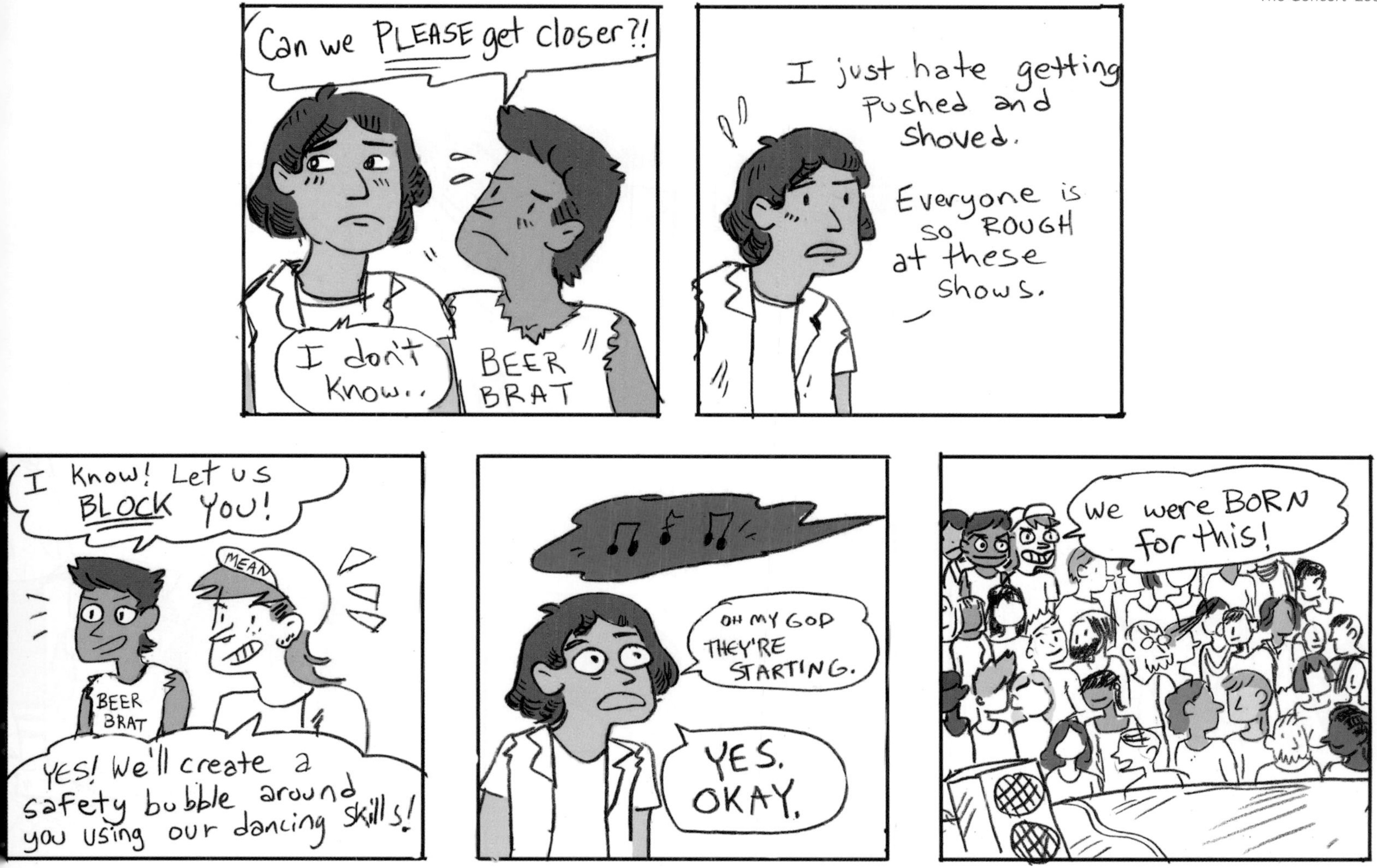
Can we PLEASE get closer?!
I don't know..
BEER BRAT
I just hate getting pushed and shoved.
Everyone is so ROUGH at these shows.
I know! Let us BLOCK you!
MEAN
BEER BRAT
YES! We'll create a safety bubble around you using our dancing skills!
OH MY GOD THEY'RE STARTING.
YES. OKAY.
We were BORN for this!

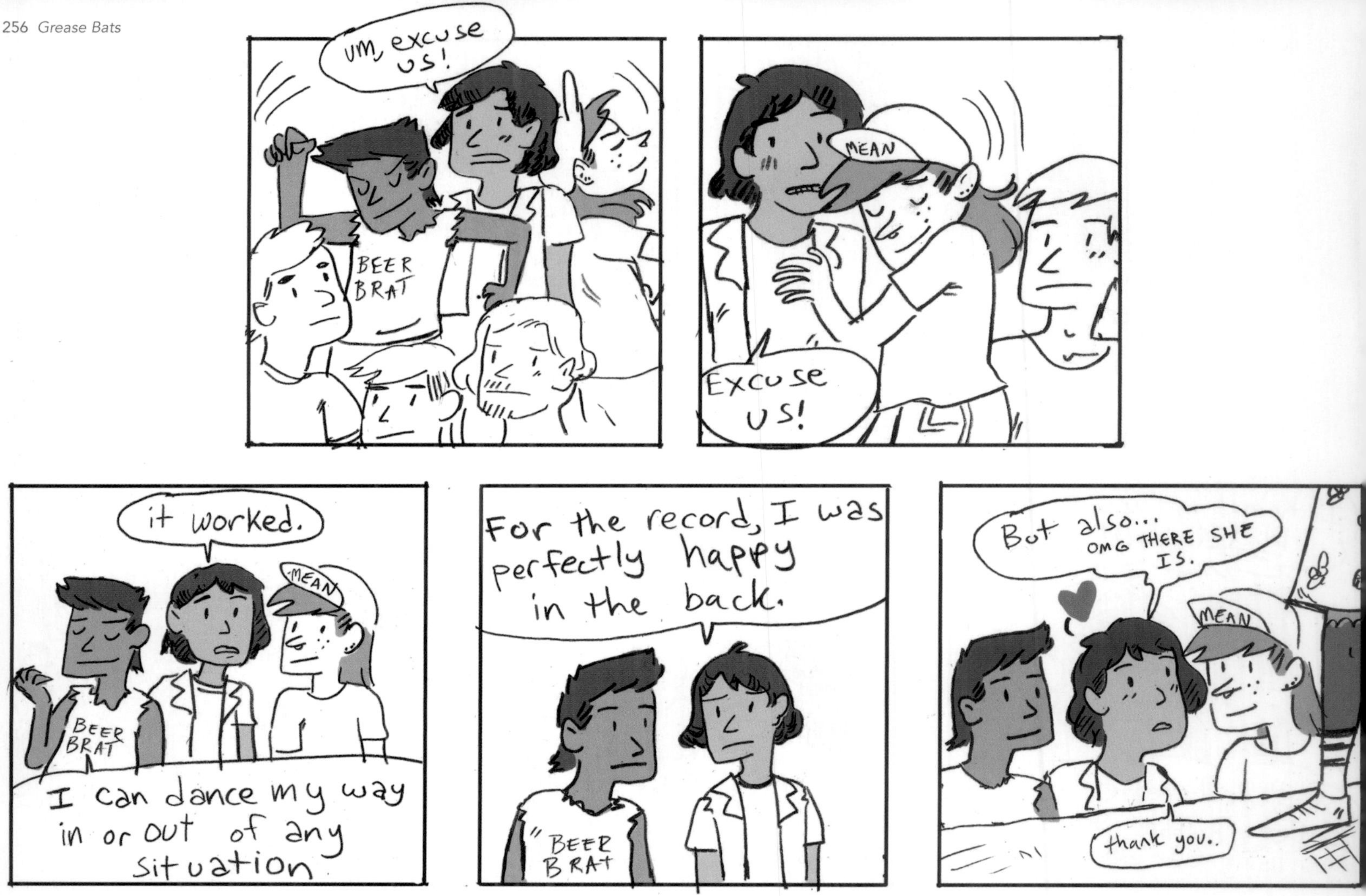
um, excuse us!
BEER BRAT
MEAN
Excuse us!
it worked.
MEAN
BEER BRAT
I can dance my way in or out of any situation
For the record, I was perfectly happy in the back.
BEER BRAT
But also... OMG THERE SHE IS.
MEAN
thank you.

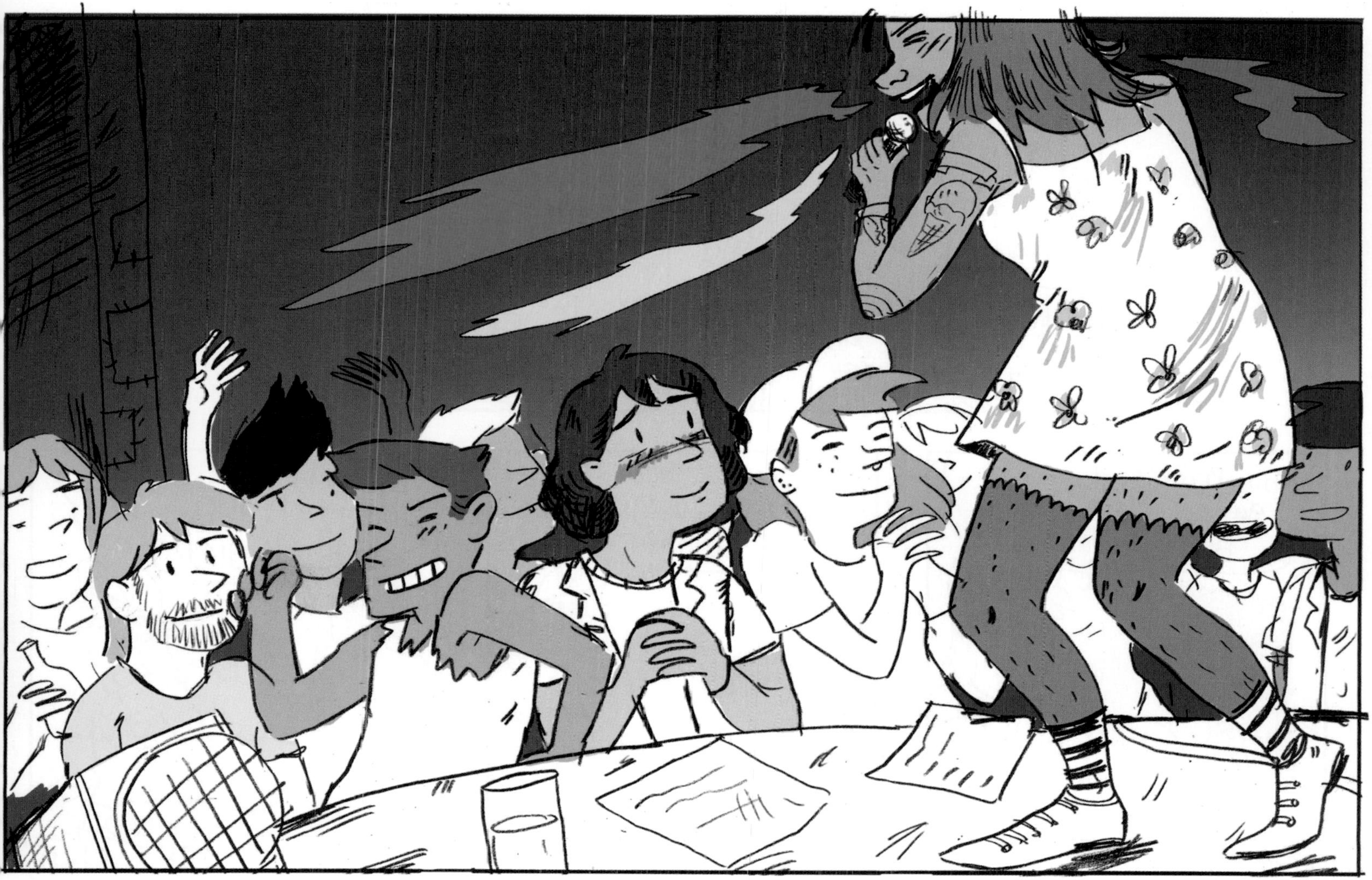

Camping

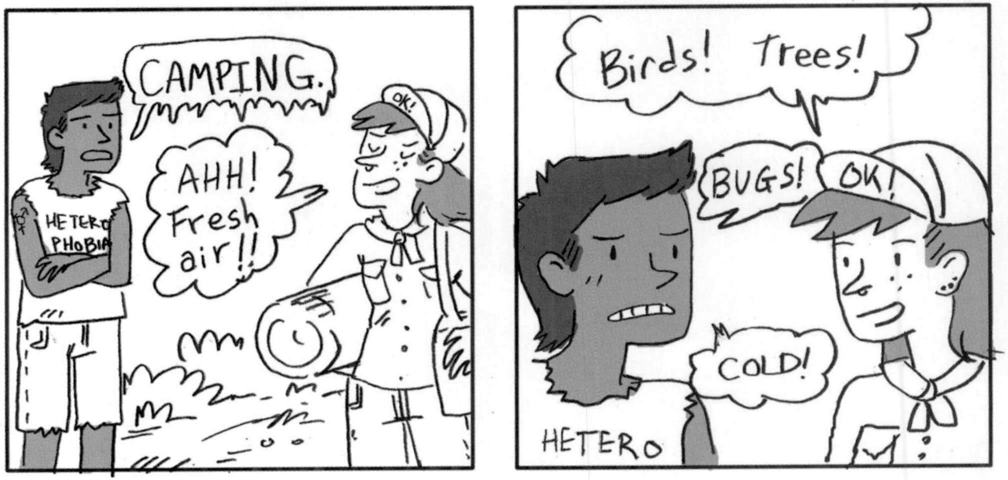
CAMPING.
AHH! Fresh air!!
HETERO PHOBIA
Birds! Trees!
BUGS!
OK!
COLD!
HETERO

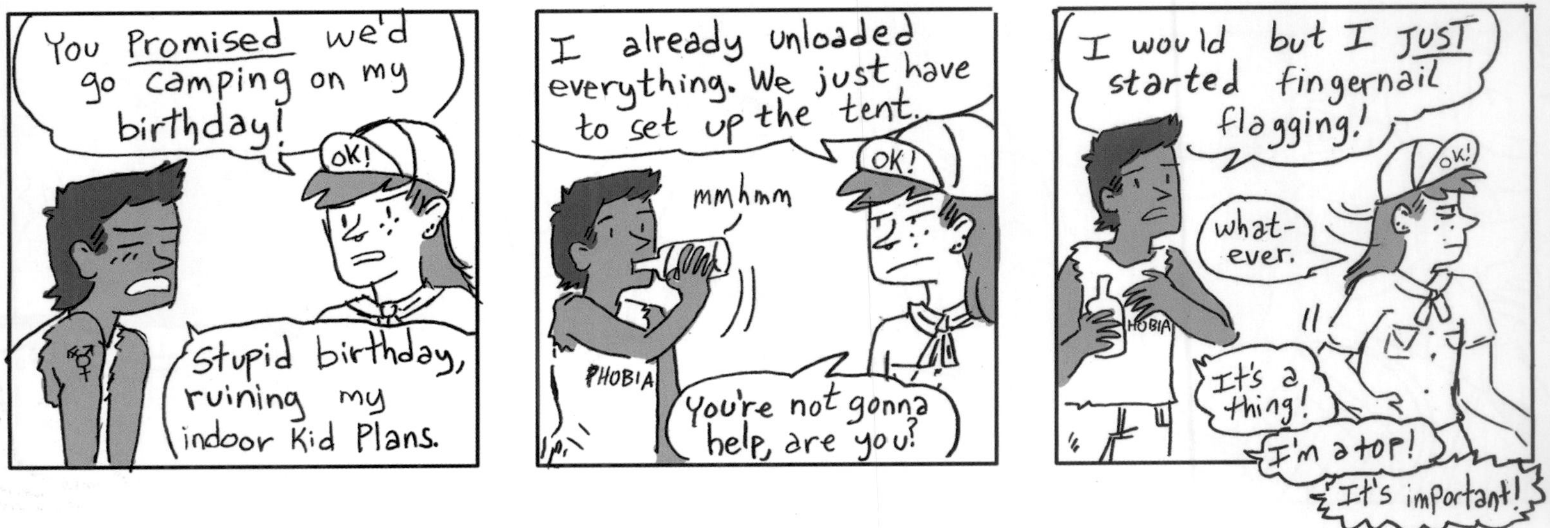
You Promised we'd go camping on my birthday!
OK!
Stupid birthday, ruining my indoor Kid Plans.
I already unloaded everything. We just have to set up the tent.
OK!
mmhmm
PHOBIA
You're not gonna help, are you?
I would but I JUST started fingernail flagging!
OK!
what-ever.
HOBIA
It's a thing!
I'm a top!
It's important!

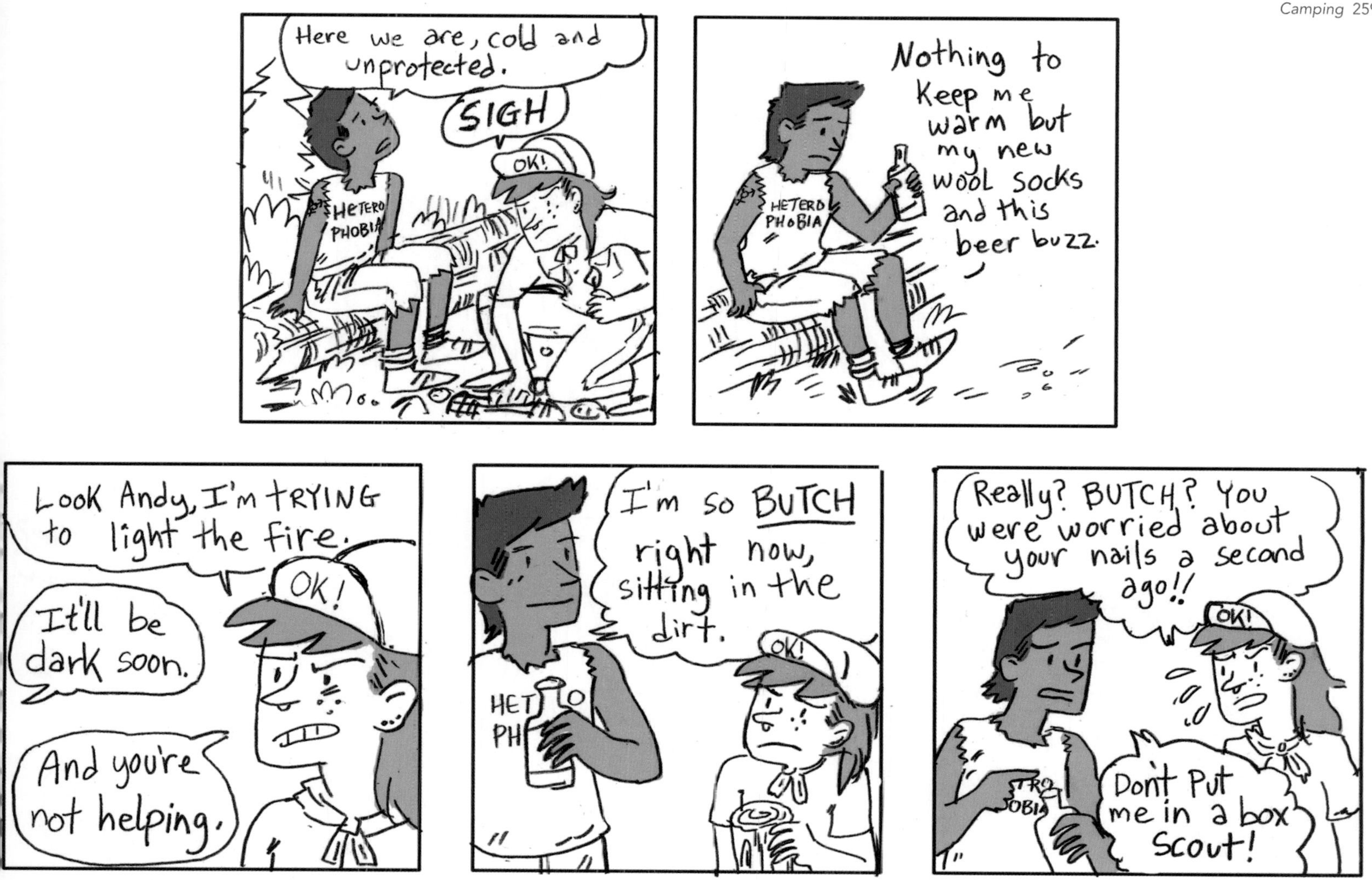
Here we are, cold and unprotected.
SIGH
OK!
HETERO PHOBIA
Nothing to Keep me warm but my new wool socks and this beer buzz.
HETERO PHOBIA
Look Andy, I'm TRYING to light the fire.
It'll be dark soon.
And you're not helping.
OK!
I'm so BUTCH right now, sitting in the dirt.
OK!
Really? BUTCH? You were worried about your nails a second ago!!
OK!
Don't Put me in a box Scout!

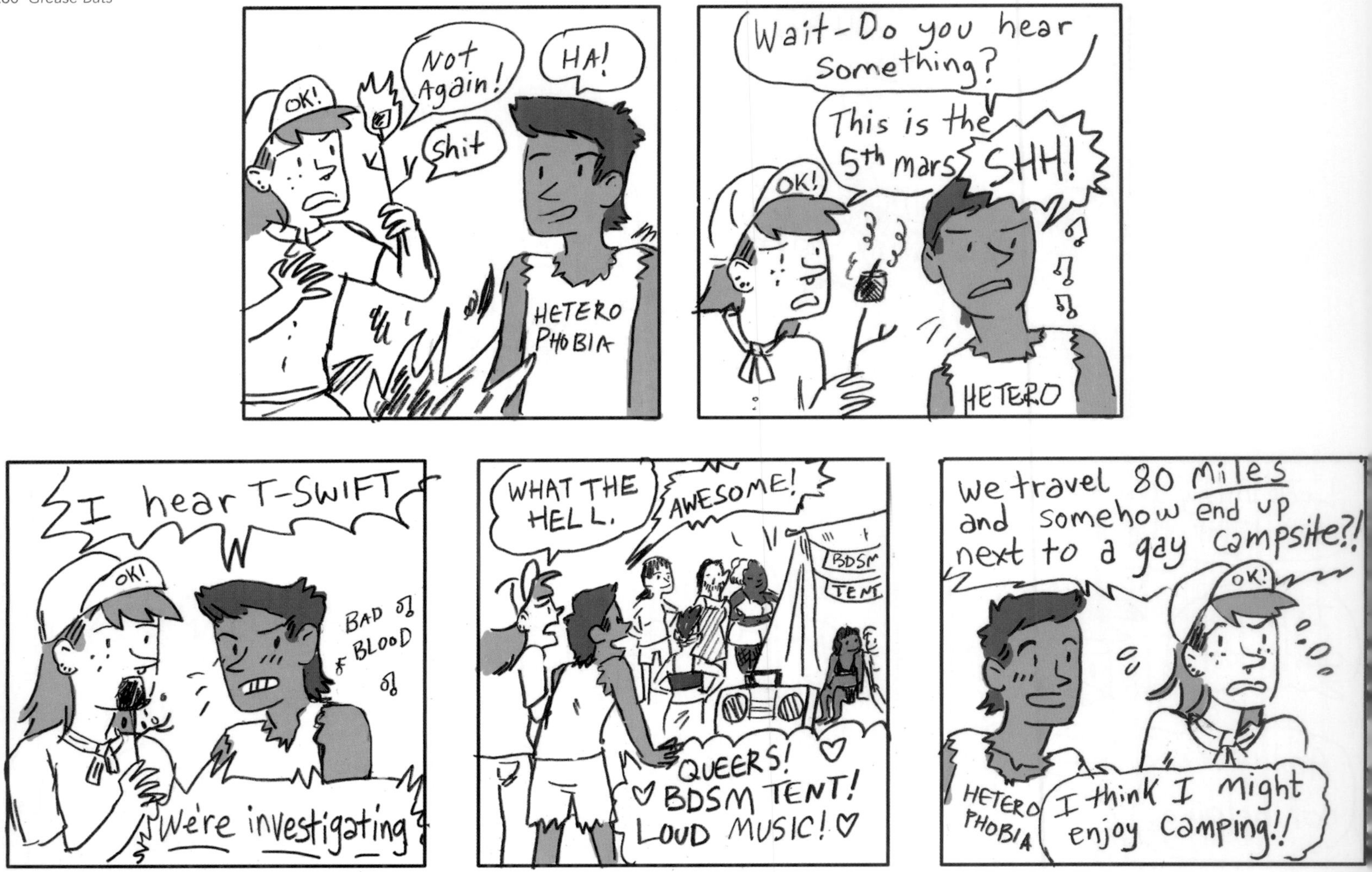
OK!
Not Again!
Shit
HA!
HETERO PHOBIA
Wait-Do you hear Something?
This is the 5th mars
SHH!
OK!
HETERO
I hear T-SWIFT
OK!
BAD BLOOD
We're investigating
WHAT THE HELL.
AWESOME!
BDSM TENT
QUEERS! BDSM TENT! LOUD MUSIC!
We travel 80 Miles and somehow end up next to a gay campsite?!
OK!
HETERO PHOBIA
I think I might enjoy camping!!

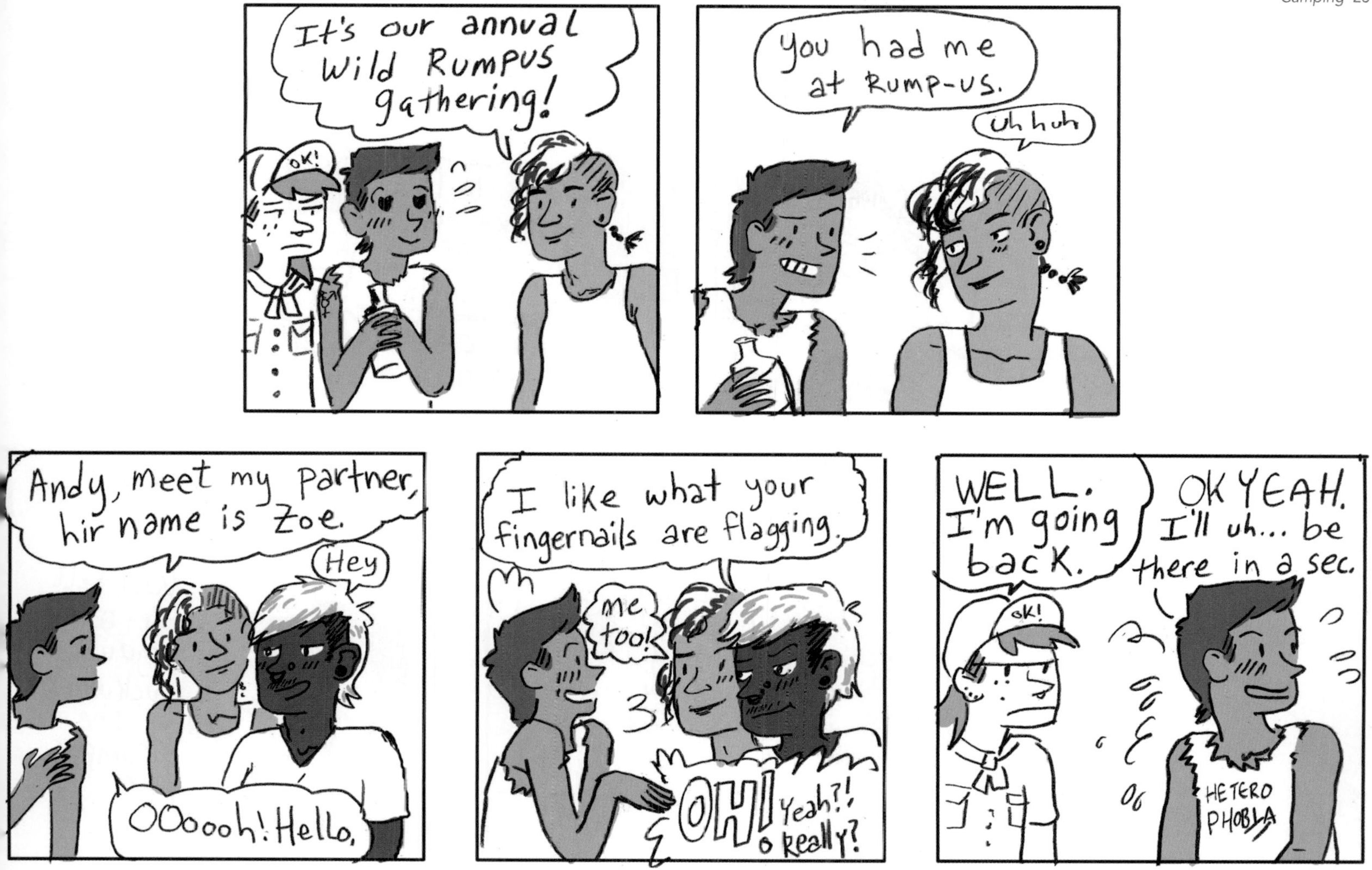
It's our annual Wild Rumpus gathering!
OK!
You had me at Rump-us.
Uh huh
Andy, meet my partner, hir name is Zoe.
Hey
OOoooh! Hello.
I like what your fingernails are flagging.
me too!
OH! Yeah?! Really?
WELL. I'm going back.
OK!
OK YEAH. I'll uh... be there in a sec.
HETERO PHOBIA

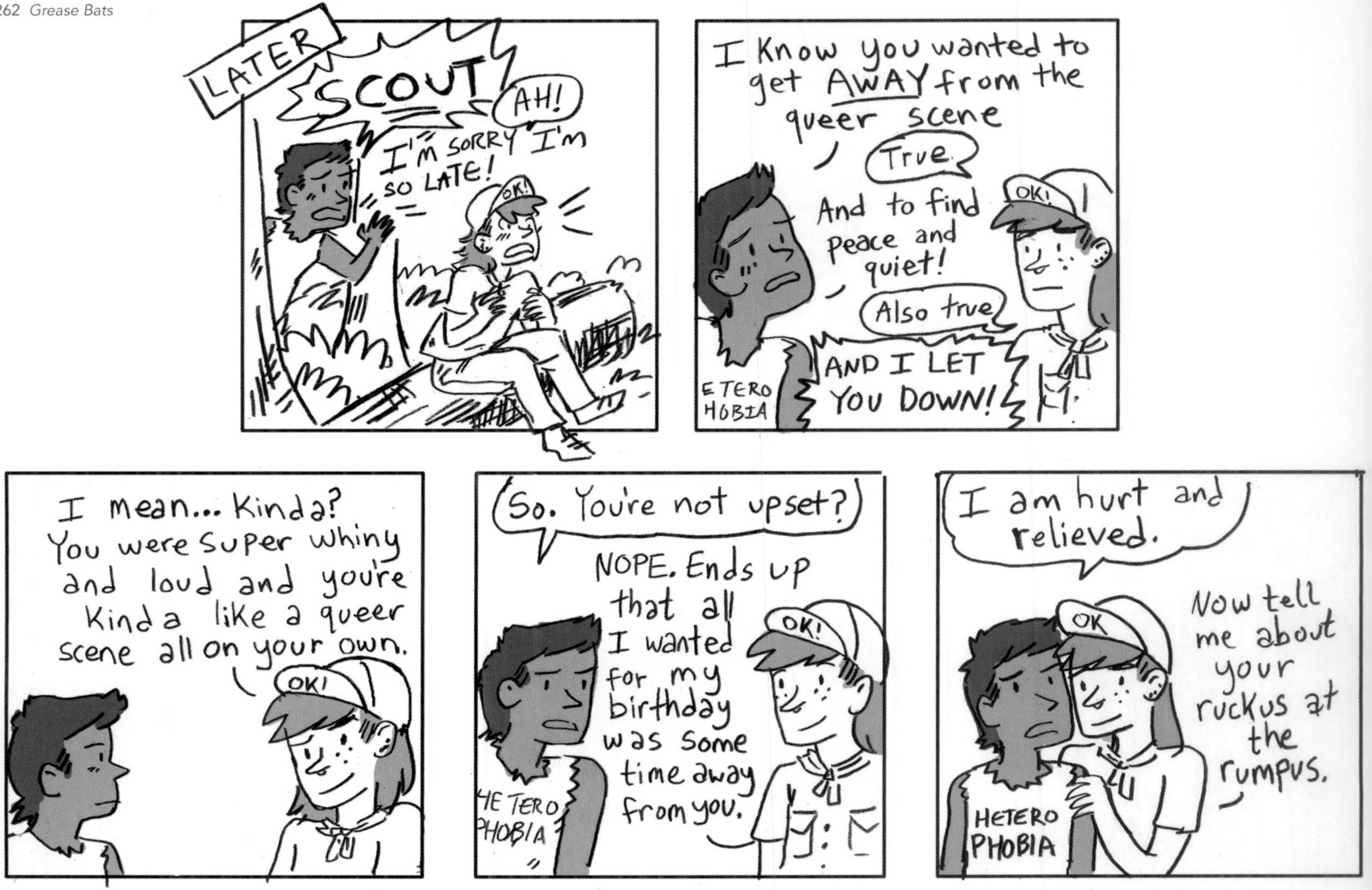
LATER
SCOUT
AH!
I'M SORRY I'M SO LATE!
OK!
I Know you wanted to get AWAY from the queer scene
True.
And to find peace and quiet!
Also true
AND I LET YOU DOWN!
ETERO HOBIA
I mean... Kinda? You were super whiny and loud and you're Kind a like a queer scene all on your own.
OK!
So. You're not upset?
NOPE. Ends up that all I wanted for my birthday was some time away from you.
OK!
HETERO PHOBIA
I am hurt and relieved.
Now tell me about your ruckus at the rumpus.
OK
HETERO PHOBIA

Can't Go Home Again

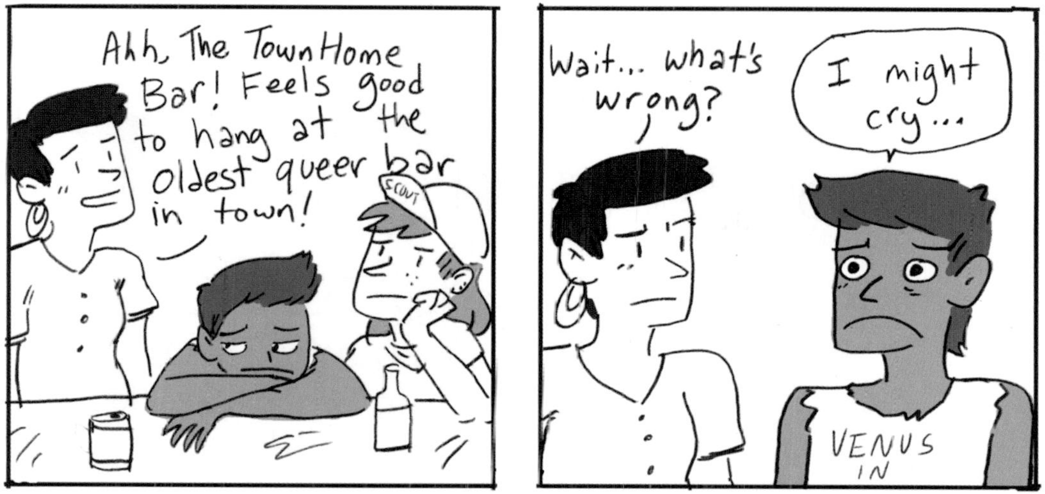
Ahh, The TownHome Bar! Feels good to hang at the oldest queer bar in town!
SCOUT
Wait... what's wrong?
I might cry...
VENUS IN

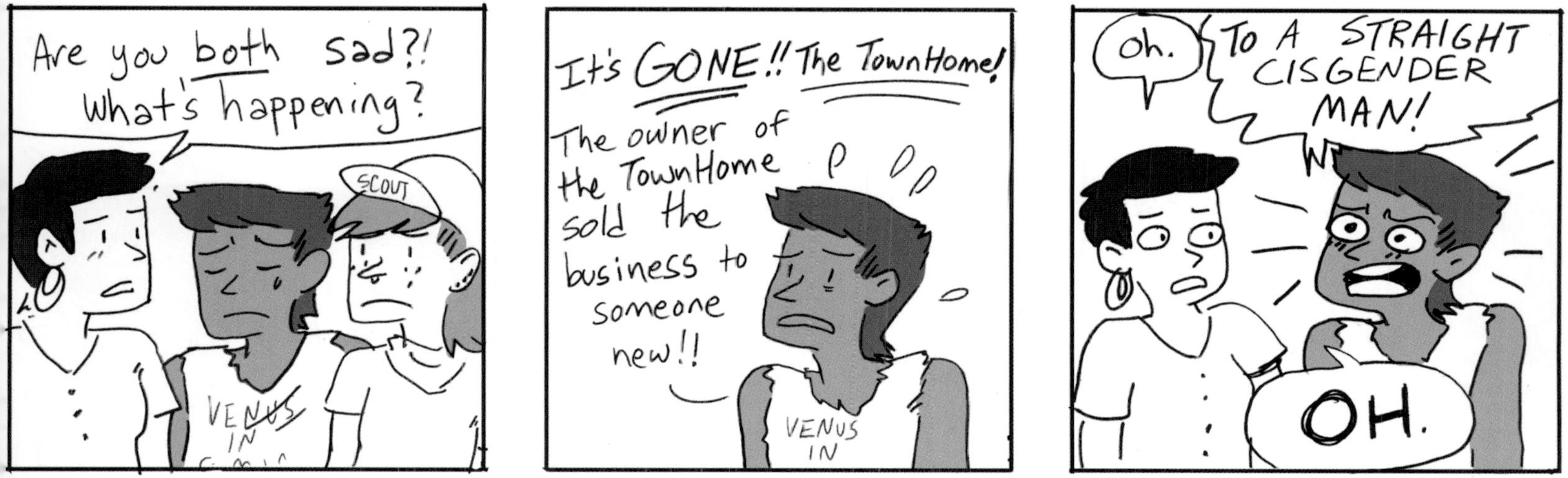
Are you both sad?! What's happening?
SCOUT
VENUS IN
It's GONE!! The TownHome!
The owner of the TownHome sold the business to someone new!!
VENUS IN
Oh.
TO A STRAIGHT CISGENDER MAN!
OH.

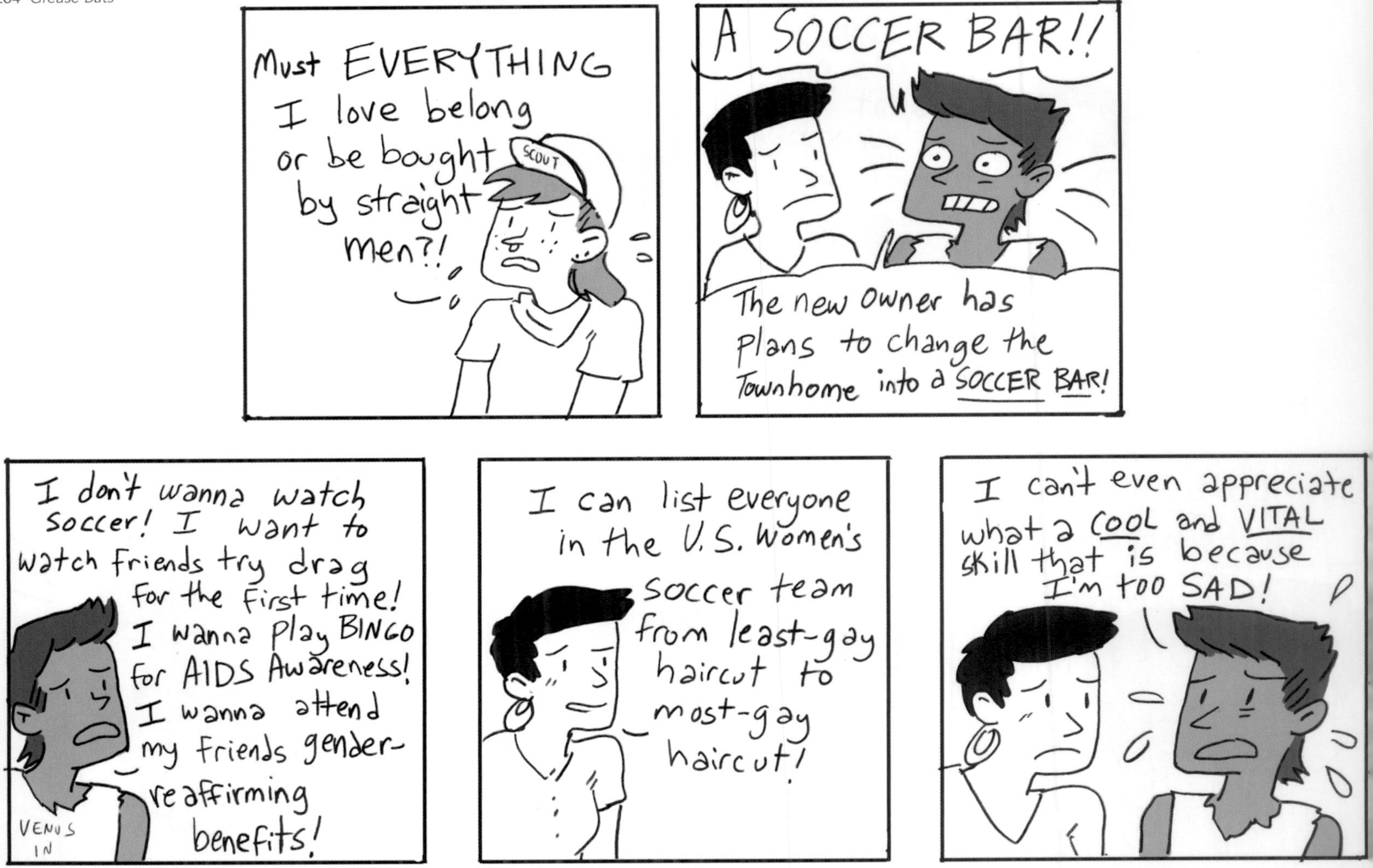
Must EVERYTHING I love belong or be bought by straight men?!
A SOCCER BAR!!
The new owner has plans to change the Townhome into a SOCCER BAR!
I don't wanna watch soccer! I want to watch friends try drag for the first time! I wanna play BINGO for AIDS Awareness! I wanna attend my friends gender-reaffirming benefits!
VENUS IN
I can list everyone in the U.S. Women's soccer team from least-gay haircut to most-gay haircut!
I can't even appreciate what a COOL and VITAL skill that is because I'm too SAD!

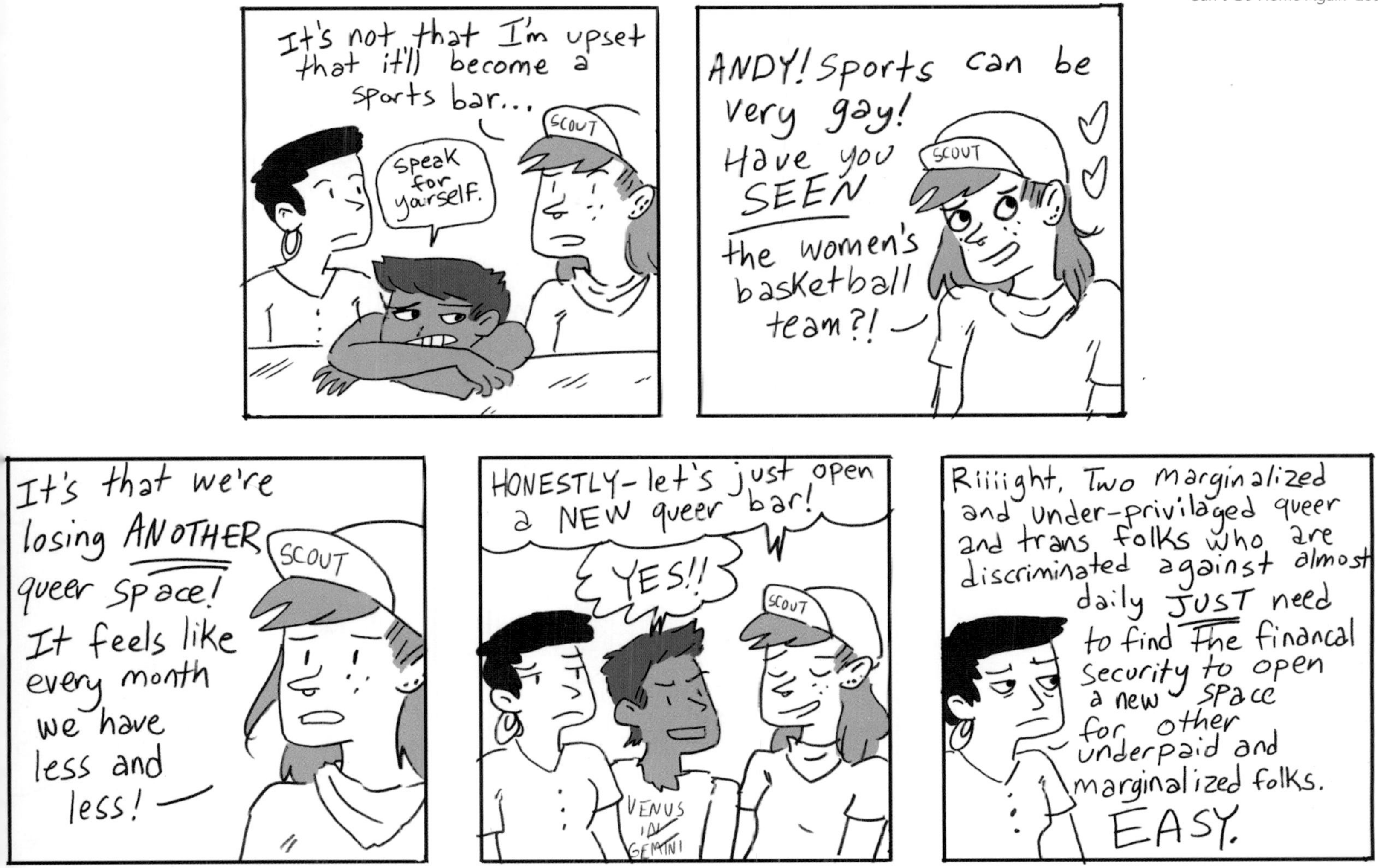
It's not that I'm upset that it'll become a sports bar...
Speak for yourself.
ANDY! Sports can be very gay! Have you SEEN the women's basketball team?!
SCOUT
It's that we're losing ANOTHER queer space! It feels like every month we have less and less!
HONESTLY- let's just open a NEW queer bar!
YES!!
VENUS IN GEMINI
Riiiiight. Two marginalized and under-privilaged queer and trans folks who are discriminated against almost daily JUST need to find the financal security to open a new space for other underpaid and marginalized folks. EASY.

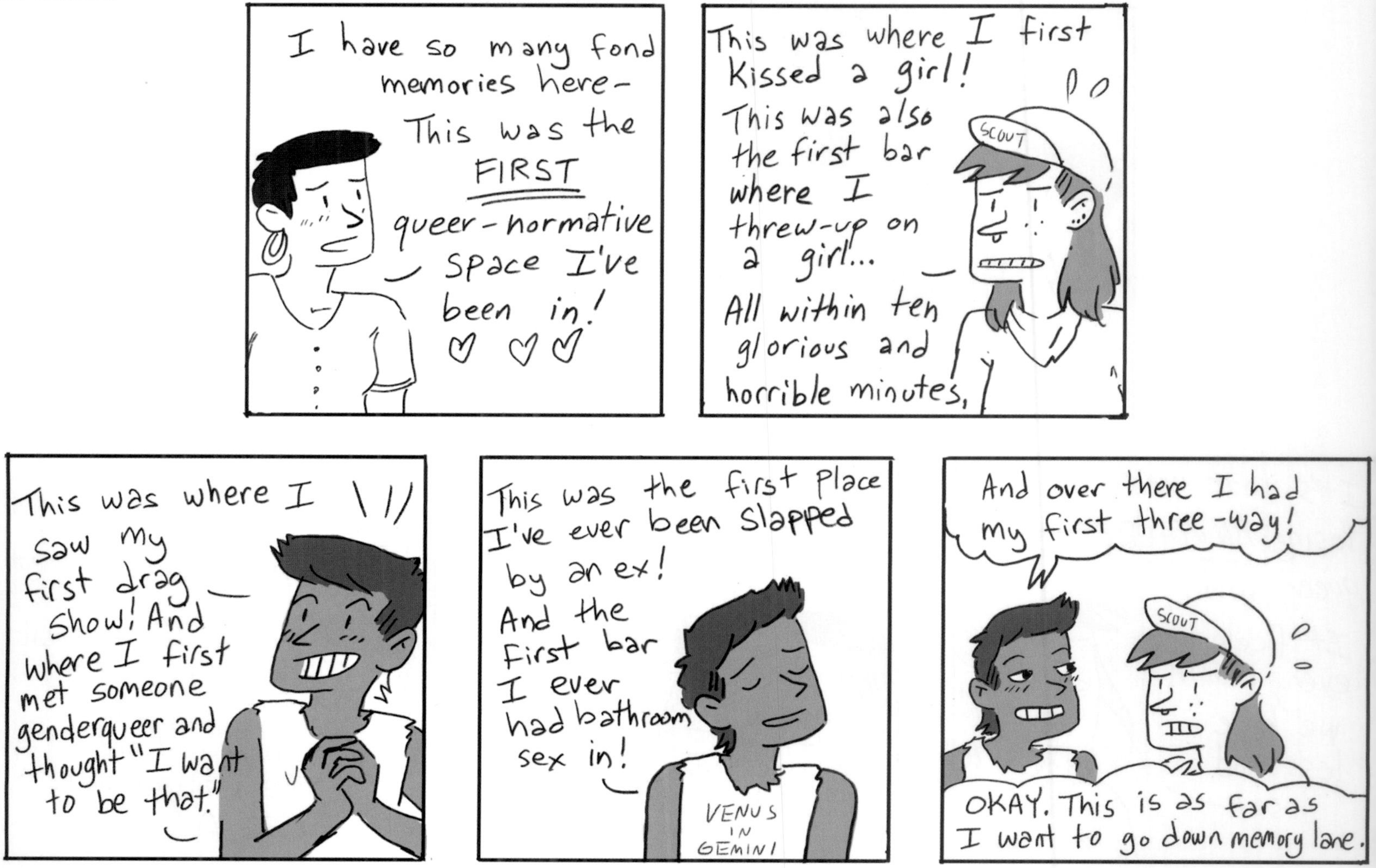
I have so many fond memories here- This was the FIRST queer-normative space I've been in!
This was where I first kissed a girl!
This was also the first bar where I threw-up on a girl...
All within ten glorious and horrible minutes,
SCOUT
This was where I saw my first drag show! And where I first met someone genderqueer and thought "I want to be that."
This was the first place I've ever been slapped by an ex!
And the first bar I ever had bathroom sex in!
VENUS IN GEMINI
And over there I had my first three-way!
SCOUT
OKAY. This is as far as I want to go down memory lane.

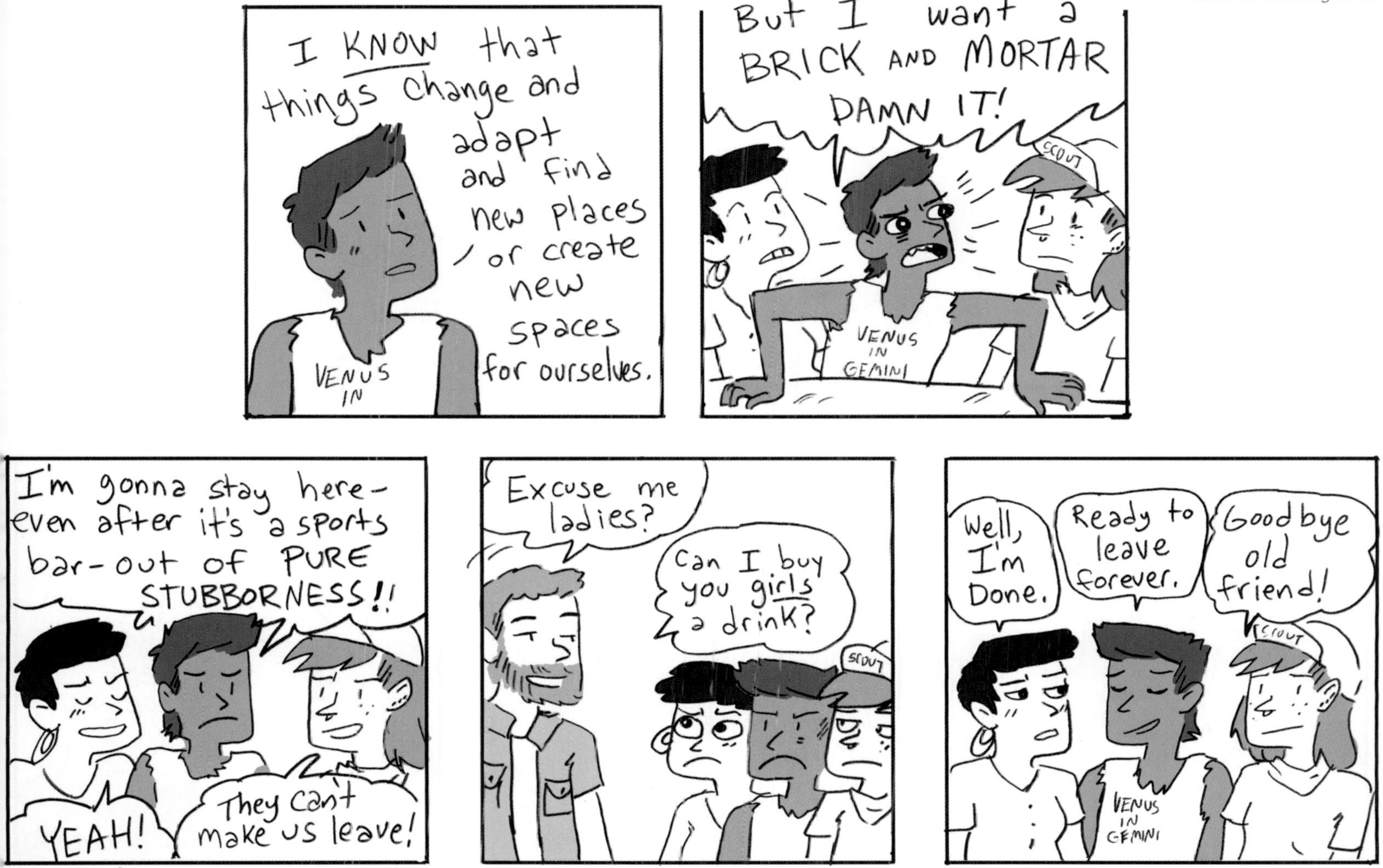
I KNOW that things change and adapt and find new places or create new spaces for ourselves.
VENUS IN
But I want a BRICK AND MORTAR DAMN IT!
SCOUT
VENUS IN GEMINI
I'm gonna stay here- even after it's a sports bar- out of PURE STUBBORNESS!!
YEAH!
They can't make us leave!
Excuse me ladies?
Can I buy you girls a drink?
SCOUT
Well, I'm Done.
Ready to leave forever.
Goodbye old friend!
SCOUT
VENUS IN GEMINI

Having a S.A.D

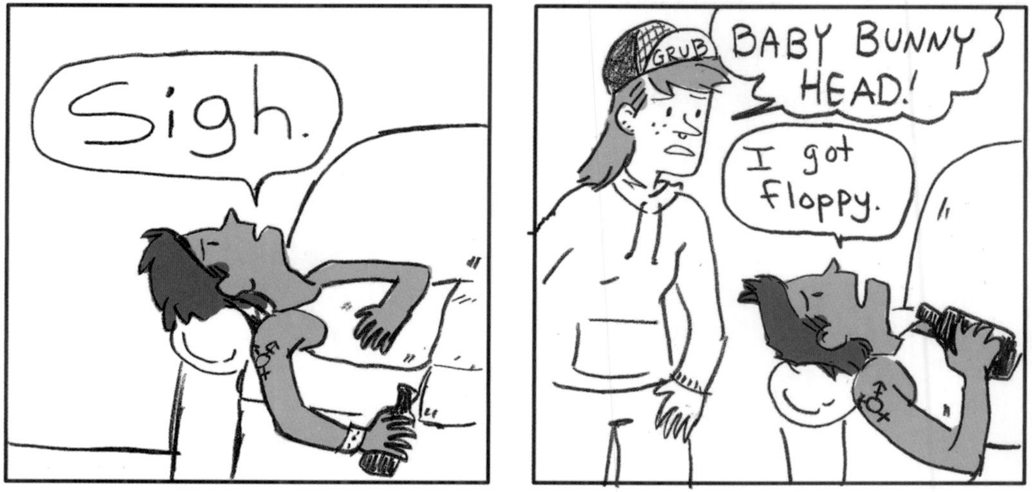
Sigh.
GRUB
BABY BUNNY HEAD!
I got floppy.

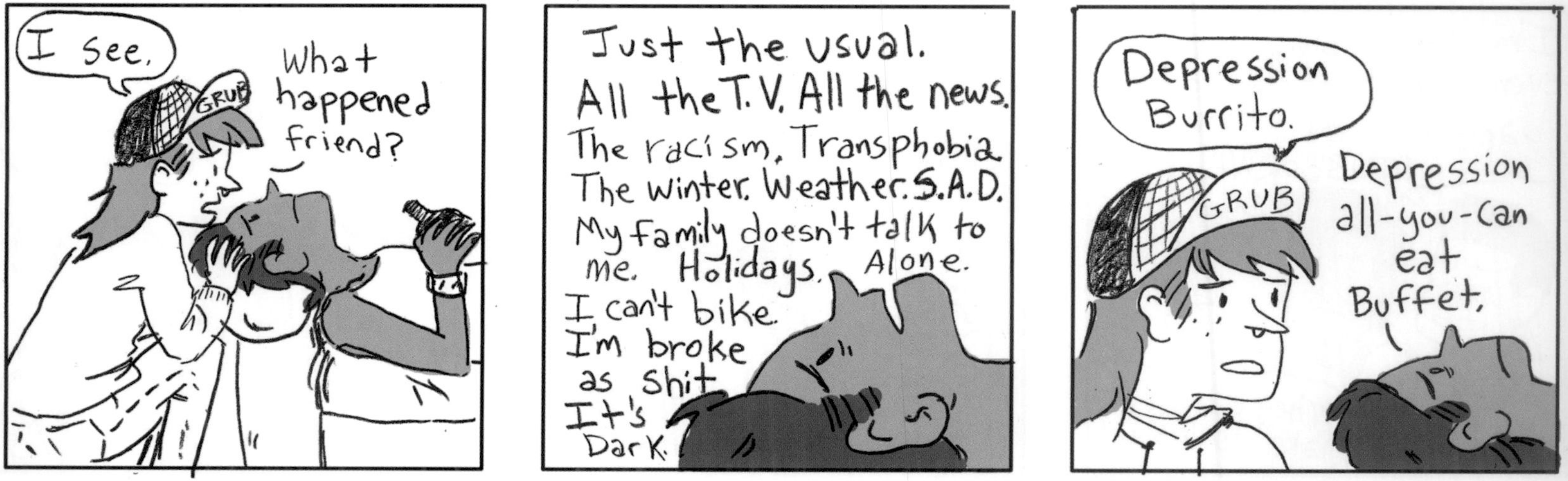
I see.
GRUB
What happened friend?
Just the usual.
All the T.V. All the news.
The racism, Transphobia
The winter. Weather. S.A.D.
My family doesn't talk to me. Holidays. Alone.
I can't bike.
I'm broke as shit
It's Dark.
Depression Burrito.
GRUB
Depression all-you-can eat Buffet.

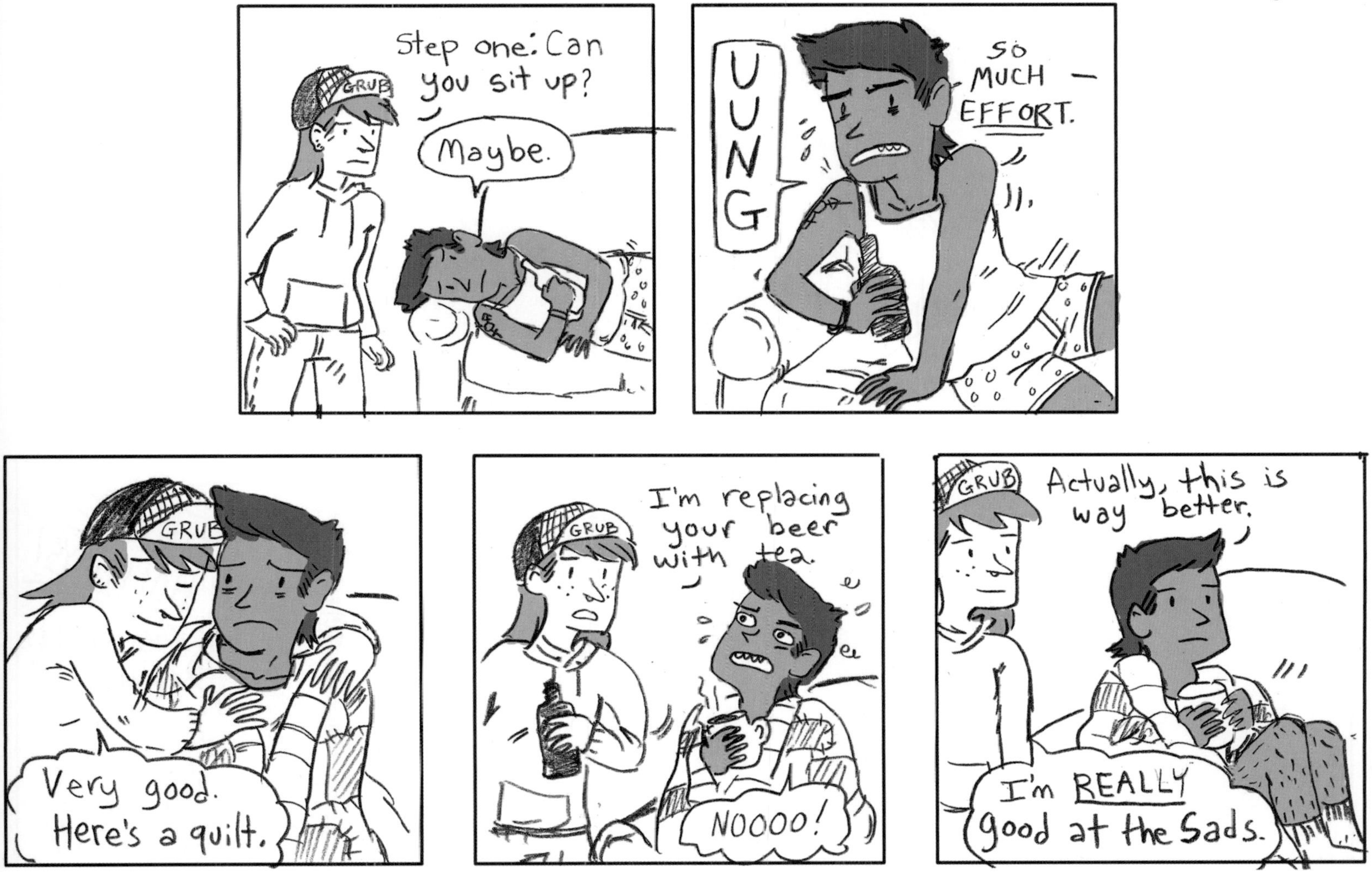
Step one: Can you sit up?
Maybe.
UUNG
SO MUCH — EFFORT.
GRUB
Very good. Here's a quilt.
I'm replacing your beer with tea.
NOOOO!
Actually, this is way better.
I'm REALLY good at the Sads.

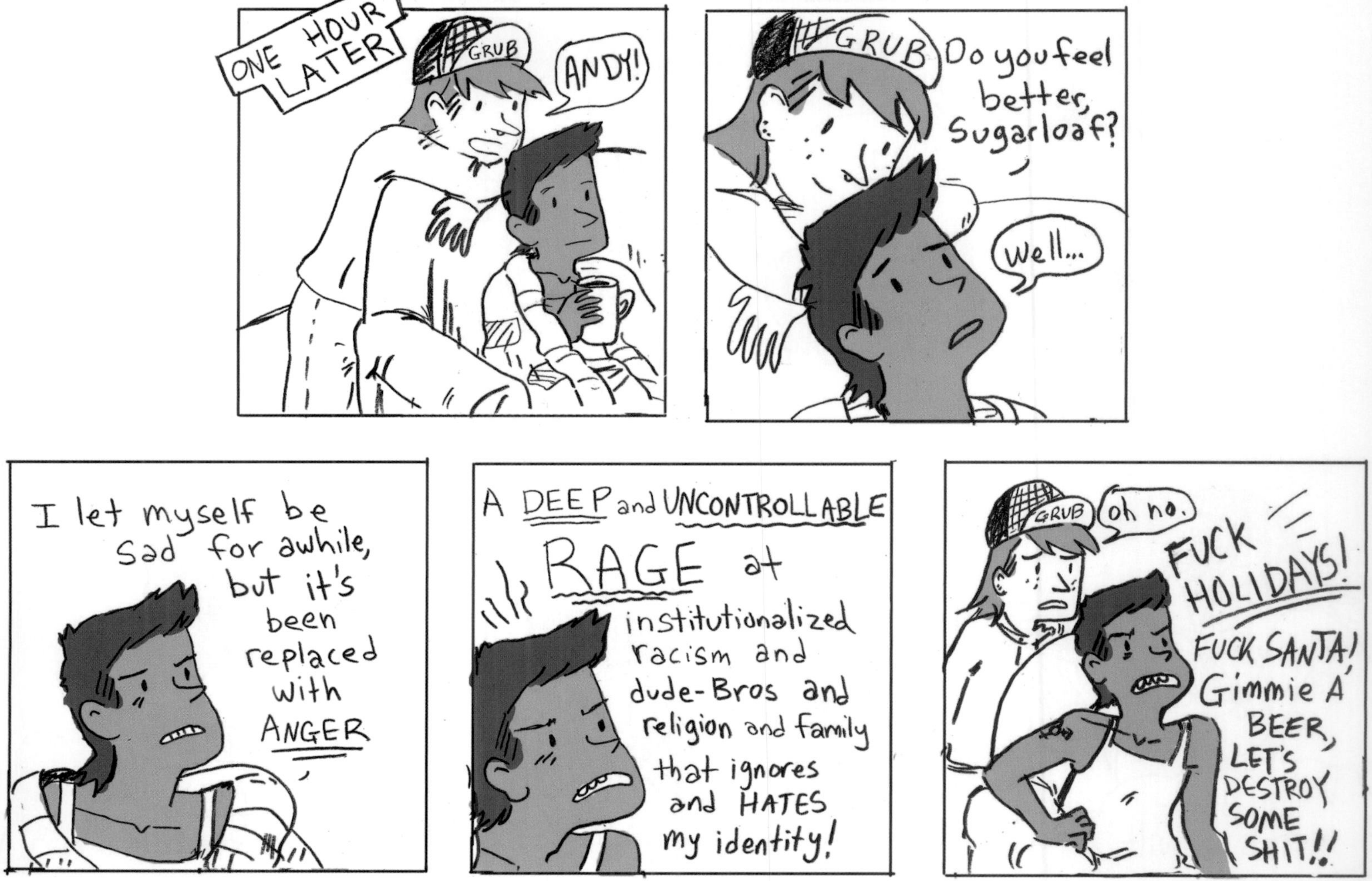
ONE HOUR LATER
GRUB
ANDY!
GRUB
Do you feel better, Sugarloaf?
Well...
I let myself be sad for awhile, but it's been replaced with ANGER
A DEEP and UNCONTROLLABLE RAGE at institutionalized racism and dude-Bros and religion and family that ignores and HATES my identity!
GRUB
oh no.
FUCK HOLIDAYS!
FUCK SANTA! Gimmie A' BEER, LET'S DESTROY SOME SHIT!!

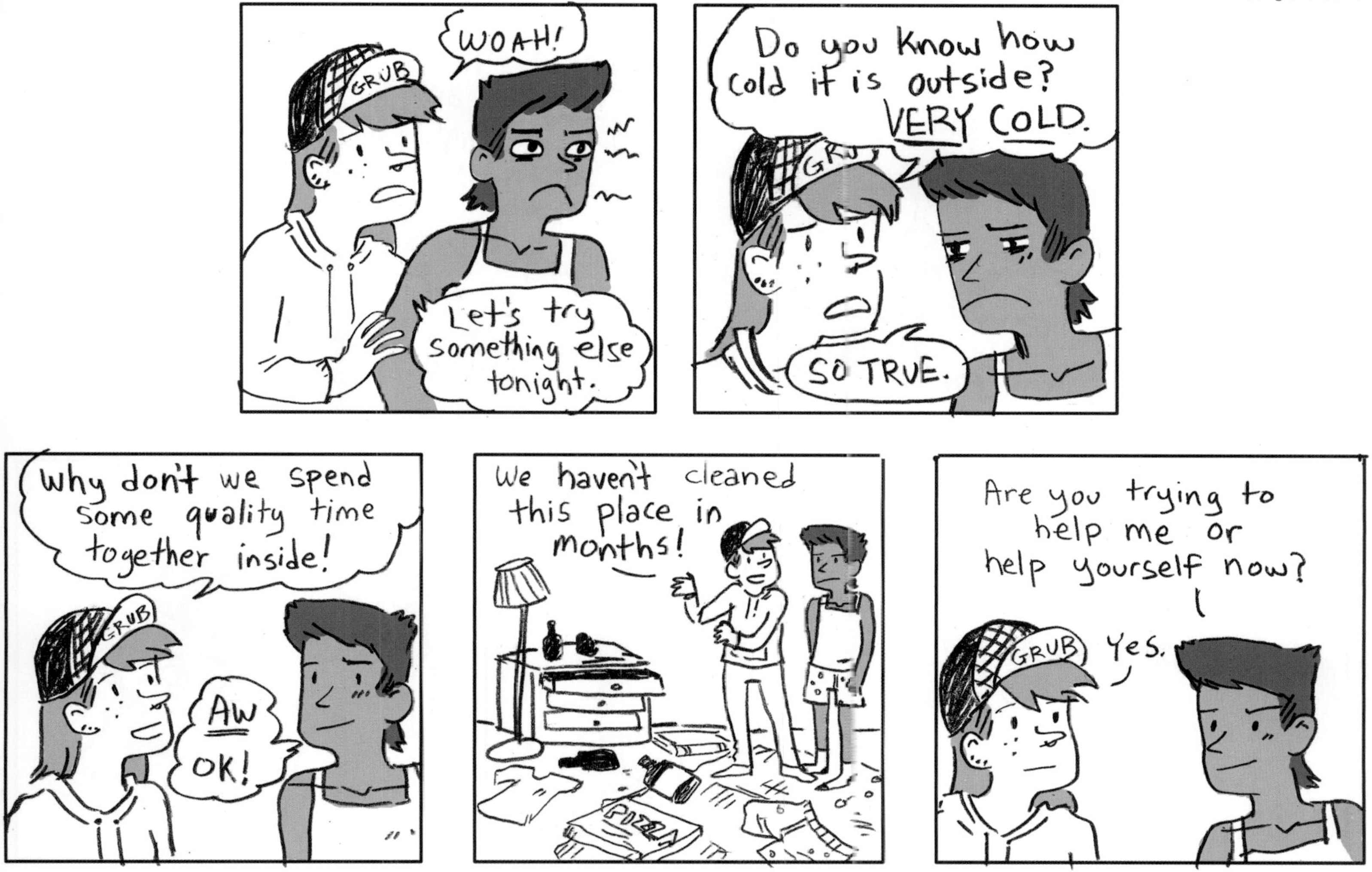
WOAH!
Let's try something else tonight.
Do you know how cold it is outside? VERY COLD.
SO TRUE.
Why don't we spend some quality time together inside!
AW OK!
We haven't cleaned this place in months!
PIZZA
Are you trying to help me or help yourself now?
Yes.

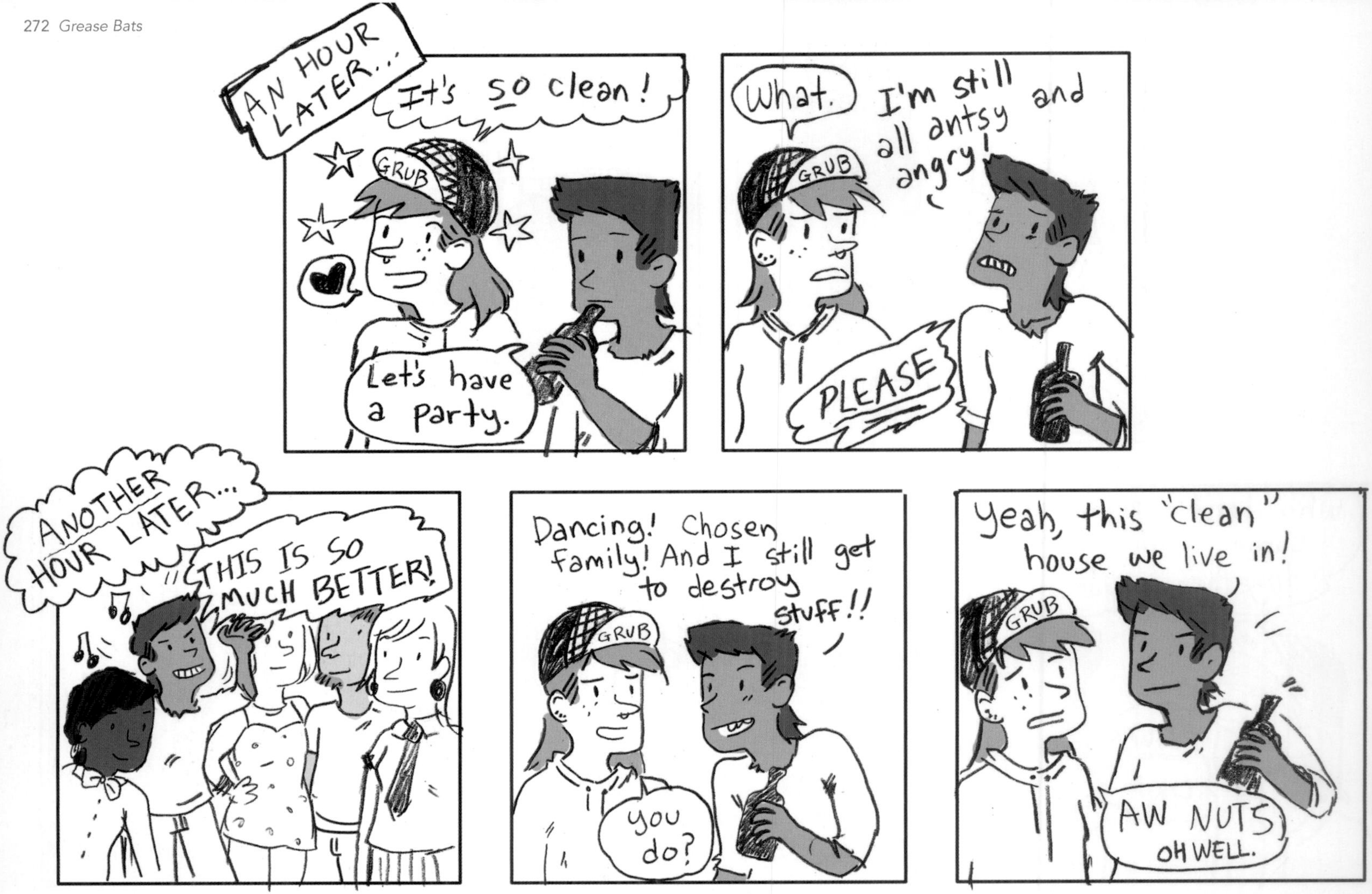
AN HOUR LATER...
It's so clean!
Let's have a party.
What.
I'm still all antsy and angry!
PLEASE
ANOTHER HOUR LATER...
THIS IS SO MUCH BETTER!
Dancing! Chosen Family! And I still get to destroy stuff!!
you do?
Yeah, this "clean" house we live in!
AW NUTS
OH WELL.

Bachelorette Party

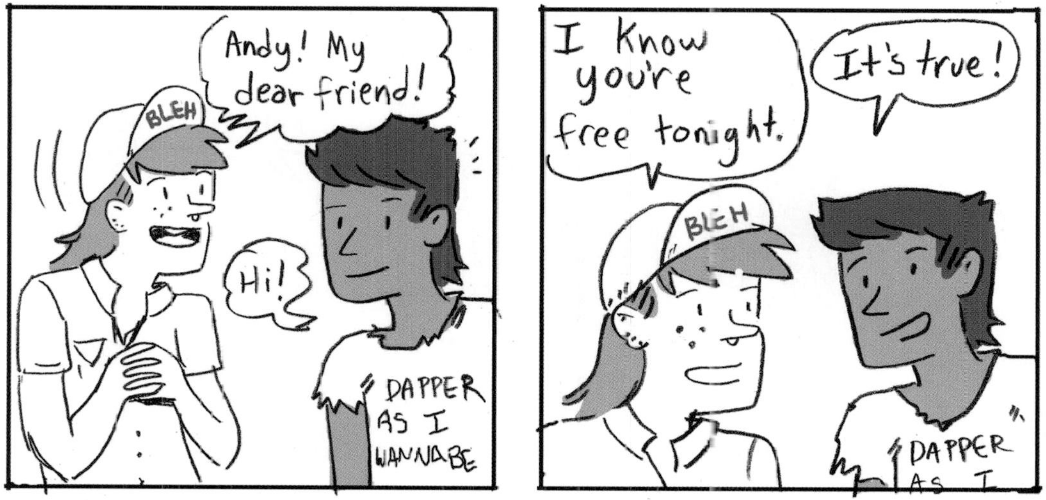
Andy! My dear friend!
Hi!
I Know you're free tonight.
It's true!
DAPPER AS I WANNABE

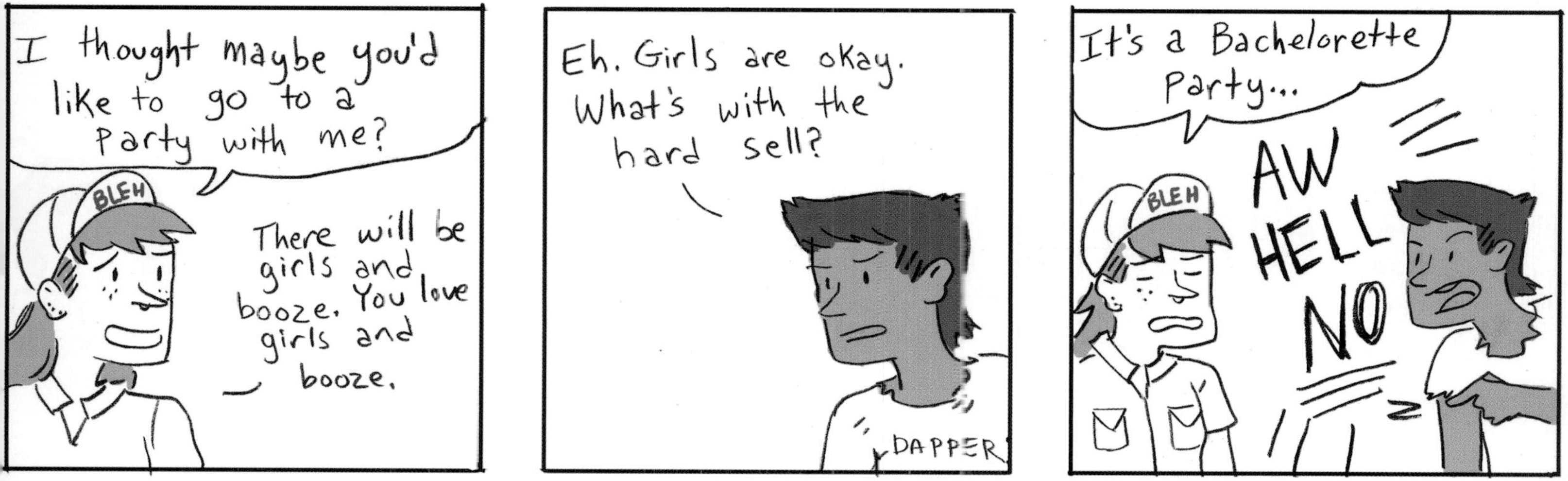
I thought maybe you'd like to go to a party with me?
BLEH
There will be girls and booze. You love girls and booze.
Eh. Girls are okay. What's with the hard sell?
DAPPER
It's a Bachelorette Party...
AW HELL NO

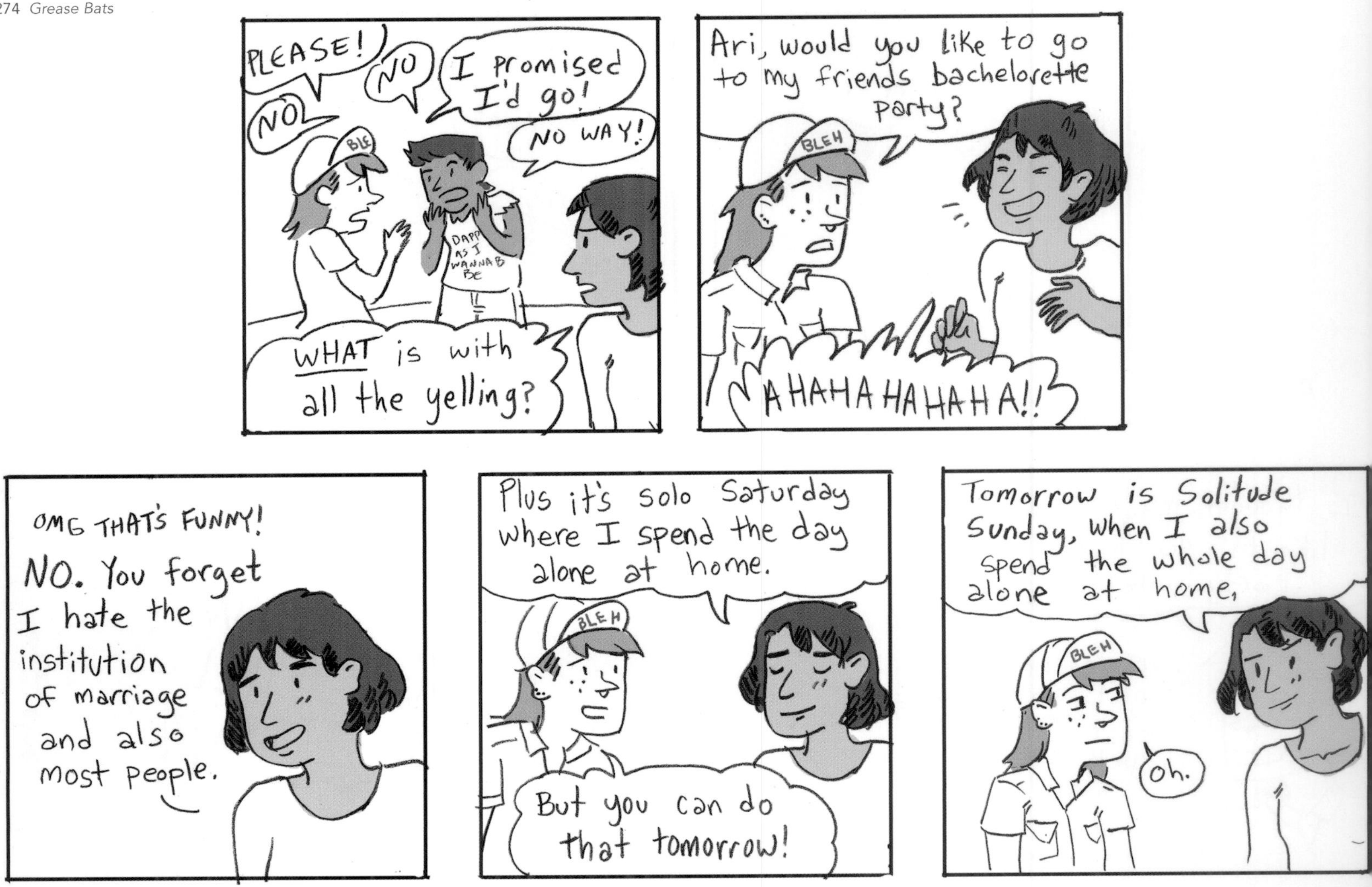
PLEASE!
NO
NO
I promised I'd go!
NO WAY!
BLE
WHAT is with all the yelling?
Ari, would you like to go to my friends bachelorette party?
BLEH
AHAHAHAHAHAHA!!
OMG THAT'S FUNNY!
NO. You forget I hate the institution of marriage and also most people.
Plus it's solo Saturday where I spend the day alone at home.
BLEH
But you can do that tomorrow!
Tomorrow is Solitude Sunday, when I also spend the whole day alone at home.
BLEH
Oh.

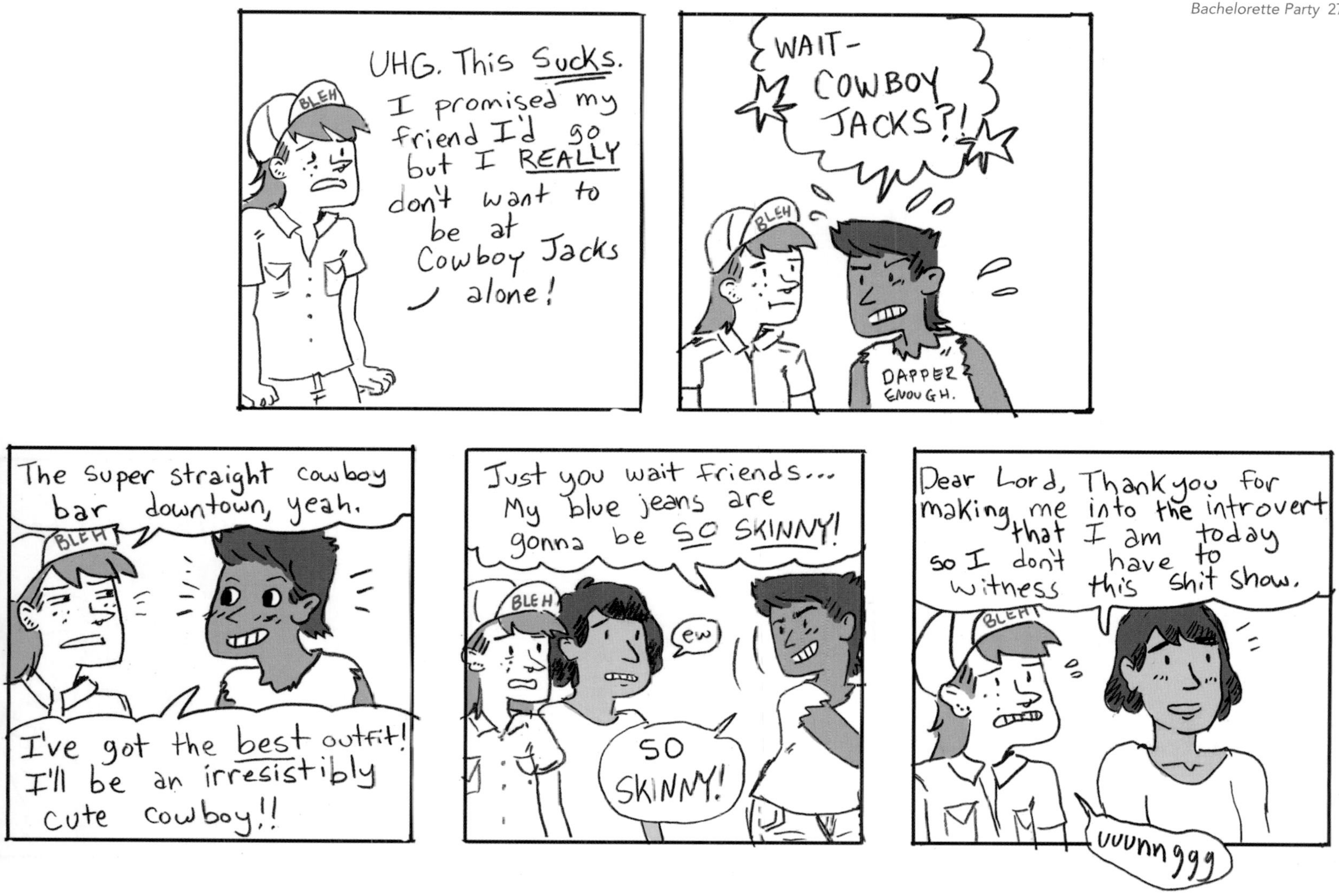
UHG. This Sucks.
I promised my friend I'd go but I REALLY don't want to be at Cowboy Jacks alone!
WAIT- COWBOY JACKS?!
DAPPER ENOUGH.
BLEH
The super straight cowboy bar downtown, yeah.
I've got the best outfit! I'll be an irresistibly cute cowboy!!
Just you wait friends... My blue jeans are gonna be SO SKINNY!
ew
SO SKINNY!
Dear Lord, Thank you for making me into the introvert that I am today so I don't have to witness this shit show.
uuunnggg

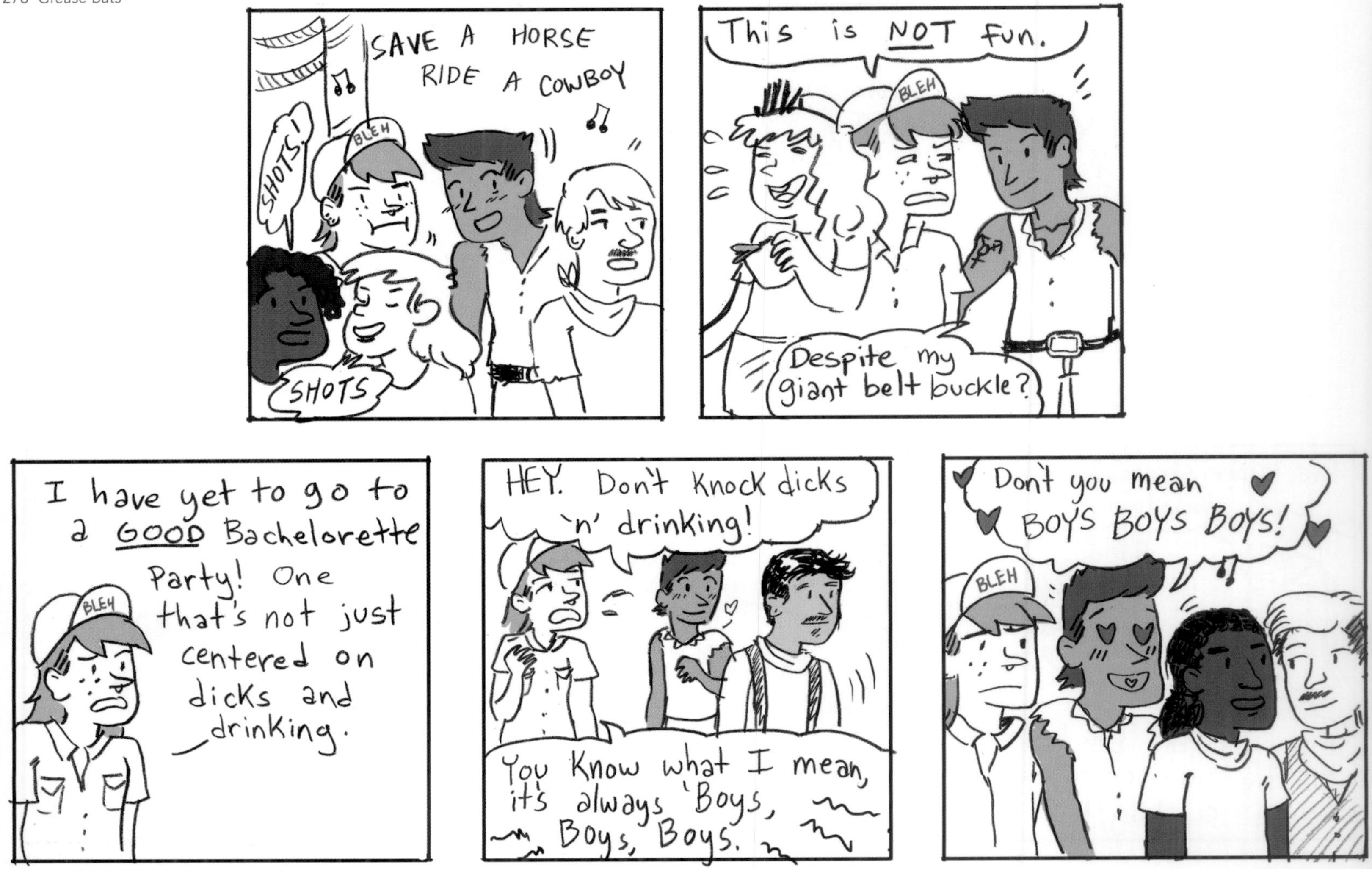
SAVE A HORSE RIDE A COWBOY
SHOTS!
SHOTS
This is NOT fun.
BLEH
Despite my giant belt buckle?
I have yet to go to a GOOD Bachelorette Party! One that's not just centered on dicks and drinking.
HEY. Don't knock dicks 'n' drinking!
You know what I mean, it's always 'Boys, Boys, Boys.'
Don't you mean BOYS BOYS BOYS!

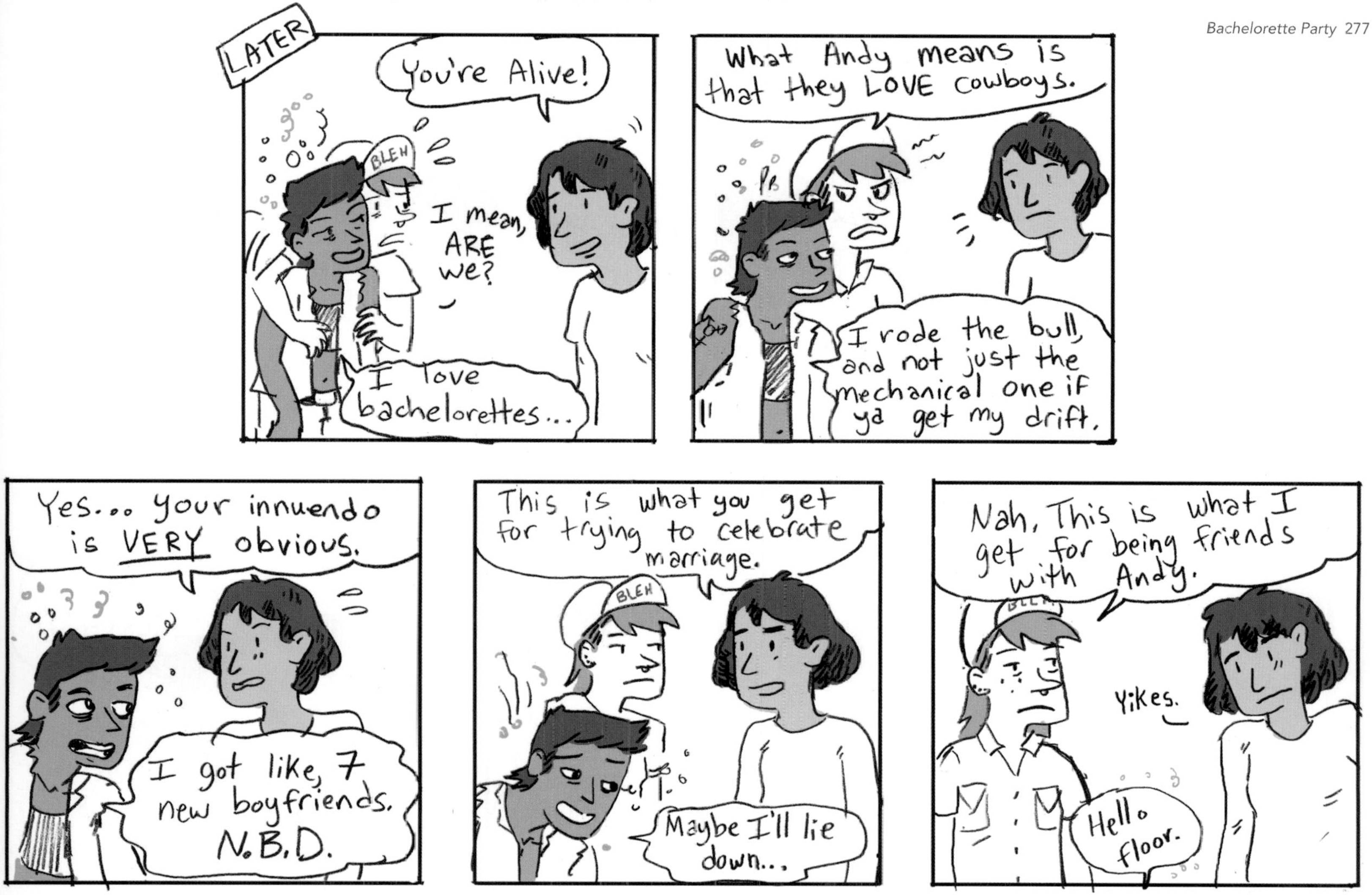
LATER
You're Alive!
I mean, ARE we?
I love bachelorettes...
What Andy means is that they LOVE cowboys.
I rode the bull, and not just the mechanical one if ya get my drift.
Yes... your innuendo is VERY obvious.
I got like, 7 new boyfriends. N.B.D.
This is what you get for trying to celebrate marriage.
Maybe I'll lie down...
Nah, This is what I get for being friends with Andy.
Yikes.
Hello floor.

Fashion Potential

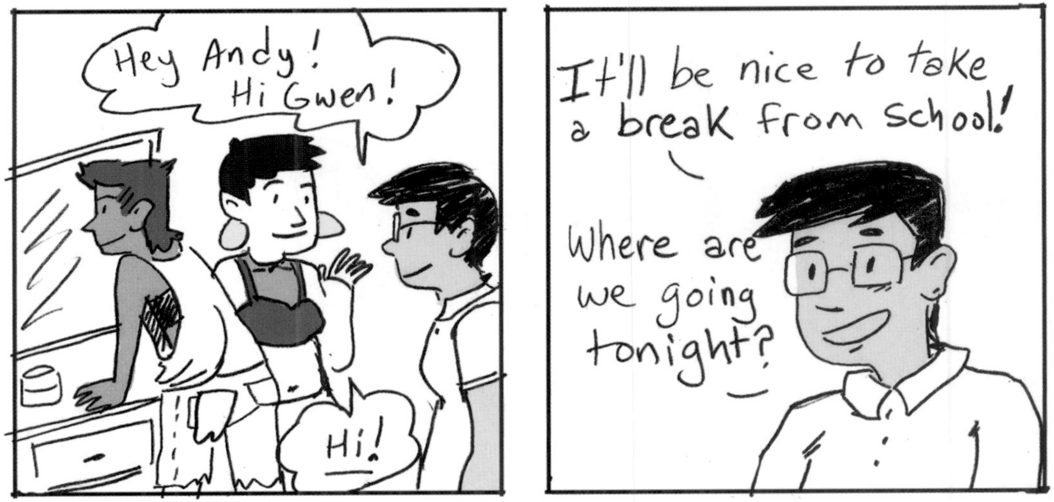
Hey Andy! Hi Gwen!
Hi!
It'll be nice to take a break from school!
Where are we going tonight?

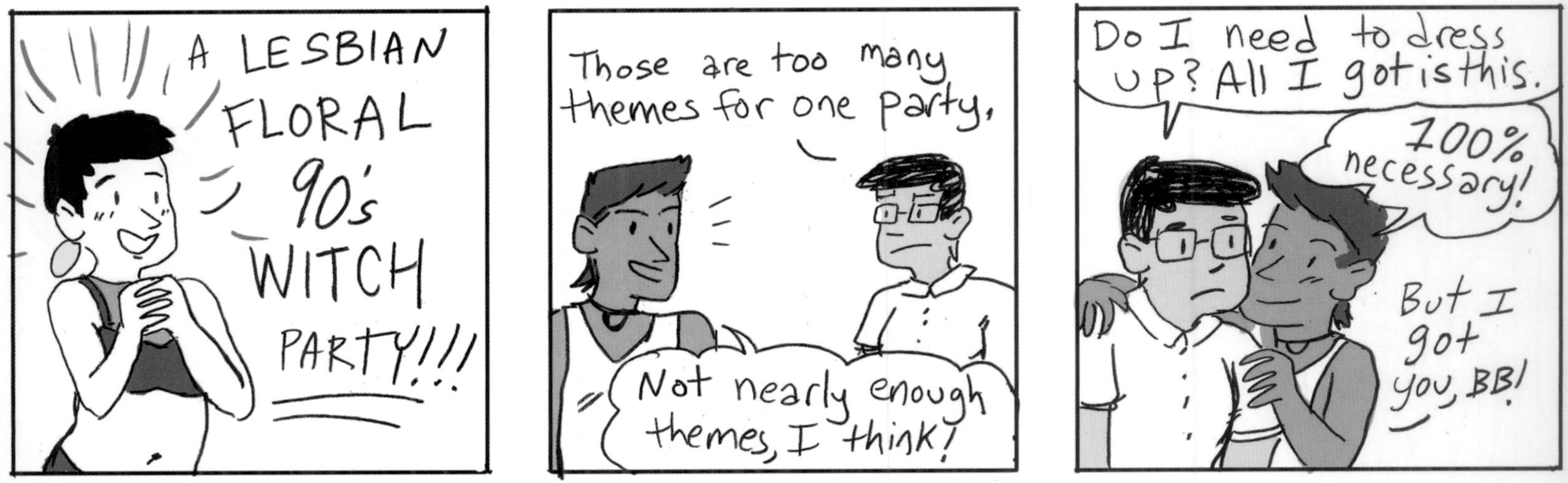
A LESBIAN FLORAL 90's WITCH PARTY!!!
Those are too many themes for one party.
Not nearly enough themes, I think!
Do I need to dress up? All I got is this.
100% necessary!
But I got you, BB!

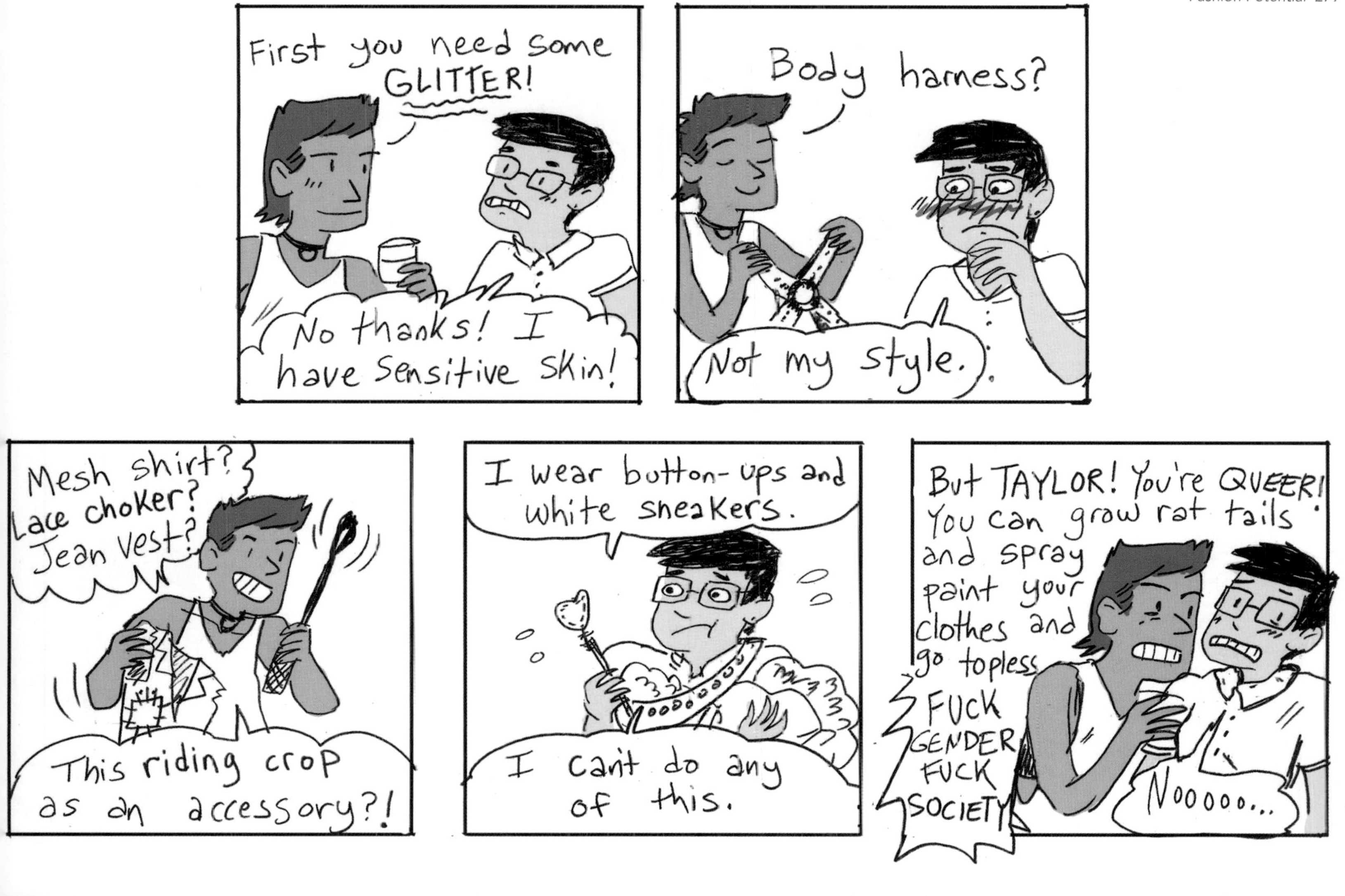
First you need some GLITTER!
No thanks! I have sensitive skin!
Body harness?
Not my style.
Mesh shirt? Lace choker? Jean vest?
This riding crop as an accessory?!
I wear button-ups and white sneakers.
I can't do any of this.
But TAYLOR! You're QUEER! You can grow rat tails and spray paint your clothes and go topless
FUCK GENDER FUCK SOCIETY
Nooooo...

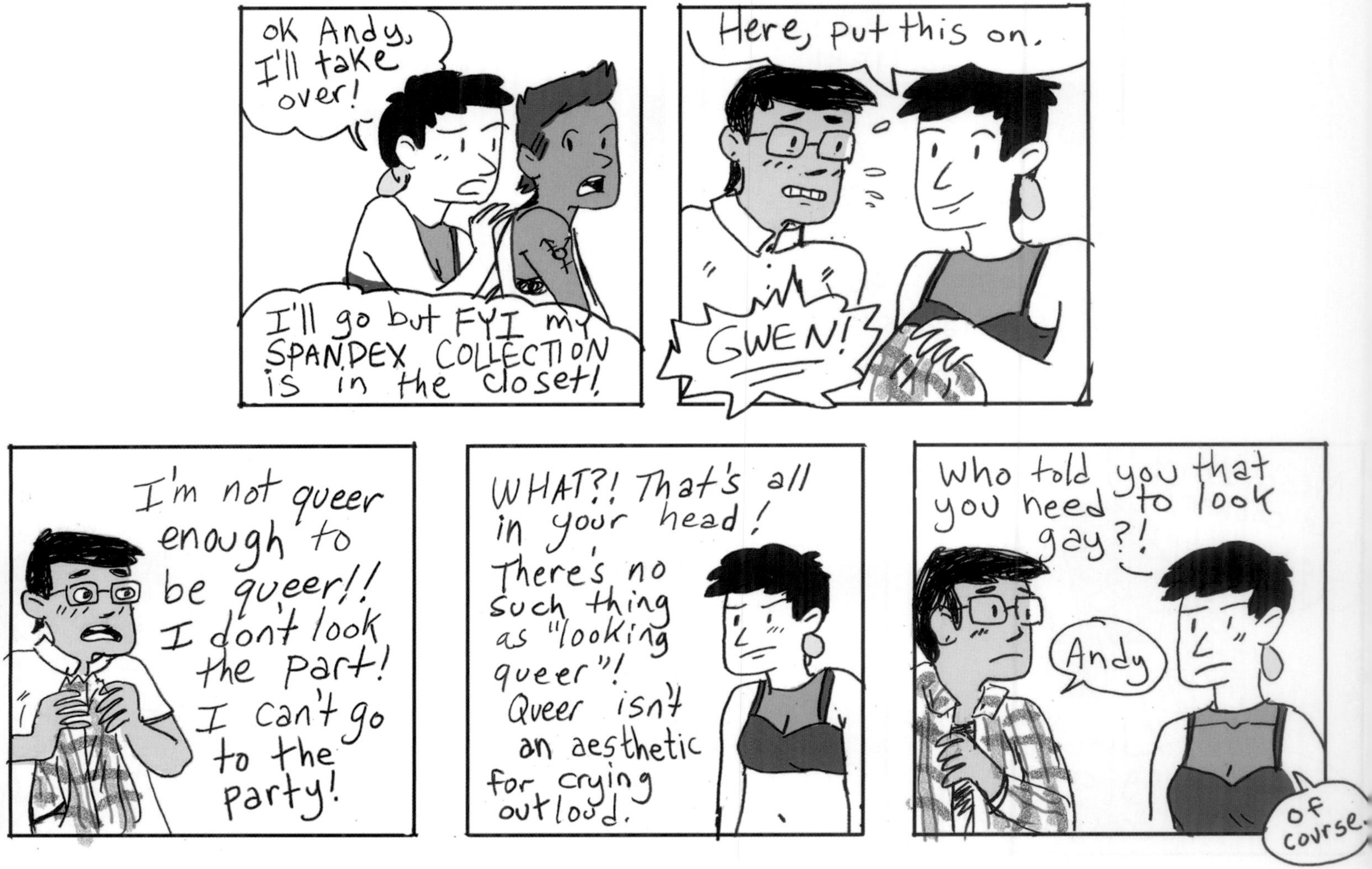
OK Andy, I'll take over!
I'll go but FYI my SPANDEX COLLECTION is in the closet!
Here, put this on.
GWEN!
I'm not queer enough to be queer!! I don't look the part! I can't go to the party!
WHAT?! That's all in your head! There's no such thing as "looking queer"! Queer isn't an aesthetic for crying outloud.
Who told you that you need to look gay?!
Andy
of course.

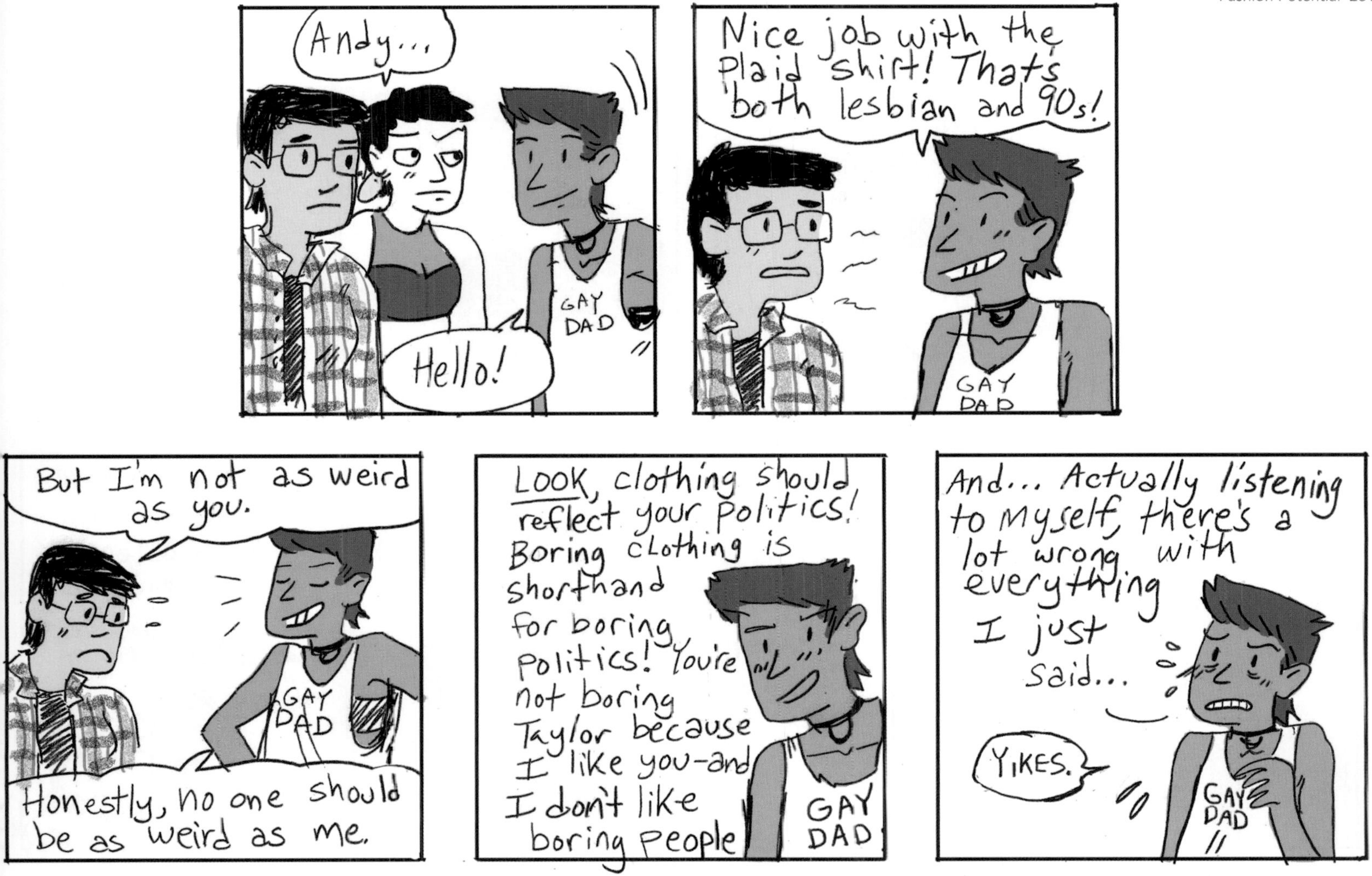
Andy...,
Hello!
GAY DAD
Nice job with the plaid shirt! That's both lesbian and 90s!
GAY DAD
But I'm not as weird as you.
GAY DAD
Honestly, no one should be as weird as me.
LOOK, clothing should reflect your politics! Boring clothing is shorthand for boring politics! You're not boring Taylor because I like you-and I don't like boring people
GAY DAD
And... Actually listening to myself, there's a lot wrong with everything I just said...
YIKES.
GAY DAD

Panel 1: I'm SORRY SORRY SORRY! Do I just get real caught up in myself! AW

Panel 2: Being queer comes from the HEART! And the HEAD! And occasionally sometimes the GROIN!

Panel 3: I just want everyone to reach their FULL FASHION POTENTIAL! But mostly I want everyone to wear what's comfortable and feels good. GAY DAD

Panel 4: GREAT! It's settled: Our differences ROCK and we're all super MEGA-BABES! Let's get to that witch party!

Panel 5: I'm gonna get so many hickeys tonight! And I'll have one beer and be asleep by midnight. So different. ♥♥♥

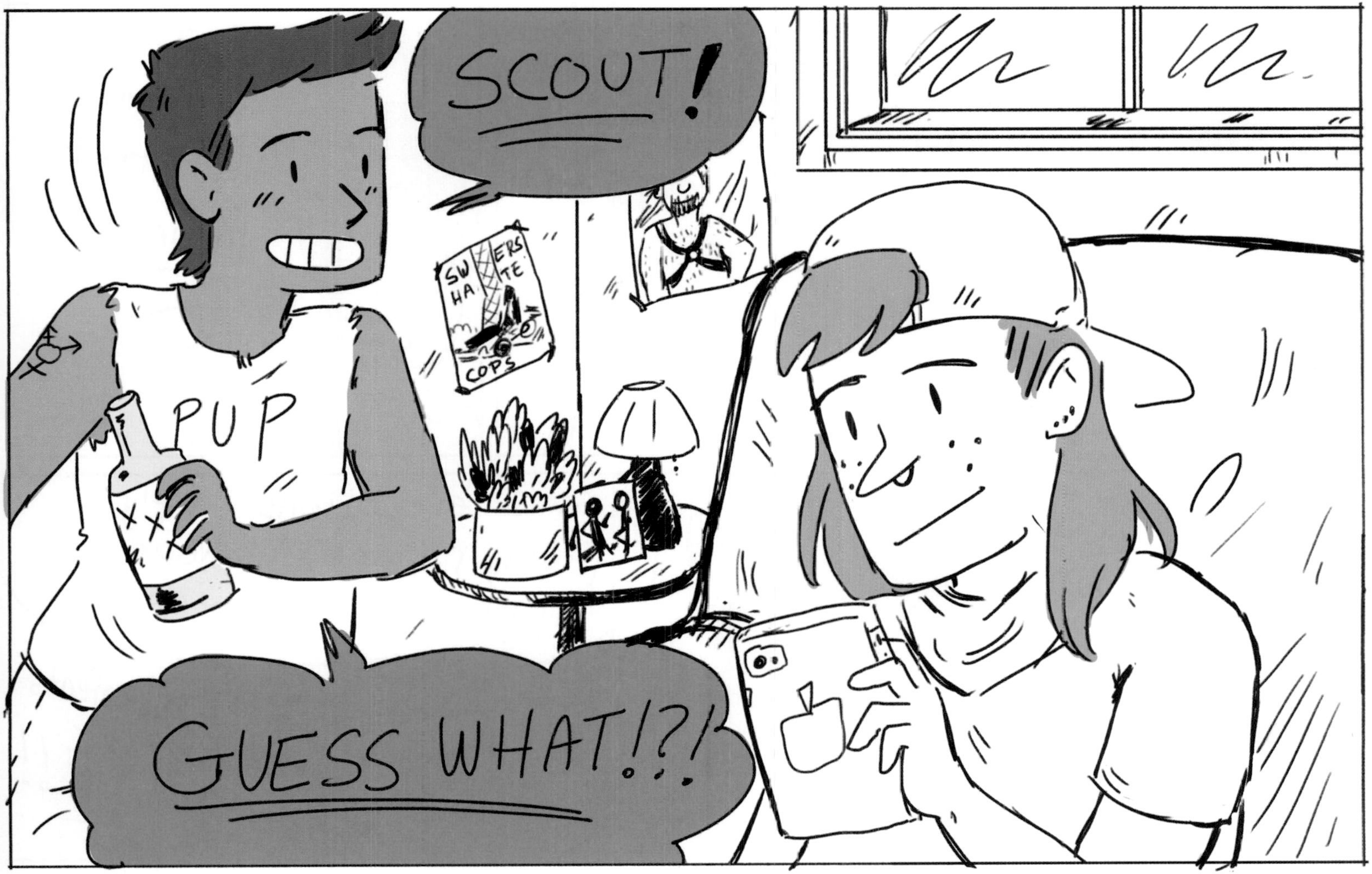
SCOUT!
GUESS WHAT!?!
PUP
COPS

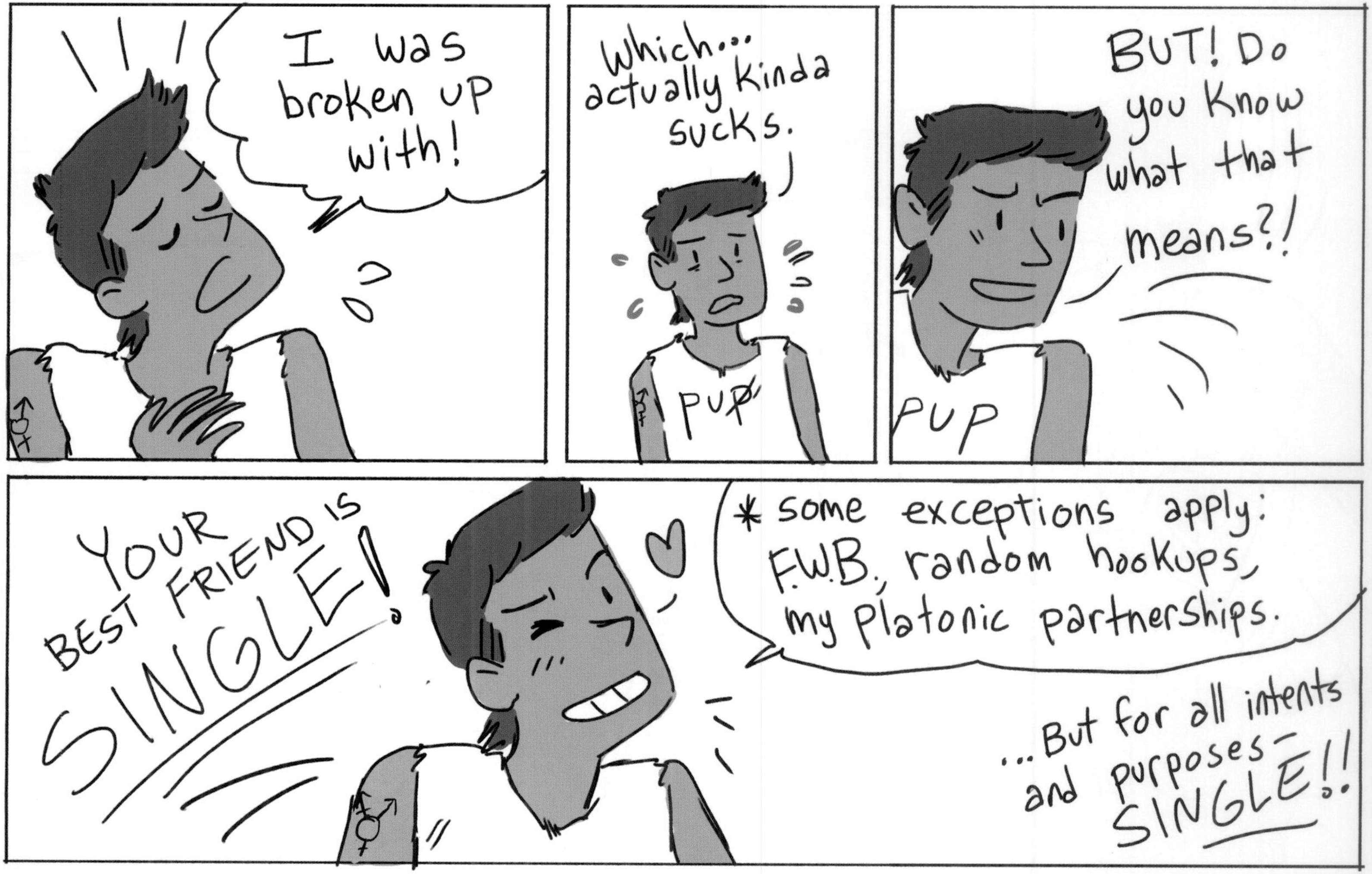
I was broken up with!
Which... actually kinda sucks.
PUP
BUT! Do you know what that means?!
PUP
YOUR BEST FRIEND IS SINGLE!
* some exceptions apply: F.W.B., random hookups, my platonic partnerships.
...But for all intents and purposes— SINGLE!!

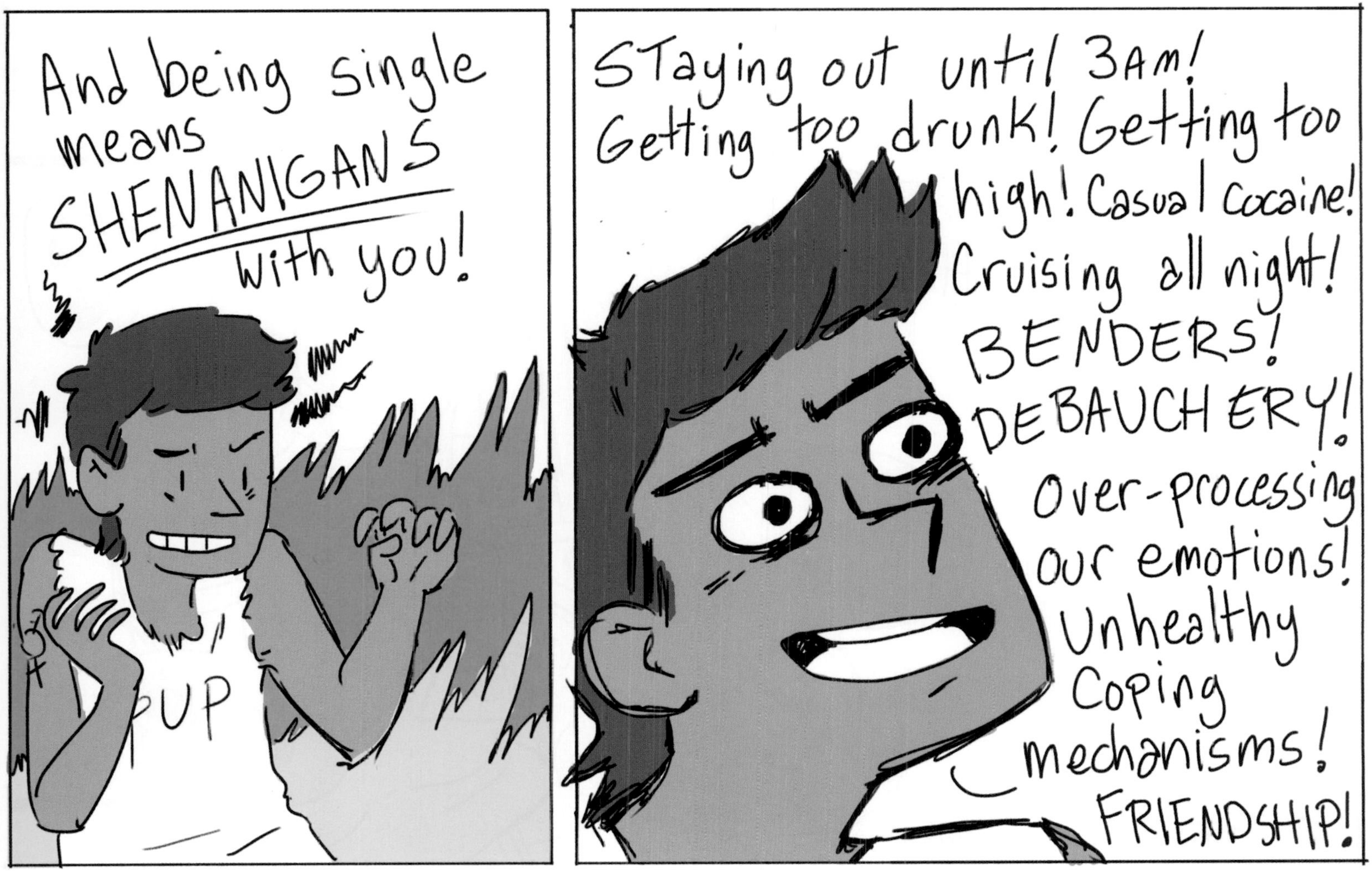
And being single means SHENANIGANS with you!
PUP
STaying out until 3AM! Getting too drunk! Getting too high! Casual cocaine! Cruising all night! BENDERS! DEBAUCHERY! Over-processing our emotions! Unhealthy Coping mechanisms! FRIENDSHIP!

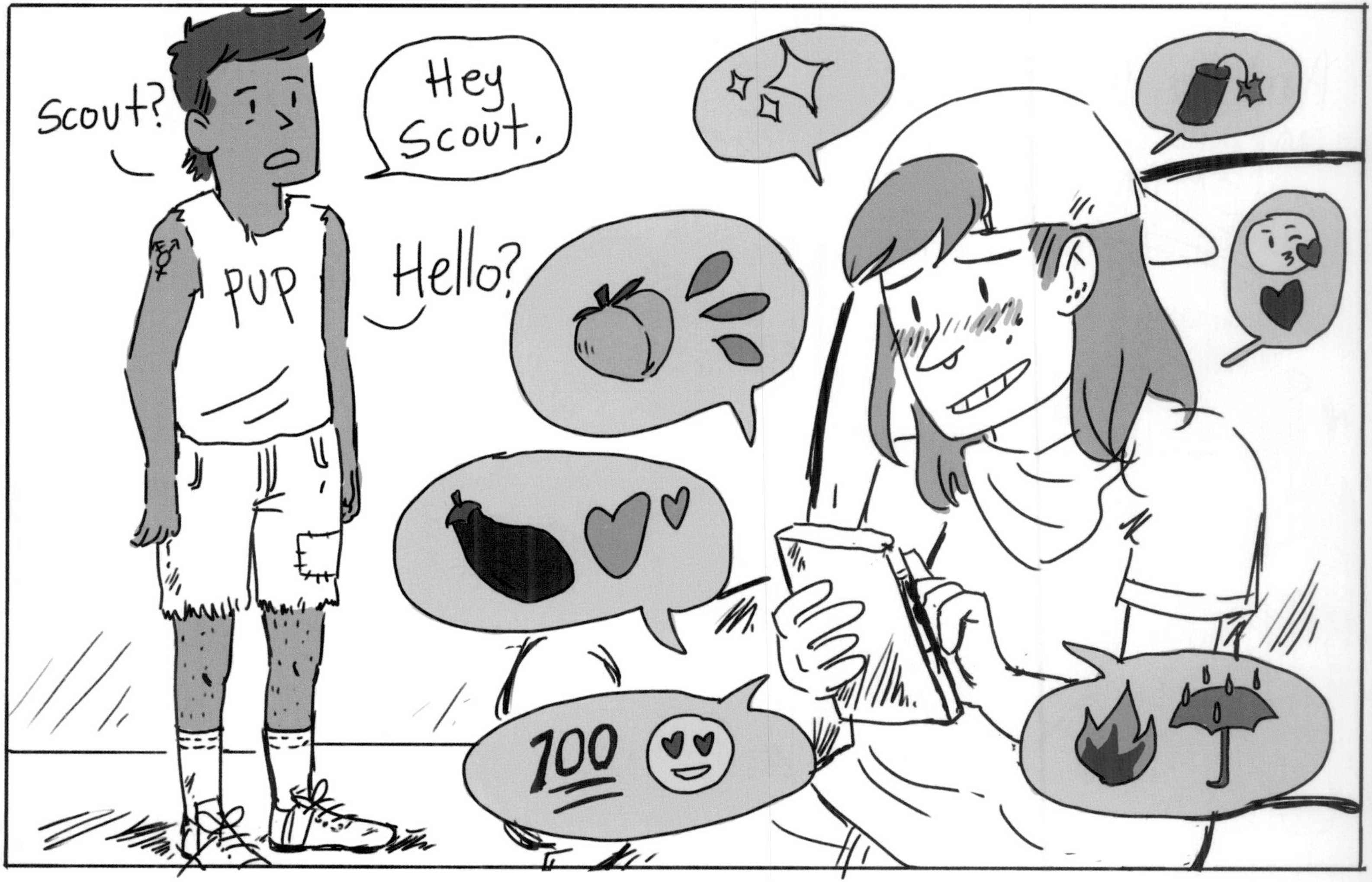

Scout?
Hey Scout.
PUP
Hello?
100

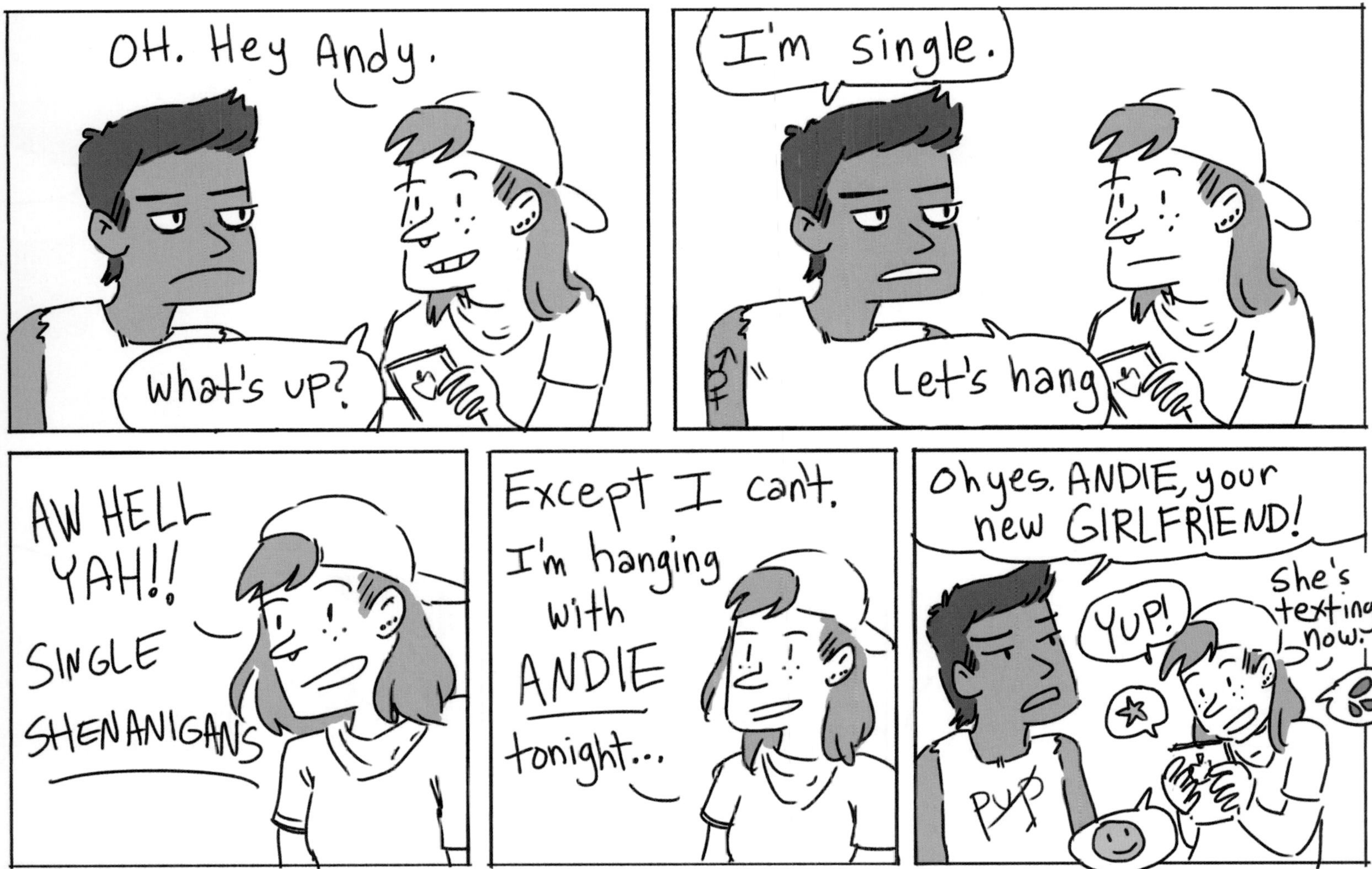
OH. Hey Andy.
what's up?
I'm single.
Let's hang
AW HELL YAH!!
SINGLE SHENANIGANS
Except I can't.
I'm hanging with ANDIE tonight...
Oh yes. ANDIE, your new GIRLFRIEND!
YUP!
she's texting now.
PUP

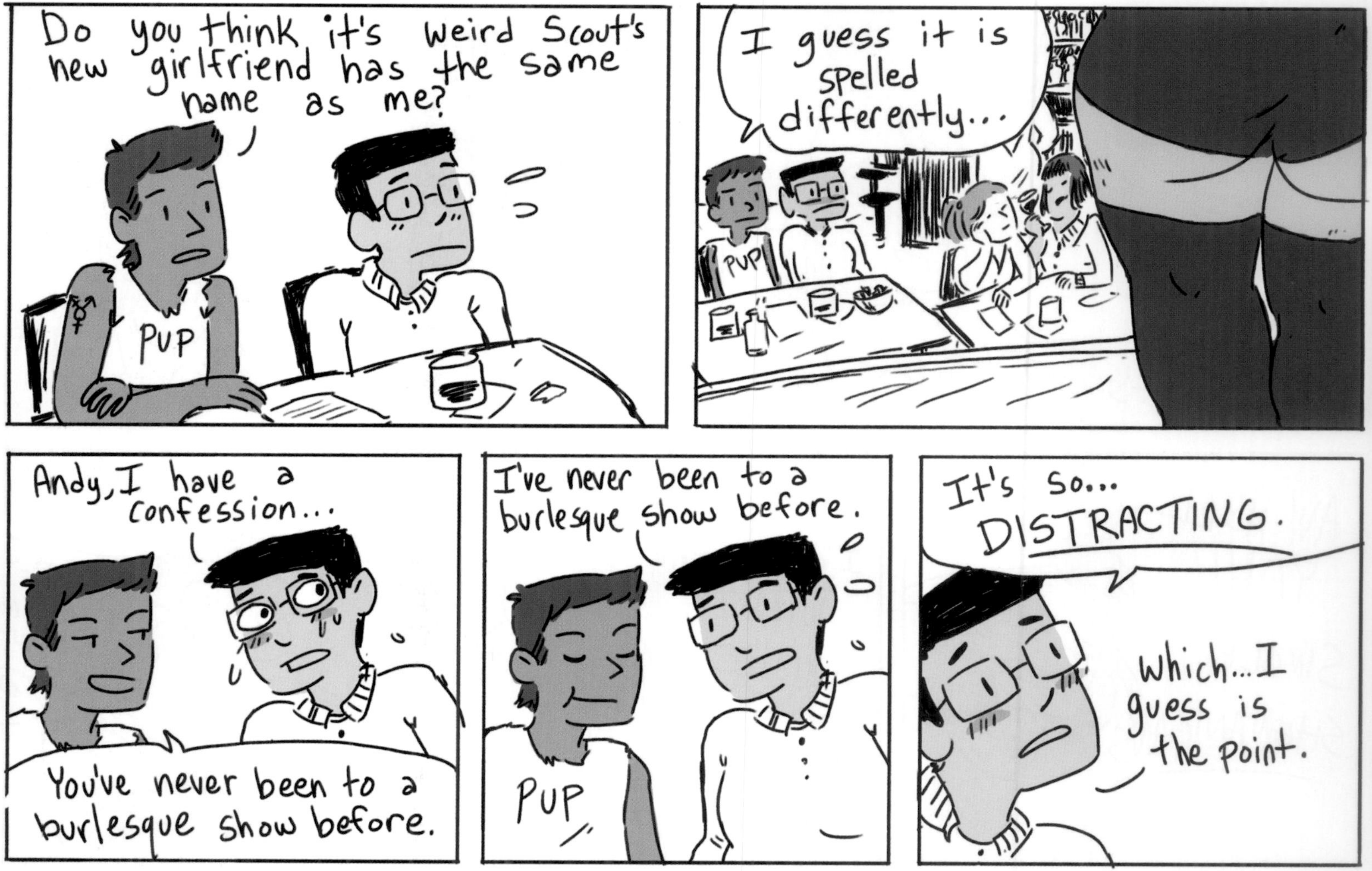
Do you think it's weird Scout's new girlfriend has the same name as me?
PUP
I guess it is spelled differently...
PUP
Andy, I have a confession...
You've never been to a burlesque show before.
I've never been to a burlesque show before.
PUP
It's so... DISTRACTING.
which... I guess is the point.

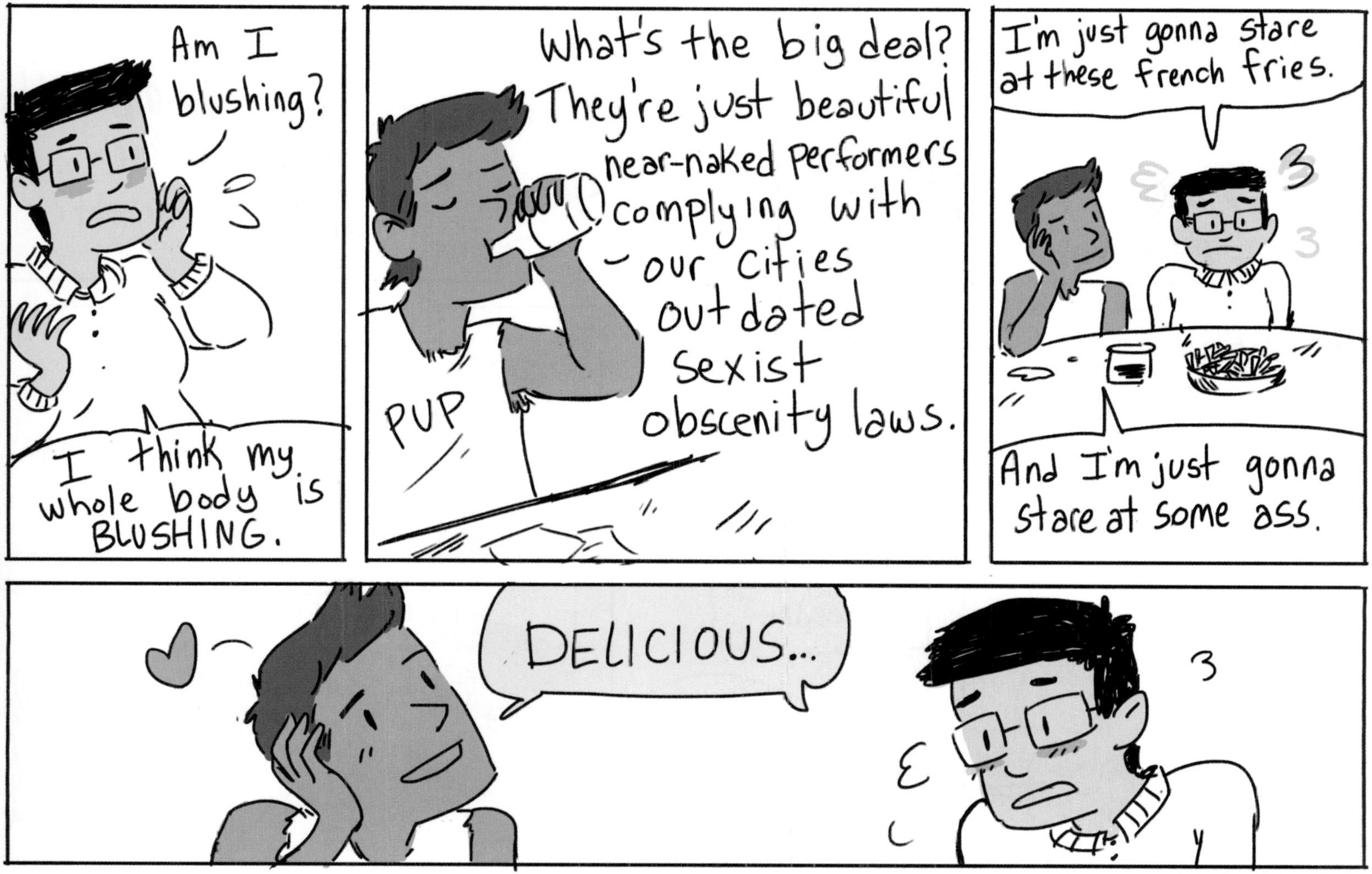
Am I blushing?
I think my whole body is BLUSHING.
What's the big deal? They're just beautiful near-naked performers complying with our cities outdated sexist obscenity laws.
PUP
I'm just gonna stare at these french fries.
And I'm just gonna stare at some ass.
DELICIOUS...

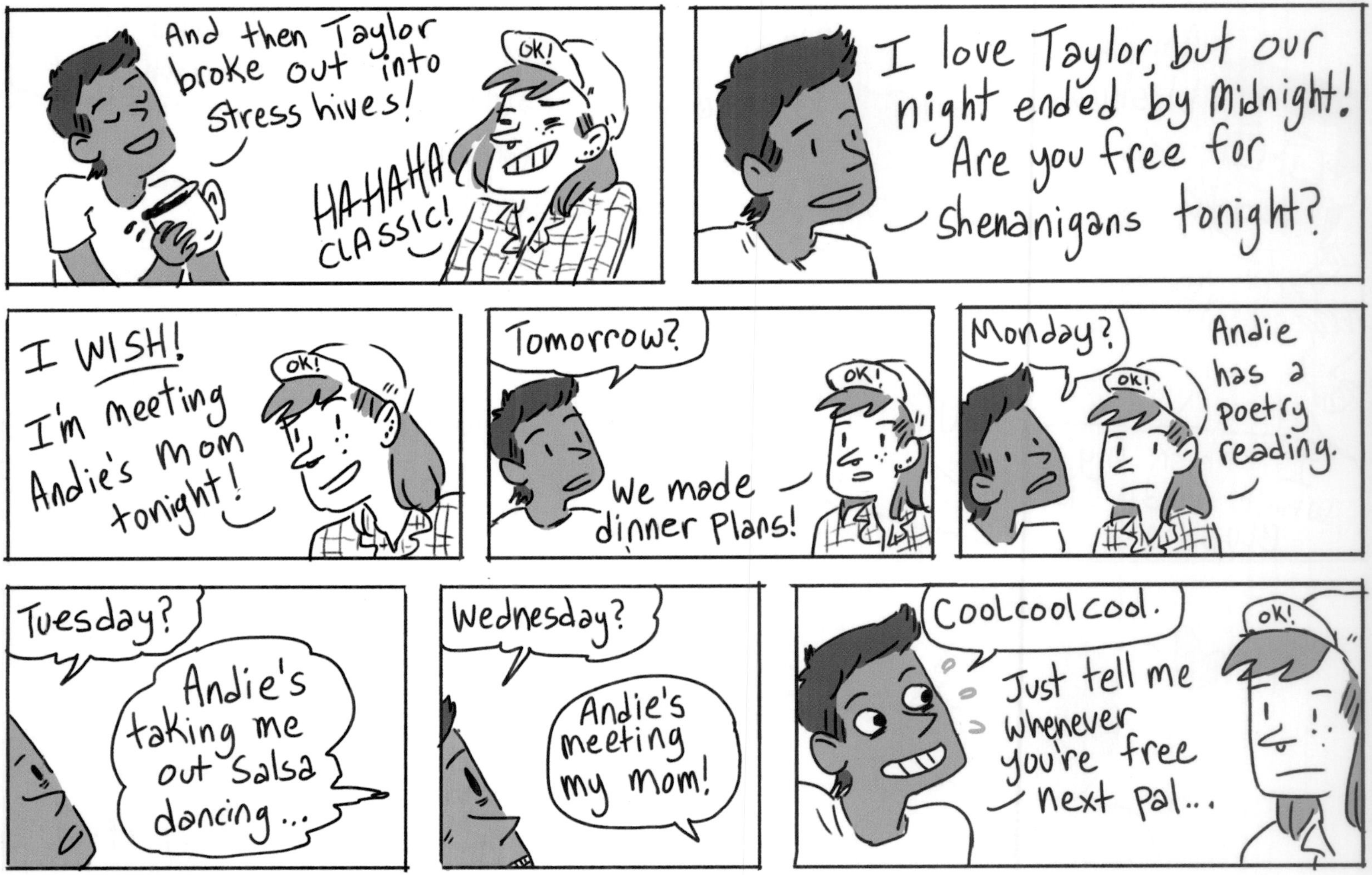
And then Taylor broke out into stress hives!
HAHAHA CLASSIC!
OK!
I love Taylor, but our night ended by Midnight! Are you free for shenanigans tonight?
I WISH! I'm meeting Andie's mom tonight!
OK!
Tomorrow?
We made dinner Plans!
OK!
Monday?
Andie has a poetry reading.
OK!
Tuesday?
Andie's taking me out Salsa dancing...
Wednesday?
Andie's meeting my mom!
Coolcoolcool.
Just tell me whenever you're free next Pal...
OK!

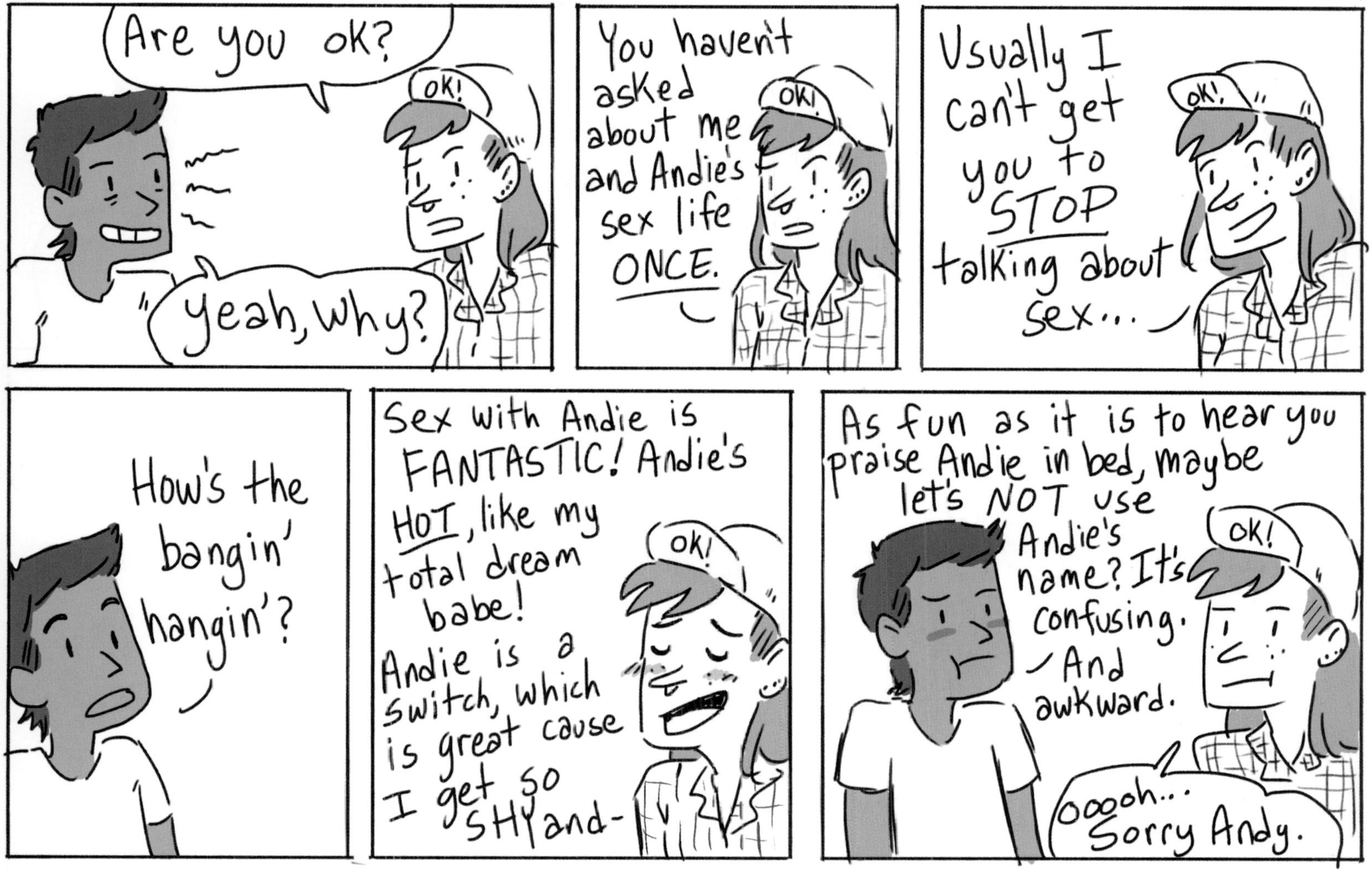
Are you ok?
OK!
Yeah, why?
You haven't asked about me and Andie's sex life ONCE.
OK!
Usually I can't get you to STOP talking about sex...
OK!
How's the bangin' hangin'?
Sex with Andie is FANTASTIC! Andie's HOT, like my total dream babe! Andie is a switch, which is great cause I get so SHY and-
OK!
As fun as it is to hear you praise Andie in bed, maybe let's NOT use Andie's name? It's confusing.
And awkward.
OK!
Ooooh... Sorry Andy.

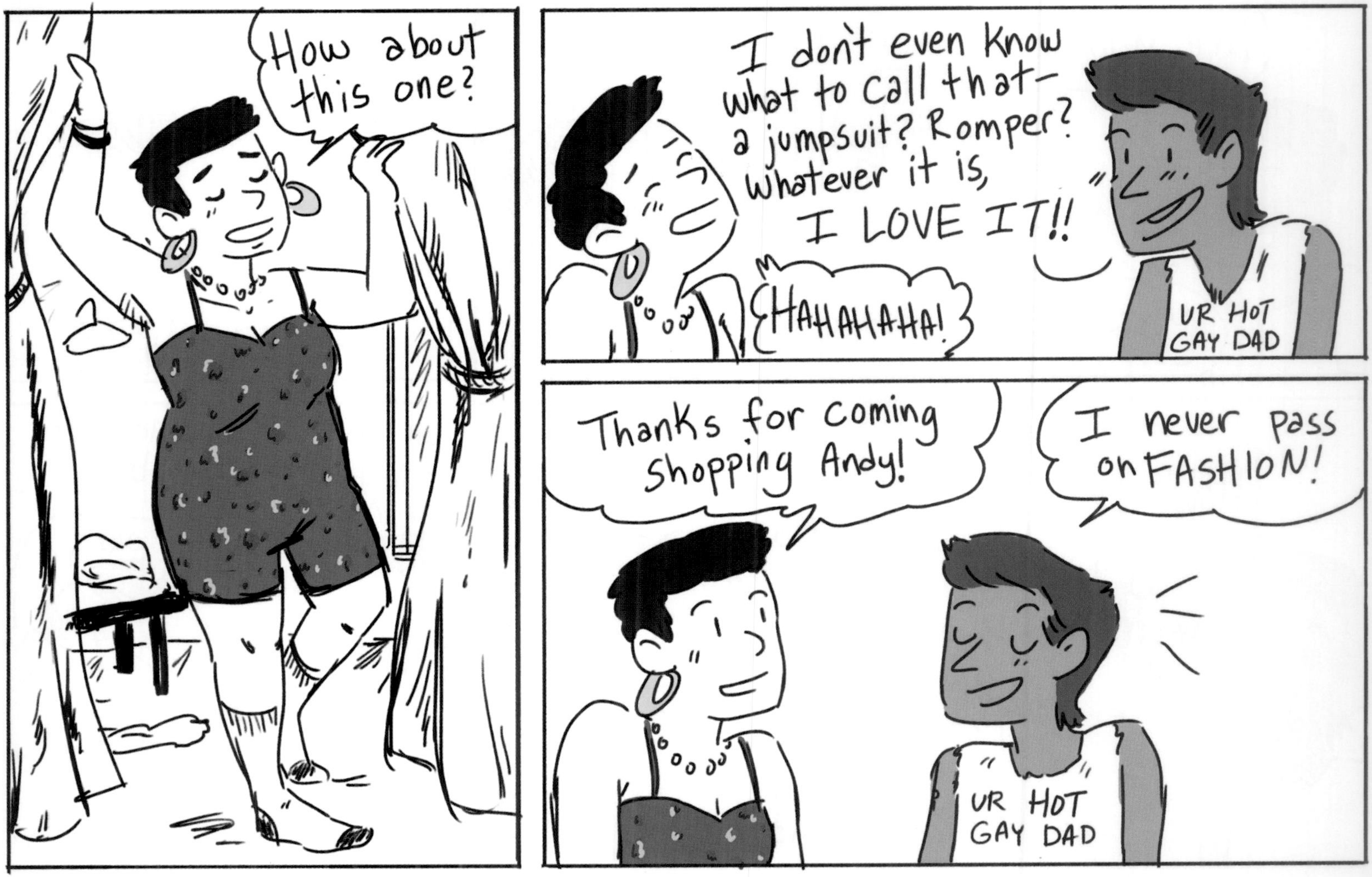
How about this one?
I don't even know what to call that—a jumpsuit? Romper? whatever it is, I LOVE IT!!
HAHAHAHA!
UR HOT GAY DAD
Thanks for coming shopping Andy!
I never pass on FASHION!
UR HOT GAY DAD

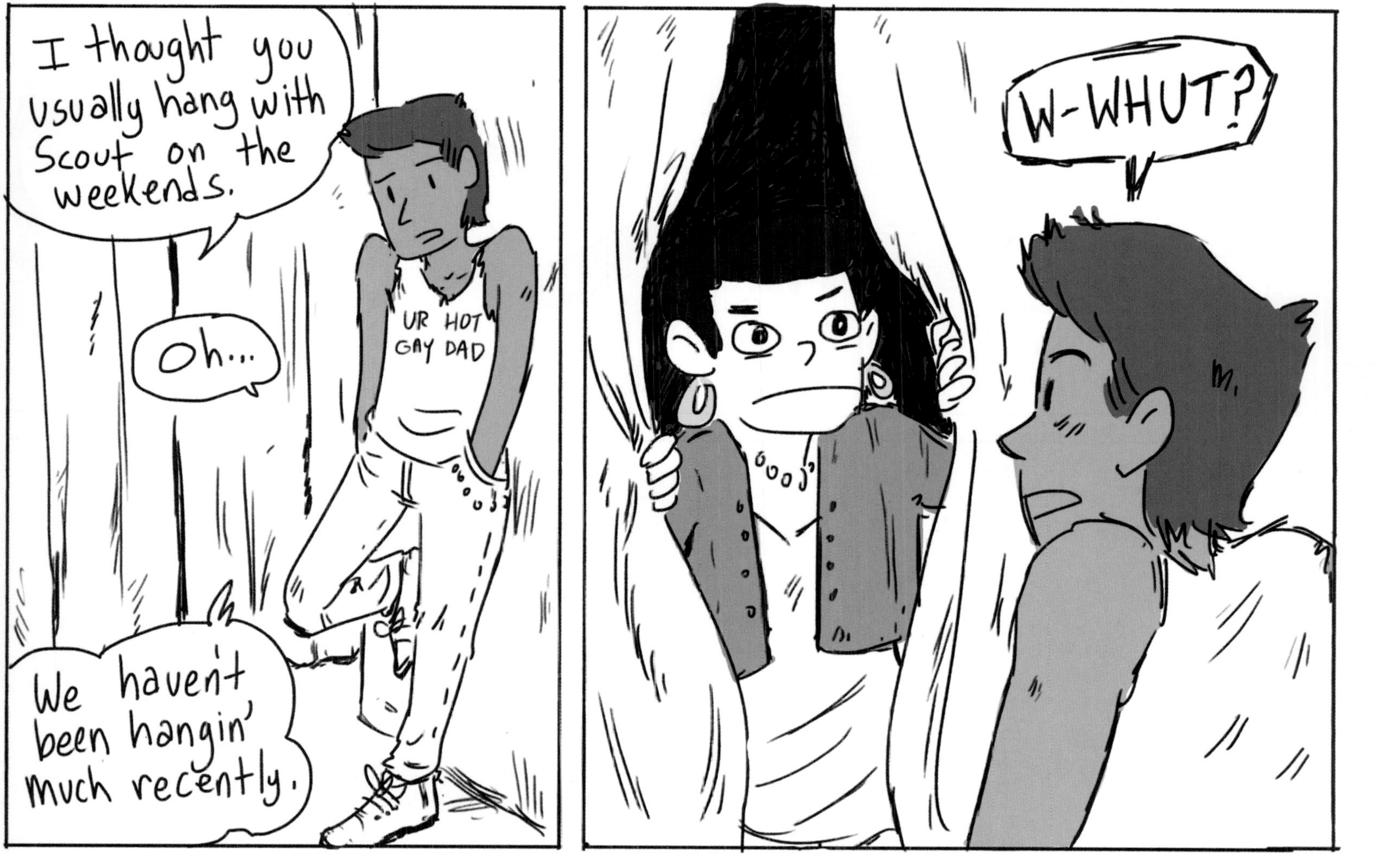
I thought you usually hang with Scout on the weekends.
Oh...
UR HOT GAY DAD
We haven't been hangin' much recently.
W-WHUT?

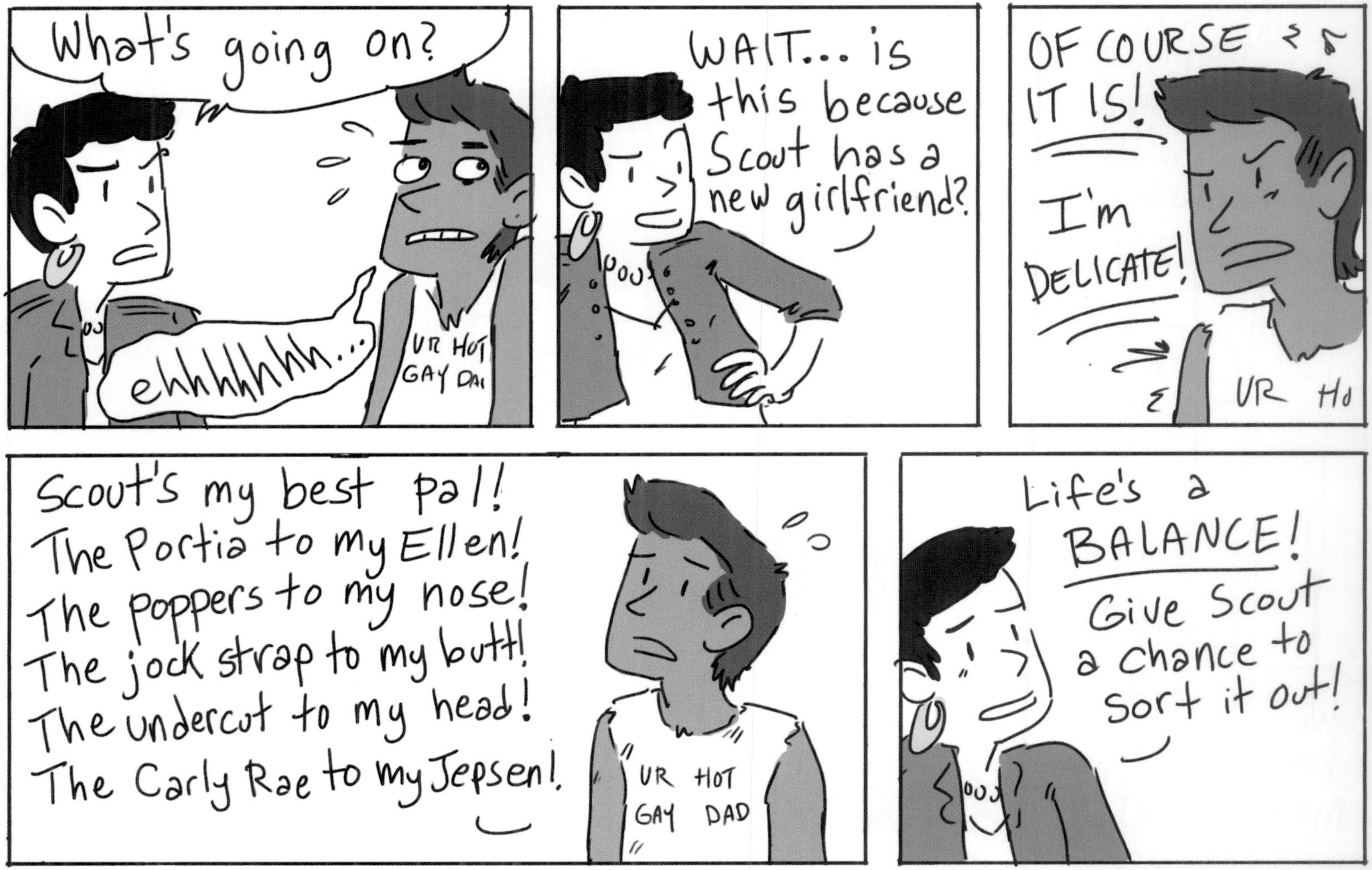
What's going on?
ehhhhhhh...
UR HOT GAY DAD
WAIT... is this because Scout has a new girlfriend?
OF COURSE IT IS!
I'm DELICATE!
UR HO
Scout's my best pal! The Portia to my Ellen! The poppers to my nose! The jock strap to my butt! The undercut to my head! The Carly Rae to my Jepsen!
UR HOT GAY DAD
Life's a BALANCE! Give Scout a chance to sort it out!

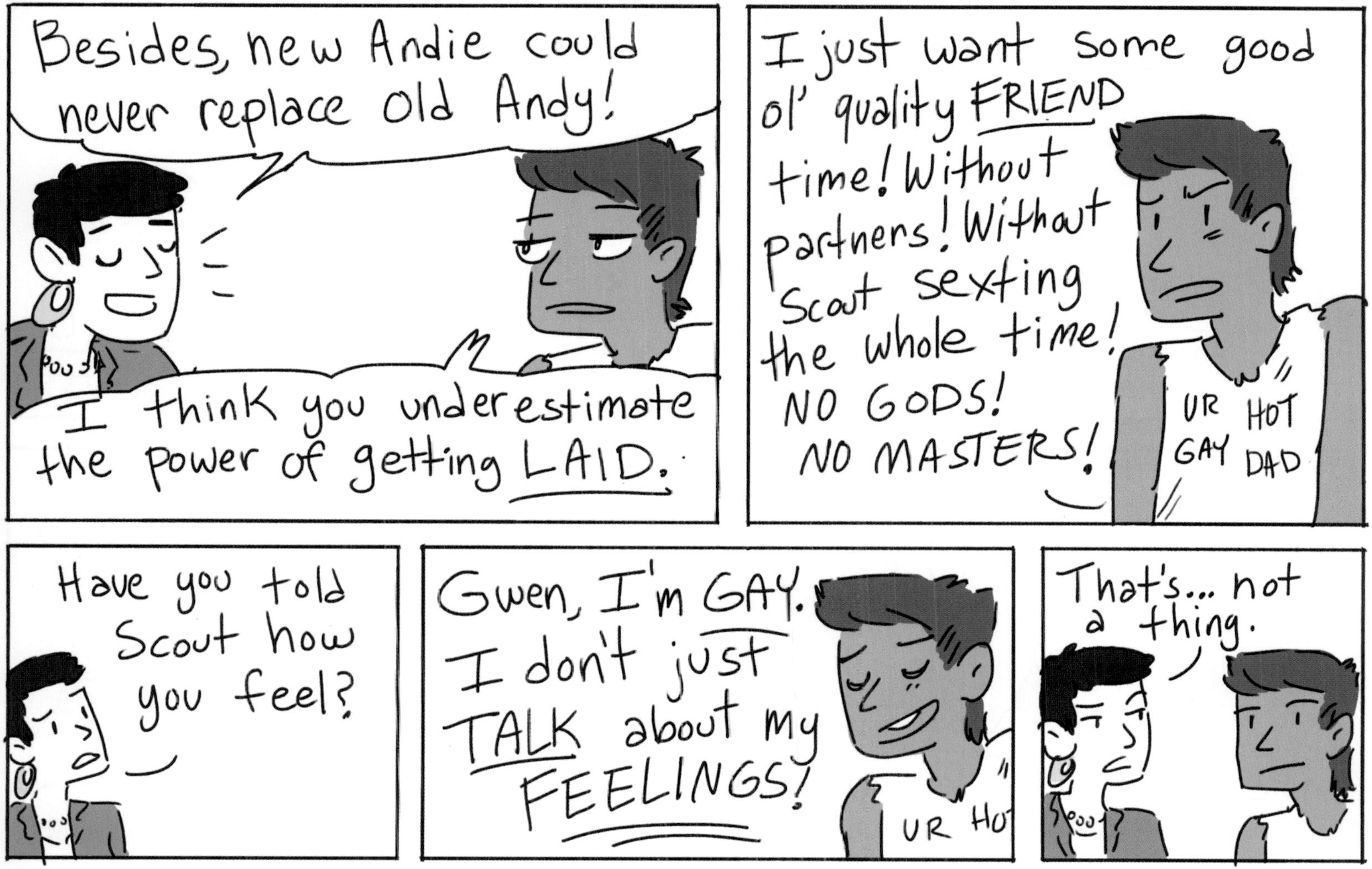
Besides, new Andie could never replace Old Andy!
I think you underestimate the power of getting LAID.
I just want some good ol' quality FRIEND time! Without partners! Without Scout sexting the whole time! NO GODS! NO MASTERS!
UR HOT GAY DAD
Have you told Scout how you feel?
Gwen, I'm GAY. I don't just TALK about my FEELINGS!
UR HO
That's... not a thing.

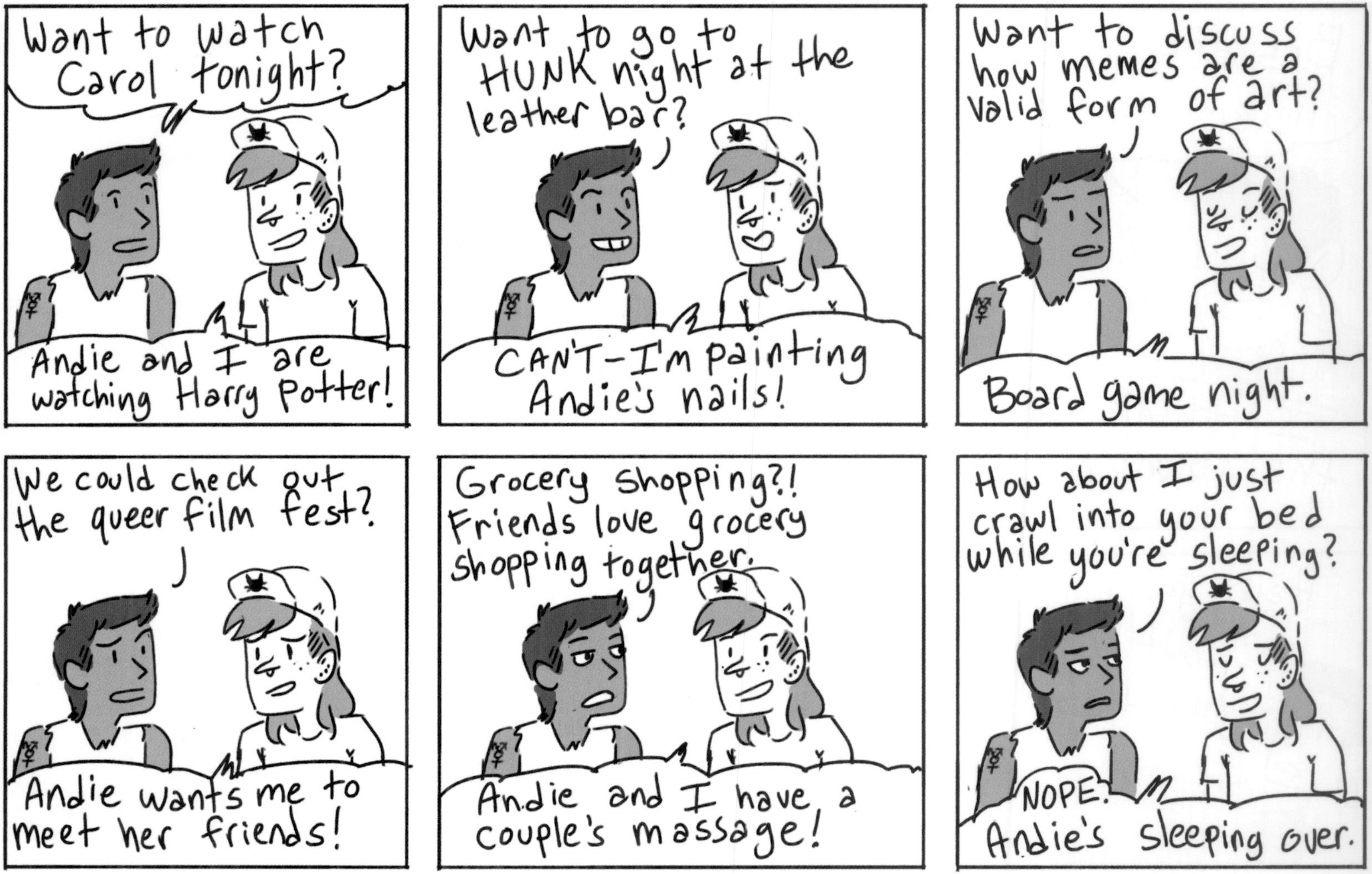
Want to watch Carol tonight?
Andie and I are watching Harry Potter!
Want to go to HUNK night at the leather bar?
CAN'T–I'm painting Andie's nails!
Want to discuss how memes are a valid form of art?
Board game night.
We could check out the queer film fest?
Andie wants me to meet her friends!
Grocery shopping?! Friends love grocery shopping together.
Andie and I have a couple's massage!
How about I just crawl into your bed while you're sleeping?
NOPE. Andie's sleeping over.

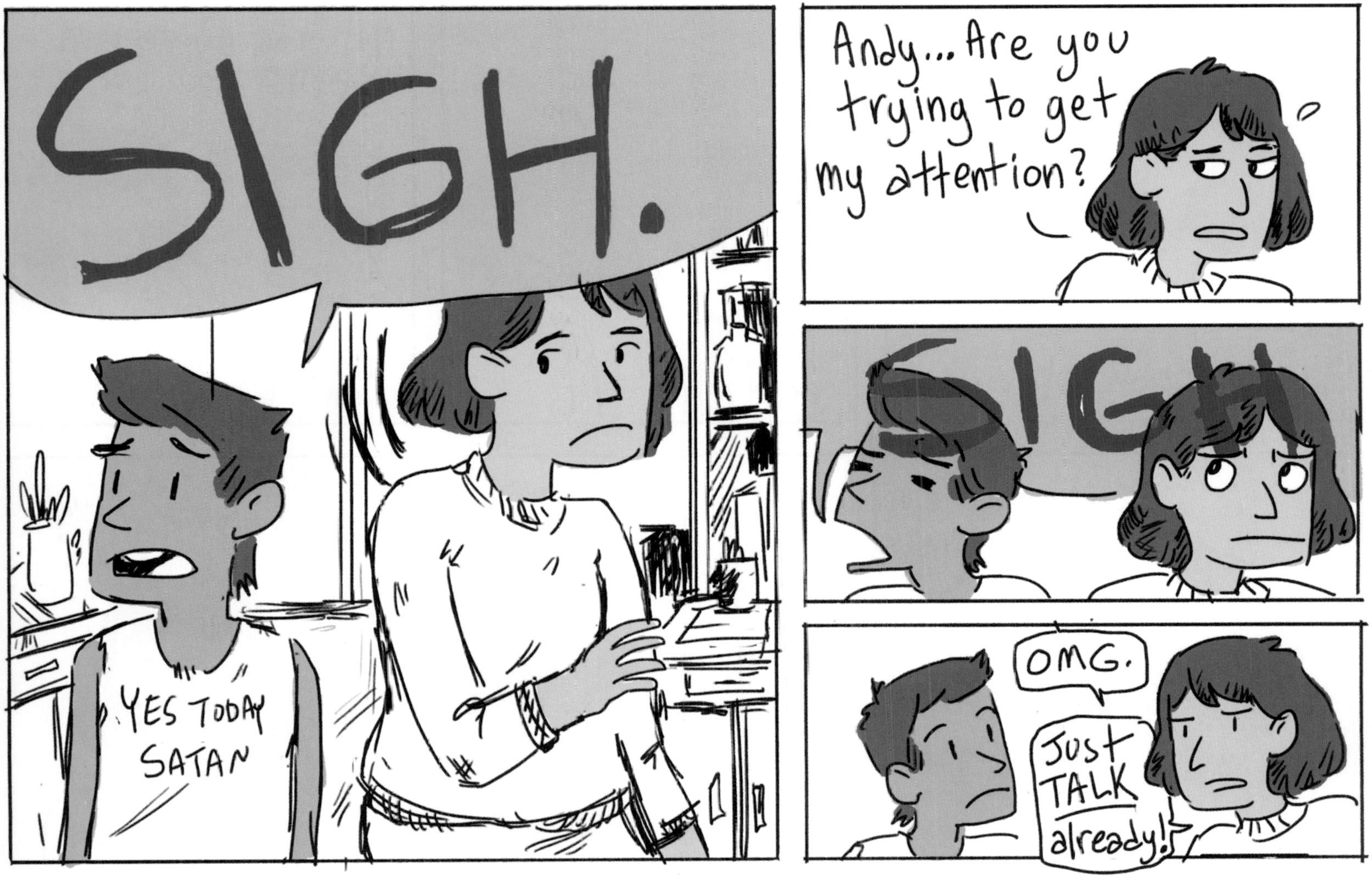
SIGH.
YES TODAY SATAN
Andy... Are you trying to get my attention?
SIGH
OMG.
JUST TALK already!

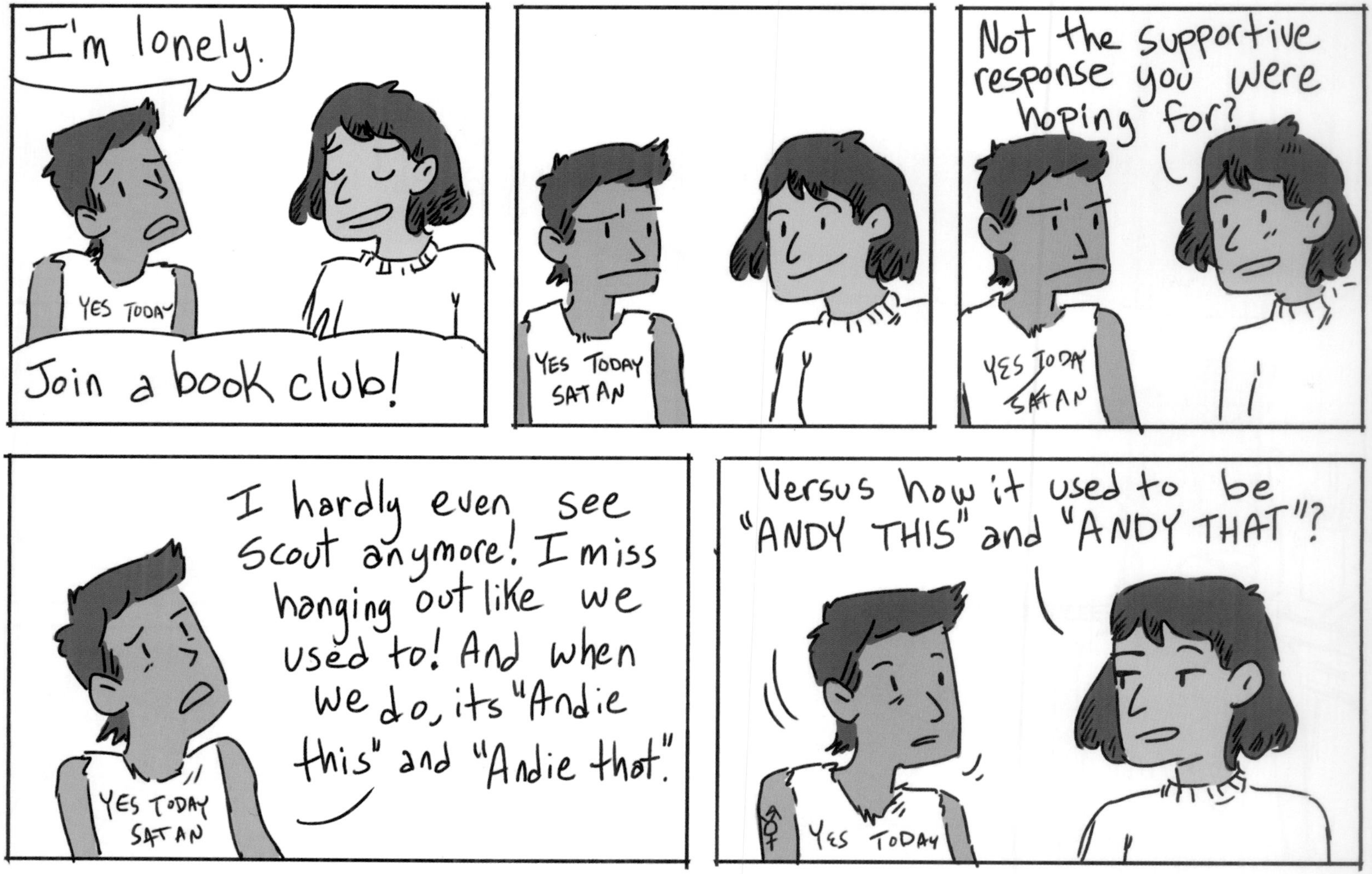
I'm lonely.
Join a book club!
YES TODAY
YES TODAY SATAN
Not the supportive response you were hoping for?
YES TODAY SATAN
I hardly even see Scout anymore! I miss hanging out like we used to! And when we do, its "Andie this" and "Andie that."
YES TODAY SATAN
Versus how it used to be "ANDY THIS" and "ANDY THAT"?
YES TODAY

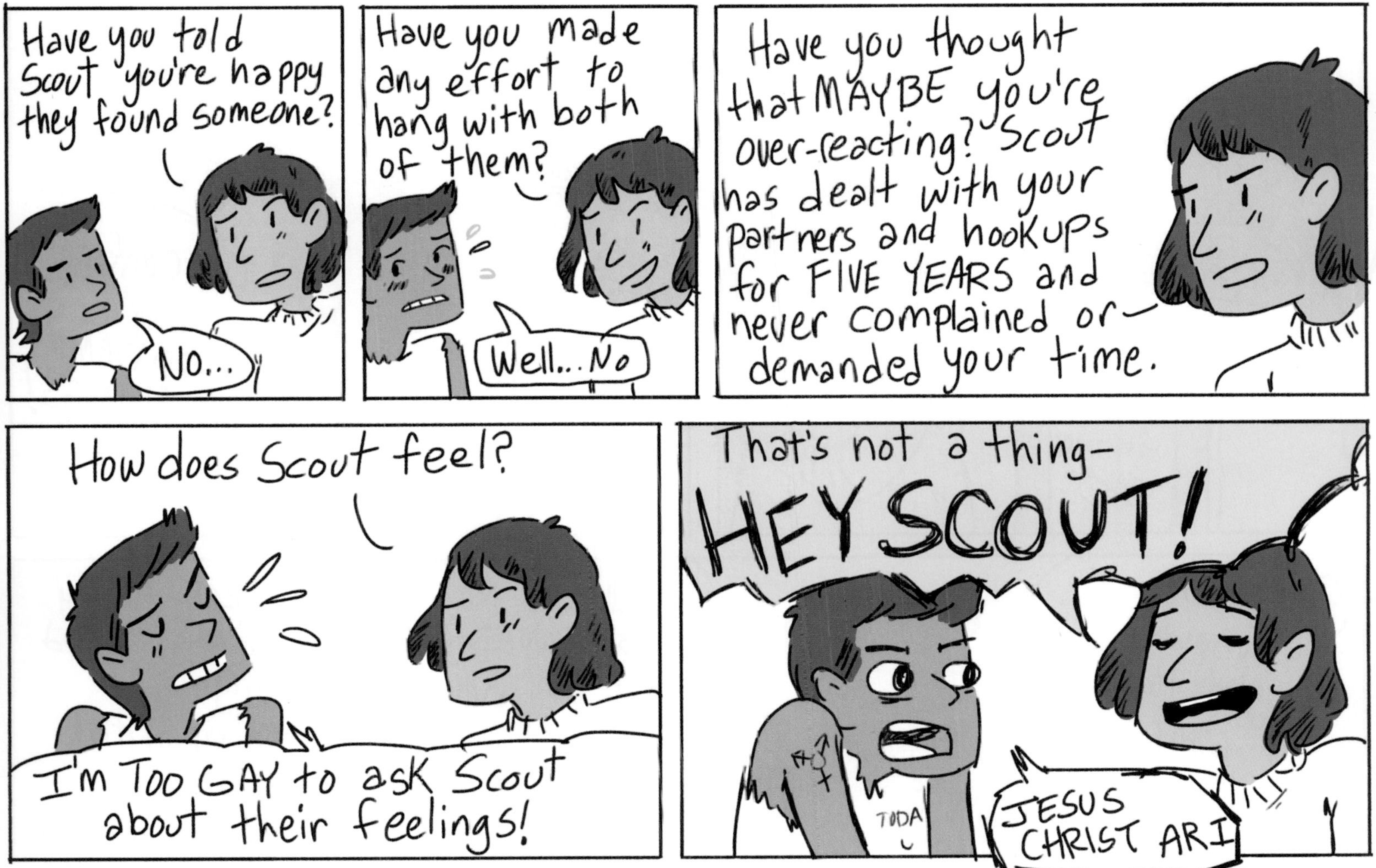
Have you told Scout you're happy they found someone?
No...
Have you made any effort to hang with both of them?
Well... No
Have you thought that MAYBE you're over-reacting? Scout has dealt with your partners and hookups for FIVE YEARS and never complained or demanded your time.
How does Scout feel?
I'm TOO GAY to ask Scout about their feelings!
That's not a thing-
HEY SCOUT!
JESUS CHRIST ARI
TODA

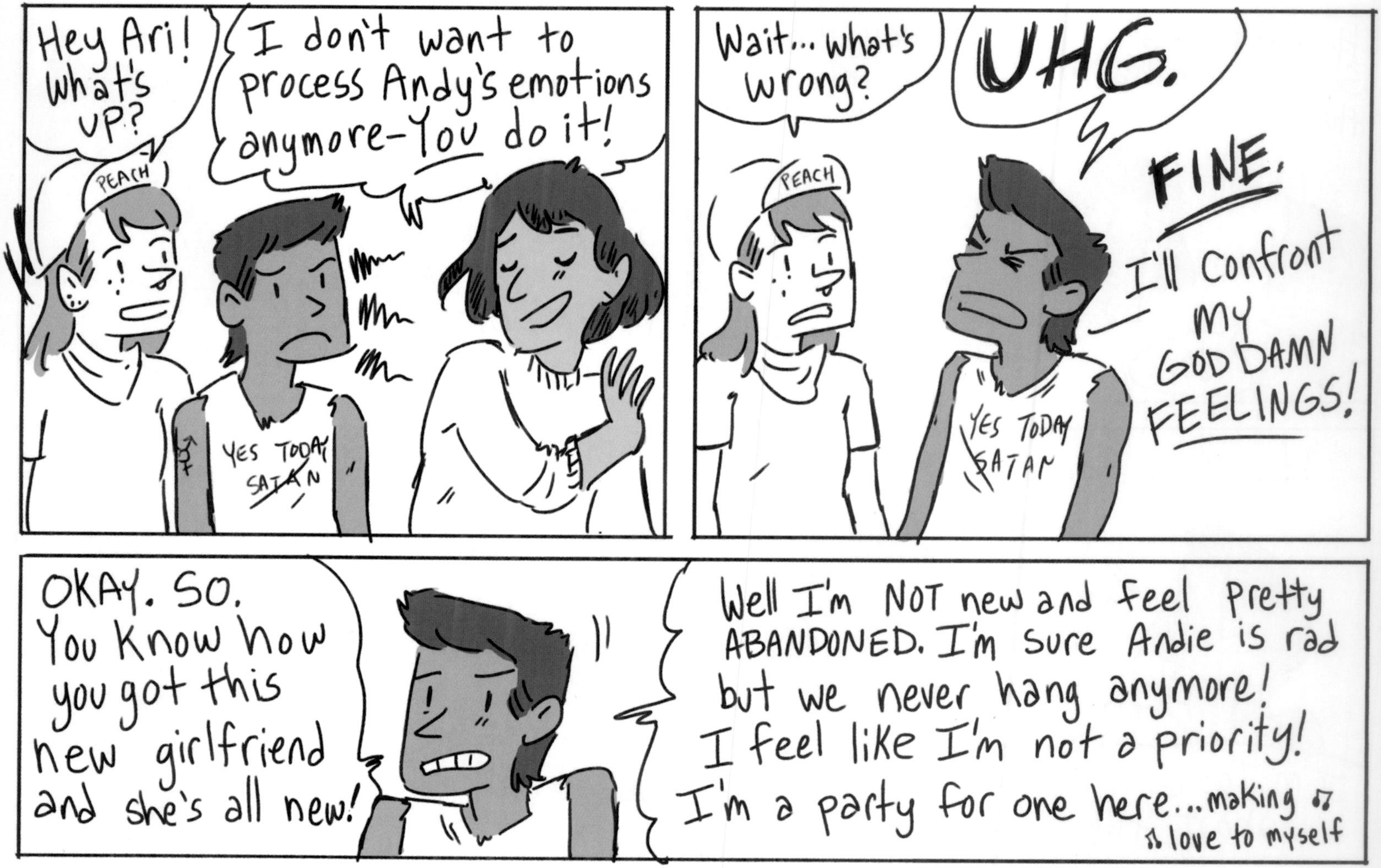
Hey Ari! What's up?
PEACH
I don't want to process Andy's emotions anymore–YOU do it!
YES TODAY SATAN
Wait... what's wrong?
PEACH
UHG.
FINE. I'll confront my GOD DAMN FEELINGS!
YES TODAY SATAN
OKAY. SO. You know how you got this new girlfriend and she's all new!
Well I'm NOT new and feel pretty ABANDONED. I'm sure Andie is rad but we never hang anymore! I feel like I'm not a priority! I'm a party for one here... making ♫ ♫ love to myself

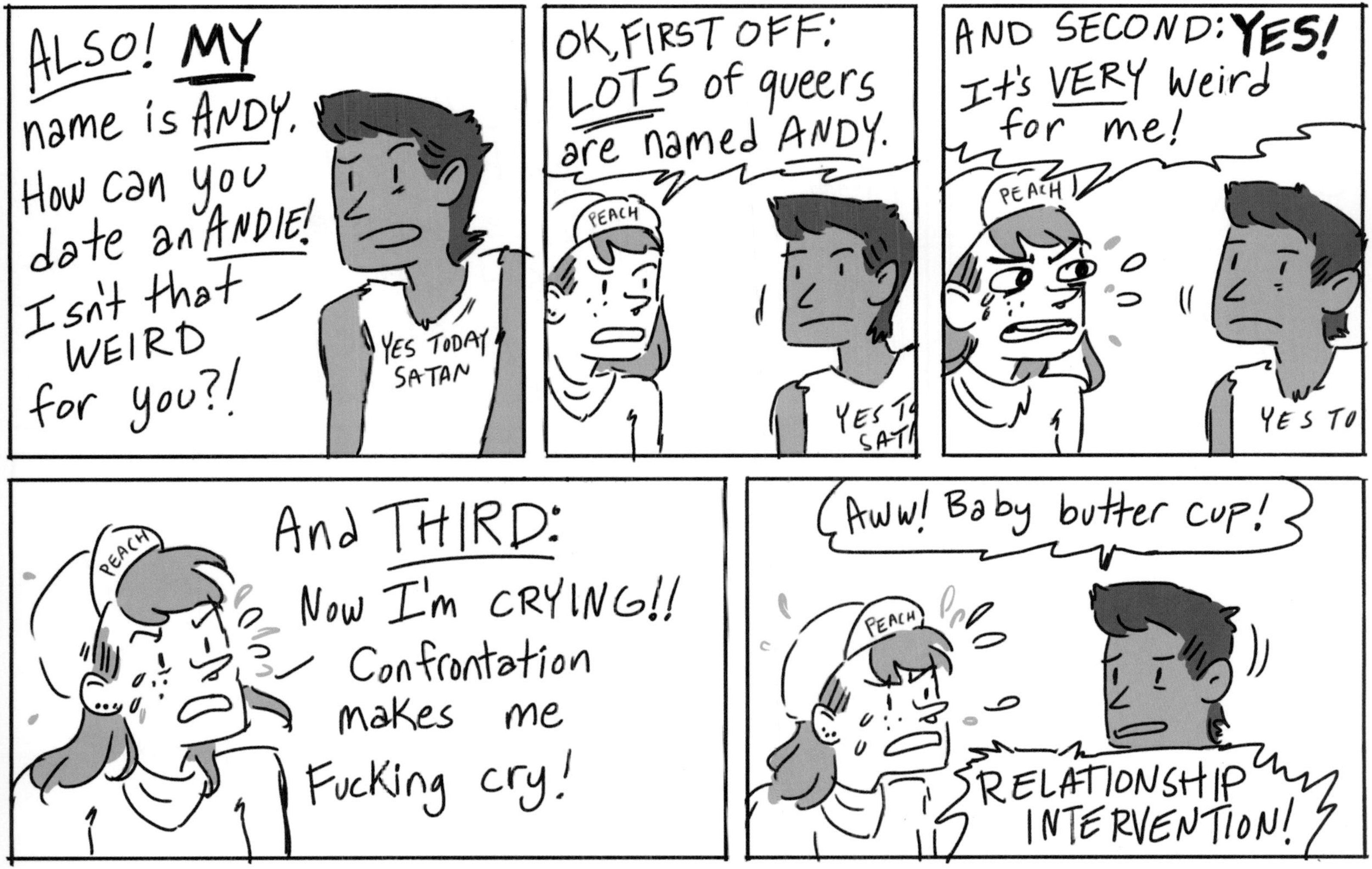
ALSO! MY name is ANDY. How can you date an ANDIE! Isn't that WEIRD for you?!
YES TODAY SATAN
OK, FIRST OFF: LOTS of queers are named ANDY.
PEACH
AND SECOND: YES! It's VERY weird for me!
PEACH
And THIRD: Now I'm CRYING!! Confrontation makes me Fucking cry!
PEACH
Aww! Baby butter cup!
PEACH
RELATIONSHIP INTERVENTION!

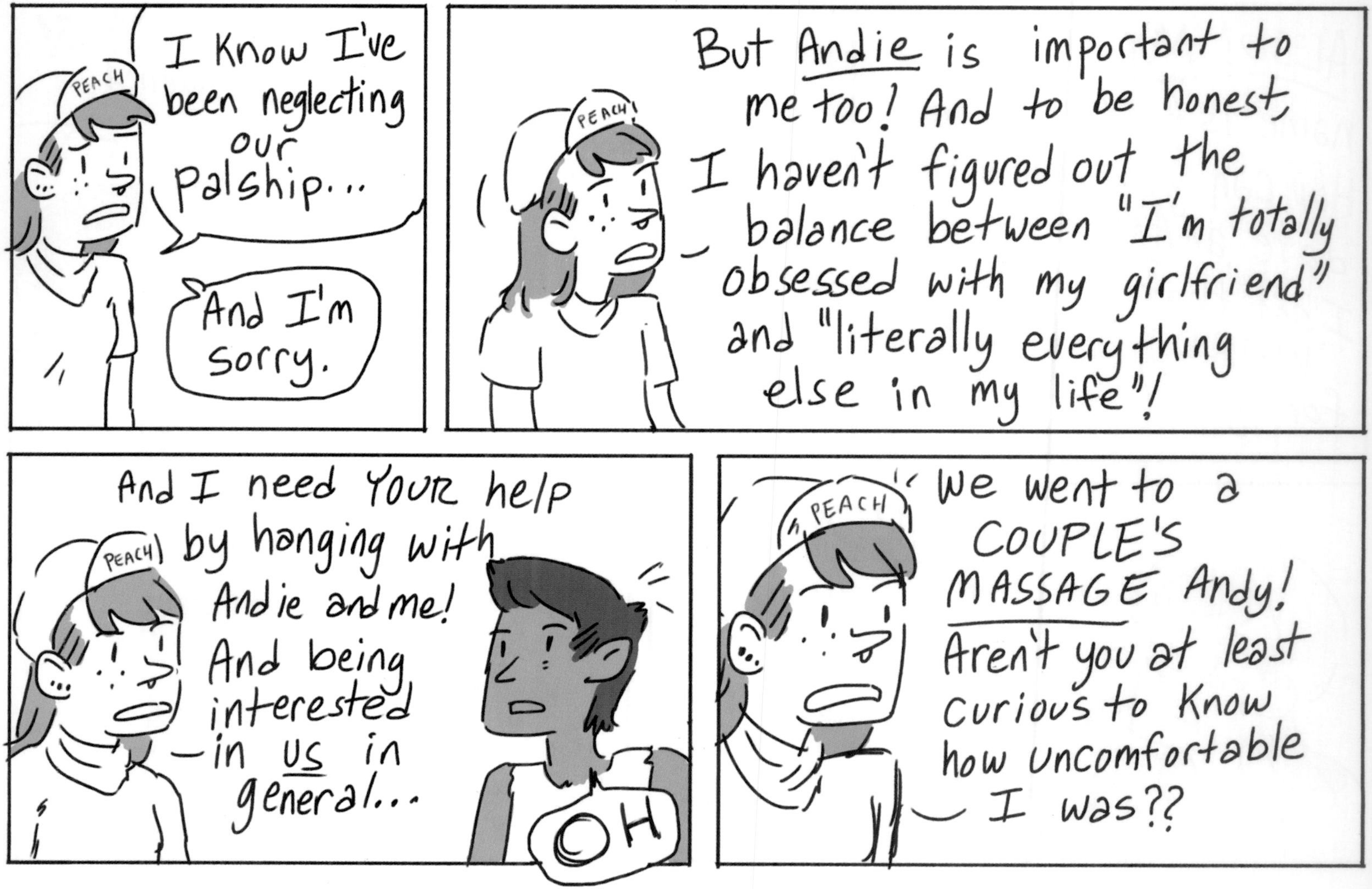
PEACH
I Know I've been neglecting our Palship...
And I'm sorry.
PEACH
But Andie is important to me too! And to be honest, I haven't figured out the balance between "I'm totally obsessed with my girlfriend" and "literally everything else in my life"!
And I need YOUR help by hanging with Andie and me! And being interested in US in general...
PEACH
OH
PEACH
We went to a COUPLE'S MASSAGE Andy! Aren't you at least curious to Know how uncomfortable I was??

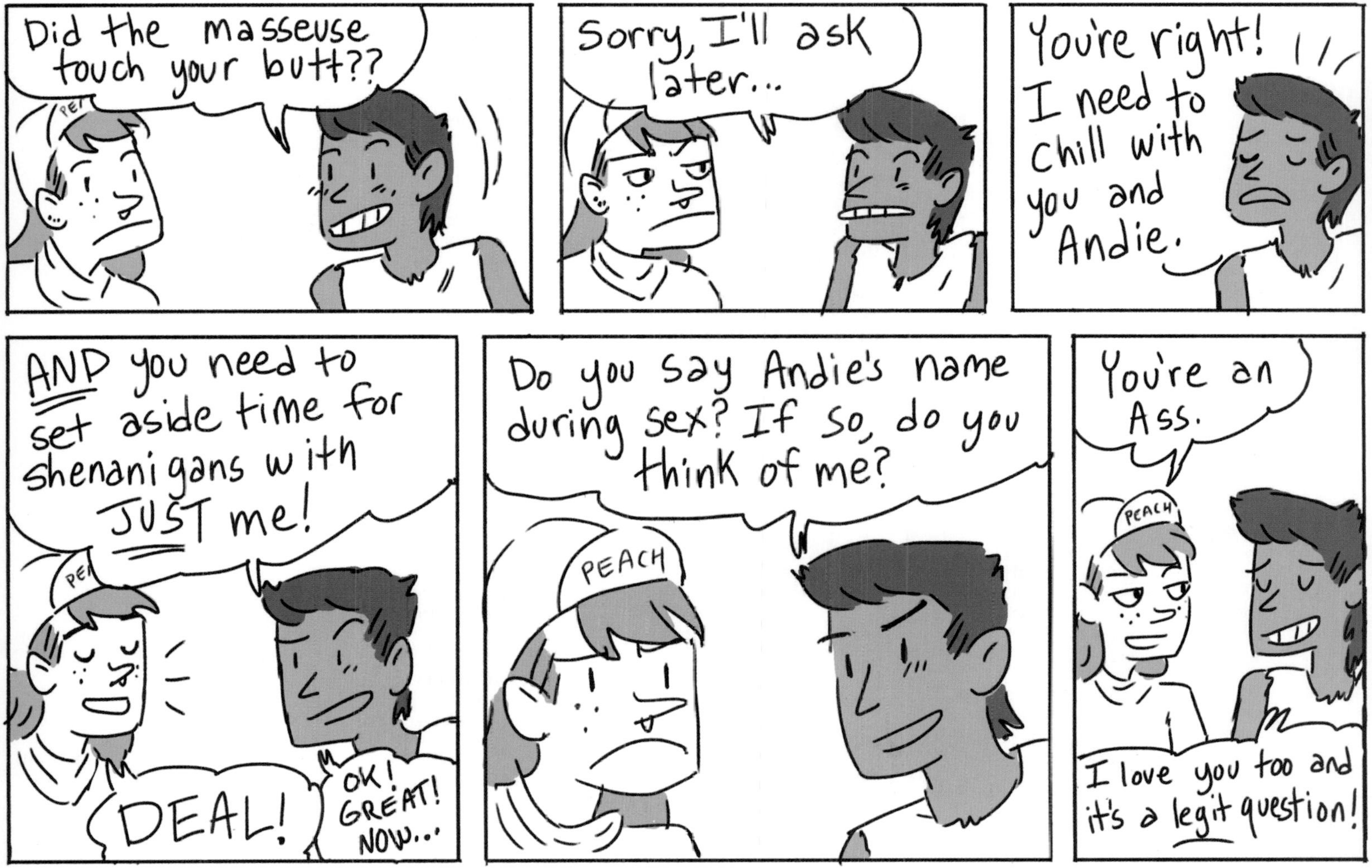
Did the masseuse touch your butt??
Sorry, I'll ask later...
You're right! I need to Chill with you and Andie.
AND you need to set aside time for shenanigans with JUST me!
DEAL!
OK! GREAT! NOW...
PEACH
Do you say Andie's name during sex? If so, do you think of me?
PEACH
You're an Ass.
I love you too and it's a legit question!

DISCOVER **ALL THE HITS**

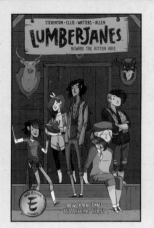

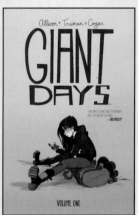

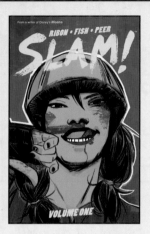

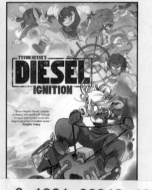

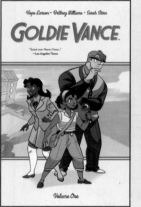

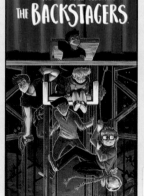

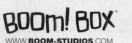

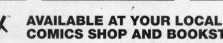

STEVENSON • ELLIS • WATTERS • ALLEN
LUMBERJANES
BEWARE THE KITTEN HOLY
NEW YORK TIMES
BESTSELLING SERIES

Allison + Treiman + Cogar
GIANT DAYS
VOLUME ONE

From a writer of Disney's Moana
RIBON • FISH • PEER
SLAM!
VOLUME ONE

Hope Larson • Brittney Williams • Sarah Stern
GOLDIE VANCE
Volume One

THE BACKSTAGERS

TYSON HESSE'S
DIESEL
IGNITION

BOOM! BOX
WWW.**BOOM-STUDIOS**.COM

AVAILABLE AT YOUR LOCAL COMICS SHOP AND BOOKSTORE

To find a comics shop in your area, visit www.comicshoplocator.com

Lumberjanes

Noelle Stevenson, Shannon Watters,Grace Ellis, Brooke Allen, and Others

Volume 1: Beware the Kitten Holy | ISBN: 978-1-60886-687-8 | $14.99 US
Volume 2: Friendship to the Max | ISBN: 978-1-60886-737-0 | $14.99 US
Volume 3: A Terrible Plan | ISBN: 978-1-60886-803-2 | $14.99 US
Volume 4: Out of Time | ISBN: 978-1-60886-860-5 | $14.99 US
Volume 5: Band Together | ISBN: 978-1-60886-919-0 | $14.99 US

Giant Days

John Allison, Lissa Treiman, Max Sarin

Volume 1 | ISBN: 978-1-60886-789-9 | $9.99 US
Volume 2 | ISBN: 978-1-60886-804-9 | $14.99 US
Volume 3 | ISBN: 978-1-60886-851-3 | $14.99 US

Jonesy

Sam Humphries, Caitlin Rose Boyle

Volume 1 | ISBN: 978-1-60886-883-4 | $9.99 US
Volume 2 | ISBN: 978-1-60886-999-2 | $14.99 US

Slam!

Pamela Ribon, Veronica Fish, Brittany Peer

Volume 1 | ISBN: 978-1-68415-004-5 | $14.99 US

Goldie Vance

Hope Larson, Brittney Williams

Volume 1 | ISBN: 978-1-60886-898-8 | $9.99 US
Volume 2 | ISBN: 978-1-60886-974-9 | $14.99 US

The Backstagers

James Tynion IV, Rian Sygh

Volume 1 | ISBN: 978-1-60886-993-0 | $14.99 US

Tyson Hesse's Diesel: Ignition

Tyson Hesse

ISBN: 978-1-60886-907-7 | $14.99 US